CLARKE & SPURRIER'S

Fine Wine Guide

WINES • GROWERS • VINTAGES

OZ CLARKE
&
STEVEN SPURRIER

• NEW EDITION •

HARCOURT, INC.

NEW YORK SAN DIEGO LONDON

www. harcourt.com

Library of Congress Cataloging-in-Publication Data available upon request

ISBN: 0-15-100918-X

K J I H G F E D C B A

Created and designed by
Websters International Publishers Limited
Axe & Bottle Court
70 Newcomen Street
London SE1 1YT
www.websters.co.uk
www.ozclarke.com

Printed and bound in Spain by Book Print, S.L., Barcelona.

HOW TO USE THIS BOOK

Glass symbols These indicate the wines
produced
R Red wine
W White wine
O Rosé wine

Star symbols These indicate ratings for
individual wines
★ A particularly good wine
★★ An excellent wine
★★★ An exceptional, world class wine

Producers' names in SMALL CAPITALS refer to
entries in the A–Z OF PRODUCERS section
within each country or region.

Telephone and fax numbers The Producer
entries include *local* telephone and fax numbers,
in that order. One number only denotes a
combined telephone and fax number. Apart
from France, the area dialling code is only
shown once, with the telephone number.

Vintage charts Detailed vintage charts and
annual assessments, with information on when
the top wines are ready to drink, can be found
within each section.

While every care has been taken in the preparation of this guide, the publishers and
authors can not accept responsibility of any kind for consequences arising from reliance
upon information contained in it.

Thanks are due to the following people for their invaluable help with this book and the generous spirit in
which they have shared their knowledge: Nicolas Belfrage MW, Andrew Caillard MW, Bob Campbell MW,
Anthony Gismondi, Dan McCarthy, Stuart Pigott, Norm Roby, Victor de la Serna, Phillip Williamson.

CONTENTS

THE WORLD OF FINE WINE

——————— REGIONAL GUIDE ———————

The following chapters include sections on the styles of wine made, the grapes used and local classification systems; Oz Clarke's and Steven Spurrier's personal selections of great wines from the region or country; an A-Z of the best appellations; an A-Z of the most interesting producers with their finest wines listed and ranked; and vintage information

THE WORLD OF FINE WINE

Looking to the Future
by OZ CLARKE

I've stopped daydreaming about how many bottles of fine wine I've got stashed away in my little cellar beneath the stairs. And I've stopped daydreaming about what vinous wonder I might purchase when I get my big win on the National Lottery.

Nowadays I muse on how to 'liberate' as many of my bottles as I can from their racks. I've become profligate, reckless. Friends are going to pop by to watch the football. Great excuse to liberate some bottles. How many can I get away with? Eight? Eight more lovely empty spaces. If I'm trying to get to sleep at night I count the spaces created in my racks. How many have I managed to organize this week? Ten? Twenty? Beautiful. And what were they? As I methodically recall each label and all the flavours of each wine, I contentedly doze.

And this is because I've changed. And the world of wine has changed. Dramatically. When I began collecting bottles, fine wine came from a handful of regions – almost all French – and from not that many properties inside those regions. The wines took a long time to mature. Squirreling them away knowing that it might be 20 years before I'd pull the cork made sense, and I could even get a curious self-denying pleasure from contemplating their tortuously slow development.

How different it is now. The reason I have this irresistible urge to haul bottle after bottle out of cellar is that if I don't get a move on in drinking my wine, I'm going to miss the boat. Nowadays fine wine comes from every half-decent wine-producing country, in ever-increasing quantities. I want to own these new and exciting creations. I want to experience and enjoy the ever-expanding range of flavours and styles that each year's new vintage brings. So I have to drink more of the bottles I've already got – otherwise where I am going to store the new ones?

Luckily the new ones won't need storing for anything like as long because winemaking has improved so dramatically during the last generation that even the finest of the fine are drinkable at an early age. Great Bordeaux red *can* be enjoyed at 5 years old, though it might be better at 15. California Cabernet, Chilean Merlot, Argentine Malbec or Australian Shiraz are thrilling to drink at 2–3 years old, though a dozen years of maturity won't do many of them any harm.

And look at the areas I've just mentioned – Australia, Argentina, Chile,

California; add to these other heavy hitters from the New World like South Africa and New Zealand as well as reformed and re-invigorated European giants, Spain, Italy, Portugal, Germany, Austria and Hungary – all make increasing amounts of fine wine in their marvellously idiosyncratic ways. And the passion and determination to excel are there for all the world to see in new stars such as Canada as well as old favourites such as Burgundy. Fine wine has become a global phenomenon in every sense, available in many forms all round the world, not merely from the few fabled sites of the European classics.

Because fine wine is about passion. A top grape variety is of no use if it is grown and vinified in a listless or cynical manner. A great vineyard site is of no value unless it is cared for and nurtured by men and women passionate in their desire to help it express its greatness. And millions spent in modernizing vineyards and wineries are millions wasted if the equipment is not controlled by producers with a passionate vision of the flavour they long to create from their grapes.

And these are the kind of people whose wines – whose fine wines – Steven and I talk about in this book. Sometimes they *do* come from vineyards that have been revered for centuries. Sometimes they *are* made by descendants of winemakers who farmed the same acres generations ago.

But sometimes the wines are from lands that are so new and untried that no-one has yet worked out a legal framework for them. Sometimes they are made by first generation winemakers, second-career winemakers, retiree winemakers – all united by the same glowing thread of passion.

The start of the new millennium sees the world of fine wine in ferment as new producers tumble over each other into the marketplace and new markets rise, flourish and fade. The emergence of newly wealthy wine drinkers in Europe, North and South America, and, above all, round the Pacific Rim, has seen the best-established and most famous wines achieve the status of luxury symbols, like branded luggage or perfume. Prices of these items are mercilessly pushed skyward as producers and traders cash in on the bonanza.

Of course, if these are fine wines – as, generally, they are – we pay tribute to them here. But with the wealth of fine wine that is judged according to the beauty of its perfumes, the richness of its fruit, the perfection of its balance – the sheer pleasure it gives to Steven and to me regardless of where it comes from, who has made it, what grape variety is used – well, that's what this book is really about. And we hope it will help you get the best out of this new, exciting, far-flung and continuously evolving world of fine wine.

THE WORLD OF FINE WINE

Building on the Past
by STEVEN SPURRIER

A fine wine is a wine with 'breed' (what the French call *race*). Breed does not happen by chance, nor can it be created purely in the cellar. Fine wine results from a determination to produce quality.

This conscious effort starts with planting selected clones of noble grape varieties on soil and sub-soil that suit them perfectly, where they will enjoy just the right climate and benefit from the correct exposure to the sun. It continues with respect for the finest time-honoured traditions in viticulture, vinification and aging, married to the best new technology judiciously applied. Such a combination will always result in the production of fine wines.

The French concept of 'terroir', which encapsulates the vine's requirements for soil, exposure and climate, is the first consideration. Next comes the choice of which grape variety or varieties to plant. In most European countries, the choice has already been enshrined in the laws of appellation (although there are interesting developments in some places where innovative and imaginative producers have found existing regulations too restricting), but in the New World, where no such rules existed, the search for quality has shown certain vineyard sites to be much better than others and such sites are now being legally recognized alongside the grape varieties most suited to them.

As long ago as the 16th century, the French author of a Treatise on Agriculture, Olivier de Serres, wrote, 'The object of vine growers is to gather their grapes *en perfection de bonté*' (i.e., when the grapes have reached their peak of perfection). Nothing has changed, and vineyard management continues the whole year (with myriad routine tasks including pruning, trellising, canopy management, combating pests and diseases and, crucially, resisting over-production), working towards the perennial goal of bringing properly ripe grapes to the winery.

Recent years have seen the application of increasingly sophisticated technical expertise but now that technical progress in winemaking seems to have reached a point where little can be improved in the cellar, the grapes themselves are receiving more attention. Traditional wisdom has it that 'fine wine is made in the vineyard', and the resurgence of this feeling is in part a reaction against excessive reliance on technology, which has, until recently, been seen as the most important part of the equation.

Good winemaking remains, however, essential to the production of fine wine. It covers every step from deciding when to harvest, through all the stages of vinification and aging, up to and sometimes beyond bottling. On small estates the vineyard and the cellar are in the same hands; on larger ones, responsibility may be divided, although the team should act as one.

Although terroir, the grapes themselves and enological expertise are what make a fine wine, the wine cannot exist without the consumer. The prescient Olivier de Serres also wrote, 'Of what value to you is a fine vineyard if there is no-one to buy your wine?' For centuries the wines produced on Church lands had their own market within the Church: this is how Burgundy and Champagne achieved greatness. Loire wines furnished the tables of the splendid royal châteaux; and Bordeaux vineyards looked to England and the Netherlands to export. Few other wines in France had any reputation.

During the 1914–18 war and again in the Depression of the 1930s demand collapsed and quality plummeted almost instantaneously. The basic ingredients to make fine wine were still there, but there was no market. Today, apparently insatiable demand at the top end of the market, and the trickledown effect that this generates as more and more producers aspire to greater achievements, mean that the outlook for the consumer is excellent.

The problem now is one of choice, and there is no getting away from the fact that the more you know the better and more pleasurable your choices will be. Reputation and price are generally a good indicator nowadays. You can usually spot the difference between a good and a very good wine if you taste them side by side but, since you can't always taste, Oz and I hope that you will find the information and advice we have included in this book will go a long way towards helping you find your way around this vast subject.

Gone are the days when the attitude of 'If it's French, it must be good' permitted wines that were in no way fine to command high prices. Challenges from California in the 1970s, Australia and New Zealand in the 1980s, and Chile and Argentina in the 1990s have served to remind the Old World that it cannot rest on its laurels. There is a surge in quality winemaking today as never before in history, and this is due as much to world competition between producers as to world demand from consumers.

A French philosopher once remarked that the future of fine wine was in the hands of the architects, meaning that if they built homes without cellars wine would not be laid down. He was right about the developments in housing but not their effects. The world may have moved on in many unpredictable ways but the future of fine wine, in the capable hands of producers and enthusiasts worldwide, has never looked more interesting.

NOBLE GRAPE VARIETIES

It has been said that the character of a wine comes from the grape, its soul from the terroir (the soil, sub-soil and mesoclimate). These are the two vital elements that make up the profile, style and character of a wine. The human input, which covers viticulture, yield control, vinification, *élevage* and bottling, must work with them as best it can. The weather will determine overall quality each year, the grapes producing more or less concentrated juice, with different degrees of ripeness, acidity and tannin according to the vintage, while retaining their innate character wherever they are planted.

Most white wines are made from white grapes, although white wine can also be made from black grapes, as in Champagne, for in all the noble grape varieties, it is only the skin that is coloured. Red wines, of course, necessarily come from black grapes.

RED GRAPES

Barbera

A prolific but late-ripening variety from north-west Italy that has a fine fruit and a high level of natural acidity. It is sold as a varietal wine and is fruity and zesty in youth, developing richness and complexity with age. It is also planted in California.

Cabernet Franc

The more fragrant of the two Cabernets, producing wine with a deep colour, a delightful aroma of raspberries or violets and a firm, sometimes earthy finish. It is at its best in France in Touraine and Anjou where it is used in Chinon, Bourgueil and Saumur-Champigny, and in the Pomerol and St-Émilion regions of Bordeaux, where it is known as Bouchet and blended with Merlot. It is a minor element in the Graves and the Médoc, and is widely planted in northern Italy. Plantings in the Southern Hemisphere have increased to blend with Cabernet Sauvignon.

Cabernet Sauvignon

The great grape of Bordeaux, this is a late-ripening variety with small, very dark berries producing a wine of intense colour, with a striking aroma of crushed red berries and blackcurrants, an intense, often tannic-backed flavour with great depth and aging potential. It is relatively easy to grow and is now found all over the world, perhaps most notably in California and Australia, but also making some very distinctive wines in Tuscany and northern Spain. Often too assertive on its own, it is regularly blended with Merlot and Cabernet Franc.

Grenache

Called Garnacha in Spain, where it originated, this is the principal grape of the southern Rhône, the major component in Châteauneuf-du-Pape, Gigondas, Tavel, Vacqueyras and the Côtes du Rhône-Villages. The second most planted grape in the Rioja, it also does well in California and Australia, particularly from old vines. The Grenache ripens early, giving fleshy fruit with high alcohol and low acidity. It quickly overripens, and is responsible for some first-class fortified wines.

Gamay

The single grape of the Beaujolais, where it is perfectly suited to the granite-based soil, producing wines with a deep violet-red colour, flavours bursting with fruit, and low tannins (but good acidity), which are best drunk young. If the best Crus in Beaujolais – Morgon, Moulin-à-Vent, Juliénas – spend several years in bottle, the wine takes on Pinot Noir characteristics. The Gamay prefers a cool climate and flourishes in the Loire Valley, Savoie and the South-West of France. It is also planted in California.

Malbec

Used for its dark colour and body in Bordeaux wines, it dominates in Cahors, where it is known as Auxerrois, and is vinified on its own in the Loire Valley. Malbec is also the most important quality grape from Argentina.

Merlot

Ripening relatively early, but very prone to rot in humid vintages, the dark-coloured Merlot is planted in Bordeaux, where it is the perfect foil for Cabernet Sauvignon in the Médoc and the Graves, and is dominant in St-Émilion and Pomerol as well as in the South-West of France and the Midi. It is also planted with great success in northern Italy, California, Washington State, South Africa, Chile, Australia and New Zealand. The wine is rich in colour, with a plummy smoothness. It needs less aging than the Cabernets, but on the right soil, not over-cropped, can produce equally impressive wine.

Mourvèdre

A late-ripening variety making intensely dark-coloured, structured wines with a firm acidity. In France it is the principal grape of Bandol and a necessity in Châteauneuf-du-Pape to add stature and aging potential to the Grenache. It is much planted in Australia and in Spain and beginning to be planted in California.

Nebbiolo

This dark-skinned grape is the principal source of the superb Barolo, Barbaresco and Gattinara wines from Piedmont. It produces highly tannic wines that need to age. It is beginning to be popular in northern California.

Pinot Noir

The traditional French grape of Burgundy and Champagne, but also planted in Alsace, the Jura and more recently in the Midi. Pinot Noir is a fragile grape that prefers a cool climate. Except in Champagne, where the juice is blended with that of Chardonnay and Pinot Meunier, it loses character if blended with other grapes. The richly delicate flavours of Pinot Noir have attracted winemakers all over the world, and it is now planted in northern California and Oregon, all over the Southern Hemisphere, with particular success in New Zealand, as well as in northern Italy, Switzerland, Germany and Austria, where it is known as Blauburgunder or Spätburgunder, and Eastern Europe.

Sangiovese

Also known as Sangioveto, this is the principal grape of Tuscany, hence the grape of Chianti. A late ripener, it gives wines with a fine ruby colour and firm acidity. In Montalcino it is known as the Brunello (producing Brunello di Montalcino) and in Montepulciano as the Prugnolo (for Vino Nobile di Montepulciano). With Nebbiolo, it is the leading Italian grape of quality, and is now being planted in the New World. (Not to be confused with Sangiovese di Romagna.)

Syrah/Shiraz

A very dark-coloured grape suited to warm climates and making rich, powerful wine with a blackcurranty, spicy aroma and concentrated fruit flavour. In France it is at its best in the northern Rhône (Hermitage, Côte-Rôtie, Cornas) and it adds backbone and style to the Grenache-based wines of the southern Rhône. Equally famous for producing rich, intensely fruity, long-lasting wines in Australia, where it is known as Shiraz, it is becoming very successful in South Africa and California.

Tempranillo

The most important variety in Rioja, where it is usually blended with Garnacha (Grenache), although excellent 100% Tempranillos are also made both there and in Navarra. The wines have a good fruit and a supple flavour that blends well with oak. Tempranillo is also becoming important in Argentina.

Touriga

The Touriga Francesa and the much rarer Touriga Nacional are the main Port grapes, producing very rich, tannic, complex and long-lived wines. They are also used for table wines in the Douro.

Zinfandel

Now acknowledged after much debate to be the same as the Primitivo of southern Italy, Zinfandel is at its best in California, where it is widely planted to make fruity, berry-like, lively wine (also rosé and even white wine). If the vines are old and yields are low, Zinfandel can produce intensely coloured, tannic wines with high alcohol, that age superbly.

WHITE GRAPES

Chardonnay

In France Chardonnay is famous for producing white Burgundy (Chablis, Meursault, the Montrachet family, Mâcon-Blanc, Pouilly-Fuissé) and Champagne, and is now successfully planted throughout the Midi. Although preferring a lightish soil and coolish climate, it adapts remarkably well to different terroirs and produces fine wines all over Europe and the New World, particularly California, Australia, New Zealand and Chile. The colour ranges from pale to full yellow, the aroma is elusive, with appley, buttery or nutty overtones, and the flavour is high in fruit, generally ripe and rounded, but with good acidity. Its versatility makes Chardonnay popular with both producers and consumers.

Chenin Blanc

Produces the finest white wines in the Loire Valley, from dry (Savennières), to fully sweet (Vouvray Moelleux, Coteaux du Layon, Quarts de Chaume), even sparkling. In very warm years, the grapes will become botrytized, producing extra concentration and richness, but never losing their crisp, lemony acidity. Also found in South Africa (where it is also called Steen), New Zealand and California.

Gewürztraminer

The best-known expression of this grape comes from Alsace, where very aromatic, heady, spicy wines, with a grapy muskiness reminiscent of lychees are made. It can be dry, but more usually has a little residual sugar, and in the Vendanges Tardives and Sélection de Grains Nobles styles, it is very concentrated and fully sweet. It is also successful in Germany, Austria, northern Italy and the New World.

Marsanne

The major white wine grape in the northern Rhône (Hermitage, St-Joseph, St-Péray), it is more reliable than the more delicate Roussanne. It is much planted in the southern Rhône too, as well as in Australia, where it makes ripe, rounded wines, whose low acidity does not prevent them from aging well.

Muscat à Petits Grains

This variety, also known as the Muscat de Frontignan, produces small berries that are packed with highly aromatic, grapy fruit. In Alsace, it is usually vinified dry, but in Beaumes-de-Venise and the Midi, it is famous for the rich, scented Vins Doux Naturels. In Italy it is important as Moscato d'Asti, and Greece's finest wines are the Muscats of Samos and Patras. It makes luscious fortified wines in the New World, especially in north-east Victoria in Australia. The more hardy Muscat of Alexandria and Muscat Ottonel are tending to supplant the Muscat à Petits Grains in New World plantings.

Palomino

The classic Sherry grape in southern Spain, producing a wine of no particular complexity, that gains its inimitable character from the way it is aged in the bodegas.

Pinot Gris

Although much planted in the Veneto, where it is known as Pinot Grigio, this grape is best in Alsace, where it produces broad-flavoured wines with rounded fruit, a suave complexity and low acidity. It is very successful in the Pfalz region of Germany, under the name of Ruländer for sweet and Grauburgunder for dry wines, where it assimilates well with new oak.

Riesling

One of the finest, perhaps *the* finest, of the white wine grapes, with the range of Chenin Blanc and the complexity of Chardonnay, Riesling has a distinctive fruit, purity of style and lemony acidity (even at its sweetest) that transcends differences in region and climate. It reaches its peak in the wines of the Mosel-Saar-Ruwer, Rheinhessen and Rheingau in Germany, and in Alsace, yet produces superb wine in Austria, California (where it may be known as Johannisberger Riesling) and Australia. Plantings are increasing in cooler spots throughout the New World.

Sauvignon Blanc

An extremely versatile grape that ripens early, but can attain noble rot in the right conditions, Sauvignon is at its most marked in the central Loire (France), where its aggressively fruity redcurrant/gooseberry aroma and crisp finish are typified by Pouilly-Fumé and Sancerre. Elsewhere in France, it is a minor element in Sauternes and the dry wines of the Graves, and is much planted in the Midi. Outside France, its greatest success has been to create a benchmark, slightly more grassy style in New Zealand, and it does well all over the New World.

Sémillon

The principal grape of the great sweet wines of Bordeaux (Sauternes, Barsac), due to its susceptibility to botrytis, Sémillon is also important in the wines of Pessac-Léognan, Graves and south-west France. Its mellow softness has made it one of the most popular wines in Australia, where, despite a low acidity, it ages remarkably well to take on great depths of flavour.

Viognier

Very fragile and previously limited to the northern Rhône, where it produced small quantities of Condrieu and Château-Grillet and played a part in the blend of (red) Côte-Rôtie, Viognier is now planted in the southern Rhône, the Midi, California and Australia for its intensely aromatic, peach-apricot bouquet and unctuous yet fine flavours.

CLASSIC WINE STYLES

Some of the classics are old, some of them are new, but all of them have proved themselves by having a particular benchmark style and personality which has frequently been copied and sometimes improved upon around the vineyards of the world.

RED WINES

Bordeaux/Cabernet
The Classed Growths of Bordeaux's Médoc are the kings here, due to their austere yet perfumed flavours and their great longevity. Most other countries – New and Old World – attempt to emulate the Bordeaux style.

Merlot
Bordeaux's St-Émilion and Pomerol set the pace here with fleshier, lusher reds, more immediately enjoyable than those of the Médoc though also good to age. There has recently been a surge of Merlot-mania worldwide. Malbec from Argentina and Chile may satisfy some of the thirst.

Juicy fruity
Early exponents, Beaujolais and Bardolino, have now been outstripped by quick-drinking styles based on a wide variety of grapes worldwide.

Low tannin
Newcomers to fine red wine often find tannins a bit severe, so low tannin, high-quality wines from grapes such as Pinot Noir, Barbera, Touriga Nacional, Tempranillo, Merlot and Shiraz are flourishing.

Cool-climate, medium-weight
Warmer global conditions have made possible a series of fine vintages in cool regions like the Loire Valley, Austria, Hungary, Canada and New Zealand.

Warm-climate, medium-weight
Increasingly popular, soft yet full-flavoured, easy-drinking reds are being made from Primitivo and Montepulciano in Italy, Grenache and Syrah in France, Tempranillo in Spain, a whole variety of grapes in Portugal, Zinfandel in California, Pinotage in South Africa and Grenache in Australia.

Burgundy/Pinot Noir
Few regions of the world can replicate Burgundy, but good, individual Pinot Noir reds are appearing in California, New Zealand, Chile and Australia as well as Spain, Italy and Germany.

Spicy blockbusters
The great reds of the Rhône Valley were the first star turns, and the main Rhône grapes – Grenache and Syrah – now make superb spicy reds worldwide. Southern Italy, Spain and Portugal use indigenous grapes to similar effect, while South Africa uses Pinotage and California Zinfandel.

Tuscan
Few producers have copied Tuscan reds worldwide, but in Tuscany itself, a far better understanding of Sangiovese, allied to improved winemaking and higher ambitions – and some classic French varieties like Cabernet – has transformed the region and its wines.

Sweet
Few successful styles, though Mavrodaphne in Greece can be good and sparkling Shiraz is often on the sweet side. Occasional Austrian and German noble-rotted reds are a batty if delicious aberration.

ROSÉ WINES

Dry
There are now lots of delicious dry rosés, full of fruit. Bordeaux and the Languedoc are excellent in France, Navarra in Spain and the Veneto in Italy have some tasty stuff and Australia's Grenache is good.

Medium-sweet
A declining category – due to the poor quality of most Portuguese rosé and Anjou rosé. The best modern-day examples often come labelled as 'White Zinfandel' from California.

FORTIFIED RED WINES

Port
The classic sweet fortified wine from the Douro Valley in Portugal. At its best, deep, rich, powerful and heady but also gentle and tawny-coloured if aged for years in oak. Australian 'ports' are first class and South Africa and California produce some good examples.

Grenache Vin Doux
Sweet, almost raisiny style epitomized by Banyuls on France's Mediterranean border with Spain. Also made elsewhere in Languedoc-Roussillon and in Rasteau in the Rhône Valley. There are occasional sightings of similar styles in Sardinia and Catalonia.

WHITE WINES

Unoaked, steely
Chablis is the classic example but many warmer areas of the world are now producing unoaked Chardonnays – admittedly a little fruitier – as some consumers move away from oak.

Oaked, ripe, spicy Chardonnay
Originally based on the barrel-fermenting methods used for top white Burgundy, warmer regions produce a richer, spicier, more blatant style which can be delicious but rarely resembles Meursault or Puligny-Montrachet.

California Chardonnay
At their best these can be dry but luscious, nutty and toasty and very similar to fine Burgundy but many examples are too sweet and lack balance.

Australian and New Zealand Chardonnay
Austalian Chardonnays are generally very fruit driven, with or without oak, though some examples approach Burgundian finesse. New Zealand's are rich, buttery, even syrupy, but refreshingly balanced with acid.

Dry Sauvignon Blanc
Though it originates in France's Loire Valley, New Zealand has made the archetypal modern snappy style. South Africa, Chile, northern Spain, Bordeaux and Hungary have shown they understand how to do it too.

Dry Chenin Blanc
Austere, reserved, slow-maturing whites from Anjou and Touraine. New Zealand, South Africa and Western Australia have also had some success.

Dry Sémillon
Initially a Bordeaux style, this was made world famous by Australia, both in oaked and unoaked styles. There are now many good examples in Bordeaux as well as increasingly in South Africa, Chile,

Argentina and New Zealand. Frequently blended with Sauvignon, sometimes with Chardonnay or Chenin.

Riesling/Mosel-Rhine

Dry The majority of German Rieslings are now dry, and a string of decent vintages have meant the balance between acid and fruit has often been good. Austria finds dry styles easier as does Australia.

Off-dry Most non-German Riesling drinkers believe that the glories of German Riesling are best revealed in Spätlese and Auslese styles that combine wonderful sweetish fruit with tingling tantalizing acidity. New Zealand makes highly successful off-dry styles; in most other countries the results are too bland.

Sweet The great German and Austrian dessert wines have long been European classics, but superb examples of truly concentrated, thickly sensuous sweet Riesling also come from New Zealand, Australia, South Africa – and, occasionally, the USA and Canada.

Sparkling wines

The greatest sparkling wines still come from the chilly northern French region of Champagne, but more and more countries have identified sites to grow suitable grapes and a mastery of the intricacies of inducing a second fermentation in the bottle have produced gorgeous biscuity, nutty fizz in California, New Zealand, Australia and South Africa and leaner but still attractive versions in Italy, Spain, England and other parts of France.

Sweet wines

The most famous sweet wines, made from overripe, nobly-rotted grapes of massively concentrated sweetness are made in France (Bordeaux, Alsace and the Loire Valley), Germany and Tokaji in Hungary. However, many other countries now make superb sweet wines, employing Sémillon or Riesling, but occasionally Sauvignon, Muscat or even Chardonnay. Italy and Austria use a variety of grape types and produce stunningly original stickies.

Eiswein/Icewine

Originally a German speciality, made from grapes picked when they are frozen to well below zero on the vine. The water freezes but the sugar and acid merely concentrate. Canada now also makes great Icewines.

FORTIFIED WHITE WINES

Sherry

Ranging from bone-dry to sumptuously sweet, these classic wines are made in Andalucía in south-west Spain. Similar wines are made in nearby Montilla. Australia and South Africa are the best New World emulators.

Madeira

Fascinating wines made on the island of Madeira. Bone-dry to intensely sweet they are marked by high acidity and a smoky burnt taste and they age brilliantly. Other countries make so-called Madeiras without conspicuous success.

Marsala

A largely forgotten but once famous fortified wine from Sicily, now primarily used for culinary purposes. More's the pity, because the occasional bottle of true Marsala Vergine reveals a superb, acid-structured, smoky, nutty wine.

Muscat Vin Doux Naturel

Made all round the Mediterranean either from partially fermented Muscat wine, or Muscat juice, barely fermented at all. The best are from southern France, Italy, Samos in Greece and Australia; South Africa and California produce pretty fair stuff.

BUYING FINE WINE

The golden rule in buying fine wine is: find a good wine merchant. There are many different ways to buy wine but no substitute for the expert you trust. Here are some of the opportunities and pitfalls inherent in the various systems. With a bit of trial and error (well worth the time, effort and expense), you will find what suits you.

Wine merchants

The advantages of a good merchant are plain: the merchant knows the wines and tastes regularly enough to know their development and relative merits; the selection will represent a personal choice; and advice on when the wines should be drunk, storage and delivery are all part of the service. All good wine merchants will take back and refund wines that are not, or are no longer, to the client's taste. In fact, it is as important for the wine merchant to know the tastes of a client as it is for the client to know the tastes of the wine merchant.

Specialist wine merchants are known for the length and erudition of their bi-annual wine lists. For many this is the ideal way to buy wine, spending an evening perusing the various lists and tasting notes before finally placing an order.

The disadvantage of this system is that one pays for this knowledge and service, and the traditional merchant is seldom the cheapest place to buy wine.

Direct from the producer

Logically, this should be the cheapest way to buy wine. In a world which has become fascinated by fine wine, where the track records of the top producers, châteaux and domaines are closely studied and vintages analysed almost daily by the various wine magazines and newsletters, it would seem that the traditional merchant is superfluous, as his much-prized knowledge

can now be acquired by any interested amateur. Yet in the last decade, while the demand for the world's best wines has outstripped their supply, the traditional merchants have flourished as never before. This is because it is the producer's job to concentrate on making the best wine he can while it is the merchant's job to provide a regular and guaranteed distribution. Merchants who buy in poor vintages will be rewarded by being first in line in the easy-to-sell good years. The finer Bordeaux châteaux and the better domaines in Burgundy and the Rhône will receive visitors, and receive them well with advance warning, particularly on the recommendation of a wine merchant, but will very rarely sell them wine. The commercial structure of importer-wholesaler-retailer/restaurateur-consumer works in the interest of all concerned, even the final consumer.

This is shown by the very logical approach of the wineries in California, where the price of a bottle sold at the winery will be, by law, the same as in a retail shop in the same state. The wholesale and retail margins are covered by a heavy discount from the winery, whose own retail sales carry a margin sufficient to cover the cost of a reception area for tastings and staff. The attractions of buying direct from the producer, being able to make a choice from wines tasted at the place where they are made, compensate the consumer for the expense in getting there and back. Once a client, you will generally be put on the winery's mailing list and given vintage reports and even pre-release offers.

En primeur

With increasing demand from consumers for the world's finest wines, you will need to think about buying 'pre-release' or 'en primeur'. The two considerations are availability and price. Tiny estates in Burgundy will see their allocations, often less than 100 cases for each export market, taken up earlier and earlier by their importers, whose customers snap them up. Such wines seldom reach the retail shelf, and rarely re-appear at auction. Here, possession is much more important than profit, as quantities are small and the purchaser has bought the wines to drink. This is not always the case for wines from the classic Bordeaux châteaux, where the 'en primeur' market has been in force for many decades. In the spring following the latest vintage, the châteaux will propose virtually all their production to the Bordeaux merchants at prices based on the quality of the vintage and the health of the market. The opening prices are referred to as *la première tranche*, and, with good wines and a healthy world economy behind them, as in the 1997 campaign for the 1996 vintage, prices may rise as much as 50%, even more, in a few weeks. Such was not the case for the lesser quality and hugely overpriced 1997 vintage, where prices later fell sharply. Despite reductions from this high level in 1998 and 1999, both good vintages, price rises from the *première tranche* have been modest. The production of Bordeaux châteaux, with few exceptions, tends to be large enough for their wines to be readily available for a few years after bottling through retailers,

and thereafter for many years at auction or through the brokers, so for Bordeaux, profit is as important as possession. It was on the blue chip wines of red Bordeaux and Vintage Port, that the equation of 'buy double what you want, sell half for double what you paid, and drink for free' was based.

Supermarkets

As popularity of wine drinking has increased in non-wine-producing countries, quality purchases have increased, and supermarkets have become more interested in the fine wine market. Often, the quality of the buyers is unrivalled, and their financial power permits them to negotiate with even the most intransigent supplier. To escape from the 'cheap and cheerful' image that launched their wine sales to the general public, such companies take pride in offering fine wines at competitive prices. The best example of this is the 'Foires aux Vins', held by all the competing supermarket chains in France and Belgium, generally each September. A huge range of wines previously associated only with specialist merchants are offered at very advantageous prices for a week or so with great success (but watch out: they are not always from the best vintages).

Retailers with multiple shops

These are midway between the specialist merchants and the supermarkets. Skilled centralized buying provides a range of wines sold by helpful and knowledgeable staff. The fact that these shops are usually found in town centres is an added convenience.

Wine clubs and mail order

There are several clubs and catalogue operations that have no retail premises and sell entirely through mail order. You need to go by word of mouth recommendations on quality and service and see whether they have reassuringly knowledgeable personnel on the end of the telephone.

The Internet

A fast-growing way to buy and sell wine is via the Internet. Websites range from wineries to retail wine merchants to Internet specialist operations to entrepreneurial brokers who tout for business by joining in wine chat forums. Buying wine via the Internet is just like buying from a wine club or by mail order and the same rules apply, except that you may be able to interrogate expert staff by e-mail as well as on the telephone and you may be offered a useful selection tool in which to enter your preferences and even what you want to eat with a given wine. Wine auctions and wine exchange over the Internet are attracting substantial amounts of business.

Wine fairs

One of the most enjoyable ways of buying wine is at local wine fairs in wine-producing countries. Many bottles will be available for tasting, and prices will generally be below retail.

Auction rooms

For anyone wishing to find a large range of the most prestigious names from mature vintages, the auction rooms are ideal. In the UK, Christie's, under Michael Broadbent, led the field from 1966 to 2000 when in the UK, at least, their great rival, Sotheby's, under Serena Sutcliffe drew ahead for the first time. Both now hold wine auctions in the US, Japan and Hong Kong, as well as various European cities. Week in, week out, a vast array of 'blue-chip' names will appear, with every minutely relevant detail the buyer could possibly need to know. The success of the auction houses is due to the fact that they provide a clearing house at any time. If the market is down, many merchants may be forced to sell stock; if it is up, many stockholders sell for a profit.

Brokers

The world demand for fine wine has been responsible for the success, perhaps even the creation, of the wine broker. This recent entry into the international trade sells from an ever-changing list at margins lower than retail, dealing mostly in 'blue-chip' wines. Many of their purchases are made at auction, others direct from the producers, some from clients they sell to. The great difference between the auctioneers and the brokers is that the latter hold stock. With the upsurge in the market for fine wines, the turnover of such companies has exploded, and the leader in the field, Farr Vintners (a UK broker), currently sells more wine than Christie's and Sotheby's combined. Anyone in a hurry to find stocks of a particular mature or rare wine should deal with the brokers.

Investment wines

Historically, an investment wine was either a top red Bordeaux or a Vintage Port, since the market for both was extremely structured and the wines had an unrivalled ability to improve with age. Recently, the concept of investment wines has expanded to cover all the world's best wines, and particularly those that are in short supply. The speculative value of each wine will vary according to several elements, but you can assume that most wines in this book given a 3-star rating are, for reasons of quality or rarity, investment wines.

MAKING THE MOST OF FINE WINE

In the realm of minor life setbacks few things are as disappointing as an anticipated great wine experience that fails to live up to expectations. You cannot always avoid this but a bit of preliminary thought about your own particular wine requirements, extra care over handling, serving and storing, and attention to when you drink a wine, the temperature you drink it at and what you drink it with will almost always pay dividends.

Tasting

It's a case of, 'Think While You Drink'. If you're spending good money on a wine it really does make sense to take a few moments to appreciate the flavour and personality of what you've paid for. I'm assuming that, having got as far as reading this book, you *do* care about the wine in your glass. In which case there are 3 stages to tasting on which we should spend a few moments each time we open a bottle.

Sight Apart from checking if the wine is clear – and with the rise of unfiltered wines, even lack of clarity *may* not be a bad thing – the colour of the wine (held against a white background for reds, catching candle- or sunlight for whites) can give us a lot of pleasure.

Smell The smell of a wine may be very similar to the taste or it may be quite different. Some wines have wonderful perfume which the palate can't quite match; some wines smell closed and withdrawn yet open up wonderfully in the mouth; the best give off a heavenly scent that is matched or improved upon by the palate. In any case swirl the wine gently around in your glass, take a full-blooded sniff of the aroma and just linger awhile enjoying it and recording the characteristics in your memory.

Taste It seems silly to have to comment on taste since we all taste so many things every day without apparent difficulty.

However, it isn't the tongue that records all the nuances of flavour, it's the nasal cavity. So take some wine in your mouth and, rather than swallow immediately, just hold it there, breathing in and out through your nose. All the facets of flavour you might have missed will reveal themselves in seconds. *Then* you swallow.

Fine wine and food

To say there are no rules anymore concerning food and wine partnership is to take the easy route. Too easy. Too facile. There are rules. Some of them work. Some of them are bunk. But whichever way you look at it, remember we're talking wine enjoyment here, not which side of the road to drive on. No-one's going to get hurt if we bend these rules a little.

Or a lot. Most wine rules date from another era when cooking cultures didn't overlap, and we either drank the relevant local wines or we drank the relatively few old classics like red Bordeaux and white Burgundy. Since most so-called fancy food was based on French cuisine, and since most classic wines were also French, rules like Chablis with oysters, Chambertin with pheasant, Médoc with spring lamb naturally became enshrined.

Well, not only has the food we eat changed but modern wine is unrecognizable from the wine of a generation ago. With a far greater understanding of fermentation methods, in particular temperature controls allowing very precise and predictable winemaking in warm areas like Australia, California and the Mediteranean basin, the ebullient natural richness of warm climate fruit as well as the scented beauty of healthy cool climate fruit can now be triumphantly captured in the glass. Wine – red, white or rosé – is now likely to be an utterly enjoyable drink in its own right, based on ripe fruit expertly vinified, rather than a difficult, frequently fruitless beverage that required sympathetic understanding and a plateful of complementary food to enjoy.

The only heart-felt piece of advice I have to give is that you should drink the wine you truly want to drink on a specific occasion, and if it is well made, from decent grapes, grown in a good vineyard, it'll get on pretty well with virtually any food you decide to marry with it.

Fine wine in restaurants

The last 10 years have seen a revolution in the way that we perceive fine food in restaurants, and galloping alongside the new wave of chefs is a bright, enthusiastic knowledgeable and radical posse of wine buyers and consultants determined to brush away the cobwebs that used to trail from the wine lists of even the world's most prestigious restaurants.

The biggest move of all in cooking has been to accept that though French cuisine is one of the great food cultures of the world, it isn't the only one, and it certainly isn't undisputed Lord of All It Surveys. The new welcome and overdue eclecticism has been mirrored in wine lists that do indeed show great respect for the French classics, but also demonstrate that other parts of the world make equally enthralling wines, that such wines may

well provide better partnerships for modern cross-cultural cooking, and that sometimes we want fine wine that leaps out of the glass at us and drags us spluttering and giggling to the trough of fun rather than fine wine that sits in solitary splendour coolly waiting for us to unpick the puzzle of its inscrutability.

So modern restaurants have become playgrounds in which we can experiment with wine more than temples at whose altar we must worship. Obviously the great classics are likely to be represented on the top wine lists, but a good restaurant is also keen to have less well-known wines that are not in general retail circulation. Consequently, many of the up-and-coming estates of France, Italy, Germany, Spain, California, Australia and elsewhere may *only* be available for us to try from the lists of leading restaurants.

And before complaining that the mark-ups are too high to make haphazard experimentation a natural option we should take a moment to check out the surrounding, survey the work done on the interior decoration, the furnishings, the glasswear and the well-turned out staff; as each course appears we should revel in the quality of the raw materials and the skill and the passion with which they have been cooked, and in a mood of contentment and good humour decide that this is precisely the time to experiment with something new and exciting.

Handling and serving fine wine

You can, of course, drink your Château Margaux 1961 out of a plastic cup. I know; I've done it – in a car park overlooking the Rhône Valley in the South of France. But even in my most iconoclastic moments, I wouldn't pretend the wine got fair treatment. A young Australian Grenache, a decent youthful Beaujolais, a chilled Spanish rosé – slurp them back whatever way you want. Château Margaux? Even I will accord it respect.

Respect covers the serving temperature and the glassware most of all. Above all, the glassware. There are lots of decent glasses on the market nowadays, and the characteristics they all share are that they are big, and they are of plain glass. Numerous experiments have been done to try to prove that a particular glass shape can transform the flavour of a wine. I've done a few of these myself, and while I would agree glass shape and size undoubtedly changes the final flavour of the wine, the effect is unpredictable, since styles of wine now vary so vastly within a region or from a single grape variety.

So buy reasonably large glasses that you can half-fill, thereby letting the aroma develop in the glass and making you feel good seeing a satisfying amount of wine swirl invitingly round the glass. And one final point. If possible, don't use detergent to wash them, just very hot water. The residue of detergent on a glass or a used drying cloth can blunt the flavour of a fine wine in no time flat.

As for temperature, too hot is always worse than too cold. Although a fine white shouldn't have more than a couple of hours in the refrigerator – and fine Chardonnay probably only needs 1 hour – at least you can warm up overchilled wine by gently cupping the glass in your hands. Wine that has got too warm often tastes dull even when you cool it and a red wine may be irrevocably stewed if served too hot. The old idea of chambré-ing red wines was conceived before the days of central heating. I wouldn't want any reds much above 15°C (60°F) and the lighter, fresher ones I'd happily cool for 40 minutes.

A couple of final points. Don't use a cheap coarse corkscrew with a rough thread on old bottles – the cork needs delicate treatment and I still haven't found a more sensitive corkscrew than the Screwpull. And if you want to decant to separate sediment and liquid in an old or unfiltered wine, go ahead, but it's not crucial – a steady hand carefully pouring will keep sediment and liquid apart except for some delicate red Burgundies with very fine deposits. Will decanting really improve the wine? Sometimes yes, sometimes no. With big glasses the wine can in any case breathe in the glass.

When to drink wine

There's no sadder moment in a wine drinker's life than to carry a treasured bottle up from the cellar cradled lovingly in his arms and present it to an enthusiastic and expectant throng of wine friends who have been hearing about its magical qualities for year upon year, too long to remember. The bottle is opened, poured carefully and equally into each waiting glass, and as the perfume rises to the nose's quivering nostrils, anticipation turns to anguish, and he mutters, 'Damn. It's past it.'

To have kept a bottle too long is far, far worse than to have drunk it before its time. To drink a wine that still can improve allows us to grow lyrical about its present quality and future brilliance; as the bottle drains away, this could be a nectar from above that we were impetuous enough to have drunk too soon, yet we still feel the glow of pleasure at having had the audacity to have done so. But to drink a wine that is past its best, whose fruit has faded and whose aromas have turned to a sour wrangling between acids and tannins with no flesh left to bind them, a wine that withers and disintegrates in bitterness, gives no pleasure at all, inspires no emotion but regret, provokes no reaction in your friends but disappointment.

The British are the worst at drinking wine too old, the French and Americans more likely to commit vinous infanticide than to be guilty of cruelty to an aged Cru. But wines of every sort from top to bottom of the quality tree are being made ready-to-drink at a far younger age than was the case a generation ago. Some will age fast; many won't. But, remember, every village has good and bad winemakers, every vintage good and bad wines. And if you are going to err – err on the side of youth.

Planning and stocking a cellar

Of course, this begs the whole question – what is a cellar nowadays? In olden times, this wouldn't be a question that needed to be answered; the homes of the middle and upper classes were built with a cellar beneath them and any gentleman with the slightest interest in wine would keep this perfect storage space amply stocked.

But that was then. Wine-drinking then, in the non-producing countries of northern Europe and much of North America, was confined to a small exclusive section of society, almost all of whom would have their own cellar. Now wine-drinking is spread across society, a society where increasingly we lead harried lives, long on stress and short on leisured pastimes. And very many of us reside in apartment blocks or modern houses built without cellars, sometimes, it seems, without space to do any thing but exist.

So we must improvise. Yet, luckily, in some ways wine is less of a challenge nowadays than before. There are vastly more good wines being made in the world, and few demand the time to mature,

though many would like it. The main streets of our cities have more good wine being sold by the bottle to take straight home and drink than ever before and the media peppers us with advice on what's hot and what's not.

So most of us don't need a cellar. But for those who do, here goes. If you have an underground cellar, cool and slightly damp it's the perfect space for storing wine because wine likes to mature lying on its side in consistent temperature, humidity and darkness. The best temperature would be somewhere between about 5 and 12°C (41-53°F) with wine maturing more slowly at the lower temperature. Even so, it is consistency that is important and a consistent temperature up to about 20°C (68°F) would do. Fluctuating temperature is likely to cause seepage through the cork and a lack of humidity dries out the cork and encourages oxidation. Bright light, especially sunlight, rapidly tires wines.

If you don't have a rigidly airconditioned/centrally-heated house or apartment, you can improvise under stairs, or beds, or anywhere undisturbed, and since cardboard is a good insulator, you can store cases of wine on their sides pretty effectively. So long as the wine is cool to start with, a thick blanket draped over it will keep it that way unless there's a tropical heatwave. If you are still worried that your wine will be affected you could try temperature-controlled cabinets (expensive) or, you can store wine with the merchant from whom you buy (not cheap, but you have the comfort of knowing it will be enjoying ideal conditions), or, you can accept that the old long-term cellar is nowadays an unnecessary, albeit charming, indulgence and you'd be better off spending the money on good restaurants and cultivating a taste for younger wine.

FRANCE

Nowadays, probably no single country can lay claim to producing the world's best wines. However, the title for being the most significant country in the production of fine wine certainly belongs to France. French wines have, quite simply, been the starting point and remain the benchmark for a vast array of wines currently produced throughout the world. France is the country first to emulate, then to beat. Competition from high-quality wines elsewhere has brought about a remarkable resurgence of French pride, which has been backed up by new investment and commitment from government, large companies and individuals.

The French contribution to the world of fine wine can be summed up under 5 major spheres of influence (see below).

The varietal influence

Outside the major wine-producing countries of Europe, most wines are varietally labelled. The following grape varieties either originated in France, or gave of their best on French soil: Cabernet Sauvignon, Merlot, Chardonnay, Pinot Noir, Sauvignon Blanc, Syrah, Chenin Blanc, Gamay, Gewürztraminer, Riesling, and to a lesser extent, Grenache, Mourvèdre, Muscat and Cabernet Franc. (For more detail on grapes, see page 8.) Over time, other countries created their own styles and benchmarks – consider New Zealand Sauvignon Blanc, Australian Shiraz (Syrah), Californian Cabernet Sauvignon or Chilean Chardonnay; nonetheless, in all these cases, the French reference point remains.

The concept of terroir

The concept of terroir, that wines have their own 'sense of place', due to where they are made, is typically French. A *vigneron* in Volnay does not make Pinot Noir wine, but Volnay, and if he plants the same clone of Pinot Noir a few metres to the north, he may be producing Pommard. The chalk of Champagne, the limestone of Burgundy, the gravel in Bordeaux are all inseparable from the character of the wine. As producers all over the world strive to make finer wine, they realize the importance of specific sites. The elegant French writer and politican, Chateaubriand, wrote that 'an original person is not someone who imitates nobody, but someone whom nobody can imitate'; this sums up the significance of terroir for the French winemaker.

The idea of style

This idea is broader than that of terroir, and has perhaps had more influence. While individual wines from a particular area will be different from each other, they will share a family likeness, born from accepted vineyard and cellar practices over the generations. While a producer in another country cannot hope to imitate a terroir, he can imitate a style. The 'Rhône Rangers' in California come to mind.

Main wine areas

The theory of Appellation Contrôlée

The laws of Appellation d'Origine Contrôlée (AC) were formulated in 1919 and finalized in 1934; they sum up the concepts of terroir, grape variety and style, and aim to combat fraud, by laying down which grape varieties can be planted where, how the vines are pruned, how large a yield each vine may produce, minimum alcohol levels and various other criteria, including the results of a tasting panel; thus a named AC wine should always have certain recognizable characteristics. The laws cannot prevent poor wine, but they do protect against fraud. Today, other European countries have similar systems, and broader-based structures, such as the American Viticultural Areas, exist in the New World.

The use of oak

Oak has been used for fermentation and aging wines in every wine-producing country for centuries. Nevertheless, French oak is the benchmark. French forests – Nevers, Tronçais and Limoges – provide tightly grained wood from trees about 200 years old, which is always split, not sawn. It is generally accepted worldwide that French oak imparts a particular sophistication and patina.

BORDEAUX

The Bordeaux region is the largest fine wine region in the world, with an annual production of around 850 million bottles (83% red, 14% white and 1% rosé), 6 times the production of Burgundy or Beaujolais, slightly less than California but almost double that of Australia. The quality of basic AC Bordeaux or Bordeaux Supérieur, known in Britain as 'claret', has improved greatly in recent years and, at the other end of the spectrum, the Crus Classés go from strength to strength and command ever-higher prices.

WINE STYLES

There is a vast range of wine across the 57 Bordeaux appellations but there are many similarities that make all these wines recognizably Bordeaux. The influences of soil, climate and history have created 3 different regions.

The left bank of the Garonne and the Gironde estuary

This area comprises the major appellations of the Médoc, northern Graves and Sauternes. The red wines are Cabernet-dominated, backed by Merlot. The whites, both sweet and dry, use mainly Sémillon.

The right bank of the Dordogne

This covers St-Émilion and Pomerol, the other Libournais wines and the Bourgeais and Blayais areas. Red wines are the story here with Merlot the dominant grape.

The Entre-Deux-Mers

This region, between the Garonne and Dordogne rivers and the southern Graves, uses mainly Merlot for red wines, and Sauvignon and Sémillon for whites.

The importance of terroir

The vineyards are ideally situated on the 45th parallel. To the west (left-bank wines), a plateau slopes gradually down to the Atlantic coast and to the east (Entre-Deux-Mers and right-bank wines), there is a lowish plateau with undulating terrain. The cool, coastal climate is moderated by the Gulf Stream, which raises and regulates the temperature. Summer and autumn tend to be warm, with occasional, damaging frost in the winter and a relatively humid spring.

The soil is naturally diverse across such a large region: the left bank consists mainly of different types of gravel, which is an efficient water filter and reflects and retains heat; on the right bank is a mixture of clay, chalk and sand, with a little gravel; in the Entre-Deux-Mers, the clayey-limestone soils favour white wine.

Unlike most other French wine regions, the average size of a Bordeaux estate is around 10ha and 45% of the properties are 20ha or more. The wine from each château will be different, but still corresponds to the style of its appellation.

Buying top-quality Bordeaux

The Bordeaux wine trade has always lived from a flourishing export market, although since the 1990s the home market has taken a larger interest in the Crus Classés, owing partly to heavy seasonal promotion by the supermarkets. Such is the volume and value of the better

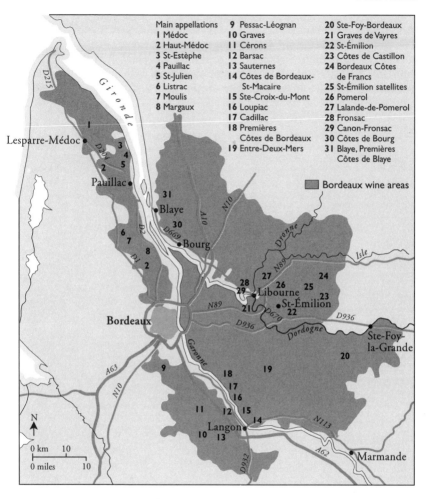

Main appellations	9 Pessac-Léognan	20 Ste-Foy-Bordeaux
1 Médoc	10 Graves	21 Graves de Vayres
2 Haut-Médoc	11 Cérons	22 St-Émilion
3 St-Estèphe	12 Barsac	23 Côtes de Castillon
4 Pauillac	13 Sauternes	24 Bordeaux Côtes
5 St-Julien	14 Côtes de Bordeaux-	de Francs
6 Listrac	St-Macaire	25 St-Émilion satellites
7 Moulis	15 Ste-Croix-du-Mont	26 Pomerol
8 Margaux	16 Loupiac	27 Lalande-de-Pomerol
	17 Cadillac	28 Fronsac
	18 Premières	29 Canon-Fronsac
	Côtes de Bordeaux	30 Côtes de Bourg
	19 Entre-Deux-Mers	31 Blaye, Premières
		Côtes de Blaye

Bordeaux wine areas

Bordeaux wines, that the historical hierarchy of middlemen is still in place: *courtiers* or brokers propose the wines to *négociants* (of whom very few are *négociants-éleveurs* in the Burgundian sense, as all classified wines and most other Bordeaux wines are château-bottled), who sell to importers or wholesalers, who in turn sell to retailers or direct to the public.

In the event of a top château selling wine direct to the public, this will generally be at the retail price, in order to maintain a stable market. To satisfy the demand of private buyers to buy as 'direct' as possible, there are now several flourishing retail shops in Bordeaux, St-Émilion and Pauillac, selling large ranges of wine at good prices.

BORDEAUX CLASSIFICATIONS

The wines of Bordeaux are well known for being classified. The appellations are not classified, but the châteaux within them are, and out of the several thousand châteaux, only the top 250 are part of the different classifications. These form a guide to relative quality within the appellations, but, as quality can rise or fall for many reasons, the real classification is often the market price.

Hierarchy of appellations

Overall, relative quality in Bordeaux can be expressed in the form of a pyramid. At the base are dry white Bordeaux and Entre-Deux-Mers and red Bordeaux and Bordeaux Supérieur, together representing about two-thirds of total production. Above them are the red and white wines from the Côtes. Above these come the regional appellations, e.g. Graves, St-Émilion, Pomerol, Médoc and Sauternes, already representing a narrower definition of terroir. From this group, but above them, are the châteaux that have been classified, beginning with the classification of the Médoc, Graves and Sauternes in 1855 and ending with the re-classification of St-Émilion in 1996. The Grands Crus and Crus Bourgeois are near the top of the pyramid, followed by the Crus Classés and finally the Premiers Crus Classés.

The Classification of 1855

This was created for the 1855 World Exhibition in Paris by the Bordeaux Chamber of Commerce. It included only red wines from the Haut-Médoc, one red wine from the Graves and the sweet white wines from Sauternes and Barsac. It was revised once in 1973, raising Mouton-Rothschild in Pauillac from 2ème Cru to 1er Cru status.

Premiers Crus Lafite-Rothschild (Pauillac); Margaux (Margaux); Latour (Pauillac); Haut-Brion (Pessac-Léognan/Graves); Mouton-Rothschild (Pauillac).

Deuxièmes Crus Rauzan-Ségla (Margaux); Rauzan-Gassies (Margaux); Léoville-Las-Cases (St-Julien); Léoville-Poyferré (St-Julien); Léoville-Barton (St-Julien); Durfort-Vivens (Margaux); Gruaud-Larose (St-Julien); Lascombes (Margaux); Brane-Cantenac (Margaux); Pichon-Longueville Baron de Longueville (Pauillac); Pichon-Longueville Comtesse-de-Lalande (Pauillac); Ducru-Beaucaillou (St-Julien); Cos d'Estournel (St-Estèphe); Montrose (St-Estèphe).

Troisièmes Crus Kirwan (Margaux); d'Issan (Margaux); Lagrange (St-Julien); Langoa-Barton (St-Julien); Giscours (Margaux); Maléscot-St-Exupéry (Margaux); Boyd-Cantenac (Margaux); Cantenac-Brown (Margaux); Palmer (Margaux); La Lagune (Haut-Médoc); Desmirail (Margaux); Calon-Ségur (St-Estèphe); Ferrière (Margaux); Marquis d'Alesme-Becker (Margaux).

Quatrièmes Crus St-Pierre (St-Julien); Talbot (St-Julien); Branaire (St-Julien); Duhart-Milon (Pauillac); Pouget (Margaux); La Tour-Carnet (Haut-Médoc); Lafon-Rochet (St-Estèphe); Beychevelle (St-Julien); Prieuré-Lichine (Margaux); Marquis de Terme (Margaux).

Cinquièmes Crus Pontet-Canet (Pauillac); Batailley (Pauillac); Haut-Batailley (Pauillac); Grand-Puy-Lacoste (Pauillac); Grand-Puy-Ducasse (Pauillac); Lynch-Bages (Pauillac); Lynch-Moussas (Pauillac); Dauzac (Margaux); d'Armailhac (Pauillac); du Tertre (Margaux); Haut-Bages-Libéral (Pauillac); Pedesclaux (Pauillac); Belgrave (Haut-Médoc); Camensac (Haut-Médoc); Cos-Labory (St-Estèphe); Clerc-Milon (Pauillac); Croizet-Bages (Pauillac); Cantemerle (Haut-Médoc).

The 1855 Classification of Barsac and Sauternes

Grand Premier Cru d'Yquem (Sauternes).
Premiers Crus La Tour-Blanche (Sauternes); Lafaurie-Peyraguey (Sauternes); Clos Haut-Peyraguey (Sauternes); Rayne-Vigneau (Sauternes); Suduiraut (Sauternes); Coutet (Barsac); Climens (Barsac); Guiraud (Sauternes); Rieussec (Sauternes); Rabaud-Promis (Sauternes); Sigalas-Rabaud (Sauternes).
Deuxièmes Crus de Myrat (Barsac); Doisy-Daëne (Barsac); Doisy-Dubroca (Barsac); Doisy-Védrines (Barsac); d'Arche (Sauternes); Filhot (Sauternes); Broustet (Sauternes); Nairac (Barsac); Caillou (Barsac); Suau (Barsac); de Malle (Sauternes); Romer de Hayot (Sauternes); Lamothe (Sauternes); Lamothe-Guignard (Sauternes).

The Classification of the Graves (since 1987 Pessac-Léognan)

This classification was carried out in 1953 encompassing only red wines and was revised in 1959 to include white wines as well. Haut-Brion features both in this and the 1855 Classification. The châteaux are listed alphabetically, followed by their commune.

Bouscaut (Cadaujac) ♥♀; Couhins (Villenave d'Ornon) ♀; Haut-Bailly (Léognan) ♥; Carbonnieux (Léognan) ♥♀; Domaine de Chevalier (Léognan) ♥♀; Fieuzal (Léognan) ♥; Olivier (Léognan) ♥♀; Malartic-Lagravière (Léognan) ♥♀; La Tour-Martillac (Martillac) ♥♀; Smith-Haut-Lafitte (Martillac) ♥; Haut-Brion (Pessac) ♥; La Mission-Haut-Brion (Talence) ♥; Laville-Haut-Brion (Talence) ♀; La Tour-Haut-Brion (Talence) ♥; Pape-Clément (Pessac) ♥.

The St-Émilion Classification

The wines of St-Émilion were first classified in 1954, and slightly modified in 1969, 1985 and 1996. The possibility of regrading can help maintain quality.

Premiers Grands Crus Classés (A) Ausone, Cheval-Blanc; **Premiers Grands Crus Classés (B)** Angélus, Beau-Séjour-Bécot, Beauséjour (Duffau-Lagarosse), Belair, Canon, Clos Fourtet, Figeac, La Gaffelière, Magdelaine, Pavie, Trottevieille.
Grands Crus Classés L'Arrosée, Balestard-La-Tonnelle, Bellevue, Bergat, Berliquet, Cadet-Bon, Cadet-Piola, Canon-La-Gaffelière, Cap de Mourlin, Chauvin, Clos des Jacobins, Clos de l'Oratoire, Clos St-Martin, La Clotte, La Clusière, Corbin, Corbin-Michotte, La Couspaude, Couvent des Jacobins, Curé Bon, Dassault, La Dominique, Faurie de Souchard, Fonplégade, Fonroque, Franc-Mayne, Grand Mayne, Les Grandes Murailles, Grand-Pontet, Guadet St-Julien, Haut Corbin, Haut-Sarpe, Lamarzelle, Laniote, Larcis-Ducasse, Larmande, Laroque, Laroze, Matras, Moulin du Cadet, Pavie-Decesse, Pavie-Macquin, Petit-Faurie-de-Soutard, Le Prieuré, Ripeau, St-Georges (Côte Pavie), La Serre, Soutard, Tertre-Daugay, La Tour Figeac, La Tour du Pin Figeac (Giraud-Bélivier), La Tour du Pin Figeac (J M Moueix), Troplong-Mondot, Villemaurine, Yon-Figeac.

The Crus Bourgeois of the Médoc

The Cru Bourgeois châteaux were first classified in 1932, listing 444 estates producing wines of regular high quality. The classification was reassessed in 1966 and in 1978 and is in the process of being revised again. The Crus Bourgeois produce almost 50% of the wine produced in the Médoc (close to 55 million bottles a year). The following Cru Bourgeois châteaux now produce wines of or near to Cru Classé standard:

d'Angludet, Charmail, Chasse-Spleen, Citran, Haut-Marbuzet, Gloria, La Gurgue, Labégorce, Labégorce-Zédé, Lilian Ladouys, Marbuzet, Meyney, Monbrison, de Pez, Phélan-Ségur, Pibran, Potensac, Poujeaux, Siran, Sociando-Mallet, La Tour Haut-Caussan.

RED BORDEAUX

The internationally recognized Cabernet Sauvignon and Merlot are well known for their individual flavours, Cabernet Franc less so, but the reputation of Bordeaux wine is built on the triple equation of climate, soil and grape varieties, whereby each region plants the grapes that best suit its soils and climate, to produce a harmonious wine with depth and character.

Cabernet Sauvignon
This late-ripening variety, with small, very dark berries, produces wines of deep colour, intense blackcurrant aromas with a firm, tannin-backed flavour that needs age to round out the fruit. Found mainly in the Médoc and the Graves, it does particularly well on their gravelly soils.

Cabernet Franc
Ripening slightly earlier than Cabernet Sauvignon, this grape provides colour, aroma and richness of fruit, combining finesse with an ability to age. It is very successful in St-Émilion and is a valuable part of the blend in the Médoc and Graves.

Merlot
This dark-coloured grape ripens relatively early, but is prone to poor setting of the fruit and to rot in humid vintages. It ripens well to provide good crops of plummy wines that may be drunk young, but age well. It is the most planted red grape, particularly in the Libournais.

Taste characteristics
Red Bordeaux, or 'claret' as it is known in Britain, is the most famous table wine in the world and it has one quality above all other wines – its 'digestibility'. A red Bordeaux is never heavy, and even the most robust styles can be drunk on any occasion. All young red Bordeaux has a deep carmine colour, a ripe berry fruit aroma with overtones of oak depending on the *élevage*, a fine fruit intensity and firm finish. The grapes' natural tannin allows even the most forward wines to age well.

The influence of winemaking
A skilled winemaker in the Côte d'Or or the Rhône Valley may produce fine wines with equipment no different from that of his father or grandfather as small volumes of fermenting wine are not difficult to control. But the relatively large average size of a Bordeaux estate, particularly of the Crus Classés, necessitates important investment in cellar equipment. Although tradition is still highly respected, Bordeaux has the most up-to-date installations in the world of wine, and there is no château of repute without a resident or consultant winemaker. Although current thinking holds that 'great wines are made in the vineyard', a totally 'hands-off' approach would not achieve the best results.

The use of oak
There are more new oak barrels in Bordeaux per hectare than in any other European wine region. Many red Bordeaux wines are entirely tank-matured, and may be most enjoyable to drink, but a classic wine will spend at least 1–2 years in small oak barrels. For the Premiers Crus and a few of the 'Super Seconds', these are 100% new every year, and for most other Crus Classés the proportion seldom drops below 50%. The ripeness and natural tannins in the wine are complemented and

GREAT RED BORDEAUX WINES

Oz Clarke's selection

Ch. Margaux
The most beautifully sculpted, the most fragrantly perfumed and the most consistently excellent of the great Médoc red wines.

Ch. Cheval-Blanc
St-Émilion's star combining richness of fruit and heady scent that is both hedonistic and intellectually stimulating.

Ch. Pétrus The rightful superstar of the Moueix stable of stars – rich, exotic, succulent red wine.

Ch. Pichon-Longueville Comtesse-de-Lalande
Brilliant, classic, yet soft-hearted Pauillac, Bordeaux's leading 'Super Second' wine.

Ch. Léoville-Barton
Austere and restrained at first but unfolding into a purist's dream of blackcurrant and cedarwood.

Ch. Grand-Puy-Lacoste
Underrated property that frequently produces one of the most exquisite Pauillacs.

Ch. Cos d'Estournel
Powerful, brooding but satisfying St-Estèphe that epitomizes Bordeaux at its most serious and impressive.

Ch. Vieux-Château-Certan
Less showy than most Pomerols, but constantly brilliant in a restrained, but deeply satisfying way.

Ch. Angélus A new star in St-Émilion promoted in the 1996 classification producing wines of irresistible sweet fruit and head-spinning scent.

Ch. Lynch-Bages A typical but marvellously sensuous Pauillac that can age to a sunshine sweetness of blackcurrant and cedar.

Ch. Gazin This is one of the most improved Pomerols – it now has a real richness and plenty of sweet ripe fruit.

Ch. Rauzan-Ségla A traditionally great Margaux château that has been continuously evolving and improving since the 1980s.

Steven Spurrier's selection

Ch. Lafite The largest of the Premiers Crus and since the mid-1980s back in its rightful position as the most elegant of all the Pauillacs – a wine of great polish and class.

Ch. Margaux Perhaps the most harmonious of the Premiers Crus, possessing the Margaux qualities – finesse, elegance and breed – to the highest degree.

Ch. Cos d'Estournel The finest St-Estèphe, for many years of Premier Cru standard, thanks to the dedication of the former owner Bruno Prats, as much as to the exceptional terroir.

Ch. Ducru-Beaucaillou This superb vineyard produces the best wine in the southern part of St-Julien, combining richness with an elegant structure.

Ch. Léoville-Barton The Médoc Cru Classé owned longest by the same family, has reached greater heights since the mid-1980s under Anthony Barton.

Ch. Léoville-Las-Cases The largest St-Julien estate produces one of the finest, most long-lived and classic red Bordeaux wines.

Ch. Grand-Puy-Lacoste Famous in the 1950s and '60s for great wines, this château has maintained its reputation under the ownership of the Bories of Ducru-Beaucaillou.

Ch. Pichon-Longueville Comtesse-de-Lalande The most smoothly textured and voluptuous Pauillac wine.

Ch. Haut-Brion This historic château produces wines of immense suavity and elegance, approachable when young, but with great power to age.

Ch. Haut-Bailly The most delicious red wine in the northern Graves, with seductive charm that belies a firm but never hard structure.

Ch. Canon-la-Gaffelière Concentrated, yet perfectly balanced St-Émilion that deserves to be elevated from Grand Cru Classé to a Premier Grand Cru Classé.

Ch. Vieux-Château-Certan Using a high proportion of Cabernet grapes, this estate produces Pomerol's most elegant and long-lived wine.

enriched by the vanillin, wood tannins, and 'roast' imparted while firing the new barrel, allowing the rough red wine to acquire a smoothness once in bottle, as well as added structure and flavour.

Top red Bordeaux appellations _____
Canon-Fronsac, Fronsac, Graves, Haut-Médoc, Lalande-de-Pomerol, Listrac-Médoc, Margaux, Médoc, Moulis, Pauillac, Pessac-Léognan, Pomerol, St-Émilion, St-Estèphe, St-Julien.

DRY WHITE BORDEAUX

The dry white wines of Bordeaux represent an average of 15% of the total production of all Bordeaux wines, down from 46% in 1960, owing to a combination of poor quality and an ever-increasing demand for red wine. The most widely planted grape variety is Sémillon, particularly in the Graves, where the finest quality is found. Sauvignon Blanc is used on its own in wines for early drinking, but is more usually blended with Sémillon to add weight and aging potential. In areas where the white wines are generally sweet, for example Barsac, a little Muscadelle is used in the dry white wine blend. The high-yielding Ugni Blanc and Colombard varieties may be included in basic Bordeaux Blanc, but not in any of the finer appellations.

Sémillon

Bordeaux's principal sweet wine grape, owing to its ability to retain natural sugar and to be affected by noble rot, is also prized for its ripeness and mellow flavours in dry white wines, especially in the Graves. This is the grape which allows the great white wines of Bordeaux, both dry and sweet, to age so gracefully.

Sauvignon Blanc

An extremely versatile, early-ripening grape which can attain noble rot in the right conditions. In dry white wines it maintains a grassy, lively style, taking its character from the soil. There is also a little Sauvignon Gris planted, giving a slightly rounder, less aggressive fruit.

Taste characteristics

The dry white Bordeaux revolution which began in the early 1970s is accredited to the *négociant* Pierre Coste of Langon, working with the enologist Denis Dubourdieu. Wines which were unbalanced by too much alcohol and acidity from the use of sulphur, became cleaner and more harmonious as the grapes were picked at natural ripeness and cool fermented in stainless steel tanks. More recently, there has been a move to ferment the whites in small oak barrels, as in Burgundy. Sauvignon characteristically gives a pale colour, fruity aroma with grassy and white berry overtones and a crisp, dry finish. Sémillon is more broad-flavoured, with less pronounced acidity. As a blend, both styles harmonize perfectly, Sauvignon giving way to Sémillon as the wine ages. There are some extremely successful wines made from Sauvignon alone, such as COUHINS-LURTON and SMITH-HAUT-LAFITTE.

The influence of winemaking

In Bordeaux, white grapes are more subject to rot than red, so while it is essential to wait for ripeness before picking, the grapes must be healthy when they arrive to be pressed. Since the bunches are not de-stemmed, pressing must be firm enough to extract the juice, but not to crush the stems and pips. The equipment plays a bigger part before fermentation starts than the winemaker, but once pressed, the juice must not oxidize before being run off into tanks or barrels. Tank fermentation is at 17–18°C, to preserve the fruit, while the more risky barrel fermentation takes place at higher temperatures, producing richer and rounder flavours.

GREAT DRY WHITE BORDEAUX WINES

Oz Clarke's selection

Pavillon Blanc de Ch. Margaux A great white wine to partner Ch. Margaux's great red with wonderful texture and a thrilling flavour of apricots, spice and the skins of still-green peaches.

Ch. Laville-Haut-Brion Slow to develop, difficult to taste young, but it opens out into a regally grand, densely textured white with age.

Ch. Smith-Haut-Lafitte This is the leader of the modern style of Pessac-Léognan white – thrilling, appetizing nectarine and passionfruit flavours when young, but aging beautifully.

Ch. de Fieuzal Heady, perfumed style that is so full of peachy fruit and luxurious aroma it almost seems sweet, but it isn't.

Dom. de Chevalier Classic dry white that is lean and austere to begin with but then develops haughty yet irresistible perfume with age.

Ch. Larrivet-Haut-Brion Underrated property consistently producing superb wines, grassy and coffee-scented to begin with but a delight of toasted nuts and cream with age.

Ch. Couhins-Lurton Tiny vineyard entirely planted with Sauvignon that makes thrillingly grassy wines spiced up with new oak.

Ch. La Tour-Martillac Behemothian property! This used to be a byword for ultra-traditional winemaking but recent modernization has transformed the white into one of Bordeaux's best.

Steven Spurrier's selection

Ch. Haut-Brion Made from mainly Sémillon, this combines nuanced flavours and sophistication to produce a supremely elegant wine. Sadly, only a tiny amount is made.

Ch. Laville-Haut-Brion From a blend of 70% Sémillon with Sauvignon and a little Muscadelle, this wine is exemplary for its aromatic richness, structure and ability to age, very much a contrast to the style of Haut-Brion.

Dom. de Chevalier Perhaps lacking the polish of Haut-Brion, or the richness of Laville-Haut-Brion, this Sauvignon-dominated wine offers great finesse and complexity, and ages slowly and beautifully.

Ch. Smith-Haut-Lafitte Under the new owners, Florence and Daniel Cathiard, this estate is now producing one of the most exciting and delicious wines of the northern Graves.

Caillou Blanc de Ch. Talbot One of the original white 'Médocs', this 100% Sauvignon has the fruit and weight of a Cru Classé Pessac-Léognan.

Pavillon Blanc de Ch. Margaux The white wine from Ch. Margaux is 100% Sauvignon, very pale, delicate and floral when young and prized for its crispness and elegance yet ages beautifully.

Clos Floridène Denis Dubourdieu has created a unique wine in the southern Graves: floral and lively, perfectly balanced.

Ch. La Louvière A classic, firm Graves from this jewel-like château that deserves to be promoted to a Cru Classé.

The use of oak

Only the more ambitious of the dry white Bordeaux wines are fermented in oak and these will generally be matured in oak as well. The search for freshness in the 1970s and early 1980s created a confidence in quality that encouraged certain châteaux to move to extract the maximum from their wines, by frequent *bâtonnage* or the periodic stirring of the lees of a very young wine, in the Burgundian manner. Such wines will benefit from wood aging, but are usually bottled before the following vintage. Vanillin flavours and the slight oxidation from the barrel are more sought after than a high-toast characteristic of some white Burgundies.

Top dry white Bordeaux appellations _____
Entre-Deux-Mers, Graves, Pessac-Léognan.

SWEET WHITE BORDEAUX

Bordeaux's sweet white wines or *vins liquoreux* come from vineyards on the left bank of the Garonne in the Graves, between Podensac and Langon, and from slopes opposite across the river on the right bank. The finest and most famous appellations are Sauternes and Barsac, yet there are some very good wines of similar style from Loupiac and Ste-Croix-du-Mont, across the river.

Taste characteristics

The grape varieties used for these wines are Sémillon (always dominant in the blend), Sauvignon Blanc and Muscadelle (to a small proportion and often omitted). The grapes are harvested as late as possible, in order to gain maximum sugar, the natural acidity in the grapes providing the necessary balance.

A fine sweet wine should have a full colour, richly yellow when young (although some Barsacs are more lemony-yellow), deepening to gold and then to amber with age. The nose should have floral, honeyed, fruity overtones, the most sought-after being ripe peaches, while the flavour should be rich, honeyed and luxurious, clean, but not cloying owing to the natural acidity.

Noble rot

The particular mesoclimate of the region, with coolish, misty mornings during the harvest, followed by the sun emerging to burn off the moisture during the day, precipitates and encourages the development of a fungus called the *Botrytis cinerea*, known as *pourriture noble* or noble rot. This fungus attacks the grapes and reduces the volume of water in each berry, with the consequent increase in sugar and potential flavour. If the weather is too cold or wet (as in 1984, '87 and '92) botrytis will not occur, and even in good years, it is seldom regular. As a result, the harvest is most often spread over several

weeks, while individual bunches, even single berries, become affected. Although early morning moisture is essential for noble rot to flourish, rain both washes off the spores and swells the grapes. No wine in Bordeaux carries more risk at harvest time than these sweet wines.

The influence of winemaking

If the harvest is the most risky in all Bordeaux, making a sweet white wine is more difficult than making a dry white or a red wine, where residual sugar is neither required, nor allowed. The grapes, botrytized if possible, are picked at a level of natural sugar beyond which the yeasts can carry the fermentation, which stops when the wine has acquired 14–15° of alcohol. It is the unfermented sugar that renders the wine sweet, while richness and concentration comes from the state of the grapes. Short cuts to obtaining high sugar levels, either by chaptalization to add sugar, which is basically illegal, or overuse of sulphur to stop the fermentation, will be evident in the wine's lack of balance. In good years, it is essential that fermentation continues for as long as is naturally possible, which requires constant supervision, to maximize complexity in the final wine.

The use of oak

All châteaux intending to make the finest wine will ferment and age their sweet wines in oak. Such is the richness of a Sauternes that it can absorb and benefit

GREAT SWEET WHITE BORDEAUX WINES

Oz Clarke's selection

Ch. d'Yquem Sublime, complex, utterly fascinating and utterly seductive sweet wine, a compelling mouthful of golden greatness from an estate totally commited to quality.

Ch. Lafaurie-Peyraguey Wonderfully balanced, beautifully rich Sauternes, usually scented with new oak to great effect, from a property currently returning to top form.

Ch. Climens This delicate Barsac wine is in no way less ripe and sensuous than its peers, but the gorgeous sweet fruit is always perfectly balanced by acid.

Ch. Rieussec Often the richest, most unctuous of Sauternes, and scented with sandalwood.

Ch. Rayne-Vigneau A great Sauternes property once more on the rise, after a long period of decline, producing sunshine-syrupy sweetness.

Ch. Gilette Remarkable Sauternes which is only released at up to 30 years old when fully mature, with rich pineapple sweetness married with barleysugar and orange marmalade.

Ch. de Fargues This small property is owned by the Lur-Saluces family of d'Yquem and run with similar perfectionist zeal. In top years it can rival d'Yquem in richness, if not in perfume and complexity.

Ch. Doisy-Védrines This rich, intensely fruity Sauternes isn't one of the most subtle, but it is one of the most reliable and has given me more pleasure over the years than almost any other – not least because it is still affordable.

Steven Spurrier's selection

Ch. d'Yquem This legendary estate makes the world's greatest sweet wine, the result of a unique terroir allied to complete attention to detail and utmost dedication to quality.

Ch. Climens From Barsac, a wine unique by virtue of its palish colour and discretion of flavour in its youth, which deepens and develops into one of the richest, most complex wines in France.

Ch. La Tour-Blanche Second only to Ch. d'Yquem in the 1855 Classification, this château is once again in the forefront of the Sauternes AC for its harmonious, honeyed wines.

Ch. Clos Haut-Peyraguey A small Sauternes estate making elegant wines, with great purity of flavour and remarkable finesse.

Ch. Gilette A tiny Sauternes estate which specializes in offering wines only when they are fully mature, often at 20 years or more. The Crème de Tête bottlings are among the finest Sauternes.

Ch. Nairac Dedication in the vineyard (very low yields) and in the cellar (high use of new oak) have resulted in wines that put this Deuxième Cru Barsac estate firmly up with the Premiers Crus.

Ch. Rieussec The 1990s saw this wine rise to the top of the Sauternes Premiers Crus, blending honeyed richness, finesse and elegance in long-lasting harmony.

Ch. Coutet Usually a more floral, earlier-maturing wine than Climens, the only other Premier Cru in Barsac. In the best vintages Coutet also produces a tiny quantity of lusciously concentrated Crème de Tête wine (selected from the finest barrels) that carries the name of Cuvée Madame.

---

from full maturation in new oak, but so unreliable are the vintages for sweet white wines and the consequent financial problems for the producers that expensive investment such as this is normally only made by a handful of Cru Classé châteaux.

Even if a sweet wine cannot benefit from the vanillin and natural tannins from new oak, the interrelation between wood and wine is deemed an advantage. Sweet wines that are fermented and aged in tanks will not have the complexity of those fermented and aged in wood.

Top sweet white Bordeaux appellations _____
Barsac, Bordeaux-Haut-Benauge, Cadillac, Cérons, Côtes de Bordeaux St-Macaire, Loupiac, Ste-Croix-du-Mont, Sauternes.

A–Z OF BORDEAUX WINE REGIONS

BARSAC AC

Sweet wine from sandy-gravelly soil north of Sauternes, producing an average of 1.75 million bottles. Only Sémillon, Sauvigon and Muscadelle grapes may be used, to be harvested with as much ripeness and concentration as can be obtained, the grapes if possible being affected by botrytis. The wines of Barsac are fully sweet, honeyed and luscious when young, with the natural acidity giving them a lemony edge. Although very attractive young, a Barsac from a fine vintage will continue to mature over 10–20 years.

Best producers Broustet, CLIMENS, COUTET, Caillou, DOISY-DAËNE, DOISY-DUBROCA, DOISY-VÉDRINES, Gravas, Guiteronde-du-Hayot, Liot, du Mayne, de Myrat, NAIRAC, Padouen, Pernaud, Piada, de Rolland, Roumieu, Roumieu-Lacoste, St-Marc, Suau.

Best years 1999, '97, '96, '95, '90, '89, '88, '86, '83, '79, '76, '75, '67.

BORDEAUX AC, BORDEAUX SUPÉRIEUR AC

The regional appellations for red, dry white and rosé wines made with the classic Bordeaux grape varieties. Much of the wine is only of average quality, but efforts are being made, especially for the Bordeaux Supérieur wines, owing to a higher natural concentration of grape sugar. The whites and rosés should be drunk the year following the vintage, while the reds are good at 2–5 years.

Best producers The Bordeaux *négociants* have made several well-known brands from these appellations, the best being Sirius, from Sichel & Cie. While such wines are reliable, the wines that are bottled at the châteaux are generally better.

Best years 1998, '96, '95.

BORDEAUX-CÔTES DE FRANCS AC

Much progress has been made in this mainly red wine appellation which was almost unknown 10 years ago. The wines are a little more supple and elegant than Côtes de Castillon, due to the higher altitude and limestone soil, and while they are ready to drink at 4–5 years, they can be kept for a decade.

Best producers de Francs, Puygueraud, Laclaverie, Marsau, la Prade.

Best years 1998, '96, '95, '94, '90.

BORDEAUX-HAUT-BENAUGE, CADILLAC, CÔTES DE BORDEAUX ST-MACAIRE, GRAVES DE VAYRES & STE-FOY-BORDEAUX ACs

Sweet and semi-sweet wines from Sémillon, Sauvignon and Muscadelle grapes in the Entre-Deux-Mers region. These are pleasant wines, less intense than Loupiac and Ste-Croix-du-Mont, for relatively young drinking but many producers make dry white wines instead.

Best producers Fayau, du Juge, Pichon-Bellevue, Toutigeac.

Best years 1999, '96, '95, '90.

CANON-FRONSAC & FRONSAC ACs

Red wine only from an area called Le Fronsadais, whose wines used to be better known than those from nearby Pomerol. Fronsac covers the lower slopes with the smaller Canon-Fronsac appellation higher up. Merlot and Cabernet Franc are the main grapes, with Cabernet Sauvignon and Malbec used for balance and colour. The wines are generally full-bodied and firm when young, needing 4–5 years to soften out, and can mature as well as a good St-Émilion or Médoc. Fronsac is generally lighter and less concentrated than Canon-Fronsac, and is ready earlier, most wines peaking before 10 years.

Best producers (Canon-Fronsac) Barrabaque, Canon de Brem, Canon-Moueix, Cassagne-Haut-Canon, Coustolle, La Fleur-Cailleau, du Gaby, du Gazin, Grand Renouil, Haut-Ballet, Haut-Mazeris, Junayme, Mazeris, Moulin-Pey-Labrie, Pichelebre, Toumalin, Vrai-Canon-Bouché; (Fronsac) de Carles, Dalem, La Dauphine, FONTENIL, La Grave, Jeandeman, Mayne-Vieil, Moulin-Haut-Laroque, La Rivière, Rouet, La Valade, La Vieille Cure, Villars.
Best years 1999, '98, '97, '96, '95, '94, '90, '89, '88, '86, '85.

CÉRONS AC

Sweet and semi-sweet white wines from a small area within the Graves appellation. In recent years, the volume has diminished in favour of the dry style, which is sold as Cérons Sec or Graves. A classic Cérons is less luscious and ripe than either Barsac or Sauternes, but is fruity and honeyed, with a pleasant acidity, for early drinking.
Best producers d'Archambeau, de Cérons, Grand Enclos du Ch. de Cérons, Haura, Mayne-Binet.
Best years 1999, '97, '96, '95, '90, '89, '88.

CÔTES DE BOURG AC

Almost entirely red wine from 3670ha on the right bank of the Gironde, opposite Haut-Médoc. The wines have more depth, colour and character than those from neighbouring Côtes de Blaye and can be both sturdy and elegant. The lighter wines may be drunk at 2–3 years, but the better ones will keep for twice as long, or longer.
Best producers de Barbe, Brulesécaille, Falfas, de la Grave, Guerry, Guionne, Lidonne, Mendoca, Nodoz, ROC DE CAMBES, Rousset, Tayac.
Best years 1998, '96, '95, '90, '89, '88.

CÔTES DE CASTILLON AC

Red wines from east of St-Émilion with an annual production of 20 million bottles.

The better wines have a deep colour and a ripe intensity of fruit, and are superior to some of the lesser St-Émilions, yet considerably less expensive. While the Merlot-based fruit allows them to be drunk young, they are best at 5–6 years.
Best producers d'Aiguilhe, de Belcier, Brehat, Cap de Faugères, Côte Montpezat, de Clotte, Moulin-Rouge, de Pitray, de Palanquey, Lacoste, Poupille, Robin.
Best years 1998, '96, '95, '94, '90, '89, '88.

ENTRE-DEUX-MERS AC

Dry whites only from a large area between the Garonne and Dordogne rivers. Sauvignon Blanc dominates Sémillon in the blend to produce 15 million bottles of floral, fruity white wine that goes perfectly with the local shellfish. The Sauvignon-based wines should be drunk young, but those with a higher proportion of Sémillon may be kept for 2–3 years. There is a small enclave known as Entre-Deux-Mers-Haut-Benauge, whose wines may be dry or semi-sweet, the only producer of note being Ch. Toutigeac.
Best producers Bonnet, Canet, Rauzan-Despagne, Ste-Marie, Thieuley, Tour de Mirambeau, Turcaud.
Best years 1999, '98, '96.

GRAVES AC

The large Graves region extends from the southern end of the Médoc at the Jalle de Blanquefort to south of Langon, where it surrounds the sweet wine appellations of Cérons, Barsac and Sauternes. The region takes its name from the nature of the soil, gravel on a sandy base with a little clay, generally flat but with excellent drainage. The actual area is roughly the same size as the Médoc, but many vineyards near Bordeaux itself have been sold for building land and the northern part of the Graves now has its own prestige appellation of Pessac-Léognan.

The Graves appellation now covers the centre and south of the region and is the only regional one in Bordeaux to cover both red and white wines. In recent years production of red wine has overtaken white and continues to grow. While most of the finest Graves wine undoubtedly comes from Pessac-Léognan, there are some excellent non-classified wines from the communes of Portets, Podensac, Illats, Langon and St-Pierre-de-Mons, which may be considered of equivalent quality to a Médoc Cru Bourgeois.

The red wines have a higher proportion of Merlot to Cabernet Sauvignon than the Pessac-Léognan wines. They consequently show a softer fruit, which makes them very attractive young, probably at their best after 6 years. The whites, dominated by Sémillon, have shown considerable improvement in recent years, with many châteaux both fermenting and aging in wood, even though most wines are still unoaked and are at their best drunk young, to capture the fruit.

Best producers d'Archambeau, d'Ardennes, d'Arricaud, Cabannieux, de Cardaillon, Cazebonne, de CHANTEGRIVE, Chicane, Duc d'Arnauton, Ferrande, CLOS FLORIDÈNE, de Landiras, Magence, Mayne-Leveque, Millet, Rahoul, de Respide, Respide-Medeville, Roquetaillade La Grange, du Seuil, Toumilon, Tourteau-Chollet.
Best years 1998, '96, '95, '94, '90, '89, '86, '85, '82.

HAUT-MÉDOC AC

The name means 'high Médoc', in terms of quality, not altitude, and the appellation, covering 4200ha, runs from the Médoc appellation south to the outskirts of Bordeaux at Blanquefort. An average of 25 million bottles of wine, all red, is produced annually. There are 5 Crus Classés and over 100 Crus Bourgeois, producing 70% of the AC. The style of wine is similar to the Médoc's, but with extra complexity and length. Cabernet Sauvignon dominates with its firm character, blended with an increasing quantity of Merlot for softness and roundness. Of the 15 communes in the appellation, those nearer to the estuary, with the highest incidence of gravel in the soil – Blanquefort, Parempuyre, Ludon, Macau, Arcins, Lamarque, Cussac and St-Seurin-de-Cadourne – tend to produce wines that have more finesse than the more solid ones from the inland communes – Le Taillan, Le-Pian-de-Médoc, Avenson, St-Lambert, St-Saveur, Cissac and Vertheuil. The wines should be drunk at 5–12 years, but the best from good vintages can last twice as long.

Best producers d'Agassac, d'Arche, d'Arcins, Arnauld, Barreyres, Beaumont, BELGRAVE, Le Bourdieu Vertheuil, du Breuil, de Camensac, Cantemerle, Charmail, Cissac, CITRAN, Clément-Pichon, COUFRAN, Dillon, Grand-Moulin, Hanteillan, Hourtin-Ducasse, La LAGUNE, Lamarque, Lanessan, Larose-Trintaudon, Lestage-Simon, Liversan, Ludon-Pomies-Agassac, Malescasse, de Malleret, Maucamps, Peyrabon, Pierbone, Ramage-la-Batisse, de Raux, Sénéjac, SOCIANDO-MALLET, de Taillan, La TOUR-CARNET, La Tour du Haut Moulin, Touteran, Verdignan, Villegeorge.
Best years 1999, '98, '96, '95, '90, '89, '88, '86, '85, '82.

LALANDE-DE-POMEROL AC

Red wine only from an area north of Pomerol. The finest wines come from the commune of Néac. The vineyards are flat, with a gravelly soil mixed with clay or sand. Merlot is dominant, as in Pomerol, and the wines have a similar deep colour and rounded flavours, but there is a leanness that needs more time in the bottle to soften out, the better wines reaching their peak after 6–8 years.

Best producers La Croix-St-André, Garraud, Grand Ormeau, Siaurac, Tournefeuille, de Viaud.

Best years 1999, '98, '96, '95, '90, '89, '88, '85, '82.

LISTRAC-MÉDOC AC

The 670ha of vines in Listrac occupy the highest parts of the Médoc, although the slopes rise to a mere 43m, north-west of Margaux. The gravelly soil has a limestone-chalk base, which encourages a deep colour and muscular firmness in the wines, described as 'grip'. The better châteaux are increasing their proportion of new oak, which gives a suppleness to these rather lean wines, which are at their best at 4–10 years old. There are 23 Cru Bourgeois châteaux.

Best producers La Bécade, Cap-Léon-Veyrin, Clarke (Rothschild), Ducluzeau, Fonréaud, Fourcas-Dupré, Fourcas-Hosten, Gobinaud, Lestage, Saransot-Dupré.

Best years 1996, '95, '90, '89, '88.

LOUPIAC AC

Sweet wine only from an area between Cadillac and Ste-Croix-du-Mont on the right bank of the Garonne. The Sémillon, Sauvignon and Muscadelle grapes are late-picked to make a rich, honeyed, Sauternes-style wine. They are generally drunk young, but can age for a decade or more.

Best producers Clos Jean, du Cros, Loupiac-Gaudiet, Mazarin, Mémoires, du Noble, de Ricaud.

Best years 1999, '97, '96, '95, '90, '89.

MARGAUX AC

Red wine only from 5 communes – Margaux, Cantenac, Labarde, Arsac and Soussans – in the southern Médoc, covering 1350ha to produce an average of 7.6 million bottles. There is a very high gravel content to the soil, which is lighter and finer than in the northern Médoc. Margaux wines have finesse and elegance, to which can be added a brilliant deep colour, complexity of aromas and capacity for aging. There are 21 Crus Classés, more than the other Médoc communes, which represent 69% of the vineyard area, and 14 Crus Bourgeois. While the wines can be appreciated at 4–5 years, their true complexity does not show until their second decade.

Best producers d'ANGLUDET, d'Arsac, Bel-Air-Marquis d'Aligre, Boyd-Cantenac, BRANE-CANTENAC, Cantenac-Brown, Charmant, DAUZAC, DESMIRAIL, DURFORT-VIVENS, FERRIÈRE, GISCOURS,

---

BUYING *EN PRIMEUR*

The majority of the 100 top châteaux in Bordeaux sell a very high proportion of their wines *en primeur*, in the spring following the vintage. The accepted rule is that the *négociants* will buy wine in less good years, on which they may well lose money, to maintain their allocations of this or that châteaux in good years, when demand outstrips supply. The top classified wines of Bordeaux are some of the few wines in the world that are traded as commodities. The large volume of wine facilitates this trade, but it is the guarantee of quality due to château-bottling that provides the confidence the market needs. The last 20 years have shown that fine wine can be a good investment. Only wines from good years with the potential for improvement over time are suitable for investment and in general the better the year and the longer the life of the wine, the more it will increase in value. A disadvantage of buying *en primeur* is that an economy that fuels demand can easily fall into recession. However good the vintage, wine is not recession-proof.

La Gurgue, d'ISSAN, KIRWAN, LABÉGORCE, LABÉGORCE-ZÉDÉ, LASCOMBES, MALÉSCOT-ST-EXUPÉRY, MARGAUX, Marquis d'Alesme-Becker, MARQUIS DE TERME, Martinens, MONBRISON, Montbrun, PALMER, Paveil de Luze, Pontac-Lynch, Pouget, PRIEURÉ-LICHINE, RAUZAN-GASSIES, RAUZAN-SÉGLA, SIRAN, Tayac, du TERTRE, La Tour de Mons.

Best years 1999, '98, '96, '95, '94, '90, '89, '88, '86, '85, '83, '82.

MÉDOC AC

From the northern part of the Médoc peninsula where the soils are gravel and clayey-limestone, a Médoc wine should have a fine ruby colour, a bouquet of red fruits, often with an overlay of oak and a good concentration of fruit on the palate. When young it can be hard, but with a clean, refreshing finish. Best drunk at 3–10 years, but can age further. There are no Crus Classés but over 100 Cru Bourgeois châteaux.

Best producers Bellerive, Bellevue, Blaignan, Le Boscq, Bournac, La Cardonne, du Castéra, Greysac, Haut-Canteloup, Haut-Rive, Laujac, Lavallière, Loudenne, du Monthil, Les Ormes-Sorbet, Patache d'Aux, POTENSAC, Rollan de By, St-Bonnet, Sestignan, Sigognac, La Tour de By, La Tour-Haut-Caussan, La Tour St-Bonnet, Vieux-Ch-Landon.

Best years 1999, '98, '96, '95, '90, '89, '88, '86, '85, '82.

MOULIS-EN-MÉDOC AC

With 600ha of vines, Moulis is the smallest of the Haut-Médoc communes, lying set back from the estuary between Margaux and St-Julien. Although the wines are often deemed similar to their neighbour Listrac, they possess a velvety texture and suppleness of fruit that Listrac lacks. There are 16 Crus Bourgeois in Moulis, the best of which are equal in quality to the Crus Classés. Moulis can be drunk at 3–4 years but can last 12–15 years longer in the best vintages.

Best producers Bel-Air Lagrave, Biston-Brillette, Branas-Grand-Poujeaux, Brillette, CHASSE-SPLEEN, Duplessis-Fabre, Dutruch-Grand-Poujeaux, Gressier-Grand-Poujeaux, MAUCAILLOU, Mauvezin, Moulin-à-Vent, POUJEAUX.

Best years 1999, '98, '96, '95, '90, '89, '88, '86, '85, '83.

PAUILLAC AC

With 1200ha of vines on undulating gravel soil, Pauillac is the heartland of Cabernet Sauvignon and is unique in possessing 3 Premiers Crus Classés – LATOUR, LAFITE-ROTHSCHILD and MOUTON-ROTHSCHILD – as well as 15 other Crus Classés to represent a total of 84% of the commune. There are 10 Crus Bourgeois. Pauillac is considered to be the most classic Médoc wine, generally austere when young, but with an intense blackcurrant fruit flavour that can take 6–10 years to develop, and can last 20–30 years in the best vintages. With very few exceptions, these wines are dominated by the Cabernet Sauvignon grape variety.

Best producers d'ARMAILHAC, BATAILLEY, La Bécasse, CLERC-MILON, La Couronne, CROIZET-BAGES, DUHART-MILON, La Fleur-Milon, FONBADET, GRAND-PUY-DUCASSE, GRAND-PUY-LACOSTE, HAUT-BAGES-LIBÉRAL, HAUT-BATAILLEY, LAFITE-ROTHSCHILD, LATOUR, LYNCH-BAGES, Lynch-Moussas, MOUTON-ROTHSCHILD, Pedesclaux, PIBRAN, PICHON-LONGUEVILLE BARON DE LONGUEVILLE, PICHON-LONGUEVILLE COMTESSE-DE-LALANDE, PONTET-CANET, La Tour Pibran.

Best years 1999, '98, '96, '95, '94, '90, '89, '88, '86, '85, '83, '82, '79, '78.

PESSAC-LÉOGNAN AC

The appellation was created in 1987 to recognize the historical superiority of the northern Graves wines from Pessac, Léognan and Martillac and covers 910ha. The red wines have much in common with the finer Médocs, possessing a more floral aroma to add charm to their natural intensity of fruit. They may be drunk even 3 years after the vintage, but mostly reach their peak after a decade; the finest wines last twice as long.

The whites are Bordeaux's finest dry white wines, and in recent years have increased in depth of flavour, owing partly to fermentation in small oak barrels. The wines are floral and fruity, often with a sappy herbaceousness and a touch of vanilla from the oak. Although pleasant to drink as soon as they are bottled, Sémillon has great aging potential, and the wines are consequently very long lived.

The Crus Classés (see page 27) are all in the northern part of the appellation. The most prestigious wines, HAUT-BRION, La MISSION-HAUT-BRION and PAPE-CLÉMENT, from the communes of Pessac and Talence, actually have their vineyards surrounded by the suburbs of Bordeaux and consequently enjoy a warmer climate. The commune of Léognan contains 6 of the 14 Crus Classés.

Best producers BOUSCAUT, Brown, CARBONNIEUX, Les Carmes-Haut-Brion, Dom. de CHEVALIER, Couhins, COUHINS-LURTON, de Cruzeau, Ferran, de FIEUZAL, de France, La Garde, HAUT-BAILLY, Haut-Bergey, HAUT-BRION, Haut-Gardère, LARRIVET-HAUT-BRION, LATOUR-MARTILLAC, LAVILLE-HAUT-BRION, La LOUVIÈRE, MALARTIC-LAGRAVIÈRE, La MISSION-HAUT-BRION, OLIVIER, PAPE-CLÉMENT, Pique-Caillou, de Rochemorin, Le Sartre, SMITH-HAUT-LAFITTE, La TOUR-HAUT-BRION, La Tour-Léognan.

Best years 1998, '96, '95, '94, '90, '89, '88, '86, '85, '83, '82, '79, '70.

POMEROL AC

Pomerol is the smallest of Bordeaux's fine red wine appellations with only 783ha of vines and produces an average of 5 million bottles of red wine a year. It is also the most fragmented, with 185 growers, one-third of whom own less than 1ha of vines. The soil is perfect for vines; a flinty, clayey gravel mixed with sand on a hard clay and iron base, the iron giving Pomerol its particular richness. The dominant grape is Merlot, often planted to 100%, with a little Cabernet Franc.

A good Pomerol will have a deep, velvety colour and robust fruit with a softness and finesse that allows it to be drunk at 2–3 years, but also a natural concentration that will enable the better wines to continue maturing for a further decade and more.

There is no classification in Pomerol, but Pétrus is universally recognized as an honorary Premier Grand Cru Classé A from neighbouring St-Émilion, and there are at least a dozen châteaux on a par with the Premiers Grands Crus Classés B.

Best producers Beauregard, de Boisset, Le BON PASTEUR, Bonalgue, Certan-Giraud, CERTAN-DE-MAY, CLINET, Clos du Clocher, Clos l'Église, Clos René, La CONSEILLANTE, La Croix, La Croix du Casse, La CROIX-DE-GAY, L'ÉGLISE-CLINET, L'Enclos, L'ÉVANGILE, Feytit-Clinet, La FLEUR-PÉTRUS, Le Gay, GAZIN, La Grave-Trignant, Guillot Clauzel, Haut-Tropchaud, LAFLEUR, Lafleur-Gazin, Lagrange, LATOUR-À-POMEROL, Moulinet, NENIN, PETIT-VILLAGE, PÉTRUS, Le PIN, Plince, La POINTE, Rouget, de Sales,

TROTANOY, VIEUX-CH.-CERTAN, Vieux-Maillet, La Violette, Vray-Croix-de-Gay. **Best years** 1999, '98, '96, '95, '90, '89, '88, '86, '85, '82, '79, '64.

PREMIÈRES CÔTES DE BLAYE AC

Mostly red wine from 4000ha on the right bank of the Gironde, opposite the northern Médoc. The Merlot grape, dominant to about 70%, produces wines with a good colour and straightforward fruit, while the limestone soil lends a touch of elegance. Drink within 5 years. **Best producers** Bourdieu, Charron, Crusquet-la-Lagarche, l'Escadre, Jonqueyres, Maine-Gazin, Peyreyre, Segonzac, Sociondo. **Best years** 1998, '96, '95, '90, '89.

PREMIÈRES CÔTES DE BORDEAUX AC

For many years the appellation, covering 3700ha along the right bank of the Garonne from the outskirts of Bordeaux south to Cadillac, was best known for its semi-sweet wines but in recent years much progress has been made with the juicy reds. Dry whites made here use the Bordeaux appellation. Merlot is the main red grape and Sémillon the white. The red wines are rounded and generously fruity, reaching their peak at around 5–6 years. **Best producers** Brethous, Cayla, de Chelivette, de la Closière, Fayau, Lagarosse, Lézongars, de la Meulière, Nenine, du Peyrat, Plaisance, Reynon, Suau. **Best years** 1998, '96, '95, '90, '89, '88.

ST-ÉMILION & ST-ÉMILION GRAND CRU ACs

St-Émilion is by far the largest fine wine area in Bordeaux, with almost 5500ha under vine, not counting the 3800ha of 'satellite' St-Émilion ACs to the north-east. The wines are red only. The main grape is Merlot, with some Cabernet Franc and a little Cabernet Sauvignon and Malbec, known locally as Pressac. Merlot gives the wine a richness and suppleness, in contrast to the rather firm intensity of the Médoc Cabernet Sauvignon-based wines. They can be drunk at 3–4 years, although the better wines will last and improve over 2 decades. St-Émilion is the basic generic AC and the best producers are found in the more tightly controlled St-Émilion Grand Cru AC category.

The 'Graves' area of sandy, gravelly soil adjacent to Pomerol gives wines with a pronounced bouquet and ripe, almost sweet fruit; and the 'Côtes', undulating vineyards with a clayey soil on a limestone base, produces wines that are rather firmer, close-knit and mature more slowly. With production nearing 40 million bottles a year, there tends to be great variation in quality.

Best producers Nowadays the top wines can come not just from the classified châteaux (see page 27) but also from the St-Émilion Grand Cru AC: ANGÉLUS, L'Arrosée, AUSONE, BEAUSÉJOUR, BEAU-SÉJOUR-BÉCOT, BELAIR, Bellefont-Belcier, BERLIQUET, CANON, CANON-LA-GAFFELIÈRE, Carteau-Côtes-Daugay, CHEVAL-BLANC, CLOS FOURTET, CLOS DE L'ORATOIRE, Cormeil-Figeac, La Couspaude, Destieux, LA DOMINIQUE, FAUGÈRES, Ferrand-Lartigue, FIGEAC, Fleur-Cardinale, La Fleur de Jaugue, La Fleur-Pourret, Fonroque, FRANC-MAYNE, LA GAFFELIÈRE, La Gomerie, Grand Corbin, GRAND-MAYNE, Haut-Segottes, LARCIS-DUCASSE, LARMANDE, Laroque, MAGDELAINE, Manuel, MONBOUSQUET, La Mondotte, Montlabert, Moulin St-Georges, PAVIE, PAVIE-DECESSE, PAVIE-MACQUIN, Peyraud, Simard, SOUTARD, LE TERTRE-RÔTEBOEUF, Teyssier, TROPLONG-MONDOT, TROTTEVIEILLE, DE VALANDRAUD, Vieux Sarpe.

Best years 1998, '96, '95, '90, '89, '88, '86, '85, '82, '79, '78, '70.

ST-ÉMILION SATELLITE ACs

Four communes north of St-Émilion, Lussac, Montagne, Puisseguin and St-Georges, have the right to the appellation, provided it is preceded by the name of the individual village. In general, these wines tend to be less concentrated than a typical St-Émilion, and are ready to drink at 2–3 years old, although the better wines are certainly worthy of the St-Émilion AC.

Best producers (Lussac) Bel-Air, Haut-Milon, de Lussac, Lyonnat, Mayne-Blanc; (Montagne) Calon, Corbin, Faizeau, Montaiguillon, Plaisance, Roudier, Vieux Ch. St-André; (Puisseguin) Bel-Air, Branda, Guibeau, Roc de Boissac; (St-Georges) Calon, La Croix-St-Georges, St-Georges, Tour-du-Pas-St-Georges.

Best years 1998, '96, '95, '90, '89.

ST-ESTÈPHE AC

The largest of the Médoc communal appellations, St-Estèphe has 5 Crus Classés, representing 20% of the commune, with 37 Crus Bourgeois. There is more sand and clay in the soil than in neighbouring Pauillac, and the wines are often more sturdy than those from the southern Médoc, always with a robust colour and fine aging potential, although they can be drunk at 4–5 years.

Best producers Beau-Site, CALON-SÉGUR, Capbern-Gasqueton, Chambert-Marbuzet, COS D'ESTOURNEL, COS-LABORY, Le Crock, HAUT-BEAUSÉJOUR, HAUT-MARBUZET, Houissant, Laffitte-Carcasset, LAFON-ROCHET, Lavillotte, Lilian Ladouys, MacCarthy, MARBUZET, Meyney, MONTROSE, Les Ormes de Pez, de PEZ, PHÉLAN-SÉGUR, Pomys, Tronquoy-Lalande.

Best years 1999, '98, '96, '95, '90, '89, '88, '86, '85, '83, '82, '78, '75.

ST-JULIEN AC

Although St-Julien possesses only 11 Crus Classés, they are all important estates, and represent 80% of the 910ha under vine. There are 6 Crus Bourgeois. The soil is the same light gravel as in Margaux, but deeper and with more clay, and the wines are correspondingly richer. They have been described as 'archetypal claret', combining a deep, velvety colour, a rich cedary, berry fruit bouquet and an intense, lingering flavour. Owing to the general ripeness of fruit, they can be approached at 4–5 years old, but the depth of flavour and fine tannins allow them to develop slowly over 10–20 years.

Best producers BEYCHEVELLE, BRANAIRE, La Bridane, DUCRU-BEAUCAILLOU, GLORIA, GRUAUD-LAROSE, Hortevie, LAGRANGE, Lalande-Borie, LANGOA-BARTON, LÉOVILLE-BARTON, LÉOVILLE-LAS-CASES, LÉOVILLE-POYFERRÉ, Moulin de la Rose, ST-PIERRE, TALBOT, Terrey-Gros-Cailloux.

Best years 1999, '98, '96, '95, '90, '89, '88, '86, '85, '83, '82, '79, '78.

STE-CROIX-DU-MONT AC

Sweet white wine only from 465ha of hillside vineyards on the right bank of the Garonne river, opposite Sauternes. The grape yields are higher than in Sauternes, producing about 2 million bottles a year, yet these wines can still acquire something of the same honeyed, rich unctuous style. They may be drunk young, but the better ones can last 20 years. As Sauternes has become justifiably more expensive, more attention is being paid to this appellation.

Best producers Laurette, LOUBENS, Lousteau-Vieil, La Rame, de Tastes.

Best years 1999, '97, '96, '95, '90, '89, '86.

SAUTERNES AC

Fully sweet white wine from 1583ha of vines from north of Barsac to Langon. The grapes are harvested when the sugar concentration is at its maximum, if possible affected by noble rot. The appellation covers 5 communes: Barsac (which is normally sold under its own appellation, or Barsac-Sauternes, but may legally also be sold under the Sauternes appellation), Bommes, Fargues, Preignac and Sauternes. These incredibly luscious, intense, honeyed, elegant wines are known mostly through their Crus Classés. Even in good years, production is very low, with each hectare yielding only one-third as much as in the Médoc or the Graves. Sauternes may be drunk young for the ripe fruit, reminiscent of peaches and apricots, but the better vintages should be kept for a decade, and the finest wines will mature for over half a century or more.

Best producers d'Arche, d'Arche-Pugneau, BASTOR-LAMONTAGNE, de la Chartreuse, CLOS HAUT-PEYRAGUEY, DE FARGUES, FILHOT, GILETTE, GUIRAUD, Les Justices, LAFAURIE-PEYRAGUEY, Lamothe, LAMOTHE-GUIGNARD, de MALLE, RABAUD-PROMIS, RAYMOND-LAFON, RAYNE-VIGNEAU, RIEUSSEC, Romer du Hayot, SIGALAS-RABAUD, SUDUIRAUT, La TOUR-BLANCHE, d'YQUEM.

Best years 1999, '97, '96, '95, '90, '89, '88, '86, '85, '83, '79, '78, '76, '70, '67.

A–Z OF BORDEAUX CHÂTEAUX

The appellation, classification – Cru Classé (CC), Grand Cru Classé (GCC) or Cru Bourgeois (CB) – and land under vines in hectares (ha) follow the château name.

CH. ANGÉLUS★★★ ? St-Émilion 1er GCC B, 23.4ha   05 57 24 71 39/05 57 24 68 56
A classy property with vines facing due south on some of the best slopes of St-Émilion. Low yields, late picking and great attention to detail in the cellars led to promotion for this château to Premier Grand Cru Classé in 1996, in recognition of the intensity and complexity of fruit the wine has shown in the last decade. Despite the soft tannins, the wine should be aged for at least 5 years to show its complexity.
Best years 1998, '97, '96, '95, '94, '93, '90, '89, '88, '86, '85

CH. D'ANGLUDET★★ ? Margaux CB, 34ha   05 57 88 71 41/05 57 88 72 52
In the commune of Cantenac, with vines surrounded by those of the Crus Classés, the Sichel family château produces well-structured wines with depth, elegance and breed.
Best years 1999, '98, '96, '95, '94, '93, '90, '89, '88, '86, '85, '83, '82

CH. D'ARMAILHAC★★ ? Pauillac 5ème CC, 50ha   05 56 73 20 20/05 56 73 20 44
This estate, under the same ownership as MOUTON-ROTHSCHILD, improved considerably in the 1990s to become one of the reliable Pauillac Cinquième Crus Classés. The wine was called Mouton-Baronne-Philippe prior to 1989.
Best years 1999, '98, '96, '95, '90, '89, '86, '85, '82

CH. AUSONE★★★ ? St-Émilion 1er GCC A, 7ha   05 57 24 68 88/05 57 74 47 39
One of the very finest wines of Bordeaux from a property named after the Roman poet Ausonius and located on the best slopes above the town of St-Émilion. There is no greater wine in St-Émilion (with the arguable exception of Ch. CHEVAL-BLANC) and none has more elegance – combining delicacy and power, taking time to mature, yet also proving the longest-lived wine of the appellation. Owner Alain Vauthier has more

than maintained standards since 1996 and with the celebrated skills of enologist Michel Rolland now at his disposal, this wine is even richer than before.
Best years 1999, '98, '96, '95, '94, '93, '90, '89, '88, '86, '85, '83, '82, '81, '79, '78

CH. BASTOR-LAMONTAGNE★ ♥ Sauternes, 58ha   05 56 63 27 66/05 56 76 87 03
A large property (for Sauternes) with all the vines in a single block around the château, producing floral, honey-sweet wines well up to the level of many Crus Classés.
Best years 1999, '98, '96, '95, '94, '90, '89, '88, '86, '85, '83, '82

CH. BATAILLEY★★ ♥ Pauillac 5ème CC, 55ha   05 56 59 01 13/05 57 87 60 30
The larger of the two Batailley châteaux, owned by the the Castéja family, is well-known for its richly coloured, early-maturing supple Pauillacs which last well for up to 15 years. With more body than finesse, the wine is nonetheless very reliable.
Best years 1999, '98, '96, '95, '94, '90, '89, '88, '86, '85, '83, '82

CH. BEAUSÉJOUR★★ ♥ St-Émilion 1er GCC B, 7ha   05 57 24 71 61/05 57 74 48 40
The smaller of the two Beau-Séjour châteaux occupies a superb site on the edge of the town. The wines have great elegance and breed and can age beautifully for 10 years.
Best years 1998, '96, '95, '94, '90, '89, '88, '86, '85

CH. BEAU-SÉJOUR-BÉCOT★★ ♥   05 57 74 46 87/05 57 24 66 88
St-Émilion 1er GCC B, 16.5ha
After its demotion from the Premiers Grands Crus Classés in 1985, this château rightly regained its position in 1996. The wine is deep-coloured with a ripe, rounded fruit style and robust tannins, suitable for a decade in the cellars.
Best years 1999, '98, '96, '95, '94, '90, '89, '88, '86, '85

CH. BELAIR★★ ♥ St-Émilion 1er GCC B, 12ha   05 57 24 70 94/05 57 24 67 11
This vineyard, on the limestone plateau on the edge of the town, produces wines of great elegance and complexity. Until the mid-1980s they lacked a little concentration, but since 1986 have produced some of the best wines in the appellation, soft yet stylish and long. The winemaker here is the much-respected Pascal Delbeck.
Best years 1999, '98, '96, '95, '94, '90, '89, '88, '86, '85, '83, '82

CH. BELGRAVE★ ♥ Haut-Médoc 5ème CC, 54ha   05 56 35 53 00/05 56 35·53 29
Since coming under the management of the Bordeaux firm Dourthe, this deep-coloured, rich wine has undergone a renaissance. It now deserves its classification.
Best years 1999, '98, '96, '95, '94, '93, '90, '89, '88

CH. BERLIQUET★★ ♥ St-Émilion GCC, 9ha   05 57 24 70 48/05 57 24·70 24
This old-established property, adjacent to Ch. Magdelaine, has seen a massive surge in quality since the arrival, in 1996, of Patrick Valette as manager. The wine is now certainly of Grand Cru quality.
Best years 1999, '98, '97, '96

CH. BEYCHEVELLE★★ ♥ St-Julien 4ème CC, 90ha   05 56 73 20 70/05 56 73 20 71
A large and famous property making classic St-Julien with deep colour and fresh, ripe flavours. After a disappointing 1990, Beychevelle has been more reliable of late. Age for 10 years or more to discover its full depth and complexity, though drinkable young.
Best years 1999, '98, '96, '95, '93, '89, '86, '85

CH. LE BON PASTEUR★★ ♥ Pomerol, 7ha   05 57 51 10 94/05 57 25 05 54
This estate is owned by Michel and Dany Rolland, the celebrated wine consultants

based in Pomerol and produces rich, dark-coloured wines with a harmonious use of new oak. Small production means high prices, but the wine is certainly worth that extra expense. Always approachable young, it matures well for 15 years. The Rollands also own Ch. FONTENIL, an excellent Fronsac property.

Best years 1999, '98, '96, '95, '94, '93, '90, '89, '88, '86, '85, '83, '82

CH. BOUSCAUT★ ❢♀ Pessac-Léognan CC, 39ha ❢, 8ha ♀   05 57 83 10 16/05 57 83 10 17

Purchased by Lucien Lurton (of BRANE-CANTENAC and DURFORT-VIVENS) in 1978, quality has been improving for both red and white wines; new investment under the guidance of his daughter Sophie has helped this estate realize its full potential.

Best years ❢1999, '98, '96, '95, '94, '90, '89, '86; ♀1999, '98, '97, '96

CH. BRANAIRE★★ ❢ St-Julien 4ème CC, 50ha   05 56 59 25 86/05 56 59 16 26

The style of wine here has been elegant but a little light in the past (despite the use of a high proportion of Cabernet Sauvignon in the wine) but became fatter and firmer during the 1990s, thanks to the new owners' investment in quality.

Best years 1999, '98, '97, '96, '95, '90, '89, '88, '86, '85, '83, '82

CH. BRANE-CANTENAC★★ ❢ Margaux 2ème CC, 85ha   05 57 88 83 33/05 57 88 72 51

One of the largest Médoc estates where superbly sited vineyards on gravelly, chalk-based soil produce an elegant wine that has improved during the last decade and is beginning to earn its classification. Now owned by Henri Lurton.

Best years 1999, '98, '97, '96, '95, '90, '89, '88, '86

CH. CALON-SÉGUR★ ❢ St-Estèphe 3ème CC, 94ha   05 56 59 30 08/05 56 59 71 51

A property with an illustrious past. The vintages of the 1970s and '80s have been irregular in quality, too often lacking ripeness and aging prematurely, but there have been signs of improvement since the mid-1990s. Top quality wines since 1997.

Best years 1999, '98, '97, '96, '95, '90, '89, '86, '82

CH. CANON★★ ❢ St-Émilion, 1er GCC B, 18ha   05 57 55 23 45/05 57 24 68 00

These wines are famous for tannic power, finesse and great aging potential. The early 1990s saw a loss in quality, which is in the process of being restored following Canon's purchase by the Wertheimer family, owners of the French fashion and perfume company, Chanel, in 1996.

Best years 1998, '96, '95, '90, '89, '88, '86, '85, '83, '82, '79, '78, '70, '66, '64, '62, '61

CH. CANON-LA-GAFFELIÈRE★★ ❢   05 57 24 71 33/05 57 24 67 95

St-Émilion GCC, 19.5ha

Purchased by the de Neipperg family in 1971, the estate did not begin to realize its true potential until Stéphan de Neipperg took over in the late 1980s. The wine is very deep-coloured and marvellously rich in extract and ripe firm fruit. See also CLOS DE L'ORATOIRE.

Best years 1999, '98, '96, '95, '93, '90, '89, '88, '85

CH. CARBONNIEUX★★ ❢♀   05 57 96 56 20/05 57 96 59 19

Pessac-Léognan CC, 45ha ❢ 42ha ♀

An impressive property, one of the oldest in the region, where vinification has greatly improved in the last decade under the guidance of the Perrin family. The white wines display purity and finesse and the reds have an appealing charm.

Best years ❢1998, '97, '96, '95, '90, '89, '88, '86; ♀1999, '98, '96, '95, '94, '90, '89, '88

CH. CERTAN-DE-MAY★★ ❢ Pomerol, 5ha   05 57 51 41 53/05 57 51 88 51
Originally part of VIEUX-CH.-CERTAN, this château is located close to CHEVAL-
BLANC and PÉTRUS on clayey-gravel soil and produces powerful but elegant wines.
Best years 1998, '97, '95, '90, '89, '88, '86, '85, '82, '79, '78

CH. DE CHANTEGRIVE★ ❢♀ Graves, 38.5ha ❢, 44ha ♀   05 56 27 17 38/05 56 27 29 42
A large property built up by the Leveque family over the past 20 years, producing fine,
supple, fruity wines. There is also a special blend of white Graves, vinified and aged in
barrel, called Cuvée Caroline.
Best years ❢1998, '96, '95, '90, '89, '88, '86; ♀1999, '98, '96, '95

CH. CHASSE-SPLEEN★★ ❢ Moulis CB, 80ha   05 56 58 02 37/05 56 58 05 70
A superb wine, deserving Cru Classé status, with a deep colour and pure Médoc
bouquet, enhanced by more than a touch of new oak, which can be enjoyed young, but
ages beautifully. There is also a tiny amount of a dry, barrel-fermented white.
Best years 1999, '98, '96, '95, '93, '90, '89, '88, '86, '83, '82

CH. CHEVAL-BLANC★★★ ❢   05 57 55 55 55/05 57 55 55 50
St-Émilion, 1er GCC A, 35ha
The leading château in St-Émilion for the stunning richness of its wines and for
exceptional and reliable quality. The high (around 60%) proportion of Cabernet Franc
from vines planted on sandy, gravelly soil opposite Pomerol lends this wine an
extraordinary sweetness of fruit and aromatic complexity, intense in flavour with rich,
ripe tannins. Cheval-Blanc is attractive in its youth, growing more splendid with age.
Best years 1999, '98, '97, '96, '95, '94, '93, '90, '89, '88, '85, '83, '82, '81, '75, '70, '66,
'64, '61, '52, '49

DOM. DE CHEVALIER★★ ❢ ★★★ ♀   05 56 64 16 16/05 56 64 18 18
Pessac-Léognan CC, 30ha ❢ 4.5ha ♀
This superb property produces the most elegant wines in the entire Graves. Often
overlooked when young, since the wines are neither overly fruity nor over-oaked, both
the white (mainly Sauvignon Blanc and both fermented and aged in oak barrels) and
the red possess incomparable balance, and continue to grow in finesse over many years.
The Bernard family, owners since 1983, have invested heavily to maintain the fine
reputation under the previous owner, Claude Ricard.
Best years ❢1999, '98, '96, '95, '94, '90, '89, '88, '85, '83, '81, '78, '70, '66, '53, '29;
♀1999, '98, '97, '96, '95, '90, '89, '88, '86, '85, '83, '82, '81

CH. CITRAN★ ❢ Haut-Médoc CB, 90ha   05 56 58 21 01/05 56 58 12 19
Japanese owners invested heavily in the vineyards, winery and cellars during the 1980s
to help produce excellent wine here. Current proprietors are the Merlaut family (of the
Taillan group) who have maintained standards and even improved this rich, plump and
attractive wine.
Best years 1999, '98, '96, '95, '90, '89, '88

CH. CLERC-MILON★★ ❢ Pauillac 5ème CC, 30ha   05 56 73 20 20/05 56 73 20 44
Clerc-Milon is part of the MOUTON-ROTHSCHILD stable. The wine has more depth
and concentration than d'ARMAILHAC, also owned by Mouton-Rothschild, owing to a
fortunate terroir on the outskirts of the town of Pauillac and increased plantings of
Cabernet Sauvignon. This is now one of Pauillac's top Cinquième Crus Classés.
Best years 1999, '98, '96, '95, '90, '89, '88, '86, '85, '83, '82

CH. CLIMENS★★★ ♀ Barsac 1er CC, 29ha   05 56 27 15 33/05 56 27 21 04

Exceptional terroir here yields a wine that, after many years' aging, is often held to be second in the region only to d'YQUEM. Pale and discreetly sweet when young, concentration and richness develop with age, and the wine continues to gain in complexity for decades after most other Sauternes have begun to fail.

Best years 1999, '98, '97, '96, '95, '90, '89, '88, '86, '83, '76, '75, '71, '62, '55

CH. CLINET★★ ❢ Pomerol, 9ha   05 56 68 55 88/05 56 30 11 45

One of the most spectacularly successful Pomerol estates during the last decade, making wine from exceptionally ripe grapes which is then left for a long maceration period to give the most rich and voluptuous of wines.

Best years 1999, '98, '97, '96, '95, '93, '90, '89, '88, '86, '85

CLOS FLORIDÈNE★★(♀only) ❢♀ Graves, 5ha❢, 12ha♀   05 56 62 96 51/05 56 62 14 89

Owned by the brilliant enologist Denis Dubourdieu, this property is renowned for the exceptional quality of its dry Sémillon-based white wine, equal to many Pessac-Léognan Crus Classés and best drunk at 4–5 years. The red wine is full and fruity.

Best years ❢1999, '98, '97, '96, '95, '94, '90; ♀1999, '98, '97, '96, '95

CLOS FOURTET★★ ❢ St-Émilion 1er GCC B, 20ha   05 57 24 70 90/05 57 74 46 52

On the limestone plateau at the edge of the town of St-Émilion, this estate produces a traditional, deep-coloured wine with dense fruit, firm in its youth, but also aging superbly. The cellars, running under the whole vineyard, are very impressive.

Best years 1998, '97, '96, '95, '94, '90, '89, '85, '82

CH. CLOS HAUT-PEYRAGUEY★★ ♀   05 56 76 61 53/05 56 76 69 65
Sauternes 1er CC, 15ha

An impeccable property, managed with love and attention by Jacques Pauly. In recent years, the wines have added concentration and richness to their honeyed purity of flavour, to emerge as one of the most elegant of the Premiers Crus Classés.

Best years 1999, '98, '97, '96, '95, '91, '90, '89, '88, '86, '85, '83, '75

CLOS DE L'ORATOIRE★★ ❢ St-Émilion GCC, 10ha   05 57 24 71 33/05 57 24 67 95

Since this property was purchased by Stéphan de Neipperg of CANON-LA-GAFFELIÈRE, the wines have taken on more richness and depth. There is also a tiny amount of a superbly extracted, complex wine called La Mondotte.

Best years 1999, '98, '97, '96, '95, '90, '89, '88

CH. LA CONSEILLANTE★★ ❢ Pomerol, 12ha   05 57 51 12 12/05 57 51 42 39

This excellent estate produces deep-coloured, smooth wines with great personality and elegance, among the longest lived in Pomerol. Age for a minimum of 5–8 years.

Best years 1999, '98, '96, '95, '94, '90, '89, '88, '86, '85, '83, '82, '81

CH. COS D'ESTOURNEL★★★ ❢   05 56 73 15 55/05 56 59 72 59
St-Estèphe 2ème CC, 65ha

With vines overlooking those of LAFITE-ROTHSCHILD, and its magnificent *chai*, Cos d'Estournel is the most prestigious property in St-Estèphe. Former owners, the Prats family, spared no expense to produce the most intensely flavoured, yet most elegant St-Estèphe. The high proportion of Merlot gives a roundness that is complemented by the ripeness of the Cabernet Sauvignon. Purchased in 1998 by the Taillan group.

Best years 1999, '98, '97, '96, '95, '94, '93, '90, '89, '88, '86, '85, '82, '79, '78, '76, '70

CH. COS LABORY★ ❢ St-Estèphe 5ème CC, 18ha   05 56 59 30 22/05 56 59 73 52
With vineyards adjacent to COS D'ESTOURNEL, this stylish, plummily fruity wine has been steadily improving. It matures relatively quickly but can last well.
Best years 1999, '98, '96, '95, '90, '89, '88, '86, '82

CH. COUFRAN★ ❢ Haut-Médoc CB, 75ha   05 56 59 31 02/05 56 81 32 35
Thanks to its high proportion of Merlot (up to 85%), Coufran has been called 'the Pomerol of the Médoc'. The wines are rich, densely fruity and of very reliable quality.
Best years 1999, '98, '97, '96, '95, '90, '89, '88, '86, '85

CH. COUHINS-LURTON★★ ♀   05 57 25 58 58/05 57 74 98 59
Pessac-Léognan CC, 5.5ha
André Lurton owns several other estates in this appellation including La LOUVIÈRE; here at Couhins-Lurton he makes a superbly rich and oaky, almost exotic, white from 100% Sauvignon, which is delicious young, becoming more complex with age.
Best years 1999, '98, '96, '95, '94, '90, '89, '88, '86, '85

CH. COUTET★★★ ♀ Barsac 1er CC, 38.5ha   05 56 27 15 46/05 56 27 02 20
Second only to CLIMENS in reputation, Coutet is once again producing top-quality wines with a honeyed sweetness and the typical Barsac lemony acidity. When the year is not appropriate for Sauternes, a proportion of the crop is made into a dry white wine, Le Blanc Sec de Ch. Coutet, sold as Graves. In great years a Crème de Tête of extraordinary richness is made in minuscule quantities under the name Cuvée Madame.
Best years 1999, '98, '97, '96, '95, '90, '89, '88, '86, '83, '81, '76, '75, '71, '59

CH. LA CROIX-DE-GAY★★ ❢ Pomerol, 12ha   05 57 51 19 05/05 57 74 15 62
A ripe, supple Pomerol that has been very successful in recent years. Alain Raynaud has taken over from his father and continues to produce a prestige cuvée, La Fleur-de-Gay.
Best years 1999, '98, '96, '95, '90, '89, '88, '85 '82

CH. CROIZET-BAGES★ ❢ Pauillac 5ème CC, 29ha   05 56 59 01 62/05 56 59 23 39
For decades one of the worst under performers of the Pauillac Crus Classés, the arrival of Jean-Louis Camp as manager has revitalized this well-located château, lying between LYNCH-BAGES and GRAND-PUY-LACOSTE.
Best years 1999, '98, '97

CH. DAUZAC★ ❢ Margaux 5ème CC, 40ha   05 57 88 32 10/05 57 88 96 00
One of the most southerly Margaux châteaux, in the commune of Labarde, Dauzac has progressed significantly since the arrival of André Lurton as manager in 1992, and is now among the successful wines of the appellation.
Best years 1999, '98, '97, '96, '95, '90

CH. DESMIRAIL★ ❢ Margaux 3ème CC, 30ha   05 57 88 34 33/05 57 88 72 51
This property has been rebuilt by Lucien Lurton (of BRANE-CANTENAC, CLIMENS and DURFORT-VIVENS fame) and is now beginning to make good wine that aims for finesse rather than weight, despite the very high (80%) proportion of Cabernet.
Best years 1999, '98, '96, '90, '89, '88, '86, '85, '83, '82

CH. DOISY-DAËNE★★ ♀ Barsac 2ème CC, 15ha   05 56 27 15 84/05 56 27 18 99
An elegant Barsac, combining vivacity and purity with honeyed sweetness, which can be appreciated after relatively brief aging. There is also an excellent dry white Bordeaux.
Best years Sweet 1999, '97, '96, '95, '94, '90, '89, '88, '86, '83; **Dry** 1999, '96, '95

CH. DOISY-DUBROCA★ ♀ Barsac 2ème CC, 3.3ha   05 56 27 15 33/05 56 27 21 04

This tiny property is owned by Lucien Lurton who also owns the more famous CLIMENS. Doisy-Dubroca produces fine quality wines with honey-sweet flavour.
Best years 1999, '97, '96, '95, '94, '90, '89, '88

CH. DOISY-VÉDRINES★★ ♀ Barsac 2ème CC, 27ha   05 56 27 15 13/05 56 27 26 76

One of the most respected châteaux in Barsac, producing a rich, unctuous wine which contrasts with the lighter style of DOISY-DAËNE; it is very well suited to long aging.
Best years Sweet 1999, '97, '96, '95, '94, '90, '89, '88, '86, '85, '83, '82, '76, '75, '70

CH. LA DOMINIQUE★★ ❗ St-Émilion GCC, 20ha   05 57 51 31 36/05 57 51 63 04

On the edge of the Pomerol AC, this estate produces rich, suave wines from very ripe old Merlot vines, with great depth of fruit and charm.
Best years 1999, '98, '96, '95, '93, '90, '86, '85, '83, '82

CH. DUCRU-BEAUCAILLOU★★★ ❗   05 56 59 05 20/05 56 59 27 37

St-Julien 2ème CC, 50ha

Ducru-Beaucaillou has a velvety-dark colour and a perfect balance of power and elegance, but needs a decade of bottle age to show its true quality. Between 1986 and 1990 some bottles suffered from mustiness due to cellar conditions but fortunately since 1992 this has disappeared. Recent vintages have been quite superb.
Best years 1999, '98, '97, '96, '95, '94, '93, '90, '89, '88, '86, '85, '83, '82, '81, '79, '78, '75, '70, '66, '62, '61, '59, '53

CH. DUHART-MILON★★ ❗   05 56 73 18 18/05 56 59 26 83

Pauillac 4ème CC, 65ha

Since the 1990s the wines of Duhart-Milon, part of the LAFITE-ROTHSCHILD stable, have taken on richness and depth, without losing their traditional Pauillac firmness.
Best years 1999, '98, '97, '96, '95, '93, '90, '89, '88, '86, '85, '83, '82, '78

CH. DURFORT-VIVENS★★ ❗ Margaux 2ème CC, 30ha   05 57 88 70 20/05 57 88 72 51

Owned by the Lurton family of BRANE-CANTENAC, Durfort-Vivens shares a liveliness of style, but is a little firmer and slower to mature. The younger generation is determined to succeed and Gonzague Lurton has made great progress in 1998 and '99.
Best years 1999, '98, '97, '96, '95, '90, '89, '86, '85, '83, '82

CH. L'ÉGLISE-CLINET★★★ ❗ Pomerol, 5.5ha   05 57 25 99 00/05 57 25 21 96

A superbly managed, tiny estate where the wines are vinified with great care and the final selection notably rigorous. The depth of fruit obtained and the elegance and the complexity of the wine as it matures put it among the very top wines of Pomerol.
Best years 1999, '98, '97, '96, '95, '94, '93, '90, '89, '88, '86, '85, '83, '82, '75, '71, '62, '61, '59, '55, '52, '50, '49, '47, '45

CH. L'ÉVANGILE★★★ ❗ Pomerol, 14ha   05 57 51 15 30/05 57 51 45 78

This estate (now part of the LAFITE-ROTHSCHILD stable) benefits from the best terroir in Pomerol to produce a superb wine that marries intensity and grace.
Best years 1999, '98, '96, '95, '94, '93, '90, '89, '88, '85

CH. DE FARGUES★★★ ♀ Sauternes, 15ha   05 57 98 04 20/05 57 98 04 21

Owned by the Lur-Saluces family, until 1999 owners of d'YQUEM, this wine receives the same care and attention. One of the most concentrated Sauternes, it ages superbly.
Best years 1999, '98, '97, '96, '95, '90, '89, '88, '86, '85, '83, '82

CH. FAUGÈRES★ ❢ St-Émilion GC, 55ha   05 57 40 34 99/05 57 40 36 14

Since 1987 Corinne Guisez and her late husband Peby have renovated this estate to
Grand Cru Classé standard. The Cuvée Peby-Faugères, created in 1998, is remarkable.
Best years 1999, '98, '96, '95, '90

CH. FERRIÈRE★★ ❢ Margaux 3ème CC, 5ha   05 56 58 02 37/05 57 88 84 40

This small property is now owned by the Merlaut family (of the Taillan group) and the
wine is made by Claire Villars (who also makes the wine at CHASSE-SPLEEN and
CITRAN) resulting in a marked improvement in quality.
Best years 1999, '98, '97, '96, '95, '94, '93

CH. DE FIEUZAL★★ ❢♀   05 56 64 77 86/05 56 64 18 88
Pessac-Léognan CC, 40ha ❢, 8ha ♀

Almost better known for the richness and concentration of its barrel-fermented white
wines than for its ripe, plummy, almost gamy reds, Fieuzal is one of the quality leaders
in the Pessac-Léognan appellation.
Best years ❢1998, '96, '95, '94, '93, '90, '89, '88, '86, '85; ♀1999, '98, '96, '95

CH. FIGEAC★★ ❢ St-Émilion 1er GCC B, 40ha   05 57 24 72 26/05 57 74 45 74

A quality estate on undulating gravelly soil which is planted 70% to Cabernet (35%
each Cabernet Franc and Cabernet Sauvignon). This gives Figeac a firmness of fruit
that contrasts with the typically Merlot-dominated wines of St-Émilion, making it
'dumb' when young but capable of showing superb complexity and elegance as it ages.
Best years 1998, '97, '96, '95, '90, '89, '88, '86, '85, '83, '82, '78, '64, '61, '59, '55, '53

CH. FILHOT★ ♀ Sauternes 2ème CC, 60ha   05 56 76 61 09/05 56 76 67 91

A large estate with a vast classical château. The wine has improved from being rather
pale and simple to more rich and complex, still without achieving the concentration of
the best Sauternes Premiers Crus. Rare bottlings of Crème de Tête Réserve are superb.
Best years 1999, '97, '96, '95, '90, '89, '86, '83, '78, '76

CH. LA FLEUR-PÉTRUS★★ ❢ Pomerol, 7ha   05 57 51 78 96/05 57 51 79 79

This estate has progressed in recent years to become one of the most elegant wines of
the appellation, especially since part of Ch. Le Gay's vines have been added to the
property, following the Moueix purchase of La Fleur-Pétrus from Mme Robin.
Best years 1999, '98, '97, '96, '95, '94, '93, '90, '89, '88, '85, '82, '78, '70

CH. FONTENIL★ ❢ Fronsac, 8ha   05 57 51 10 94/05 57 51 66 08

A splendidly rich and smooth wine from a property owned by Michel Rolland, the
well-known wine consultant, and his wife Dany. See also le BON-PASTEUR.
Best years 1999, '98, '97, '96, '95, '90, '89

CH. FRANC-MAYNE★ ❢ St-Émilion GCC, 7ha   05 57 24 62 61/05 57 24 68 25

Well-placed vineyards on the limestone plateau north-west of the town of St-Émilion
produce sophisticated wines with body and elegance.
Best years 1998, '97, '95, '94, '90, '89, '88

CH. LA GAFFELIÈRE★★ ❢ St-Émilion 1er GCC B, 22ha   05 57 24 72 15/05 57 24 65 24

One of the finest vineyards in the St-Émilion area. This estate has belonged to the de
Malet-Roquefort family for over 400 years and its wine has robust colour, depth and
charm. Since 1994 there has been a quantum leap in quality.
Best years 1999, '98, '97, '96, '95, '94, '90, '89, '88, '86, '85

CH. GAZIN★★ ❢ Pomerol, 26ha   05 57 51 07 05/05 57 51 69 96

One of the largest and most impressive estates in Pomerol, with vines in a single block, is now once again making wines of power and elegance and capable of long aging – a benchmark for the appellation which has begun to justify its substantial price.
Best years 1999, '98, '97, '96, '95, '94, '90, '89, '88, '82, '78

CH. GILETTE★★★ ♀ Sauternes, 4.5ha   05 56 76 28 44/05 56 76 28 43

This legendary property is owned by Christian Médeville, known as *l'antiquaire du Sauternais* because of his policy of selling wines after they have been aged for at least 15 years in concrete vats (as opposed to the more normal wooden *barriques*), by which time they have already begun to acquire the patina and concentration of age.
Best years 1979, '78, '76, '75, '70, '67, '59, '55, '53, '49

CH. GISCOURS★★ ❢ Margaux 3ème CC, 83ha   05 57 97 09 09/05 57 97 09 00

After a period of glory in the 1970s, the wines went through an uneven patch. Recent investment in the vineyards has raised the quality back to Troisième Cru Classé.
Best years 1999, '98, '96, '95, '90, '86, '83, '82, '81, '79, '76, '70

CH. GLORIA★★ ❢ St-Julien CB, 47ha   05 56 59 08 18/05 56 59 16 18

This vineyard was put together, for the most part, in the 1950s and '60s by purchases of parcels of St-Julien from the surrounding Crus Classés. Thus, although only a Cru Bourgeois, its deeply fruity wines are recognized as the equal of the Crus Classés.
Best years 1999, '98, '96, '95, '94, '93, '90, '89, '88, '86, '85, '83, '82

CH. GRAND-MAYNE★★ ❢ St-Émilion GCC, 19ha   05 57 74 42 50/05 57 24 68 34

Situated on one of the finest slopes in the appellation, this estate has a perfectionist approach both in the vineyards and the cellars. The wines have great depth of colour and flavour. Quality has been particularly good since 1990. Keep for 5 years or more.
Best years 1999, '98, '97, '96, '95, '94, '90, '89, '88, '86, '85, '82

CH. GRAND-PUY-DUCASSE★ ❢   05 56 01 30 10/05 56 79 23 57
Pauillac 5ème CC, 40ha

With vines next to GRAND-PUY-LACOSTE and PONTET-CANET, this château made disappointing wines throughout the 1980s, but since the early 1990s they have become richer, fuller-bodied and more classically Pauillac with ripe blackcurrant fruit.
Best years 1999, '98, '96, '95, '90, '89, '88, '86, '85, '83, '82

CH. GRAND-PUY-LACOSTE ★★★ ❢   05 56 59 05 20/05 56 59 27 37
Pauillac 5ème CC, 50ha

Owned by the Borie family of DUCRU-BEAUCAILLOU since 1978, this estate is now a source of deeply coloured and intensely flavoured Pauillac for long aging. The vines are in a single block surrounding the château, producing wines of quality far outweighing its Cinquième Cru Classé status. Recent vintages have been superb.
Best years 1999, '98, '96, '95, '90, '89, '88, '86, '85, '83, '82, '81, '79, '78, '70

CH. GRUAUD-LAROSE ★★★ ❢ St-Julien 2ème CC, 82ha   05 56 73 15 20/05 56 59 64 72

This large property has most of its vines in a single block planted on deep gravel around the château in the southern part of St-Julien. The wines are dark-coloured, rich, even gamy, with superb potential for aging. Gruaud-Larose was bought from Cordier in 1997 by the Taillan group, assuring its quality under George Pauli's continuing management.

Best years 1999, '98, '96, '95, '94, '93, '92, '91, '90, '89, '88, '86, '85, '84, '83, '82, '81, '79, '78

CH. GUIRAUD★★ ♈♈ Sauternes 1er CC, 118ha   05 56 76 61 01/05 56 76 67 52

Guiraud is the largest estate in Sauternes and makes one of the most honeyed, fully sweet examples of this appellation, capable of improving over very many years. The property also produces a dry white and a supple red wine. Investment continues with a new *cuverie* completed in 1999 and the wines are likely to improve even further.
Best years 1999, '97, '98, '96, '95, '90, '89, '88, '86, 85, '83

CH. HAUT-BAGES-LIBÉRAL★ ♈   05 56 58 02 37/05 56 59 29 82
Pauillac 5ème CC, 28ha

With vines bordering LATOUR and PICHON-LONGUEVILLE COMTESSE-DE-LALANDE, this is one of the most stylish Pauillacs. Purchased by the Taillan group in 1983, the improvements to the vineyards and the cellar are now bearing results.
Best years 1999, '98, '96, '95, '93, '90, '89, '86, '85, '83, '82

CH. HAUT-BAILLY★★★ ♈ Pessac-Léognan CC, 28ha ♈   05 56 64 75 11/05 56 64 53 60
Jean Sanders, responsible for the exceptional quality here for over two decades, has retired, leaving his granddaughter Véronique as manager for the new American owner. The wines have perfect balance, showing deep, charming fruit and then aging superbly.
Best years 1999, '98, '97, '96, '95, '94, '93, '90, '89, '88, '86, '85, '82

CH. HAUT-BATAILLEY★★ ♈ Pauillac 5ème CC, 20ha   05 56 59 05 20/05 56 59 27 37
The smaller of the two Batailley châteaux, Haut-Batailley produces an elegant wine, showing more finesse but less weight than BATAILLEY. A problem of mustiness that affected many bottles from 1986–1992 has now been solved. This charming wine may be drunk younger than many Pauillacs, at 4–5 years old, but it will also last longer.
Best years 1999, '98, '96, '95, '85, '82, '81, '75, '70, '66, '61

CH. HAUT-BERGEY★ ♈♈ Pessac-Léognan, 26ha   05 56 64 05 22/05 56 64 06 98
The vineyard and *chai* have been entirely renovated since 1994 and the result is one of the best non-classified northern Graves reds. There is a tiny amount of Sauvignon-based white which is very fruity and attractive and for early drinking.
Best years ♈1999, '98, '96, '95; ♀1999, '98, '97

CH. HAUT-BRION★★★ ♈♀   05 56 00 29 30/05 56 98 75 14
Pessac-Léognan 1er CC, 43.2ha ♈, 2.7ha ♀

The gravel-based vineyards of this famous château are now totally surrounded by the city of Bordeaux and it was the only Graves property to be honoured in the great 1855 Classification of Bordeaux red wines. In 1959 Haut-Brion was the first estate in Bordeaux to install stainless steel vats, to control the temperature during fermentation, an example of the forward-looking policy that continues to this day. The red wine has a depth of bouquet and textural flavour as well as a longevity unrivalled in Bordeaux. A tiny quantity of white wine is made. It is equally superb with an extraordinary capacity for aging and a fascinating rich flavour yet with a marvellously dry finish. The estate's second wine, Ch. Bahans-Haut-Brion, is supple and elegant, and may be drunk relatively young.
Best years ♈1999, '98, '97, '96, '95, '94, '93, '90, '89, '88, '86, '85, '83, '82, '81, '78, '75, '64, '61, '59, '55, '53, '52, '45, '29, '28, '26, '21; ♀1999, '98, '97, '96, '95, '94, '92, '90, '89

CH. HAUT-MARBUZET★★ ❢ St-Estèphe CB, 50ha   05 56 59 30 54/05 56 59 70 87

A wine of richness and complexity, seemingly soft, even exotic, for a St-Estèphe due to the high proportion of new oak, but which also ages remarkably well.

Best years 1999, '98, '96, '95, '90, '89, '88, '86, '85, '83, '82, '78

CH. D'ISSAN★★ ❢ Margaux 3ème CC, 30ha   05 57 88 35 91/05 57 88 74 24

One of the most historic Bordeaux châteaux, d'Issan makes a deep-coloured Margaux with soft tannins. Quality improved considerably in the 1990s, especially from 1996.

Best years 1999, '98, '97, '95, '90, '89, '85, '83, '82

CH. KIRWAN★★ ❢ Margaux 3ème CC, 35ha   05 57 87 64 55/05 57 87 57 20

This well-known property underwent a change of direction in the early 1990s. The wines here are now rich in extract, without losing the delicate essence of Margaux.

Best years 1999, '98, '97, '96, '95, '94, '93, '90, '89, '88, '86, '85, '83, '82

CH. LABÉGORCE★ ❢ Margaux CB, 38ha   05 57 88 71 32/05 57 88 35 01

One of the best Crus Bourgeois in Margaux, producing ripe, supple wine from a fine vineyard north of the village itself. It is always one of the best Crus Bourgeois.

Best years 1999, '98, '96, '95, '90, '89, '88, '86, '85, '83, '82

CH. LABÉGORCE-ZÉDÉ★ ❢ Margaux CB, 38ha   05 57 88 71 31/05 57 88 72 54

A quality Cru Bourgeois, in the hands of Luc Thienpont of the Libournais family (VIEUX-CH-CERTAN), which combines deep fruit and elegance with quite firm tannin.

Best years 1999, '98, '96, '95, '90, '89, '88, '86, '85, '83, '82

CH. LAFAURIE-PEYRAGUEY★★★ ♀   05 56 95 53 09/05 56 95 53 01

Sauternes 1er CC, 40ha

A well-situated property capable of producing one of the finest wines in this appellation. The balance of richness to acidity in the wine is perfect and the botrytis element is noticeable. This wine shows its quality after only a few years, yet also ages superbly in the manner of all great Sauternes. At 15 years they are perfect.

Best years 1999, '98, '97, '96, '95, '90, '89, '88, '86, '85, '83

CH. LAFITE-ROTHSCHILD★★★ ❢   05 56 73 18 18/05 56 59 26 83

Pauillac 1er CC, 100ha

The most elegant of the Pauillac Premiers Crus, Lafite is at the northern end of the commune. Sometimes deceptive if drunk too young, the wine needs several years for its violet aroma and its true breed to appear. Although a very large property, it is rare for more than half the wine produced to be made as Lafite, the rest being used for the fine second wine, Les Carruades de Ch. Lafite, and for the simple Pauillac that also includes wine from the younger vines of the neighbouring DUHART-MILON.

Best years 1999, '98, '97, '96, '95, '94, '90, '89, '88, '86, '85, '83, '82, '81, '79, '76, '75, '62, '61, '59, '53, '49, '48, '45

CH. LAFLEUR★★ ❢ Pomerol, 4.5ha   05 57 84 44 03/05 57 84 83 31

From half Cabernet Franc and half Merlot vines, this small estate produces supremely elegant, intensely coloured wines that age magnificently over 2 and even 3 decades and they can even rival PÉTRUS for depth of fruit and style. A true collector's wine.

Best years 1999, '98, '97, '96, '95, '90, '89, '88, '86, '85, '83, '82, '78, '75

CH. LAFON-ROCHET★★ ❢ St-Estèphe 4ème CC, 40ha   05 56 59 32 06/05 56 59 72 43

This estate borders LAFITE-ROTHSCHILD. Both the château and the vineyard were reconstituted in the 1970s by Guy Tesseron, who later purchased PONTET-CANET. Since the late 1980s, the wines have succeeded in marrying intensity of St-Estèphe fruit with finesse and breed. Generally offers excellent value for money.

Best years 1999, '98, '97, '96, '95, '94, '90, '89, '88, '86, '85, '83

CH. LAGRANGE★★ ❢ St-Julien 3ème CC, 112ha 05 56 73 38 38/05 56 59 26 09

The largest property in St-Julien and the largest of all the Crus Classés, Lagrange produces a classic St-Julien of great reliability, thanks to a fine terroir and large investment by the Japanese group Suntory, owners since 1983. Quality is ensured by declassifying a high proportion of the crop into the second wine, Les Fiefs de Lagrange.

Best years 1999, '98, '97, '96, '95, '90, '89, '88, '86, '85

CH. LA LAGUNE★★ ❢ Haut-Médoc 3ème CC, 72ha 05 57 88 82 77/05 57 88 82 70

The Haut-Médoc's southernmost Cru Classé has a more sandy soil than the rest of the Crus Classés. Owned by the Champagne house of Ayala, La Lagune produces round, velvety wines which are aged in a high proportion of new oak.

Best years 1999, '98, '96, '95, '90, '89, '88, '86, '85, '83, '82, '81, '79, '78, '76, '75

CH. LANGOA-BARTON★★ ❢ St-Julien 3ème CC, 15ha 05 56 59 06 05/05 56 59 14 29

This property has belonged to the Barton family for 6 generations, and is, with LÉOVILLE-BARTON, the Cru Classé with the longest history of private ownership in the Médoc. The wine is a traditional St-Julien, deep, velvety in colour, with ripe red fruits and a smoothness that is pleasing young, but which ages very well. Anthony Barton is one of the most-liked and respected figures in Bordeaux.

Best years 1999, '98, '97, '96, '95, '90, '89, '88, '86, '85, '82, '78, '62, '59, '45

CH. LARCIS-DUCASSE★★ ❢ St-Émilion GCC, 11ha 05 57 24 70 84/05 57 24 64 00

With vines at the foot of the famous southern Côtes just below Ch. PAVIE, this property produces wines of great refinement that have an excellent capacity for aging.

Best years 1999, '98, '96, '95, '94, '90, '89, '88

CH. LARMANDE★★ ❢ St-Émilion GCC, 25ha 05 57 24 71 41/05 57 74 42 80

One of the largest and the most reliable in quality of the Grands Crus Classés, Larmande produces rich, densely extracted wines with deep, smooth fruit.

Best years 1999, '98, '97, '96, '90, '89, '88, '86, '85, '83, '82

CH. LARRIVET-HAUT-BRION★★ ❢♀   05 56 64 75 51/05 56 64 53 47

Pessac-Léognan, 33ha ❢, 9ha ♀

Unlike HAUT-BRION which lies in the commune of Pessac, Larrivet-Haut-Brion is located in Léognan. Much improvement has occurred in the wines since the early 1990s, the reds acquiring a riper fruit and more new oak, the whites becoming more fruity and elegant.

Best years ❢1999, '98, '96, '95, '94, '90, '89, '88, '86, '85, '82, '78; ♀1999, '98, '96

CH. LASCOMBES★★ ❢ Margaux 2ème CC, 50ha 05 57 88 70 66/05 57 88 72 17

A fine and reliable Margaux, always showing ripe blackcurrant fruit and deep flavours, if lacking an edge of finesse. Overall, a very satisfying wine that ages for 10–15 years.

Best years 1999, '98, '96, '95, '90, '89, '88, '86, '85, '83, '75, '70, '66, '62, '61

CH. LATOUR★★★ ❢ Pauillac 1er CC, 65ha 05 56 73 19 80/05 56 73 19 81

The most structured and the most regular in quality of the 3 Pauillac Premiers Crus Classés. Latour's vineyards lie near to the Gironde estuary, and benefit from the superb gravel soil, as well as being relatively protected from frost. The wine is almost unique in combining firmness and richness and needs, even in recent years, over a decade to open up and even then it is capable of improving for many more decades. Only the best parts of the vineyard and the oldest vines are used for Latour itself, the remainder being declassified into the superb second wine, Les Forts de Latour, or into a simple Pauillac wine. Its reputation for making fine wine in less successful vintages is well deserved. After 30 years in British hands, the estate was purchased by François Pinault in 1993.

Best years 1999, '98, '97, '96, '95, '94, '93, '91, '90, '89, '88, '82, '79, '78, '75, '70, '66, '62, '61, '59, '49, '45, '34, '29, '28, '26, '24

CH. LATOUR-MARTILLAC★ ❢★★ ♀   05 57 97 71 11/05 57 97 71 17

Pessac-Léognan CC, 30ha ❢, 8ha ♀

An organically run estate that has been in the hands of the well-known Kressmann family since 1929. The red wines have good, smoky fruit from old vines and the elegant whites are continuing to progress in quality thanks to modern vinification methods. This estate is a fine example of the general wine renaissance currently taking place in the northern Graves.

Best years ❢1999, '98, '96, '95, '94, '90, '88, '86, '85; ♀1999, '98, '96, '95, '94, '90

CH. LATOUR-À-POMEROL★★ ❢ Pomerol, 8ha   05 57 51 78 96/05 57 51 79 79

One of the most famous and most concentrated wines of the appellation, with ownership shared (as at PÉTRUS) between the Lacoste and the Moueix families. These wines have great power and concentration, yet remain beautifully elegant as they age.

Best years 1999, '98, '97, '96, '95, '94, '90, '89, '88, '85, '83, '82, '81, '79, '70, '61, '59, '47

CH. LAVILLE-HAUT-BRION★★★♀   05 56 00 29 30/05 56 98 75 14

Pessac-Léognan CC, 3.7ha

Laville-Haut-Brion is La MISSION-HAUT-BRION's superb white wine, made from 70% Sémillon. In recent years, the grapes have been picked at optimum balance between ripeness and acidity to showcase this remarkable terroir.

Best years 1999, '98, '97, '96, '95, '94, '90, '89, '88, '85, '76, '71, '62

CH. LÉOVILLE-BARTON★★★ ❢   05 56 59 06 05/05 56 59 14 29

St-Julien 2ème CC, 46ha

Purchased by the Barton family in 1826, this is the smallest and most traditional of the 3 Léoville estates. The wines are classic St-Julien, with beautiful, dense fruit, never too heavy nor too extracted, and they age superbly. Outstanding in the 1990s, it is no longer the relative bargain it used to be but its price reflects its quality.

Best years 1999, '98, '97, '96, '95, '94, '90, '89, '88, '86, '85, '82, '81, '61, '59, '55, '45

CH. LÉOVILLE-LAS-CASES★★★ ❢   05 56 59 25 26/05 56 59 18 33

St-Julien 2ème CC, 97ha

The leading estate in St-Julien, with some of the vines running alongside those of LATOUR. The quality of the terroir, the age of the vines, the attention to detail, all combine to make a great wine, which continues to develop in bottle over 20 years or more. The well-known second wine, Clos du Marquis, is of Cru Classé quality. Currently the Grand Vin sells for the same price as a Pauillac Premier Cru. From a good year the wine really does need 15 years of aging.

Best years 1999, '98, '97, '96, '95, '93, '90, '89, '88, '86, '85, '83, '82, '81, '79, '78, '75

CH. LÉOVILLE-POYFERRÉ★★ ❢　　　　　05 56 59 08 30/05 56 59 60 09
St-Julien 2ème CC, 80ha

This powerful, deep-coloured wine, from one of the finest parts of the appellation, used to lack a little finesse. Many improvements in the 1980s, and the arrival of Michel Rolland as consultant in 1994, have had very positive effects.

Best years 1999, '98, '97, '96, '95, '90, '89, '88, '86, '85, '83, '82, '61, '59, '53, '47, '45

CH. LOUBENS★★ ♀ Ste-Croix-du-Mont, 17ha ♀　　　05 56 62 01 25/05 56 76 71 65

With its honeyed fruit, this is one of the best sweet white wines made outside Sauternes.

Best years 1999, '98, '97, '96, '95, '90, '89, '88, '86, '85, '83

CH. LA LOUVIÈRE★★ ❢♀ Pessac-Léognan, 33ha ❢, 15ha ♀　　05 56 64 75 87/05 56 64 71 76

Owned and revived by André Lurton, the most fervent supporter of the wines of the northern Graves, this estate is recognized as being equal to the better Pessac-Léognan Crus Classés. The deep-coloured, meaty reds benefit from long aging and the whites have fine fruit and grip, also needing a few years to show at their best.

Best years ❢1998, '97, '96, '95, '94, '90, '89, '88, '86, '85; ♀1999, '98, '96, '95, '90, '89, '88

CH. LYNCH-BAGES★★ ❢ Pauillac 5ème CC, 90ha　　　05 56 73 24 00/05 56 59 26 42

One of the most famous wines in Pauillac, and one which performs on the level of a Deuxième Cru Classé more often than that of a Cinquième. Lynch-Bages is always robust and plummy, but with an impressive concentration and complexity.

Best years 1999, '98, '97, '96, '95, '90, '89, '88, '87, '86, '85, '82, '70, '61, '59, '55, '53

CH. MAGDELAINE★★ ❢ St-Émilion 1er GCC B, 10ha　　05 57 55 05 80/05 57 25 13 30

From vines located near AUSONE and BELAIR on the high plateau above the town itself, Ch. Magdelaine produces wines of great refinement, delicate compared to more robustly extracted St-Émilions, but still capable of aging beautifully.

Best years 1999, '98, '97, '96, '95, '90, '89, '88, '85, '83, '82, '75, '70, '61

CH. MALARTIC-LAGRAVIÈRE★★ ❢♀　　　　　05 56 64 75 08/05 56 64 99 66
Pessac-Léognan CC, 15ha ❢, 4ha ♀

One of the most prestigious estates in the appellation which has recently returned to private hands after a period as part of the LAURENT-PERRIER group. The finesse of the Sauvignon-dominated white is now being equalled by the depth of fruit in the reds.

Best years ❢1999, '98, '96, '95, '90, '89; ♀1999, '98, '97, '96, '95

CH. MALÉSCOT ST-EXUPÉRY★★ ❢　　　　　05 57 88 70 68/05 57 88 35 80
Margaux 3ème CC, 23.5ha

After a period of decline in the 1970s and early '80s, this wine is now one of the most elegant in the appellation, spurred on by the younger generation of the Zuger family.

Best years 1999, '98, '97, '96, '95, '94, '93, '90, '89, '88, '70, '61, '59, '55, '47, '45

CH. DE MALLE★★ ♀ Sauternes 2ème CC, 27ha　　　05 56 62 36 86/05 56 76 82 40

Always known for its rich, almost barley-sugared wine, de Malle has risen far above its classification since the 1986 vintage, making wines with true botrytis richness and length. There is also a good, dry white Graves called M de Malle.

Best years 1999, '97, '96, '95, '94, '91, '90, '89, '88

CH. MARBUZET★ ❢ St-Estèphe CB, 7ha　　　　05 56 73 15 50/05 56 59 72 59

Owned by the Prats family, who were owners of COS D'ESTOURNEL until 1998, this wine was also Cos' second wine until the creation of Les Pagodes de Cos in 1994. This is a fruity, rounded but firm St-Estèphe, of top Cru Bourgeois quality. It is not cheap, but the wine is good enough to justify the extra expense.

Best years 1999, '98, '97, '96, '95, '94, '90, '89, '88, '86, '85

CH. MARGAUX★★★ ❢ ★★ ♀   05 57 88 83 83/05 57 88 31 32
Margaux 1er CC, 78ha ❢, 10ha ♀

The only château in the Médoc to give its name to an appellation, Ch. Margaux is the quintessential Premier Cru Classé. As much as 50% of the crop is declassified each year into the splendid second wine, Pavillon Rouge, so that the Grand Vin never disappoints. This wine is the perfect combination of power and elegance and shows the extraordinary quality of the terroir of Margaux. Even the lightest vintages age superbly. Planted entirely to Sauvignon Blanc and vinified in a separate *chai* from the red wine, Pavillon Blanc is a sophisticated floral, crisp white wine, delightful young but delicious with a little age. Ch. Margaux is rare in Bordeaux in possessing its own cooperage.

Best years ❢1999, '98, '97, '96, '95, '93, '90, '89, '88, '86, '85, '83, '82, '81, '80, '79, '78, '61, '59, '53, '52, '47, '45, '28, '26

CH. MARQUIS DE TERME★ ❢   05 57 88 30 01/05 57 88 32 51
Margaux 4ème CC, 35ha

With superb terroir near LASCOMBES, this estate produces deep-coloured wines with a richness of fruit and has been performing well since the early 1980s. It produced one of the best wines of the Margaux appellation in 1990.

Best years 1999, '98, '97, '96, '95, '90, '89, '88, '86, '85, '83

CH. MAUCAILLOU★ ❢ Moulis CB, 80ha   05 56 58 01 23/05 56 58 00 88

A fine, supple wine, always rich in colour with smooth tannins and ripe fruit, made with the use of a high proportion of new oak (up to 60% new casks each year).

Best years 1999, '98, '97, '96, '95, '90, '89, '88, '86, '85, '83, '82, '81

CH. LA MISSION-HAUT-BRION★★★ ❢   05 56 00 29 30/05 56 98 75 14
Pessac-Léognan CC, 20.9ha

Although separated by only a narrow road from HAUT-BRION, the styles of wine are quite different, even though both of these superb vineyards have been under the same ownership since 1983. La Mission has perhaps a greater depth of colour and a fuller-bodied earthiness with a menthol hint, and while it lacks the supple smoothness of HAUT-BRION, it equals it in complexity and aging potential.

Best years 1999, '98, '97, '96, '95, '94, '93, '90, '89, '88, '85, '83, '82, '81, '79, '78, '75, '66, '64, '61, '59, '55, '49, '48, '47, '46, '45, '29, '28

CH. MONBOUSQUET★ ❢ St-Émilion GC, 31ha   05 57 24 67 19/05 57 74 41 29

One of the larger estates in St-Émilion, Monbousquet has undergone a transformation since being purchased by Gérard Perse in 1995. Changes include harvesting late to obtain very ripe grapes and the vinification is now overseen by the renowned enologist, Michel Rolland. The wine has now begun to equal the better Grands Crus Classés.

Best years 1999, '98, '96, '95, '94, '93, '90, '89, '88, '85, '83, '82, '79, '78

CH. MONBRISON★★ ❢ Margaux CB, 21ha   05 56 58 80 04/05 56 58 85 33

One of the most concentrated, aromatic and complex of the Margaux Crus Bourgeois, regularly superior to many of the appellation's Crus Classés.

Best years 1999, '98, '97, '96, '95, '90, '89, '88, '86, '85, '83, '82

CH. MONTROSE★★★ ! St-Estèphe 2ème CC, 68ha   05 56 59 30 12/05 56 59 38 48
With all the vines in a single block near the Gironde estuary, like those of LATOUR, Montrose was famous for producing the most intense, longest-lived wines of the Médoc. Recent vintages have been rounder, more approachable in their youth, but with no loss of concentration. Montrose, with COS D'ESTOURNEL, could become the Premier Cru of St-Estèphe, given its privileged site and dedication to quality. The second wine is called La Dame de Montrose.
Best years 1999, '98, '97, '96, '95, '94, '90, '89, '86, '85, '82, '76, '70, '64, '61, '59, '55, '53, '49, '47, '45, '29, '28

CH. MOUTON-ROTHSCHILD★★★ !   05 56 73 21 29/05 56 73 21 28
Pauillac 1er CC, 75ha
With a reputation as one of the world's greatest wines, Mouton-Rothschild is the most explosively fruity of the Pauillac Premiers Crus Classés, but also the least reliable. The wine can possess a dense, almost exotic ripeness of fruit, backed by the firmness of old Cabernet Sauvignon vines, which seduces when young but can improve for several decades. Since 1993, there has been an official second wine called Le Petit Mouton.
Best years 1999, '98, '97, '96, '95, '94, '90, '89, '88, '86, '85, '83, '82, '78, '70, '66, '62, '61, '59, '55, '53, '49, '48, '47, '45, '34, '29, '28

CH. NAIRAC★★ ! Barsac 2ème CC, 17ha   05 56 27 16 16/05 56 27 26 50
One of the properties in the region most devoted to quality. When the wine is not good enough for the owners, none of it is sold under the château label. Such meticulous dedication in the vineyard and the cellar has placed Nairac at the top of the Deuxième Crus Classés. Use of new oak means the wine can age for 10–15 years.
Best years 1999, '98, '97, '96, '95, '90, '89, '88, '86, '83, '82, '81, '80, '76, '75

CH. NENIN★★ ! Pomerol, 27ha   05 57 51 00 01/05 57 51 77 47
A large property for Pomerol, and one that has seen a marked improvement in quality following its sale in early 1998 to the Delon family of LÉOVILLE-LAS-CASES.
Best years 1999, '98, '96, '95, '90, '89, '88, '85

CH. OLIVIER★ !♀ 　　　　　　　　　　　05 56 64 73 31/05 56 64 54 23
Pessac-Léognan CC, 33ha !, 12ha ♀
One of the oldest châteaux in the Graves region, the wines were for many years less impressive than the buildings. Investment and selection have brought improvement, but it is still not in the forefront of this very progressive appellation.
Best years !1998, '97, '96, '90, '89, '88, '86, '85; ♀1999, '96, '95

CH. LES ORMES SORBET★ ! Médoc CB, 21ha   05 56 73 30 30/05 56 73 30 31
This wine is a classic Médoc, showing typical Cabernet Sauvignon depth and finesse, along with sensible use of oak. It is at its best with at least 5 years' aging.
Best years 1999, '98, '97, '96, '95, '90, '89, '88

CH. PALMER★★★ ! Margaux 3ème CC, 45ha   05 57 88 72 72/05 57 88 37 16
Generally recognized for years as second only to Ch. MARGAUX in this appellation (and often superior in the 1960s and '70s), Palmer's high proportion of Merlot and habitual late-harvesting gives it an almost untypical roundness, yet the wine has an aging capacity that is almost unrivalled. Keep good vintages for 30 years or more to taste at their best. The vinification cellars were completely modernized in 1995.

Best years 1999, '98, '96, '95, '90, '89, '88, '86, '85, '83, '82, '79, '78, '75, '70, '66, '61, '59, '55, '52, '49, '48, '47, '45, '29

CH. PAPE-CLÉMENT★★★ ▮♀   05 57 26 38 38/05 57 26 38 39

Pessac-Léognan CC, 30ha ▮, 2.5ha ♀

The red wines of Pape-Clément are among the most flavourful of the appellation, with firm but velvety fruit matching the superb colour. Famous for quality until the mid-1970s, a period of unevenness followed but since 1985 there has been a string of very successful vintages. A tiny amount of delicate, fragrant white wine is also produced.

Best years ▮1999, '98, '96, '95, '94, '90, '89, '86, '85, '62, '61, '53; ♀1999, '98, '97, '96, '95

CH. PAVIE★★ ▮ St-Émilion 1er GCC B, 37ha   05 57 55 43 43/05 57 24 63 99

One of the most respected estates in St-Émilion, producing a firm, long-lived, complex wine, from south-facing vines, which sadly lost a little of its concentration during the 1990s. At its best this wine can age for at least 20 years. Now owned by Gérard Perse of Ch. MONBOUSQUET, who is producing a wine of elegance and intensity.

Best years 1999, '98, '96, '95, '90, '89, '88, '86, '85, '83, '82, '81

CH. PAVIE-DECESSE★★ ▮ St-Émilion GCC, 10ha   05 57 55 43 44/05 57 24 63 99

The vines are situated above those of PAVIE and face directly south, producing a wine of depth and finesse, although in recent years quality had seen a slight decline. Under the new ownership of Gérard Perse of Ch. MONBOUSQUET, in 1997, quality has improved substantially, making the château worthy of Premier Grand Cru status. Drink between 5 and 10 years of aging.

Best years 1999, '98, '96, '95, '90, '89, '88, '86, '85, '83, '82, '81, '78, '75

CH. PAVIE-MACQUIN★★ ▮ St-Émilion GCC, 15ha   05 57 24 74 23/05 57 24 63 78

With vineyards located between PAVIE and TROPLONG-MONDOT and farmed on biodynamic lines, this estate made great strides in the late 1980s. The wine has become very impressive with good concentration of fruit and depth.

Best years 1999, '98, '97, '96, '95, '94, '93, '90, '89, '88

CH. PETIT-VILLAGE★★ ▮ Pomerol, 11ha   05 57 51 21 08/05 57 51 87 31

Located at the highest point of Pomerol's gravel plateau, this estate (owned by the AXA insurance group) produces very fine wine with great richness and finesse.

Best years 1999, '98, '97, '96, '90, '89, '88, '85, '83, '82, '81, '75, '70, '66, '61

CH. PÉTRUS★★★ ▮ Pomerol, 11.5ha   05 57 51 78 96/05 57 51 79 79

The most famous estate in Pomerol and also one of the most famous wines in the world, Pétrus has vines facing those of CHEVAL-BLANC in neighbouring St-Émilion. From this fortunate terroir it continues to produce wines of unmatched opulence and complexity. Despite the very high (95–100%) proportion of Merlot, which allows this great wine to be drunk at 5 years old, Pétrus also ages exceptionally well long-term.

Best years 1999, '98, '97, '96, '95, '90, '89, '88, '86, '85, '82, '80, '79, '75, '71, '70, '64, '61, '59, '48, '47, '45

CH. DE PEZ★ ▮ St-Estèphe CB, 24ha   05 56 59 30 07/05 56 59 39 25

These wines were among the best of the St-Estèphe Crus Bourgeois in the 1970s and early '80s. The estate was recently purchased by Jean-Claude Rouzaud of Champagne ROEDERER, and the new owner has succeeded in restoring much of its former glory.

Best years 1999, '98, '97, '96, '95, '90, '89, '88, '86, '85, '83, '82, '79, '78, '75

CH. PHÉLAN-SÉGUR★★ ❢ St-Estèphe CB, 64ha   05 56 59 74 00/05 56 59 74 10

One of the most classically beautiful châteaux in the Médoc, situated in a vast park overlooking the Gironde estuary, Phélan-Ségur has received substantial investment from the Gardinier family since they purchased the property in 1985. As a result the wine, a Cru Bourgeois, is now showing the finesse, depth and breed of a Cru Classé with elegant, lush fruit. It is best at 6 or 7 years.

Best years 1999, '98, '97, '96, '95, '94, '90, '89, '88

CH. PIBRAN★ ❢ Pauillac CB, 9.5ha   05 56 73 17 17/05 56 73 17 28

Owned by the AXA insurance group, this small estate near PONTET-CANET produces very ripe, deep-coloured wines and is one of the best Crus Bourgeois in the Médoc. In 1997 it won the coveted 'Coupe des Crus Bourgeois'.

Best years 1999, '98, '97, '96, '95, '94, '90, '89, '88

CH. PICHON-LONGUEVILLE BARON DE LONGUEVILLE★★★ ❢

Pauillac 2ème CC, 68ha   05 56 73 17 17/05 56 73 17 28

With some of the best land in Pauillac, Pichon-Baron, as it is commonly known, produces very deep-coloured wines with superb intensity from Cabernet Sauvignon. They need several years to soften out, but can continue to improve for 20 years or more. The successes since 1988 are due to the investments of the AXA insurance group, under the direction of Jean-Michel Cazes of LYNCH-BAGES.

Best years 1999, '98, '97, '96, '95, '94, '90, '89, '88, '86, '82, '59, '53, '49

CH. PICHON-LONGUEVILLE COMTESSE-DE-LALANDE★★★ ❢

Pauillac 2ème CC, 75ha   05 56 59 19 40/05 56 59 29 78

Quite different in style from PICHON-BARON, owing partially to the high proportion of Merlot in the vineyard as well as to the influence of its owner, Mme de Lencquesaing, Pichon-Longueville-Lalande produces the finest, most seductive Pauillac that has the ability of showing well at an early age, but lasting as long as its peers. The rivalry between the 2 Pichons has served to keep both at an exceptionally high level of quality.

Best years 1999, '98, '97, '96, '95, '94, '89, '88, '86, '85, '83, '82, '81, '79, '78, '75, '62, '61, '59, '55, '52, '49, '45

CH. LE PIN★★★ ❢ Pomerol, 2ha   Tel 05 57 51 33 99

This tiny estate was made famous by Jacques Thienpont, co-owner of VIEUX-CH.-CERTAN, in the early 1980s. The wines are a model of ripeness, concentration and finesse and now rival those of PÉTRUS for record prices at auction.

Best years 1999, '98, '97, '96, '95, '94, '90, '89, '88, '87, '86, '85, '83, '82, '81

CH. LA POINTE★★ ❢ Pomerol, 25ha   05 57 51 02 11/05 57 51 42 33

A large estate for Pomerol, managed with dedication by the d'Arfeuille family, producing warm, rounded, supple wines, that showed much improvement in the 1990s with more weight and lush Pomerol character.

Best years 1999, '98, '97, '96, '95, '90, '89

CH. PONTET-CANET★★ ❢ Pauillac 5ème CC, 78ha   05 56 59 04 04/05 56 59 26 63

This vineyard adjoins MOUTON-ROTHSCHILD. Bought in 1975 by the Tesseron family, owners of LAFON-ROCHET, it took over 10 years before the investment in both the vineyard and cellars translated into the quality of rich, blackcurrant wine which had once put Pontet-Canet near the top of the Pauillac Cinquième Crus Classés, a position it once more shares since the 1994 vintage. The deep, tannic wine needs 5-10 years of aging.

Best years 1999, '98, '97, '96, '95, '94, '90, '89, '88, '86, '85, '83, '82, '75, '61, '45

CH. POTENSAC★★ ❢ Médoc CB, 51ha   05 56 73 25 26/05 56 59 18 33

Owned by the Delon family of LÉOVILLE-LAS-CASES, this is the best wine in this appellation, famed for its consistency year on year. Drink the wine either after 4–5 years or age for at least 10 years.

Best years 1999, '98, '97, '96, '95, '94, '93, '90, '89, '88, '86, '85, '83, '82, '81

CH. POUJEAUX★★ ❢ Moulis CB, 52ha   05 56 58 02 96/05 56 58 01 25

This is the finest wine of Moulis, which regularly outclasses many Crus Classés. The estate is located on excellent terroir. Its wine is very deep in colour and subject to extremely careful vinification and aging. Good vintages can easily last for 20 years.

Best years 1999, '98, '97, '96, '95, '94, '93, '90, '89, '88, '86, '85, '83, '82, '81, '78

CH. PRIEURÉ-LICHINE★★ ❢ Margaux 4ème CC, 69ha   05 57 88 36 28/05 57 88 78 93

A wine which will always be associated with Alexis Lichine, a great promoter of top-quality French wines in the twentieth century, who rebuilt and expanded the vineyard during almost 40 years from 1952 until his death in 1989. His son, Sacha sold the estate to a Bordeaux *négociant* group in 1999, but quality remains very high.

Best years 1999, '98, '97, '96, '95, '93, '90, '89, '88, '86, '85, '83, '82, '78, '64, '61

CH. QUINAULT★ ❢ St-Émilion GC, 12ha   05 57 74 19 42/05 57 25 91 20

Dr Alain Raymaud of La CROIX-DE-GAY purchased the estate in 1997 since when yields have fallen and quality risen dramatically. L'Enclos is the Grand Vin, La Fleur the lighter, second wine.

Best years 1999, '98

CH. RABAUD-PROMIS★★ ♀ Sauternes 1er CC, 30ha   05 56 76 67 38/05 56 76 63 10

A very reliable estate, making fully sweet wines with true richness and purity of fruit, which improve over 20 years of keeping.

Best years 1999, '98, '97, '96, '95, '94, '90, '89, '88, '86, '83, '67

CH. RAUZAN-GASSIES★ ❢ Margaux 2ème CC, 30ha   05 57 88 71 88/05 57 88 37 49

After more than 2 decades of producing mediocre wines, the arrival of a new director, Jean-Louis Camp from Ch. Loudenne, saw an immediate improvement. Although not yet of Deuxième Cru Classé standard, the wines are much better than in the past.

Best years 1999, '98, '97, '96, '95, '90, '83, '79, '78, '75

CH. RAUZAN-SÉGLA★★★ ❢ Margaux 2ème CC, 51ha   05 57 88 82 10/05 57 88 34 54

Since its purchase by the Chanel group in 1994, Rauzan-Ségla has regained its second place behind Ch. MARGAUX in the appellation. The wine is very elegant with precise fruit flavours and now possesses great complexity and fruit. Replanting in the vineyards along with a new *chai* and cellar show that this property is very much in the ascendant.

Best years 1999, '98, '97, '96, '95, '94, '90, '89, '88, '86, '85, '83, '82

CH. RAYMOND-LAFON★★ ♀ Sauternes, 18ha   05 56 63 21 02/05 56 63 19 58

Owned by a former manager of d'YQUEM, this wine is made in a similar style and can even rival that classic wine for quality and honeyed richness of fruit. The vines are surrounded by Premiers Crus and the wine is certainly of matching quality.

Best years 1999, '98, '97, '96, '95, '90, '89, '88, '86, '85, '83, '82, '81, '80, '78, '76, '75

CH. DE RAYNE-VIGNEAU★★ ♀ Sauternes 1er CC, 79ha   05 56 01 30 01/05 56 79 23 57
A large property for Sauternes, possessing possibly the finest soil and mesoclimate after d'YQUEM. The wine possesses elegance and purity of fruit but sometimes lacks the concentration and richness of the best Premiers Crus Classés.
Best years 1999, '98, '97, '96, '95, '90, '89, '88, '86, '83

CH. RIEUSSEC★★★ ♀ Sauternes 1er CC, 100ha   05 56 62 20 71/05 56 76 27 82
Now part of the LAFITE-ROTHSCHILD holdings. Recent investment has allowed Rieussec to regain its position as a leading Sauternes Premier Cru Classé. The wine has a honeyed-floral richness and great persistence of flavour. Age for at least 10 years.
Best years 1999, '98, '97, '96, '95, '90, '89, '88, '86, '85, '83, '81, '75, '71, '67, '62, '59, '45

CH. ROC DE CAMBES★ ❗ Côtes de Bourg, 9.5ha   05 57 24 70 57/05 57 74 42 11
Owned by the Mitjaville family of Le TERTRE-RÔTEBOEUF in St-Émilion, these wines share the same depth of colour and richness derived from late-harvested grapes.
Best years 1999, '98, '97, '96, '95, '94, '93, '91, '90, '89

CH. ST-PIERRE★★ ❗ St-Julien CC, 17ha   05 56 59 08 18/05 56 59 16 18
Always reliable in the past, St-Pierre, the smallest of the St-Julien Crus Classés, has been producing splendid wine in the 1990s with deep, robust fruit and fine structure.
Best years 1999, '98, '96, '95, '90, '88, '86

CH. SIGALAS-RABAUD★★ ♀ Sauternes 1er CC, 14ha   05 56 95 53 00/05 56 95 53 01
A well-situated vineyard, part-owned by Cordier, the *négociants* who own LAFAURIE-PEYRAGUEY, making elegant, sophisticated wines which can be enjoyed young.
Best years 1999, '98, '97, '96, '95, '91, '90, '89, '88, '86, '85, '83, '81, '79, '75, '71, '67, '62

CH. SIRAN★★ ❗ Margaux CB, 25ha   05 57 88 34 04/05 57 88 70 05
For many years considered the equal of a Cru Classé, Siran continues to produce very deep-coloured wines with charm and depth from its well-drained gravel soil. The wines, which have a high proportion of new oak, age very well.
Best years 1999, '98, '96, '95, '90, '89, '86, '85, '83, '82

CH. SMITH-HAUT-LAFITTE★★ ❗♀   05 57 83 11 22/05 57 83 11 21
Pessac-Léognan CC, 44ha ❗, 11ha ♀
This famous estate is a shining example of the improvement dedicated new owners can bring in only a few years. Good before, both the red and the white are now superb. One of the rare châteaux in Bordeaux to have its own cooperage.
Best years ❗1999, '98, '96, '94, '90, '89, '88, '86, '85; ♀1996, '95, '94, '93

CH. SOCIANDO-MALLET★★ ❗   05 56 73 38 80/05 56 73 38 88
Haut-Médoc CB, 58ha
Known as 'the LATOUR of the Haut-Médoc', this château produces intense, classic Cabernet wine which repays aging over 10–15 years. The finest Cru Bourgeois, its quality surpasses that of many Crus Classés and it also commands a premium price.
Best years 1999, '98, '97, '96, '95, '94, '93, '91, '90, '89, '88, '86, '85, '83, '82, '79

CH. SOUTARD★★ ❗ St-Émilion GCC, 22ha   05 57 24 72 23/05 57 24 66 94
An old family estate with a lovely 18th-century château, producing traditional, long-lived wines, now benefiting from more new oak than in the past. The wine is agreeable young, yet can age for up to 20 years.
Best years 1999, '98, '97, '96, '95, '94, '90, '89, '88, '86, '85, '83, '82, '78, '70, '66, '64

FRANCE/BORDEAUX

CH. SUDUIRAUT★★★ ♀ Sauternes 1er CC, 88ha   05 56 63 61 80/05 56 63 61 93

One of the largest estates in Sauternes and perhaps the only wine to have rivalled d' YQUEM in several vintages, for concentration of fruit from fully botrytized grapes. Undergoing a renaissance under the auspices of the AXA insurance group, these are some of the very richest, most unctuous Sauternes easily worthy of their classification.
Best years 1999, '98, '97, '96, '95, '90, '89, '88, '82, '80, '79, '76, '75, '70, '67, '62, '59, '28

CH. TALBOT★★ ♥ St-Julien 4ème CC, 102ha ♥, 6ha ♀   05 56 73 21 50/05 56 73 21 51

The Cordier family has owned Talbot since the early 1900s. Always rich in colour, this wine is most attractive when young, showing a deep smoothness of fruit but also balancing tannins which permit long aging. Since 1994 the quality has improved further. The oak-aged dry white called Caillou Blanc is very attractive.
Best years ♥1999, '98, '97, '96, '95, '94, '90, '89, '88, '86, '85, '83, '82, '79, '66, '62, '61, '59, '45

CH. DU TERTRE★ ♥ Margaux 5ème CC, 48ha   05 57 97 09 09/05 97 09 00

Lying on some of the highest ground in Margaux, du Tertre was sold in 1998 after many decades in the hands of the Capbern Gasqueton family of CALON-SÉGUR. The wines are classic Margaux with colour and complexity and will age for 10-15 years.
Best years 1999, '98, '97, '96, '95, '90, '89, '88, '86, '85, '83, '82

CH. LE TERTRE-RÔTEBOEUF★★ ♥ St-Émilion, 4.5ha   Fax 05 57 74 42 11

A wine of extraordinary concentration and depth from an immaculately run estate known for harvesting as late as possible in order to obtain exceptionally ripe grapes.
Best years 1999, '98, '97, '96, '95, '94, '93, '90, '89, '88, '86, '85, '83, '82, '81

CH. TEYSSIER★ ♥ St-Émilion GC, 18ha   05 57 84 64 22/05 57 84 63 54

Since purchasing the estate in 1994, Jonathan and Lyn Malthus have raised the quality of Ch. Teyssier to rival that of the Crus Classés. The two special cuvées, Le Dôme★★ and La Forge★★, are remarkable.
Best years 1999, '98, '96, '95

CH. LA TOUR-BLANCHE★★ ♀ Sauternes 1er CC, 35ha   05 57 98 02 73/05 57 98 02 78

La Tour-Blanche, placed second to d'YQUEM in the 1855 Classification, went through a long period of decline until the mid-1980s. Under new direction and benefiting from investment in new oak, the wines are now full-flavoured and concentrated.
Best years 1999, '98, '97, '96, '95, '94, '90, '89, '88, '86

CH. LA TOUR-CARNET★ ♥   05 57 22 28 00/05 57 22 28 05
Haut-Médoc 4ème CC, 43ha

La Tour-Carnet has much increased in quality since 1990 and should improve still further under the new ownership of Bernard Magrez of Ch. PAPE-CLÉMENT.
Best years 1999, '98, '96, '95, '90, '89, '88, '86

CH LA TOUR-HAUT-BRION★★ ♥   05 56 00 29 30/05 56 98 75 14
Pessac-Léognan, 4.9ha ♥

A wine of very deep colour and rich, smoky aromas, this is one of the finest, but least-known red Graves. The vineyards were part of the La MISSION-HAUT-BRION holdings purchased from the Woltner family by the Duc and Duchesse de Mouchy of HAUT-BRION in 1983. Jean-Bernard Delmas of Haut-Brion oversees the winemaking.
Best years 1999, '98, '97, '96, '95, '94, '90, '89, '88, '82, '78, '75

CH. TROPLONG-MONDOT★★ ❗
05 57 55 32 05/05 57 55 32 07
St-Émilion GCC, 30ha

A large estate for St-Émilion, at the highest point of the appellation above Ch. PAVIE, which has been producing superb, deeply concentrated, yet elegant and long-lasting wines over the past decade. It was a strong contender for elevation to Premier Grand Cru Classé status in the revised St-Émilion classification of 1996.

Best years 1999, '98, '97, '96, '95, '94, '93, '90, '89, '88, '86, '85

CH. TROTANOY★★ ❗ Pomerol, 7.5ha
05 57 51 78 96/05 57. 51 79 79

Another of the prestigious châteaux owned or managed by J-P Moueix in Pomerol, Trotanoy has vines near those of PÉTRUS, but on more clayey soil. The wine is very dark in colour, robust and firm when young and needing 10 years to fully open up and become one of the longest-lived wines of this appellation.

Best years 1999, '98, '97, '96, '95, '90, '89, '88, '82, '79, '78, '76, '75, '71, '70, '67, '66, '64, '61, '59, '45, '28

CH. TROTTEVIEILLE★ ❗ St-Émilion 1er GCC B, 10ha
05 57 24 71 34/05 57 87 60 30

A traditionally made wine from mainly old vines, generally full-bodied and robust but not always possessing the depth and finesse expected from a Premier Grand Cru Classé.

Best years 1999, '98, '97, '96, '95, '94, '90, '89, '88, '86, '85

CH. DE VALANDRAUD★★ ❗ St-Émilion, 2.5ha
05 57 24 65 60/05 57 24 67 03

This tiny estate made its first wine only in 1992 – of great concentration and using 100% new wood, it was one of the great surprises of the vintage. It has become one of St-Émilion's most sought-after wines, as well as one of Bordeaux's most expensive.

Best years 1999, '98, '97, '96, '95, '94, '93, '92

VIEUX-CHÂTEAU-CERTAN★★★ ❗ Pomerol, 13.5ha
05 57 51 17 33 /05 57 25 35 08

With vines adjoining those of PÉTRUS, this superb estate produces Pomerol's most elegant wines. The high proportion of Cabernet Sauvignon and Cabernet Franc for the appellation (up to 45%) allows it to age more gracefully than any other Pomerol. Wines made during the last decade have been superlative.

Best years 1999, '98, '97, '96, '95, '94, '93, '90, '89, '88, '86, '85, '83, '82, '78, '75, '70, '66, '64, '61, '59, '53, '52, '50, '48, '47, '45, '29

CH D'YQUEM★★★ ♀ Sauternes 1er CC, 102ha
05 57 98 07 07/05 57 98 07 08

This renowned wine is the quintessence of great Sauternes. No effort is spared to make the most concentrated wine possible from botrytis-affected grapes with the vintage sometimes spreading over 6 weeks or more. Production, from old vines, is rarely more than one glass of wine per vine, compared to one whole bottle in the Médoc. The intense and exotic flavour improves with keeping for anything up to half a century. Although this is the largest estate in Sauternes, world demand outstrips supply to ensure that Yquem is rare, and sold only in the most select places. Although very expensive, this unique wine is generally less expensive than the Médoc Premiers Crus Classés, a situation some view as unjust. There is also a stylish, quite rich, honeyed dry white called 'Y' or Ygrec produced in certain years. The giant LVMH group has recently taken over the estate from the Lur-Saluces family, owners for 406 years.

Best years 1995, '93, '90, '89, '88, '86, '83, '81, '80, '79, '76, '75, '71, '70, '67, 62, '59, '55, '53, '49, '47, '45, '43, '37, '29, '28, '21

BORDEAUX'S SECOND WINES

The existence of 'second wines' is not new, but it was only in the 1980s that they began to exist on a large scale, and to acquire an economic validity of their own. The purpose of a second wine is to allow châteaux that wish to maintain high standards for their flagship wine to declassify a proportion of the crop each year but still bottle it at the château, selling it under a different label to that of the main label or 'Grand Vin'.

Second wines

Generally, second labels used to be reserved for wines made either from young vines, or from grapes picked too early or too late. In the last decade, however, it has become an obligation for the top châteaux to make a more and more rigorous selection as to what is bottled as their Grand Vin, with the result that second wines have to some extent lost their 'declassified' image, and have become demanded in their own right. All second wines are château-bottled.

Pricing second wines

The price of a second wine begins at not more than 50% of that of the Grand Vin, and since there is much less speculative value in a second wine, the gap will normally widen as the wine matures. From quality producers, a second wine is a very good way to appreciate the vintage and the appellation, as well as the style of the particular château, but, however attractive the price in relation to its big brother, second wines will not have the depth of the Grand Vin. The list below is of the better known châteaux with the names of their second wines.

Angélus (Carillon de l'Angélus); Beychevelle (Amiral de Beychevelle, Réserve de l'Amiral); Branaire (Duluc); Brane-Cantenac (Ch. Notton, Dom. de Fontarney); Calon-Ségur (Marquis de Ségur); Canon (Clos J. Kanon); Canon-La-Gaffelière (Côte Migon-La-Gaffelière); Cantemerle (Villeneuve de Cantemerle); Cantenac-Brown (Canuet); Chasse-Spleen (L'Hermitage de Chasse-Spleen); Cheval-Blanc (Le Petit Cheval); Climens (Les Cyprès de Climens); Clos Fourtet (Dom. de Martialis); Cos d'Estournel (Les Pagodes de Cos); Ducru-Beaucaillou (La Croix); Duhart-Milon (Le Moulin de Duhart); de Fieuzal (L'Abeille de Fieuzal); Figeac (Les Grangeneuves de Figeac); La Gaffelière (Clos La Gaffelière); Gloria (Haut-Beychevelle-Gloria); Grand-Puy-Ducasse (Artigues-Arnaud); Grand-Puy-Lacoste (Lacoste-Borie); Gruaud-Larose (Sarget de Gruaud-Larose); Guiraud (Le Dauphin); Haut-Bailly (La Parde de Haut-Bailly); Haut-Batailley (Le Tour d'Aspic); Haut-Brion (Bahans Haut-Brion); Lafite-Rothschild (Carruades de Ch. Lafite); Lafleur (Pensées de Lafleur); Lafon-Rochet (No 2 de Lafon-Rochet); La Lagune (Ludon-Pomies-Agassac); Langoa-Barton (Lady Langoa); Lascombes (Ségonnes); Latour (Les Forts de Latour); Léoville-Barton (La Réserve de Léoville-Barton); Léoville-Poyferré (Moulin-Riche); Lynch-Bages (Haut-Bages-Avérous); Margaux (Pavillon Rouge de Ch. Margaux); Montrose (La Dame de Montrose); Mouton-Rothschild (Le Petit Mouton); Palmer (Réserve du Général); Pape-Clement (Le Clementin du Pape-Clement); Phélan-Ségur (Franck Phelan); Pichon-Longueville-Baron (Les Tourelles de Pichon); Pichon-Longueville-Lalande (Réserve de la Comtesse); Pontet-Canet (Les Hauts de Pontet); Poujeaux (La Salle de Poujeaux); Prieuré-Lichine (Clairefont); Rauzan-Ségla (Lamouroux); Smith-Haut-Lafitte (Les Hauts de Smith-Haut-Lafitte); Talbot (Connétable de Talbot); Troplong-Mondot (Mondot); Valandraud (Virginie de Valandraud); Vieux-Château-Certan (Clos de la Gravette).

Red Bordeaux is one of the longest-lived wines in the world, thanks to the dense fruit and tannins of the Cabernet and Merlot grapes and to its excellent balance. It is as impossible to disassociate these fine wines from their vintage date as it is to separate them from their appellation.

Aging qualities

Modern vineyard management and winemaking mean that red Bordeaux may be consumed earlier than in the past. Grapes are picked when they are more fully ripe, when the tannins are rounder, and when improved cellar techniques can provide depth of fruit extraction without hardness. Yet although such wines, even in great years, are enjoyable younger than before, they age as well as they did in the past.

Given proper cellarage conditions, well-made wines from good vintages are still in the prime of life at 20–25 years and the very greatest wines will last for a further 20, even 30 years. Cabernet Sauvignon and Cabernet Franc have more natural tannin than Merlot, but it is ripeness as much as tannin that allows a wine to age well. Up to the early 1970s, even including '78, most wines possessed a firmness of style that gave the wine backbone and 'grip', but progress both in the cellar and in the vineyard, the latter seemingly helped by global warming, has produced wines with riper tannins, which can be enjoyed even after 4–5 years. Since balance is as important to a wine's aging

Maturity charts

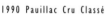

1990 was a very hot, dry year and produced superb wines in the Médoc. The top Pauillac wines have wonderful ripeness, giving intensity of fruit, rounded tannins and balanced acidity. In St-Émilion the wines were rich and intensely fruity with excellent balance.

1990 Pauillac Cru Classé

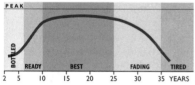

1990 St-Émilion 1er Cru Classé

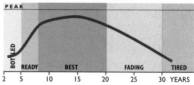

VINTAGE CHART

	99	98	97	96	95	94	93	91	90	89	88	87
Northern Haut-Médoc (inc. St-Estèphe, Pauillac, St-Julien)	8○	8○	7○	9○	8○	7○	6●	5●	10◑	9◑	8◑	6●
Southern Haut-Médoc (inc. Margaux, Listrac, Moulis)	8○	8○	7○	8○	8○	6○	6●	5●	9●	8◑	7◑	5●
Graves, Pessac-Léognan	7○	8○	7○	8○	8○	7○	6●	5●	8●	8◑	8●	5●
St-Émilion, Pomerol	8○	10○	7○	7○	8○	7○	6●	3●	10◑	9◑	8●	6●

KEY ○= needs more time ◑= ready but will improve ●= at peak ◑= fading or tired

potential as concentration, there is no reason to suppose that they will age any less well, although today's wines, even in great years, may be drunk younger.

Even a region with a temperate climate like Bordeaux will suffer from poor vintages as well as profit from good ones. A poor vintage is when the grapes do not ripen properly, thus not producing sufficient colour, fruit and tannin to make a very successful wine. Progress in the vineyards and in the cellar, rather than changes in the climate, have ensured that disastrous vintages like 1968, '65 and '63 are now a thing of the past. As a rule, wines from the right bank (St-Émilion, Pomerol and the Libournais) mature earlier than wines from the left bank (Médoc and Graves).

Annual vintage reports

1999★★ Heavy rain spoiled a second superb year for the right bank, but the thicker skins of the Cabernets ensured good overall quality on the left bank.
1998★★-★★★ A magnificent vintage for Pomerol and St-Émilion, the best since 1990, and very good but not great in the Médoc and the Graves.
1997★★ The most drawn-out vintage in recent times, running from mid-September to mid-October. Generally more successful in the Merlot-based Libournais than in the Cabernet-based Médoc, but good wines overall.

1996★★-★★★ Very good in the Médoc, with perfect Cabernet Sauvignon; good, but not great, on the right bank.
1995★★ Despite some rain during the vintage, the grapes had good ripeness and thick skins at the start, to provide good colour and concentration.
1994★-★★ A rainy vintage, but generally more successful than first thought. The earlier-ripening Merlot-based right bank fared better than the Médoc and Graves.
1993★ Almost continuous rain during the vintage diluted what looked like a good year, although there were some attractive wines made on both banks.
1992 Rain throughout the harvest washed any concentration out of the grapes. Very few successful wines.
1991★ A severe frost in late April caused major damage to Merlot, and October rains dashed hopes for a successful, late harvest. A small and difficult vintage, but with more character than '92.
1990★★★ A very hot, dry year, where the vines narrowly avoided being starved of water, but rain in early September saved the day to produce wines with immense concentration yet also excellent balance. The Médocs are probably the finest since '82. The Graves, St-Émilion and Pomerol are also very good.
1989★★★ Intense heat and near-drought conditions produced the earliest vintage this century. Spectacularly rich, opulent wines were made throughout the

Libournais and the Graves, only the Médocs being a little over-concentrated.

1988★★ A very fine vintage producing deep-coloured wines with fine tannic structure. Although surpassed by both '90 and '89 in volume and richness of fruit, this is a very good year for classic wines.

1987★ A year of almost continuous rain, where the Merlot suffered more than the Cabernet. Some attractive, light wines were made, but not for keeping.

1986★★-★★★ A classic Médoc vintage and a very large crop, with more colour, body and tannin than the '85s. The Graves were also very good, but quality tended to be much more variable in St-Émilion and Pomerol on the right bank.

1985★★★ An almost unparalleled stretch of sunny, dry weather from August to October produced a large crop of extremely healthy, very ripe grapes. The quality of the wines was consistently good throughout the region.

1983★★ A large crop of firm, tannic wines, less successful in St-Émilion and Pomerol than in the Graves and the Médoc, and very successful in Margaux.

1982★★★ A very large crop of sun-filled, perfectly ripe grapes that produced plummy wines with great richness and depth of fruit. An extraordinarily impressive vintage, particularly in the Libournais. In very many cases, the best vintage since '61, but with softer tannins.

1981★-★★ Well-balanced wines, but without the opulent fruit of '82, and less depth than '79 and '78. Very good Graves.

1979★★ Very large crop from a late harvest that produced wines with excellent colour, fruit and depth from St-Émilion, Pomerol and the Graves, and a little lighter in the Médoc.

1978★★ A fine, warm autumn saved this vintage, to produce wines with good colour and concentration of fruit. The tannins were firmer than in '79, giving the wines a leaner, more classic appearance.

1976★ A very hot dry summer was broken by autumn rains, which the skins were thick enough to resist, to produce solid, robust wines rather lacking in finesse.

1975★-★★ Initially considered to be a great year, but the tannins proved to be excessive in many cases, although the wines had better length than '76.

1971★★ A large crop. Much better in St-Émilion and Pomerol than on the left bank.

1970★★★ A very large crop for the time, and an encouragingly high concentration of fruit thoughout. The best wines are still supported by their deep tannins.

1966★★★ Fine, classically structured wines, particularly good in the Médoc.

1964★-★★★ Superb in St-Émilion and Pomerol, good in the Graves, but very inconsistent in the Médoc, due to rain spoiling the vintage.

1962★★ Very well balanced wines, over-shadowed by the '61s.

1961★★★ Rightly considered one of the classic vintages of this century, producing intense, concentrated and beautifully balanced wines, many of legendary quality.

1959★★-★★★ A very hot year, with some quite outstanding wines that rival, even surpass the '61s, but less consistent overall.

Other good years 1955 produced fine, stylish wines, particularly in the Graves and the Médoc; '53 was a year of great finesse and charm whose wines have aged very well; '52 was more sturdy and powerful, but less balanced. The wines of the late '40s, with the exception of '46, were all very good: classic, intense wines from '49, slightly leaner ones from '48, splendidly opulent and rich wines from '47 and magnificently concentrated wines from the famous vintage of 1945.

WHITE BORDEAUX VINTAGES

Both dry and sweet Bordeaux wines age extremely well. Dry wines, at least those of quality, generally have a high proportion of Sémillon and almost all hail from the Graves and Pessac-Léognan appellations. These mature well for up to a decade, with the best examples keeping longer. Sweet white wines with high levels of sugars and alcohol from Barsac, Sauternes, Ste-Croix-du-Mont or Loupiac, can be some of Bordeaux's longest-lived wines.

Aging dry white wines

If Sauvignon is planted in the well-drained, gravelly soil of the Graves, it will be less overtly fruity, but possess finesse and length, and age well for up to 10 years. Sémillon is less aromatic and far less showy in its youth, but ages superbly, acquiring waxy, lanolin characteristics, blended with a toastiness if it has been in new oak. While the best dry white has the fruit to be attractive soon after bottling, it does need 2–3 years more to show its full dimensions, and ages slowly thereafter. Although these wines can be kept longer, the fruit begins to fade after 10 years. Only the very best wines will improve into their second decade.

Aging sweet white wines

Owing to their high alcohol and sugar content, sweet wines age very well. The lighter ones may be drunk when bottled and kept for 1–2 years, but the finer, richer wines (usually affected by botrytis) will show beautifully at 10 years old and continue to mature over 20–30 years or even longer. The very best, if properly stored and re-corked when necessary, will last for over 50 years. A good vintage for sweet white wine depends, however, on the appearance of *Botrytis cinerea*, or noble rot, and this does not happen every year. On average, the quality of the grapes is good enough only 5 years in a decade to make a good nobly rotted sweet wine.

Maturity charts

1996 was a fine year for top white Pessac-Léognan wines and very fine for Sauternes, the best vintage since the glorious trio of 1990, '89 and '88.

1996 Pessac-Léognan Cru Classé
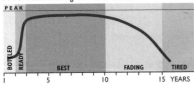

1996 Sauternes 1er Cru Classé
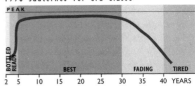

VINTAGE CHART

	99	98	97	96	95	94	93	91	90	89	88	87
Dry Graves, Pessac-Léognan	9○	8○	5◑	8◑	8●	9●	5◑	5◑	9●	8◑	9●	5◑
Sauternes	9○	8○	9○	9○	7○	6●	4◑	3◑	10◑	9◑	9●	3◑

KEY ○= needs more time   ◑= ready but will improve   ●= at peak   ◐= fading or tired

VINTAGES AT A GLANCE

Vintages for dry white Bordeaux are more reliable than for reds because Sémillon and Sauvignon ripen before the red varieties at the beginning of the harvest when there is less risk of adverse weather.

	Dry White Bordeaux	Sweet White Bordeaux
Great Years ★★★	1996, '94, '90, '88, '83	1999, '97, '96, '90, '89, '88, '86, '83, '67, '61, '59, '55, '53, '49, '47, '45
Good Years ★★	1999, '98, '96, '95, '89, '85	1998, '95, '88, '81, '79, '76, '75, '71
Moderate Years ★	1997, '93, '91, '87, '86, '84, '82, '81	1995, '94, '85, '84, '82, '78
Poor Years (No Stars)	1992	1993, '92, '91, '87

Annual vintage reports

1999 Dry★★ Picked generally before the mid-September rains, the wines have fine balance and elegant fruit. **Sweet★★★** A remarkable vintage that survived the rain to make rich, concentrated wines.

1998 Dry★★ Well-extracted, well-balanced wines. **Sweet★★** Good, rich wines overall.

1997 Dry★ The earliest harvest this century, the first grapes being picked in mid-August, but great problems with grey rot. **Sweet★★★** A very long, drawn-out harvest produced some excellent wines, though in very small quantities.

1996 Dry★★-★★★ Elegant wines with stylish fruit and good acidity. **Sweet★★★** Very good conditions for botrytis.

1995 Dry★★ Wines with ripeness and weight, which will mature well. **Sweet★-★★** Rich, powerful wines.

1994 Dry★★★ A good year, despite rain during the harvest. Finely balanced wines. **Sweet★** A small but good-quality vintage.

1993 Dry★ Despite the rain, some attractive wines were made. **Sweet** Very little wine, owing to wet weather.

1991 Dry★ A very small vintage, owing to frost, but some good wines. **Sweet** Spring frost and October rains spoiled the vintage.

1990 Dry★★★ Very good ripeness, due to the hot summer, but also good balancing acidity. **Sweet★★★** A great, rich vintage.

1989 Dry★★ An even hotter year than '90

gave the wines more weight than acidity. **Sweet★★★** A great vintage, even more concentration, but less botrytis than '90.

1988 Dry★★★ A classic vintage that produced elegant, long-lasting wines. **Sweet★★-★★★** A fine, classic year giving wines with structure and concentration.

1987 Dry★ The dry whites escaped the rain that spoilt the rest of Bordeaux. **Sweet** A light year, spoilt by rain.

1986 Dry★ Floral and well balanced wines. **Sweet★★★** A splendid year, with richness and real elegance.

1985 Dry★★ Good wines, but less impressive than the reds. **Sweet★** This dry, sunny vintage produced much better red wines than whites.

1984 Dry★ Crisp, lively wines, a little lacking in weight. **Sweet★** Some passable wine was made.

1983 Dry★★★ Wines of concentration and elegance. **Sweet★★★** A great year, the first of such quality for 16 years.

1982 Dry★ Large crop of supple, quick-maturing wines. **Sweet★** Potential richness was spoilt by rain in the Sauternes region.

1981 Dry★ Lively, attractive wines. **Sweet★★** Elegant wines, with good sweetness and concentration.

Other good years Dry Most are past their best. **Sweet** 1979, '76, '75 and '71 but none have the quality of '90/'89/'88 and '97/'96/'95. Also excellent were 1967, '61, '59, '55, '53, '49, '47 and '45.

BURGUNDY

The vineyards of Burgundy extend across 4 *départements* south-east of Paris: the Yonne, the Côte d'Or, the Saône-et-Loire and the Rhône. Burgundy's wines are less uniform in style than those of, say, Alsace or Champagne, but at the same time less diverse than wines from the Loire or Rhône valleys. One obvious reason for this is the tight focus on Pinot Noir and Chardonnay. In complete contrast to Bordeaux, that age-old rival as a producer of fine wine, Burgundy has a vast number of appellations, in many cases smaller than a single Médoc Cru Classé. A Burgundy appellation tends to be divided up between a whole multitude of growers, who may sell their produce in bulk to merchants or else opt to bottle the wine themselves.

WINE REGIONS

The Burgundy region is generally divided into distinct areas where the wines, although largely made from the same grapes, have very different characters which reflect varying climates and soil types.

Chablis and the Auxerrois
This is the northern limit for making red wines in France, with the exception of the rare reds in Champagne and Alsace. Pinot Noir is the main red grape but the finest wines are white, from Sauvignon Blanc which thrives on the chalky limestone soil, Aligoté and above all Chardonnay, the grape used for world-famous Chablis.

Côte de Nuits
The northern part of the famous Côte d'Or, which is almost exclusively red wine country. The vineyards stretch from the outskirts of Dijon to south of the town of Nuits-St-Georges and villages here produce some of the world's most sought-after red wines, all from Pinot Noir, which achieves magical results here.

Côte de Beaune
Beginning at the great hill of Corton, north of the town of Beaune, the vineyards continue south to Santenay, near Chagny, with white wines gradually taking over from red, Chardonnay from Pinot Noir. Top vineyards are all on the west side of the N74 and vines on heavier soils on the other side of the road must use the regional Bourgogne appellation, rather than the village name.

Côte Chalonnaise
Vineyards continue south from the Côte de Beaune almost without interruption and this area has gained enormously in importance in recent years. Chardonnay and Pinot Noir are still the main grapes, with some excellent whites from Aligoté.

The Mâconnais
Three-quarters of the vineyards are planted with Chardonnay. Pouilly-Fuissé is the best-known wine, with some fine estates.

Beaujolais
The most southerly and most scenic vineyards of Burgundy, stretching from just south of Mâcon to the edge of Lyon. Just under half the wines carry the basic

Beaujolais appellation and are light reds to be drunk within months of the harvest. The finest wines come from 10 villages or Crus in the northern part of the region. Gamay is the only grape allowed for red Beaujolais and Chardonnay is used for the tiny production of white Beaujolais.

Terroir

Terroir has really created the Burgundy appellations with the soil rather than climate distinguishing the different wines. In Chablis it is the same chalk as in Champagne that gives Chardonnay such minerality and firmness; in the Côte d'Or it is limestone that brings elegance to Pinot Noir and Chardonnay; and in Beaujolais granite-based soil lends character to the Gamay grape.

Buying top-quality Burgundy

More than in any other region of France, it is the name of the bottler on the label – whether *négociant*, grower or co-operative – that is the guide to quality. Quality and price are so variable within each appellation that it is important to have the guarantee of a good producer.

Négociants and growers

The *négociants* of Burgundy, based historically in Nuits-St-Georges and Beaune, forged the reputation of this region's wines. They not only negotiate contracts to buy in grapes, must or finished wine from growers, bring them on and bottle them, but many of them also own large holdings in some of the most prestigious vineyards in Burgundy.

However good their skills in vinification, *élevage* and distribution, the key to quality is a supply of good grapes. In recent years, larger *négociants* have been adding to their vineyard holdings in order

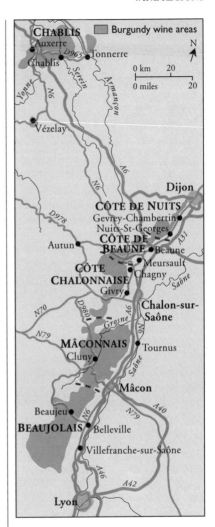

to obtain a guaranteed supply of grapes and produce wines to rival those made by the best growers in each appellation.

Quality rose substantially during the 1990s, the final guarantee being careful bottling. Choose wines bottled at the domaine or in the region itself.

BURGUNDY'S APPELLATIONS AND CLASSIFICATIONS

The French system of Appellation d'Origine Contrôlée is at its most precise in Burgundy, especially in the Côte d'Or, where a minutely accurate classification of vineyards, *climats* and Crus has evolved down the centuries.

Generic appellations

The appellation Bourgogne covers the basic level of red and white wines made from Pinot Noir or Chardonnay grapes planted anywhere in Burgundy. There are massive differences in style and quality but some fine wines can be found under this label, from good producers with vineyards in good locations. If a rosé wine is made – always from the Pinot Noir grape – the appellation is Bourgogne Rosé, and there is some good sparkling wine under the name Crémant de Bourgogne. While the white Aligoté grape may be planted anywhere in the region, the wine must be called Bourgogne-Aligoté, to distinguish it from white Burgundy made with Chardonnay. The newly created appellations of Bourgogne-Côte d'Auxerre, Bourgogne-Hautes-Côtes de Nuits, Bourgogne-Hautes-Côtes de Beaune and Bourgogne-Côte Chalonnaise are geographically more specific.

Regional appellations

These are generally very large appellations representing a specific region, such as Chablis, Côte de Nuits-Villages, Côte de Beaune-Villages, Beaujolais and Mâcon.

Village or communal appellations

In the Côte d'Or and the Côte Chalonnaise each village has its vineyards legally defined. Those with no special reputation, which do not qualify for the higher levels of Premier and Grand Cru, are usually sold under the village name. The wine may be blended from more than one *climat* or vineyard within the village. Wines labelled Volnay, Meursault, Fixin or Rully, for example, may be from any part of the appellation. If such a wine comes from a single *climat* or *lieu-dit* ('named place') this may be added on the label below the appellation name, but only in letters half the size.

Premiers Crus

Certain specific vineyard sites in a communal appellation, generally with a long-established reputation, have been classified as Premier Cru or First Growth. On the label, the site may be hyphenated with the village name, as in Meursault-Charmes, or put below the appellation, as in Vosne-Romanée Les Malconsorts. If two or more Premiers Crus are blended together, the label will state Premier Cru, but may not use the individual names. The names of the best Premiers Crus in each village can be found on pages 78–94. The Mâconnais and Beaujolais have no Premiers Crus.

Grands Crus

Even though Premier Cru does mean First Growth, it is the Grands Crus or Great Growths that represent the pinnacle of quality in Burgundy. The Grands Crus of the Côte d'Or have their own individual appellations and use only their name on the label, omitting the village they come from, since their name is already superior to the village appellation. In Chablis, the appellation is used with the name of the Grand Cru. With the exception of Corton in the Côte de Beaune, all the red Grands Cru are in the Côte de Nuits, and apart from a few white vines in Musigny, all the white Grands Crus are either in the Côte de Beaune or in Chablis. As may be seen from the map, the Grands Crus tend to be clustered together, where soil, vine location and mesoclimate are particularly favourable. Many of the best Premiers Crus immediately adjoin the Grands Crus, in only marginally less-favoured sites.

The size of each individual Grand Cru is small, and there are both legal and voluntary restrictions on yield to reduce the quantity produced from these superb sites still further. While low yields (below 35hl/ha) do not in themselves create depths of flavour in a Grand Cru wine, excess yields will certainly dilute it and willingness to sacrifice quantity for quality is the hallmark of every good producer, not just in Burgundy.

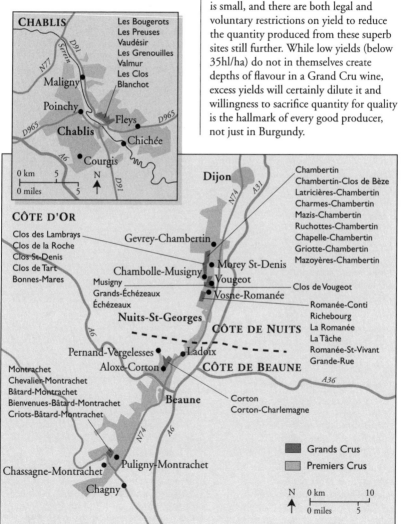

RED BURGUNDY

Red Burgundy is made exclusively from Pinot Noir, arguably the most temperamental of the world's noble grape varieties, both to grow and to vinify. During the 1990s there was a marked increase in quality at all levels, and although really great red Burgundy is still only available in tiny quantities, from a very few vineyards, most of which are in the Côte d'Or, there are undoubtedly many more good wines available than ever before.

Taste characteristics

In the right hands, fine red Burgundy can be the most seductive of all red wines. When young, it should be fragrant and fruity, with tones of raspberry, strawberry, cherry or plum, sometimes with a hint of chocolate and often a touch of new oak. As it matures, primary fruits give way to flavours from the soil, showing the terroir, mingling with aromas of *sous bois*, or autumnal undergrowth, sometimes truffles and well-hung game.

All great red Burgundy should have concentration and depth, remarkable nuance and complexity of flavour and impressive texture and structure, but it should not be heavy. Pinot Noir does not have to be dark in colour and deeply extracted to show flavour, and while really fine colours are to be admired, over-extraction is not.

Grands and Premiers Crus and the best village wines should do honour to their appellations. While lesser communes can provide wines with flavour and character, they do tend to be lighter.

The influence of winemaking

A number of factors over which the winemaker has real control can influence both the wine's flavour and structure. The skill lies in allowing the maximum potential of the raw material to be expressed. At the top estates, the approach is the most 'hands off' – with the finest grapes available, the winemaking process only requires a guiding hand.

The use of oak

New oak has become almost universal in the aging of fine red Burgundy. The proportion used can vary from 10–15%, through 50% to 100% for the grandest wines, and, on very rare occasions, where the wine undergoes malolactic fermentation in a new barrel, and then matures in a different new barrel, 200%!

Wines usually spend 18 months in wood before bottling, but this, and the percentage of new to second- and third-year oak depends both on the vintage and the style of wine sought by the producer.

Since a producer should not waste expensive new barrels on an inferior wine, a rule of thumb could be that 'new oak equals quality'. However, it is vital that the wood does not completely overwhelm the wine once it is in bottle.

Fining and filtration

These practices, once seen as necessary to the wine's long-term stability, are no longer thought to be essential, particularly if the wine is to be bottled in its most natural state. Unfiltered wines throw a deposit, and their storage and handling require more care, but the complex flavours of the wine will be retained in the bottle. Wines bottled unfiltered are often top quality, in need of careful handling.

GREAT RED BURGUNDIES

Oz Clarke's selection

Échézeaux (Emmanuel Rouget) Beautiful perfumed Burgundy with a red cherry-like richness and a deep but delicate soft texture.

Clos de Vougeot (Méo-Camuzet) Irresistible, fleshy Vougeot style with sweet ripe dark fruit, scented oak and an achingly beautiful perfume of violets.

Richebourg (Mongeard-Mugneret) Powerful but beautiful wine, strongly oaked but with a heavenly texture, oozing ripeness, and a richness of blackberry and strawberry syrup.

Charmes-Chambertin (Dugat) Excellent wine that combines the typical muscularity of Chambertin with a heady scent of ripe black cherries.

Vosne-Romanée Les Suchots (Jean Grivot) Fine example of a vineyard in Vosne-Romanée that always exhibits a savoury meatiness adding excitement to the dark chocolate and black plum fruit.

Volnay Santenots (Lafon) Lafon's white wine expertise clearly influences his reds which exhibit irresistible cherry scent and lush texture.

Vosne-Romanée Aux Réas (A-F Gros) Fabulously fragrant red with gorgeous succulent fruit and a savoury mineral texture.

Nuits-St-Georges Les Hauts-Poirets (Jayer-Gilles) Heavily oaked but sublimely textured red, full of ripe cherry fruit and black chocolate richness.

Volnay Taillepieds (Marquis d'Angerville) Marvellous scented Volnay but with weight and structure, too, and a core of ripe morello cherry jam.

Nuits-St-Georges Les St-Georges (Robert Chevillon) Rich style of Nuits packed with lovely ripe cherry and plum fruit and a beguiling floral scent.

Gevrey-Chambertin Lavaux-St-Jacques (Denis Mortet) Classic Gevrey-Chambertin combining considerable structure with rich chocolaty fruit and cherry perfume.

Nuits-St-Georges Hauts Pruliers (Rion) My favourite wine from a domaine that seems to improve with each vintage and now mixes dark plum fruit with a sensuous fat texture and toasty oak.

Steven Spurrier's selection

Chambertin Clos-de-Bèze (Rousseau) The jewel in the crown of this impeccable family domaine.

Bonnes-Mares (Roumier) Under the brilliant Christophe Roumier, this estate has reasserted itself at the top of the Burgundy tree.

Richebourg (Dom. de la Romanée-Conti) For those who cannot afford the

sublime La Tâche or the elegant Romanée-St-Vivant, the Richebourg is always richly rewarding.

Chambolle-Musigny Les Amoureuses (de Vogüé) The finest wine in Chambolle from this superb domaine, back on form since 1989.

Clos Vougeot (Jean Grivot) The Grivot vines, in the best part of Le Clos, give a true expression of this famous Grand Cru.

Nuits-St-Georges Les Vaucrains (Gouges) A classic, family-run domaine, where respect for the vineyard counts more than flashy winemaking.

Corton Clos des Cortons (Faiveley) The epitome of the richly structured, long-lived wines from Corton.

Corton Cuvée Docteur Peste (Hospices de Beaune) Rich and robust wine from one of the finest of the Hospices' many vineyards.

Pommard Clos des Epeneaux (Armand) One of the most impressive and deeply flavoured Pommards.

Volnay-Santenots (Lafon) A fabulous Volnay, from vines in the commune of Meursault.

Volnay Clos des Ducs (d'Angerville) One of the oldest estates in Volnay, producing majestically elegant, long-lasting wines.

Beaune Clos des Mouches (Drouhin) This stylishly oaked red from the family's prized vineyard in Beaune illustrates Drouhin's international reputation for good quality.

Top red Burgundy villages

Aloxe-Corton, Auxey-Duresses, Beaune, Chambolle-Musigny, Chassagne-Montrachet, Fixin, Gevrey-Chambertin, Givry, Mercurey, Monthélie, Morey-St-Denis, Nuits-St-Georges, Pernand-Vergelesses, Pommard, St-Aubin, Santenay, Savigny, Volnay, Vosne-Romanée.

WHITE BURGUNDY

White Burgundy is made (almost) exclusively from Chardonnay, the world's most popular grape variety and comes mainly from the Côte de Beaune. Pinot Gris, known locally as Pinot Beurot, can be found in parts of the Côte de Beaune and there is still some Pinot Blanc in Pernand-Vergelesses. Aligoté is planted throughout the region.

Taste characteristics

Chardonnay can produce an attractive wine wherever it is planted, but Chablis' chalky soils and the Côte de Beaune's limestone happen to suit it perfectly, as do Burgundy's cool springs and warm autumns for long, slow ripening.

The style varies according to the various sub-regions and appellations, with added concentration of bouquet and flavour for the Premiers and the Grands Crus, but white Burgundy should always be a blend of floral and fruit aromas – hawthorn, melon, white peaches – with honeyed, nutty, buttery qualities appearing as the quality increases, followed by supple, rounded fruit flavours on the palate, with a balancing acidity.

Chardonnay, like Pinot Noir, becomes bland and diffuse if over-produced, and incapable of passing the vital message of terroir from the vine to the glass. Minor white Burgundies are refreshing and attractive, but also have a presence and weight that are seldom found in lesser varietal Chardonnays.

Great white Burgundies will have a complex bouquet, many layers of flavour and always a roundness of fruit, but also good structure. Colours vary from pale, buttery yellow, often with hints of green, to a richer, pale gold for the riper wines.

The influence of winemaking

Chardonnay can 'make itself', the juice from the pressed grapes being run off into barrels or vats for the alcoholic and malo-lactic fermentations, and then racked into vats or barrels for further aging, but recent studies have emphasized the importance of the lees during the wine's early life.

The system of *bâtonnage*, which involves forcibly stirring up the lees once or twice a day while in barrel, 'feeds' the wine and balances high acidity. Since this is an expensive, manual process, it is only carried out by producers wanting this extra element of flavour.

The use of oak

It is not necessary for white Burgundy to be made with any new oak, and indeed many growers in Chablis and the Mâconnais firmly disapprove of it, saying that it clouds Chardonnay's pure fruit.

Most fine whites, however, are aged for a time in oak, the percentage of new barrels depending on the domaine and the quality of the wine, and the finest ones will be barrel-fermented as well. The vanillin flavours from new oak blend beautifully with the Chardonnay fruit, and the wine gains complexity from the minuscule oxidation during barrel-aging.

Fining and filtration

Although choosing not to filter red Burgundy is *de rigueur* among many top domaines, white Burgundies are likely to be filtered at the bottling stage, for limpidity and clarity is essential to the way these wines appear at the time of drinking.

GREAT WHITE BURGUNDIES

Oz Clarke's selection

Corton-Charlemagne (Coche-Dury) Coche-Dury makes some of Meursault's greatest wines, but his interpretation of Corton-Charlemagne is magnificent even by his standards.

Meursault Les Charmes (Lafon) Wonderful rich and self-confident style of Meursault from one of Burgundy's leading winemakers.

Meursault Genevrières (Michelot) Deep honeyed wine from one of Meursault's great traditionalists.

Bâtard-Montrachet (Vincent Leflaive) This great Burgundy estate triumphantly returned to form during the 1990s. Its Bâtard is a connoisseur's dream of savoury *pain grillé* and roasted cashews intensity.

Bienvenues-Bâtard-Montrachet (Carillon) Carillon's traditional wine-making style brings out all the richness but also the haughty reserve of this top vineyard.

Corton-Charlemagne (Rollin) Succulent wine swathed in toasty oak, but always suitable for long aging.

Bâtard-Montrachet (J-N Gagnard) Excellent deep, nutty wine, rich but with a most individual muscular meatiness.

Meursault Perrières (Roulot) Top Meursault sometimes streaked with a mineral ruthlessness but always wrapped in intense, long-lasting fruit.

Pouilly-Fuissé Vieilles Vignes (Ch. Fuissé) Super-ripe Burgundy dripping with honey, peach and angelica and proof that Pouilly-Fuissé can be a great wine.

Chablis Les Clos (J-M Brocard) One of Chablis' most go-ahead, quality-conscious growers produces thrilling, ripe wines from the great Grand Cru Les Clos.

Pouilly-Fuissé Hors Classe (Ferret) A fine old Pouilly-Fuissé estate making rich yet dry wines full of nuts and cream but always revealing a touch of wild 'Sauvage'.

Chablis Vaillons (Defaix) Classic wine from a top Premier Cru, ripe yet minerally and benefiting from 18 months' aging on the lees.

Steven Spurrier's selection

Chablis Les Clos (Raveneau) Les Clos is generally the richest of Chablis' Grands Crus and this example comes from Chablis' most reputed domaine.

Chablis Les Preuses (Dauvissat) Produced by another exceptional family domaine, this wine comes from the Chablis Grand Cru with the most finesse.

Chablis Vaudésir (Droin) The use of oak heightens the complexities of this superb Grand Cru.

Nuits-St-Georges Les Perrières (Gouges) A very rare white Nuits-St-Georges, combining finesse and body.

Meursault Clos de la Barre (Lafon) A wine worthy of Premier Cru status from Meursault's top domaine.

Meursault-Genevrières (Pierre Morey) One of the most elegant Premiers Crus from a supremely talented winemaker.

Meursault-Perrières (Coche-Dury) Coche-Dury stands alongside Lafon and Morey, at the peak of quality in Meursault.

Puligny-Montrachet Les Pucelles (Leflaive) This estate is the world reference for elegant Chardonnay.

Puligny-Montrachet Les Combettes (Sauzet) This Premier Cru in the hands of Gérard Boudot can equal a Bâtard-Montrachet.

Puligny-Montrachet Les Folatières (Jadot) Rich and voluptuous, this is a flagship wine of this fine *négociant*.

Corton-Charlemagne (Bonneau du Martray) The largest and best-situated holding combined with careful winemaking produces a great wine that has few rivals.

Mâcon-Pierreclos La Chavigne Vieilles Vignes (Guffens-Heynen) Probably the finest wine from the Mâconnais region.

Top white Burgundy villages

Auxey-Duresses, Bâtard-Montrachet, Bienvenues-Bâtard-Montrachet, Blagny, Chablis, Chablis Premier Cru, Chablis Grand Cru, Chassagne-Montrachet, Chevalier-Montrachet, Corton-Charlemagne, Mercurey, Meursault, Montagny, Le Montrachet, Pernand-Vergelesses, Pouilly-Fuissé, Puligny-Montrachet, Rully, St-Véran.

A–Z OF BURGUNDY WINE REGIONS

ALOXE-CORTON AC

An important village at the northern end of the Côte de Beaune, Aloxe-Corton produces almost entirely red wine. One-third of its vines are Premiers Crus, but it is most famous for the Grand Cru vineyards of Corton and Corton-Charlemagne. The village wine has a full colour and a meaty, robust fruitiness and is at its best from 6–12 years old.

Premiers Crus Partly located in the commune of Ladoix-Serrigny, these lie on the slopes below the Grands Crus and above the village wines. The best are Les Vazolières, Les Maréchaudes, Les Fournières, Les Paulands and Les Chaillots.

Best producers BOUCHARD Père et Fils, Denis Boussey, CHAMPY, Marc COLIN, DROUHIN, Antonin GUYON, LATOUR, Prince Florent de Mérode, Comte SENARD, TOLLOT-BEAUT, Michel Voarick.

Best years 1999, '98, '96, '95, '93, '90, '89, '88, '85.

AUXEY-DURESSES AC

This small village just below Monthélie and north-west of Meursault produces both red and white wine. The white wines are lively and stylish, comparable to a minor Meursault, and should be drunk at 2–4 years of age. The reds have more finesse than Monthélie, and are also softer and quicker-maturing.

Premiers Crus There are 9 Premiers Crus. The best ones are Clos du Val, Les Duresses (shared with Monthélie) and Les Grands Champs.

Best producers d'AUVENAY, Comte ARMAND, BOUCHARD Père & Fils, BOUZEREAU, Boyer-Martenot, COCHE-DURY, Alain Creusefond, Jean-Pierre Diconne, DROUHIN, JADOT, Jaffelin, André & Bernard Labry, Henri Latour &

Fils, Olivier LEFLAIVE, Jean-Pierre Prunier, Pascal Prunier, Michel Prunier, Philippe Prunier-Damy, Dominique & Vincent Roy, Philippe Taupenot.

Best years ♥1999, '98, '96, '95, '93, '90; ♀1999, '96.

BÂTARD-MONTRACHET AC

This world-famous white Grand Cru is almost equally divided between the communes of Puligny and Chassagne and lies directly below Le Montrachet. The wine has great richness and intensity of flavour, yet can sometimes lack elegance. Drink at 5–10 years, although the best wines can improve for a few years longer.

Best producers Bachelet-Ramonet, BLAIN-GAGNARD, Jean-Marc BOILLOT, Henri Clerc, Fernand Coffinet, COLIN-DELÉGER, DROUHIN, Richard FONTAINE-GAGNARD, Jean-Noël GAGNARD, Jacques GAGNARD-DELAGRANGE, HOSPICES DE BEAUNE, JADOT, LATOUR, LEFLAIVE, Olivier LEFLAIVE, Louis Lequin, Marc Morey, Pierre MOREY, NIELLON, Paul Pernot, RAMONET, SAUZET, VERGET.

Best years 1999, '96, '95, '93, '92, '90, '89, '88, '86, '85.

BEAUNE AC

The town of Beaune gives its name to the southern part of the Côte d'Or and also to this appellation for red and white wine from one of the largest communes in the Côte d'Or. The Premier Cru vines tend to far exceed the village wines; the latter have good colour with straightforward Pinot fruit and are attractive at 4–8 years. Many Beaune *négociants* have holdings in the appellation, making high-quality wines.

Premiers Crus These lie adjacent to Savigny-lès-Beaune in the north and to Pommard in the south. The wines have more depth, intensity of bouquet, flavour and velvety fruit than straight Beaune and are still maturing at 12–15 years. The best ones are: (north) Les Marconnets, Clos du Roi, Les Perrières, Clos des Fèves, Les Cents Vignes, Les Bressandes, Les Greves, La Vigne de l'Enfant Jésus, Les Teurons and Les Cras; (south) La Montée Rouge, Clos de la Mousse, Les Champimont, Les Avaux, Les Aigrots, Clos des Ursules, Les Vignes Franches, Clos des Mouches, Les Boucherottes and Les Epenottes. The HOSPICES DE BEAUNE own the largest holding of fine Premiers Crus.

Best producers Robert Ampeau, Bernard Bescancenot, Vincent Bitouzet-Prieur, BOUCHARD Père & Fils, Henri Cauvard, CHAMPY, CHANSON, Ch. de Chorey-lès-Beaune, DROUHIN, Camille GIROUD, HOSPICES DE BEAUNE, JADOT, Michel LAFARGE, Daniel Largeot, LATOUR, Albert MOROT, Mussy, Parent, Jacques PRIEUR, Jean-Claude Rateau, Thomas-Moillard, TOLLOT-BEAUT, Léon Violland.

Best years ❦1999, '98, '96, '95, '93, '92; ♀1999, '96, '95.

BIENVENUES-BÂTARD-MONTRACHET AC

This small white Grand Cru in Puligny lies below the Premier Cru Les Pucelles. The wines have more finesse, but less weight than Bâtard-Montrachet, and mature a little sooner, within 5–8 years.

Best producers Bachelet-Ramonet, CARILLON et Fils, Henri Clerc, Guillemard-Clerc, LATOUR, LEFLAIVE, Paul Pernot, RAMONET, SAUZET.

Best years 1999, '96, '95, '93, '92, '90, '89.

BLAGNY AC

The vineyards of this small hamlet are actually situated mostly in Meursault and Puligny, yet use the name Blagny for the red wine. Any white produced here, nearly all Premier Cru, is sold as Meursault, Puligny-Montrachet or Meursault-Blagny. The red wine is lively and quite robust.

Premiers Crus Of the red Premiers Crus, La Pièce-sous-le-Bois produces the longest lived wine; keep for up to 10 years. Red wines from the Premier Cru Hameau-de-Blagny in Puligny are sold as Blagny Premier Cru.

Best producers Robert Ampeau, Gilles Bouton, Henri Clerc, François JOBARD, René Lamy, Lamy-Pillot, Olivier LEFLAIVE, MATROT, Paul Pernot.

Best years ❦1999, '98, '96, '95, '92; ♀1999, '96.

BONNES-MARES AC

A large red Grand Cru partly in Morey-St-Denis and partly in Chambolle-Musigny. Compared to the velvety finesse of the neighbouring Musigny Grand Cru, Bonnes-Mares is almost tannic, and has a greater capacity for aging.

Best producers d'AUVENAY, BOUCHARD Père et Fils, DROUHIN, Drouhin-Laroze, DUJAC, Fougeray de Beauclair, Robert GROFFIER, JADOT, Dominique LAURENT, J F Mugnier, ROUMIER, de VOGÜÉ.

Best years 1999, '98, '96, '95, '93, '90, '89, '88, '85, '83, '80, '78.

BOURGOGNE-ALIGOTÉ AC

A dry white wine with high acidity made from the Aligoté grape planted throughout the Burgundy region. The best Aligoté wine comes traditionally from Bouzeron in the Côte Chalonnaise where the vines do well on the local limestone-clay soil.

Best producers (Bouzeron) BOUCHARD Père & Fils, Chanzy, de VILLAINE.

Best years 1999, '98, '97, '96.

BOURGOGNE CÔTE CHALONNAISE AC

These are red and white wines from an appellation created in 1990 to recognize the specific characteristics of the local

Chardonnay and Pinot Noir. The red wines have a fine cherry colour, a lively, fruity aroma and authentic Pinot flavour. The whites are fruit-dominated, gaining complexity with age. Both can be drunk young, up to 5 years old.

Best producers Cave des Vignerons de Buxy, Michel Derain, Michel Goubard & Fils, Gouffier, Jean-Hervé Jonnier, Jean-Michel & Laurent Pillot, de VILLAINE.

Best years 1999, '98, '96, '95, '93, '90.

BOURGOGNE-HAUTES CÔTES DE BEAUNE AC

These are red, white and rosé wines, from an AC only created in the 1970s; these higher-altitude vines give of their best in warmer vintages.

Best producers Denis Carré, François Charles, Caves des Hautes-Côtes, Lucien Jacob, Robert JAYER-GILLES.

Best years 1999, '98, '96, '95, '93, '90, '89.

BOURGOGNE-HAUTES CÔTES DE NUITS AC

These are pleasant red wines and much better whites from vines grown in the hills behind the Côte de Nuits.

Best producers Cornu, FAIVELEY, Caves des Hautes-Côtes, MÉO-CAMUZET.

Best years 1999, '98, '96, '95, '93, '90.

BROUILLY & CÔTE DE BROUILLY ACs

Two Beaujolais Crus on the slopes of Mont Brouilly. Côte de Brouilly, on the higher slopes, makes a deeper and more vigorous red than Brouilly, needing 2 years to open up and lasting for 5–7 years. Brouilly should be drunk within 3 years.

Best producers (Brouilly) la Chaize; (Côte de Brouilly) J-C Pivot, Ch. Thivin, la Voûte des Crozes.

Best years 1999, '98.

CHABLIS AC

Planted on Kimmeridgian chalk, the Chardonnay grape produces wines that are floral and fresh in good years, but still have persistence, weight and good acidity. These wines are good at 1 year old and the better examples can last 5 years or more.

Best producers Christian Adine, Billaud-Simon, Pascal Bouchard, Jean-Marc Brocard, La CHABLISIENNE, de Chantemerle, Jean Collet, Jean Dauvissat, René & Vincent DAUVISSAT, E & D Defaix, Jean-Paul DROIN, DROUHIN, Gérard Duplessis, Jean Durup, Alain Geoffroy, Jean-Pierre Grossot, LAROCHE, Long-Depaquit, de la MALADIÈRE, des Malandes, des Marronniers, Louis Michel, J. Moreau, Gilbert Picq, Louis Pinson, Denis Race, RAVENEAU, Michel Régnard, Guy Robin, Francine et Olivier Savary, Simonnet-Febvre, Gérard Tremblay, Laurent Tribut, Vocoret.

Best years 1999, '98, '96, '95, '92, '90, '89.

CHABLIS GRAND CRU AC

Planted on the south-facing slopes above the right bank of the Serein at the north-east edge of the town, the 7 Grands Crus cover only 105ha. Chardonnay ripens perfectly on these chalky slopes and yields

---

THE USE OF OAK IN CHABLIS

The use of oak in Chablis has become a contentious issue over the last 20 years. Some producers use oak to give an extra complexity to their wines, while others do not want the true character of Chablis to be in any way obscured by vanillin and oaky flavours. One camp has stayed with the traditional tank fermentation and aging in old wood, another keeps the wine from start to finish in stainless steel, while a third group both ferment and mature the wine in barrel, a high proportion of which will be new.

Oak's main protagonists La Chablisienne, Jean-Paul Droin, Drouhin.

Old-fashioned use of oak René & Vincent Dauvissat, Raveneau.

Stainless steel preferred to oak Brocard, Jean Durup, Louis Michel, Régnard.

are kept low to give the wine the necessary weight and presence to reflect the unique terroir. The Grands Crus are Blanchots, Bougros, Les Clos, Grenouilles, Preuses, Valmur and Vaudésir. Each one has its own character and the growers' different methods of vinification and aging also affect the final style of wine. A Grand Cru wine begins to show well at 5 years old and can last two decades or more.

Best producers La CHABLISIENNE, René & Vincent DAUVISSAT, E & D Defaix, Jean-Paul DROIN, DROUHIN, Gérard Duplessis, JADOT, LAROCHE, de la MALADIÈRE, Louis Michel, RAVENEAU, Guy Robin, Marcel Servin, Simonnet-Febvre, VERGET, Vocoret.

Best years 1999, '98, '96, '95, '92, '90, '89, '88, '86, '85, '82.

CHABLIS PREMIER CRU AC

The Premier Cru vineyards are limited to 581ha surrounding the town of Chablis, on both banks of the river Serein. The best vineyards are to the north and east of the town, on either side of the Grands Crus. There are 29 officially recognized Premiers Crus, but only a dozen are well-known. Montée de Tonnerre can equal a Grand Cru and is recognized as the finest, but very good wines also come from Beugnons, Côte de Lechet, Les Forêts, Fourchaume, Montmains, Mont de Milieu, Sechets, Vaulorent and Vaillons. They are good value as they cost only 20–30% more than straight Chablis, but can be twice as good. Even the lightest wines should be kept for a year after bottling and the best will last for 10 years.

Best producers see Chablis AC page 80.

Best years 1999, '98, '96, '95, '92, '90, '89, '88, '86.

CHAMBERTIN AC

This Grand Cru produces one of the most famous red wines in the world. It is a big wine, powerful but never heavy and the best vintages need 10 years to show their true qualities, and may last half a century.

Best producers Camus, CHARLOPIN, Pierre DAMOY, DROUHIN, JADOT, LATOUR, LEROY, Denis MORTET, Jacques PRIEUR, Henri REBOURSEAU, Rossignol-Trapet, Armand ROUSSEAU.

Best years 1999, '98, '97, '96, '95, '93, '90, '89, '88, '85, '83, '80, '78.

CHAMBERTIN-CLOS-DE-BÈZE AC

Adjacent to and slightly larger than Chambertin, the Clos-de-Bèze Grand Cru is thought to be more stylish and elegant than its neighbour, but at this level of quality differences are negligible.

Best producers CHAMPY, Bruno CLAIR, Pierre DAMOY, DROUHIN, Drouhin-Laroze, FAIVELEY, Gelin, Robert GROFFIER, JADOT, Dominique LAURENT, PRIEURÉ-ROCH, Jean RAPHET, Armand ROUSSEAU, Thomas-Moillard.

Best years 1999, '98, '97, '96, '95, '93, '91, '90, '89, '88, '85, '83, '80, '78.

CHAMBOLLE-MUSIGNY AC

The qualities of wine from this commune – charm, elegance, suppleness, ripeness and length – have made Chambolle-Musigny one of the most sought-after red Burgundies. The almost delicate fruit makes the wine very attractive when young, but the underlying structure allows the best wines to last for 2 decades.

Premiers Crus There are 24 Premiers Crus, some so tiny as to be rarely mentioned by name on the label, some so famous (Les Amoureuses and Les Charmes) that they sell for almost as much as Grands Crus. Other good Premiers Crus are Les Feusselottes, Les Fuées, Les Cras, Les Sentiers, Les Chabiots and La Combe d'Orveau.

Best producers Bernard Amiot, AMIOT-SERVELLE, BARTHOD, Pierre Bertheau, Ch. de CHAMBOLLE-MUSIGNY,

DROUHIN, Drouhin-Laroze, FAIVELEY, Robert GROFFIER, Hudelot-Baillet, HUDELOT-NOËLLAT, JADOT, Dominique LAURENT, Moine-Hudelot, MUGNERET-GIBOURG, Georges ROUMIER, Hervé Roumier, Bernard Serveau, de VOGÜÉ.
Best years 1999, '98, '97, '96, '95, '93, '90, '89, '88, '85, '80.

CHAPELLE-CHAMBERTIN AC
What this red Grand Cru sometimes lacks in weight, it makes up for in delicacy. The wine may be drunk as young as 5 years old but can also last for 2 decades.
Best producers Pierre DAMOY, Drouhin-Laroze, Rossignol-Trapet, Jean Trapet.
Best years 1999, '98, '97, '96, '95, '93, '90, '89, '85, '83, '80, '78.

CHARMES-CHAMBERTIN AC
The largest of Gevrey-Chambertin's red Grands Crus produces supple, elegant wine that is often surpassed in quality by the top Gevrey Premiers Crus such as Clos St-Jacques. It is considerably less expensive than Chambertin and is best at 10 years.
Best producers Camus, CHAMPY, CHARLOPIN, Claude Dugat, Bernard DUGAT-PY, DUJAC, Géantet-Pansiot, Frédéric Magnien, MAUME, Henri Perrot-Minot, Jean Raphet, Joseph ROTY, Armand ROUSSEAU, Tortochot.
Best years 1999, '98, '97, '96, '95, '93, '90, '89, '85.

CHASSAGNE-MONTRACHET AC
The village red wines are full-bodied, satisfying, but sometimes slightly rustic. However, it is the white wines which are more prized and some of the finest white Burgundies come from the commune's Grand Cru vineyards. Around 60% of the village wine is red, but only 30% of the Premiers Crus, proving that the finer soils are planted with Chardonnay. Drink the village reds at 4–7 years. The whites are less stylish than those from Puligny, but have an added weight and structure and even the village wines can be most impressive at 3–5 years old.
Premiers Crus Drink both the red and white wines at 6–10 years. The best Crus are Abbaye de Morgeot, Les Baudines, Bois-de-Chassagne, La Boudriotte, En Cailleret, Le Champ-Gain, Les Chaumes, Les Chevenottes, Clos St-Jean, Les Embrazées, La Maltroie, La Grande Montagne, Les Morgeots, En Remilly, La Romanée and En Virondot.
Best producers Guy AMIOT et Fils, Bachelet-Ramonet, Joseph Belland, BLAIN-GAGNARD, BOUCHARD Père et Fils, CHAMPY, CHARTON ET TRÉBUCHET, COLIN-DELÉGER, Delagrange-Bachelet, DROUHIN, Richard FONTAINE-GAGNARD, J-N GAGNARD, Jacques GAGNARD-DELAGRANGE, JADOT, Labouré-Roi, Marquis de Laguiche (DROUHIN), René Lamy-Pillot, LATOUR, Duc de Magenta (JADOT), Ch de la Maltroye, Bernard Moreau, Bernard MOREY, Jean-Marc Morey, Marc MOREY, Morey-Coffinet, Michel NIELLON, Fernand & Laurent Pillot, Jean-Marc PILLOT, Paul Pillot, RAMONET, Rodet, Roux et Fils, VERGET.
Best years ♥1999, '98, '96, '95, '93, '90, '89; ♀1999, '98, '96.

CHÉNAS AC
The smallest Beaujolais Cru produces full-coloured, generous reds with a floral aroma which are very good at 2–3 years.
Best producers Michel Benon & Fils, Guy Braillon, des Bruyères, Louis Champagnon, de Chénas, Daniel Robin, Bernard Santé.
Best years 1999, '98, '97, '96, '95.

CHEVALIER-MONTRACHET AC
A superb Grand Cru for white wines, situated on poorer soil above Le Montrachet and second only to this Cru for quality, possessing great depth of

flavour. Drink the wines at 5–15 years old.
Best producers d'AUVENAY, BOUCHARD
Père et Fils, Jean Chartron, Henri Clerc,
JADOT, Louis LATOUR, Dom. LEFLAIVE,
Michel NIELLON, Ch. de PULIGNY-
MONTRACHET, SAUZET.
Best years 1999, '98, '96, '95, '93, '92,
'90, '89, '86, '85.

CHOREY-LÈS-BEAUNE AC

A small commune with vineyards generally
east of the N74 road, producing almost
entirely red wine. These wines are supple
and elegant, to be drunk within 4–7 years.
Often sold as Côte de Beaune-Villages, but
more and more under the Chorey label.
Best producers Arnoux Père et Fils,
Ch. de Chorey-lès-Beaune, François Gay,
Maillard Père et Fils, TOLLOT-BEAUT.
Best years 1999, '98, '96, '95, '93, '90.

CLOS DES LAMBRAYS AC

High above the village of Morey-St-Denis,
this small site was awarded Grand Cru
status as recently as 1981 and has seen
necessary improvements in the last decade.
Solely owned by the Freund family from
Koblenz, the wines are elegant and age well.
Best years 1999, '98, '96, '95, '93, '90, '85.

CLOS DE LA ROCHE AC

This is the largest of Morey St-Denis'
5 red Grands Crus and is supposed to

produce the finest wine, combining lush,
bright fruit and a firm structure. It is best
at around 10 years, but can last for 20.
Best producers Pierre Amiot, DUJAC,
HOSPICES DE BEAUNE, LEROY, Georges
Lignier, Hubert LIGNIER, PONSOT,
Louis Rémy, Armand ROUSSEAU.
Best years 1999, '98, '97, '96, '95, '93,
'90, '89, '88, '85, '80.

CLOS ST-DENIS AC

Although this Grand Cru gave its name to
the village of Morey, it covers only 6.60ha.
The wine is more elegant but lighter than
Clos de la Roche, and matures earlier –
drink within 10 years.
Best producers Bertagna, CHARLOPIN,
DUJAC, JADOT, Georges Lignier, PONSOT.
Best years 1999, '98, '96, '95, '90, '89, '85.

CLOS DE TART AC

This Morey Grand Cru, owned solely by
Mommessin, merchants from Mâcon, lies
between Clos des Lambrays and Bonnes-
Mares. The quality is good, but not great.
Best years 1999, '98, '96, '95, '93, '90, '85.

CLOS DE VOUGEOT AC

This enclosed Clos or 'walled vineyard',
has an ancient medieval château which is
home to the Chevaliers de Tastevin wine
fraternity, and encompasses 50ha of vines,
making it the largest Grand Cru in the
Côte de Nuits. It is split between 80
owners, some bottling all their wine, some
selling to *négociants* and all eager to exploit
the vineyard's famous name. When it's
good, the wine is wonderfully fleshy,
turning dark and exotic at 7–15 years.
Best producers AMIOT-SERVELLE, Robert
ARNOUX, Bertagna, BOUCHARD Père et
Fils, CHAMPY, CONFURON-COTÉTIDOT,
DROUHIN, Drouhin-Laroze, René
ENGEL, FAIVELEY, Jean GRIVOT, Anne
GROS, Gros Frère et Soeur, Jean Gros,
HUDELOT-NOËLLAT, JADOT, François
Lamarche, LEROY, MÉO-CAMUZET,

CHOOSE CLOS DE VOUGEOT WITH CARE
Surrounded by its magnificent wall, the
Clos de Vougeot is one of Burgundy's most
famous wine names and seems to many to
epitomize Burgundy. Indeed it does, for the
Clos is divided between 80 owners, all
eager to exploit the famous name, the
choice of grower is, therefore, crucial.
While the land at the top of the slope is
very fine, that down by the road is not – it
is considerably lower and more alluvial
than any other Grand Cru – but somehow
not many people admit to owning land
down by the roadside!

MONGEARD-MUGNERET, Denis
MORTET, Jacques PRIEUR, Jean RAPHET,
Henri REBOURSEAU, RION, Ch. de la Tour,
de la VOUGERAIE.
Best years 1999, '98, '97, '96, '95, '93,
'90, '89, '88, '85.

CORTON AC

Red wines from almost 120ha in the
communes of Aloxe-Corton and Ladoix-
Serrigny, which are either sold as Corton
Grand Cru, or with the name of a specific
climat as in Corton-Bressandes. The
vineyards on the hill of Corton are some
of the most impressive in Burgundy, and
produce deep-coloured, full-bodied wines,
with a richness and gamyness that can
rival anything from the Côte de Nuits for
structure, yet retain the smoothness typical
of the Côte de Beaune. They are at their
best after 10 years and in the great vintages
capable of lasting for several decades.

The best-known *climats* are Le Corton,
Clos-des-Cortons-Faiveley, Les Clos du
Roi, Les Renardes, Les Bressandes, Les
Pougets, Les Maréchaudes, Les Languettes,
Les Greves, Clos-de-La-Vigne-au-Saint
and Les Perrières.
Best producers Adrien Belland, BONNEAU
DU MARTRAY, BOUCHARD Père et Fils,
Henri et Gilles Buisson, Cachat-Ocquidant,
CHANDON DE BRIAILLES, Marius
Delarche, DROUHIN, Dubreuil-Fontaine,
FAIVELEY, Michel Gaunoux, Antonin
GUYON, HOSPICES DE BEAUNE, JADOT,
Michel JUILLOT, LATOUR, Olivier
LEFLAIVE, LEROY, Maillard Père et Fils,
Prince de Mérode, RAPET Père et Fils,
Comte SENARD, Thomas-Moillard,
TOLLOT-BEAUT, Michel Voarick.
Best years 1999, '98, '97, '96, '95, '93,
'90, '89, '88, '85, '80, '78.

CORTON BLANC AC

This white wine should not be confused
with Corton-Charlemagne. There is only a
small amount made and the finest *climat* is
Les Vergennes, part owned by the
HOSPICES DE BEAUNE. JADOT also
produces a few barrels from the same Cru.
Best producers CHANDON DE
BRIAILLES, JADOT.
Best years 1999, '98, '96, '95, '92, '90, '89.

CORTON-CHARLEMAGNE AC

This white wine from the high, south-
west-facing slopes of Aloxe-Corton and
Pernand-Vergelesses, on 49ha of clay and
limestone soil, is often compared to
Bâtard-Montrachet. It is one of the
firmest, most structured white Burgundies,
needing 5 years to show its complexity and
usually reaching its peak at 10 years.
Best producers BONNEAU DU MARTRAY,
BOUCHARD Père et Fils, CHAMPY,
CHANDON DE BRIAILLES, CHARTRON &
TRÉBUCHET, Bruno CLAIR, COCHE-
DURY, Marius Delarche, DROUHIN,
Dubreuil-Fontaine, FAIVELEY, Robert et
Raymond Jacob, JADOT, Michel JUILLOT,
Laleure-Piot, LATOUR, Olivier LEFLAIVE,
Pierre Marey, André & Jean-René
Nudant, RAPET Père & Fils, Rollin Père et
Fils, Baron Thenard, TOLLOT-BEAUT,
Louis Violland, Michel Voarick, de la
VOUGERAIE.
Best years 1999, '98, '97, '96, '95, '92,
'90, '89, '88, '86.

CÔTE DE BEAUNE AC

A small appellation of under 30ha for
pleasant, early-maturing, mainly red wines
from the hills above Beaune.
Best producers Jean Allexant, Dom.
Cauvard, Machard de Gramont.
Best years 1999, '98, '96, '95, '90.

CÔTE DE BEAUNE-VILLAGES AC

Red wine only from 16 villages in the
Côte de Beaune, made singly or blended
with others. This is a fruity wine, mostly
used by local *négociants*.
Best years 1999, '98, '96, '95, '93, '90.

CÔTE DE NUITS-VILLAGES AC

This appellation is almost exclusively for red wines from either end of the Côte de Nuits and is generally used by the local merchants such as Labouré-Roi.

Best producers Huguenot, Quillardet.

Best years 1999, '98, '97, '96, '95, '93, '90.

CRIOTS-BÂTARD-MONTRACHET AC

The smallest of the Montrachet white Grands Crus, with 1.57ha within the commune of Chassagne and immediately below Bâtard-Montrachet. The wines are the least ripe of the Grands Crus, but can be very fine. Drink at 5–10 years.

Best producers d'AUVENAY, Joseph Belland, BLAIN-GAGNARD, FONTAINE-GAGNARD.

Best years 1999, '98, '97, '96, '95, '92, '90, '89.

ÉCHÉZEAUX AC

With 37.69ha in the commune of Flagey-Échézeaux, this is one of the largest Grands Crus in Burgundy. The red wines are supple with good fruit and generally mature at 5–10 years. They are sometimes declassified into Vosne-Romanée Premier Cru, whose quality they often resemble.

Best producers CONFURON-COTÉTIDOT, DUJAC, René ENGEL, FAIVELEY, Jean GRIVOT, JADOT, JAYER-GILLES, LAMARCHE, MONGEARD-MUGNERET, MUGNERET-GIBOURG, Dom. des PERDRIX, Jacques PRIEUR, Dom. de la ROMANÉE-CONTI, Emmanuel ROUGET.

Best years 1999, '98, '97, '96, '95, '93, '90, '89, '85.

FIXIN AC

This appellation (pronounced 'Fissin') is the second most northerly in the Côte d'Or and produces mainly red wines. These should be deep-coloured and full-bodied and can be sold under the Côte de Nuits-Villages appellation, although Fixin is now well established in its own right.

Premiers Crus There are 8 Premiers Crus. The best ones are Les Arvelets, Clos de la Perrière, Clos du Chapitre, Clos Napoléon and Les Hervelets.

Best producers Vincent & Denis Berthaut, Pierre Gelin, Guyard, Philippe Joliet.

Best years 1999, '98, '96, '95, '93, '90, '88.

FLEURIE AC

Red wine from perhaps the finest Beaujolais Cru, covering 800ha on granite-based soil that is perfect for the Gamay grape. Fleurie is known as 'the Queen of the Beaujolais'. The best-known *climat* is La Madonne, overlooking the village. The wine can be drunk at 1–3 years but the best keep for 5 years or more.

Best producers Berrod, Michel Chignard, Clos la Chapelle des Bois, Clos des Moriers, Clos de la Roilette, Jean-Marc Després, DUBOEUF, Pierre Ferraud, Mehu, André Métrat.

Best years 1999, '98, '97, '96, '95.

GEVREY-CHAMBERTIN AC

The largest commune in the Côte de Nuits, with almost 500ha under vines, which includes 86ha of Premiers Crus and 87ha of Grands Crus, producing wine with deep colour, a bouquet of fruit mingled with spice and a long velvety finish. One of the most reliable red Burgundies, at its best aged for 7–15 years.

Premiers Crus There are 26 Premiers Crus, the best ones lying on the slopes behind the village. The wines have more vigorous fruit than the village wines, and the best are equal to Gevrey's Grands Crus. The best Premiers Crus are Les Cazetiers, La Petite-Chapelle, Clos du Chapitre, Clos St-Jacques, Clos des Varoilles, La Combe-aux-Moines, Aux Combottes, Les Estournelles-St-Jacques and Lavaux-St-Jacques.

Best producers Denis Bachelet, Vincent & Denis Berthaut, Lucien Boillot, Pierre Bourée, Burguet, Camus, CHARLOPIN, Bruno CLAIR, Pierre DAMOY, DROUHIN, Drouhin-Laroze, Claude Dugat, Bernard DUGAT-PY, DUJAC, Frédéric Esmonin, Michel Esmonin, FAIVELEY, Geantet-Pansiot, Heresztyn, JADOT, Labouré-Roi, Philippe Leclerc, René Leclerc, Henri Magnien, MAUME, Denis MORTET, Henri REBOURSEAU, Rossignol, Rossignol-Trapet, Joseph ROTY, Armand ROUSSEAU, Christian Serafin, Jean Trapet, Varoilles.
Best years 1999, '98, '97, '96, '95, '93, '90, '89, '88, '85.

GIVRY AC
Red and white wines from 120ha in the Côte Chalonnaise which improved steadily during the 1990s. The fresh, nutty whites should be drunk at 2–3 years old and the fruity reds at 3–5 years.
Best producers René Bourgeon, Chofflet-Valdenaire, du Gardin, Joblot, François Lumpp, Gérard Mouton, Gérard & Laurent Parize, Ragot, Sarrazin, Steinmeyer.
Best years ❚1999, '98, '96, '95, '93, '90; ♀1999, '98, '97.

LA GRANDE RUE AC
Vosne-Romanée's newest Grand Cru (elevated from Premier Cru in 1992) lies between La Tâche and La Romanée-Conti. With 1.65ha of Pinot Noir vines, it is solely owned by LAMARCHE.
Best years 1999, '98, '96, '95, '93, '90, '89, '85.

GRANDS-ÉCHÉZEAUX AC
This Grand Cru, adjoining the best part of Clos de Vougeot, produces red wine richer than its neighbour, Échézeaux, more structured with greater intensity of fruit, and consequently tending to mature more slowly. It is ready after 8-10 years.
Best producers DROUHIN, René ENGEL, Gros Frère et Soeur, LAMARCHE,

MONGEARD-MUGNERET, Baron Thénard (Remoissenet), de la ROMANÉE-CONTI.
Best years 1999, '98, '97, '96, '95, '93, '90, '89, '88, '85, '80.

GRIOTTE-CHAMBERTIN AC
With only 2.73ha, this is the smallest of Gevrey's Grands Crus. The wine is deep-flavoured and most entrancing, and shows brilliantly at 10 years.
Best producers DROUHIN, Claude Dugat, Frédéric Esmonin, JADOT, PONSOT.
Best years 1999, '98, '97, '96, '95, '93, '90, '89, '88, '85.

JULIÉNAS AC
A Beaujolais Cru of 580ha producing deep-coloured, exciting red wines with a bouquet of raspberries and flavours of ripe berry fruit. Juliénas can be drunk young at 1–2 years, or left to age for 4–5 years.
Best producers Gérard Descombes, Thierry Descombes, Pierre Ferraud, Ch. de Juliénas, René Monnet, Jean-François Perraud, Bernard Santé, Michel Tête.
Best years 1999, '98, '97, '96, '95, '93, '90.

LADOIX AC
Ladoix-Serrigny is the most northern Côte de Beaune commune, producing mostly solid red wines, which have a slight resemblance to those from Aloxe-Corton, plus a very little white wine.
Best producers Cachat-Ocquidant et Fils, Chevalier Père et Fils, Edmond Cornu, André & Jean-René Nudant.
Best years 1999, '98, '96, '95, '93, '90, '89.

LATRICIÈRES-CHAMBERTIN AC
This 7.35-ha red Grand Cru lies between Le Chambertin and the Premier Cru Les Combottes in Gevrey-Chambertin, and produces a sturdy wine that ages well.
Best producers Camus, Drouhin-Laroze, FAIVELEY, LEROY, PONSOT, Rossignol-Trapet, Trapet.
Best years 1999, '98, '97, '96, '95, '93, '91, '90, '89, '85, '83, '80.

MÂCON BLANC AC, MÂCON-VILLAGES AC

An AC for red, rosé and white wines. The white wines must be 100% Chardonnay, the reds and rosés may be from either Gamay or Pinot Noir. Although the quality of the red wines is improving, their reputation is overshadowed both by the white Mâconnais wines, and by red wines from the neighbouring Beaujolais Crus. Mâcon-Villages is of superior quality to plain Mâcon, and the name of an individual commune may be hyphenated to Mâcon on the label. Look for the following commune names: Charnay, Fuissé, Igé, Loché, Lugny, Peronne, Pierclos, Prissé, La Roche Vineuse and Uchizy. A new AC, Viré-Clessé, was created in 1998 to group the region's two best communes. The wines are at their best at 1–3 years. The local co-operatives handle 80% of the production.

Best producers Dom. de la BONGRAN, André Bonhomme, Cordier, Deux Roches, Francis Fichet, Cave des Grands Crus Blancs, GUFFENS-HEYNEN, Roger Lassarat, Lugny co-operative, Roger Luquet, Manciat-Poncet, Olivier Merlin, Rousset, Saumaize-Michelin, Talmard, Thibert, Jean Thévenet, Viré co-operative.

Best years ♀1999, '98, '97, '96.

MARANGES AC

An appellation created in 1988 to regroup 3 villages at the southern end of the Côte de Beaune whose red wines had previously been sold as Côte de Beaune-Villages. This is a good honest red, with rather tannic edges. There is a tiny amount of white.

Best producers Bernard Bachelet, Maurice Charleux, Vincent GIRARDIN, Edmund Monnot, Claude Nouveau.

Best years 1999, '98, '96, '95, '90.

MARSANNAY AC

This commune on the southern outskirts of Dijon is well known for the rosé first popular in the 1920s. It now also produces firm red wines and a very little white.

Best producers CHARLOPIN, Bruno CLAIR, Bernard Coillot, Fougeray de Beauclair, JADOT, Denis MORTET.

Best years 1999, '98, '97, '96, '95, '93, '90.

THE HOSPICES DE BEAUNE

The Hospices de Beaune (or Hôtel-Dieu) is the 15th-century hospital in the centre of Beaune to which vineyards have been bequeathed over the centuries. The holdings now comprise 38 different *cuvées* of wine from over 60ha. The vineyards are almost all in Premiers and Grands Crus and are tended by local *vignerons*, the wines being made in the new cellars on the edge of Beaune. Whatever the date of the vintage, the wines are sold (following a tasting by *négociants*, international buyers and the press) on the third Sunday in November, the second day of the Trois Glorieuses festival. The *négociants* who have purchased the wines, generally on behalf of clients, will collect the wine in barrel from the Hospices' cellars the following January, and barrel mature and bottle the wines themselves. The prices paid at the Hospices' sale are viewed as an indication of the state of the market, but, since the auction is for charity and receives international coverage, prices tend to be considerably higher than the average.

The wines are always known by the name of the person or family who donated them. The best-known are: Mazis-Chambertin, Cuvée Madeleine Collignon; Corton, Cuvée Charlotte Dumay; Corton, Cuvée Docteur Peste; Beaune, Cuvée Nicolas Rolin; Beaune, Cuvée Guigone de Salins; Beaune, Cuvée Dames Hospitalières; Pommard, Cuvée Dames de la Charité; Volnay, Cuvée Général Muteau; Meursault-Genevrières, Cuvée Baudot; Corton-Charlemagne, Cuvée François de Salins.

MAZIS-CHAMBERTIN AC

The Mazis- (or Mazy-) Chambertin Grand Cru covers 9ha extending from Clos-de-Bèze north towards the village of Gevrey. The red wine is fine and elegant and may be drunk in its first decade.

Best producers d'AUVENAY, Frédéric Esmonin, FAIVELEY, HOSPICES DE BEAUNE (Cuvée Madeleine Collignon), Dominique LAURENT, MAUME, Philippe NADDEF, Henri REBOURSEAU, Joseph ROTY, Armand ROUSSEAU, Tortochot.

Best years 1999, '98, '97, '96, '95, '93, '90, '89, '88, '85.

MAZOYÈRES-CHAMBERTIN AC

This is an alternative name for Charmes-Chambertin, mainly used by Dom. Camus.

MERCUREY AC

This is the most important appellation in the Côte Chalonnaise and covers red and a very little white wine from over 600ha. The white is lively and fruity, while the red has a deep colour and firm fruit, often needing a few years to soften. Before the AC laws, the reds were grouped with Côte de Beaune, an indication of their quality.

Premiers Crus There are several very fine ones, whose wines can last a decade or more. The best are Clos du Roi, Les Crets, En Sazenay and Les Veleys.

Best producers Brintet, Ch. de Chamilly, Ch. de Chamirey (Rodet), Jean-Pierre Charton, FAIVELEY, Jeannin-Naltet Père & Fils, Émile Juillot, Michel JUILLOT, Meix-Foulot, Jean Raquillet, Michel Raquillet, SUREMAIN, Émile Voarick.

Best years ❚1999, '98, '96, '95, '90, '89, '88; ♀1999, '98, '97.

MEURSAULT AC

Mainly white and a very little red from just under 420ha, making Meursault the third-largest commune in the Côte d'Or after Beaune and Gevrey. The red wines come from the borders of Volnay, but retain a Meursault vigour and robustness as opposed to the elegance normally associated with Volnay. The rest of the appellation is perfect for Chardonnay, and Meursault is one of the most characteristic and expressive white Burgundies, the style showing a lively fruit, taking on honeyed and nutty aspects as it matures. The village wines, generally of good quality, can be drunk at 2–3 years, while certain *climats*, notably Le Clos de la Barre, Les Casse-Têtes, Les Chevaliers, Les Narvaux, Les Tillets, Les Luchets and Les Tessons, produce much superior wines, often on the level of a Premier Cru, which need longer aging for 5–8 years. Because of the large amount of wine produced, *négociants* can find reliable sources of wine both at village and Premier Cru levels.

Premiers Crus There are 29 Premiers Crus, the most famous being Les Poruzots, Les Bouchères, La Goutte d'Or, and, of Grand Cru quality, Les Charmes, Les Genevrières and Les Perrières.

Best producers ALBERT-GRIVAULT, Robert Ampeau, d'AUVENAY, Bitouzet-Prieur, Guy Bocard, Jean-Marc Boillot, BOUCHARD Père et Fils, BOUZEREAU, Boyer-Martenot, Hubert Chavy-Chouet, Coche-Debord, COCHE-DURY, Henri Darnat, Jean-Philippe Fichet, Jean-Paul Gauffroy, Jean-Michel Gaunoux, Henri Germain, Patrick JAVILLIER, Charles & Rémi JOBARD, François JOBARD, LAFON, LATOUR, Latour-Giraud, MATROT, Dom. Michelot, François Mikulski, Pierre Millot-Battault, René Monnier, Pierre MOREY, Jacques PRIEUR, Guy ROULOT, VERGET, Virely-Rougeot.

Best years ♀1999, '97, '96, '95, '92, '90, '89, '88.

MONTAGNY AC

White wine only from the most southern appellation in the Côte Chalonnaise. The wines are more similar to those from the Mâconnais than the Côte de Beaune and the Premier Cru wines acquire a nutty complexity with age. Generally the wines are best drunk at 2–3 years.

Best producers Cave des Vignerons de Buxy, Ch de la Saule, LATOUR, Bernard Michel.

Best years 1999, '98, '96, '95.

MONTHELIE AC

Mainly red wine from 140ha, nearly a quarter of which are Premier Cru, on limestone soil west of Volnay. The wine combines Volnay's elegance with Pommard's firmness along with a certain rusticity, and can be drunk at 5–8 years. *Négociants* have made a speciality of this appellation.

Premiers Cru There are 11 Premiers Crus, but only Les Champs Fuillot and Les Duresses are much used.

Best producers Jacques & Eric Boigelot, BOUCHARD Père & Fils, Denis Boussey, Maurice Deschamps, DROUHIN, Dupont-Fahn, Paul Garaudet, Jaffelin, Ch. de Monthelie, Monthelie-Douhairet, Ropiteau.

Best years 1999, '98, '96, '95, '90, '89, '88.

LE MONTRACHET AC

This is the grandest of all Burgundy's white Grands Crus, with 8ha shared between the communes of Puligny and Chassagne, making what should be Chardonnay at its most sublime. Even compared to Chevalier-Montrachet, Le Montrachet has extra power and concentration, without losing any elegance and finesse. It needs 10 years' aging to show its full qualities.

Best producers Guy AMIOT et Fils, BOUCHARD Père et Fils, Marc COLIN et Fils, Delagrange-Bachelet, GAGNARD-DELAGRANGE, LAFON, de Laguiche (DROUHIN), LEFLAIVE, Jacques PRIEUR, Ch. de PULIGNY-MONTRACHET, RAMONET, de la ROMANÉE-CONTI, Baron Thénard (Remoissenet).

Best years 1999, '98, '97, '96, '95, '93, '92, '90, '89, '88, '86, '85.

MOREY-ST-DENIS AC

This is the smallest Côte de Nuits commune, after Vougeot, with 109ha of vines, including 43ha of Premiers Crus. The red wines have a full colour and intense bouquet, without the spiciness of Gevrey-Chambertin, nor the smoothness of Chambolle-Musigny, but are firm and structured and age well.

Premiers Crus There are 20 Premiers Crus, but they tend to be overshadowed by the Grands Crus. The wine is generally of high quality, needing 5 years to begin to open out. The best are Le Clos des Ormes, Les Sorbès, Clos Sorbé, Les Montluisants, Les Charmes, Clos de la Bussière and Les Ruchottes.

Best producers Pierre Amiot, Arlaud, CLOS DE TART, DUJAC, Heresztyn, Lécheneaut, Dom. des LAMBRAYS, Georges Lignier, Hubert LIGNIER, Frédéric Magnien, Jean-Paul Magnien, Henri Perrot-Minot, PONSOT, Jean RAPHET, Louis Rémy, Georges ROUMIER, Christian Sérafin, Bernard Serveau.

Best years 1999, '98, '97, '96, '95, '93, '90, '89, '88, '85.

MORGON AC

The second largest Beaujolais Cru, with 1030ha and producing wines with full fruit, even meaty and robust, which age very well, taking on a Burgundy-like flavour after 5–6 years. The best *climats* are Le Py, Le Clachet and Les Charmes.

Best producers Georges Brun, François Calot, Gérard Charvet, Jean Descombes (DUBOEUF), Louis-Claude Desvignes, Jean Foillard, Dominique Piron, Pierre Savoye, Jacques Trichard.

Best years 1998, '97, '96, '95, '93, '90.

MOULIN-À-VENT AC

Red wine from the most prestigious

Beaujolais Cru, with 670ha on granite soil which imparts more intensity of bouquet and flavour to the wine than in the other Crus. The wine possesses a rich velvety fruitiness which has gained the appellation the title 'King of the Beaujolais'. These wines are good at 2–3 years, but can last for a decade.

Best producers François Bergeron, Louis Champagnon, Jules Chauvet, DUBOEUF, Gay-Coperet, Ch. des JACQUES, Paul Janin & Fils, Hubert Lapierre.

Best years 1998, '97, '96, '95, '93, '90.

MUSIGNY AC

From this Grand Cru with 10.86ha of vines comes one of the very greatest red Burgundies and one of the rarest whites (exclusive to de VOGÜÉ). A good red Musigny is silky and velvety when compared to a Chambertin, but lacks none of Chambertin's underlying power. Wines from good years should be kept for a decade and the best can improve for 20–30 years.

Best producers DROUHIN, GROFFIER, LEROY, J-F Mugnier, Jacques PRIEUR, Georges ROUMIER, de VOGÜÉ.

Best years 1999, '98, '97, '96, '95, '93, '91, '90, '89, '88, '85, '78.

NUITS-ST-GEORGES AC

The southernmost appellation in the Côte de Nuits covers 375ha and produces almost exclusively red wine. A good Nuits-St-Georges is a sturdy, serious wine, containing minerally, gamy flavours, robust but not heavy, and slow to mature. Recent vintages have shown real class in the wines, which gain a little softness when from the commune of Prémeaux south of the town of Nuits itself.

Premiers Crus The 37 Premiers Crus run south of the village of Vosne, past Nuits-St-Georges, to Prémeaux. The wines are more elegant in the north, softer in the

south, and perhaps most typical of the appellation in the middle. The best are: (north) Aux Boudots, Aux Chaignots, Aux Champs Perdrix, Aux Cras, Les Damodes, Aux Thorey, Les Vignes-Rondes; (middle) Les Cailles, Les Perrières, Les Porrets, Les Pruliers, Les Hauts Pruliers, Les Roncières, Les St-Georges, Les Terres Blanches, Les Vaucrains; (south) Clos des Argillières, Clos de l'Arlot, Clos de la Maréchale, Les Forets, Clos des Corvées, Les-Corvées-Pagets, Clos St-Marc.

Best producers Bertrand Ambroise, de l'Arlot, Robert Arnoux, Daniel Bocquenet, Lucien Boillot, BOUCHARD Père et Fils, Jean Chauvenet, Robert CHEVILLON, A Chopin et Fils, Chopin-Groffier, Jean-Jacques CONFURON, DROUHIN, FAIVELEY, Henri GOUGES, Jean GRIVOT, JADOT, JAYER-GILLES, Labouré-Roi, LAURENT, Lécheneaut, LEROY, Alain Michelot, Dom. de PERDRIX, PRIEURÉ ROCH, Henri et Gilles Remoriquet, RION, Thomas-Moillard, Charles Vienot, Dom. de la VOUGERAIE.

Best years 1999, '98, '97, '96, '95, '93, '90, '89, '88, '85.

PERNAND-VERGELESSES AC

Red and white wines from 194ha, of which nearly one-quarter are Premiers Crus. The red wines, often rather toasted in the past, have fine colour and firm flavours needing 4–5 years to show well, while the whites, with a lively fruit and attractive acidity, are some of the best value from the Côte de Beaune.

Premiers Crus These are of high quality, in particular Les Fichots, Les Vergelesses and Île de Vergelesses.

Best producers CHANDON DE BRIAILLES, CHANSON, DROUHIN, Dubreuil-Fontaine, Claude Cornu, Doudet, GUYON, JADOT, Laleure-Piot, LATOUR, Pierre Marey, RAPET Père et Fils, Rollin Père et Fils.

Best years ♦1999, '98, '96, '95, '93;
♀1999, '98, '97, '96, '95.

POMMARD AC
Red wine only from 337ha (more than
one-third of which are Premiers Crus)
between Beaune and Volnay. The wines
are full-coloured and firm, quite high in
tannin, a little ungracious when young,
but age well. Quality has been improving
recently, as the growers are no longer
relying on the popularity of the
appellation to sell their wine.
Premiers Crus There are no Grands Crus
but Les Rugiens can rival the finest
Corton, combining intensity and
elegance. Other good ones are Les
Arvelets, Les Bertins, Clos Blanc, Clos de
la Commaraine, Clos des Epeneaux, Les
Petits Epenots, Les Grands Epenots, Les
Fremiers, Les Jarolières, Les Argillières and
Les Pezerolles.
Best producers ARMAND, Billard-
Gonnet, J-M BOILLOT, Coste-Caumartin,
de Courcel, Paul Garaudet, Michel
Gaunoux, Germain Père & Fils, Vincent
GIRARDIN, Lahaye Père et Fils, Olivier
LEFLAIVE, Lejeune, René Monnier, de
MONTILLE, Mussy, Parent, Ch. de
Pommard, Pothier-Rieusset, Dom. de la
POUSSE D'OR, le Royer-Girardin, Virely-
Rougeot. Most Burgundy *négociants* sell
wine from this world-famous appellation.
Best years 1999, '98, '97, '96, '95, '93, '90,
'89, '88.

POUILLY-FUISSÉ, POUILLY-LOCHÉ
& POUILLY-VINZELLES ACs
Pouilly-Fuissé is by far the best and best-
known of these 3 white wine appellations.
The appellation covers 5 communes, all of
which may use the name Fuissé. Here
Chardonnay produces heady, sappy wines,
with a floral bouquet and almost exotic
fruit, often enhanced by new oak. It can
be drunk at 1–2 years, but this is too
young to show its full complexity and the
wines are much improved after 2–3 years
in bottle. The very best ones can rival
Côte d'Or whites in intensity of fruit.
Wines from Pouilly-Loché and Pouilly-
Vinzelles are less complex and can be
drunk younger than Pouilly-Fuissé.
Best producers Daniel Barraud,
Collovray-Terrier, Cordier, Corsin,
DROUHIN, DUBOEUF, J-A FERRET,
Ch. FUISSÉ, des Gerbeaux, GUFFENS-
HEYNEN, JADOT, Labouré-Roi, Roger
Lassarat, Louis LATOUR, Robert-Denogent,
St-Philibert, Saumaize-Michelin, de la
Soufrandise, Valette, VERGET.
Best years 1999, '98, '97, '96, '95, '92,
'90.

PULIGNY-MONTRACHET AC
Although smaller than neighbouring
Meursault and Chassagne-Montrachet,
Puligny-Montrachet, with 246ha of vines,
including 100ha of Premier Cru and 21ha
of Grand Cru, can fairly claim to be the
greatest white wine commune in
Burgundy. A very small amount of red
wine is made, but it is the superb white
wines that are world famous. Even the
village wines (in the right hands) show
more refined fruit than Meursault and
more elegance than Chassagne, combining
floral aromas with firmness of flavour.
Drink at 2–4 years.
Premiers Crus There are 23 in all. The
wines will just be coming into their own as
the village wines fade, and can last for a
decade. The best are Les Caillerets,
Les Chalumeaux, Les Champs-Canet,
Le Champ-Gain, Le Clavoillon,
Les Combettes, Les Folatières,
La Garenne, Les Perrieres, Les Pucelles,
Les Referts and La Truffière.
Best producers Guy Amiot,
J-M BOILLOT, BOUCHARD Père et Fils,
CARILLON et Fils, CHARTRON ET

TRÉBUCHET, Gérard Chavy et Fils,
Philippe Chavy, Henri Clerc, COCHE-
DURY, DROUHIN, JADOT, Louis LATOUR,
LEFLAIVE, Olivier LEFLAIVE, Duc de
Magenta (JADOT), Roland Maraslovac-
Léger, MATROT, Pascal, Paul Pernot et Fils,
Ch. de PULIGNY-MONTRACHET, Rodet,
SAUZET, VERGET.
Best years 1999, '98, '97, '95, '92, '90, '89,
'88.

RICHEBOURG AC
With 8.03ha, the Richebourg Grand Cru
produces the richest, most sumptuous red
wine in all Burgundy, needing 10 years to
mature properly, but already explosively
fruity from a much earlier age.
Best producers Jean GRIVOT, A-F Gros,
Anne GROS, Jean Gros, Gros Frère et
Soeur, HUDELOT-NOËLLAT, LEROY,
MÉO-CAMUZET, MONGEARD-
MUGNERET, Denis Mugneret, Dom. de la
ROMANÉE-CONTI.
Best years 1999, '98, '97, '96, '95, '93,
'91, '90, '89, '88, '85, '83, '80, '78.

LA ROMANÉE AC
The smallest AC in France, at just 0.85ha,
the Romanée Grand Cru lies just above La
Romanée-Conti. Owned solely by the
Liger-Belair family, the wines are made and
distributed by BOUCHARD Père et Fils.
Best years 1999, '98, '96, '95, '90, '89, '88.

LA ROMANÉE-CONTI AC
The 1.81ha of this jewel in Burgundy's
crown produce an average of 6000 bottles
in a good year. Like La Tâche, this Grand
Cru belongs to Dom. de la ROMANÉE-
CONTI which spares no effort nor expense
to produce a very great wine indeed. It
needs 10–20 years to show its true quality.
Best years 1999, '98, '97, '96, '95, '93,
'91, '90, '89, '88, '85, '80, '78.

ROMANÉE-ST-VIVANT AC
With 9.44ha, situated close to the village
of Vosne, this is the lightest in texture of
the Vosne Grands Crus, with a similar
breed and length to Musigny. Drink
between 10 and 20 years old.
Best producers ARNOUX, Jean-Jacques
CONFURON, DROUHIN, HUDELOT-
NOËLLAT, LATOUR, LEROY, Dom. de la
ROMANÉE-CONTI, Thomas-Moillard.
Best years 1999, '98, '97, '96, '95, '93, '90,
'89, '88, '85.

RUCHOTTES-CHAMBERTIN AC
The second-smallest and most northern of
Gevrey's Grands Crus with 3.3ha, the
name derives from *rochers* (rocks); the
wine is correspondingly firm and well-
structured, and can age well.
Best producers Frédéric Esmonin,
JADOT, MUGNERET-GIBOURG, Georges
ROUMIER, ROUSSEAU.
Best years 1999, '98, '97, '96, '95, '93,
'91, '90, '89, '88, '85, '80.

RULLY AC
Red and white wines from an appellation
in the Côte Chalonnaise. Here the white
wines are better known than the reds, and
they can achieve a complexity and depth
resembling a minor Meursault. In recent
years the reds have gained colour and
weight while keeping their suppleness.
Premiers Crus There are 2 well-known
ones – Les Cloux and La Pucelle.
Best producers Belleville, Jean-Claude
Brelière, DROUHIN, FAIVELEY, Jaffelin, la
Folie, JACQUESON, Olivier LEFLAIVE, de
la Renarde (Delorme), Ch. de Rully
(Rodet), de VILLAINE.
Best years ▮1999, '98, '95; ♀1999, '98.

ST-AUBIN AC
Red and white wines from 236ha, more
than half of which are Premiers Crus, on
the high slopes above Puligny and
Chassagne-Montrachet. The whites have
great finesse, with a refreshing acidity and
round fruity finish that can rival more
important appellations, yet may be drunk

at 3–4 years. The reds, with their fine cherry colour and lively fruit, are supple wines to drink at 3–5 years.

Premiers Crus There are 29 Premiers Crus, and the best known are Les Frionnes, Les Murgers des Dents de Chien, En Remilly and Les Perrières.

Best producers Jean-Claude Bachelet, Gilles Bouton, Marc COLIN, Hubert Lamy, Larue, Daniel Nicvert, Henri Prudhon, Roux Père et Fils, Thomas.

Best years ❦1999, '98, '96, '95, '93, '90; ♀1999, '98, '96.

ST-ROMAIN AC

Red and white wines from 135ha in the hills above Auxey-Duresses. The higher altitude means that the red wines are sometimes on the light side, but the natural acidity benefits the whites, especially in warm years. Both should be drunk relatively young, at up to 5 years.

Best producers H & G Buisson, Denis Carré, Germain Père & Fils, Alain Gras, René Gras-Buisson, Thévenin-Monthélie.

Best years ❦1998, '96, '95; ♀1999, '96.

ST-VÉRAN AC

White wines from an AC created in 1991, to recognize some superior communes in the Mâconnais, having a little more vivacity and fruit than a straight Mâcon Blanc, but none of the richness of a Pouilly-Fuissé. Drink young, at 1–4 years.

Best producers Georges Burrier, Corsin, Denuziller, Deux Roches, DUBOEUF, Ch. FUISSÉ, Gonon, Roger Lassarat, Roger Luquet, Olivier Merlin, Jacques & Nathalie Saumaize, Saumaize-Michelin, des Valanges, VERGET.

Best years 1999, '98, '97.

SANTENAY AC

Red and a little white wine from the southern end of the Côte de Beaune, with 378ha of vines, of which 124ha are Premiers Crus. The white wines are rounded with a little acidity and are ready at 2–3 years; the reds are more similar to those from Chassagne, but a little smoother and drink well at 4–7 years.

Premiers Crus These wines have more finesse and depth and are at their peak at 5–10 years. Of the 14 Crus the best known are Beauregard, Clos des Tavannes, Les Gravières, Clos Rousseau, Grand Clos Rousseau, La Comme, La Maladière and Le Passe-Temps.

Best producers L'Abbaye de Santenay, Adrien Belland, Roger Belland, Hautes Cornières, Vincent GIRARDIN, René Lequin-Colin, Mestre, Lucien Muzard & Fils, POUSSE D'OR, Prieur-Brunet.

Best years ❦1999, '98, '96, '95, '93, '90.

SAVIGNY-LÈS-BEAUNE AC

Red and a little white wine from 383ha, nearly one-third of which are Premiers Crus. The white is stylish and lively, the red lightly elegant and smooth. Both can be enjoyed at 2–3 years, but keep well for up to 5 years.

Premiers Crus These are almost entirely Pinot Noir and have more depth, enhancing the hallmark elegance of this commune. The Premiers Crus (Les Clous, Les Serpentières, Les Guettes, Les Lavières and Aux Vergelesses) and the village wines from the Pernand-Vergelesses side of Savigny have firm fruit yet develop a silky texture and floral bouquet. Drink at around 5 years old. Those closer to Beaune (La Dominode, Les Jarrons, Les Marconnets and Les Rouvrettes) are more complete and mature more quickly.

Best producers Arnoux Père & Fils, Pierre Bitouzet, Simon BIZE, BOUCHARD Père et Fils, Camus-Bruchon, CHAMPY, CHANDON DE BRIAILLES, CHANSON, Bruno CLAIR, DROUHIN, Philippe Dubreuil-Fontaine, Maurice ÉCARD, Louis Écard-Guyot, Girard-Vollot, Pierre

Guillemot, JADOT, Jean-Marc Pavelot, Thomas-Moillard.

Best years ❢1999, '98, '93, '95, '93, '90, '89, '88; ♀1999, '98, '97, '96, '95.

LA TÂCHE AC

The 6.06ha of this superb Grand Cru in Vosne-Romanée belong to the famous Dom. de la ROMANÉE-CONTI. It is unquestionably one of the greatest French red wines, thanks to its ripeness, and although its silky fruit allows it to be drunk young, it can also last for decades.

Best years 1999, '98, '97, '96, '95, '93, '91, '90, '89, '88, '85, '78.

VOLNAY AC

Red wine only from 235ha, nearly half of which are Premiers Crus, on gentle slopes overlooking the Saône valley. This wine is considered to have the most bouquet and expression of all Côte de Beaune wines and is often compared to Chambolle-Musigny. Quality is due as much to the individual producers as to the vineyards. Drink at 4–7ʾ years. Many Beaune *négociants* own land in Volnay, especially BOUCHARD; the HOSPICES DE BEAUNE own several parcels of Premier Cru vines.

Premiers Crus Some of these are equal to the Côte de Beaune Grands Crus and need aging for 10–15 years. The best are Les Angles, Caillerets-Dessus (including Clos des 60 Ouvrées), En Cailleret, En Champans, Carelle-sous-la-Chapelle, En Chevret, Clos de la Bousse d'Or, Clos des Chênes, Clos des Ducs, Les Fremiets, Les Mitans, Les Taillepieds, Les Pitures-Dessus and Les Santenots (in Meursault).

Best producers d'ANGERVILLE, Bitouzet-Prieur, J-M BOILLOT, Lucien Boillot, BOUCHARD Père et Fils, Jean-Marc Bouley, Reyanne & Pascal Bouley, François Buffet, Yvon Clerget, DROUHIN, Vincent GIRARDIN, Bernard & Louis Glantenay, HOSPICES DE BEAUNE,

Michel LAFARGE, LAFON, de MONTILLE, POUSSE D'OR, Rossignol-Changarnier, Rossignol-Fevrier, Vaudoisey-Mutin, Voillot.

Best years 1999, '98, '96, '95, '90, '89, '88.

VOSNE-ROMANÉE AC

Red wine only from 240ha, of which just half is Premier or Grand Cru. The wines are firmer than those of Chambolle-Musigny, lighter than Gevrey-Chambertin and Nuits-St-Georges, but more elegant than both. It is best at 7-12 years.

Premiers Crus With 7 Grands Crus in the communes of Vosne and Flagey, the 13 Premiers Crus have had to be very good to gain their reputation. The best known are Aux Malconsorts, Clos des Réas, Cros-Parentoux, Aux Brûlées, Les Beaux-Monts (or Beaumonts) and Les Suchots.

Best producers ARNOUX, Cacheux, Sylvain Cathiard, Bruno Clavelier, Jack CONFURON-COTÉTIDOT, René ENGEL, Forey Père et Fils, François Gerbet, Jean GRIVOT, A-F Gros, Anne GROS, Jean Gros, Gros Frère et Soeur, LAMARCHE, LEROY, Manière-Noirot, Machard de Gramont, MÉO-CAMUZET, MONGEARD-MUGNERET, Gérard Mugneret, MUGNERET-GIBOURG, des PERDRIX, Pernin-Rossin, PRIEURÉ-ROCH, RION, Emmanuel ROUGET, Jean Tardy, Thomas-Moillard, Fabrice Vigot, Ch. de Vosne-Romanée.

Best years 1999, '98, '97, '96, '95, '93, '90, '89, '88, '85.

VOUGEOT AC

There are only 12ha of vines outside the walls of Clos de Vougeot qualifying for the Vougeot AC, including a tiny amount of Premier Cru. The wine is mainly red, of good village standard and a lot cheaper than any Clos de Vougeot.

Best producers Bertagna, l'Héritier-Guyot.

Best years 1999, '98, '96, '95, '90, '89, '88.

GUY AMIOT ET FILS, Chassagne-Montrachet   03 80 21 38 62/03 80 21 90 80

A steadily improving estate with vineyards in the best parts of Chassagne-Montrachet. The red wines are finely structured, the whites floral and elegant, with a hint of honey.
Best wines ★★ Chassagne-Montrachet 1er Cru Les Caillerets ♀, ★ Chassagne-Montrachet 1er Cru Les Champs Gain ♀, Puligny-Montrachet 1er Cru Les Demoiselles ♀, Montrachet ♀, Chassagne-Montrachet 1er Cru Clos St-Jean ♥ and Chassagne-Montrachet 1er Cru La Maltroye ♥
Best years ♥1999, '98, '96, '95, '93, '90; ♀1999, '98, '96, '95, '93, '90

AMIOT-SERVELLE, Chambolle-Musigny   03 80 62 80 39/03 80 62 84 16

This estate has vines in some of the best parts of Chambolle-Musigny and makes wines that are full-bodied yet graceful, and age well.
Best wines ★★ Chambolle-Musigny 1er Cru Derrière La Grange ♥ and 1er Cru Les Amoureuses ♥, ★ Chambolle-Musigny 1er Cru Les Charmes ♥ and Clos de Vougeot ♥
Best years 1999, '98, '96, '95, '93, '90, '88

MARQUIS D'ANGERVILLE, Volnay   03 80 21 61 75/03 80 21 65 07

One of the pioneers of domaine-bottling, this historic estate makes benchmark Volnay – wines that are often sturdy when young, but age superbly. Keep for at least 5 years.
Best wines ★★★ Volnay 1er Cru Clos des Ducs (monopole) ♥, ★★ Volnay 1er Cru Les Taillepieds ♥ and Volnay 1er Cru Les Champans ♥, ★ Volnay ♥
Best years 1999, '98, '97, '96, '95, '93, '91, '90, '89, '88, '85

COMTE ARMAND, Pommard   03 80 24 70 50/03 80 22 72 37

This renowned estate, previously limited to Pommard, has now grown to 10ha. The whites are ripe and fruity and the reds dense and tannic and built to last.
Best wines ★★ Pommard 1er Cru Clos des Epeneaux (monopole) ♥, ★ Volnay 1er Cru Les Fremiets ♥, Auxey-Duresses ♀ and Pommard ♥
Best years ♥1999, '98, '96, '95, '94, '93, '91, '90, '88; ♀1999, '98, '96, '95

ROBERT ARNOUX, Vosne-Romanée   03 80 61 09 85/03 80 61 36 02

A large estate, now run by Pascal Lachaux, making ripe, complex wines which age well.
Best wines ★★ Vosne-Romanée 1er Cru Les Suchots ♥ and Romanée-St-Vivant ♥, ★ Nuits-St-Georges Les Poizets ♥ and Vosne-Romanée 1er Cru Aux Reignots ♥
Best years 1999, '98, '96, '95, '93, '90, '88, '85

DOM. D'AUVENAY, Meursault   03 80 21 23 27

This tiny estate with vines in both the Côte de Nuits and Côte de Beaune is Mme Bize-Leroy's personal holding, separate from Dom. LEROY. Both the red and white wines are the epitome of concentration and purity and mature superbly.
Best wines ★★★ Meursault Les Narvaux ♀, Puligny-Montrachet 1er Cru Les Folatières ♀, Chevalier-Montrachet ♀, Bonnes-Mares ♥ and Mazis-Chambertin ♥, ★★ Auxey-Duresses ♀
Best years ♥1999, '98, '97, '96, '95, '93, '90, '89, '88, '85; ♀1999, '98, '97, '96, '95, '92, '90

GHISLAINE BARTHOD,   03 80 62 80 16/03 80 62 82 42
Chambolle-Musigny

This estate produces elegant, supple and not over-oaked wines from the village of Chambolle-Musigny, with a fine selection of 7 Premiers Crus and good AC Bourgogne.
Best wines ★★ Chambolle-Musigny 1er Cru Les Charmes ♥, ★ Chambolle-Musigny 1er

Cru aux Beaux Bruns ♥ and Chambolle-Musigny 1er Cru Les Fuées ♥, ★ Bourgogne ♥
Best years 1999, '98, '97, '96, '95, '93, '90, '89

SIMON BIZE ET FILS, Savigny-lès-Beaune   03 80 21 50 57/03 80 21 58 17
An important estate of 23ha, making wines of great purity and distinction.
Best wines ★★ Savigny-lès-Beaune 1er Cru Les Vergelesses ♥, ★★ Corton-Charlemagne ♀,
★ Savigny-lès-Beaune 1er Cru Les Guettes ♥ and Savigny-lès-Beaune 1er Cru Les Marconnets ♥
Best years 1999, '98, '96, '95, '93, '90, '88

BLAIN-GAGNARD, Chassagne-Montrachet   03 80 21 34 07/03 80 21 90 07
These wines are designed to aim for finesse and elegance, avoiding over-ripeness.
Best wines ★★ Criots-Bâtard-Montrachet ♀, ★ Chassagne-Montrachet 1er Cru Les Morgeots ♀,
Chassagne-Montrachet 1er Cru Les Boudriottes ♀ and Bâtard-Montrachet ♀
Best years ♥1999, '98; ♀1997, '96, '95, '92

JEAN-MARC BOILLOT, Pommard   03 80 22 71 29/03 80 24 98 07
Jean-Marc Boillot is related to the late Étienne SAUZET and his vineyards in Puligny-
Montrachet bear the family stamp of quality – these white wines are oaky but
excellent. There are also some notable and characterful reds from Volnay and Beaune.
Best wines ★★ Puligny-Montrachet 1er Cru Les Combettes ♀ and Pommard 1er Cru Les
Rugiens ♥, ★ Puligny-Montrachet ♀, Bâtard-Montrachet ♀ and Volnay ♥
Best years ♥1999, '98, '96, '95, '90, '89, '88; ♀1999, '98, '97, '96, '95, '93, '90

DOM. DE LA BONGRAN, Clessé   03 85 36 94 03/03 85 36 99 25
This estate benefits from a superb mesoclimate, which permits its owner, Jean
Thévenet, to produce some of the most impressive wines in the Mâconnais.
Best wines ★★ Mâcon-Clessé Cuvée Levroutée ♀ and Mâcon-Clessé ♀
Best years 1999, '98, '97, '96, '95

BONNEAU DU MARTRAY, Pernand-Vergelesses   03 80 21 50 64/03 80 21 57 19
An historic estate, the finest by far in Corton-Charlemagne, with 9.5ha in Grand Cru
white and 1.5ha in Corton red. After many successful vintages in the 1980s, quality in
the 1990s has been even more spectacular. The whites can last for 10–20 years.
Best wines ★★★ Corton-Charlemagne ♀, ★★ Corton ♥
Best years ♥1999, '98, '96, '95, '94, '93; ♀1999, '98, '97, '96, '95, '92, '90, '89, '88, '86

BOUCHARD PÈRE ET FILS, Beaune   03 80 24 80 24/03 80 24 97 56
Bouchard Père et Fils are the largest vineyard owners among the Burgundy *négociants*
owning 130ha, including some of the finest Grands and Beaujolais Crus in Burgundy.
During the 1980s the quality of the wine had declined and in 1995 Joseph HENRIOT
from Champagne bought the company from the Bouchard family. Since then the
quality has improved to match the quality of the vineyards.
Best wines ★★★ Meursault 1er Cru Les Genevrières ♀, Chevalier-Montrachet ♀, Beaune 1er
Cru Les Grèves Vigne de l'Enfant Jésus (monopole) ♥, Volnay 1er Cru Les Caillerets Ancien
Cuvée Carnot ♥ and Bonnes-Mares ♥, ★★ Nuits-St-Georges 1er Cru Clos St-Marc ♥,
Corton-Charlemagne ♀ and Montrachet ♀
Best years ♥ 1999, '98, '97, '96, '95, '90; ♀1999, '98, '97, '96, '95, '90

DOM. MICHEL BOUZEREAU ET FILS, Meursault   03 80 21 20 32/03 80 21 64 34
A 12-ha estate, mostly for white wine, with a fine selection of Premiers Crus in
Beaune, Meursault and Puligny.

Best wines ★★ Meursault 1er Cru Les Charmes ♀, Meursault 1er Cru Les Genevrières ♀, Meursault Les Tessons ♀ and Bourgogne Chardonnay ♀
Best years 1997, '96, '95, '94, '93, '92

LOUIS CARILLON ET FILS, Puligny-Montrachet 03 80 21 30 34/03 80 21 90 02
A sometimes underrated estate, two-thirds planted to Chardonnay, producing wines of great finesse and concentration, which may be aged for up to 15 years.
Best wines ★★ Bienvenues-Bâtard-Montrachet ♀, Puligny-Montrachet 1er Cru Les Perrières ♀ and Puligny-Montrachet 1er Cru Les Referts ♀, ★ Puligny-Montrachet ♀
Best years 1999, '98, '96, '95, '92, '90, '89

LA CHABLISENNE, Chablis 03 86 42 89 89/03 86 42 89 90
This large co-operative makes nearly one third of all Chablis and enjoys a fine reputation, with some wines rivalling those from much smaller top estates. Best are the oaky Grands Crus. Age the Grands Crus for 7–8 years.
Best wines ★★★ Chablis Grand Cru Ch. Grenouille ♀, ★★ Chablis Grand Cru Blanchot ♀, Chablis 1er Cru Mont de Milieu ♀ and Chablis Vieilles Vignes ♀
Best years 1999, '98, '97, '96, '95, '92, '90, '89

CH. DE CHAMBOLLE-MUSIGNY, Chambolle-Musigny 03 80 62 85 39/03 80 62 87 36
A tiny estate producing wines with finesse and elegance.
Best wines ★★★ Musigny 🍷, ★★ Bonnes-Mares 🍷, Chambolle-Musigny 1er Cru Les Fuées 🍷 and Chambolle-Musigny 1er Cru Les Amoureuses 🍷
Best years 1996, '95, '94, '93, '90

CHAMPY, Beaune 03 80 25 09 99/03 80 25 09 95
Established in 1720, Champy is the oldest *négociant* in Burgundy. JADOT acquired the company for its vineyards and sold the name and stock in 1990 to Henri and Pierre Meurgey, Beaune wine brokers. A range of fine, elegant wines is produced.
Best wines ★★ Charmes-Chambertin 🍷, Chambertin Clos-de-Bèze 🍷 and Corton-Charlemagne ♀, ★ Savigny-lès-Beaune 1er Cru 🍷, Côte de Beaune-Villages 🍷 and Pernand-Vergelesses ♀
Best years 🍷1999, '98, '96, '95, '93, '91, '90; ♀1999, '98, '97, '96, '95

CHANDON DE BRIAILLES, Savigny-lès-Beaune 03 80 21 52 31/03 80 21 59 15
Steady improvement at this elegant estate during the 1980s has been followed by exceptional wines in the 1990s from a mother and daughter winemaking team.
Best wines ★★★ Corton-Charlemagne ♀, ★★ Pernand-Vergelesses 1er Cru Île de Vergelesses 🍷, Corton Clos du Roi 🍷, Savigny-lès-Beaune 1er Cru Les Lavières 🍷 and Corton-Bressandes 🍷
Best years 🍷1999, '98, '97, '96, '95, '93, '90, '89; ♀1999, '98, '97

CHANSON PÈRE ET FILS, Beaune 03 80 22 33 00/03 80 24 17 42
A fine, rather old-fashioned *négociant*, with mostly Pinot Noir vines in some of the best Premiers Crus in Beaune and Savigny. The wines are very elegant and long-lasting, and should improve further following the 1990 purchase by BOLLINGER.
Best wines ★★ Beaune 1er Cru Clos des Marconnets Monopole 🍷 and Beaune 1er Cru Clos des Feves 🍷, ★ Savigny-lès-Beaune 1er Cru La Dominode 🍷
Best years 1999, '98, '96, '95, '93, '92, '90, '89, '88

PHILIPPE CHARLOPIN, Gevrey-Chambertin 03 80 51 81 18/03 80 51 81 27
A fine 12-ha estate, making deep-coloured, fleshy wines, full of depth and flavour.

FRANCE/BURGUNDY

Best wines ★★ Clos-St-Denis ♥, Gevrey-Chambertin Vieilles Vignes ♥ and Charmes-Chambertin ♥, ★ Marsannay-en-Montchenevoy ♥
Best years 1999, '98, '97, '96, '95, '93, '90

CHARTRON ET TRÉBUCHET, Puligny-Montrachet   03 80 21 32 85/03 80 21 36 35
Based on the Chartron family's estate in the best Puligny-Montrachet sites, the strength of this *négociant* lies in light, stylish white wines. Age the best wines for 5–10 years.
Best wines ★★ Puligny-Montrachet 1er Cru Clos de la Pucelle (monopole) ♀, Puligny-Montrachet 1er Cru Les Folatières ♀ and Chassagne-Montrachet 1er Cru Les Morgeots ♀
Best years 1999, '98, '97, '96, '95, '90

ROBERT CHEVILLON, Nuits-St-Georges   03 80 62 34 88/03 80 61 13 31
This producer owns 8 Premiers Crus in Nuits-St-Georges. All the wines share deep colour, ripe fruit, structure and elegance. A comprehensive tasting of the different Crus shows perfectly the differences in terroir.
Best wines ★★★ Nuits-St-Georges 1er Cru Les St-Georges ♥, ★★ Nuits-St-Georges 1er Cru Les Roncières ♥, Nuits-St-Georges 1er Cru Les Perrières ♥, Nuits-St-Georges 1er Cru Les Cailles ♥, Nuits-St-Georges 1er Cru Les Pruliers ♥ and Nuits-St-Georges 1er Cru Les Vaucrains ♥
Best years 1999, '98, '97, '96, '95, '93, '90, '89, '88, '85

BRUNO CLAIR, Marsannay-La-Côte   03 80 52 28 95/03 80 52 18 14
From his share in the break-up of the famous Clair-Dau domaine, Bruno Clair has built up an estate across several appellations, but concentrating on the northern Côte de Nuits. The vines are old, yields are low and the wines are models of concentration.
Best wines ★★★ Corton-Charlemagne ♀ and Chambertin Clos de Bèze ♥, ★★ Marsannay Les Longeroies ♥, Gevrey-Chambertin 1er Cru Les Cazetiers ♥, Morey-St-Denis En la Rue de Vergy ♥ and Savigny-lès-Beaune 1er Cru Les Dominodes ♥
Best years ♥1999, '98, '97, '96, '95, '93, '90, '89, '88; ♀1999, '98, '97, '96, '95

CLOS DE TART, Morey-St-Denis   03 80 34 30 91/03 80 24 60 01
The Clos de Tart Grand Cru belongs entirely to Mommessin. This light, dry red wine needs 10 years' aging in fine vintages.
Best wines ★★ Morey-St-Denis 1er Cru ♥ and Clos de Tart ♥
Best years 1999, '98, '96, '95, '93, '90

JEAN-FRANÇOIS COCHE-DURY, Meursault   03 80 21 24 12/03 80 21 67 65
A highly sought-after estate, with vines (80% Chardonnay) in the best Meursault *climats* and one of the leading winemakers in the Côte de Beaune. The white wines, although superb young, should really be aged for 5–10 years. The red wines can be drunk from their fourth year.
Best wines ★★★ Corton-Charlemagne ♀, Puligny-Montrachet 1er Cru Les Enseigneres ♀ and Meursault 1er Cru Les Perrières ♀, ★★ Meursault Les Rougeots ♀, Meursault Les Chevalières ♀ and Auxey-Duresses ♥
Best years ♥1999, '98, '96, '95, '90; ♀1999, '98, '97, '96, '95, '92, '90, '89, '88, '86, '85

MARC COLIN ET FILS, St-Aubin   03 80 21 30 43/03 80 21 90 04
An important estate making remarkably pure and distinctive wines, especially whites.
Best wines ★★ St-Aubin 1er Cru En Rémilly ♀, St-Aubin 1er Cru Les Charmois ♀, Chassagne-Montrachet 1er Cru Les Caillerets ♀ and Santenay Vieilles Vignes ♥
Best years ♀1999, '98, '97, '96, '95, '92, '90, '89

COLIN-DELÉGER, Chassagne-Montrachet   03 80 21 32 72/03 80 21 32 94
Production is split equally between white and red wines; the character and rich fruit of the whites puts them in the first rank. The reds are good, if not great.
Best wines ★★ Bâtard-Montrachet ♀, Chassagne-Montrachet 1er Cru Les Chevenottes ♀ and Chassagne-Montrachet 1er Cru Les Vergers ♀, ★ Chassagne-Montrachet Vieilles Vignes ❢
Best years ❢1999, '98, '96, '95, '90; ♀1999, '98, '97, '96, '95, '92

JEAN-JACQUES CONFURON, Nuits-St-Georges   03 80 62 31 08/03 80 61 34 21
Small estate making elegant, concentrated wines, the best aged in 100% new oak.
Best wines ★★★ Romanée-St-Vivant ❢, ★★ Chambolle-Musigny 1er Cru ❢, Clos de Vougeot ❢ and Nuits-St-Georges 1er Cru Les Boudots ❢, ★ Bourgogne ❢
Best years 1999, '98, '97, '96, '95, '93, '90, '88

JACKY CONFURON-COTÉTIDOT, Vosne-Romanée   03 80 61 03 39/03 80 61 17 85
Late picking and long maturation at this domaine produce wines with deep colour and powerful personality from low-yielding vines, among the oldest in the appellation.
Best wines ★★ Vosne-Romanée 1er Cru Les Suchots ❢, ★★ Chambolle-Musigny ❢ and Nuits-St-Georges 1er Cru ❢
Best years 1999, '98, '97, '96, '95, '93, '90, '88, '85

PIERRE DAMOY, Gevrey-Chambertin   03 80 34 30 47/03 80 58 54 79
An important estate owning most of the Chambertin Clos-de-Bèze Grand Cru.
Best wines ★★ Chambertin ❢ and Chambertin Clos-de-Bèze ❢
Best years 1999, '98, '96, '95, '93, '90

RENÉ ET VINCENT DAUVISSAT, Chablis   03 86 42 11 58/03 86 42 85 32
Noted domaine, arguably the finest in Chablis, with vineyards in the best Crus producing carefully made, concentrated wines which can last for 15–20 years.
Best wines ★★★ Chablis Grand Cru Les Clos ♀ and Chablis Grand Cru Les Preuses ♀, ★ Chablis 1er Cru La Forêt ♀ and Chablis 1er Cru Séchet ♀
Best years 1999, '98, '97, '96, '95, '92, '90, '89, '88

JEAN-PAUL DROIN, Chablis   03 86 42 16 78/03 86 42 42 09
This young producer has finely situated vines in both Premiers and Grands Crus. These ripe, buttery wines are vinified in oak and the best can age from 5–8 years.
Best wines ★★★ Chablis Grand Cru Valmur ♀, Chablis Grand Cru Les Clos ♀ and Chablis Grand Cru Vaudésir ♀, ★★ Chablis 1er Cru Vosgros ♀ and 1er Cru Montée de Tonnerre ♀
Best years 1999, '98, '97, '96, '95, '93, '90

JOSEPH DROUHIN, Beaune   03 80 24 68 88/03 80 22 43 14
One of the very top Burgundy houses. The elegance, depth and finesse of these wines is world renowned. Many of the best wines come from their own vines, but the quality of winemaking and the fine use of oak is the same across the full range of wines.
Best wines ★★★ Montrachet Marquis de Laguiche ♀ and Grands-Échézeaux ❢, ★★ Beaune 1er Cru Clos des Mouches ❢, Volnay 1er Cru En Chevret ❢, Chablis Grand Cru Les Preuses ♀, Chambolle-Musigny 1er Cru ❢ and Chassagne-Montrachet Marquis de Laguiche ♀
Best years ❢1999, '98, '97, '96, '95, '93, '90, '89, '88; ♀1999, '98, '97, '96, '95, '90

GEORGES DUBOEUF, Romanèche-Thorins   03 85 35 34 20/03 85 35 34 25
The *négociant* Georges Duboeuf has been the most important influence in Beaujolais
• for the last 30 years. Even with a production of 25 million bottles a year, quality remains

high. Many of the Beaujolais Cru wines are bottled under the name of the grower.

Best wines ★★ Morgon Jean Descombes 🍷, Juliénas Dom. de la Seigneurie 🍷, Moulin-à-Vent Clos des Maréchaux 🍷, Pouilly-Fuissé 🍷 and Brouilly Dom. de Combillaty 🍷

Best years 🍷1998, '97, '96, '95

BERNARD DUGAT-PY, Gevrey-Chambertin   03 80 51 82 46/03 80 34 16 45

The 5.6-ha estate produces some of the most sumptuously rich and intensely flavoured wines in the Côte de Nuits.

Best wines ★★★ Charmes-Chambertin 🍷 and Mazis-Chambertin 🍷, ★★ Gevrey-Chambertin Vieilles Vignes Coeur du Roi 🍷 and Gevrey-Chambertin 1er Cru Lavaux St-Jacques 🍷

Best years 1999, '98, '97, '96, '95, '93, '90

DOM. DUJAC, Morey-St-Denis   03 80 34 01 00/03 80 34 01 09

One of Burgundy's leading winemakers with holdings in various ACs, Jacques Seysses is very influential among younger producers. The best reds will age for 2 decades.

Best wines ★★ Morey-St-Denis 🍷, Gevrey-Chambertin 1er Cru Les Combottes 🍷, Clos de La Roche 🍷 and Bonnes-Mares 🍷

Best years 1999, '98, '97, '96, '95, '93, '90, '89, '88, '85, '78

MAURICE ECARD ET FILS, Savigny-lès-Beaune   03 80 21 50 61/03 80 26 11 05

A family estate producing perhaps the most robust and structured wines of this village.

Best wines ★★ Savigny 1er Cru Les Narbantons 🍷, ★ Savigny 1er Cru Les Peuillets 🍷, Savigny 1er Cru Les Jarrons 🍷 and Savigny 1er Cru Les Serpentières 🍷

Best years 1999, '98, '97, '96, '95, '90

RENÉ ENGEL, Vosne-Romanée   03 80 61 10 54/03 80 62 39 73

A splendid family estate making elegant wines which age well for 5–10 years.

Best wines ★★ Grands-Échézeaux 🍷 and Clos de Vougeot 🍷, ★ Vosne-Romanée 1er Cru Les Brûlées 🍷 and Échézeaux 🍷

Best years 1999, '98, '97, '96, '95, '93, '91, '90, '89, '88

JOSEPH FAIVELEY, Nuits-St-Georges   03 80 61 04 55/03 80 62 33 37

This *négociant* owns 120ha of vines, mainly in the Côte Chalonnaise. The whites are lively and honeyed and the reds dense and relatively tannic. Both age well. François Faiveley was one of the pioneers of hand-bottling unfiltered wines for his best Crus.

Best wines ★★★ Corton Clos des Cortons 🍷, Latricières-Chambertin 🍷, Mazis-Chambertin 🍷, Chambertin Clos-de-Bèze 🍷, Corton-Charlemagne 🍷, ★★ Nuits-St-Georges 1er Cru Clos de la Maréchale (monopole) 🍷

Best years 🍷1999, '98, '97, '96, '95, '93, '90, '88, '85, '78; 🍷1999, '98, '97, '96, '95

DOM. J-A FERRET, Pouilly-Fuissé   03 85 35 61 56/03 85 35 62 74

A family estate with some of the oldest vines in the region, making rich, honeyed wines.

Best wines ★★ Pouilly-Fuissé Tête du Cru 🍷 and Pouilly-Fuissé Hors Classe 🍷

Best years 1999, '98, '97, '96, '95, '90

RICHARD FONTAINE-GAGNARD,   03 80 21 35 50/03 80 21 90 78
Chassagne-Montrachet

One of the many Gagnard families in Chassagne, with well-situated vineyards.

Best wines ★★ Criots-Bâtard-Montrachet 🍷, Bâtard-Montrachet 🍷 and Chassagne-Montrachet 1er Cru Les Caillerets 🍷, ★ Chassagne-Montrachet 1er Cru La Maltroie 🍷

Best years 1999, '98, '97, '96, '95, '92

CH. FUISSÉ, Pouilly-Fuissé   03 85 35 61 44/03 85 35 67 34
This large estate, owned by Jean-Jacques Vincent, serves as a benchmark for other producers in Pouilly-Fuissé. Age the best of these ripe, concentrated wines for 5 years.
Best wines ★★ Pouilly-Fuissé Vieilles Vignes ♀ and Pouilly-Fuissé Le Clos ♀
Best years 1999, '98, '97, '96, '95, '94, '93, '92, '90, '89, '88

JEAN-NOËL GAGNARD, Chassagne-Montrachet   03 80 21 31 68/03 80 21 33 07
This important estate makes both red and white wine and is also known as Ch. de la Maltroye. Quality is improving every year and the list of Premiers Crus is impressive.
Best wines ★★★ Chassagne-Montrachet 1er Cru Les Caillerets ♀ and Bâtard-Montrachet ♀,
★★ Chassagne-Montrachet 1er Cru Les Morgeots ♀ and Chassagne-Montrachet 1er Cru La Maltroie ♀, ★ Santenay 1er Cru Clos de Tavannes ❢ and Chassagne-Montrachet ♀
Best years ❢1999, '98, '96, '95, '90; ♀1999, '98, '97, '96, '95, '92, '90, '89

JACQUES GAGNARD-DELAGRANGE,   03 80 21 31 40/03 80 21 91 59
Chassagne-Montrachet
A small estate owned by Jean-Noël Gagnard's younger brother 'Jacky' Gagnard. The wines are rich and complex and repay aging for at least 7–10 years.
Best wines ★★★ Montrachet ♀, Bâtard-Montrachet ♀ and Chassagne-Montrachet 1er Cru Les Morgeots ♀, ★★ Chassagne-Montrachet 1er Cru Les Boudriottes ♀
Best years 1999, '98, '97, '96, '95, '93, '92, '90, '89

VINCENT GIRARDIN, Santenay   03 80 20 64 29/03 80 20 64 88
Built up in the 1980s, this estate produces rich, succulent reds and whites with a high percentage of new oak. Recently a *négociant* business has added wines to the range.
Best wines ★★ Chassagne-Montrachet 1er Cru Les Morgeots ❢, ★ Santenay 1er Cru Les Gravières ❢ and Santenay 1er Cru Clos du Beauregard ♀
Best years ❢1999, '98, '96, '95; ♀1999, '98, '97, '96, '95

CAMILLE GIROUD, Beaune   03 80 22 12 65/03 80 22 42 84
Owner of just 1ha of vines in Beaune, this company specializes in purchasing small lots of deep-coloured red wines for slow aging in barrels in their cellars.
Best wines ★★ Vosne-Romanée 1er Cru Les Suchots ❢, Beaune 1er Cru Les Cras ❢ and Nuits-St-Georges 1er Cru Les Perrières ❢, ★ Volnay ❢
Best years 1999, '98, '96, '95, '94, '93, '90, '88

HENRI GOUGES, Nuits-St-Georges   03 80 61 04 40/03 80 61 32 84
This family was one of the first in Burgundy to practise estate bottling back in the 1920s. The wines are understated when young, but mature to show superb complexity. Age the reds for 8–10 years. The white Nuits St-Georges, from Pinot Noir, is a rarity.
Best wines ★★ Nuits-St-Georges Les Perrières ♀, Nuits-St-Georges 1er Cru Les Pruliers ❢, Nuits-St-Georges 1er Cru Les Vaucrains ❢, Nuits-St-Georges 1er Cru Clos des Porrets ❢ and Nuits-St-Georges 1er Cru Les St-Georges ❢
Best years ❢1999, '98, '97, '96, '95, '93, '91, '90, '89, '88; ♀1999, '98, '97, '96, '95

DOM. ALBERT GRIVAULT, Meursault   03 80 21 23 12/03 80 21 24 70
A small family estate producing quality wines which are discreet yet powerful.
Best wines ★★ Meursault 1er Cru Clos des Perrières (monopole) ♀, ★ Meursault ♀, Meursault 1er Cru Les Perrières ♀ and Pommard 1er Cru Clos Blanc ❢
Best years ❢1999, '98, '96, '95, '93, '90, '88; ♀1999, '98, '97, '96, '95, '94, '92

JEAN GRIVOT, Vosne-Romanée 03 80 61 05 95/03 80 61 32 99
Now run by Étienne Grivot, this estate owns vines in the best Côte de Nuits appellations and is making some truly classic Burgundies in a velvety, silky style.
Best wines ★★★ Vosne-Romanée 1er Cru Les Suchots 🍷, and Richebourg 🍷, ★★ Vosne-Romanée 1er Cru Les Brûlées 🍷, Nuits-St-Georges 1er Cru Les Boudots 🍷 and Clos de Vougeot 🍷
Best years 1999, '98, '97, '96, '95, '93, '90

ROBERT GROFFIER, Morey-St-Denis 03 80 34 31 53/03 80 34 15 48
This estate has most of its vines in Chambolle-Musigny, producing wines with great elegance and purity of fruit and with fine aging potential.
Best wines ★★ Chambolle-Musigny 1er Cru Les Amoureuses 🍷 and Chambolle-Musigny 1er Cru Les Sentiers 🍷, ★ Chambolle-Musigny 1er Cru Les Haut Doix 🍷
Best years 1999, '98, '97, '96, '95, '93, '90, '88

ANNE GROS, Vosne-Romanée 03 80 61 07 95/03 80 61 23 21
This estate has been reduced through family shareholdings, but still has superbly placed vines around Vosne-Romanée, making intensely fruity wines. Age the wines for 8 years or more. One of the purest expressions of Pinot Noir fruit in the whole of Burgundy.
Best wines ★★★ Clos de Vougeot 🍷 and Richebourg 🍷, ★★ Vosne-Romanée Les Barraux 🍷 and Chambolle-Musigny La Combe d'Orveau 🍷
Best years 1999, '98, '97, '96, '95, '93, '90, '88

DOM. GUFFENS-HEYNEN, Vergisson 03 85 35 84 22/03 85 35 82 72
A tiny (3-ha) estate whose very old, low-yielding vines, combined with brilliant winemaking, produce wines that surpass their appellations. See VERGET.
Best wines ★★★ Pouilly-Fuissé ♀ and Mâcon-Pierreclos En Chavigne Vieilles Vignes ♀
Best years 1999, '98, '97, '96, '95, '93, '92

ANTONIN GUYON, Savigny-lès-Beaune 03 80 67 13 24/03 80 66 85 87
This very large family estate has half its vines in the Hautes Côtes de Nuits. The wines, from many of the major appellations of the Côte d'Or, are well-made and reliable.
Best wines ★★ Chambolle-Musigny 🍷, Meursault 1er Cru Les Charmes ♀, Corton-Charlemagne ♀, Volnay 1er Cru Clos des Chênes 🍷 and Corton-Bressandes 🍷
Best years 🍷1999, '98, '96, '95, '93, '90, '88; ♀1999, '98, '97, '96, '95

HOSPICES DE BEAUNE See page 87

ALAIN HUDELOT-NOËLLAT, Vougeot 03 80 62 85 17/03 80 62 83 13
This Côte de Nuits estate posseses vines in no fewer than 5 Premiers Crus and 3 Grands Crus, making wines with amazing richness and ripe fruit for drinking after 7–10 years or more.
Best wines ★★ Romanée-St-Vivant 🍷 and Richebourg 🍷, ★ Vosne-Romanée 1er Cru Les Suchots 🍷, Vosne-Romanée 1er Cru Les Malconsorts 🍷, Vosne-Romanée 1er Cru Les Beaumonts 🍷 and Clos de Vougeot 🍷
Best years 1999, '98, '97, '96, '95, '93, '90, '89, '88

CH. DES JACQUES, Romanèche-Thorins 03 85 35 51 64/03 85 35 59 15
A large Beaujolais estate, now owned by the Beaune *negociant* JADOT. The wines are deep-coloured and with fine tannins, and are best at 3–10 years old. It is one of the rare Beaujolais cellars to use a high proportion of new oak in the winemaking.

Best wines ★★ Moulin-à-Vent Grand Clos de Rochegrès ❢ and Moulin-à-Vent Clos de Champ de Coeur ❢

Best years 1999, '98, '97, '96, '95

HENRI ET PAUL JACQUESON, Rully   03 85 91 25 91/03 85 87 14 92

An estate of 8ha, producing wines with depth of fruit and great finesse that are almost always the best in the Rully appellation.

Best wines ★★ Rully 1er Cru La Pucelle ♀ and Rully 1er Cru Les Cloux ❢

Best years ❢1999, '98, '96, '95, '93, '90; ♀1999, '98, '97, '96, '95

LOUIS JADOT, Beaune   03 80 22 10 57/03 80 22 56 03

The overall quality of the Jadot range puts it at the head of the Burgundy *négociants*. From a fine base of vineyards, Jadot has been expanding its range, and now owns 51ha of Pinot Noir across the best Crus in the Côte d'Or, 27ha of Gamay – the Ch. des JACQUES estate in Moulin-à-Vent – and 19ha of Chardonnay. The white wines have a rich, honeyed fruit with a balancing acidity and the reds deeply extracted colours, dense fruit but rounded tannins. Both styles are made for long aging.

Best wines ★★★ Chablis Grand Cru Les Preuses ♀, Chassagne-Montrachet 1er Cru Les Caillerets ♀, Puligny-Montrachet 1er Cru Les Folatières ♀, Chevalier-Montrachet Les Demoiselles ♀, Clos Vougeot ❢, Bonnes-Mares ❢ and Chambertin Clos-de-Bèze ❢, ★★ Beaune 1er Cru Les Vignes Franches Clos des Ursules (monopole) ❢

Best years ❢1999, '98, '97, '96, '95, '93, '90, '89, '88, '85; ♀1997, '96, '95, '94, '93, '92

PATRICK JAVILLIER, Meursault   03 80 21 27 87/03 80 21 29 39

A 9.5-ha estate which has made a speciality of single-*climat* Meursaults. The wines are fine, elegant and typical and may be drunk quite young (between 3 and 7 years).

Best wines ★★ Meursault 1er Cru Les Charmes ♀, Meursault Les Murgers ♀, Meursault Clos du Cromin ♀ and Meursault Les Tillets ♀

Best years 1999, '98, '97, '96, '95

ROBERT JAYER-GILLES, Magny-Les-Villers   03 80 62 91 79/03 80 62 99 77

This domaine with Pinot Noir vines around Vosne-Romanée and in the Hautes Côtes makes very high-quality wines, though there is some criticism of too much new oak.

Best wines ★★★ Échézeaux ❢, ★★ Nuits-St-Georges 1er Cru Les Hauts-Poirets ❢, Bourgogne-Aligoté ♀, Bourgogne Hautes-Côtes de Nuits ❢ and Nuits-St-Georges 1er Cru Les Damodes ❢

Best years 1999, '98, '97, '96, '95, '93, '90, '88

FRANÇOIS JOBARD, Meursault   03 80 21 21 26/03 80 21 26 44

This excellent, small estate (5.5ha) has a reputation for making firm, long-lived Meursaults that require 5 years of aging to show them at their complex best.

Best wines ★★ Meursault 1er Cru Les Genevrières ♀, Meursault 1er Cru Les Charmes ♀ and Meursault 1er Cru Les Poruzots ♀, ★ Meursault ♀

Best years 1999, '98, '97, '96, '95, '92, '90

RÉMI JOBARD, Meursault   03 80 21 20 23/03 80 21 67 69

This father-and-son team makes some fine, well-balanced classic Meursaults that are best after 3–5 years of aging, when their natural acidity has blended with the fruit.

Best wines ★★ Meursault 1er Cru Les Charmes ♀, Meursault 1er Cru Les Genevrières ♀ and Meursault 1er Cru Les Poruzots-Dessus ♀, ★ Meursault En Luraule ♀

Best years 1999, '98, '97, '96, '95, '92, '90

MICHEL JUILLOT, Mercurey   03 85 45 27 27/03 85 45 25 52
A well-established 30-ha estate known for its impressive wines from low-yielding vines
that produce richly structured wines with a marked use of oak.
Best wines ★★ Corton-Charlemagne ♀, Mercurey Clos Tonnerre (monopole) ❗ and
Mercurey Clos des Barraults ❗, ★ Mercurey ♀
Best years ❗1999, '98, '96, '95, '93, '90; ♀1999, '98, '97, '96, '95

MICHEL LAFARGE, Volnay   03 80 21 61 61/03 80 21 67 83
Lafarge is the doyen of the Volnay AC, now handing over to his equally competent son
Frédéric and maintaining top quality in these concentrated wines which show purity
and finesse, and age as well as the best wines from the Côte de Nuits.
Best wines ★★★ Volnay 1er Cru Clos des Chênes ❗ and Beaune 1er Cru Les Grèves ❗, ★★
Côte de Beaune-Villages ❗, Volnay 1er Cru ❗, Pommard 1er Cru Les Pezerolles ❗ and Bourgogne ❗
Best years 1999, '98, '97, '96, '96, '95, '93, '91, '90, '89, '88, '85

DOM. DES COMTES LAFON, Meursault   03 80 21 22 17/03 80 21 61 64
With holdings across the finest vineyards in the Côte de Beaune, this world-famous
estate has a justified reputation for producing the very best that terroir and the grapes
can offer. Despite a forward quality when they are young, both the reds and whites are
made for aging longer than their neighbours. Keep the whites and top reds for 10 years
or more. The vineyard is almost 100% biodynamic, for enhanced expression of 'terroir'.
Best wines ★★★ Meursault 1er Cru Les Charmes ♀, Meursault 1er Cru Les Genevrières ♀,
Meursault 1er Cru Les Perrières ♀, Meursault Clos de la Barre ♀, Montrachet ♀ and Volnay
1er Cru Les Santenots ❗, ★★ Volnay 1er Cru Clos des Chênes ❗ and Meursault ♀
Best years ❗1999, '98, '97, '96, '95, '93, '90, '89, '88, '85; ♀1999, '98, '97, '96, '95, '93, '92,
'90, '89

FRANÇOIS LAMARCHE, Vosne-Romanée   03 80 61 07 94/03 80 61 24 31
An important estate, owning 4 Premiers Crus and 4 Grands Crus in Vosne-Romanée.
The quality of the wines show much needed improvement since 1990.
Best wines ★★ Vosne-Romanée 1er Cru Les Malconsorts ❗, Vosne-Romanée 1er Cru Les
Suchots ❗, Grands-Échézeaux ❗ and La Grande Rue ❗
Best years 1999, '98, '97, '96, '95, '93, '90

DOM. DES LAMBRAYS, Morey-St-Denis   03 80 51 84 33/03 80 51 81 97
A famous 'monopole', this 10.65-ha estate owns all but 420 square metres of the Clos
des Lambrays Grand Cru. The new owners are beginning to improve quality here.
Best wines ★★ Clos des Lambrays ❗ and Morey-St-Denis 1er Cru ❗
Best years 1999, '98, '96, '95, '93, '90, '85

DOM. LAROCHE, Chablis   03 86 42 89 00/03 86 42 89 29
With 100ha of vines, and as one of Chablis' larger *négociants*, Laroche is known around
the world for steely, fruity wines combining purity and complexity.
Best wines ★★★ Chablis Grand Cru Réserve de l'Obédiencerie ♀, ★★ Chablis 1er Cru
Vaudevey ♀ and Chablis 1er Cru Fourchaume ♀, ★ Chablis St-Martin ♀
Best years 1999, '98, '96, '95, '93, '92, '90, '89

LOUIS LATOUR, Beaune   03 80 24 81 00/03 80 22 36 21
With particularly fine vineyards in Corton and Corton-Charlemagne, Louis Latour is
one of the longest established Burgundian *négociants*. In general, the white wines are

rich, unctuous and oaky, while the reds tend to lack persistence and depth.

Best wines ★★ Meursault 1er Cru Les Genevrières ♀, Corton-Charlemagne, Romanée-St-Vivant Les Quatres Journaux ♀, Chevalier-Montrachet Les Demoiselles ♀, Mâcon-Lugny ♀ and Corton-Grancey ♀

Best years ♀1999, '98, '96, '95, '93, '90; ♀1999, '98, '97, '96, '95, '92, '90, '89, '88

DOMINIQUE LAURENT, Nuits-St-Georges   03 80 61 49 94/03 80 61 49 95

Established at the beginning of the 1990s, Dominique Laurent is the newest *négociant* house in Burgundy, yet one of the most impressive. Grapes are bought from vineyards with very old vines and the wines are made to retain the maximum colour and concentration, intensity of flavour being added by a very high proportion of new oak.

Best wines ★★★ Nuits-St-Georges 1er Cru Les St-Georges ♀, Mazis-Chambertin ♀, Chambertin Clos-de-Bèze ♀ and Bonnes-Mares ♀, ★★ Pommard Vieilles Vignes ♀ and Échézeaux ♀

Best years 1999, '98, '97, '96, '95, '94, '93

DOM. LEFLAIVE, Puligny-Montrachet   03 80 21 30 13/03 80 21 39 57

Along with LAFON, the reputation of this estate has reached mythic proportions. No other domaine in Burgundy can approach it for the perfection of expression of the whole range of wines from Puligny-Montrachet. The estate is now run on biodynamic lines by Anne-Claude Leflaive, with Pierre Morey from Meursault as manager.

Best wines ★★★ Montrachet ♀, Chevalier-Montrachet ♀, Bienvenues-Bâtard-Montrachet ♀, Bâtard-Montrachet ♀, Puligny-Montrachet 1er Cru Les Folatières ♀ and Puligny-Montrachet 1er Cru Les Pucelles ♀, ★★ Puligny-Montrachet 1er Cru Les Clavoillons ♀

Best years 1999, '98, '97, '96, '95, '94, '93, '92, '90, '85

OLIVIER LEFLAIVE, Puligny-Montrachet   03 80 21 37 65/03 80 21 33 94

This *négociant,* once manager at Dom. LEFLAIVE, also owns vines in the Côte de Beaune and produces elegant wines which are generally good value for money.

Best wines ★★ Pommard 1er Cru Les Rugiens ♀, Corton-Charlemagne ♀, Chassagne-Montrachet 1er Cru La Romanée ♀, Volnay 1er Cru Les Champans ♀, Chassagne-Montrachet 1er Cru Les Morgeots ♀ and Meursault Les Narvaux ♀

Best years ♀1999, '98, '97, '96, '95, '93, '90; ♀1999, '98, '97, '96, '95, '93

DOM. LEROY, Vosne-Romanée   03 80 21 21 10/03 80 21 63 81

This estate has vines in some of the greatest vineyards of the Côte d'Or. Owned by Lalou Bize-Leroy, who has a part-interest in Dom. de la ROMANÉE-CONTI, the vines are cultivated to produce far lower yields than those demanded by other high-quality estates, and the wines reflect this concentration of true flavours. Every tiniest detail is attended to and these exceptional wines are, justifiably, very expensive.

Best wines ★★★ Corton-Charlemagne ♀, Vosne-Romanée 1er Cru Les Beaumonts ♀, Nuits-St-Georges 1er Cru Aux Boudots ♀, Clos de la Roche ♀, Clos de Vougeot ♀, Latricières-Chambertin ♀, Chambertin ♀ and Musigny ♀

Best years ♀1999, '98, '97, '96, '95, '93, '92, '91, '90, '89, '88

HUBERT LIGNIER, Morey-St-Denis   03 80 34 31 79/03 80 51 80 97

This estate has only recently begun to bottle all its wines. The wines are deep-coloured, quite heavily-oaked and firm but elegant. They need aging for 10–12 years.

Best wines ★★ Clos de la Roche ♀, ★ Morey-St-Denis ♀, Morey-St-Denis 1er Cru Vieilles

Vignes ❗ and Gevrey-Chambertin 1er Cru Les Combottes ❗
Best years 1999, '98, '97, '96, '95, '93, '90, '88, '85

DOM. DE LA MALADIÈRE, Chablis   03 86 42 12 51/03 86 42 19 14
One of the leading Chablis estates with vines in all 7 Grands Crus and purchased from
William Fèvre by Joseph HENRIOT of Champagne. The wines flaunt both the qualities
of the Kimmeridgian chalk soil from around the town and the virtues of oak-aging.
Best wines ★★ Chablis 1er Cru Vaulorent ♀, Chablis Grand Cru Grenouilles ♀, Chablis
Grand Cru Bougros ♀ and Chablis Grand Cru Vaudésir ♀
Best years 1999, '98, '97, '96, '95, '93, '92

DOM. MATROT, Meursault   03 80 21 20 13/03 80 21 29 62
This family estate produces slightly austere wines that have great persistence and
balance, needing a few years' aging to show at their natural best.
Best wines ★★ Meursault 1er Cru Blagny ♀, Puligny-Montrachet 1er Cru Les Chalumeaux ♀
and Blagny 1er Cru La Pièce-sous-le-Bois ❗, ★ Meursault ♀
Best years ❗1999, '98, '96, '95, '93, '90, '88; ♀1999, '98, '97, '96, '95, '92, '90, '89, '88, '86

DOM. MAUME, Gevrey-Chambertin   03 80 34 33 14/03 80 34 16 82
A tiny (4.25ha) estate producing fine, robust wines for long aging.
Best wines ★★★ Mazis-Chambertin ❗, ★★ Gevrey-Chambertin 1er Cru Lavaux St-Jacques ❗
and Charmes-Chambertin ❗, ★ Bourgogne ❗
Best years 1999, '98, '97, '96, '95, '93, '90, '88

DOM. MÉO-CAMUZET, Vosne-Romanée   03 80 61 11 05
This top estate is managed by Jean-Nicolas Méo, who learnt winemaking from the
great Henri Jayer. New oak and lush fruit combine to give ageworthy wines.
Best wines ★★★ Richebourg ❗, Clos de Vougeot ❗ and Vosne-Romanée 1er Cru Les Brûlées ❗,
★★ Vosne-Romanée 1er Cru Cros Parantoux ❗ and Bourgogne Hautes Côtes de Nuits ♀
Best years 1999, '98, '97, '96, '95, '93, '92, '90, '89, '88

DOM. MONGEARD-MUGNERET, Vosne-Romanée   03 80 61 11 95/03 80 62 35 75
After a slight dip in the mid-1980s, this large family estate has regained its place as a
top estate, due partly to lower yields from the now organically farmed vineyards.
Best wines ★★ Grands-Échézeaux ❗ and Richebourg ❗, ★ Vosne-Romanée 1er Cru En
Orveaux ❗ and Nuits-St-Georges 1er Cru Les Boudots ❗
Best years 1999, '98, '97, '96, '95, '93, '91, '90

HUBERT DE MONTILLE, Volnay   03 80 21 62 67/03 80 21 67 14
One of the very best producers of Volnay and Pommard, making elegant, pure wines,
which are a little lean when young, but age superbly over 10 years or more. A small
parcel of Puligny-Montrachet 1er Cru Les Cailleret was acquired in 1993.
Best wines ★★★ Volnay 1er Cru Les Taillepieds ❗ and Volnay 1er Cru Les Champans ❗,
★★ Pommard 1er Cru Les Rugiens ❗ and Volnay 1er Cru Les Mitans ❗
Best years 1999, '98, '97, '96, '95, '93, '90, '89, '88, '85, '83

BERNARD MOREY, Chassagne-Montrachet   03 80 21 32 13/03 80 21 39 72
A particularly good source of red wine in a village better known for its whites.
Best wines ★★ Chassagne-Montrachet Vieilles Vignes ❗, Chassagne-Montrachet Vide Bourse ♀ and
Chassagne-Montrachet 1er Cru Morgeot ♀, ★ Santenay 1er Cru Grand Clos Rousseau ❗
Best years ❗1999, '98, '96, '95, '93, '92, '90; ♀1999, '98, '97, '96, '95, '93

MARC MOREY ET FILS, Chassagne-Móntrachet   03 80 21 30 11/03 80 21 90 20
This estate is the best of the Morey domaines in Chassagne-Montrachet. The wines have great fruit and length due to low yields and impeccable winemaking.
Best wines ★★ Chassagne-Montrachet 1er Cru Les Virondots ♀, 1er Cru Les Chenevottes ♀, 1er Cru Morgeot ♀ and Puligny-Montrachet 1er Cru Les Pucelles ♀
Best years 1999, '98, '97, '96, '95, '93, '92

PIERRE MOREY, Meursault   03 80 21 21 03/03 80 21 66 38
Pierre Morey is one of the most respected producers of white Burgundy as well as making the wine for Domaine LEFLAIVE. His wines have great precision, concentration and depth, and age well. He also makes wines under the *négociant* label of Morey-Blanc.
Best wines ★★★ Bâtard-Montrachet ♀ and Meursault Les Tessons ♀, ★★ Meursault 1er Cru Les Perrières ♀ and Meursault 1er Cru Les Genevrières ♀
Best years 1999, '98, '97, '96, '95, '92, '90, '89, '88

DOM. ALBERT MOROT, Beaune   03 80 22 35 39/03 80 22 47 50
This estate now only bottles wine from its own vines, all in Premiers Crus.
Best wines ★★★ Beaune 1er Cru Les Teurons ❢, ★★ Beaune 1er Cru Les Marconnets ❢, Beaune 1er Cru Les Bressandes ❢ and Savigny-lès-Beaune 1er Cru Les Vergelesses ❢
Best years 1999, '98, '96, '95, '93, '90, '88, '85

DENIS MORTET, Gevrey-Chambertin   03 80 34 10 05/03 80 58 51 32
A young producer specializing in ripe, concentrated wines from low-yielding, old vines. This 9.5ha estate includes appellations from Marsanny to Chambolle-Musigny, where each vine is treated with care to produce the finest possible grapes.
Best wines ★★★ Gevrey-Chambertin 1er Cru Lavaux St-Jacques ❢, Clos de Vougeot ❢ and Chambertin ❢, ★★ Gevrey-Chambertin En Motrot (monopole) ❢ and Gevrey-Chambertin Au Velle ❢, ★ Bourgogne ❢
Best years 1999, '98, '97, '96, '95, '94, '93, '90

DOM. MUGNERET-GIBOURG, Vosne-Romanée   03 80 61 01 57/03 80 61 33 08
This estate is now managed by the daughters of the late Dr Mugneret. The wines retain a distinctive velvety quality and have potential for aging.
Best wines ★★★ Ruchottes-Chambertin ❢, ★★ Vosne-Romanée ❢, Nuits-St-Georges 1er Cru Les Chaignots ❢, Chambolle-Musigny 1er Cru Les Feusselottes ❢ and Échézeaux ❢, ★ Bourgogne ❢
Best years 1999, '98, '97, '96, '95, '93, '90, '88

PHILIPPE NADDEF, Couchey   03 80 51 45 99/03 80 58 83 62
Very small estate producing wines with great colour, richness and aging potential.
Best wines ★★★ Mazis-Chambertin ❢, ★★ Gevrey-Chambertin 1er Cru Les Cazetiers ❢, Gevrey-Chambertin Vieilles Vignes ❢ and Fixin ❢
Best years 1999, '98, '97, '96, '95, '94, '93, '90

MICHEL NIELLON, Chassagne-Montrachet   03 80 21 30 95/03 80 21 92 93
This small estate produces some of the most concentrated yet balanced white wines in Burgundy. They repay aging for 5–10 years.
Best wines ★★★ Chevalier-Montrachet ♀, Bâtard-Montrachet ♀ and Chassagne-Montrachet 1er Cru Les Vergers ♀, ★★ Chassagne-Montrachet 1er Cru Les Champs Gain ♀
Best years 1999, '98, '97, '96, '95, '92, '90

DOM. DES PERDRIX, Nuits-St-Georges　　　03 85 98 12 12/03 85 45 21 61
This fine domaine was purchased in 1997 by Bertrand Devillard, head of the *négociants* Antonin Rodet, whose ★★ Ch. de Rully ♀ and ★★ Ch. de Chamirey ❢♀ are benchmarks of the Mercurey appellation. The Perdrix wines have all the richness and depth expected from top Côte de Nuits wines.
Best wines ★★★ Échézeaux ❢, ★★ Nuits-St-Georges 1er Cru Aux Perdrix ❢ and Vosne-Romanée ❢

JEAN-MARC PILLOT ET FILS, Chassagne-Montrachet　　03 80 21 33 35/03 80 21 92 57
The smallest of the 3 Pillot domaines in Chassagne is also the best one, producing wines with excellent fruit and depth for medium-term aging.
Best wines ★★ Chassagne-Montrachet 1er Cru Morgeot ❢♀, Chassagne-Montrachet 1er Cru Les Caillerets ♀ and Chassagne-Montrachet 1er Cru Les Vergers ♀
Best years ❢1999, '98, '96, '95, '93, '90; ♀1999, '98, '97, '96, '95, '93, '92

DOM. PONSOT, Morey-St-Denis　　　03 80 34 32 46/03 80 58 51 70
Old-fashioned wines from top vineyards – the grapes are picked late and aged with very little new oak. Age the top reds for 8–10 years and the white wine for 3–4 years.
Best wines ★★ Clos St-Denis ❢, Clos de la Roche ❢, Morey-St-Denis Cuvée des Grives ❢ and Morey-St-Denis Les Monts Luisants ♀
Best years ❢1999, '98, '97, '96, '95, '93, '90, '89, '88

DOM. DE LA POUSSE D'OR, Volnay　　　03 80 21 61 33/03 80 21 29 97
A splendid estate in Volnay managed until 1997 by the late Gérard Potel, producing some of the purest, most elegant Volnays. Age for 3–5 years or more.
Best wines ★★★ Volnay 1er Cru Clos de la Bousse d'Or ❢, ★★ Volnay 1er Cru Les Caillerets Clos des 60 Ouvrées (monopole) ❢, Pommard 1er Cru Les Jarollières ❢ and Santenay 1er Cru Les Gravières ❢
Best years 1999, '98, '96, '95, '93, '91, '90

JACQUES PRIEUR, Meursault　　　03 80 21 23 85/03 80 21 29 19
An exceptional estate with vines in some of the most prestigious Côte d'Or sites. These splendid wines are made and sold in partnership with the *négociant* Rodet.
Best wines ★★★ Musigny ❢, Meursault 1er Cru Les Perrières ♀ and Montrachet ♀,
★★ Chambertin ❢, Beaune 1er Cru Clos de la Féguine ❢ and Puligny-Montrachet 1er Cru Les Combettes ♀
Best years ❢1999, '98, '97, '96, '95, '94, '93, '90; ♀1999, '98, '97, '96, '95, '93, '92

DOM. PRIEURÉ ROCH, Vosne-Romanée　　　03 80 62 00 00/03 80 61 00 01
An important estate run by the co-manager of the Dom. de la ROMANÉE-CONTI, producing wines with intense aromas and concentrated fruit from very low-yielding vines.
Best wines ★★★ Vosne-Romanée 1er Cru Les Suchots ❢ and Chambertin Clos-de-Bèze ❢,
★★ Clos de Vougeot ❢ and Nuits-St-Georges 1er Cru Clos des Corvées (monopole) ❢
Best years 1999, '98, '97, '96, '95, '94, '93, '90

CH. DE PULIGNY-MONTRACHET, Puligny-Montrachet　03 80 21 39 14/03 80 21 39 07
One of the largest Côte de Beaune estates with deeply fruity, powerful wines.
Best wines ★★ Chevalier-Montrachet ♀, ★ Puligny-Montrachet 1er Cru La Garenne ♀, Puligny-Montrachet 1er Cru Les Folatières ♀ and Meursault 1er Cru Les Poruzots ♀
Best years 1999, '98, '97, '96, '95, '93

DOM. RAMONET, Chassagne-Montrachet 03 80 21 30 88/03 80 21 35 65
Father and sons produce white wines that are especially complex and expensive. The reds are less impressive. Age the fine whites for 10 years or more.
Best wines ★★★ Chassagne-Montrachet 1er Cru Les Ruchottes ♀ and Montrachet ♀, ★★ Bâtard-Montrachet ♀ and Chassagne-Montrachet 1er Cru Les Caillerets ♀, ★ Chassagne-Montrachet 1er Cru Clos St-Jean ▮
Best years ♀1999, '98, '97, '96, '95, '94, '93, '92, '90, '89, '86, '85

RAPET PÈRE ET FILS, Pernand-Vergelesses 03 80 21 50 05/03 80 21 53 87
An important estate whose wines are now replacing rusticity with elegance.
Best wines ★★ Corton-Charlemagne ♀, Pernand-Vergelesses 1er Cru Île de Vergelesses ▮ and Beaune 1er Cru Clos du Roi ▮, ★ Pernand-Vergelesses ♀
Best years ▮1999, '98, '96, '95, '93, '90; ♀1999, '98, '97, '96, '95, '93, '92

JEAN RAPHET, Morey-St-Denis 03 80 34 31 67/03 80 58 51 79
This estate has 12ha of magnificent vineyards in Morey and Gevrey, producing wines noted for their purity and balance.
Best wines ★★★ Morey-St-Denis ▮ and Chambertin Clos-de-Bèze ▮, ★★ Gevrey-Chambertin 1er Cru Les Combottes ▮ and Clos de Vougeot ▮
Best years 1999, '98, '97, '96, '95, '93, '90

JEAN-MARIE RAVENEAU, Chablis 03 86 42 17 46/03 86 42 45 55
This small estate is Chablis' most traditional, making wines that bring out the honeyed, minerally qualities of each Cru to perfection. They can age for up to 20 years.
Best wines ★★★ Chablis 1er Cru Montée de Tonnerre ♀, Chablis 1er Cru Beugnons ♀ and Chablis Grand Cru Les Clos ♀, ★★ Chablis 1er Cru Chapelot ♀
Best years 1999, '98, '97, '96, '95, '93, '92, '90, '89, '88, '86

HENRI REBOURSEAU, Gevrey-Chambertin 03 80 51 88 94/03 80 34 12 82
This important estate has vines in 4 Grands Crus and makes rich, rounded wines.
Best wines ★★ Clos de Vougeot ▮, Chambertin ▮ and Mazis-Chambertin ▮
Best years 1999, '98, '97, '96, '95, '93, '90, '88, '85

DANIEL RION ET FILS, Prémeaux-Prissey 03 80 62 31 28/03 80 61 13 41
A top producer offering a wide range of immaculately made wines. The reds are supple and rounded and there is also some good white wine from Nuits-St-Georges.
Best wines ★★ Vosne-Romanée 1er Cru Les Beaux-Monts ▮, Chambolle-Musigny 1er Cru Les Charmes ▮, Nuits-St-Georges Les Vignes Rondes ▮, Nuits-St-Georges Hauts Pruliers ▮, Nuits-St-Georges Les Terres Blanches ♀, ★ Côte de Nuits-Villages ▮ and Vosne-Romanée ▮
Best years ▮1999, '98, '97, '96, '95, '94, '93, '91, '90, '88

DOM. DE LA ROMANÉE-CONTI, Vosne-Romanée 03 80 62 48 80/03 80 61 05 72
The most famous Burgundy estate, with 24ha of Pinot Noir and 0.85ha of Chardonnay, all in the very finest Grands Crus including the whole of La Tâche and La Romanée-Conti. These vineyards are run biodynamically and the grapes are picked as late as possible for maximum ripeness. Prices are very high, but at their best the wines justify their price with incomparable complexity after 15 years' aging.
Best wines ★★★ Grands-Échézeaux ▮, Romanée-St-Vivant ▮, Richebourg ▮, La Tâche ▮, Romanée-Conti ▮ and Montrachet ♀, ★★ Échézeaux ▮
Best years ▮1999, '98, '97, '96, '95, '93, '90, '89, '88, '85, '78; ♀1999, '98, '97, '96, '95, '93

JOSEPH ROTY, Gevrey-Chambertin   03 80 34 38 97/03 80 34 13 59
Roty is one of Burgundy's finest winemakers and known as a great enthusiast, producing rich, deeply extracted yet elegant wines, with good aging potential.
Best wines ★★★ Charmes-Chambertin ▮ and Mazis-Chambertin ▮, ★★ Gevrey-Chambertin 1er Cru Clos des Fontenys ▮ and Marsannay ▮
Best years 1999, '98, '97, '96, '95, '93, '91, '90, '89, '88, '85

EMMANUEL ROUGET, Flagey-Échézeaux   03 80 62 83 38/03 80 62 86 61
Emmanuel Rouget makes wines from vineyards once owned by the legendary Henri Jayer. His style is both elegant and powerful, with supple oak flavours enhancing the deep fruit. A period of about 7–8 years' aging is needed to enhance these flavours.
Best wines ★★★ Vosne-Romanée 1er Cru Cros Parantoux ▮ and Échézeaux ▮, ★★ Vosne-Romanée ▮, Savigny-lès-Beaune ▮ and Nuits-St-Georges ▮
Best years 1999, '98, '97, '96, '95, '93, '92, '90, '89, '88

GUY ROULOT, Meursault   03 80 21 21 65/03 80 21 64 36
Jean-Marc Roulot, actor-turned-winemaker, is known for the purity and liveliness of his white wines, especially the Meursaults which are impressive (but expensive).
Best wines ★★ Meursault Les Vireuils ♀, Meursault Les Meix Chavaux ♀, Meursault Les Tillets ♀, Meursault Perrières ♀, and Bourgogne Chardonnay ♀
Best years 1999, '98, '97, '96, '95, '93, '92, '90, '89

GEORGES ROUMIER, Chambolle-Musigny   03 80 62 86 37/03 80 62 83 55
A superb estate managed with great flair by Christophe Roumier, one of Burgundy's most respected young winemakers whose main interest is terroir. Age the wines for 5–15 years.
Best wines ★★★ Ruchottes-Chambertin ▮, Bonnes-Mares ▮, Musigny ▮, Morey-St-Denis 1er Cru Clos de la Bussière ▮ and Chambolle-Musigny 1er Cru Les Amoureuses ▮
Best years 1999, '98, '97, '96, '95, '94, '93, '90, '88

ARMAND ROUSSEAU, Gevrey-Chambertin   03 80 34 30 55/03 80 58 50 25
One of the best-known Burgundy estates continues to make elegant wines which are classics in their appellations. They may be drunk quite young or kept for 5–15 years.
Best wines ★★★ Gevrey-Chambertin 1er Cru Clos St-Jacques ▮, Ruchottes-Chambertin ▮, Chambertin Clos-de-Bèze ▮ and Chambertin ▮, ★★ Clos de la Roche ▮, ★ Gevrey-Chambertin 1er Cru Les Cazetiers ▮
Best years 1999, '98, '97, '96, '95, '93, '92, '91, '90, '89, '88, '85

ÉTIENNE SAUZET, Puligny-Montrachet   03 80 21 32 10/03 80 21 90 89
This famous estate produces some of the finest white Burgundies. Full-flavoured and opulent, they show well in their youth but also age well for 5–12 years.
Best wines ★★★ Puligny-Montrachet 1er Cru Les Combettes ♀, Bienvenues-Bâtard-Montrachet ♀, Bâtard-Montrachet ♀ and Chevalier-Montrachet ♀, ★★ Puligny-Montrachet 1er Cru Les Champs Canets ♀ and Puligny-Montrachet 1er Cru Les Referts ♀
Best years 1999, '98, '97, '96, '95, '93, '92, '90, '89, '88, '86

COMTE SENARD, Aloxe-Corton   03 80 26 41 65/03 80 26 45 99
A superb historic estate producing classic, deep-coloured red wines for long aging.
Best wines ★★ Corton Clos du Roi ▮, Corton-Bressandes ▮, Corton Clos des Meix ▮ and Aloxe-Corton 1er Cru Les Valozieres ▮
Best years 1999, '98, '96, '95, '93, '90, '89, '88

DOM. DE SUREMAIN, Mercurey   03 85 45 20 87/03 85 45 17 88
One of the oldest estates, with some of the best vineyards in the Côte Chalonnaise.
Best wines ★★ Mercurey 1er Cru Clos du Roy ▮, Mercurey Clos l'Evêque ▮, Mercurey Clos
Voyen ▮ and Mercurey Sazenay ▮
Best years 1999, '98, '96, '95, '93, '90

TOLLOT-BEAUT & FILS, Chorey-lès-Beaune   03 80 22 16 54/03 80 22 12 61
Top-quality estate producing ripe, supple red wines with plenty of new oak character
that give pleasure early, but also mature well over 5–10 years.
Best wines ★★ Corton-Bressandes ▮, Beaune 1er Cru Les Grèves ▮, Aloxe-Corton 1er Cru ▮
and Savigny-lès-Beaune 1er Cru Les Lavières ▮
Best years 1999, '98, '97, '96, '95, '93, '92, '90, '88

VERGET, Mercurey   03 85 51 66 02/03 85 51 66 09
This relatively new *négociant* produces white wine only, mostly from grapes bought in
from the finest vineyards. The wines are made by Jean-Marie Guffens, of GUFFENS-
HEYNEN, and they have good depth of fruit and character.
Best wines ★★★ Chablis Grand Cru Valmur ♀, Chablis 1er Cru Fourchaume Vieilles Vignes ♀,
St-Véran Tête de Cuvée ♀ and Meursault Rougeot ♀, ★★ Chassagne-Montrachet 1er Cru
Les Morgeots Vieilles Vignes ♀ and Corton-Charlemagne ♀
Best years 1999, '98, '97, '96, '95, '92, '91, '90

A & P DE VILLAINE, Bouzeron   03 85 91 20 50/03 85 87 04 10
This estate at the northern end of the Côte Chalonnaise is owned by Aubert de
Villaine, the co-director of Dom. de la ROMANÉE-CONTI and produces fine Aligoté
(now sold under the new Bouzeron AC), as well as some very pure red and white
Burgundies. Recently, vineyards have been added in Rully.
Best wines ★★ Bouzeron ♀, ★ Bourgogne Les Clous ♀ and Bourgogne-Côte Chalonnaise ▮
Best years ▮1999, '98, '96, '95, '93, '90; ♀1999, '98, '97, '96, '95

COMTE GEORGES DE VOGÜÉ, Chambolle-Musigny   03 80 62 86 25/03 80 62 82 38
The most famous estate in Chambolle is probably the second most renowned in
Burgundy after the Dom. de la ROMANÉE-CONTI. The domaine owns three-quarters
of the Grand Cru Musigny as well as most of the famous Chambolle 1er Cru les
Amoureuses. After a fall-off in quality between 1970 and 1988, these wines are back to
their earlier impeccable standard, combining elegance and depth to the highest degree.
Age for at least 5–10 years and the best wines for 30 years.
Best wines ★★★ Musigny ▮, Bonnes-Mares ▮ and Chambolle-Musigny 1er Cru Les
Amoureuses ▮, ★★ Chambolle-Musigny 1er Cru ▮
Best years 1999, '98, '97, '96, '95, '94, '93, '92, '91, '90

DOM. DE LA VOUGERAIE, Nuits-St-Georges   03 80 62 61 61 /03 80 62 37 38
The finest vineyards of the Jean-Claude Boisset company, comprising 29 appellations,
mostly in Grands and Premiers Crus vineyards, are grouped under this name. The first
vintage was 1999, made by Pascal Marchand, whose winemaking at the Comte
ARMAND estate in Pommard had been so successful.
Best wines ★★ Clos Blanc de Vougeot ♀ and Corton-Charlemagne ♀, ★ Clos de Vougeot ▮,
Gevrey-Chambertin 1er Cru Bel-Air ▮ and Nuits-St-Georges 1er Cru Les Damodes ▮
Best years 1999

RED BURGUNDY VINTAGES

The last years of the 1990s were very kind to Burgundy, with a run of fine vintages since 1995. Whereas 1990 is the greatest of the 1988, '89 and '90 trio, 1995 and 1996 are still neck and neck. Suffice it to say that the Burgundians have taken full advantage of their good fortune to ensure that the quality of their wine has never been better.

Aging qualities

The Pinot Noir is a grape giving great delicacy of fruit. In good years, when the grapes are fully ripe, the wines have a deep fruit that masks the natural tannic acidity; in lesser years, not only will the colour be less intense, but so will the fruit and length, yet in the hands of capable winemakers, the charm will remain. The wines from such light vintages should be drunk before they are 10 years old, and preferably earlier. Better vintages may (and are) drunk young, for their impressive fruit, but become immeasurably more complex in their second decade.

Site, the age and clone of the vines, vineyard management, vintage conditions and the rigours of yield and selection, all contribute directly to quality and potential for aging. Added to this, the style of wine favoured by a given producer will have a marked effect on the final wine.

The trend in Burgundy now is to make more extracted wines than in the 1980s, helped by a series of good vintages with top-quality fruit.

Maturity charts _____

1996 was a large harvest, with grapes in perfect health, producing wines with remarkable purity of fruit. At first seen as rather lean, especially after the more robust 1995s, but the persistence of flavour makes it certainly the best vintage since 1990. 1998 was a great Beaujolais vintage.

1996 Volnay 1er Cru

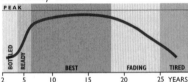

1996 Nuits-St-Georges 1er Cru

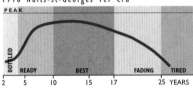

1996 Fleurie (Beaujolais Cru)

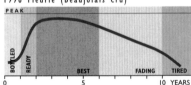

VINTAGE CHART												
	99	**98**	**97**	**96**	**95**	**94**	**93**	**92**	**91**	**90**	**89**	**88**
Côte de Nuits	8○	8○	7◐	9○	9○	6●	9◐	6◐	7●	10◐	7●	8●
Côte de Beaune	8○	8○	7◐	9○	8○	5●	8●	6●	7●	10●	8◐	8●
Côte Chalonnaise	8○	8○	7○	9◐	8●	5●	8●	6◐	7◐	10●	8◑	8◑
Beaujolais Crus	8○	9◐	7●	9●	9●	7●	8●	5◑	9●	6◑	7◑	8◑

KEY ○= needs more time   ◐= ready but will improve   ●= at peak   ◑= fading or tired

VINTAGES AT A GLANCE

There have been several great vintages in recent years. It is as much to do with the determination to produce the best wine possible as to do with the vagaries of nature. Poor years now seem to be a thing of the past in Burgundy.

Great Years ★★★   1996, '95, '93, '90, '88, '85, '64, '61, '59, '53, '47, '45
Good Years ★★   1999, '98, '97, '95, '91, '89, '88, '85, '83, '80, '78, '72, '71, '69, '62, '55, '52, '49, '48
Moderate Years ★   1994, '92, '87, '86, '83, '82, '80, '79, '76, '72; '70
Poor Years (No Stars)   1984, '83, '81

Annual vintage reports

1999★★ A very large harvest with very good wines from the estates that restricted yields. Rain from mid-September means the Côte de Nuits, which picked later, may be more patchy than the Côte de Beaune.

1998★★ A small harvest with good balance and concentration of fruit.

1997★★ A smaller crop than in '96 and '95, with uneven ripening of the grapes, saved by a dry, sunny autumn. The wines have a good colour and lively fruit for medium-term aging.

1996★★★ A large harvest with grapes in superb health, producing wines with remarkable purity of fruit; elegant wines that are made to last.

1995★★-★★★ A good-sized vintage, but smaller than '94, producing well-extracted wines with good structure and firm tannins, best in the Côte de Nuits.

1994★ A large crop of uneven quality, with many wines lacking colour and character, but some successes among the top estates. Most wines are ready to drink.

1993★★★ A good vintage, both in quantity and quality, with excellent colour, fruit and acidity, not as rich as the 1990s, but full of flavour and character.

1992★ A large vintage of mostly pleasant wines, but many were diluted from over-production. They were ready for drinking in 1995 but the best will keep until 2000.

1991★★ A medium-size vintage, producing firm, structured wines, better in the Côte de Nuits than the Côte de Beaune. Can be drunk or kept.

1990★★★ A superb year for red Burgundy with a very large crop, which produced surprisingly deep-coloured, full-bodied wines, rich in fruit and ripe tannins. Can be drunk or kept.

1989★★ A good crop from a very hot vintage which produced warmly fruity wines with sweetness and elegance, a little better in the Côte de Beaune. The wines are mature, but will keep.

1988★★-★★★ An average-sized crop of firm, classic wines, with deep, restrained fruit. The best wines can still be kept.

1987★ A small crop from a cold vintage, yet the wines had good colour and some fruit and charm.

1986★ A very large vintage, with some fruit but no concentration.

1985★★-★★★ A small crop of deep-coloured, rich and fruity wines that are now fully mature.

1983★-★★ A good-sized crop of concentrated wines that were very variable due to vintage conditions causing rot. The best are very rich and concentrated, but many more collapsed early on.

1982★ A huge crop, inevitably bringing dilution of fruit and only serious winemakers produced wines that held flavour and character. Now past their best.

1980★-★★ A large crop, with more fruit and structure in the Côte de Nuits than the Côte de Beaune.

1979★ A large crop of balanced, fruity wines that matured quickly.

1978★★ A small crop of close-knit, firm wines with good, if not exceptional fruit. The best wines are fine examples of classic red Burgundy.

1976★ Highly concentrated wines from a heatwave vintage, often with exaggerated tannins.

1972★-★★ A very large and very late vintage, producing wines with firm fruit and high acidity. The best are still drinking well.

1971★★ The smallest vintage of the 1970s, producing rich, concentrated wines that are now fully mature.

1970★ A very big vintage, making wines that were agreeable young, but without the concentration to last.

1969★★ A small, successful vintage, with good intensity of fruit and ripe tannins.

1964★★★ A very hot vintage with wines of great warmth and concentration.

Other good years 1962 had fine balance and '61 great concentration; 1959 was superb from a hot year, 1955, '53 and '52 were all very fine. 1949, '48, '47 and '45 were classic years.

WHITE BURGUNDY VINTAGES

Chardonnay is a hardy grape that generally ripens early and is seldom subject to rot, so vintages are more regular in quality than for red Burgundies.

Aging qualities
Despite being drinkable at a young age, far too much fine white Burgundy is drunk before it has had time to show all its qualities. The lightest Chablis or Mâconnais wines will be attractive at less than a year and wines with more weight and flavour will benefit from further aging. The best village wines and the Premiers Crus should be drunk from their third year, the Grands Crus as much again. Many top white Burgundies are vinified as well as aged in oak, which brings added fruit, flesh and structure and therefore more aging potential, but it is the fruit/acidity balance of the vintage that defines aging. Wines with low acidity are not made for a long life.

Maturity charts
1996 was a superb vintage for Chablis, with the fruit and acidity in perfect balance. In the Côte de Beaune 1998 was a fine vintage in Meursault with enough acidity to keep the wines fresh as they age. Further south, in Pouilly-Fuissé, ripe fruit with good acidity made 1999 a great year.

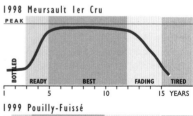

1998 Meursault 1er Cru

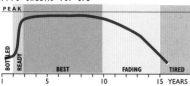

1996 Chablis 1er Cru

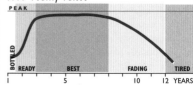

1999 Pouilly-Fuissé

VINTAGE CHART

	99	98	97	96	95	94	93	92	91	90	89	88
Chablis	9O	8O	7◑	10◐	8O	6●	7●	6●	6◑	9●	8●	8◑
Côte de Beaune	8O	7O	7◑	9O	9O	6◑	7●	8●	6◑	8●	9●	8◑
Côte Chalonnaise	8O	7O	7◑	8●	8●	6◑	7●	8●	6◑	8●	9◑	7●
Mâconnais, Pouilly-Fuissé	8O	7O	8◑	8◑	8●	6◑	7◑	8●	6◑	7◑	8●	8◑

KEY O = needs more time   ◑ = ready but will improve   ● = at peak   ◐ = fading or tired

VINTAGES AT A GLANCE

There are few poor years as Chardonnay ripens early and generally an honourable result can be achieved. Yet, as the wines age, the deficiencies in fruit and balance become only too evident.

Great Years ★★★ 1999, '97, '96, '90, '89, '88, '85
Good Years ★★ 1999, '98, '95, '93, '92, '90, '89, '88, '86, '82, '79, '78
Moderate Years ★ 1994, '91, '87, '83
Poor Years (No Stars) 1984, '81, '80

Annual vintage reports

1999★★-★★★ Large crop of very healthy grapes. Excellent in Chablis.

1998★★ Well-balanced, attractive, fruity wines. Small crop in Meursault due to hail.

1997★★★ A good-sized crop, offering the perfect balance between maturity and acidity, to produce wines of great clarity of flavour and ripeness, that will last well.

1996★★★ A good crop of superb ripeness and concentrated fruit flavours, very fine overall and superb in Chablis.

1995★★ An average crop of wines with elegance and structure, not exceptionally ripe, but very well balanced.

1994★ A large crop spoiled by rain, but the wines harvested early have lively fruit.

1993★★ A good crop of wines with good fruit and acidity, depth and character.

1992★★ An average to large crop of wines with roundness and fruit, slightly lacking the backbone of acidity. They are bigger, but less elegant than the 1993s.

1991★ An average crop of pleasant wines, lacking concentration and character.

1990★★-★★★ A large crop of full-bodied, fruity wines with ripeness but lowish acidity, generally very successful, but not as great as the red wines.

1989★★-★★★ A low average crop from an almost heatwave vintage, producing full, opulent wines with high alcohol but good acidity. Impressive rather than elegant.

1988★★-★★★ A large vintage with clean wines, fruity but lacking in concentration.

1987★ A small crop lacking in ripeness of fruit, but attractive young.

1986★★ A very large crop with variable wines, but the best had very good fruit and balancing acidity.

1985★★★ An average crop of firm, classic wines that developed superbly and the best may still be kept.

1983★ A largish crop, totally in contrast to 1984, being overly fruity, alcoholic and even sweet, now past their best.

1982★★ A huge crop and very attractive during the 1980s, now past their best.

1979★★ A very large crop with surprising concentration and elegance.

1978★★ A small crop with firm fruit and acidity, opposite to the 1979s.

Older vintages These wines are, with very rare exceptions, too old to be enjoyable.

THE RHÔNE VALLEY

This vast region begins with steeply terraced vineyards at Côte-Rôtie, just south of Lyon, and ends on the edge of Provence, with the extensive plains of vines around Avignon. The location of the vines and the grape varieties planted divide the valley into the much smaller North, where wines are usually made from one variety, either Syrah, Viognier or Marsanne (the fragile Roussanne is now rarely planted); and the South, where Grenache is a dominant variety, and even the great wines are blends. Vintages during the l990s have heralded a new era for Rhône wines after some difficult decades.

GREAT RHÔNE RED WINES

Oz Clarke's selection
Côte-Rôtie Cuvée du Plessy (Gilles Barge) The very essence of Côte-Rôtie delicacy and fragrance, with sweet loganberry fruit and creamy texture enveloped in woodsmoke and floral scent.
Côte-Rôtie (Jamet) Another brilliant exponent of Côte-Rôtie's remarkable ability to be well-structured yet also rich in fruit and perfume.
Cornas (Verset) A great producer, harnessing the sun-broiled intensity of the fruit with freshness and fragrance.
Crozes-Hermitage La Guiraude (Graillot) This wine equals Hermitage with its tannic structure, dark chocolate richness and brooding smoky scent.
Crozes-Hermitage Clos des Grives (Combier) Another stunning new wave Crozes, bursting with rich, dark fruit but hemmed in with tannin and new oak.
Crozes-Hermitage (Entrefaux) Excellent and fairly priced domaine making classic Syrah reds, bursting with mulberrry and loganberry fruit and scented with woodcutter's smoke.
Châteauneuf-du-Pape (Le Vieux Donjon) Excellent,

traditional property with super-ripe Grenache creating dark, brooding yet balanced reds with elegant fruit and tannin for long aging.
Châteauneuf-du-Pape Vieilles Vignes (Janasse) Powerful, baked reds balancing deep blackcurrant-loganberry fruit with tannic sternness and beguiling perfume.
Châteauneuf-du-Pape (La Mordorée) Rich, almost cooked style but the fruit is so good and the spicy scent so irresistible.
Côtes-du-Rhône-Villages-Rasteau (Gourt de Mautens) Astonishing wine from one of the southern Rhône's trailblazers with its heady violet and sandalwood scent and concentrated richness.

Steven Spurrier's selection
Crozes-Hermitage La Guiraude (Graillot) With depth of fruit and elegance, this is one of Crozes' best.
Cornas (Clape) Recognized as the 'father' of Cornas,

sometimes severely tannic when young, but superb in its second decade.
Côte-Rôtie La Mouline (Ch. d'Ampuis) The smoothest, most velvety and enveloping of Marcel Guigal's 'Grands Crus', more seductive than his superb La Landonne.
Côte-Rôtie La Landonne (Rostaing) The classic Côte-Rôtie Côte Brune, made from low-yielding, old Syrah vines.
Hermitage (Chave) The 500-year-old family holdings in the best Hermitage sites are faithfully reflected in this magnificent wine.
Hermitage La Chapelle (Paul Jaboulet Aîné) Another grandiose wine from this prestigious Rhône *négociant*.
Châteauneuf-du-Pape (Rayas) Very old Grenache vines on a sandy soil produce this hedonistic wine with superb potential for aging.
Châteauneuf-du-Pape (Beaucastel) The Perrin brothers have continued the heroic tradition of their father, making multi-faceted, concentrated wines.
Châteauneuf-du-Pape (Clos des Papes) Almost Bordeaux-like, this wine is all elegance and finesse.

Appellations

Despite using many of the same grape varieties, the Rhône appellations are distinctively different from one another, due to varying soils and location. There are no Grands or Premiers Crus, each wine using the basic AC, sometimes with a named vineyard site. Perhaps the best known of these are the Côte Brune and Côte Blonde from the middle slopes of the Côte-Rôtie appellation.

GREAT RHÔNE WHITE WINES

Oz Clarke's selection

Condrieu Les Chaillets Vieilles Vignes (Cuilleron) Heavenly, exotic-scented white, crème fraîche and apricot blossom married with divine oak scent.

Hermitage (Chave) Remarkable white, full of strange bedfellows like stewed apricots, pepper and celery, and positively demanding long aging.

Condrieu Puyvert (Ch. de St-Cosme) Irresistible, perfumed white full of apricot and Christmas jellies wrapped round with allspice that nonetheless leaves a scent of mayblossom hovering above the wine.

Steven Spurrier's selection

Condrieu Coteau de Vernon (Vernay) The leading Condrieu estate, making wines perhaps less explosively aromatic than Marcel Guigal's La Doriane, but with fabulous flavour and finesse.

Hermitage (Chave) The finest Rhône white begins to blossom at 5 years and continues to improve for another 20.

Châteauneuf-du-Pape Roussanne Vieilles Vignes (Beaucastel) A magnificent, dry yet intensely aromatic wine, made entirely from the rare and fragile Roussanne grape and vinified in small oak barrels.

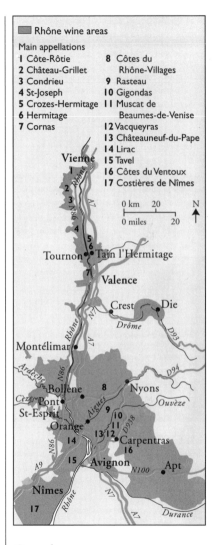

Rhône wine areas

Main appellations
1 Côte-Rôtie
2 Château-Grillet
3 Condrieu
4 St-Joseph
5 Crozes-Hermitage
6 Hermitage
7 Cornas
8 Côtes du Rhône-Villages
9 Rasteau
10 Gigondas
11 Muscat de Beaumes-de-Venise
12 Vacqueyras
13 Châteauneuf-du-Pape
14 Lirac
15 Tavel
16 Côtes du Ventoux
17 Costières de Nîmes

GRAPE VARIETIES

Cinsaut

Full-flavoured red variety with good fruit and acidity which is frequently blended with Grenache in the southern Rhône; also used for quality rosé in Tavel and Lirac.

Grenache

Originating from north Spain, where it is called Garnacha, Grenache needs a hot climate to ripen, giving full-bodied, alcoholic, 'warm' red wines. It is especially important in Châteauneuf-du-Pape where

117

it combines great alcoholic strength with rich raspberry fruit.

Marsanne

The major white varietal in the northern Rhône produces fine, scented, full-bodied wines. It is at its best in Hermitage. It is also planted in the southern Rhône.

Mourvèdre

A late-ripening red varietal making dark-coloured, firmly structured wines with a welcome acidity; a good foil to Grenache.

Roussanne

Once the north's major white varietal, now being replaced by the more robust and more reliable Marsanne.

Syrah

This very dark-coloured grape thrives in warm climates to make rich, powerful wine with a blackcurranty, spicy aroma and concentrated fruit. It is at its best in the northern Rhône and also adds backbone and style to the best wines from the South. If yields are kept low, the wine is very intense and long-lived.

Viognier

A very fragile variety (poor yields and prone to disease), it was once only found in Condrieu but now is increasingly planted in the southern Rhône and Provence, where its intense, aromatic qualities make it popular as a single varietal or as part of a blend.

Top Rhône appellations _____

Red wines Châteauneuf-du-Pape, Cornas, Costières de Nîmes, Côte-Rôtie, Côtes du Rhône, Côtes du Rhône-Villages, Côtes du Ventoux, Crozes-Hermitage, Gigondas, Hermitage, Lirac, St-Joseph, Vacqueyras.
White wines Château-Grillet, Châteauneuf-du-Pape, Condrieu, Costières de Nîmes, Côtes du Rhône, Côtes du Rhône-Villages, Côtes du Ventoux, Crozes-Hermitage, Hermitage, Lirac, St-Joseph.
Rosé wines Costières de Nîmes, Côtes du Rhône, Côtes du Rhône-Villages, Gigondas, Lirac, Tavel, Vacqueyras.
Fortified wines Muscat de Beaumes-de-Venise, Rasteau.

A–Z OF RHÔNE WINE REGIONS

CHÂTEAU-GRILLET AC

This tiny appellation of 3ha is represented by a single estate of the same name. As at neighbouring Condrieu, only Viognier is planted but the wines are denser, less exotic, and may be aged for 5–6 years.
Best years 1999, '98, '97, '96, '95.

CHÂTEAUNEUF-DU-PAPE AC

This famous AC is spread across 5 communes and several soil types and consequently produces many different styles of wine. Almost all are red, mainly from Grenache, with Syrah and Mourvèdre adding spice and structure.

Cinsaut, Counoise, Muscardin, Terret Noir and Vaccarese are also planted by a few estates. The red wines are among the most full-bodied and alcoholic in France, but have a warmth of flavour and richness of fruit that carries this well. A good red Châteauneuf needs 5–10 years to show its true qualities, and very good vintages can last 2–3 decades. The white wines are principally from Grenache Blanc, Clairette and Bourboulenc, with a little Roussanne. They should be drunk young, except for the rare 100% Roussanne wines. Overall quality of the whites is high.

Best producers BEAUCASTEL, de
BEAURENARD, BONNEAU, BOSQUET
DES PAPES, les CAILLOUX, CHAPOUTIER,
CLOS DU MONT OLIVET, CLOS DES
PAPES, FONT DE MICHELLE, FORTIA,
la GARDINE, GUIGAL, JANASSE,
de MARCOUX, MONT-REDON,
la MORDORÉE, Nalys, la NERTHE,
du PEGAU, PÈRE PAPE, RAYAS, SABON,
ST-BENOÎT, de la SOLITUDE, TARDIEU-
LAURENT, le VIEUX DONJON, VIEUX
TÉLÉGRAPHE.
Best years 1999, '98, '95, '90, '89, '88,
'85, '81, '79, '78, '72, '70, '69, '67.

CONDRIEU AC

Here on the right bank of the Rhône the
Viognier grape yields headily aromatic
peachy/apricotty wines, rich in texture,
but generally dry. Plantings have increased
substantially in the past 20 years, due to
Viognier's growing popularity. Its low
acidity means the wine should be drunk
within 2–3 years.
Best producers Ch. d'AMPUIS (La
Doriane), du Chêne, CHÈZE, CLUSEL-
ROCH, CUILLERON, DELAS, DUMAZET,
GAILLARD, Yves Gangloff, GUIGAL, du
Monteillet, PERRET, VERNAY, VILLARD.
Best years 1999, '98, '97, '96, '95.

CORNAS AC

These red wines are classic Syrah – deep-
coloured and robust. Lighter wines are
made from vines on the plain and may be
drunk at 3–4 years old; more concentrated
wines come from the higher vineyards,
and in good years can last a decade or more.
Best producers ALLEMAND, CLAPE,
COLOMBO, Laurent Courbis, DELAS,
JABOULET, LIONNET, MICHEL, Noël
Verset, Alain VOGE.
Best years 1999, '98, '96, '95, '91, '90,
'89, '85, '79, '78.

COSTIÈRES DE NÎMES AC

An appellation created in 1989, now

covering 10,000ha. The wines are mainly
red, a cross between those of the Rhône
and the Languedoc, and increasingly
interesting owing to the efforts of some
small quality estates.
Best producers Beaubois, Campuget,
Mourgues du Grès, de la Tuilerie.
Best years 1999, '98, '96, '95, '94, '93, '90.

CÔTE-RÔTIE AC

These are red wines only from mostly
steeply terraced, south-west-facing slopes
on the right bank of the Rhône. Up to
20% of white Viognier may be used in the
blend with Syrah and it adds an exotic
fragrance quite unexpected in a red wine.
Many wines are 100% Syrah, and where
Viognier is added, it is usually only to 5%.
Viognier is planted on the lighter soils of
the Côte Blonde site; the more northerly
Côte Brune, with more clay and iron in
the soil, is 100% Syrah. These wines
should be deep-coloured with good
aromatic concentration, rich, suave,
complex flavours and an elegant finish.
Lighter vintages need only 2–3 years to
show their charm, while better years need
twice that, and the best can last for 20 years.
Best producers Ch. d'AMPUIS, BARGE,
Bernard Burgaud, CHAMPET,
CHAPOUTIER, CLUSEL-ROCH, DELAS,
GAILLARD, Henri Gallet, Vincent Gasse,
GÉRIN, GUIGAL, JAMET, Patrick & Robert
JASMIN, Michel Ogier, René ROSTAING,
de VALLOUIT, VIDAL-FLEURY.
Best years 1999, '98, '97, '96, '91, '90,
'89, '88, '85, '83, '78.

CÔTES DU RHÔNE AC

This AC covers a few communes in the
southern part of the northern Rhône, but
the quantity produced there is very small.
In the southern Rhône, however, it is the
largest AC, producing about 200 million
bottles of red and rosé wine and 4 million
of white. Much of the wine is of good

THE 'RHÔNE RANGERS'
This phrase was coined in the 1980s in California, to describe the emergence of winemakers such as Randall Grahm of Bonny Doon Vineyards, who were fascinated with the traditional grapes varieties of the Rhône Valley. Now, Syrah is one of the most admired of wines in America, and Viognier certainly the most fashionable. Grenache and Mourvèdre for reds, and Marsanne for whites, are now being planted in regions where the climate is similar to that of the Rhône. Shiraz is, of course, the backbone to Australian wines and well-known in South Africa and the success of Rhône varietals in California has underlined the benchmark qualities of these grapes. The Perrin brothers of Ch. de Beaucastel must agree, for they have invested heavily in California, using only French rootstocks for the same grape varieties they use back home in Châteauneuf-du-Pape.

commercial quality, but there are also some exceptional wines, often from vineyards adjoining grander appellations.
Best producers des AMOURIERS, BEAUCASTEL, de FONSALETTE, la GARDINE, GRAMENON, GUIGAL, JABOULET, JANASSE, la MORDORÉE, l'ORATOIRE ST-MARTIN, la RÉMÉJEANNE, ST-GAYAN, STE-ANNE, SANTA DUC, TARDIEU-LAURENT, des TOURS, VIDAL-FLEURY.
Best years 1999, '98, '95.

CÔTES DU RHÔNE-VILLAGES AC
Sixteen specific communes in the Vaucluse, Gard and southern Drôme departments have the right to add 'Villages' to the basic Côtes du Rhône AC, provided the yield is lowered to a base of 35hl/ha. For the reds and rosés, Grenache is by far the dominant varietal, followed by Syrah, Mourvèdre, Cinsaut and Carignan. Better vintages will improve for 3–5 years. The whites, principally from

Grenache Blanc, Clairette, Bourboulenc and recent plantings of Roussanne and Viognier, should, with few exceptions, be drunk young. The best communes are Beaumes-de-Venise, Cairanne, Laudon, Rasteau, Sablet and Séguret.
Best producers de Baumalric, de BEAURENARD, des Bernardins, BRESSY-MASSON, Daniel BRUSSET, des Buisserons, de Cabasse, COYEUX, Cros de la Mure, DURBAN, de Fenouillet, les GOUBERT, Gourt de Mautens, JABOULET, l'ORATOIRE ST-MARTIN, PELAQUIÉ, Perrin, de PIAUGIER, RABASSE-CHARAVIN, Marcel RICHAUD, ST-GAYAN, STE-ANNE, la SOUMADE.
Best years 1999, '98, '97, '95, '90, '89.

CÔTES DU VENTOUX AC
Mostly red wines from around Mont Ventoux, planted with Grenache, Syrah, Cinsaut and Carignan. These are pleasant, fruity wines with some character.
Best producers des Anges, Dom. de Champaga, JABOULET, la Vieille Ferme.
Best years 1999, '98, '95.

CROZES-HERMITAGE AC
The largest of the northern Rhône ACs and, along with Hermitage, located on the left bank of the Rhône. Most of the wine is red, from Syrah. It may be soft and fruity from vines grown on the plain, but an increasing number of growers have reduced yields to make more concentrated, full-coloured wines that show Syrah at its best. From good vintages and the best sites, such wines can last for a decade. The whites are pleasant, but no rival to St-Joseph.
Best producers Albert Belle, CHAPOUTIER, du Colombier, COMBIER, Entrefaux, FERRATON, GRAILLOT, JABOULET, POCHON, SORREL, Caves de Tain, TARDIEU-LAURENT, VIDAL-FLEURY.
Best years ♥1999, '98, '97, '96, '95, '90, '89, '88, '85, '78; ♀1999, '98, '97.

GIGONDAS AC

These full-bodied, Grenache-based red wines come from the foot of the Dentelles de Montmirail, east of Orange. Syrah, Mourvèdre and Cinsaut can be used to make up not more than 20% of the blend. Gigondas should be deep coloured, with a spicy, herby, red berry aroma and structure, length and firmness on the palate. Best wines should ideally be kept for 5 years and will last a decade more.

Best producers Daniel BRUSSET, BURLE, de CAYRON, de FONT-SANE, de la Garrigue, les GOUBERT, GUIGAL, de LONGUE-TOQUE, Ch. de MONTMIRAIL, Moulin de la Gardette, les PALLIÈRES, de PIAUGIER, RASPAIL-AY, Ch. Redortier, de ST-COSME, ST-GAYAN, SANTA DUC, TARDIEU-LAURENT, du Terme, VIDAL-FLEURY.

Best years 1999, '98, '95, '90, '89, '85.

HERMITAGE AC

In the 19th century, Hermitage was the most expensive wine in France and in recent years its reputation has justifiably returned. The red wine (from Syrah) should always be very deep in colour, with a concentrated bouquet and flavour of ripe red fruits, and sufficient fruit and tannin to allow aging for 20–30 years. White Hermitage, mostly from Marsanne, represents about 20% of the AC and needs 3–4 years in bottle to show its real qualities. Overall, quality here is very high.

Best producers Albert Belle, CHAPOUTIER, CHAVE, DELAS, FAURIE, FERRATON, GRIPPAT, GUIGAL, JABOULET, SORREL, TARDIEU-LAURENT, de VALLOUIT.

Best years 1999, '98, '96, '95, '91, '90, '89, '85, '83, '79, '78, '76, '71, '70.

LIRAC AC

Red, rosé and white wines from an underrated appellation adjacent to Tavel. The reds do not have Châteauneuf-du-Pape's power but they are fruity and elegant. The whites and rosés have an attractive acidity and should be drunk young.

Best producers d'AQUÉRIA, Assémat, Fermade, Maby, la MORDORÉE, PÉLAQUIÉ, ST-ROCH, Ségriès.

Best years 1999, '98, '95, '91, '90.

MUSCAT DE BEAUMES-DE-VENISE AC

A fortified wine made with the Muscat de Frontignan grape, which captures a grapy essence of ripe peaches and apricots with a rich, floral finish. Drink young.

Best producers de Beaumalric, COYEUX, DURBAN, de la Pigeade, VIDAL-FLEURY.

RASTEAU AC

A fortified wine made from the Grenache grape that can appear golden, or tawny red if fermented on the skins. Aged Rasteau left in barrels for 2 years or more takes on a flavour known as 'rancio'. Rasteau is also one of the best villages in the Côtes-du-Rhône-Villages appellation.

Best producer BRESSY-MASSON.

ST-JOSEPH AC

A rather fragmented AC producing both red and white wines. Syrah is used for the fine, fruity reds; Marsanne, and even a little Roussanne, for the dry, aromatic whites. Unlike most Syrah wines, St-Joseph can be lively and charming, to be drunk at 2–3 years, when the fruit is still dominant, while the more robust wines can last twice as long. The whites have an attractive floral freshness and should be drunk young.

Best producers CHAPOUTIER, CHAVE, CHÈZE, Pierre Coursodon, FAURIE, GAILLARD, GRAILLOT, GRIPPAT, JABOULET, PERRET, Trollat, VILLARD.

Best years 1999, '98, '97, '96, '95, '90.

ST-PÉRAY AC

Marsanne is grown here for a sparkling wine that is much appreciated locally, as

well as some aromatic but dry still wine.
Best producers Jean-François Chaboud,
Jean LIONNET, Jean-Louis Thiers.
Best years 1999, '98, '97, '96, '95.

TAVEL AC

Tavel is the only French AC limited to a
dry rosé. Made mainly from Grenache and
Cinsaut, the wine is full-bodied and
sometimes headily fruity. With its high
alcoholic content of about 13%, it is best
drunk with food, and also young, while it
still retains its fruit.
Best producers d'AQUÉRIA, de la
Genestière, la MORDORÉE, Trinquevedel.
Best years 1999, '98.

VACQUEYRAS AC

Granted its own AC in 1989, Vacqueyras
is mostly planted with Grenache, with
Syrah and Mourvèdre becoming
fashionable. This is a robust, deep-
coloured red wine that in good years can
hold its own against Gigondas or
Châteauneuf-du-Pape, provided it is
allowed 5–6 years to mature.
Best producers des AMOURIERS, BURLE,
le Clos des Cazaux, la Fourmone,
JABOULET, MONTMIRAIL, de Montvac,
SANG DES CAILLOUX, TARDIEU-
LAURENT, des Tours.
Best years 1999, '98, '97, '95, '90, '89, '88.

A–Z OF RHÔNE PRODUCERS

THIERRY ALLEMAND, Cornas   04 75 81 06 50
A small, new domaine, but one of the best and most modern in Cornas. These relatively
low-tannin wines do not need long keeping. Le Chaillot is from younger vines.
Best wines ★★★ Cornas Le Reynard ! and Cornas Le Chaillot !
Best years 1999, '98, '97, '96, '95, '94, '91

DOM. DES AMOURIERS, Vacqueyras   04 90 65 83 22/04 90 65 84 13
This domaine is currently producing some of the best wines in Vacqueyras.
Best wines ★★★ Vacqueyras Les Genestres !, ★★ Vacqueyras Cuvée Signature !, ★ Côtes du
Rhône ! and Vacqueyras !   **Best years** 1999, '98, '97, '95, '90, '89, '88

CH. D'AMPUIS, Ampuis   04 74 56 10 22/04 74 56 18 76
This handsome building on the banks of the Rhône has recently been bought by
Marcel GUIGAL. The first cuvée to carry the name of the château will be from the
superb 1995 vintage and will be released in 1999. In the meantime, Guigal has
regrouped his famous 'Grands Crus' wines under the Ch. d'Ampuis banner.
Best wines ★★★ Condrieu La Doriane ♀, Côte-Rôtie La Mouline !, Côte-Rôtie La
Landonne !, Côte-Rôtie La Turque ! and Côte-Rôtie Ch. d'Ampuis !
Best years 1999, '98, '97, '96, '95, '90, '89, '88, '85, '83, '79, '78

CH. D'AQUÉRIA, Tavel   04 66 50 04 56/04 66 50 18 46
This is one of the largest properties in Tavel; it also owns vines in Lirac.
Best wines ★★ Lirac !♀ and Tavel ♀   **Best years** !1999, '98, '95; ♀1999, '98

GILLES BARGE, Ampuis   04 74 56 13 90/04 74 56 10 98
These fine Côte-Rôties are made traditionally, with 5% Viognier, 2 years' aging in oak
and bottling without filtration. Although they age well, they also have a perfumed
elegance when compared with some more powerful wines from this appellation.
Best wines ★★ Côte-Rôtie Cuvée du Plessy ! and Côte-Rôtie Côte Brune !
Best years 1999, '98, '97, '96, '95, '91, '90, '89, '88, '85, '83, '80, '78

CH. DE BEAUCASTEL, Courthézon   04 90 70 41 00/04 90 70 41 19
One of the largest, and certainly one of the most famous estates in the southern Rhône, where Jean-Pierre and François Perrin have continued the extraordinary work of their father, Jacques. He is commemorated with a special cuvée of rare concentration. Organic farming, old vines, with less Grenache and more Mourvèdre than is usual, and specialized vinification all combine to make some of the region's longest-lived wines.
Best wines ★★★ Châteauneuf-du-Pape Roussanne Vieilles Vignes ♀, Châteauneuf-du-Pape ❢ and Châteauneuf-du-Pape Hommage à Jacques Perrin ❢, ★★ Côtes du Rhône Coudoulet de Beaucastel ❢ and Châteauneuf-du-Pape ♀, ★ Côtes du Rhône Coudoulet de Beaucastel ♀
Best years ❢1999, '98, '96, '95, '93, '90, '89, '88, '86, '85, '82, '81; ♀1999, '98, '97, '96, '95, '94, '93, '90, '89, '88

DOM. DE BEAURENARD, Châteauneuf-du-Pape   04 90 83 71 79/04 90 83 78 06
This domaine, managed by Paul and Daniel Coulon, is one of the region's most modern for vinification. The Cuvée Boisrenard, from 50–90 year old vines, uses 20% new wood and needs 4-5 years' aging to show at its best.
Best wines ★★ Châteauneuf-du-Pape Boisrenard ♀, Châteauneuf-du-Pape Boisrenard ❢, ★ Châteauneuf-du-Pape ❢ and Côtes du Rhône-Villages Rasteau ❢
Best years 1999, '98, '96, '95, '93, '90, '89

DOM. HENRI BONNEAU, Châteauneuf-du-Pape   04 90 83 73 08
Tiny Châteauneuf estate of 5ha run by an unconventional producer. The wines, made from very old and very low-yielding Grenache vines, have extraordinary concentration and length; Bonneau does not rate Syrah, as the grape is not native to the region.
Best wines ★★★ Châteauneuf-du-Pape Réserve des Celestins ❢, ★★ Châteauneuf-du-Pape Marie Beurrier ❢
Best years 1999, '98, '96, '95, '90, '89, '88, '86, '85, '83, '79, '78, '70

DOM. BOSQUET DES PAPES, Châteauneuf-du-Pape   04 90 83 72 33/04 90 83 50 52
A sizeable Châteauneuf estate of 30ha using mainly low-yielding Grenache vines and producing traditional, solid wines that age beautifully.
Best wines ★★ Châteauneuf-du-Pape Cuvée Chantemerle ❢, ★ Châteauneuf-du-Pape ❢
Best years 1999, '98, '96, '95, '94, '90, '89, '88, '86, '85, '83, '79, '78, '70

DOM. BRESSY-MASSON, Rasteau   04 90 46 10 45/04 90 46 17 78
A very traditional estate, one of the rare producers of Rasteau Rancio.
Best wines ★★★ Rasteau Rancio ❢, ★ Côtes du Rhône-Villages Rasteau ❢
Best years 1999, '98, '96, '95, '90

DANIEL BRUSSET, Cairanne   04 90 30 82 16/04 90 30 73 31
Almost one-quarter of the Brusset vines are located on superb terraces above the town of Gigondas. Unusually for the appellation, the top wine is aged in 100% new oak.
Best wines ★★★ Gigondas Les Hauts de Montmirail ❢, ★★ Côtes du Rhône-Villages Cairanne ❢
Best years 1999, '98, '95, '90, '89, '88

EDMONDE BURLE, Gigondas   04 90 70 94 85/04 90 70 94 61
A small estate with 4ha in Vacqueyras and 2ha in Gigondas, producing rich, classically concentrated wines.
Best wines ★★ Gigondas Les Pallieroudas ❢, ★ Vacqueyras ❢
Best years 1999, '98, '96, '95, '90, '89, '88

DOM. LES CAILLOUX, Châteauneuf-du-Pape   04 90 83 72 62/04 90 83 51 07
A fine estate, well-known for its classic Châteauneuf wines, which has now planted more Mourvèdre and is beginning to use new oak.
Best wines ★★ Châteauneuf-du-Pape Cuvée Centenaire ▮, ★ Châteauneuf-du-Pape ▮
Best years 1999, '98, '96, '95, '94, '90, '89, '88, '78

DOM. DU CAYRON, Gigondas   04 90 65 87 46/04 90 65 88 81
A well-run estate making superbly rich wines from a blend based on 70% Grenache. Low yields from the stony soil enhance the quality of this supple, rounded Gigondas.
Best wine ★★ Gigondas ▮   **Best years** 1999, '98, '96, '95, '94, '93, '90, '89, '86, '85, '83

ÉMILE & JOËL CHAMPET, Ampuis   Tel 04 74 56 10 88
A 2.5-ha vineyard on the steepest slope in Côte-Rôtie is used by father, Émile, and son, Joël, to make separate wines. Émile uses more traditional winemaking techniques.
Best wines ★★ Côte-Rôtie La Vallière (Joël Champet) ▮, ★ Côte-Rôtie (Émile Champet) ▮
Best years 1999, '98, '95, '91, '90, '89, '88

CHAPOUTIER, Tain-l'Hermitage   04 75 08 28 65/04 75 08 81 70
A large family *négociant* with vines across the best northern Rhône appellations as well as in Châteauneuf-du-Pape. Since Michel and Marc Chapoutier took over in 1987, quality has improved dramatically: low yields, long vinification, intelligent use of oak and the conversion of the domaine into 'culture biodynamique' have all combined to make some of the most impressive Rhône wines around.
Best wines ★★★ Hermitage La Sizéranne ▮, Ermitage Le Pavillon ▮, Côte-Rotie La Modorée ▮, Châteauneuf-du-Pape Barbe Rac ▮, ★★ St-Joseph Les Granits ♀▮, Hermitage Chante-Alouette ♀ and Crozes-Hermitage Les Varonniers ▮, ★ St-Joseph Deschants ▮ and Châteauneuf-du-Pape La Bernadine ▮
Best years ▮1999, '98, '96, '95, '94, '90. '89; ♀1999, '98, '97, '96, '95, '90

CHÂTEAU-GRILLET, Verin   04 75 53 57 08/04 75 53 68 92
The Rhône's most famous white wine estate covers just 3.4ha and has its own appellation. It has been in the hands of the Néyrat-Gachet family since 1830 and the wine is bottled in a distinctive brown *flûte*. The general feeling has been that quality from this extraordinary vineyard could be improved and since 1995 this has been the case, but the great reputation has yet to be regained.
Best wine ★ Château-Grillet ♀   **Best years** 1999, '98, '97, '96, '95

DOM. JEAN-LOUIS CHAVE, Mauves   04 75 08 24 63/04 75 07 14 21
The Chave family have been growing grapes on the Hermitage hill since 1481 and Gérard Chave, a modern wine superstar, now shares the winemaking with his son Jean-Louis, who trained in California. This is not the largest domaine in the northern Rhône, but it is at the very top in terms of quality and, above all, consistency. The vines are mainly old and in all the best Hermitage sites (Les Baumes, Les Bessards, Le Méal, Péleat and Les Rocoules). The grapes are picked and vinified separately, then blended into a single red or white wine. Almost no new oak is used except in the Cuvée Cathelin; all these Hermitage wines are examples of Syrah at its spicy, complex best. A rare sweet Vin de Paille is made when vintage conditions permit.
Best wines ★★★ Hermitage ▮♀, Hermitage Cuvée Cathelin ▮ and Hermitage Vin de Paille ♀, ★★ St-Joseph ▮

Best years ❢1999, '98, '97, '96, '95, '94, '91, '90, '89, '88, '86, '85, '83, '82, '78, '67; ♀1999, '98, '97, '96, '95, '94, '91, '90, '89, '88, 83

LOUIS CHÈZE, Limony   04 75 34 02 88/04 75 34 13 25

A forward-looking domaine, where the wines are overseen by Jean-Luc COLOMBO.
Best wines ★★ Condrieu Coteau de Brèze ♀ and St-Joseph Cuvée de Caroline ❢
Best years 1999, '98, '97, '96, '95

AUGUSTE CLAPE, Cornas   04 75 40 33 64/04 75 81 01 98

Auguste Clape, who has now passed the winemaking over to his son, Pierre-Marie, is to Cornas what Georges VERNAY is to Condrieu. His domaine is justly famous for classic, uncompromising, long-lasting wines which are redolent of fine blackcurrants.
Best wine ★★★ Cornas ❢, ★ Côtes du Rhône ♀ and St-Péray ♀
Best years 1999, '98, '97, '97, '96, '95, '94, '91, '90, '89, '88, '87, '86, '85, '83, '78

CLOS DU MONT OLIVET, Châteauneuf-du-Pape   04 90 83 72 46 /04 90 83 51 75

This estate has 90% plantings of Grenache of an average age of 60 years which yield powerful, traditionally tannic red wines that can last for 2 decades. Despite the name Clos, the estate is very split up, with parcels of vines covering all the soil types in the AC.
Best wines ★★ Châteauneuf-du-Pape Cuvée du Papet ❢, ★ Châteauneuf-du-Pape ❢
Best years 1999, '98, '96, '95, '90, '89, '88, '85

CLOS DES PAPES, Châteauneuf-du-Pape   04 90 83 70 13/04 90 83 50 87

The Avril family are one of the oldest families in Châteauneuf. Their estate is broken up into 17 different parcels, allowing them to create the balanced, elegant wine on which their reputation rests. This is not a massive wine, more a 'claret in Châteauneuf'. The white wine takes on a nutty character with age and resembles fine, aged Burgundy. Vintages since 1990 have produced wines with more concentration.
Best wines ★★★ Châteauneuf-du-Pape ❢, ★★ Châteauneuf-du-Pape ♀
Best years ❢1999, '98, '97, '96, '95, '93, '90, '89, '88, '87, '86, '85, '83, '78

DOM. CLUSEL-ROCH, Ampuis   04 74 56 15 95/04 74 56 19 74

Tiny domaine which produces some polished wines in Condrieu and Côte-Rôtie with superb, velvety concentration. Their finest vineyard, Les Grandes Places, superbly sited on the Coteau de Verenay in Côte-Rôtie, is generally bottled separately.
Best wines ★★★ Côte-Rôtie Les Grandes Places ❢, ★★ Condrieu ♀ and Côte-Rôtie ❢
Best years 1999, '98, '97, '96, '95, '91, '90, '89, '88

JEAN-LUC COLOMBO, Cornas   04 75 40 36 09/04 75 40 16 49

Jean-Luc Colombo has built up a modest domaine specializing in Cornas and has recently created a small *négociant* company, Les Terroirs du Rhône. His wines are ripe and rich without harsh tannins and use up to 100% new oak for the best wines.
Best wines ★★★ Cornas Les Ruchets ❢, Cornas Cuvée JLC ❢, ★★ Cornas Les Terres Brûlées ❢, Cornas La Louvée ❢ and Cornas Les Mejeans ❢
Best years 1999, '98, '97, '96, '95, '91, '90

DOM. COMBIER, Tain l'Hermitage   04 75 84 61 56/04 75 84 53 43

A modern estate in Crozes-Hermitage, whose wines are attracting justified attention. A high level of new oak for the region gives the wines added richness and depth.
Best wines ★★ Crozes-Hermitage Clos des Grives ❢, ★ Crozes-Hermitage ❢
Best years 1999, '98, '97, '96, '95, '90, '89

DOM. DE COYEUX, Beaumes-de-Venise   04 90 12 42 42/04 90 12 42 43

With 50ha of Muscat vines, this is one of the largest producers in the appellation, creating seductively aromatic wines with a rich honeyed fruit.

Best wines ★★ Muscat de Beaumes-de-Venise ♀, ★ Côtes du Rhône-Villages Beaumes-de-Venise ❢

Best years Muscat de Beaumes-de-Venise 1999, '98

YVES CUILLERON, Chavanay   04 74 87 02 37/04 74 87 05 62

This young producer has plantings of Syrah, Viognier and Marsanne vines, producing some of the best northern Rhône whites, as well as good red Côte-Rôtie and St-Joseph.

Best wines ★★★ Condrieu Les Chaillets ♀, ★★ Condrieu La Petite Côte ♀, St-Joseph Lyseras ♀, St-Joseph Cuvée Réserve ❢, St-Joseph Le Bois Lombard ♀, ★ Côte-Rôtie ❢

Best years ♀1999, '98, '97, '96, '95, '94; ❢1999, '98, '96, '95, '94, '93

DELAS, St-Jean-de-Muzols   04 75 08 60 30/04 75 08 53 67

A family firm now owned by the Champagne house ROEDERER. Some vineyard holdings have been sold, retaining 4ha in Côte-Rôtie, 10ha in the best parts of Hermitage and 2ha in Condrieu. After a period of decline in the early 1990s, the wines from these superb vineyards are some of the best in these appellations.

Best wines ★★★ Condrieu Clos Boucher ♀ and Hermitage Les Bessards ❢, ★★ Condrieu ♀ and Hermitage Marquis de la Tourette ❢

Best years ❢1999, '98, '97, '96, '95, '90, '89, '88, '85, '83, '78; ♀1999, '98, '97, '96, '95, '94

PIERRE DUMAZET, Limony   04 75 34 03 01/04 75 34 14 01

A tiny estate with just over 1ha of vines in the best Condrieu sites. The vines from the Coteau de Côte Fournet vineyard are over 65 years old.

Best wines ★★★ Condrieu Coteau de Côte Fournet ♀, ★★ Condrieu ♀, Condrieu Coteau Rouelle Midi ♀ and Condrieu La Myriade ♀

Best years 1999, '98, '97, '96, '95

DOM. DE DURBAN, Beaumes-de-Venise   04 90 62 94 26/04 90 65 01 85

An intense, lusciously aromatic and headily concentrated Muscat.

Best wine ★★★ Muscat de Beaumes-de-Venise ♀   **Best years** 1999, '98

BERNARD FAURIE, Tournon   04 75 08 55 09

A very small estate of just over 3ha split between Hermitage and St-Joseph. The Hermitage Cuvée Le Méal comes from vines over 80 years old.

Best wines ★★★ Hermitage Le Méal ❢, ★★ St-Joseph Vieilles Vignes ❢ and Hermitage Greffieux ❢, ★ St-Joseph Jeunes Vignes ❢

Best years 1999, '97, '96, '95, '91, '90, '88

MICHEL FERRATON, Tain l'Hermitage   04 75 08 59 51/04 75 08 81 59

A well-run small estate with well-placed vines in Hermitage and Crozes-Hermitage.

Best wines ★★ Hermitage Cuvée Les Miaux ❢ and Crozes-Hermitage La Matinière ❢

Best years 1999, '98, '96, '95, '90, '85

CH. DE FONSALETTE, Lagarde-Pareol   04 90 83 73 09/04 90 83 51 17

This small estate belongs to the Reynaud family (of Ch. RAYAS) and the white and red wines produced here are almost as delicious and long-lived as their Châteauneuf wines.

Best wines ★★★ Côtes du Rhône ❢♀ and Côtes du Rhône Syrah ❢

Best years ❢1999, '98, '97, '96, '95, '93, '90, '89, '88, '86, '85; ♀1999, '98, '97, '96, '95

FONT DE MICHELLE, Bédarrides   04 90 33 00 22/04 90 33 20 27

Owned by the Gonnet brothers, whose uncle is Henri Brunier of VIEUX TÉLÉGRAPHE; there is some resemblance in the wines' concentrated fruit flavours and southern herbal fragrance. Both the red and white wine benefit from aging for a minimum of 3 years.
Best wines ★★★ Châteauneuf-du-Pape Cuvée Étienne Gonnet ♀, ★ Châteauneuf-du-Pape ♀♀
Best years ♀1999, '98, '96, '95, '93, '90, '89, '88; ♀1999, '98, '97, '96, '95

DOM. DE FONT-SANE, Gigondas   04 90 65 86 36/04 90 65 81 71

This estate has low-yielding vines in the best parts of the Gigondas appellation. The wines are always deep in colour and densely fruity.
Best wines ★★★ Gigondas Cuvée Futee ♀, ★★ Gigondas ♀
Best years 1999, '98, '96, '95, '90, '89, '88, '86

CH. FORTIA, Châteauneuf-du-Pape   04 90 83 72 25/04 90 83 51 03

Once the most respected estate in the region – a former owner, Baron Pierre Le Roy, laid down the strict production rules that later became the Appellation Contrôlée laws – Ch. Fortia has recently emerged from a 20-year decline in quality and is now under the control of Bruno Le Roy, aided by the enologist Jean-Luc COLOMBO.
Best wines ★★ Châteauneuf-du-Pape ♀, ★ Châteauneuf-du-Pape ♀
Best years 1999, '98, '96, '95, '90, '89, '88, '86, '85, '83, '81, '78

PIERRE GAILLARD, Malleval   04 74 87 13 10/04 74 87 17 66

Producer of fine wines in St-Joseph, Condrieu and Côte-Rôtie. The white St-Joseph is 100% Roussanne and the red St-Joseph is aged in 20% new oak.
Best wines ★★ St-Joseph ♀, ★ St-Joseph Clos de Cuminaille ♀, Côte-Rôtie ♀ and Condrieu ♀
Best years ♀1999, '97, '96, '95, '90, '89; ♀ 1999, '98, '97

CH. LA GARDINE, Châteauneuf-du-Pape   04 90 83 73 20/04 90 83 77 24

A large 92-ha estate making Châteauneuf-du-Pape in the modern style, with the accent on fruit and balance. The special cuvées finish their aging in new oak, and the white Cuvée des Générations is barrel-fermented as well as barrel-aged.
Best wines ★★★ Châteauneuf-du-Pape Cuvée des Générations ♀, ★★ Châteauneuf-du-Pape Cuvée des Générations ♀, Côtes du Rhône-Villages ♀ and Châteauneuf-du-Pape Cuvée Tradition ♀
Best years ♀1999, '98, '95, '90, '89, '88; ♀ 1999, '98

JEAN-MICHEL GÉRIN, Ampuis   04 74 56 16 56/04 74 56 11 37

This is an important new wave Côte-Rôtie estate, using sophisticated winemaking methods. The top wine, Les Grandes Places, is made chiefly from 80-year-old vines, spends 2 years in 100% new oak and has masses of soft, concentrated fruit.
Best wines ★★★ Côte-Rôtie Les Grandes Places ♀, ★★ Côte-Rôtie Champin Le Seigneur ♀
Best years 1999, '98, '97, '96, '95, '94, '91, '90

DOM. LES GOUBERT, Gigondas   04 90 65 86 38/04 90 65 81 52

A well-respected domaine, where the best red wines are bottled without filtration. The owner, Jean-Pierre Cartier is passionate about his hillside vineyards, which produce densely fruity, slow-maturing wines. Cuvée Florence will age for at least 10 years.
Best wines ★★★ Gigondas Cuvée Florence ♀, ★★ Gigondas ♀, ★ Côtes du Rhône Viognier ♀ and Côtes du Rhône-Villages Sablet ♀
Best years 1999, '98, '95, '90, '89, '88, '85

ALAIN GRAILLOT, Pont-de-l'Isère   04 75 84 67 52/04 75 84 79 33
Founded in 1985, this estate produces powerful, concentrated reds and well-balanced, characterful white wines. An emphasis on low yields and careful vinification has led to recognition for Graillot as one of the very best producers of Crozes-Hermitage.
Best wines ★★★ Crozes-Hermitage La Guiraude ❢, ★★ Crozes-Hermitage ❢ and St-Joseph ❢, ★ Hermitage ❢ and Crozes-Hermitage ♀
Best years ❢1999, '97, '96, '95, '91, '90, '89, '88

DOM. GRAMENON, Montbrison-sur-Lez   04 75 53 57 08/04 75 53 68 92
This domaine is farmed organically and wines are made from low-yielding, old vines in the most meticulous, traditional manner to give unparalleled depth and complexity.
Best wines ★★★ Côtes du Rhône Cuvée des Laurentides ❢ and Côtes du Rhône Ceps Centénaires ❢, ★★ Côtes du Rhône ❢
Best years 1999, '98, '96, '95, '93, '90

JEAN-LOUIS GRIPPAT, Tournon   04 75 08 15 51/04 75 07 00 97
This estate is justly more famous for its elegant whites than for its reds, which are attractive but can lack concentration. The white Hermitage comes from 70-year-old vines to produce a wine of floral elegance that can be drunk when bottled.
Best wines ★★ St-Joseph ♀, St-Joseph Cuvée des Hospices ❢ and Hermitage ♀, ★ Hermitage ❢
Best years ❢1999, '98, '97, '96, '95, '90, '89, '88; ♀1999, '98, '97, '96, '95

GUIGAL, Ampuis   04 74 56 10 22/04 74 56 18 76
Inheriting from his father a passion for Rhône wines, especially those of Côte-Rôtie, the brilliant Marcel Guigal has expanded the firm his father created to become the largest *négociant* in the region, while revitalizing the appellations of Côte-Rôtie and Condrieu. The Guigal wines from the southern Rhône are as impressive as those from the north owing to very careful sourcing from the best producers. See also Ch. d'AMPUIS.
Best wines ★★ Côtes du Rhône ❢♀, Châteauneuf-du-Pape ❢, Gigondas ❢, Côte-Rôtie Brune et Blonde ❢, Hermitage ❢♀ and Condrieu ♀
Best years ❢1999, '98, '96, '95, '90, '89, '88, '85, '83, '78; ♀1999, '98, '97, '96, '95

PAUL JABOULET AÎNÉ, La Roche-de-Glun   04 75 84 68 93/04 75 84 56 14
A top-quality *négociant*/grower and one of the largest producers in the northern Rhône, Jaboulet has been a source of the best Rhône wines for decades. Despite the early death in 1997 of Gérard Jaboulet, who represented his family's wines so well all around the world, the vineyards and the cellars are well looked after by various brothers and cousins with Nicolas Jaboulet taking over the export market. The flagship wine, red Hermitage La Chapelle, heads a fine range of Rhône wines down to Côtes du Ventoux.
Best wines ★★★ Hermitage La Chapelle ❢, ★★ Crozes-Hermitage Dom. de Thalabert ❢ and Cornas Dom. de St-Pierre ❢, ★ Côtes du Rhône-Villages ❢ Vacqueyras ❢, Hermitage Le Chevalier de Stérimberg ♀ and Côte-Rôtie Les Jumelles ❢
Best years ❢1999, '98, '97, '96, '95, '91, '90, '89, '88, '83, '82, '81, '79, '78, '76, '72, '70, '66, '61; ♀1999, '98, '97, '96, '95

DOM. JEAN-PAUL & JEAN-LUC JAMET, Le Vallin   04 74 56 12 57/04 74 56 02 15
New temperature-controlled cellars are one factor in the success of this impresssive Côte-Rôtie estate run by 2 young brothers. The wines are rich and concentrated, from low yields and a long maceration, and are bottled without filtration.

Best wine ★★ Côte-Rôtie 🍷
Best years 1999, '98, '97, '96, '95, '91, '90, '89, '88, '85, '83, '82

DOM. DE LA JANASSE, Courthézon 04 90 70 86 29/04 90 70 75 93

A notable estate near BEAUCASTEL, sharing the same forward-looking approach to quality, while retaining the best traditional values. The vines here average 60 years of age, producing ripe, velvety wines that blend elegance and power.

Best wines ★★★ Châteauneuf-du-Pape Cuvée Chaupin 🍷 and Châteauneuf-du-Pape Vieilles Vignes 🍷, ★★ Côtes du Rhône Cuvée Tradition 🍸, Côtes du Rhône Les Garrigues 🍷 and Châteauneuf-du-Pape 🍸, ★ Châteauneuf-du-Pape 🍷
Best years 🍷1999, '98, '96, '95, '90, '89 🍸 1999, '98, '97

PATRICK & ROBERT JASMIN, Ampuis 04 74 56 11 41/04 74 56 01 78

Well-sited vineyards offer low yields and there is plenty of exuberant fruit in these fine wines when young. They also age gracefully. Robert Jasmin sadly died in 1999.

Best wines ★★ Côte-Rôtie 🍷
Best years 1999, '98, '96, '95, '91, '90, '89, '88, '85, '83, '78

JEAN LIONNET, Cornas 04 75 40 36 01/04 75 81 00 62

Lionnet has vineyards in Cornas and in St-Péray and makes supple, modern reds with plenty of fruit and enough tannin to age well.

Best wines ★★ Cornas Dom. de Rochepertuis 🍷 and St-Péray 🍸
Best years 🍷1999, '98, '97, '96, '95, '91, '90, '89, '88, '85, '83; 🍸1999, '98, '97, '96, '95

DOM. DE LONGUE-TOQUE, Gigondas 04 90 12 39 31/04 90 12 39 32

A medium-sized estate with vines ranging from 50 to 100 years old. The wines are a blend of 80% Grenache and 20% Syrah.

Best wines ★★ Gigondas Cuvée Prestige 🍷 and Gigondas Cuvée Excellence 🍷
Best years 🍷1999, '98, '97, '95, '90, '89, '88

DOM. DE MARCOUX, Orange 04 90 34 67 43/04 90 51 84 53

Located in the northern part of the Châteauneuf-du-Pape appellation, the Armenier family have run this estate on biodynamic lines since 1990. Some of the vines here are almost 100 years old, and yields are consequently low. As a result, these wines are warm and concentrated.

Best wines ★★★ Châteauneuf-du-Pape Vieilles Vignes 🍷, ★★ Châteauneuf-du-Pape 🍷🍸
Best years 🍷1999, '98, '95, '93, '90, '89

ROBERT MICHEL, Cornas 04 75 40 38 70/04 75 40 58 57

This traditional Cornas estate has 5ha of well-placed, old vines.

Best wines ★★ Cornas La Geynale 🍷, ★ Cornas 🍷
Best years 1999, '98, '96, '95, '90, '89, '88

CH. DE MONTMIRAIL, Vacqueyras 04 90 65 86 72

This large estate practises traditional winemaking with a touch of sophistication.

Best wines ★★ Vacqueyras Cuvée des Deux Frères 🍷, Vacqueyras Cuvée de l'Ermite 🍷 and Gigondas Cuvée Beauchamp 🍷
Best years 1999, '98, '97, '96, '95, '90, '89, '88, '85

DOM. DE MONT-REDON, Châteauneuf-du-Pape 04 90 83 72 75 /04 90 83 77 20

One of the largest estates in Châteauneuf, producing red and white wines, and the only one, along with BEAUCASTEL, to plant all 13 permitted varieties. For many years it was a benchmark for the appellation and after 2 decades of slight decline, the most recent vintages have shown a return to the classic, ripe and concentrated style.

Best wines ★★ Châteauneuf-du-Pape ❢♀

Best years ❢1999, '98, '95, '90, '89, '85, '83, '81, '78; ♀1999, '98, '97, '96, '95

DOM. DE LA MORDORÉE, Tavel   04 66 50 00 75/04 66 50 47 39

This relatively new organic estate has its main vineyards in Lirac and Tavel, but also some superbly placed, 60-year old vines in Châteauneuf. One of the southern Rhônes new stars, whose Tavel and Lirac are regularly the finest of their respective ACs.

Best wines ★★★ Tavel ♀, Lirac Cuvée de la Reine des Bois ❢ and Châteauneuf-du-Pape Cuvée de la Reine des Bois ❢, ★★ Côtes du Rhône ❢, Lirac Cuvée de la Reine des Bois ♀, Lirac ❢ and Châteauneuf-du-Pape ❢

Best years ❢1999, '98, '96, '95; ♀1999, '98

CH. LA NERTHE, Châteauneuf-du-Pape   04 90 83 70 11/04 90 83 79 69

One of the largest and most famous estates in Châteauneuf, certainly the one with the most impressive château and park, La Nerthe makes wines of great concentration and elegance and is now back on form after massive recent investment by new owners.

Best wines ★★★ Châteauneuf-du-Pape Cuvée des Cadettes ❢ and Châteauneuf-du-Pape Clos de Beauvenir ♀, ★★ Châteauneuf-du-Pape ❢

Best years ❢1999, '98, '95, '90, '89; ♀1999, '98, '97, '96, '95

DOM. DE L'ORATOIRE ST-MARTIN, Cairanne   04 90 30 82 07/04 90 30 74 27

Exciting wines, both red and white, from old vines.

Best wines ★★ Côtes du Rhône ♀, Côtes du Rhône-Villages-Cairanne ♀, Côtes du Rhône-Villages Cairanne Réserve des Seigneurs ❢ and Côtes du Rhône-Villages-Cairanne Cuvée Prestige ❢

Best years 1999, '98, '96, '95

DOM. LES PALLIÈRES, Gigondas   04 90 65 85 07

Perhaps the most perfectly situated, and certainly the most traditional estate in the Gigondas appellation, with 50-year-old vines planted on terraces below the Dentelles de Montmirail. Quality is now back after a dip.

Best wine ★ Gigondas ❢   **Best years** 1999, '98, '95, '90, '89, '88, '85

DOM. DU PÉGAÜ, Châteauneuf-du-Pape   04 90 83 72 70/04 90 83 53 02

Old, low-yielding vines in some of the best Châteauneuf sites and uncompromising winemaking combine to produce some of the most powerful wines in the appellation.

Best wines ★★★ Châteauneuf-du-Pape Cuvée Réserve ❢ and Cuvée Laurence ❢

Best years 1999, '98, '97, '96, '95, '90, '89, '88, '86, '85, '83, '81, '78

DOM. DE PÉLAQUIÉ, Laudun   04 66 50 06 04/04 66 50 33 32

Producer of exceptional white wines which do credit to the Côtes-du-Rhône AC. The Laudun Blanc is consistently one of the best white wines produced in the Gard.

Best wines ★★★ Côtes du Rhône-Villages Laudun ♀, ★ Lirac ❢

Best years ♀1999, '98, '97, '96, '95; ❢1999, '98, '97, '96, '95

DOM. DU PÈRE PAPE, Châteauneuf-du-Pape   04 90 83 70 16/04 90 83 50 47

A substantial estate, most of it put together in the last 20 years. The Clos de Calvaire is a superb vineyard site between Nalys and VIEUX TÉLÉGRAPHE.

Best wines ★★ Châteauneuf-du-Pape ❢ and Châteauneuf-du-Pape Clos de Calvaire ❢

Best years 1999, '98, '94, '90, '89, '88, '85

ANDRÉ PERRET, Chavanay   04 74 87 24 74/04 74 87 05 26
André Perret is one of the stars of both Condrieu and St-Joseph. Old vines in the 2 best
sites in Condrieu, the Coteau de Chéry and the Clos Chanson, combined with
brilliant winemaking, are the secrets of the success of this sought-after estate.
Best wines ★★★ Condrieu Coteau du Chéry ♀ and Condrieu Clos Chanson ♀, ★★ St-Joseph
Les Grisières ❢ and Condrieu ♀
Best years ♀1999, '98, '97, '96, '95; ❢1999, '98, '97, '96, '95, '91, '90, '89, '88

DOM. DE PIAUGIER, Sablet   04 90 46 96 49/04 90 46 99 48
A superb estate brought to new heights in the hands of Jean-Marc Autran.
Best wines ★★★ Côtes du Rhône-Villages Sablet Les Briguières ❢, ★★ Côtes du Rhône-
Villages Sablet Montmartel ❢, Côtes du Rhône-Villages Sablet Tenebi ❢ and Gigondas ❢
Best years 1999, '98, '96, '95, '90, '89

DOM. ÉTIENNE POCHON, Chanos-Curson   04 75 07 34 60/04 75 07 30 27
Concentrated but elegant wines, the best of which have a good proportion of new oak.
Best wines ★★ Crozes-Hermitage Ch. Curson ❢, ★ Crozes-Hermitage Ch. Curson ♀
Best years 1999, '98, '96, '95, '90

DOM. RABASSE-CHARAVIN, Cairanne   04 90 30 70 05/04 90 30 74 42
A fine family domaine with old vines in the wine villages of Cairanne and Rasteau.
Best wines ★★ Côtes du Rhône-Villages-Cairanne Cuvée Estevenas ❢ and Côtes du Rhône-
Villages-Rasteau Cuvée Corinne Couturier ❢
Best years 1999, '98, '97, '96, '95, '90

DOM. RASPAIL-AY, Gigondas   04 90 65 83 01/04 90 65 89 55
A 18-ha estate planted to 70% Grenache, making wines with dense fruit and a capacity
for long aging. Not to be confused with the less good Ch. Raspail.
Best wine ★★★ Gigondas ❢   **Best years** 1999, '98, '97, '96, '95, '90, '89, '88, '86, '85

CH. RAYAS, Châteauneuf-du-Pape   04 90 83 73 09/04 90 83 51 17
An estate unique in the region both for the eccentricity of its owners, the Reynaud
family, and for its remarkable rich, heady Châteauneuf from 100% old-vine Grenache,
harvested as late as possible. Emmanuel Reynaud succeeded to the estate following the
death of his renowned uncle Jacques in 1996, while keeping his own property in
Vacqueyras, the 36-ha Ch. des Tours. The quality of the white wine is equally
extraordinary, but it is made on an irregular basis. See also FONSALETTE.
Best wines ★★★ Châteauneuf-du-Pape ❢, ★★ Châteauneuf-du-Pape ♀ and Châteauneuf-du-
Pape Clos Pignan ❢
Best years ❢1998, '95, '93, '90, '89, '88, '86; ♀1999, '98, '97, '96, '95, '90, '89

DOM. LA RÉMÉJEANNE, Sabran   04 66 89 44 51/04 66 89 64 22
A medium-sized domaine whose best wines are ripe and velvety.
Best wines ★★ Côtes du Rhône Les Genevriers ❢ and Côtes du Rhône Les Eglantiers ❢
Best years 1999, '98, '97, '95

DOM. MARCEL RICHAUD, Cairanne   04 90 30 85 25/04 90 30 71 12
Marcel Richaud makes very ripe, fruit-driven wines of great quality. They are not
wood-aged and are usually released young but age remarkably well in bottle.
Best wines ★★ Côtes du Rhône-Villages Cairanne ❢♀
Best years ❢1999, '98, '96, '95

DOM. RENÉ ROSTAING, Ampuis   04 74 56 12 00/04 74 56 62 56

Having taken over the splendid vineyards of his father-in-law Albert Dervieux and of his uncle Marius Gentax, René Rostaing now has 7ha in the best Côte-Rôtie sites, planted mainly with old vines. In good years, 4 different blends are made, all of exceptional quality, with ripe fruit and deep colour.

Best wines ★★★ Côte-Rôtie La Viallière 🍷, Côte-Rôtie Côte Blonde 🍷 and Côte-Rôtie La Landonne 🍷, ★★ Côte-Rôtie 🍷

Best years 1999, '98, '97, '96, '95, '91, '90, '89, '88, '85

DOM. ROGER SABON, Châteauneuf-du-Pape   04 90 83 71 72/04 90 83 50 51

A superbly situated estate making solidly traditional wines with no new oak and no filtration. The vines that produce the Cuvée Prestige are almost 100 years old.

Best wines ★★★ Châteauneuf-du-Pape Cuvée Prestige 🍷, ★★ Lirac 🍷, Châteauneuf-du-Pape Les Olivets 🍷 and Châteauneuf-du-Pape Cuvée Réserve 🍷, ★ Lirac 🍸

Best years 1999, '98, '96, '95, '93, '90

DOM. ST-BENOÎT, Châteauneuf-du-Pape   04 90 83 51 36/04 90 83 51 37

A domaine created in 1989 by 3 growers pooling their vineyard holdings. The vines are between 40 and 70 years old, giving low yields and the wine is made in the modern, fruit-concentrated style.

Best wines ★★ Châteauneuf-du-Pape Soleil et Festins 🍷, Châteauneuf-du-Pape Grande Garde 🍷, Châteauneuf-du-Pape La Truffière 🍷, ★ Châteauneuf-du-Pape Cuvée Élise 🍷

Best years 1999, '98, '96, '95, '90, '89

CH. DE ST-COSME, Gigondas   04 90 65 86 97/04 90 65 81 05

An estate that once sold most of its wine in bulk, but now bottles its ripe, fruity Gigondas, using new oak for the most exceptional cuvées. Also makes superb Condrieu.

Best wines ★★★ Condrieu 🍸, ★ Gigondas Cuvée Valbelle 🍷 and Gigondas 🍷

Best years 🍷1999, '96, '95, '90; 🍸1999, '98, '97

DOM. ST-GAYAN, Gigondas   04 90 65 86 33/04 90 65 85 10

This domaine, with holdings in the best parts of Gigondas, has always been one of the leaders of the appellation. Roger Meffre's family has been at St-Gayan since 1400. The vines average 60 years old, producing a classic deep, meaty Gigondas. The wines have 3 years' aging in large, wooden casks before they are bottled and released for sale.

Best wines ★★★ Gigondas 🍷, ★★ Côtes du Rhône 🍷 and Côtes du Rhône-Villages Rasteau 🍷, ★ Côtes du Rhône 🍸

Best years 🍷1999, '98, '97, '96, '95, '90, '89, '88, '86, '85

CH. DE ST-ROCH, Roquemaure   04 66 82 82 59/04 66 82 83 00

Established 40 years ago, this is one of the leaders in Lirac. The Verda family also own the fine adjoining estate, Ch. de Cantegril.

Best wines ★★ Lirac Cuvée Ancienne Viguerie 🍷, ★ Lirac 🍷🍸

Best years 1999, '98, '97, '95, '90

DOM. STE-ANNE, St-Gervais   04 66 82 77 41/04 66 82 74 57

An innovative estate owned by Guy Steinmaier whose wines have explosively ripe fruit.

Best wines ★★★ Côtes du Rhône Viognier 🍸 and Côtes du Rhône-Villages Cuvée Notre Dame des Cellettes 🍷, ★★ Côtes du Rhône Cuvée St-Gervais 🍷

Best years 🍷1999, '98, '96, '95; 🍸 1999, '98, '97

DOM. LE SANG DES CAILLOUX, Sarrians　　　　04 90 65 88 64/04 90 65 88 75

As the name 'blood from the stones' suggests, this estate is the source of red wines with great depth and concentration.

Best wine ★★ Vacqueyras ▮　　　　　　**Best years** 1999, '98, '95, '90

DOM. SANTA DUC, Gigondas　　　　04 90 65 84 49/04 90 65 81 63

An estate now producing concentrated, rich wines with dense colours and ripe fruit that are among the very best in this appellation.

Best wines ★★ Côtes du Rhône ▮, Gigondas Cuvée Classique ▮ and Gigondas Prestige des Hautes Garrigues ▮

Best years 1999, '98, '97, '96, '95, '93, '90

DOM. DE LA SOLITUDE, Châteauneuf-du-Pape　　　　04 90 83 71 45/04 90 83 51 34

This estate has been making wine continuously since 1604 and owns some of the best terroir in the appellation. Quality has returned since 1990.

Best wine ★★ Châteauneuf-du-Pape ▮♀　　　　**Best years** 1999, '98, '97, '95, '90

MARC SORREL, Tain l'Hermitage　　　　04 75 07 10 07/04 75 08 75 88

An estate evenly split between Crozes-Hermitage and Hermitage. Winemaking is traditional, with no new oak, and the wines are dark, opaque and powerful, with a great capacity for aging. The Crozes-Hermitage wines are some of the best in the AC.

Best wines ★★★ Hermitage Les Rocoules ♀ and Hermitage Le Gréal ▮, ★★ Hermitage Classique ♀, Hermitage Classique ▮ and Crozes-Hermitage ▮

Best years ▮1999, '98, '97, '96, '95, '91, '90, '89, '88, '85, '84, '83, '78; ♀1999, '98, '97, '96, '95, '90, '89

DOM. LA SOUMADE, Rasteau　　　　04 90 83 72 62/04 90 83 51 07

Old vines yield wine of great concentration and extraordinary quality for the Côtes du Rhône-Villages appellation.

Best wines ★★★ Côtes du Rhône-Villages Rasteau Cuvée Prestige ▮ and Côtes du Rhône-Villages Rasteau Cuvée Confiance ▮

Best years 1999, '98, '97, '96, '95

TARDIEU-LAURENT, Loumarin　　　　04 90 08 32 07/04 90 08 41 11

This company, founded in 1994, specializes in buying juice from producers known for concentration of flavour. The already impressive wines are then aged in small oak barrels, a high proportion of which are new, and are bottled without filtration to produce wines of immense richness and complexity.

Best wines ★★★ Gigondas Vieilles Vignes ▮, Crozes-Hermitage Vieilles Vignes ▮ and Hermitage ▮, ★★ Côtes du Rhône Cuvée Guy-Louis ▮, Vacqueyras ▮ and Châteauneuf-du-Pape ▮

Best years 1999, '98, '97, '96, '95

CH. DES TOURS, Vacqueyras　　　　04 90 65 41 75/04 90 65 38 46

A fine estate owned by Emmanuel Reynaud, nephew of the late Jacques Reynaud of Ch. RAYAS, who shares the same philosophy of using old vines and low yields.

Best wines ★★ Côtes du Rhône ▮ and Vacqueyras Réserve ▮

Best years 1999, '98, '96, '95, '90, '89

LOUIS DE VALLOUIT, St-Vallier　　　　04 75 23 10 11/04 75 23 05 58

This family company owns a large holding of vines in Côte-Rôtie, as well as some in Hermitage and St-Joseph, and also makes wines from many other Rhône appellations.

Unsurprisingly, those from the estate's own vineyards are the best.

Best wines ★★★ Hermitage Les Greffières ❗ and Côte-Rôtie La Vonière ❗, ★★ Côte-Rôtie Les Roziers ❗

Best years 1999, '98, '97, '96, '95, '91, '90, '89, '88, '85, '83, '78.

GEORGES & LUC VERNAY, Condrieu   04 74 59 52 22/04 74 56 60 98

Georges Vernay can be credited with saving the Condrieu AC from extinction over 2 decades ago, at a time when his own 6-ha estate represented almost 50% of the appellation. Now, at over 70, he and his son, Luc, are producing some of the best Condrieus today – rich and opulent, with tropical fruit flavours.

Best wines ★★★ Condrieu Les Chaillées de l'Enfer ♀ and Condrieu Coteaux du Vernon ♀, ★★ Condrieu ♀

Best years 1999, '98, '97, '96, '95

VIDAL-FLEURY, Ampuis   04 74 56 10 18/04 74 56 19 19

Founded in 1781, and by far the oldest of the *négociant/*growers in the region, Vidal-Fleury was taken over by Marcel GUIGAL in 1985. With substantial holdings in Côte-Rôtie, the company is well-placed, under Guigal's dynamic guidance, to produce some of the finest wines from this appellation, as well as respectable wines from the others.

Best wines ★★★ Côte-Rôtie La Chatillonne ❗, ★ Côte-Rôtie Brune et Blonde ❗, Gigondas ❗ and Muscat de Beaumes-de-Venise ♀

Best years ❗1999, '98, '97, '96, '95, '91, '90, '89, '85, '83, '78

LE VIEUX DONJON, Châteauneuf-du-Pape   04 90 83 70 03/04 90 83 50 38

On the plateau near MONT-REDON, this estate has mostly 80-year old vines. Wine-making is very traditional, producing dark, long-lasting reds and ageworthy whites.

Best wines ★★★ Châteauneuf-du-Pape ❗, ★ Châteauneuf-du-Pape ♀

Best years ❗1999, '98, '96, '95, '90, '89, '88, '85, '83, '81, '78; ♀1999, '98, '97, '96, '95

DOM. DU VIEUX TÉLÉGRAPHE, Bédarrides   04 90 33 00 31/04 90 33 18 47

One of the best-known Châteauneuf estates, owing to its superbly situated vineyards, favourable mesoclimates and meticulous winemaking by the Brunier family. The 1978 was one of the greatest wines produced in that magnificent vintage, and since 1990 these accessible Grenache-based wines have returned to that standard.

Best wines ★★★ Châteauneuf-du-Pape ❗, ★★ Châteauneuf-du-Pape ♀ and Châteauneuf-du-Pape Vieux Mas des Papes ❗

Best years ❗1999, '98, '95, '94, '90, '89, '88, '81, '79

FRANÇOIS VILLARD, St-Michel-sur-Rhône   04 74 53 11 25/04 74 53 38 32

In less than 5 years, this estate, with 2.25ha on the opposite slope to Château-Grillet, has acquired a fine reputation. The Condrieus are powerful and concentrated but not heavy. Cuvée Quintessence is an outstandingly rich, late-harvest wine.

Best wines ★★★ Condrieu Coteaux de Poncin ♀ and Condrieu Quintessence ♀, ★★ Condrieu Les Terrasses de Palat ♀, St-Joseph Reflet ❗ and Côte-Rôtie La Brocade ❗

Best years ❗1999, '98, '97, '96, '95; ♀1999, '98, '97

ALAIN VOGE, Cornas   04 75 40 32 04/04 75 81 06 02

A large estate for Cornas, and the wines are ripe and plump, aging well.

Best wines ★★ Cornas Vieilles Vignes ❗, ★ Cornas ❗

Best years ❗1999, '98, '97, '96, '95, '91, '90, '89, '88, '85, '83, '80, '78

Although the Rhône Valley, in general, has few very poor vintages, the region's situation in the warmer southern half of France does not guarantee fully ripe grapes. Rain and lack of sun can be a problem in the North, and too much sun can shrivel the grapes in the South. Syrah, and particularly Mourvèdre, need a fine late summer in order to ripen fully, while the early-ripening Grenache is subject to rot. Nevertheless, the great vintages of the Rhône are very great indeed.

Aging qualities

For all red wines of the Rhône, it is the producer's winemaking style rather than the particular vintage that determines whether a wine will be long-lasting or not. In the North only Hermitage and Cornas should be kept for up to 20 years, while Côte-Rôtie reaches its peak at 10 years. St-Joseph and Crozes-Hermitage are usually drunk before their fifth birthday.

In the South, Châteauneuf-du-Pape, Gigondas and Vacqueyras are at their best between 5 and 15 years. Lirac and Côtes du-Rhône-Villages mature at 2–3 years, but can last longer.

White wines, especially those from the South, should be drunk while still young at 1–2 years. The exception is white Hermitage, which can age like the red version; and the rare Château-Grillet.

Maturity charts _____

1995 was a fine, even great year in the northern Rhône and the best Hermitage should last for up to 25 years. In the South it was a very hot year, producing concentrated wines that will age well.

1995 Hermitage red

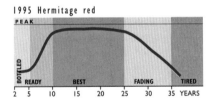

1995 Châteauneuf-du-Pape red

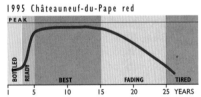

VINTAGE CHART

	99	98	97	96	95	94	93	92	91	90	89	88
Côte-Rôtie	9○	7○	7○	7○	9○	7●	4●	6○	9●	7●	8○	9○
Condrieu	9○	8●	7○	9○	8●	8◐	5◐	7○	9◐	8◐		
Hermitage reds	9○	8○	4◑	8○	9○	7◑	3●	6○	8●	10◑	9○	9●
Cornas, St-Joseph reds	9○	7○	7○	7◑	9○	8◑	4●	6○	8●	9○	8●	8●
Hermitage, Crozes-Hermitage and St-Joseph whites	9○	8○	7◑	9○	8○	7◑	5●	7○	9●	8●	8●	8●
Southern reds especially Châteauneuf-du-Pape and Gigondas	9○	10○	6◑	6●	9○	7◑	6●	5○	5●	9●	10●	8●
Southern whites	9○	9◑	6◑	7●	8●	7●	6●	6◐	7◐	8◐	8◐	8◐

KEY ○= needs more time   ◑= ready but will improve   ●= at peak   ◐= fading or tired

VINTAGES AT A GLANCE

In the 1970s, even into the early 1980s, the problem was not poor vintages but often inadequate winemaking. Since then there has been dramatic improvements in the cellar combined with greater commitment from the producers.

Great Years ★★★	North	1999, '95, '91, '90, '85, '83, '78, '61, '59, '52
	South	1998, '95, '90, '89, '81, '78, '70, '67, '61
Good Years ★★	North	1998, '97, '96, '94, '92, '91, '89, '88, '85, '83, '82, '79, '76, '70, '66, '64
	South	1999, '97, '95, '88, '86, '85, '83, '81, '79, '72, '71, '66, '64, '62, '61
Moderate Years ★	North	1997, '92, '87, '82, '80, '75, '73, '72, '71
	South	1997, '96, '94, '93, '86, '80, '83, '76, '75, '73
Poor Years (No Stars)	North	1993, '86, '84, '81, '77, '68, '65, '63; South 1992, '91, '87, '84, '82, '77, '68, '65, '63

Annual vintage reports

1999 North★★★ Perfect growing season produced dark-coloured, sumptuous wines. **South★★** Fine, ripe wines, but rain at vintage time lightened concentration.

1998 North★★ Good depth of fruit and firm tannins, but not quite great. **South★★★** Exceptional concentration and ripeness resulted in a very great year.

1997 North★-★★ A very dry and sunny September allowed growers to wait for optimum ripeness in both the white and red grapes. The results should be good. **South★-★★** A wet August was followed by a hot, dry September, causing uneven ripeness; selection in the vineyards was the key to success. The white wines are good whereas maturity in the reds was more variable.

1996 North★★ A year with good concentration in the grapes owing to the Mistral blowing during September, drying them out. Not as easy a vintage as 1995, but successful overall. The white wines were very good. **South★** A rainy, cold year, saved by dry weather at the end. Rigorous producers made good wines but without the concentration of the 1995s. Choose carefully.

1995 North★★★ A very good year for red wines, especially Côte-Rôtie, and they are full of ripeness and concentration. The reds will develop early, but have the

structure to last. Also an excellent year for whites. **South★★-★★★** A very hot year, where, despite rain in mid-September, the wines were rich and ripe and capable of aging well. Particularly good in Gigondas.

1994 North★★ A good year from a difficult, rainy vintage. Better for firm, structured Hermitage reds and richly aromatic whites than in Côte-Rôtie. **South★** A very hot summer was followed by heavy September rain, so this vintage turned out to be good, not great.

1993 North Constant rainfall in September with warm temperatures caused widespread rot. Only the very best growers produced good wine. **South★** A moderately good year, with pleasantly fruity wines for early drinking.

1992 North★-★★ September rains meant a large crop of lightish wines for relatively early drinking. Stick to the top producers. The whites were better than the reds. **South** Torrential rain during the harvest generally ruined the vintage.

1991 North★★-★★★ A lower than average crop produced wines of great depth and concentration. Initially underrated, these are very good, especially in Côte-Rôtie. The whites are excellent too. **South** A year lacking in ripeness, producing thin wines.

1990 North★★★ A spectacular vintage, especially in Hermitage. Almost all appellations produced their best wines

since 1983. Côte-Rôtie was affected by rain after a summer of drought.
South★★★ A hot year, producing wines with rich concentration and warm flavours, with extract, alcohol and tannin all in balance.

1989 North★★ A drought-affected vintage, like 1990, that produced wines with concentration and high levels of alcohol, but without the balance of the 1990s. Condrieu was a great success. **South★★★** An exceptionally hot year, producing wines with great power and concentration for long-term aging. Châteauneuf-du-Pape was a great success.

1988 North★★ A very good year, producing wines strong in colour, extract and tannin. Some are a little too hard. **South★★** A good crop of solid, foursquare wines, with ripe, firm flavours. Overshadowed by both 1989 and '90.

1986 North A large crop of wines generally lacking in concentration. **South★-★★** A difficult vintage, with great irregularity in quality, the best wines coming from Châteauneuf-du-Pape.

1985 North★★-★★★ A year when exceptionally ripe grapes produced wines with a huge colour and dense fruit, exceptional in Côte-Rôtie. There was also superb white Hermitage. **South★★** A rich, ripe vintage, with very good fruit but low in acidity for current drinking.

1983 North★★-★★★ A year of great concentration producing tannic wines for long-term aging. Hermitage is the star here, both red and white. **South★-★★** This was a small crop owing to the failure of Grenache, which produced untypically tannic wines.

1982 North★-★★ A very hot vintage produced a large crop of very ripe grapes, but lacking the tannins needed for a very long life. **South** A very large crop where the Grenache became overripe in the heat at vintage time. Unbalanced wines.

1981 North A very difficult year plagued by rot and unripeness. **South★★-★★★** An average vintage in quantity, whose reputation has increased with time. Some exceptional wines were made, especially in Châteauneuf-du-Pape.

1980 North★ A good crop of underrated wines with attractive fruit. **South★** An average crop of attractive, fruity wines.

1979 North★★ A very good vintage both for quality and quantity. **South★★** A large crop of well-balanced wines with good fruit, overshadowed by the 1978s.

1978 North★★★ An exceptional vintage with rich wines of depth and concentration, still youthful after 2 decades. **South★★★** An average crop of very full-bodied, concentrated wines of exceptional quality.

1977–1970 North A span of unexciting vintages, the best being 1972 and '70. **South** The mid-1970s were not very successful in the southern Rhône, but 1972, poor in most other regions of France, produced some firmly structured wines. 1970 was very good, especially in Châteauneuf-du-Pape.

1969–1960 North Apart from the general disasters of 1968, '65 and '63, a decade of good to very good vintages, the best by far being '61. **South** The rained-out vintages of 1968, '65 and '63 affected the south as well as the rest of France. 1967 was quite exceptional, perhaps the best vintage of the decade. 1966, '64, '62 and '61 were all very good. 1961 was quite exceptional and with '78 and '67 is the only year to unquestionably rate ★★★.

1959–1945 These vintages are rare, and most of the wines will be past their best, The best were 1959, '57, '55, '52, '49, '48, '47, '45.

THE JURA

Lying on attractive slopes in farming country between Burgundy and Switzerland, the Jura vineyards are some of the oldest in France and the wines are certainly some of the most individual, including the very rare Vin Jaune and Vin de Paille. The Burgundian grapes, Pinot Noir and Chardonnay, are used to make attractive wines but the real quality comes from the interesting local grape varieties such as Savagnin and Poulsard.

Vin Jaune

Found only in Jura, this wine style is named after the deep yellow colour it acquires through its unique aging process. Only Savagnin can be used, picked as late as possible, and after fermentation the wine matures in oak barrels where it remains, with no topping-up, for at least 6 years. The end result is a wine with a heady, nutty bouquet and the flavour of a concentrated fino sherry. Once bottled (in a special 62-cl bottle called a *clavelin*) it can outlast a human lifespan.

Vin de Paille

Mainly found in Jura, this style of wine is sometimes made in Hermitage. Whole bunches of grapes are picked and placed on straw mats or suspended from rafters for 3 months to become almost raisin-like with highly concentrated sugars. A very slow, difficult fermentation will produce an astoundingly rich, amber-coloured nectar. Aged for 3–4 years in wood before bottling, it lasts almost indefinitely.

ARBOIS AC

The reds tend to be light while the whites from the local Savagnin grape have a nutty, almost sherry-like bouquet. Chardonnay is increasingly used.
Best producers FRUITIÈRE VINICOLE D'ARBOIS, Aviet, Dugois, Désiré, de la Pinte, Puffeney, ROLET, Tissot.
Best years 1999, '98, '96, '95, '90.

CÔTES DU JURA AC

In the southern Jura, the local Poulsard and Trousseau grapes make some fruity reds and whites similar to Arbois but supposedly better. Some superb Vins Jaunes and Vins de Paille are made too.
Best producers d'ARLAY, Baud, Berthet-Bondet, Boilley, Bourdy, Chalandard, COURBET, DELAY, Reverchon.
Best years 1999, '98, 96, '95, '93, '90.

CHÂTEAU-CHALON AC

A unique 50-ha area of vines split between many growers, planted on steep slopes to produce low yields of concentrated juice for Vin Jaune. Only the local Savagnin grape can be used and it is harvested as late as possible, sometimes even when snow is on the ground. The wine can last 50 years or more.
Best producers Baud, Berthet-Bondet, Chalandard, COURBET, DURAND-PERRON, MACLE.
Best years 1995, '92, '90, '89, '88.

L'ÉTOILE AC

White wines only from a small, 64-ha appellation just north of Lons-le-Saunier, with more finesse than those from Arbois. There is also some Vin Jaune and Vin de Paille as well as some good Champagne-method sparkling wine.
Best producers Baud, Chalandard, de l'Étoile, Geneletti, Montbourgeau.
Best years 1999, '98, '96, '95, '93, '90, '89.

CH. D'ARLAY, Arlay   03 84 85 04 22/03 84 48 17 96
One of the most historic and important estates in the Jura. The quality is very reliable.
Best wines ★★ Côtes du Jura Vin Jaune ♀ and Vin de Paille ♀, ★ Côtes du Jura ♥♀
Best years 1999, '98, '96, '95, '93, '90

JEAN-MARIE COURBET, Nevy-sur-Seille   03 84 85 28 70/03 84 44 68 88
A small family domaine making uncompromising, traditional wines.
Best wines ★★ Château-Chalon ♀ and Vin de Paille ♀
Best years 1995, '90, '89

RICHARD DELAY, Gevingey   03 84 47 46 78/03 84 43 26 75
One of the rare Jura growers to make a superb red Pinot Noir wine.
Best wines ★★ Côtes du Jura Pinot Noir ♥ and Côtes du Jura Savagnin-Chardonnay ♀
Best years 1999, '98, '96, '95, '93, '90

DURAND-PERRON, Voiteur   03 84 44 66 80/03 84 44 62 75
A small (4.5-ha) estate with vines in the best part of Château-Chalon.
Best wine ★★★ Château-Chalon ♀   **Best years** 1995, '90, '89

FRUITIÈRE VINICOLE D'ARBOIS, Arbois   03 84 66 11 67/03 84 37 48 80
With 200ha of vines, this is the largest co-operative in the Jura.
Best wines ★★ Arbois Vin Jaune ♀ and Arbois Vin de Paille ♀
Best years 1999, '98, '96, '95, '93, '90, '89

JEAN MACLE, Château-Chalon   03 84 85 21 85/03 84 85 27 38
A superb 14-ha estate, which has replanted its original vineyard on the steepest slopes
of Château-Chalon. It now produces wines of incredible finesse.
Best wines ★★★ Château-Chalon ♀, ★ Côtes du Jura ♀
Best years 1999, '98, '96, '95, '90, '89

DOM. ROLET, Arbois   03 84 66 00 05/03 84 37 47 41
With 60ha, this family domaine is one of the most important in the Jura. Modernism
and traditionalism blend to produce a consistent range of wines.
Best wines ★★ Arbois Mémorial ♥, Côtes du Jura Chardonnay/Savagnin ♀, Arbois Tradition ♀,
★ Arbois Chardonnay ♀
Best years 1999, '98, '96, '95, '93, '90, '89

GREAT JURA WINES

Oz Clarke's selection
Vin Jaune ♀ (Ch. d'Arlay)
One of the behemoths of French wine – angular, aggressive yet inexplicably fascinating.
Château-Chalon ♀ (Jean Macle) Also quite unlike anything else made in France, but more fragrant and almost approachable!

Vin Jaune ♀ (Reverchon)
Great blast of mountain man's wild intensity to match the pungency of his excellent Comté cheese.
Steven Spurrier's selection
Château-Chalon ♀ (Jean Macle) A Vin Jaune of incredible finesse from the steepest slopes in the appellation.

Côtes du Jura
Chardonnay-Savagnin ♀ (Rolet) One of the many superb wines from the Rolet family. The typicity of the Savagnin is heightened by the Chardonnay fruit.
Vin de Paille ♀ (Ch. d'Arlay) A classic Vin de Paille, rich and raisiny, from the Jura's most historic estate.

CHAMPAGNE

Marie Antoinette, that ill-fated Queen of France, once said that 'Champagne is the only wine that leaves a woman beautiful after drinking it' and today it is still the world's leading 'fizz', the wine of choice for special occasions, or just for elegant enjoyment. Legally, it may only come from the region of Champagne in northern France, at the northern limits for grape-ripening. Good Champagne is not cheap to produce, so it will not be cheap to purchase, yet the Champenois are aware of their obligation to provide value for money. They are also ultra-conscious of the value of their brands, so a non-vintage Champagne with a well-respected name will have to live up to the reputation of the house that produced it.

CHAMPAGNE STYLES

The Champagne region produces more than 250 million bottles of Champagne a year, all sold under one regional appellation, regardless of style. Most of the vines are in the Marne *département*, followed by the Aube and the Aisne, and the region's soil is deep chalk, rich in minerals, which brings finesse and liveliness to the wine. Champagne is usually a blended wine, from Pinot Noir, Pinot Meunier and Chardonnay, or, more rarely, it is made from a single variety. There are two minor appellations for still wines.

Non-vintage

This style covers 80% of all Champagne made and is in theory based on a blend of wines from several years. However, 80–90% of the base wine for this style will usually come from a single vintage, the balance being added at the time of blending from 'reserve' wines. In this way, the Champagne blenders manage to maintain a 'house style', which is always consistent. It is usually released for sale 2–3 years after bottling.

Vintage

Champagne from a single, good vintage, made only in the best years, usually averaging not more than one year in two, and not released for sale until at least 5 years after the harvest. Most vintage Champagne will continue to gain complexity well into its second decade.

Blanc de Blancs

Light, delicate Champagne made with 100% Chardonnay. The finest examples are produced from vines grown on the Côte des Blancs.

Blanc de Noirs

Complex, flavourful Champagne made from the juice of Pinot Noir and/or Pinot Meunier grapes. The best examples come from the Montagne de Reims.

Champagne rosé

Champagne rosé is the only French wine where red and white wine (as opposed to grapes) may be blended. Rosés vinified as such are very rare: most Champagne rosé has 10–15% of still red wine added at the blending stage to create the desired colour. This wine is often derived from the aptly-named wine village of Bouzy.

Luxury or prestige cuvées

Most major Champagne houses produce a *cuvée de prestige*, in which as much thought has gone into the packaging as into the wine. As a house's most expensive Champagne it should be, though is not always, its best. Both vintage and non-vintage styles are made. The most famous ones include MOËT ET CHANDON's Dom Pérignon, ROEDERER's Cristal, TAITTINGER's Comtes de Champagne and LAURENT-PERRIER's Grand Siècle.

Levels of sweetness

Champagne is made in varying levels of sweetness. Brut on the label means very dry Champagne, Extra Dry is confusingly less dry than Brut, Sec is literally dry but indicates medium-dry Champagne, Demi-sec is medium-sweet, Doux is sweet and Rich is the sweetest style of all.

Coteaux Champenois AC

These are still red, white or rosé wines from the Champagne region. A village name may be stated on the label and Bouzy is one of the best. Production varies with each vintage, but is never more than 1% of the total crop.

Rosé des Riceys AC

A still, deep-coloured rosé wine made from Pinot Noir at les Riceys in the Aube department. Has good aging potential but tends to be expensive for the style of wine.

Classifications

In Champagne the best villages rather than individual vineyards are classified as 100% or Grand Cru. There are 17 in all. The 41 Premier Cru villages come next and are graded between 99 and 90%. Usually only growers or co-operatives use these descriptions on their labels.

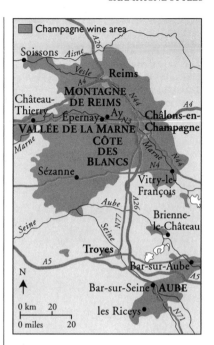

Producers

Production is divided between growers, who own their vineyards and may only produce Champagne from their own grapes; *négociants*, who may and usually do own vineyards, but buy in grapes as well; and co-operatives, who group the grapes of their members, and produce Champagnes sold under a variety of labels.

Labelling

The following codes appear in tiny print on the labels. R.M. = Récoltant-Manipulant, a grower making his own Champagne; R.C. = Récoltant-Co-opérateur, Champagne made at the co-opérative, but sold by the grower; C.M. = Co-opérative-Manipulant, Champagne made and sold by the co-operative; N.M. = Négociant-Manipulant, a Champagne house; M.A. = Marque d'Acheteur, a 'buyers own brand', bought from a *négociant* or co-operative.

GREAT CHAMPAGNES

Oz Clarke's selection

Krug Clos du Mesnil ♀
Krug's top Champagne – a creamy delight from the village of Le Mesnil-sur-Oger in the Côte des Blancs.

Billecart-Salmon Cuvée Nicolas-François Billecart ♀
Gently, yet richly satisfying nutty vintage wine from my favourite Champagne house.

Charles Heidsieck Vintage ♀ Beautifully ripe, balanced wine from the most improved leading Champagne house.

Alfred Gratien Vintage ♀
An old favourite of mine for classically deep, densely textured wines for long aging.

Jacques Selosse Vintage ♀
A great original – very traditional wine, slow to mature, yet boasting a thrilling scent of cedar.

Louis Roederer Vintage ♀
Elegant, sophisticated wine of incomparable finesse – and consistent too.

R de Ruinart Vintage ♀
Delightful, honeyed style of Champagne, both in classic and non-classic years.

Pol Roger Vintage ♀
Elegant, rather restrained style of Champagne that nonetheless coats its reserve with an irresistible veneer of cream.

Laurent-Perrier Grand Siècle ♀ An old favourite now back on form for smooth, creamy fizz.

Veuve Clicquot Vintage ♀
Another old trusty style of Champagne and triumphantly back on form.

Lanson Vintage ♀ Always a tiptop wine for long-aging. The most recent vintages are more immediately approachable without losing any personality.

Deutz Blanc de Blancs Vintage ♀ Sleek, elegant, almost austere wine of exquisite balance and ethereal cedar fragrance.

Gosset Grand Rosé Vintage ♀ My choice when I want to combine the style of vintage wine with the naughtiness of a glass of pink.

Steven Spurrier's selection

Bollinger Grande Année ♀
From 70% Pinot Noir and 30% Chardonnay, this vintage Champagne ages beautifully.

Krug Vintage ♀ No Champagne house makes wines that keep their freshness as long as Krug. This wonderfully complex vintage Champagne needs keeping for 5–10 years after release.

Billecart-Salmon Cuvée Nicolas-François Billecart ♀
This vintage Champagne is the

most complex among the many fine Billecart-Salmon Champagnes.

Jacquesson Blanc de Blancs ♀ A classic vintage Blanc de Blancs based on wines from the Grand Cru Avize.

Louis Roederer Brut Premier ♀ A brilliant non-vintage wine from some of the best vineyards in Champagne.

Roederer Cristal ♀ The ultimate in luxury vintage Champagne.

Moët et Chandon Cuvée Dom Pérignon ♀ The great rival to Roederer Cristal, a wine of incomparable finesse and length.

Charles Heidsieck Cuvée des Millénaires ♀ A simply beautiful vintage Blanc de Blancs, almost creamily soft on the palate.

Laurent-Perrier Grand Siècle 'La Cuvée' ♀ A Blanc de Blancs Champagne with liveliness and grip which ages superbly.

Salon ♀ A firm vintage Blanc de Blancs, reminiscent of the Grands Crus of Burgundy.

Pol Roger White Foil ♀
One of the very best non-vintage blends, known for its lively elegance.

Veuve Clicquot Yellow Label ♀ Another classic non-vintage blend based on Pinot Noir, a complete contrast to the Pol Roger.

Top Champagne producers

Négociants Ayala, BILLECART-SALMON, BOLLINGER, Cattier, Charbaut, Comte Audoin de Dampierre, DELAMOTTE, DEUTZ, Nicolas Feuillatte, GOSSET, Alfred GRATIEN, Charles HEIDSIECK, HENRIOT, JACQUESSON, KRUG, LANSON, LAURENT-PERRIER, MOËT ET CHANDON, MUMM, PAILLARD, Joseph Perrier, PERRIER-JOUËT, PHILIPPONNAT, Piper Heidsieck, POL ROGER, POMMERY, Louis ROEDERER, RUINART, SALON, TAITTINGER, de Venoge, VEUVE CLICQUOT.
Growers BARA, BARNAUT, Beerens, Cattier, ÉGLY-OURIET, GATINOIS, GIMONNET, Gremillet, Launois, MONCUIT, SELOSSE, A Vessele, G Vesselle, J Vesselle, VILMART.
Co-operatives Blin, Jacquart, MAILLY, PALMER, Pannier, UNION CHAMPAGNE.

PAUL BARA, Bouzy   03 26 57 00 50/03 26 57 81 24

A highly regarded estate from this top village, producing some of the finest wines, which combine Bouzy's richness and structure with finesse and harmony.

Best wines ★★ Special Club ♀ and Coteaux Champenois Bouzy Rouge !, ★ Brut Réserve ♀
Best years 1996, '95, '89, '88, '85

EDMOND BARNAUT, Bouzy   03 26 57 01 54/03 26 57 09 97

A 14-ha domaine using mostly Pinot Noir and Pinot Meunier to make full-flavoured Champagnes with power and richness.

Best wines ★ Brut Réserve ♀ and Brut Rosé !   **Best years** 1996, '95, '90, '89, '88, '85

BILLECART-SALMON, Mareuil-sur-Ay   03 26 52 60 22/03 26 52 64 88

A family firm with only 10ha of vines for its 650,000-bottle production, but purchases of top-quality grapes from the Montagne de Reims and the upper Vallée de la Marne, thoughtful, enlightened winemaking and careful aging produce Champagnes that are as fine as they are reliable.

Best wines ★★★ Blanc de Blancs ♀V and Nicolas-François Billecart ♀V, ★ Brut Réserve ♀ and Brut Réserve Rosé !
Best years 1996, '95, '91, '90, '89, '88, '86, '85, '82

BOLLINGER, Ay   03 26 53 33 66/03 26 54 85 59

One of the most famous and highly regarded Champagne houses, still family run and very traditional. Bollinger is one of the few houses still to ferment its base wine in barrels. Each bottle features the famous Bollinger 'Charter of Quality', which led the way for many *négociants* to improve their wines after the excesses of the 1980s.

Best wines ★★★ Grande Année ♀V and RD ♀V, ★★ Coteaux Champenois Ay Rouge la Côte aux Enfants ! and Special Cuvée Brut ♀
Best years 1992, '90, '89, '88, '85, '82, '81

DELAMOTTE, Le Mesnil-sur-Oger   03 26 57 51 65/03 26 57 79 29

Owned by LAURENT-PERRIER, Delamotte specializes in Blanc de Blancs Champagnes from the renowned Côte des Blancs villages of Le Mesnil and Avize.

Best wines ★★ Blanc de Blancs ♀V, ★ Brut Blanc de Blancs ♀
Best years 1995, '90, '85

DEUTZ, Ay   03 26 56 94 00/03 26 56 94 10

Taken over by ROEDERER in 1993, this medium-sized, well-regarded house has fine vineyards in the Grand Cru villages of Ay and Le Mesnil. The wines are elegant, firm and long-lasting. William Deutz is the prestige, weightier *cuvée.*

Best wines ★★ Cuvée William Deutz ♀V and Blanc de Blancs ♀V, ★ Brut Classic ♀
Best years 1995, '90, '89, '88, '85, '82

ÉGLY-OURIET, Ambonnay   03 26 57 00 70/03 26 57 06 52

A small 7-ha domaine with vines in the superb Grand Cru village of Ambonnay, one of the best for Pinot Noir, at the junction of the Montagne de Reims and the Vallée de la Marne. The Blanc de Noirs is balanced by skilful use of oak-aging.

Best wines ★★ Brut Blanc de Noirs ♀ and Brut Réserve ♀
Best years 1995, '90, '89, '88, '85

GATINOIS, Ay   03 26 55 14 26/03 26 52 75 99

A small domaine in the very best part of Ay, a village in the Montagne de Reims renowned for producing the finest Pinot Noir grapes in Champagne, and home to some of Champagne's most famous names.

Best wines ★★ Coteaux Champenois Ay Rouge ♀V and Brut Grand Cru Reserve ♀V

Best years 1995, '90, '89, '88, '85

PIERRE GIMONNET, Cuis   03 26 59 78 70/03 26 59 79 84

This Côte des Blancs grower has vines in the Grands Crus of Cramant and Chouilly and the Premier Cru Cuis and makes a lively, dry Blanc de Blancs Champagne. The large size of the estate, 26ha, helps to ensure a reliably high standard.

Best wines ★★ Spécial Club ♀V, ★ Brut Cuis Premier Cru ♀

Best years 1996, '95, '93, '90, '89, '88, '85

GOSSET, Ay   03 26 56 99 56/03 26 51 55 88

The oldest producer of still wines in Champagne, Gosset is now in the energetic hands of Béatrice Cointreau. The Champagnes are cask-fermented and the style is heavily influenced by Pinot Noir, with an old-fashioned, rich and sumptuous quality.

Best wines ★★ Grande Millésime Brut ♀V and Cuvée Célébris ♀, ★ Grande Réserve ♀

Best years 1995, '90, '89, '88, '85, '82

ALFRED GRATIEN, Épernay   03 26 54 38 20/03 26 54 53 44

A small but respected house, owned by Gratien & Meyer of Saumur, Alfred Gratien still makes its Champagne in wooden casks, rare now in Champagne, and keeps its wines for a long time on the lees to yield individual and attractive Champagne. Vintage Champagnes are released at 10 years old when they are properly mature.

Best wines ★★ Brut ♀ and Cuvée Paradis ♀V, ★ Brut Réserve ♀V

Best years 1990, '89, '88, '87, '85, '83, '82

CHARLES HEIDSIECK, Reims   03 26 84 43 50/03 26 84 43 86

Purchased by the Rémy-Cointreau group in 1985, Charles Heidsieck has, thanks largely to their brilliant winemaker Daniel Thibault, emerged as one of the best Champagne brands, with a mature, creamy style derived from use of stocks of quality 'reserve' wines.

Best wines ★★★ Blanc des Millénaires ♀V, ★★ Brut Vintage ♀V, ★ Brut Non-Vintage ♀

Best years 1995, '90, '89, '85

HENRIOT, Reims   03 26 89 53 00/03 26 89 53 10

Joseph Henriot returned his company to independence in 1994, buying it back from its owners, the LVMH group, but not the vineyards. The wines are elegant and slightly austere, with, unusually, no Pinot Meunier in the blend. They age beautifully.

Best wines ★ Brut Blanc de Blancs ♀ and Brut Vintage ♀V

Best years 1995, '90, '89, '85, '82, '79

JACQUESSON, Dizy   03 26 55 68 11/03 26 51 06 25

Once Napoleon's favourite, today this is one of Champagne's finest small houses, with holdings in top Grands Crus, especially Avize in the Côte des Blancs. It has a rigorous approach to quality.

Best wines ★★ Blanc de Blancs Grands Crus ♀V and Signature Brut ♀V

Best years 1995, '90, '89, '88, '85, '83, '82, '79

KRUG, Reims   03 26 84 44 20/03 26 84 44 49

Although part of the LVMH group, Krug is still run by Henri and Rémi Krug, and their children. Apart from Gratien it is the only house to ferment all its wines in small barrels. Krug's long-lived Champagnes are the epitome of quality. Limited production and the high price make them a luxury but they are well worth the expense. Large stocks of reserve wines have helped create the Krug style.

Best wines ★★★ Grande Cuvée ♀, Clos du Mesnil Blanc de Blancs ♀V and Vintage ♀V, ★★ Grande Cuvée Rosé ♀V

Best years 1990, '89, '88, '85, '83, '82, '81, '79

LANSON, Reims   03 26 78 50 50/03 26 78 50 99

Bought in 1990 by the LVMH group and later sold to the giant Marne et Champagne company, since when quality has actually improved. The non-vintage Black Label Brut has kept its lively, light style and vintage wines are made solely from Grand Cru grapes.

Best wines ★★ Noble Cuvée ♀V, ★ Black Label ♀

Best years 1994, '93, '90, '89, '88, '85, '83, '82, '79

LAURENT-PERRIER, Tours-sur-Marne   03 26 58 91 22/03 26 58 77 29

Family-owned house, with a production of 6 million bottles which are extremely well vinified by winemaker Alain Terrier. The very reliable non-vintage Champagne contains a high proportion of Pinot Noir and Pinot Meunier while the prestige cuvée Grand Siècle is 100% Chardonnay. The Grand Siècle La Cuvée is a blend of declared vintages.

Best wines ★★ Grand Siècle Blanc de Blancs ♀V, Grand Siècle Blanc de Blancs 'La Cuvée' ♀ and Grand Siècle Alexandra Rosé ♀V, ★ Vintage ♀V and Brut ♀

Best years 1995, '90, '88, '85, '82, '79

MAILLY, Mailly-Champagne   03 26 49 41 10/03 26 49 42 27

This small co-operative in the Mailly Grand Cru in the Montagne de Reims has a good reputation for fully flavoured wines that age well.

Best wines ★ Extra Brut ♀ and Cuvée Echansons ♀V

Best years 1995, '90, '89, '88, '86, '85

MOËT ET CHANDON, Épernay   03 26 51 20 20/03 26 51 20 10

With an annual production of 23 million bottles, even the 768ha of vines owned by Moët et Chandon only meet 20% of their needs. For a company this size, the quality is uniformly high. The world-famous deluxe Cuvée Dom Pérignon, a blend of 50% Chardonnay and 50% Pinot Noir, is at its best at 10 years old.

Best wines ★★★ Dom Pérignon ♀V, ★ Brut Impérial ♀ and Brut Impérial Rosé ♀V

Best years 1995, '93, '92, '90, '88, '86, '85, '83, '82

PIERRE MONCUIT, Le Mesnil-sur-Oger   03 26 57 52 65/03 26 57 97 89

An important domaine in Le Mesnil, the finest of the Côte des Blancs Grands Crus.

Best wines ★★ Brut ♀ and Cuvée Nicole Moncuit Vieilles Vignes ♀V

Best years 1995, '93, '91, '90, '89, '88

MUMM, Reims   03 26 49 59 69/03 26 40 46 13

Mumm is the second largest brand in Champagne after MOËT. Quality is slowly improving, but the wines still tend to have more weight than finesse.

Best wines ★ Mumm de Cramant Blanc de Blancs ♀ and Cuvée René Lalou ♀V

Best years 1995, '90, '89, '88, '85

BRUNO PAILLARD, Reims · 03 26 36 20 22/03 26 36 57 72

In the last 15 years the youthful Bruno Paillard has created one of the most dynamic, quality houses in Champagne. Contrary to other houses, Paillard owns no vineyards, concentrating efforts on creating a range of individual wines, under the banner of *Je signe les Champagnes rares*. Over 90% of the production is exported and the winemaking is meticulous.

Best wines ★★ Brut ♀V, ★ Brut Réserve ♀ and Brut Blanc de Blancs Crémant ♀
Best years 1995, '90, '89, '88, '85, '82

PALMER, Reims · 03 26 07 35 07/03 26 07 45 24

A Champagne co-operative which has has access to 350ha of vines. The house style is dominated by the full flavours of Pinot Noir.

Best wines ★★ Cuvée Amazone ♀V, ★ Brut Réserve ♀
Best years 1996, '95, '90, '89, '88, '86, '85, '82, '79, '78, '75, '70

PERRIER-JOUET, Épernay · 03 26 53 38 00/03 26 54 54 55

Formerly part of the Canadian multinational Seagram group, this large house produces reliable but not currently inspiring Champagnes. An exception is the luxury *cuvée*, Belle Époque, in its famous Art Nouveau bottle.

Best wines ★ Blason de France Brut ♀ and Belle Époque ♀V
Best years 1990, '88, '86, '85, '82

PHILIPPONNAT, Mareuil-sur-Ay · 03 26 56 93 00/03 26 56 93 18

The fame of this house comes from its superb vineyard, le Clos des Goisses, which borders the Marne canal. Bought by Bruno PAILLARD in 1998.

Best wines ★★ Clos des Goisses ♀V, ★ Royal Réserve ♀
Best years 1995, '90, '86, '85, '82, '79, '75

POL ROGER, Épernay · 03 26 59 58 00/03 26 55 25 70

A traditional, family-run house, whose reputation is very high in English-speaking countries. With the exception of the robust vintage Cuvée Sir Winston Churchill (his favourite Champagne), the house style tends to elegance rather than weight.

Best wines ★★ Brut Vintage ♀V, Chardonnay Vintage Blanc de Blancs ♀V and Cuvée Sir Winston Churchill ♀V, ★ White Foil Brut ♀
Best years 1995, '93, '90, '89, '88, '86, '85, '82, '79

POMMERY, Reims · 03 26 61 62 63/03 26 61 63 97

Now part of the LVMH group, the Pommery style is still in the hands of Prince Alain de Polignac, whose family once owned the company. The Pommery facilities are among the most modern in Reims. Lively and elegant, the wines age well.

Best wines ★ Pommery Brut ♀, ★★ Cuvée Louise Pommery ♀V
Best years 1995, '93, '90, '89, '88, '85, '82, '81, '80

LOUIS ROEDERER, Reims · 03 26 40 42 11/03 26 47 66 51

The most successful company in Champagne due to its unwavering commitment to quality. Despite demand, production is kept around 2.5 million bottles a year. Vintage wines drink well after 10 years' aging. The deluxe brand Cristal is world-famous and it is hard to imagine a non-vintage wine better than the Brut Premier.

Best wines ★★★ Vintage ♀V, Cristal ♀V and Cristal Rosé ♀V, ★★ Brut Premier ♀
Best years 1993, '90, '89, '88, '86, '85, '82

RUINART, Reims   03 26 77 51 51/03 26 82 88 43

One of the oldest Champagne firms, with vines in the Montagne de Reims. The house specializes in attractive, full-bodied wines, but retains its low profile in spite of increased production and being part of the giant LVMH group.

Best wines ★★★ Dom Ruinart Blanc de Blancs ♀V and Dom Ruinart Rosé ♀V, ★ R de Ruinart Brut ♀

Best years 1995, '93, '92, '90, '88, '86, '85, '83, '82

SALON, Le Mesnil-sur-Oger   03 26 57 51 65/03 26 57 79 29

Owned by LAURENT-PERRIER, this tiny house makes only one Champagne – a superb vintage Blanc de Blancs from Le Mesnil Grand Cru grapes which is aged for many years before disgorgement. Generally, Salon vintages are not released for 10 years.

Best wine ★★ Vintage ♀V   **Best years** 1990, '88, '85, '83, '82, '79, '76, '73, '71, '69

JACQUES SELOSSE, Avize   03 26 57 53 56/03 26 57 78 22

A tiny domaine managed by the brilliant Anselme Selosse, who experiments, unusually for Champagne, with new oak to enhance the flavours of his Grand Cru Chardonnay wines. As they mature, they resemble great white Burgundy from the Côte d'Or.

Best wines ★★ Blanc de Blancs Grand Cru ♀V and Grand Cru Tradition ♀

Best years 1995, '90, '89, '88, '85

TAITTINGER, Reims   03 26 85 45 35/03 26 85 17 46

One of the few large independently-owned Champagne houses, with vineyards in some of the best Crus, especially in the Côte des Blancs, which explains why its Champagnes are particularly creamy and elegant.

Best wines ★★★ Comtes de Champagne Blanc de Blancs ♀V and Comtes de Champagne Rosé ♀V, ★ Brut Réserve ♀

Best years 1995, '93, '91, '90, '89, '88, '86, '85, '82, '79

UNION CHAMPAGNE, Avize   03 26 57 94 22/03 26 57 57 98

A fine co-operative in this famous Grand Cru village in the Côte des Blancs which specializes in making Champagne for other houses such as Comte Audoin de Dampierre. Their own label is called St-Gall.

Best wines ★★ Cuvée Orpale ♀V, ★ Blanc de Blancs Grand Cru ♀V

Best years 1995, '90, '89, '88, '85

VEUVE CLICQUOT, Reims   03 26 89 54 40/03 26 40 60 17

The vineyards owned by Veuve Clicquot are dominated by Pinot Noir, with the result that their wines tend to be full-bodied and rich. The non-vintage Yellow Label is one of the most distinctive and reliable brands in Champagne.

Best wines ★★★ La Grande Dame Rosé ♀V, ★★ Vintage Reserve ♀V and La Grande Dame ♀V, ★ Yellow Label ♀

Best years 1993, '90, '89, '88, '85, '82, '79

VILMART, Rilly-La-Montagne   03 26 03 40 01/03 26 03 46 57

A long-established family domaine with vineyards in the best parts of the Montagne de Reims, producing small quantities of robust Champagne from cask-fermented wine which ages very well, owing to the long lees contact.

Best wines ★★ Grand Cellier d'Or ♀V and Coeur de Cuvée ♀V

Best years 1995, '93, '90, '88, '85

CHAMPAGNE VINTAGES

A vintage Champagne is named after the year in which the grapes were picked, and has to be made from unblended wines of that year. Generally, only the finest years are selected to be 'vintaged', although in times of high demand, some less-than-great years may be selected. Not more than 80% of the total crop may be vintaged, leaving 20% of this quality base wine to be incorporated in subsequent non-vintage blends.

Aging qualities

A non-vintage Champagne is ready to drink when it is released for sale. The wine will be on average 3 years old and will taste fresh and lively. However, such is the balance of most carefully made, non-vintage wines that they continue to mature for a further 1–3 years after release. If you want the creamy nuttiness generally only found in vintage Champagne buy non-vintage and allow it to mature further. In contrast, non-vintage rosé Champagne should not be aged after release.

A vintage Champagne is kept for 3 years before sale, but good Champagne houses keep their wines for at least 5 years. Good vintage Champagne will improve for a few more years after release, reaching true maturity at 10 years old. A fine vintage Champagne is fully mature at 10 years old, but it should still taste well after 15 years or more, displaying a rounded, slightly nutty character and perhaps losing a little sparkle. The Champagne houses themselves have much older wines still in very good condition, but these will have been stored in their own cellars since birth. Vintage rosé Champagne can age as well as classic vintage Champagne.

To enjoy Champagne at its best, the bottles should always be stored in a cool cellar. Champagne, more than any other wine, is particularly sensitive to direct light and warm temperatures.

Maturity chart _____
1995 was the first year of proper vintage quality since 1990. The wine will be best at around 10 years old.

1995 Vintage Champagne

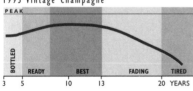

CHAMPAGNE BOTTLE SIZES

Champagne is sold in all sizes from the quarter or 'split' to the 20-bottle Nebuchadnezzer, but the more usual sizes are the half-bottle, bottle and magnum. As with all wines, Champagne once disgorged will age more quickly in a half-bottle than in a bottle, and more slowly in a magnum than a bottle. All Champagne houses carry out the secondary fermentation in bottles and magnums. The best will extend this to half-bottles and Jereboams. Quarter bottles are always decanted, as are the very large ones.

VINTAGE CHART

Vintage Champagne	96	95	93	90	89	88	86	85	83	82	81	79
	10○	8◑	7◑	10●	8●	8●	7●	9○	7◑	9●	8●	8●

KEY ○= needs more time   ◑= ready but will improve   ●= at peak   ◐= fading or tired

VINTAGES AT A GLANCE

Vintage Champagne is made only in the best years and it is rare to have more than 5 vintages a decade. Individual houses may sometimes vintage a lesser year, but the best years are generally declared by all.
Years in bold = generally declared vintage

Great Years ★★★	1996, **'95, '90, '89, '88, '85, '82**, '70
Good Years ★★	1997, '86, '81, **'83, '79, '76, '75**, '69
Moderate Years ★	1994, '93, '92, '91, '78, **'73**
Poor Years (No Stars)	1987, '84

Annual vintage reports

1999★★ The largest crop ever recorded in Champagne and of overall good quality, but rather low acidity.

1998★★ Well-structured wines with fruit and freshness. Vintage wines are likely.

1997★★ A good to very good year, with grapes in good condition (especially Pinots Noir and Meunier) and high sugar levels.

1996★★★ The hot summer produced good quality grapes, which were turned into great quality by a warm month of September, said by some to be the finest quality in living memory. Sure to be generally declared.

1995★★★ A good summer produced a large crop of ripe grapes, the first year of proper vintage quality since 1990. Many houses now releasing vintage wines with good aging potential.

1994★ A cool year, spoiled by rain during the harvest.

1993★ Another year spoiled by rain at vintage time, but a handful of surprisingly attractive vintage wines are appearing.

1992★ A large vintage of average quality. Some vintage wine was made.

1991★ A large crop (especially when compared to the rest of France) of only average quality.

1990★★★ A very hot summer produced wines with body, structure and more elegance than the even hotter 1989. A superb year for vintage wines.

1989★★★ A very hot summer and almost tropical September produced wines that are full bodied and overtly fruity for Champagne. The vintage wines are showing very well now.

1988★★★ A fine year, producing firm, concentrated wines that have more acidity than the more 'showy' '89s, and need to be kept for some years.

1986★★ An above average, but not great, year, with some good vintage Champagne.

1985★★★ A very good year, producing excellent ripe, elegant vintage wines.

1983★★ A year good enough for most houses to declare as a vintage, but rather overshadowed by 1982.

1982★★★ A splendid, rich vintage, certainly the finest of the decade, the best of which are still drinking very well today.

1981★★ A small crop of good, firm wine. A few houses declared a vintage.

1979★★ A large crop of ripe, well-balanced wines. A very successful, attractive vintage.

1978★ A small crop of firm, rather hard wines, less good than elsewhere in France.

1976★★ A heatwave year, with some vintage wines being very impressive.

1975★★ A very fine vintage making elegant, classic wines.

1973★ Vintage too large to be great.

1970★★★ A fine, classic year, with vintage wines of structure and depth.

1969★★ A very hot vintage which suited those houses specializing in Pinot Noir-based blends.

ALSACE

The scenic vineyards of Alsace cover a long, narrow stretch between the Rhine Valley and the Vosges Mountains. These mountains protect the vines from the wind and rain coming from the north-west, to the extent that Alsace has one of the driest climates in France, with sunny days lasting well into the autumn. The northern Bas-Rhin *département* is less protected than the Haut-Rhin, where the wines tend to be richer and more aromatic. Soil is variable, with a mix of limestone, clay, silt, sandy-gravel, sandstone and granite running through the vineyards. Some grape varieties grown here are equally renowned in nearby Germany, but Alsatian wines have a distinct and subtle fruity character which is all their own. Most wines are labelled by variety and there is a fine wine from this region to suit almost any cuisine.

GRAPE VARIETIES

White grapes predominate and 4 varieties – Muscat, Pinot Gris, Gewurztraminer and Riesling – are the finest or 'noble' varietals, and the only ones allowed for the Grand Cru AC.

Gewurztraminer
Produces wines with exceptional body and fruit as well as being highly aromatic, with an aroma of lychees or roses and an exotic spiciness on the palate.

Muscat
Aromatic wines, with a pronounced 'grapiness', usually dry, but can ripen to make a heady, 'musky' wine, often with residual sugar.

Pinot Auxerrois
Rich and characterful wines, midway in style between Pinot Blanc and Pinot Gris.

Pinot Blanc
Fruity wines of regular quality year to year and rarely exceptional. They are much used in sparkling Crémant d'Alsace.

Pinot Gris
Formerly sold under the name of Tokay, this grape, originating from Burgundy, now uses its own name. Rather neutral in poor years, it takes on a luxurious richness in ripe vintages, and is particularly impressive in Vendange Tardive and Sélection des Grains Nobles wines.

Pinot Noir
The only Alsace red grape and historically vinified as a rosé. The riper grapes of recent vintages have produced some interesting red wines.

Riesling
Fine vibrant wines, with distinctive lemony fruit and a purity of style that reflects perfectly any differences in soil and vineyard site. These wines can attain great richness, but they also always retain an underlying acidity.

Sylvaner
A straightforward, light-coloured, refreshing wine, often moderately priced, and pleasant to drink alone or with food.

CLASSIFICATIONS

Vin d'Alsace AC
This is the generic AC covering wines from any of the 8 permitted grape varieties. Great variation in yields and winemaking make it essential to choose one of the better producers.

Alsace Grand Cru AC
Fifty vineyard sites have now been recognized as regularly producing wines of quality and individuality. Only the 4 'noble' grape varieties may use this AC, and the maximum yield of 55 hl/ha, rarely attained, further enhances their character.

Main Grands Crus _____

Altenberg de Bergheim, Brand, Eichberg, Froehn, Furstentum, Geisberg, Goldert, Hengst, Kastelberg, Kessler, Kirchberg de Barr, Kirchberg de Ribeauvillé, Kitterlé, Mambourg, Moenchberg, Muenchberg, Osterberg, Pfersigberg, Rangen, Rosacker, Saering, Schlossberg, Schoenenbourg, Sommerberg, Sonnenglanz, Sporen, Steinert, Vorbourg, Wiebelsberg and Zotzenberg.

Vendange Tardive
Wine with a higher degree of natural sugar and greater concentration of flavours from one of the 4 'noble' varieties. Usually made from sweet, late-picked grapes and most wines will have residual sugar.

Sélection des Grains Nobles
Very sweet wines from botrytized grapes from the 4 'noble' varieties. Tiny quantities are made, and only from the best vineyards in the very top years.

Crémant d'Alsace
Good Champagne-method sparkling wines – the whites are usually from Pinot Blanc and the rosés from Pinot Noir.

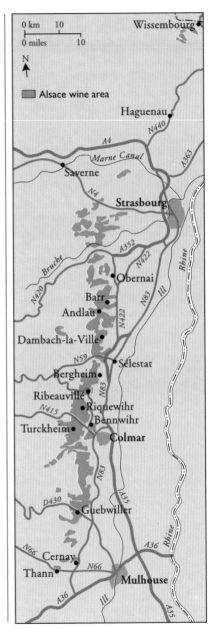

Alsace wine area

GREAT ALSACE WINES

Oz Clarke's selection

Pinot Gris Clos Jebsal ♀ (Zind-Humbrecht) Made in both sweet and relatively dry styles, this is a glorious demonstration of the Pinot Gris grape at its finest.

Gewurztraminer Rangen de Thann Clos St-Urbain ♀ (Zind-Humbrecht) Great vineyard producing a spicy, rich Gewurztraminer which explodes in the mouth.

Tokay Pinot Gris Furstentum ♀ (Mann) Superb, honeyed Pinot Gris with perfect balance right up to rich Sélection de Grains Nobles level.

Riesling Schlossberg ♀ (Paul Blanck) The Blanck family are some of Alsace's most inspired Riesling producers, each vineyard site thrillingly expressing its personality under their care.

Gewurztraminer ♀ (Charles Schléret) This grower has a most sensitive touch with dry wines of great perfume and intensity.

Gewurztraminer Kaefferkopf ♀ (Martin Schaetzel) Everything you could ever want from Gewurztraminer – lush, sensuous, heavily perfumed but perfectly balanced.

Riesling Schlossberg Ste-Cathérine ♀ (Weinbach) Few domaines in Alsace manage to blend so brilliantly the fundamental austerity of Riesling with depth, complexity and seductive aromas.

Muscat Spiegel ♀ (J P Dirler) A long-time favourite for the marvellous crunchy fresh fruit of the Muscat allied to an amazing ability to age.

Pinot Gris Hinterberg ♀ (Meyer-Fonné) Wonderful, luscious, honeyed fruit that retains its fresh balance despite awesome weight.

Riesling Muenchberg ♀ (Ostertag) New-wave winemaker producing impressive, honeyed Riesling.

Riesling Schoenenbourg ♀ (Marcel Deiss) Masterful expression of Riesling's ability to challenge the palate, yet caress it at the same time.

Steven Spurrier's selection

Pinot Auxerrois 'H' ♀ (Josmeyer) 50-year-old vines on the Grand Cru Hengst produce a marvel of peach, citrus and apricot fruit with minerally acidity.

Muscat Vorbourg Clos St-Landelin ♀ (Muré) A fabulous Muscat wine, heady and ripe, from vineyards facing due south.

Riesling Cuvée Frédéric-Émile ♀ (Trimbach) A fine, complex, serious Riesling, yet approachable quite young.

Riesling Clos Ste-Hune ♀ (Trimbach) The perfect Riesling: steely and minerally when young, yet developing complexity and power.

Riesling Vendange Tardive ♀ (Hugel) A classic Riesling, almost old-fashioned in avoiding explosive aromas.

Riesling Furstentum ♀ (Blanck) Definitive Riesling but richer and fatter than their Schlossberg Riesling.

Riesling Schlossberg Ste-Cathérine ♀ (Weinbach) Explosively expressive, yet a pure reflection of this marvellous Grand Cru.

Riesling Rangen de Thann Clos St-Urbain ♀ (Zind-Humbrecht) Rich, opulent, perfumed Riesling, from low yields in a great vineyard.

Pinot Gris Rangen de Thann Clos St-Urbain ♀ (Zind-Humbrecht) Rich and unctuous and, like the Riesling, the perfect explanation of grape variety and terroir.

Gewurztraminer Cuvée Anne Sélection de Grains Nobles ♀ (Schlumberger) A great example of this style.

Gewurztraminer Quintessence de Grains Nobles ♀ (Weinbach) Equally rich but less massive and more ethereal. An elixir.

Top Alsace producers _____

Merchants Jean-Baptiste ADAM, Léon BEYER, Dopff & Irion, DOPFF AU MOULIN, HUGEL, JOSMEYER, KUENTZ-BAS, Gustave Lorentz, A Seltz, Pierre Sparr, TRIMBACH, Willm.

Growers Lucien Albrecht, BARMÈS-BUECHER, Jean Becker, BLANCK, BOTT-GEYL, Albert BOXLER, BURN, Théo Cattin, DEISS, Jean-Pierre Dirler, Pierre Frick, André Hartmann, Alfred Heim, Bruno Hunold, KIENTZLER, KREYDENWEISS, Seppi Landmann, MANN, MEYER-FONNÉ, MITTNACHT-KLACK, MURÉ, OSTERTAG, Paul Reinhardt, SCHAETZEL, SCHLÉRET, SCHLUMBERGER, SCHOFFIT, Schueller, SIPP, SORG, Wantz, WEINBACH, ZIND-HUMBRECHT.

Co-operatives Cleebourg, Kientzheim-Kaysersberg, Pfaffenheim, Turckheim, Wolfberger.

JEAN-BAPTISTE ADAM, Ammerschwihr   03 89 78 23 21/03 89 47 35 91
A merchant with 100ha of his own vines, including Pinot Noir, making dry, lively wines which are best appreciated young. There is also very good Crémant d'Alsace.
Best wines ★★ Muscat Réserve ♀ and Crémant d'Alsace Extra Brut ♀, ★ Tokay-Pinot Gris Cuvée Jean-Baptiste ♀, and Pinot Noir ❢, Gewurztraminer Vendange Tardive ♀, and Riesling ♀
Best years 1998, '96, '95, '94, '90, '89, '88

BARMÈS-BUECHER, Wettolsheim   03 89 80 62 92/03 89 79 30 80
A fine estate with 15ha of vines including 3 Grands Crus (Hengst, Pfersigberg and Steingrubler) producing expansive, aromatic wines often retaining some residual sugar. Their Gewurztraminer is particularly good in this style.
Best wines ★★ Gewurztraminer Grand Cru Hengst Vendange Tardive ♀, Gewurztraminer Grand Cru Pfersigberg Vendange Tardive ♀ and Tokay-Pinot Gris Rosenberg Sélection de Grains Nobles ♀, ★ Tokay Pinot Gris Vendange Tardive ♀
Best years 1998, '96, '95, '94, '90, '89, '88

LÉON BEYER, Eguisheim   03 89 41 41 05/03 89 23 93 63
One of the best known families in Alsace (they have made wine since 1580), the Beyers supply most of their wines to top restaurants around the world. Their brand Comtes d'Eguisheim is very reliable and the Vendanges Tardives and Sélections de Grains Nobles are wines of real quality and repay at least 6–8 years of aging.
Best wines ★★ Tokay-Pinot Gris Vendange Tardive ♀, ★ Gewurztraminer Comtes d'Eguisheim ♀ and Riesling Cuvée Particulière ♀
Best years 1998, '96, '95, '94, '93, '90, '89, '88, '85, '83, '76

DOM. PAUL BLANCK, Kientzheim   03 89 78 23 56/03 89 47 16 45
A fine domaine of 30ha, painstakingly built up by Paul Blanck and his sons, Marcel and Bernard, and now run by their sons, Philippe and Frédéric. Their holdings of old vines (*vieilles vignes*) in the Grands Crus of Schlossberg and Furstentum produce some of the finest wines in Alsace that remain youthful for many years. The Blancks are a fine example of the dedication of Alsace families to their terroir.
Best wines ★★★ Riesling Grand Cru Schlossberg Vieilles Vignes ♀ and Riesling Grand Cru Furstentum Vieilles Vignes ♀, ★★ Pinot Auxerrois Vieilles Vignes ♀ and Gewurztraminer Grand Cru Furstentum Vieilles Vignes ♀, ★ Sylvaner Vieilles Vignes ♀
Best years 1998, '96, '95, '94, '93, '90

DOM. BOTT-GEYL, Beblenheim   03 89 47 90 04/03 89 47 97 33
This small domaine owns some superb Grand Cru vineyards and aims to pick the grapes at their ripest and then further increase the richness and depth by extended contact with the lees. In good vintages, the wines will have kept some residual sugar.
Best wines ★★ Gewurztraminer Grand Cru Sonnenglanz Vieilles Vignes ♀, Tokay-Pinot Gris Grand Cru Sonnenglanz ♀ and Riesling Grand Cru Mandelberg ♀
Best years 1998, '96, '95, '94, '90, '89, '88

ALBERT BOXLER, Niedermorschwihr   03 89 27 11 32/03 89 27 70 14
A small 10-ha domaine, but one of the best producers in the granite-based Grands Crus Brand and Sommerberg. The Rieslings are especially renowned for their finesse.

Best wines ★★ Riesling Grand Cru Brand ♀ and Riesling Grand Cru Sommerberg ♀
Best years 1998, '96, '95, '94, '90, '89, '88

DOM. ERNEST BURN, Gueberschwihr   03 89 49 20 68/03 89 49 28 56
Although the Burn family's domaine covers only 9ha of vines, they are important
owners in the Grand Cru Goldert, incuding all the Clos St-Imer, a terraced vineyard
on Goldert's upper slopes. Their wines have great concentration, without losing any
finesse. This is one of the rare domaines in Alsace specializing in Muscat. Always
impressive, in good years the wines can be exceptional.
Best wines ★★★ Muscat Grand Cru Goldert Clos St-Imer Cuvée de La Chapelle ♀,
★★ Riesling Grand Cru Goldert Clos St-Imer Cuvée de La Chapelle ♀ and Gewurztraminer
Grand Cru Goldert Clos St-Imer Cuvée de La Chapelle Vendange Tardive ♀
Best years 1998, '96, '95, '94, '90, '89, '88

MARCEL DEISS, Bergheim   03 89 73 63 37/03 89 73 32 67
Marcel Deiss is committed to allowing the terroir to express itself from every part of his
20-ha domaine (biodynamic since 1998) through low yields and brilliant winemaking.
Such is the quality of his Grand Cru wines that the lesser wines suffer unfairly in
comparison. This domaine has few rivals in Alsace for the quality of its Rieslings.
Best wines ★★★ Riesling Grand Cru Altenberg de Bergheim ♀ and Riesling Grand Cru
Schoenenbourg ♀, ★★ Pinot Noir Vieilles Vignes Burlenberg de Bergheim ❢, Pinot Gris Grand
Cru Altenberg de Bergheim ♀ and Gewurztraminer Grand Cru Altenberg de Bergheim ♀
Best years 1998, '96, '95, '94, '90, '89, '88, '85, '83, '76

DOPFF AU MOULIN, Riquewihr   03 89 47 92 23/03 89 47 83 61
This large grower-merchant, best-known for its Crémant d'Alsace, has recently
returned to form. Holdings in some of the best Grands Crus (Brand, Sporen and
Schoenenbourg) produce their most successful wines.
Best wines ★★ Gewurztraminer Grand Cru Sporen ♀, ★ Riesling Grand Cru
Schoenenbourg ♀ and Gewurztraminer Grand Cru Brand ♀
Best years 1998, '96, '95, '94, '90, '89, '88, '85, '83

HUGEL ET FILS, Riquewihr   03 89 47 92 15/03 89 49 00 10
This is probably the name wine-drinkers associate most readily with Alsace, thanks to
expert marketing. Run by an unbroken line of the family since 1639, this very
traditional grower-merchant is a by-word for quality in Alsace. Although it has vines in
Grands Crus, notably Sporen, the Hugel family prefers to label its wines according to
their own hierarchy: Tradition, Jubilee, Réserve Personelle and so on. Once at
Vendange Tardive or Sélection de Grains Nobles level, the quality is quite superb. The
patriarch, Johnny Hugel, is a vociferous defender of Alsace wines.
Best wines ★★★ Riesling Sélection de Grains Nobles ♀, Tokay-Pinot Gris Sélection de Grains
Nobles ♀ and Gewurztraminer Sélection de Grains Nobles ♀, ★★ Riesling Vendange Tardive ♀,
Tokay-Pinot Gris Vendange Tardive ♀ and Gewurztraminer Vendange Tardive ♀, ★ Pinot
Noir Jubilée Réserve Personnelle ❢, Riesling Jubilee ♀ and Tokay-Pinot Gris Jubilée ♀
Best years 1998, '96, '95, '94, '93, '90, '89, '88, '85, '83

JOSMEYER, Wintzenheim   03 89 27 91 90/03 89 27 91 99
Jean Meyer makes wines with delicacy and finesse that can be drunk young, but age
well. His holdings in the Grand Cru Hengst include some magnificent old Pinot

Auxerrois vines. He also makes the best Chasselas in the region, also from old vines.

Best wines ★★ Pinot Auxerrois Vieilles Vignes 'H' ♀, Riesling Les Pierrets ♀, Gewurztraminer Grand Cru Hengst ♀ and Chasselas ♀

Best years 1998, '96, '95, '94, '93, '90, '89, '88, '85, '83

ANDRÉ KIENTZLER, Ribeauvillé   03 89 73 67 10/03 89 73 35 81

From vines perfectly sited in 2 Grands Crus surrounding the town of Ribeauvillé, the epicentre of fine Riesling in Alsace, Kientzler makes wines with fine-tuned fruit and a certain austerity when young, which then show beautifully as they age. The Muscat Ottonel is a benchmark in the region for this fragile grape.

Best wines ★★ Riesling Grand Cru Geisberg ♀, ★ Pinot Auxerrois 'K' ♀ and Muscat Grand Cru Kirchberg ♀

Best years 1998, '96, '95, '94, '93, '90, '89, '88

MARC KREYDENWEISS, Andlau   03 88 08 95 83/03 88 08 41 16

From the northern section of the Alsace vineyards, these wines are finely chiselled and elegant. Since 1991, the entire domaine has been farmed organically, and now biodynamically, which adds to the wines' purity of expression and length of flavour.

Best wines ★★ Pinot Noir Andlau ❢, Pinot Gris Moenchberg ♀ and Riesling Kastelberg ♀, ★ Riesling Wiebelsberg ♀

Best years 1998, '96, '95, '94, '90, '89, '88, '85

KUENTZ-BAS, Husseren-les-Châteaux   03 89 49 30 24/03 89 49 23 39

A small grower-merchant producing quality throughout the range of wines. Wines from their own vineyards are labelled as Réserve Personnelle.

Best wines ★★ Pinot Gris Réserve Personnelle ♀, ★ Riesling Grand Cru Pfersigberg ♀ and Gewurztraminer Grand Cru Eichberg ♀

Best years 1998, '96, '95, '94, '90, '89, '88, '85

DOM. ALBERT MANN, Wettolsheim   03 89 80 62 00/03 89 80 34 23

With 19ha of vines, most of them situated in Grands Crus, this is currently one of the best domaines in Alsace. In lesser years the wines are bone dry, but when sugar levels permit, the natural ripeness of the grapes will produce more richness and concentration. Owned by Maurice and Jacky Barthelme.

Best wines ★★ Gewurztraminer Grand Cru Steingrubler ♀, Riesling Grand Cru Furstentum ♀ and Tokay-Pinot Gris Grand Cru Furstentum ♀

Best years 1998, '96, '95, '94, '90, '89, '88

MEYER-FONNÉ, Katzenthal   03 89 27 16 50/03 89 27 34 17

This small domaine produces consistently good wines with an emphasis on finesse. Félix Meyer is a rising star among Alsace winemakers.

Best wines ★★ Pinot Blanc Vieilles Vignes ♀ and Riesling Grand Cru Wineck-Schlossberg ♀

Best years 1998, '96, '95, '94, '90, '89, '88

DOM. MITTNACHT-KLACK, Riquewihr   03 89 47 92 54/03 89 47 89 50

This 10-ha estate has vines entirely on the best slopes of Riquewihr, Hunawihr and Ribeauvillé and produces finely aromatic wines very typical of their grape variety. Their richly complex Gewurztraminer is a speciality.

Best wines ★★ Riesling Grand Cru Schoenenbourg ♀ and Gewurztraminer Sporen ♀

Best years 1998, '96, '95, '94, '90, '89, '88

RENÉ MURÉ, Rouffach   03 89 78 58 00/03 89 78 58 01

Most of the 14ha owned by the Muré family are in the Grand Cru Vorbourg, where clayey-chalky soil produces opulent wines that age well. Even the lesser grape varieties from the Clos St-Landelin parcel within Vorbourg are fine and concentrated, the natural ripeness of grapes in the Clos very often reaching Vendange Tardive standards.

Best wines ★★★ Muscat Grand Cru Vorbourg Vendange Tardive, ♀ **★★** Pinot Gris Grand Cru Vorbourg Vendange Tardive ♀ and Riesling Grand Cru Vorbourg Vendange Tardive ♀, **★** Sylvaner Clos St-Landelin Cuvée Oscar ♀

Best years 1998, '96, '95, '94, '90, '89, '88

OSTERTAG, Epfig   03 88 85 51 34/03 88 85 58 95

André Ostertag has brought a creative artist's vision to his family domaine in the northern section of Alsace vineyards, making wines full of character that reflect his personality as much as the soil. Some of his Pinot Gris wines are vinified and matured in new oak *barriques*, a rarity in the region.

Best wines ★★ Riesling Grand Cru Muenchberg ♀ and Gewurztraminer Vignobles d'Epfig ♀, **★** Pinot Gris Barriques ♀

Best years 1998, '96, '95, '94, '93, '90, '89, '88, '85, '83

MARTIN SCHAETZEL, Ammerschwihr   03 89 47 11 39 /03 89 78 29 77

A tiny domaine of only 4.5ha whose output is increased by purchasing grapes from local growers, particularly in Ammerschwihr's Kaefferkopf vineyard. These very fine wines are fairly quick-maturing.

Best wines ★★ Riesling Kaefferkopf Cuvée Isabelle ♀ and Gewurztraminer Kaefferkopf Cuvée Catherine ♀, **★** Sylvaner Vieilles Vignes ♀

Best years 1998, '96, '95, '94, '90, '89, '88

CHARLES SCHLÉRET, Turckheim   Tel 03 89 27 06 09

A fine domaine whose best wines come from the Grand Cru Herrenweg.

Best wines ★★ Riesling Grand Cru Herrenweg Cuvée Prestige ♀, Muscat d'Alsace VV ♀ and Gewurztraminer Grand Cru Herrenweg Cuvée Spéciale ♀

Best years 1998, '96, '95, '94, '90, '89, '88

DOM. SCHLUMBERGER, Guebwiller   03 89 74 27 00/03 89 74 85 75

The largest domaine in Alsace with 140ha of vines, Schlumberger is family-owned and based in the south of the region. Grand Cru wines, from its own spectacularly steeply terraced vineyards, are far superior to the basic Alsace AC wines. Each vintage of Cuvée Anne (Sélection de Grains Nobles) and Cuvée Christine (Vendage Tardive) becomes a collector's item.

Best wines ★★★ Gewurztraminer Grand Cru Cuvée Anne Sélection de Grains Nobles ♀ and Gewurztraminer Cuvée Christine Vendange Tardive ♀, **★★** Gewurztraminer Grand Cru Kessler ♀, **★** Pinot Gris Grand Cru Kitterlé ♀ and Riesling Grand Cru Saering ♀

Best years 1998, '96, '95, '94, '93, '90, '89, '88, '85, '83, '76

DOMAINE SCHOFFIT, Colmar   03 89 24 41 14/03 89 41 40 52

This 15-ha domaine is based just outside Colmar but Schoffit's best vineyards are further south in the Grand Cru Rangen outside Thann and rival in quality those of ZIND-HUMBRECHT, the other major owner in this Grand Cru. Very low yields produce wines with intensity as well as elegance. They age magnificently.

Best wines ★★★ Pinot Gris Grand Cru Rangen de Thann Clos St-Théobald ♀, ★★ Muscat Cuvée Alexandre ♀ and Pinot Gris Cuvée Alexandre ♀

Best years 1998, '96, '95, '94, '90, '89, '88

JEAN SIPP, Ribeauvillé   03 89 73 60 02/03 89 73 82 38

One of the first producers in Alsace to use organic viticulture. The wines reflect the essence of their terroir as well as their grape variety.

Best wines ★★ Tokay-Pinot Gris Trottacker ♀ and Riesling Grand Cru Kirchberg de Ribeauvillé ♀

Best years 1998, '96, '95, '94, '90, '89, '88

BRUNO SORG, Eguisheim   03 89 41 80 85/03 89 41 22 64

A high-quality domaine, whose wines are true examples of their particular grape variety and Cru, balancing alcohol and acidity to achieve great purity of expression.

Best wines ★★ Muscat Grand Cru Pfersigberg ♀ and Gewurztraminer Grand Cru Eichberg ♀

Best years 1998, '96, '95, '94, '90, '89, '88

F E TRIMBACH, Ribeauvillé   03 89 73 60 30/03 89 73 89 04

Admired above all for its Rieslings, Trimbach is one of the finest grower-merchants in Alsace. The house style is dry to the point of crispness, which allows the wines to accompany food more easily than some of Alsace's more weighty wines without sacrificing fruit and flavour. The personality of the grape and the terroir comes to affirm itself over time. Clos Ste-Hune is Alsace's definitive Riesling.

Best wines ★★★ Riesling Clos Ste-Hune ♀, ★★ Riesling Cuvée Frédéric-Émile ♀, Pinot Gris Réserve Personelle ♀ and Gewurztraminer Cuvée des Seigneurs de Ribeaupierre ♀

Best years 1998, '96, '95, '94, '93, '90, '89, '88, '85, '83

WEINBACH, Kaysersberg   03 89 47 13 21/03 89 47 38 18

One of the most famous domaines in Alsace, admirably managed by Colette Faller and her two daughters, of whom the younger, Laurence, now makes the wine. The granite soils of Kaysersberg and Kientzheim help ripen the grapes earlier, so acidity is not lost. The wines are supremely elegant and show their quality early on.

Best wines ★★★ Riesling Grand Cru Schlossberg Ste-Cathérine ♀, Gewurztraminer Quintessence de Grains Nobles ♀, ★★ Pinot Gris Ste-Cathérine ♀, Gewurztraminer Cuvée Laurence ♀, Riesling Cuvée Théo ♀ and Muscat Réserve ♀

Best years 1998, '96, '95, '94, '93, '90, '89, '88, '85

ZIND-HUMBRECHT, Turckheim   03 89 27 02 05/03 89 27 22 58

Léonard Humbrecht is the great name in post-war Alsace. He was the first grower in Alsace to understand that the terroir was of equal importance to grape variety. His insistence on the special qualities of his soil in the Rangen, Hengst and Brand vineyards paved the way for the creation of the Grand Cru system in Alsace. Based in Turckheim, this domaine has the finest vineyards in Alsace, from which it obtains reduced yields to concentrate quality. Léonard's son, Olivier, the first Master of Wine in France, is as brilliant a winemaker as was his famous father.

Best wines ★★★ Riesling Clos Windsbuhl ♀, Gewurztraminer Grand Cru Hengst ♀, Pinot Gris Grand Cru Rangen de Thann ♀, Riesling Grand Cru Rangen de Thann Clos St-Urbain ♀ and Pinot Gris Clos Jebsal ♀

Best years 1998, '96, '95, '94, '93, '90, '89, '88, '85, '83

ALSACE VINTAGES

Alsace's very dry climate gives it an advantage over the rest of France in that the vintages are very rarely 'rained off'. Perhaps the only drawback of the climate is that the vines may overproduce, leading to dilution of quality through high yields, but the better producers prepare against this.

Aging qualities

Wines from the 'minor' Alsace grape varieties – Sylvaner, Pinot Blanc, Pinot Auxerrois and Pinot Noir – are generally best drunk at 1–4 years, but exceptions abound: late-harvest Auxerrois and wood-aged Pinot Noir being the best examples.

Muscat is best drunk young to appreciate its grapy charm, but more concentrated versions will improve for 2–3 years. Riesling is the most long-lived grape in Alsace, perhaps the world, and the only one that really needs at least 5 years to show its true complexity. Recent tastings have shown that Rieslings can keep their freshness for half a century. Both Gewurztraminer and Pinot Gris wines,

due to their intrinsic lack of acidity, show well young, but the better ones have the natural sugar and concentration to last for a decade or more.

No chaptalization is allowed for Vendange Tardive and Sélection de Grains Nobles wines. The extra intensity and higher natural degree of alcohol of Vendange Tardive wines means that they need 2–3 years to fully open up (more for Riesling) and will continue to improve over the next 10 years. Sélection de Grains Nobles are some of the most concentrated wines in the world, the very high sugar content allowing them to be appreciated early, while the high acidity will preserve them for 25 years, and beyond.

Maturity charts _____

Along with the rest of northern France, 1996 was a good year for Alsace. The long, dry autumn allowed producers to wait until the grapes were fully ripe. The wines are classic in style, including superb Riesling, allowing it to show the maximum fruit, while enhancing the evidence of terroir.

1996 Gewurztraminer

1996 Riesling Grand Cru

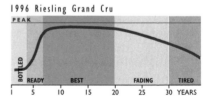

VINTAGE CHART

	99	98	97	96	95	94	93	91	90	89	88	85	83
Riesling (esp. Grand Cru)	7○	7○	7◐	8◑	7○	6●	6●	6◐	9●	8○	9●	9●	9●
Gewurztraminer	7○	8○	7●	8◑	7●	7●	5●	5●	9●	9●	9●	9●	9●
Pinot Gris	7○	7○	7●	8◑	7●	7●	5●	5●	9●	10●	9●	9●	9●

KEY ○= needs more time   ◑= ready but will improve   ●= at peak   ◐= fading or tired

VINTAGES AT A GLANCE

Alsace's clement climate and the wide range of grape varieties with their different ripening patterns means that even in poor years it is very rare to have a vintage that is an all-round disappointment.

Great Years ★★★	1996, '90, '88, '85, '83, '76
Good Years ★★	1999, '98, '97, '95, '94, '89, '71
Moderate Years ★	1999, '97, '93, '91, '86, '82
Poor Years (No Stars)	1992, '87, '84

Annual vintage reports

1999★-★★ A cool, wet summer was saved by a warm, dry September. A very large crop meatnt that only serious growers with well-managed sites produced wines with proper concentration.

1998★★ Good vintage but high yields and fairly quick-maturing. Many first-rate Rieslings and some late-harvest wines.

1997★-★★ High degrees at vintage time hid a lack of concentration. These are pretty wines with up-front fruit.

1996★★★ A normal flowering, except for Gewurztraminer, which suffered from the wet spring. An early October harvest followed a year with less heat than 1995, the wines combining the richness of a warm vintage with the austerity of a cool one. Very fine results, especially Riesling.

1995★★ A very late flowering and a cold summer resulted in a late vintage, which was particularly good in Pinot Gris and Gewurztraminer. Fine, concentrated wines, many with high sugars.

1994★★ In contrast to the rest of France, Alsace had a rapid, early flowering, a hot summer and a cool autumn. A large vintage of very good ripeness, the best wines being those harvested late.

1993★ A very hot, dry summer, followed by rain at the end of August that refreshed the vines and also added to the crop. Quality was uneven, with Muscat and Gewurztraminer doing best.

1992 A hot, almost tropical summer was followed by a very wet September. A difficult vintage, where it paid to be patient. Many wines were dilute, but the late-harvest wines were more successful.

1991★ A difficult year owing to spring frost affecting the quantity and a cold summer affecting the ripening, Nevertheless, some fine wines were made.

1990★★★ A dry summer of almost tropical heat, with very little rain, right through to beyond a normal vintage date. Over-ripening or blocked ripening caused heavy losses for Gewurztraminer and Muscat, but some superb Rieslings were made, which will last well. Many quality Vendange Tardive wines were made, but it was too dry to produce much botrytis.

1989★★ An early flowering was followed by a warm, humid summer and autumn. An overall lack of consistency in this vintage where total ripeness, even botrytis, came early, producing rich, opulent wines.

1988★★★ A textbook vintage, with the right weather at the right time, resulting in a medium-size crop of well-balanced, concentrated wines that will last.

1987 A difficult vintage.

1986★ A vintage of good, average quality.

1985★★★ A good volume crop of healthy grapes provided wines of excellent fruit and balance and the best will still keep a while longer.

1983★★★ A very good year, with all the concentration that had been lacking in 1982. Superb late-harvest wines, but too much production to be good overall.

Other good years 1976 and '71.

THE LOIRE VALLEY

The Loire is the longest river in France, rising in the Massif Central, and joining the Atlantic Ocean 1000 km later at Nantes. More than 80,000ha of vines are grown here in this temperate climate to produce some 450 million bottles of wine each year.

Wine styles

Virtually every style of wine is found in the Loire: from the driest whites to extraordinarily long-lived, rich, honeyed desssert wines; from light, fruity reds for early drinking, to more serious reds; from rosés to fine sparkling wine. The river rises in the Auvergne, on the same latitude as Beaujolais, so it is not surprising that Gamay is widely planted here. As it winds northward, the Burgundy grapes, Pinot Noir, Chardonnay and Aligoté, are found alongside Sauvignon Blanc. As the river enters the Nivernais, the beginning of what is recognized as the proper Loire Valley, Pinot Noir is still found but Sauvignon Blanc is now the dominant grape. When the river turns westward at Orléans, it enters Touraine and château country, and vines are planted with hardly a break on both banks right to Nantes. Touraine whites show the change from Sauvignon to Chenin Blanc, and Pinot Noir disappears in favour of the Cabernet family. Gamay and Chardonnay are also widely planted. The finest red wines come from Chinon and Bourgueil and the best whites from Montlouis and Vouvray.

As the river enters Anjou, the style changes again. With the exception of Saumur-Champigny and Anjou-Villages, the reds become less interesting, the rosés are well-known, but white wines from Savennières, Bonnezeaux, Coteaux du Layon and Quarts de Chaume, all from Chenin Blanc and mostly very sweet, are the jewels of the Loire.

In the Pays Nantais the wines are dry and almost exclusively white, the most famous wine being Muscadet.

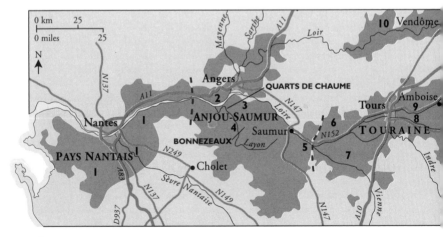

GRAPE VARIETIES

Cabernet Franc
More fragrant than Cabernet Sauvignon, this grape makes wine with a fine, deep carmine colour, a delightful aroma of raspberries or violets and a firm, fruit finish. In the Loire Valley, this grape is at its best in Touraine and Anjou.

Cabernet Sauvignon
Plays second fiddle to Cabernet Franc in Anjou, and rarely ripens fully.

Chenin Blanc
Known locally as Pineau de la Loire, this underrated grape produces fine, complex wines in the Loire Valley, ranging from a lemony dryness to a luscious richness. In good vintages, the grapes may become botrytized, to produce rich sweet wines to rival a classed growth Sauternes or an Alsace Sélection de Grains Nobles.

Cot
Makes firm, fruity wines, with more character than charm. Better known in Bordeaux and Argentina as Malbec.

Gamay
In the Loire, this variety produces very attractive, fruity red wines for drinking young, with less alcohol than those from Beaujolais.

Melon de Bourgogne
The single grape used for Muscadet, now synonymous with this appellation.

Pineau d'Aunis
Planted in Touraine and Anjou as a blending grape for red wines, but more successful on its own as a rosé.

Pinot Noir
The noble grape of Burgundy also makes attractively fruity red and rosé Sancerre, Reuilly and Menetou-Salon.

Sauvignon Blanc
This variety is at its most marked in the Loire Valley. It has an aggressively fruity redcurrant/gooseberry aroma, sometimes grassy and herbaceous, typified in the popular wines of Sancerre and Pouilly-Fumé, with their crisp, acidic finish.

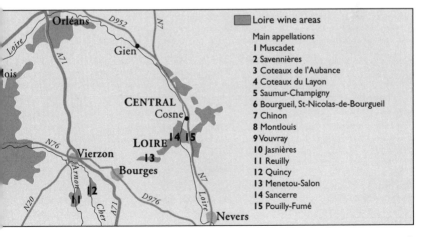

GREAT LOIRE WINES

Oz Clarke's selection

Coteaux du Layon-St-Aubin Cuvée Marie Jauby ♀ (Baudoin) A world class sweet wine from an exciting grower at Coteaux du Layon-St-Aubin making wines of intense concentration.

Coteaux du Layon-St-Aubin Cuvée Eléanore ♀ (Cady) Almost aggressively rich wine from another outstanding St-Aubin grower.

Saumur Blanc ♀ (Clos Rougeard) Primarily makers of excellent red Saumur-Champigny, but now also producing the acme of dry Chenin – ripe but balanced and perfumed with goldengage and nectarine.

Quarts de Chaume ♀ (Joseph Renou) Classic, slow-developing sweet wine of great syrupy intensity and high natural acid from the Layon Valley.

Coteaux du Layon ♀ (Claude Branchereau) Rich, powerful sweet wines that reach their perfumed peak with Cuvée des Forges and Les Onnis.

Anjou Chavigné Sec ♀ (Richou) For some time the maker of good sweet Coteaux de l'Aubance and fine Anjou Villages reds. Now making some of Anjou's greatest dry whites.

Vouvray ♀ (Ch. Gaudrelle) Producer of fine, dry Vouvray whose top sweet wines,

under the labels of Réserve Spéciale and Réserve Personelle, are thrilling drinks.

Vouvray ♀ (Champalou) Excellent Vouvray wines ranging from bone dry and assertive through to deep syrupy sweet examples perfumed with apple blossom and smooth as lanolin.

Vouvray ♀ (Aubusières) Traditional producer of single-vineyard Vouvrays – sensational when sweet, but in some vintages even better when Demi-Sec, showing a memorable mix of honey, quince and a sprinkling of salt.

Sancerre ♀ (Lucien Crochet) Classic, tangy Sancerre, ripe yet acid and full of gooseberry, coffeebean and watercress freshness.

Steven Spurrier's selection

Savennières Becherelle ♀ (Ch. de la Roche-aux-Moines) Nicolas Joly was the precursor of biodynamic viticulture in France and his white Chenin Blanc wines now have a complexity and length beyond compare, lasting for decades.

Bonnezeaux ♀ (de Fesles) The finest estate in this

undervalued tiny sweet wine AC, making sublimely honeyed wine from incredibly low yields.

Quarts de Chaume ♀ (Baumard) Classically rich, wines from this historic AC.

Vouvray Moelleux ♀ (Clos Naudin) One of the finest Vouvrays: floral, unctuous, but never heavy.

Vouvray Clos du Bourg Sec ♀ (Huet) White wine with incredible purity and depth of flavour owing to biodynamic viticulture allied to brilliant winemaking.

Sancerre Chavignol La Grande Côte ♀ (Cotat) Not a modern style of Sancerre, but the finest expression of the terroir and with excellent aging potential.

Pouilly-Fumé ♀ (Tracy) One of Pouilly's grand old estates, producing a wine of breed and elegance.

Bourgueil Grand Mont ! (Druet) Although a relative newcomer, Pierre-Jacques Druet is recognized as the best grower in Bourgueil.

Chinon Les Varennes du Grand Clos ! (Joguet) The finest, most long-lived Chinon from one of the Loire's most famous estates.

Touraine Premières Vendanges ! (La Charmoise) The purest expression of the Gamay grape in Touraine, perhaps in all France.

Top Loire appellations _____

Red wines Anjou-Villages, Bourgueil, Chinon, St-Nicolas-de-Bourgueil, Sancerre, Saumur-Champigny.

White wines Chinon, Jasnières, Menetou-Salon, Montlouis, Muscadet des Coteaux de la Loire, Muscadet Côtes de Grand Lieu, Muscadet de Sèvre-et-Maine, Pouilly-Fumé, Sancerre, Saumur, Savennières, Vouvray.

Rosé wines Anjou Rosé, Bourgueil, Chinon, Sancerre.

Sweet wines Bonnezeaux, Coteaux de l'Aubance, Coteaux du Layon, Jasnières, Montlouis, Quarts de Chaume, Savennières, Vouvray.

Sparkling wines Montlouis, Vouvray.

ANJOU AC, ANJOU-VILLAGES AC

Anjou is the regional AC for a range of red, white and rosé wines. Semi-sweet and sweet rosés are AC Cabernet d'Anjou or Rosé d'Anjou and the best white wines have their own ACs. The best reds, made only from Cabernets Franc and Sauvignon, come under the newish Anjou-Villages AC; in good years these wines can age for 3–4 years.

Best producers du Closel, de FESLES, Jean-Yves Lebreton, Lecointre, OGEREAU, de Passavant, PIERRE-BISE, de Putille, RICHOU, des Rochettes.

Best years 1999, '98, '97, '96, '95.

BONNEZEAUX AC

Some of the Loire's finest sweet whites are produced here from Chenin Blanc. Past quality was high enough to earn Bonnezeaux Grand Cru status in the Coteaux du Layon appellation, yet only in the 1990s have conscientious growers begun to make the most of their superb terroir.

Best producers de FESLES, GODINEAU, Petits Quarts, Petit Val, RENOU.

Best years 1999, '97, '96, '95, '94, '93, '90, '89, '88, '85, '83, '78, '76, '71, '64, '59, '47, '21.

BOURGUEIL AC

Red and some refreshing rosé wines made mainly from Cabernet Franc. In the past, these were rustic wines with high acidity, but dedicated growers, helped by good vintages and increasing demand, are now achieving more depth and fruit. In good vintages, Bourgueil can age like a Médoc.

Best producers AMIRAULT, Thierry Boucard, Breton, de la Butte, Chevalière, Max Cognard, Delaunay, DRUET, Lamé-Delille-Boucard, des Raguenières.

Best years 1999, '98, '97, '96, '95, '93, '90, '89, '88, '86.

CHINON AC

The largest of the red Loire appellations, Chinon is also the best known. A tiny amount of crisp white wine is made from Chenin Blanc, and a little rosé, but its fame comes from the aromatic, elegant red wines that show Cabernet Franc's fruit and the quality of the terroir to perfection.

Best producers ALLIET, Bernard BAUDRY, COULY-DUTHEIL, Jean-Marie Dozon, de la Grille, JOGUET, de Ligré, Dom. du Raifault, Olga Raffault.

Best years 1999, '98, '97, '96, '95, '93, '90, '89, '88, '85, '83, '82, '78.

COTEAUX DE L'AUBANCE AC

Semi-sweet and sweet Chenin white from vines along the banks of the river Aubance. The wines are more lively than Coteaux du Layon, but of almost equal quality. Production has been falling in favour of dry white wines, which are sold under the Anjou label.

Best producers Bablut, Jean-Yves Lebreton, Montgilet, RICHOU.

Best years 1999, '98, '97, '96, '95, '94, '93, '90, '89, '88.

COTEAUX DU LAYON AC

After the superb vintages of 1997, '96, '95, '90, and '89, combined with a new generation of winemakers, this appellation for semi-sweet and sweet wines from Chenin Blanc is undergoing a renaissance. The fully ripe grapes are ideally affected by botrytis, to make a pale golden wine with a summery, honeyed, spicy bouquet and sweet but not generally cloying finish. High natural sugars allow the wines to age superbly for 20 or more years. The best communes – Beaulieu, Chaume (the finest), Faye, Rablay, Rochefort, St-Aubin and St-Lambert – can now use the Coteaux du Layon-Villages AC.

Best producers Pierre Aguilas, Patrick Baudoin, de la Bergerie, Branchereau, du Breuil, Cady, DELESVAUX, de la Genaiserie, GODINEAU, OGEREAU, PIERRE-BISE, PITHON, des Rochettes, de la Roulerie, des SABLONNETTES, Soucherie, la Varière.

Best years 1999, '98, '97, '96, '95, '94, '93, '90, '89, '88, '85, '83, '76, '75, '59, '47, '21.

JASNIÈRES AC
Mainly dry but also semi-sweet or *moelleux* whites from a small Chenin Blanc appellation. In good years, Jasnières can rival the honey and flowers of Vouvray.

Best producers de Cézin, Joël Gigou, Jean-Jacques Maillet.

Best years 1998, '97, '96, '95, '93, '90, '89.

MENETOU-SALON AC
From near Bourges, these are mainly attractive Sauvignon whites, with some fresh and fruity Pinot Noir reds and rosés.

Best producers de Chatenoy, Jean-Paul Gilbert, Henri Pellé.

Best years 1999, '98, '97, '96, '95.

MONTLOUIS AC
Dry, semi-sweet, sweet and sparkling Chenin Blanc wines that resemble, and sometimes rival, those of Vouvray, though ripening the grapes can be more difficult.

Best producers Berger (Dom. des Liards), Chidaine, Olivier Delétang, Christian Galliot, Levasseur, TAILLE AUX LOUPS.

Best years 1999, '98, '97, '96, '95, '90, '89, '88, '86, '85.

MUSCADET ACs
South of Nantes 3 ACs (Muscadet des Coteaux de la Loire, de Sèvre-et-Maine and Côtes de Grand Lieu) produce the best Muscadet. This dry white wine, from grapes harvested early to keep as much freshness and fruit as possible, has finesse and a crisp, dry finish. The top wines use the traditional method of bottling (*sur lie*) and have the most character.

Best producers Beaurenard, du Cléray, des Dorices, Jean Douillard, de l'ÉCU, de la Galissonière, de Goulaine, Guindon, Métaireau, Henri Poiron, de la Preuille, de la Ragotière.

Best years 1999, '98, '97, '96, '95.

POUILLY-FUMÉ AC
These bone-dry whites, from Sauvignon grown on chalky clay soil with a touch of limestone, are more elegant than Sancerre and improve in bottle for 2–3 years.

Best producers Henri Bourgeois, Cailbourdin, Jean-Claude Chatelain, Didier DAGUENEAU, Jean-Claude Dagueneau, de Favray, Pascal Jolivet, Masson-Blondelet, du Nozet, Saget, TRACY.

Best years 1999, '98, '97, '96, '95, '93, '90.

MAKING THE DESSERT WINES OF THE LOIRE EVEN RICHER
There is a trend, particularly among the younger generation of growers in the best areas of Anjou, to pick as late as possible, berry by berry, to retain extraordinary levels of natural sugar in the grapes. The wines of Quarts de Chaume, Bonnezeaux and Coteaux du Layon have always, in good years, been honeyed and luscious, but this new band of growers, known by their detractors as Les Chasseurs de Sucre or 'Sugar Hunters', are intent in pushing ripeness and concentration to the maximum, as far as an Alsace Sélection de Grains Nobles or Riesling Trockenbeerenauslese, and even further. However, at this point, the natural lemony acidity of Chenin Blanc is lost and some wines have difficulty in fermenting, leaving the liquid as more of a syrup than a wine. These 'super wines' have attracted a good deal of interest from wine lovers and command exceptionally high prices, which is good for the region as well as for the risk-taking producer, but they can only be made in the best vintages.

QUARTS DE CHAUME AC

Tiny AC for fully sweet wine from Chenin Blanc to a maximum yield of 22 hectolitres (under 3000 bottles per hectare), the lowest in France. There has been a resurgence of interest in these rich, honeyed wines, which, in great vintages, have few rivals in the world.

Best producers BAUMARD, BELLERIVE, Laffourcade, des Maurières, PIERRE-BISE, RENOU, Suronde.

Best years 1999, '97, '96, '95, '94, '93, '90, '89, '88, '85, '83, '81, '78, '76, '70, '69, '66, '64, '59, '47.

ST-NICOLAS-DE-BOURGUEIL AC

An enclave within the greater BOURGUEIL AC making reds that are generally lighter and less long-lived than Bourgueil itself.

Best producers Max Cognard, Mabileau.

Best years 1999, '98, '97, '96, '95, '90, '89.

SANCERRE AC

One of the best-known wines of France, Sancerre is almost 90% white, from Sauvignon Blanc; the rest are Pinot Noir reds and rosés. The dry white wine is recognized as a benchmark expression of the grape worldwide. Openly fruity, with good acidity, it has more obvious fruit than Pouilly-Fumé, but ages less well. The most expressive wines come from the communes of Chavignol, Bué and Verdigny and the town of Sancerre itself.

Best producers Bailly-Reverdy, Balland-Chapuis, Philippe de Benoist, Henri Bourgeois, Cherrier, COTAT, CROCHET, Vincent Delaporte, Gitton, MELLOT, de Montigny, Vincent Pinard, Prieur, Jean Reverdy, Jean-Max Roger, Vacheron.

Best years 1999, '98, '97, '96, '95, '90.

SAUMUR-CHAMPIGNY AC

Red wine from Cabernet Franc planted on the best limestone-chalk soils on the left bank of the Loire east of Saumur. These wines have a fine aroma of crushed raspberries and generous fruit and depth. The Parisians love this wine, so plantings have increased to more than 1300ha and quality is high. The dry white wine, sold as AC Saumur Blanc, can also be excellent and is best drunk at 1–3 years.

Best producers Cave des Vignerons de Saumur, de Chaintre, CLOS ROUGEARD, Filliatreau, du HUREAU, René-Noël Legrand, de la Paleine, ROCHES NEUVES, de Targé, de VILLENEUVE.

Best years 1999, '98, '97, '96, '95, '90, '89.

SAVENNIÈRES AC

On the right bank of the Loire west of Angers Chenin Blanc makes dry or semi-sweet whites. A good Savennières has some honey and spice on the nose, is dry and firm when young, and needs up to 20 years' bottle age. There are 2 Grand Cru vineyards with their own ACs: la Coulée-de-Serrant and la Roche-aux-Moines.

Best producers BAUMARD, la Bizolière, de CHAMBOUREAU, CLOS ROUGEARD, Closel, d'ÉPIRÉ, aux Moines, PIERRE-BISE, de la ROCHE-AUX-MOINES.

Best years 1999, '98, '97, '96, '95, '93, '90, '89, '88, '85, '83, '82, '78, '76, '71, '70, '67, '66.

VOUVRAY AC

These dry, semi-sweet (*moelleux*) and sweet wines are known worldwide, but the fine sparkling wine is rarely exported. All Vouvray has a floral, honeysuckle aroma, even the dry wines, becoming richer as the wines get sweeter, but never losing Chenin's typical lemony acidity. The finest wines can age for 50 years or more.

Best producers Allias, AUBUISIÈRES, Brisebarre, Champalou, CLOS BAUDOIN, CLOS NAUDIN, Clos de Nouys, Ch. Gaudrelle, HUET, F Mabille, Pichot.

Best years 1998, '97, '96, '95, '93, '90, '89, '88, '85, '83, '78, '76, '75, '70, '59, '47, '21.

A–Z OF LOIRE PRODUCERS

PHILIPPE ALLIET, Cravant-les-Coteaux   02 47 93 17 62

This small estate, now expanded to 9ha of Cabernet Franc, produces deep-fruited wines.
Best wines ★★ Chinon Coteaux de Noire ❗, ★ Chinon Vieilles Vignes ❗
Best years 1999, '98, '97, '96, '95, '90, '89, '88

YANNICK AMIRAULT, Bourgueil   02 47 97 78 07/02 47 97 94 78

Wines of complexity and class from a well-kept, 16-ha estate.
Best wines ★★ Bourgueil Le Grand Clos ❗ and St-Nicolas-de-Bourgueil Les Malgagnes ❗
Best years 1999, '98, '97, '96, '95, '90, '89, '88

DOM. DES AUBUISIÈRES, Vouvray   02 47 52 61 55/02 47 52 67 81

A highly regarded estate, run by Bernard Fouquet, with a devotion to quality.
Best wines ★★★ Vouvray Moelleux Le Marigny ♀, ★★ Vouvray Sec Le Marigny ♀
Best years 1998, '97, '96, '95, '93, '90, '89, '88

BERNARD BAUDRY, Cravant-les-Coteaux   02 47 93 15 79/02 47 98 44 44

A superb 25-ha estate with vines in the best parts of Cravant producing rich, fruity wines.
Best wines ★★ Chinon Signature ❗ and Chinon Les Grézeaux ❗, ★ Chinon Les Granges ❗
Best years 1999, '98, '97, '96, '95, '90, '89

DOM. DES BAUMARD, Rochefort-sur-Loire   .   02 41 78 70 03/02 41 78 83 82

Family-owned 44-ha estate with several centuries' experience of making high-quality
wine. Current vintages have been exemplary for these rare white wines.
Best wines ★★ Savennières Clos du Papillon ♀, Savennières Clos St-Yves ♀, Quarts de
Chaume ♀ and Coteaux du Layon Clos de Ste-Cathérine ♀
Best years 1999, '98, '97, '96, '95, '90, '89, '88, '85, '83, '82, '78, '76, '71, '69, '66

CH. BELLERIVE, Rochefort-sur-Loire   02 41 78 33 66/02 41 78 68 47

For many years owned by the Lalanne family and still managed by Jacques Lalanne,
this estate, with 100% Chenin Blanc vines, is rediscovering its former glory.
Best wine ★★ Quarts de Chaume ♀   **Best years** 1999, '98, '97, '96, '95, '90, '89, '88

CH. DE CHAMBOUREAU, Savennières   02 41 77 20 04/02 41 77 27 78

A substantial estate for this AC, run by Pierre Soulez, a member of a renowned local
winemaking family. It produces fine examples of the style.
Best wines ★★ Savennières-Roches aux Moines Chevalier Buhard ♀, ★ Savennières ♀
Best years 1999, '98, '97, '96, '95, '90, '89, '88

DOM. DE LA CHARMOISE, Soings   02 54 98 70 73/02 54 98 75 66

Henri Marionnet makes brilliant Gamay and Sauvignon wines. As well as being the
king of *en primeur* wines in Touraine, he is the leading researcher into Gamay.
Best wines ★★ Touraine Premières Vendanges ❗, Touraine M de Marionnet ♀, Touraine
Gamay Dom. de la Charmoise ❗ and Gamay Vinifera ❗
Best years 1999, '98, '97, '96, '95

CLOS BAUDOIN, Vouvray   02 47 52 71 02/02 47 52 60 94

A splendid 19-ha property, enclosed by walls (*clos* means a walled vineyard in French).
Meticulously managed by Prince Philippe Poniatowski, it is famous for its old vintages.
Best wines ★★★ Vouvray Moelleux Clos Baudoin ♀, ★★ Vouvray Aigle Blanc ♀
Best years 1998, '97, '96, '95, '93, '90, '89, '88, '85, '82, '78, '76, '64, '61, '59, '47

DOM. DU CLOS NAUDIN, Vouvray   02 47 52 71 46/02 47 52 73 81
The Foreau family produce some of the greatest wines of France from their perfectly situated 12ha of vines. Depending on the vintage a range of styles is made.
Best wines ★★★ Vouvray Demi-Sec ♀ and Vouvray Moelleux Réserve ♀, ★★ Vouvray Sec ♀
Best years 1998, '97, '96, '95, '93, '90, '89, '88, '85, '82, '78, '76, '64, '61, '59, '47

CLOS ROUGEARD, Chacé   02 41 52 92 65/02 41 52 98 34
This Saumur estate is impeccably managed by the Foucault brothers, who have had considerable influence in the region, particularly with their white wines.
Best wines ★★★ Coteaux de Saumur Liquoreux ♀ and Saumur-Champigny Les Poyeux ❗,
★★ Saumur Blanc ♀
Best years 1999, '98, '97, '96, '95, '90, '89, '88

COTAT FRÈRES, Sancerre   02 48 54 04 22/02 48 78 01 41
This minute 1.5-ha domaine makes Sancerres of incredible complexity from very low grape yields, with excellent aging potential. Great vintages will easily keep for 10 years or more, thus defying the view that Sauvignon Blanc should be drunk young.
Best wines ★★★ Sancerre La Grande Côte ♀ and Sancerre Les Monts Damnés ♀
Best years 1999, '98, '97, '96, '95, '90, '89, '88, '85

DOM. COULY-DUTHEIL, Chinon   02 47 97 20 20/02 47 97 20 25
The Couly-Dutheil family has been upholding the finest traditions of this large Chinon merchant house for generations and the quality level is always high, even though Couly-Dutheil is responsible for 10% of the Chinon appellation. The domaine uses its own vineyards for their top wines, particularly Clos de l'Écho.
Best wines ★★★ Chinon Clos de l'Écho ❗, ★★ Chinon Domaine René Couly ❗, ★ Chinon Les Gravières ❗ and Chinon Blanc ♀
Best years 1999, '98, '97, '96, '95, '90, '89, '88, '86, '85, '83, '82, '76

LUCIEN CROCHET, Bué   02 48 54 08 10/02 48 54 27 66
A fine Sancerre estate with 25ha of Sauvignon Blanc and 8ha of Pinot Noir.
Best wines ★★ Sancerre Prestige ♀❗   **Best years** 1999, '98, '97, '96, '95, '90

DIDIER DAGUENEAU, St-Andelin   03 86 39 15 62/03 86 39 07 61
Very complex wines with a high proportion of new wood for both fermentation and aging, from an iconoclast winemaker in Pouilly-Fumé who has done much to raise quality levels in a far too complacent region. Quality is high but so are the prices.
Best wines ★★★ Pouilly-Fumé Pur Sang ♀, ★★ Pouilly-Fumé Silex ♀
Best years 1999, '98, '97, '96, '95, '90, '89, '88

PHILIPPE DELESVAUX, St-Aubin-de-Luigné   02 41 78 18 71/02 41 78 68 06
From his first vintage in 1989, Philippe Delesvaux has produced sweet wines of great richness and purity. Recently, he has made wines of greater concentration but with no loss of elegance. He is one of the band of 'Sugar Hunters' (see box page 164).
Best wines ★★★ Coteaux du Layon Anthologie ♀ and Coteaux du Layon Grains Nobles ♀,
★★ Coteaux du Layon-St-Aubin ♀
Best years 1999, '98, '97, '96, '95, '90, '89

PIERRE-JACQUES DRUET, Benais   02 47 97 37 34/02 47 97 46 40
Created in the 1980s, Pierre-Jacques Druet's estate is now a leader in the Bourgueil appellation. These complex red wines have deep fruit and can age superbly.

Best wines ★★★ Bourgueil Vaumoreau ❢ and Bourgueil Grand Mont ❢, ★★ Bourgueil Cents Boisselées ❢ and Chinon ❢

Best years 1999, '98, '97, '96, '95, '90, '89, '88, '85, '83

DOM. DE L'ÉCU, Le Landreau   02 40 06 40 91/02 40 06 46 79

This is one of the rare Muscadet estates to practise biodynamic viticulture. The wines are quintessential Muscadet: refreshing young, but gaining character with 1 year in bottle.

Best wines ★★ Muscadet de Sèvre-et-Maine Hermine d'Or ♀ and Muscadet de Sèvre-et-Maine finement boisé Guy Bossard ♀

Best years 1999, '98, '97, '96, '95, '90

CH. D'ÉPIRÉ, Savennières   02 41 77 15 01/02 41 77 16 23

A fine estate with vines next to the famous Coulée-de-Serrant AC whose Savennières wine has been first rate since 1995. There is also a little Anjou red from Cabernet Franc.

Best wines ★★ Savennières ♀ and Savennières Réserve ♀

Best years 1999, '98, '97, '96, '95, '90, '89, '88

CH. DE FESLES, Thouarcé   02 41 68 94 00/02 41 68 94 01

Now in the hands of the Germain family of Bordeaux, this famous estate is once again making top-class wines after ownership changes in the late 1980s saw a marked decline in quality. The sublimely honeyed Bonnezeaux is a benchmark for sweet Anjou wines.

Best wines ★★★ Bonnezeaux ♀, ★ Anjou F de Fesles ♀

Best years Sweet 1999, '98, '97, '96, '95, '90, '89, '88, '85, '83, '78, '76, '64, '59, '47, '21

DOM. GODINEAU, Fayé d'Anjou   02 41 54 03 00/02 41 54 25 36

A large (50-ha) estate making aromatic and luscious Coteaux du Layon-Faye and 2 special Bonnezeaux wines, Mellarisses and Malabé.

Best wines ★★ Coteaux du Layon-Faye ♀ and Bonnezeaux ♀

Best years 1999, '98, '97, '96, '95, '90, '89, '88, '85

DOM. HUET, Vouvray   02 47 52 78 87/02 47 52 66 51

With 33ha of vines, this has always been one of the leading Vouvray estates. It now practises biodynamic viticulture and enjoys most intelligent winemaking from Noël Pinguet, son-in-law of the great Gaston Huet. Three vineyards, Le Mont, Le Haut Lieu and Le Clos du Bourg, make the full Vouvray range and some wines can last for 50 years.

Best wines ★★★ Vouvray Clos du Bourg Moelleux ♀ and Demi-Sec ♀, Vouvray Le Mont Moelleux ♀ and Demi-Sec ♀, and Vouvray Le Haut Lieu Moelleux ♀ and Demi-Sec ♀, ★★ Vouvray Clos du Bourg Sec ♀, Vouvray Le Mont Sec ♀ and Le Haut Lieu Sec ♀

Best years 1999, '98, '97, '96, '95, '93, '90, '89, '88, '85, '76, '64, '61, '59, '47

CH. DU HUREAU, Saumur   02 41 67 60 40/02 41 50 43 35

Fine, elegant wines with great depth of fruit from a superbly managed 18-ha estate.

Best wines ★★ Coteaux de Saumur Liquoreux ♀ and Saumur-Champigny Grande Cuvée ❢

Best years 1997, '96, '95, '90, '89

CHARLES JOGUET, Sazilly   02 47 58 55 53/02 47 58 52 22

Charles Joguet is one of the most celebrated winemakers in the Loire Valley and his estate has been a benchmark for 20 years. The wines benefit from 5–10 years' aging.

Best wines ★★★ Chinon Clos de la Dioterie ❢, ★★ Chinon Clos de la Cure ❢ and Chinon Les Varennes du Grand Clos ❢

Best years 1999, '98, '96, '95, '90, '89, '88, '85, '83, '82, '81, '76

ALPHONSE MELLOT, Sancerre   02 48 54 07 41/02 48 54 07 62

Alphonse Mellot has been one a leading Sancerre producer for many generations, with a 50-ha estate on the slopes surrounding the town; there is also a *négociant* business. La Moussière is unoaked and Cuvée Edmond is vinified and aged in new oak.

Best wines ★★ Sancerre Cuvée Edmond ♀, Sancerre Dom. La Moussière ♀ and Sancerre La Moussière Géneration XIX ❢

Best years 1999, '98, '96, '95, '90, '89

DOM. OGEREAU, St-Lambert-du-Lattay   02 41 78 30 53/02 41 78 43 55

A meticulously managed 24-ha estate, producing good red Anjou as well as excellent whites, both dry and sweet, from superbly sited vines in St-Lambert.

Best wines ★★ Coteaux du Layon Prestige, ★ Anjou Sec ♀ and Anjou-Villages ❢

Best years 1999, '98, '97, '96, '95, '90, '89, '88

CH. PIERRE-BISE, Beaulieu-sur-Layon   02 41 78 31 44/02 41 78 41 24

This estate is owned by the Papin family whose intimate knowledge of their terroir puts them at the forefront of the Anjou wine renaissance. They pick their grapes as ripe as possible and their sweet wines have few rivals in the region. There is also good Anjou Blanc.

Best wines ★★★ Coteaux du Layon Chaume ♀ and Quarts de Chaume ♀, ★★ Savennières Clos de Coulaine ♀

Best years Sweet 1999, '98, '97, '96, '95, '90, '89, '88, '86, '85; **Dry** 1999, '98, '97, '96, '95

JO PITHON, St-Lambert-du-Lattay   02 41 78 40 91/02 41 78 46 37

This small estate is the leader of the 'Sugar Hunters' (see box page 164), producing sweet wines with an extraordinary concentration of fruit and flavour.

Best wines ★★★ Coteaux du Layon-St-Lambert Clos des Bonnes Blanches ♀ and Coteaux du Layon-St-Lambert Ambrosie, ★★ Coteaux du Layon-Beaulieu ♀

Best years 1999, '98, '97, '96, '95, '93, '90, '89, '88

RENÉ RENOU, Bonnezeaux   02 41 54 11 33/02 41 54 11 34

René Renou, a seventh-generation *vigneron*, now concentrates on Bonnezeaux alone.

Best wines ★★★ Bonnezeaux Cuvée Zenith ♀, ★★ Bonnezeaux Beauregard ♀

Best years 1999, '98, '97, '96, '95, '93, '90, '89, '88

RICHOU, Mozé-sur-Louet   02 41 78 72 13/02 41 78 76 05

Finest estate in the small Coteaux de l'Aubance AC. The wines can age up to 20 years.

Best wines ★★★ Coteaux de l'Aubance Les Trois Demoiselles ♀, ★★ Anjou Chavigné Sec ♀

Best years Sweet 1999, '98, '97, '96, '95, '94, '93, '90, '89, '88

CH. DE LA ROCHE-AUX-MOINES, Savennières   02 41 72 22 32/02 41 72 28 68

Owned by Nicolas Joly, this estate has been run for the last 20 years according to strict biodynamic principles and is the uncontested leader in Savennières. These fine Chenin Blanc wines can last for decades.

Best wines ★★★ Savennières Becherelle ♀ and Savennières-Clos de la Coulée-de-Serrant ♀

Best years 1999, '98, '97, '96, '95, '90, '89, '88, '85, '83, '82, '78, '76, '71, '70, '69, '66

DOM. DES ROCHES NEUVES, Varrains   02 41 52 94 02/02 41 52 49 30

The Germain family of Bordeaux recently bought this 15-ha estate from Denis Duveau and continues to make the richest, most velvety wines in the appellation.

Best wines ★★ Saumur Blanc Insolite ♀ and Saumur-Champigny Terres Chaudes ❢

Best years 1999, '98, '97, '96, '95, '93, '90, '89, '88, '85

DOM. DES SABLONETTES, Rablay-sur-Layon   02 41 78 40 49/02 41 78 61 15

An up-and-coming estate producing classic, pure wines with race and elegance.
Best wines ★★ Coteaux du Layon-Rablay Noblesse ♀ and Coteaux du Layon-Rablay Les
Erables Sélection de Grains Nobles ♀
Best years 1999, '98, '97, '96, '95, '93, '90, '89, '88, '85

TAILLE AUX LOUPS, Montlouis-sur-Loire   02 47 45 11 11/02 47 45 11 14

The best wines of the often underrrated AC Montlouis come from this estate.
Best wines ★★ Montlouis Sec ♀ and Montlouis Moelleux ♀
Best years 1998, '97, '96, '95, '90, '89, '88, '86, '85, '83, '82, '78, '76, '70

CH. DE TRACY, Tracy-sur-Loire   03 86 26 15 12/03 86 26 10 73

One of the finest family estates in Pouilly, producing impeccable wines that age well.
The 1996 vintage celebrated Tracy's 600th anniversary.
Best wine ★★ Pouilly-Fumé ♀   **Best years** 1999, '98, '97, '96, '95, '90, '89

CH. DE VILLENEUVE, Sousay-Champigny   02 41 51 14 04/02 41 50 58 24

This superb estate makes the best Saumur Blancs, plus good Saumur-Champigny from
low-yielding old vines and vinified with great care. Les Cormiers is fermented in oak.
Best wines ★★★ Saumur-Champigny Le Grand Clos ❢ and Saumur Les Cormiers ♀,
★★ Saumur-Champigny Vieilles Vignes ❢
Best years ❢1999, '98, '97, '96, '95, '90, '89; ♀1999, '98, '97, '96, '95

LOIRE VINTAGES

Vintages in the Loire tend to follow a similar pattern across all the widely
differing styles of wine. A poor vintage will be poor with few exceptions,
owing to the temperate climate, and a good vintage tends to be universally
successful throughout the region. Hot summers are rare but when they
appear, they always produce great wine.

Aging qualities

The Loire knew lean times in the early
1990s, but recovered with 3 excellent
vintages during the mid-1990s. Except in
great years, the red wines do not improve
beyond 5 years and their lively fruit is best
appreciated when the wines are young.

With their high sugars and relatively
high acids, the sweet whites can keep for
many decades. Recent tastings have shown
sweet Vouvrays still to be beautifully
evocative at 80 years, and similar sweet
wines from Anjou, Quarts de Chaume for
example, can last almost as long.

Muscadet and Sancerre/Pouilly-Fumé,
the two dry white wine styles found at the
western and eastern ends of the Loire
Valley, tend to make wines that survive
poor weather at harvest time, as both the
Melon de Bourgogne (used for Muscadet)
and Sauvignon Blanc (used for Sancerre
and Pouilly-Fumé) grapes can be picked
early. These wines should, for the most
part, be drunk while still young.

Anjou and Touraine's fine red wines,
and especially the superb sweet wines from
these two regions, do need a good vintage
to show their true qualities. Such vintages
came in 1989 and '90 and again in the
wonderful trilogy of 1995, '96 and '97.
International recognition of their quality
has resulted in a justified price increase.

VINTAGE CHART

	99	98	97	96	95	94	93	92	91	90	89
Dry Anjou/Touraine whites	8○	7○	9◑	9●	8●	6●	7●	6●	5●	10●	9●
Anjou/Touraine reds	8○	8○	8◑	10◑	8●	5●	6●	5●	4◑	10●	8◑
Sweet Anjou/Touraine whites	7○	7○	9◑	8◑	9◑	8◑	6◑	5●	4●	9◑	10◑
Central Loire whites Sancerre, Pouilly-Fumé	8○	8○	9●	9●	9●	7●	7●	6●	7●	8●	8◑

KEY ○= needs more time   ◑= ready but will improve   ●= at peak   ◐= fading or tired

Maturity charts
1996 was the best year for reds since 1990, producing wines with enough body to last for 2 decades, as well as for sweet whites whose natural acidity will help them last for 25 years or so.

1996 Chinon

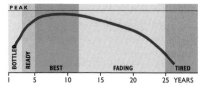

1996 Quarts de Chaume

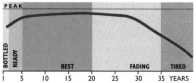

Annual vintage reports

1999★★ Very good dry whites and reds, but rain affected the sweeter wines in Vouvray and Montlouis.

1998★★ Fine, fruity, supple wines lacking just a little richness; some very good reds.

1997★★★ A year of extraordinary concentration in the sweet wines, and superb fruit and elegance in the dry whites and reds. The reds are soft and forward.

1996★★★ A very dry year, with little botrytis for the sweet wines, but wonderful concentration. The red

VINTAGES AT A GLANCE

The Loire Valley enjoyed 3 excellent vintages during the mid-1990s.

Great Years ★★★	1997, '96, '95, '90, '89, '85, '76, '71, '64, '59, '49, '47
Good Years ★★	1999, '98, '88, '86, '82, '62
Moderate Years ★	1993, '94
Poor Years (No Stars)	1994, '92, '91, '87

Cabernet Franc wines were superb and will age well.

1995★★★ A splendid long autumn, lasting well into November, created some superb sweet whites as well some aromatic dry whites. The reds were good, if a little tannic.

1994 0-★ A difficult vintage, with passable quality in Sancerre.

1993★ A wet harvest, but even so, it turned out satisfactorily. Quite good reds, good dry whites and some very surprisingly good sweet whites.

1992 A very difficult year.

1991 A year generally devasted by frost.

1990★★★ Quite superb for red wines and very fine for sweet whites, although these were maybe less concentrated than the '89s.

1989★★★ A stupendous year for sweet wines, compared immediately to the historic vintages of 1947 and '21. The reds were very concentrated, but a little overripe. **Other good years** 1988, '85, '82, '76, '71, '64, '62, '59, '55, '49, '47.

THE SOUTH AND SOUTH-WEST

These regions share a long history of wine production that has been saved from obscurity by a growing group of dedicated producers. Thanks to the blending of the best of the old (historic terroirs and grape varieties) with modern viticulture and winemaking, both these regions are transformed.

Provence and Languedoc-Roussillon

This vast area extends in an almost unbroken sea of vineyards along the full length of the French Mediterranean coast. The vineyards are some of France's oldest, having been planted by the Romans.

Two thousand years later, the region was known mostly for its oxidized whites over-alcoholic rosés and heavy reds. In the past 3 decades, however, there has been a growing movement for quality at the expense of quantity, a complete re-thinking of what the vineyards can produce, and so much investment in cellar equipment that the region has been labelled the 'California of France'. Along with all these innovations, the best of the old traditions have been preserved, to create an exciting vineyard area.

The South-West

Covering a vast area from the Atlantic coast across to Languedoc-Roussillon, the South-West makes a wide variety of wines. In terms of wine style, they are midway between the elegant wines of Bordeaux and the sun-filled wines of the Midi.

Not surprisingly, Bordeaux grape varieties are common for both the reds (Cabernet Sauvignon, Merlot and Cabernet Franc) and the whites (Sauvignon Blanc, Sémillon and Muscadelle) and there are many interesting local varieties, such as Tannat in Madiran, Petit Manseng in Jurançon and Mauzac in Gaillac. Even though there is little resemblance in style between some

of the wines, there are common characteristics; for example, red Bergerac and Madiran share a certain earthy robustness, despite being made from different varieties.

The most striking red wines are Cahors and Madiran – big, tannic wines, now softened with new oak, yet still requiring several years in bottle to be at their best. Lighter red wines and rosés are made from Merlot and Gamay. Dry whites vary from crisp modern Sauvignons to more interesting Gaillacs from the local Mauzac, while the sweet wines of Monbazillac and Jurançon are on a par with those from Bordeaux and the Loire.

Top wines _____

Red wines Bandol, les Baux-de-Provence, Bergerac, Cahors, Collioure, Corbières, Coteaux d'Aix-en-Provence, Coteaux de Languedoc, Côtes de Bergerac, Côtes de Provence, Côtes du Roussillon, Côtes du Roussillon-Villages, Faugères, Fitou, Gaillac, Madiran, Minervois, Palette.

White wines Bergerac Sec, Cassis, Corbières, Coteaux d'Aix-en-Provence, Côtes de Provence, Faugères, Gaillac, Jurançon Sec, Minervois, Pacherenc du Vic Bilh.

Rosé wines Bandol, les Baux-de-Provence, Bergerac, Collioure, Corbières, Coteaux d'Aix-en-Provence, Coteaux du Languedoc, Côtes de Provence, Gaillac.

Sweet wines Côtes de Bergerac Moelleux, Jurançon, Monbazillac.

Sparkling wines Blanquette de Limoux, Gaillac.

Fortified wines Banyuls, Maury, Muscat de Frontignan, Muscat de St-Jean-de-Minervois, Muscat de Lunel, Muscat de Rivesaltes, Rivesaltes.

GREAT SOUTHERN FRENCH WINES

Oz Clarke's selection

Collioure ! (La Tour-Vieille) Stupendous, 'both feet on the gas', burly southern red that oozes concentrated sun-saturated, deep dark fruit.

Madiran ! (d'Aydie) Powerful, brooding red wine, needing long aging but now a little softer than previously.

Coteaux du Languedoc ! (de Fontareche) Wonderful marriage between ancient and modern – from old, low-yield terraced vineyards, farmed virtually organically and vinified to a fabulous, herb-scented beauty.

Côtes du Roussillon ! (Gauby) The top estate in the AC, producing perfumed whites and structured, oaky but densely fruity reds.

Coteaux du Languedoc ! (Dom. du Granoupiac) Marvellous unfiltered red that mixes loganberries and blueberries with tar and floral scent. Heady stuff.

Muscat de Rivesaltes ♀ (de Jau) Excellent grapy Muscat dripping with orange, apple and crystallized lemon peel.

Limoux Prestige ♀ (Begude) Superb Chardonnay from one of Limoux's best single estates.

Vin de Pays de l'Hérault ♀ (Mas de Daumas Gassac) Irresistible blossom-perfumed white based on Viognier from this inspirational property at Aniane north of Montpellier.

Steven Spurrier's selection

Jurançon Sec Cuvée Marie ♀ (Clos Uroulat) Charles Hours vinifies his Petit and Gros Manseng grapes in small oak, which adds richness and body, without losing the freshness inherent in Jurançon.

Madiran Cuvée Prestige ! (Montus) This superb wine from Alain Brumont has magnificent richness, helped by 100% new oak.

Vin de Pays des Bouches-du-Rhône ! (Trévallon) This dense, long-lived Cabernet Sauvignon and Syrah blend is as good as any in Provence.

Bandol ! (Pibarnon) From 95% Mourvèdre, this wine has deep fruit and classic structure.

Vin de Pays de l'Hérault ! (Mas de Daumas Gassac) Created in 1970, the terroir of this renowned domaine is perfect for making long-lasting Bordeaux lookalikes. The early vintages were overly tannic, but now the depth of fruit and terroir is supremely evident.

Rivesaltes Cuvée Aimé ! (Cazes) The ultimate wood-aged Rivesaltes. The current vintage, 1975, has a bright amber colour, an aroma of orange peel and spices and intense, complex fruit.

Jurançon Quintessence du Petit Manseng ♀ (Cauhapé) This barrel-fermented sweet wine has wonderful concentrated sweetness with underlying new oak and has plenty of aging potential.

Coteaux du Languedoc ! (Prieuré de St-Jean-de-Bébian) Classic Provençal grape varieties, old vines, tiny yields and uncompromising winemaking, all combine to create a unique wine which has become more polished in recent vintages.

A–Z OF WINE REGIONS

BANDOL AC

Mainly red wine, with a little rosé and even less white, from coastal vineyards west of Toulon. The full-bodied, fruity red wine must have a minimum of 50% Mourvèdre, the remainder being Syrah, Grenache, Cinsault and Carignan, and repays keeping for 5-10 years.

Best producers Bastide Blanche, Dom. Bunan (Ch. de la Rouvière), de Frégate, Moulin des Costes, OTT (Ch. Romassan),

PIBARNON, PRADEAUX, Ray Jane, TEMPIER, Dom. de Terrebrune, Dom. de la Tour de Bon, Vannières.

Best years 1999, '98, '97, '96, '95, '94, '93, '91, '90, '89, '88, '85, '83, '82.

BANYULS VDN

Red and aged tawny fortified wines from terraced vineyards on the border with Spain. There are 2 styles of wine: those aged in barrel (often placed outside in the sun to accelerate aging) for many years to acquire a tawny colour and complex 'rancio' flavours, and those bottled young like a Vintage Port, to mature in bottle. The general level of quality is very high.

Best producers CELLIER DES TEMPLIERS, Clos des Paulilles, l'Étoile, MAS BLANC, la Rectorie, Vial Magnères.

LES BAUX-DE-PROVENCE AC

In 1995 this AC detached itself from the Coteaux d'Aix, setting strict rules for vineyards around the historic village of Les Baux to ensure that the wines (80% red) are of uniformly high quality. This idea has succeeded, the only casualty being Dom. de TRÉVALLON, by far the best estate, that has been excluded from the appellation because it has a high proportion of the non-traditional Cabernet Sauvignon in its blend.

Best producers Hauvette, Mas de la Dame, Mas de Gourgonnier, Mas Ste-Berthe, Romanin, Terres Blanches.

Best years 1999, '98, '97, '96, '95, '94, '93, '91, '90.

BERGERAC, BERGERAC SEC, CÔTES DE BERGERAC, CÔTES DE BERGERAC MOELLEUX ACs

The Bergerac appellations cover red, rosé, dry and sweet white wines from the Dordogne department near Bordeaux. The reds have attractive fruit and light tannins, the rosés are supple and fruity and the whites are light and fresh. Overall, quality is improving in the region.

Best producers Bélingard, de la Colline, Combrillac, Court-les-Mûts, du Gouyat, la Jaubertie, le Mayne, de Panisseau, le Raz, la Rayre, Richard, Theulet, Tour de Grangemont, TOUR DES GENDRES.

Best years 1998, '96, '95, '94, '93, '91, '90, '89.

BLANQUETTE DE LIMOUX AC

Attractively fresh sparkling wines from south-west of Carcassonne, made chiefly from Mauzac, and generally high quality.

Best producers l'Aigle, Antech, Laurens, Sieur d'Arques co-operative.

Best years 1999, '98, '97, '96, '95.

CAHORS AC

A red wine of Gallo-Roman origins, from the banks of the river Lot around Cahors, currently undergoing a resurgence in quality. The Malbec grape produces a robust, tannic wine, softened by the addition of Merlot and in some cases aging in new wood. The expression 'Vieux Cahors' is for wines aged 3 years in wood.

Best producers du CÈDRE, CLOS TRIGUEDINA, la Coutale, de Gamot, Gautoul, des Grauzils, Haute-Serre, LAGREZETTE, des Savarines.

Best years 1999, '98, '96, '95, '94, '92, '90, '89, '88, '86, '85.

CASSIS AC

Mainly white wine from 175ha of vines above the little port of Cassis to the east of Marseille. The best are both aromatic and refreshing, dry but with a low acidity, and should be drunk young.

Best producers Caillol, CLOS STE-MAGDELEINE, Ferme Blanche, Fontcreuse.

LA CLAPE

The vineyards between Narbonne and the coast are a Cru within the sprawling Coteaux du Languedoc appellation and the chalky soil gives the wines an unexpected elegance. The whites have a fine floral fruit and the reds, usually from a blend of Carignan and Grenache, have good body and depth.

Best producers Moujan, Pech-Céleyran, Pech-Redon, la Roquette-sur-Mer.

Best years 1999, '98, '97, '96, '95.

COLLIOURE AC

Collioure is a tiny appellation for the Midi, producing red and rosé wines from steeply terraced vineyards near the Spanish border. Grenache is the dominant grape

(60%), backed by Syrah, Mourvèdre and Cinsaut. The wines have finesse as well as body, and can age well.

Best producers CELLIER DES TEMPLIERS, Clos des Paulilles, MAS BLANC, la Rectorie, la Tour-Vieille.

Best years ❢1999, '98, '95, '94, '93, '90, '89, '88.

CORBIÈRES AC

Mainly red wines from south-east of Carcassonne. The reds and rosés are made with at least 90% classic Mediterranean grape varieties to give a deep colour and a concentrated flavour from the grapes and the sun. The whites, mostly for drinking young, are from Clairette and Malvoisie, and there is also some rosé.

Best producers la Baronne, Caraguilhes, l'Étang des Colombes, Grand Moulin, Haut-Gléon, Hélène, de Lastours, les Palais, du Réverend, St-Auriol, Salvagnac, de Villemajou, Vaugelas, la Voulte-Gasparets.

Best years ❢1999, '98, '95, '94, '93, '90, '89, '88.

CORSICA

Vines were first planted in Corsica by the Greeks and the island continues to make fine wines from the local Nielluccio and Sciacarello grapes for reds and rosés, and Vermentino (also known as Rolle) for aromatic whites. The basic AC is Vin de Corse, with various sub-regions: the best are Calvi (aromatic whites and rosés from Clos Culombu and Clos Landry); Cap Corse, famous for its fortified Muscats and Clos Nicrosi's superb white; and Porto-Vecchio (from Torraccia). Ajaccio (from Comte Peraldi and Clos Capitoro) and Patrimonio (from ARENA, de Catarelli, Gentile and Leccia) have their own ACs.

Best years 1999, '98, '95, '96, '95, '90.

COTEAUX D'AIX-EN-PROVENCE AC

The full range of Provençal grape varieties are planted in the vineyards around Aix, as well as Cabernet Sauvignon, which is permitted up to a limit of 60%. The rosés are fresh and attractive, the whites aromatic and refreshing, and the reds lively and fruity.

Best producers de Beaulieu, de Beaupré, Calissanne, Fonscolombe, Revelette, du Seuil, Vignelaure.

Best years ❢1999, '98, '96, '95.

COTEAUX DU LANGUEDOC AC

Red and rosé wines from right across the Hérault department, which must be made from at least 80% of the accepted Mediterranean varieties. Quality is improving rapidly, especially from the Cru villages (best ones are Cabrières, la Clape, Coteaux de la Méjanelle, Montpeyroux, Picpoul-le-Pinet, Pic-St-Loup, Quatourze, St-Drézery and St-Georges-d'Orques).

Best producers Abbaye de Valmagne, de l'Aiguelière, d'Aupilhac, Cabrières, Carrion-Nizas, de Cazeneuve, la Condamine-Bertrand, du Granoupiac, de l'Hortus, Mas Bruguière, Mas de Chimeres, Mas Jullien, Pech-Céleyran, Peyre Rose, PRIEURÉ DE ST-JEAN-DE-BÉBIAN, St-Germain, St-Martin de la Garrigue.

Best years ❢1999, '98, '96, '95, '94, '93.

CÔTES DE PROVENCE AC

Red, white and rosé (80%) wines from the Var department. Quality has improved dramatically in the last decade, owing to the commitment of the growers. The rosés are perfect as an apéritif, or with food, the whites now more sophisticated and elegant, and the reds showing firm fruit.

Best producers l'Aumerade, Barbeyrolles, de la Bastide Neuve, de la Bernarde, de Berne, Clos Mireille (OTT), Commanderie de Peyrassol, de la COURTADE, d'Esclans, Ferrey-Lacombe, Gavoty, de Galoupet, les Maîtres

Vignerons de St-Tropez, de Marchandise, Mas Cadenet, Minuty, Réal Martin, Rimauresq, St-André-de-Figuière, St-Baillon, Ste-Marguerite, de Selle (OTT).
Best years ❢1999, '98, '97, '96, '95.

CÔTES DU ROUSSILLON, CÔTES DU ROUSSILLON-VILLAGES ACs

Two appellations for mainly red wine from some of the best sites between Perpignan and the Pyrenees. The whites are lively and fruity, the rosés a bit heady and the reds robust, yet smooth. Carignan is used to 70% for the reds, the rest being Grenache, Cinsaut, Syrah and Mourvèdre.
Best producers CAZES, de Corneilla, Força-Réal, Gauby, de Jau, Jaubert-Noury, de Joliette, Mas Crémat, Dom. Parcé, Les Pins, Piquemal, Sarda-Malet.
Best years ❢1999, '98, '95, '94, '93.

FAUGÈRES AC

Red and dry white wines from one of the finest parts of the Languedoc, just north of Béziers. The red wines, earthy but smooth, can be very good.
Best producers ALQUIER, Estanilles, de Fenouillet, du Fraisse, Grézan, Haut-Fabrègues, Roque.
Best years ❢1999, '98, '96, '95, '94, '90.

FITOU AC

Fitou is the oldest appellation in the Midi, dating from 1948. The solid, robust reds are Carignan-based, and many are now being improved by new-oak aging. They are warm, welcoming and mature well.
Best producers Bertrand-Bergé, Colomer, les Fenals, de Nouvelles, les Producteurs du Mont Tauch.
Best years 1999, '98, '96, '95, '93, '90, '89.

GAILLAC AC

One of the oldest wine areas of France, Gaillac's reputation was founded on sparkling wines, made mainly from Mauzac, but recent interest has focused on the fruity reds from the local Duras and

Fer grapes, often blended with Syrah for improved flavour.
Best producers Jean Cros, de Lastours, Mas d'Aurel, de Mayragues, Robert PLAGEOLES, des Terrisses.
Best years ❢1999, '98, '96, '95, '94, '90.

JURANÇON AC

This appellation is known for its sweet white wines which have come back into vogue recently, thanks to the dedication of a new generation of growers. Despite a concentrated honeyed richness, Jurançon always retains a balancing lemony acidity. The rapidly improving dry white, called Jurançon Sec, is attractive and refreshing.
Best producers Bellegarde, BRU-BACHÉ, CAUHAPÉ, Cinquau, Clos Lapeyre, Clos Thou, CLOS UROULAT, Cru Lamouroux.
Best years Sweet 1999, '98, '95, '94, '93, '90.

MADIRAN AC

Powerful and often over-tannic, Madiran is currently the finest red wine in the South-West. Made mainly from the rather rustic Tannat grape, Cabernet (both Franc and Sauvignon) is used to add an aromatic elegance. The wines are solid, well-structured, with great depth of fruit and age superbly. Madiran's success has forced the recent improvement in the rival wines of Cahors.
Best producers d'AYDIE, Barréjat, Berthoumieu, BOUSCASSÉ (Ch. Montus), Capmartin, du Crampilh, Ducournau (Chapelle-Lenclos, Mouréou), Laffitte-Teston, de PEYROS.
Best years 1999, '98, '96, '95, '94, '93, '90, '89, '88, '85.

MAURY VDN

Red and aged tawny fortified wines made from Grenache. The vineyards have a similar schistous soil to that at Banyuls, and the style is similar, if not as complex.
Best producers MAS AMIEL, la Pléïade.

MINERVOIS AC

Mainly red wine, with a little white and rosé, from an area between Narbonne and Carcassonne. These robust, fruity reds age well – the top wines for 5 years or so.

Best producers Borie de Maurel, Domergue, du Donjon, Fabas, de Gourgazaud, Maris, d'Oupia, Paraza, Piccinini, Ste-Eulalie, la Tour-Boisée, Villerambert-Julien.

Best years 1999, '98, '96, '95, '93, '90.

MONBAZILLAC AC

This is Bergerac's leading sweet white wine and after decades of poor quality, standards have improved to rival or even outperform generic Sauternes.

Best producers le Fagé, Grande Maison, TIRECUL LA GRAVIÈRE.

Best years 1999, '98, '97, '96, '95, '94, '93, '90, '89, '88, '86.

MUSCAT VDNs

There are several areas in Languedoc making aromatic fortified wine from the Muscat grape, to be drunk young. Some of the best comes from Frontignan.

Best producers de Barroubio, la Capelle, Clos Bellevue, La Côte du Mazet, du Gres St-Paul, Mas Neuf, de Mereville, de la Peyrade, les Vignerons de Septimanie.

PACHERENC DE VIC BILH AC

Dry and sweet white wines from the Madiran region. Local grape varieties are blended with Sauvignon and Sémillon for fruit and character and the wines have a lively acidity.

Best producers d'AYDIE, BOUSCASSÉ, Producteurs Plaimont.

Best years 1999, '98, '96, '95, '94, '93.

PALETTE AC

A tiny appellation on predominantly chalky soil just south of Aix-en-Provence, making excellent wines. There are only 2 producers: SIMONE and Crémade.

Best years ▮1999, '98, '96, '95, '90, '89, '88, '85.

RIVESALTES & MUSCAT DE RIVESALTES VDNs

Fortified reds and rosés from at least 50% Grenache, which rarely have the complexity of Banyuls, but some wines aged 20 years or more in barrel can be exceptional. There are also Muscats of very high quality, to be drunk young.

Best producers CAZES, de Corneilla, Garria, de Jau (Mas Christine), Piquemal, Sarda-Malet, de Villeneuve.

VIN DE PAYS

The rise in quality in the Midi has been the recent success story of French viticulture. Most Vins de Pays now carry the name of 1 or sometimes 2 grape varieties. Most are inexpensive, of honest quality with good varietal characteristics but some are exceptional (MAS DE DAUMAS GASSAC and de TRÉVALLON), and justifiably more expensive.

FRANCE'S VINS DOUX NATURELS (VDNs) OR FORTIFIED WINES

These naturally sweet, fortified wines are not to be confused with *vins liquoreux* which are naturally sweet from the over-maturity of botrytized grapes when harvested. A VDN is the result of the fermentation being stopped early by the addition of alcohol, a neutral grape brandy of at least 90°, before the must has fermented out all the sugar. This operation is called *mutage* and occurs when the must has reached around 7° of alcohol with the same amount remaining as natural grape sugar and the alcohol itself adding a further 6°–10°. The finest ones come from the southern Rhône and the Midi. Those from Muscat (Beaumes-de-Venise and Frontignan) have a pale gold to light amber colour, depending on the aging after fermentation. The Grenache-based ones vary from deep purple when young to tawny when fully aged, the best of which take on a highly prized flavour called 'rancio'.

A–Z OF WINE PRODUCERS

JEAN-MICHEL ALQUIER, Faugères   04 67 23 07 89/04 67 95 30 51
This 30-ha estate is the best in Faugères. The balance between fruit and extract in these Syrah-based wines is perfect and there is sophisticated use of new oak.
Best wines ★★ Faugères Les Bastides ❢, ★ Faugères ❢
Best years 1999, '98, '95, '90

DOM. ANTOINE ARENA, Patrimonio   04 95 37 08 27/04 95 37 01 14
This estate proves that great wines can come from Corsica. The indigenous Nielluccio grape yields a smoothly robust red wine, and the Muscat a superbly aromatic sweet white, both flourishing on Patrimonio's unique chalky soil.
Best wines ★★ Patrimonio ❢ and Muscat du Cap Corse Grotte di Sole ♀
Best years ❢1999, '98, '97, '96, '95, '90

CH. D'AYDIE, Aydie   05 59 04 01 17/05 59 04 01 53
The Laplace family has made this one of the most reliable estates in the Madiran region, for both red and white wines. It was among the first to estate-bottle Madiran.
Best wines ★★ Madiran ❢ and Pacherenc du Vic Bilh Moelleux ♀
Best years ❢1999, '98, '96, '95, '94, '90, '89, '88, '85; ♀1999, '98, '97, '96, '95

CH.BOUSCASSÉ/CH. MONTUS, Maumusson   05 62 69 74 67/05 62 69 70 46
The wines of Alain Brumont introduced the Madiran appellation to an international clientele. He has been compared, with reason, to GUIGAL of the Rhône Valley, because of his voluptuous concentration of fruit and sophisticated use of new oak.
Best wines ★★★ Madiran Ch. Montus Cuvée Prestige ❢ and Madiran Ch. Bouscassé Vieilles Vignes ❢, ★★ Pacherenc du Vic Bilh Doux Bouscassé Vendémiaire ♀, Pacherenc du Vic Bilh Doux Bouscassé Brumaire ♀ and Madiran Ch. Montus ❢, ★ Pacherenc du Vic Bilh Sec ♀
Best years ❢1999, '98, '96, '95, '94, '93, '90, '89, '88, '85; ♀1999, '98, '97, '96, '95,

DOM. BRU-BACHÉ, Monein   05 59 21 36 34/05 59 21 32 67
A small 7-ha estate in Jurançon making top-quality rich, sweet wines.
Best wines ★★★ Jurançon La Quintessence ♀, ★★ Jurançon Casterrasses ♀ and Jurançon L'Éminence ♀, ★ Jurançon Traditionnel ♀
Best years 1999, '98, '97, '96, '95, '94, '93, '90, '89, '88

DOM. CAUHAPÉ, Monein   05 59 21 33 02/05 59 21 41 82
This is, without doubt, the leading estate in Jurançon. The dry, and especially the sweet wines are of exceptional quality.
Best wines ★★★ Jurançon Noblesse du Petit Manseng ♀ and Jurançon Quintessence du Petit Manseng ♀, ★★ Jurançon Sec Noblesse du Petit Manseng ♀, ★ Jurançon Sec Traditionnel ♀
Best years Dry 1999, '98, '97, '96, '95, '90; **Sweet** 1998, '97, '96, '95, '94, '93, '90, '89, '88

DOM. CAZES, Rivesaltes   04 68 64 03 26/04 68 64 69 79
One of Roussillon's leading domaines, with 160ha of vines spread over several appellations. The finest wines are the headily aromatic fortified ones, some of which are aged for over 20 years in wood. In contrast, the pale grapy Muscat is bottled 6 months after the vintage.
Best wines ★★★ Rivesaltes Cuvée Aimé Cazes ❢, ★★ Muscat de Rivesaltes ♀
Best years ❢1999, '98, '96, '95, '94, '93

DOM. DU CÈDRE, Viré-sur-Lot   05 65 36 53 87/05 65 24 64 36
A 25-ha estate, planted to 80% Malbec, produces 3 different *cuvées* of intense, oaky
Cahors that ages well, beginning to show true complexity after 3–4 years.
Best wines ★★ Le Cèdre ❢, Cahors Le Prestige ❢ **Best years** 1999, '98, '96, '95, '90, '89, '88
CELLIER DES TEMPLIERS, Banyuls   04 68 98 36 70/04 68 98 36 91
This is the largest co-operative in Banyuls, whose top-of-the range fortified wines
include superb, single-vintage wines known as Rimage. There is also good Collioure.
Best wines ★★★ Banyuls Grand Cru Président Henri Vidal ❢, **★★** Banyuls Grand Cru
Amiral F Vilarem ❢
Best years 1999, '98, '96, '95, '94, '93, '92, '88, '86, '82
CLOS STE-MAGDELEINE, Cassis   04 42 01 70 28/04 42 01 15 51
A 12-ha estate perched above the port of Cassis, producing full-bodied and vivacious
white wines that possess a floral aroma.
Best wine ★★ Cassis ♀   **Best years** 1999, '98, '97
CLOS TRIGUEDINA, Puy l'Evêque   05 65 21 30 81/05 65 21 39 28
A well-known family-owned estate renowned for quality and attention to detail, whose
Prince Probus wine is regularly one of the best wines in Cahors.
Best wines ★★ Cahors Prince Probus ❢, **★** Cahors ❢
Best years 1999, '98, '96, '95, '90, '89, '88, '86, '85
CLOS UROULAT, Monein   05 59 21 46 19/05 59 21 46 90
Although he has only 7.5ha of vines, Charles Hours bears comparison with Henri
Ramonteu of CAUHAPÉ, for his elegant, barrel-fermented wines, both dry and sweet.
Best wines ★★ Jurançon Sec Cuvée Marie ♀ and Jurançon (*moelleux*) ♀
Best years Dry 1999, '98, '97, '96, '95 **Sweet** 1999, '98, '97, '96, '95, '93, '90, '89, '88, '83
DOM. DE LA COURTADE, Île de Porquerolles   04 94 58 31 44/04 94 58 34 12
A recently created estate, idyllically located on this tranquil island with its favourable
mesoclimate, making sophisticated wines that accurately reflect their grapes and terroir.
Best wine ★★ Côtes de Provence ❢♀   **Best years** ❢1999, '98, '95, '90
CH. LAGREZETTE, Caillac   05 65 20 07 42/05 65 20 06 95
Since 1994, the wines at this 54-ha estate in Cahors have been vinified by Michel
Rolland, the famous Bordeaux enologist, and have taken on added richness and depth.
Best wine ★★ Cahors ❢
Best years 1999, '98, '96, '95, '94, '90, '89
MAS AMIEL, Maury   04 68 29 01 02/04 68 29 17 82
This is the best estate in the Maury appellation, west of Perpignan, making fortified
wines in various styles. These are generally ready to drink on release.
Best wines ★★ Maury 15 years old ❢ and Maury Vintage ❢
Best years Vintage 1998, '96, '95, '94, '93, '90
DOM. DU MAS BLANC, Banyuls   04 68 88 32 12/04 68 35 03 95
The late Dr André Parcé was the most revered producer in the region and the
domaine's old vines, low yields and constant search for excellence result in wines of the
highest quality. The limited Cuvées of Collioure are among the appellation's best wines.
Best wines ★★★ Banyuls Rimage ❢ and Banyuls de Solera ❢, **★★** Collioure Clos du Moulin ❢
Best years Collioure 1999, '98, '96, '95, '94, '93

MAS DE DAUMAS GASSAC, Aniane   04 67 57 71 28/04 67 57 41 03
The soil on this celebrated estate, created from nothing in the early 1970s, is uniquely rich in minerals and perfectly suited to producing densely fruity wines from Cabernet Sauvignon, Chardonnay and Viognier and other varieties.
Best wines ★★★ Vin de Pays de l'Hérault ¶, ★★ Vin de Pays de l'Hérault ♀
Best years ¶1999, '98, '96, '95, '94, '93, '90, '89, '88, '87, '85, '83, '82

CH. MONTUS See Ch. Bouscassé page 178

DOM. OTT/CH. ROMASSAN, le Castellet   04 94 98 71 91/04 94 98 65 44
One of the most important and influential winemaking families in Provence, the Otts produce the finest Bandol rosé on their 65-ha estate.
Best wines ★★ Bandol Longue Garde ¶, ★ Bandol Coeur de Grain ¶
Best years ¶1999, '98, '97, '97, '96, '95, '90, '89

CH. DE PEYROS, Corbère-Abères   05 59 02 45 90/05 59 84 06 71
This old estate, which used to make Bordeaux-style wines, has now rediscovered its Madiran roots and extracts more colour and body from the local Tannat grape.
Best wines ★★★ Madiran Le Couvent du Château ¶, ★ Madiran ¶
Best years 1999, '98, '96, '95, '90, '89

CH. DE PIBARNON, la Cadière d'Azur   04 94 90 12 73/04 94 90 12 98
An estate with terraced vines on the highest slopes of Bandol. The red, from 95% Mourvèdre, is classically structured and ages beautifully, and the white and rosé are fruity and elegant.
Best wines ★★★ Bandol ¶, ★★ Bandol ♀, ★ Bandol ¶
Best years ¶1999, '98, '96, '95, '90, '89, '88, '85

ROBERT PLAGEOLES, Cahuzac-sur-Vère   05 63 33 90 40/05 63 33 95 64
The Plageoles family has been making wine in Gaillac for 500 years. The brilliant Robert Plageoles runs the estate with his son. The reds are fruity and earthy, but the whites are unique, for Plageoles has resurrected several almost extinct local varieties.
Best wines ★★ Gaillac Vin de Voile ♀ and Gaillac Vin d'Autan ♀, ★ Gaillac Muscadelle ♀, Gaillac Ondenc ♀ and Gaillac Duras ¶
Best years ♀1999, '98, '97, '96, '95, '94

CH. PRADEAUX, St-Cyr-sur-Mer   04 94 32 10 21/04 94 32 16 02
A 14.5-ha estate, family-owned for generations, producing some of the most long-lived and concentrated wines in Bandol from old Mourvèdre, Grenache and Cinsaut vines.
Best wines ★★★ Bandol ¶, ★ Bandol ¶
Best years ¶1999, '98, '95, '93, '90, '89, '88, '85, '82

PRIEURÉ DE ST-JEAN-DE-BÉBIAN, Pézenas   04 67 98 13 60/04 67 98 22 24
This estate used to be renowned for its powerful wines from low-yielding, old vines. New proprietors have kept the tradition, while adding polish to the winemaking.
Best wines ★★ Coteaux du Languedoc ¶♀
Best years ¶1999, '98, '96, '95, '89, '88, '85

CH. SIMONE, Meyreuil   04 42 66 92 58/04 42 66 80 77
The original and the largest domaine in the tiny Palette appellation produces wines that have the sophistication of a fine Bordeaux, but maintain their Provençal character.
Best wines ★ Palette ¶♀¶   **Best years** ¶1998, '96, '95, '89, '88, '85

DOM. TEMPIER, le Plan-du-Castellet   04 94 98 70 21/04 94 90 21 65
The late Lucien Peyraud made Tempier the benchmark for Bandol. The estate now
bottles several different cuvées, all using a high proportion of Mourvèdre. Their Bandol
rosé is now second only to that made by OTT.
Best wines ★★ Bandol Cuvée Classique ❗, Bandol Cabassaou ❗ and Bandol La Tourtine ❗,
★ Bandol ❗
Best years ❗1999, '98, '96, '95, '93, '90, '89, '88, '85, '83, '82

CH. TIRECUL-LA-GRAVIÈRE, Monbazillac   05 53 57 44 75/05 53 24 85 01
This estate benefits from a great terroir. The search for concentrated flavour is pushed
to the maximum and the resulting sweet wines have even been compared with d'YQUEM.
Best wines ★★★ Monbazillac Cuvée Madame ♀, ★★ Monbazillac ♀
Best years 1999, '98, '97, '96, '95, '90, '89, '88, '86

CH. TOUR DES GENDRES, Ribagnac   05 53 57 12 43/05 53 58 89 49
Now one of the best properties in Bergerac with 43 ha of vines. The owner, Luc de
Conti, vinifies with as much sophistication as found in the Bordeaux Crus Classés.
Best wines ★ Côtes de Bergerac La Gloire de Mon Père ❗ and Moulin des Dames ❗♀
Best years ❗1999, '98, '97, '96, '95, '90, '89

DOM. DE TRÉVALLON, St-Étienne-du-Grès   04 90 49 06 00/04 90 49 02 17
Since its first vintage in 1977, the de Trévallon estate, owned by Eloi Dürrbach, has
regularly made one of southern France's best red wines. Since the 1994 vintage it has
ludicrously been prevented from using the local Les Baux-de-Provence AC because of
the untraditional blend of 55% Cabernet Sauvignon and 45% Syrah.
Best wines ★★★ Vin de Pays du Bouches-du-Rhône ❗, ★★ Vin de Pays du Bouches-du-Rhône ♀
Best years ❗1999, '98, '97, '96, '95, '93, '90, '89, '88, '85, '83, '82

SOUTH AND SOUTH-WEST VINTAGES

Although southern France has a reputation for sun-filled holidays, it would
be quite wrong to suppose that the wine producers always had an easy time
at vintage. This is a vast region and overall quality is by no means uniform.

PROVENCE, LANGUEDOC-ROUSSILLON AND CORSICA

The vintages here follow, to a large extent,
the pattern of those in the southern Rhône
with the additional factor of the maritime
element which can both hinder as well as
help the grapes to ripen.

Fortified wines

The lively and aromatic Muscat vins doux
naturels that are bottled the spring after
the vintage, and the Grenache-based wines
that are expressly aged in wood to attain

the *rancio* flavour, should both be drunk
within 1-2 years of bottling. Vintage (or
rimage in Catalan) wines are bottled 1-2
years after the vintage, with the intention
that they mature slowly in bottle like a
Vintage Port.

THE SOUTH-WEST

In general, the vintages are broadly similar
to those of Bordeaux. Such is the variation
and style from producer to producer that
the vintage is often more an indication of
age than of quality.

GERMANY

German Rieslings possess a marriage of intensity and delicacy, subtlety and effusiveness unique among the world's white wines. This was long obscured by the flood of cheap generic wines, dismal 'sugar-water' caricatures of the real thing. However, during the 1990s a new generation of German winemakers instigated a Riesling renaissance and their experiments with the Pinot family of grapes for dry white and red wines are also yielding results.

Taste characteristics

Germany's cool climate decisively marks the wines from the valleys of the Rhine and its tributaries, the Mosel, Nahe and Main. Riesling is the only grape that can translate this climate and steep vineyards with stony soils into great white wines, because its personality precisely matches these conditions. It gives wines light in body that possess an extraordinary aromatic intensity and complexity. Peach may be the hallmark aroma of ripe Riesling grapes, but depending upon the vineyard location and vintage they can show all manner of fruit notes – from green apple to passion fruit – along with a broad range of mineral, spice and herbal notes.

Selective harvesting

This tradition means that growers frequently produce a handful of different Riesling wines from a single vineyard in one vintage. Today these range from a dry wine – German dry Rieslings dramatically improved in quality during the 1990s – up to a lusciously sweet dessert wine, either Auslese, Beerenauslese or Trockenbeerenauslese (these will be made from stringently selected berries affected by noble rot and shrivelled to a raisin-like appearance). In spite of being among the world's most concentrated whites, the best have a purity and brilliance few other dessert wines can match.

Viticulture and winemaking

During the 1970s and '80s yields, even at the top estates, were generally too high to make truly first-class wines. One of the first principles of the new generation of winemakers to emerge during the 1990s was to dramatically reduce yields, and today Germany's finest Rieslings are picked at yields comparable with the great wines of France. Most of the new star estates are small compared to the leaders of 30 or more years ago, most of whom have fallen behind. While some co-operatives are good sources for everyday wines, none plays a serious role in the fine wine field.

Low yields and improved winemaking have also greatly benefited the dry wines from the Pinot family (Weissburgunder/ Pinot Blanc, Grauburgunder/Pinot Gris and Spätburgunder/Pinot Noir) and Chardonnay. In recent years a group of growers in the warm, southerly regions of the Pfalz and Baden has begun to make exciting dry white wines from the first two of these grapes and serious reds from the latter. They have mastered the aging of these wines in small new oak casks or barriques, though not all Weissburgunder or Grauburgunder needs to – or receives – new oak. The best examples have as much body and alcohol as comparable wines from France or the New World, but are more restrained in style.

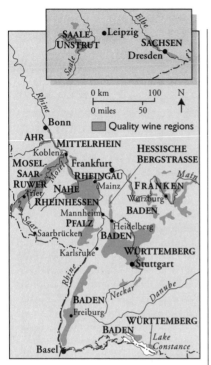

WINE REGIONS

Ahr
Best known for light, pale Spätburgunder reds. Some recent wines are more serious.

Baden
The best wines are Spätburgunder reds and dry Grauburgunder, which are even weightier than those from the Pfalz. Good dry Riesling and Traminer from Ortenau.

Franken
Specializes in full-bodied, earthy, dry Riesling and Silvaner.

Hessische Bergstrasse
Tiny region making some good dry and sweet Rieslings, but few remarkable wines.

Mittelrhein
The slate soils in the Rhine gorge can yield Rieslings as aromatic as the Mosel's, but slightly softer in style.

Mosel-Saar-Ruwer
The Mosel's steep vineyards and slate soils produce Germany's most elegant and refined Rieslings. Nearly all the exciting wines have some natural sweetness.

Nahe
This geologically complex region gives intensely minerally, racy Rieslings in the 'classic' sweet style. Both Weissburgunder and Grauburgunder can produce good medium-bodied dry whites.

Pfalz
Germany's richest Rieslings, full-bodied dry Weissburgunder, Grauburgunder, improving Spätburgunder reds and aromatic Scheurebe and Gewürztraminer.

Rheingau
Famous for aristocratic Rieslings, both sweet and dry, now emerging from a period of under-performance.

Rheinhessen
Large region with one fine wine 'island' at Nackenheim-Nierstein making rich, silky dry and classic sweet Riesling wines.

Saale-Unstrut
Good dry Weissburgunder, Traminer and Riesling. Full potential not yet realized.

Sachsen
Aromatic dry Riesling and Traminer.

Württemberg
Few highlights except for some earthy dry Riesling and occasional serious reds.

WINE LAWS AND CLASSIFICATIONS

The German wine law of 1971 defines wine quality solely by the grape sugar content at harvest, the location of the vineyard having no significance for the legal classification of the wines grown there. Since the passing of this law experts have been calling it an ass. Now, a steadily growing number of Germany's leading winemakers are working to establish an alternative that gives back to the top vineyards the importance they enjoyed until 1971.

Problems of the German wine law

Until 1971 the hierarchical Prädikat system of the German wine law was almost exclusively used for Rieslings from traditional vineyards that were sold under this string of designations for unchaptalized wines, (in ascending order) Spätlese, Auslese, Beerenauslese and Trockenbeerenauslese. The 1971 wine law added Tafelwein/Landwein, QbA and Kabinett to the bottom of this ladder and legitimized the use of these terms for all grape varieties and vineyards so long as the grapes had enough sugar. Together with rampant commercialism this led to a vast expansion of Germany's vineyard area. Most of the new vineyards are poorly sited, planted with inferior modern grapes and the mass-produced 'sugar-water' they yielded in the 1970s and '80s all but destroyed Germany's reputation for quality.

Vineyard classifications

Quality-orientated German growers have long argued that in their ultimate cool-climate wine country the difference in potential between ideally exposed and poorly sited vineyards is immense, and that the wine law must recognize this. They insist that it is no coincidence that vineyards such as the Mosel's Brauneberger Juffer-Sonnenuhr have enjoyed special reputations for centuries. Today vineyard classification is the rallying call of Germany's new generation of winemakers.

Classifications (in ascending order)

Tafelwein Most is thin and cheap, but some winemakers sell their new oak-aged wines under this designation, as in Tuscany.

QbA (Qualitätswein bestimmter Anbaugebeite) If sold without vineyard designation, these ought to be dryish for everyday drinking; if with a vineyard name, then of some depth and sophistication.

QmP (Qualitätswein mit Prädikat) wines:

Kabinett Light-bodied (7.5–10° alcohol) but vibrant, aromatic wines with a balance just off dryness. The lowest legal designation for non-chaptalized wines.

Spätlese A medium-bodied, late-harvest wine which, however intense in aroma and flavour, should still have a certain lightness but also be capable of long aging.

Auslese Full and rich with a pronounced natural sweetness and balancing acidity, and at least a decade's aging potential. Some estates sell Auslesen as either Trocken (bone dry) or Halbtrocken (off-dry).

Beerenauslese (BA) Rich, luscious dessert wines made from selected botrytized grapes, the acidity preventing an impression of heaviness or cloyingness, and always slow developers.

Trockenbeerenauslese (TBA) Massively concentrated dessert wines with intense raisiny botrytis character that need decades of aging for their full riches to unfold.

Eiswein Made from naturally frozen grapes, Eisweins have a tense sweet-sour balance and rich tropical fruit flavours.

GREAT GERMAN WINES

Oz Clarke's selection
Oberhäuser Brücke Riesling Eiswein ♀ **(Dönnhoff)** A concentrated mouthful of intense fruit from the Nahe's top grower.
Erdener Prälat Riesling Auslese 'Gold Cap' ♀ **(Loosen)** Tiny vineyard and minuscule production provides an unexpected but unforgettable element of sensuality to a great Mosel.
Nackenheimer Rothenberg Riesling Auslese 'Gold Cap' ♀ **(Gunderloch)** Fritz Hasselbach's handling of Rothenberg Riesling fruit produces one of Germany's most recognizable single-vineyard wines.
Serriger Schloss Saarstein Riesling ♀ From Kabinett to Eiswein the estate produces searingly focused Rieslings that grip the palate and gladden the heart.
Haardter Herrenletten Grauburgunder BA ♀ **(Müller-Catoir)** Southern Germany's greatest winemaker shows what fabulous quincy, honeyed succulence he can coax from the Pinot Gris grape.
Escherndorfer Lump Riesling TBA ♀ **(Horst**

Sauer) Brilliant, super-sweet wine from one of Franken's star producers, but all Sauer's wines, from bone dry to succulent, are excellent.
Ürziger Würzgarten Riesling Auslese 'Gold Cap' ♀ **(Mönchhof)** Exciting, spicy, wild-eyed wine packed with fruit and intensity, from one of the Mosel's most individual single vineyards.
Maximin Grünhäuser Abtsberg Riesling Auslese single Füder ♀ Fragrant, elegant, hauntingly beautiful style — sublime honey mingled with limeflower scent and slate acidity.

Steven Spurrier's selection
Rüdesheimer Berg Schlossberg Riesling Charta ♀ **(Breuer)** Classic Rheingau dry Riesling from a medium-sized estate run by Bernhard Breuer.
Forster Pechstein Riesling Auslese ♀ **(Bürklin-Wolf)** One of Germany's largest

private wine estates, over 4 centuries old, making superb wines in the Pfalz region.
Brauneberger Juffer-Sonnenuhr Riesling Auslese ♀ **(Fritz Haag)** A famous Mosel estate, with vines in the famous 'Sundial' vineyard, making superb, elegant wines.
Wehlener Sonnenuhr Riesling Spätlese ♀ **(Loosen)** The young Ernst Loosen has continued to make benchmark wines from this famous estate.
Maximin Grünhäuser Abtsberg Riesling Spätlese ♀ Carl von Schubert has made this the finest estate in the Ruwer.
Scharzhofberger Riesling Spätlese ♀ **(Müller-Scharzhof)** One of the best estates in the Saar, Egon Müller's wines are famed for their clarity of fruit.
Mülheimer Helenenkloster Riesling Eiswein ♀ **(Richter)** Dr Dirk Richter is Germany's foremost producer of Eiswein, a rare speciality among his other fine wines.
Serriger Schloss Saarstein Riesling Spätlese ♀ One of the most elegant and longest lived wines in the region.

Top German producers _____

Riesling von Bassermann-Jordan, BECKER, BIFFAR, BREUER, BÜRKLIN-WOLF, CHRISTOFFEL, Schlossgut DIEL, DÖNNHOFF, GUNDERLOCH, Fritz HAAG, HAART, HEYL ZU HERRNSHEIM, HEYMANN-LÖWENSTEIN, von HÖVEL, JOHANNISHOF, JOST, KARLSMÜHLE, KARTHÄUSERHOF, KELLER, von KESSELSTATT, KOEHLER-RUPRECHT, KÜNSTLER, LEITZ, LOEWEN, LOOSEN, MAXIMIN GRÜNHAUS, Georg Mosbacher, MÜLLER-CATOIR, MÜLLER-SCHARZHOF, J J PRÜM, REBHOLZ, Max. Ferd. RICHTER, ST ANTONY, SCHAEFER, SCHLOSS REINHARTSHAUSEN, SELBACH-OSTER, WAGNER, WEIL, WOLF, ZILLIKEN.
Dry Weissburgunder/Grauburgunder/Chardonnay Fritz Becker, BERCHER, BERGDOLT, FÜRST, HEGER, HEYL ZU HERRNSHEIM, HUBER, JOHNER, Franz Keller, Messmer, MÜLLER-CATOIR, REBHOLZ, Salwey, Wehrheim, WOLF.
Spätburgunder reds BERCHER, HEGER, HUBER, JOHNER, Knipser, KOEHLER-RUPRECHT, Meyer-Näkel, REBHOLZ.
Aromatic grapes BERCHER, HUBER, Andreas LAIBLE, MÜLLER-CATOIR, REBHOLZ.

A–Z OF GERMAN WINE VILLAGES

BACHARACH

The most important Mittelrhein village for fine Riesling. Dry wines can be good, but it is with some natural sweetness that these wines reveal their full racy charm.

First growth vineyards Hahn, Posten.

Best producers Toni JOST, Randolf Kauer, Helmut Mades, Jochen Ratzenberger.

Best years 1999, '98, '97, '96, '95, '93, '92, '90, '89.

BERNKASTEL

Medieval town on the Mittel Mosel reputed for wines of classical elegance, but the vineyards are of widely varying quality. At their rare best they can produce wines of great subtlety. The lesser wines, however, can be hard and earthy.

First growth vineyards Alte Badstube am Doctorberg, Doctor, Graben, Lay.

Best producers Hansen-Lauer, LOOSEN, Joh Jos PRÜM, SELBACH-OSTER, WEGELER.

Best years 1999, '98, '97, '95, '93, '90, '88, '83.

BRAUNEBERG

A century ago Brauneberg's wines were considered the finest in the entire Mosel, and not without good reason. They marry minerally power with ripe peachy fruit and firm structure; these are Rieslings which can impress when young, but also possess enormous aging potential.

First growth vineyards Juffer, Juffer-Sonnenuhr.

Best producers Bastgen, Fritz HAAG, Willi HAAG, Max Ferd. RICHTER.

Best years 1999, '98, '97, '95, '93, '90, '88, '85, '83, '79, '75, '71.

DEIDESHEIM

This old town in the heart of the Pfalz produces full, aromatic Rieslings with silky acidity (therefore they are also good as dry wines). Drought-stressed vines can be a problem in very hot years.

First growth vineyards Grainhübel, Hohenmorgen, Kalkofen, Leinhöhle.

Best producers von Bassermann-Jordan, Josef BIFFAR, von Buhl, J L WOLF.

Best years 1999, '98, '97, '96, '93, '92, '90, '89.

DORSHEIM

This village has some of the best vineyards on the Lower Nahe. Stony soils and steep slopes result in Rieslings that can easily be mistaken for great Mosel wines, but are rather more forthright and assertive.

First growth vineyards Burgberg, Goldloch, Pittermännchen.

Best producer Schlossgut DIEL.

Best years 1999, '98, '97, '96, '95, '93, '90, '89, '86, '83, '79, '76, '75, '71.

DURBACH

Wine town in Baden's Ortenau district with excellent vineyards for Riesling (local name Klingelberger), which is unusual for Baden, as well as Traminer (here called Klevner) and Scheurebe. Poor granitic soil and steep inclines give the wines a delicacy and freshness rare in Baden.

First growth vineyards Plauelrain, Schlossberg, Schloss Grohl.

Best producer Andreas LAIBLE.

Best years 1999, '98, '97, '96, '94.

ERBACH

A single vineyard, the Marcobrunn, has made this Rheingau village famous, although it possesses a handful of fine sites. Austere in their youth, the Rieslings with natural sweetness become classics after 3–5 years of aging but in great vintages can last for 20 years or more.

First growth vineyards Marcobrunn, Schlossberg, Siegelsberg.

Best producers von Knyphausen,

SCHLOSS REINHARTSHAUSEN.
Best years 1999, '97, '95, '94, '92, '90, '89.

ERDEN

The massive red-slate cliffs of Erden stand out from the grey-slate hillsides typical of the Mittel Mosel. This soil and an extremely favourable exposition result in substantial wines with a firm minerally core. The site at Prälat produces the richest and most exotic of all Mosel-Saar-Ruwer wines.

First growth vineyards Prälat, Treppchen.
Best producers J J CHRISTOFFEL, LOOSEN, Meulenhof, Mönchhof.
Best years 1999, '98, '97, '96, '95, '94, '93, '90.

FORST

Historically regarded as the premier wine village of the Pfalz, Forst has a string of great vineyards whose Riesling wines marry power and firm structure with an elegance rare in this region. Quality has much improved in recent years.

First growth vineyards Jesuitengarten, Kirchenstück, Pechstein, Ungeheuer.
Best producers von Bassermann-Jordan, BÜRKLIN-WOLF, Georg Mosbacher, Werlé, J L WOLF.
Best years 1999, '98, '97, '96, '94, '90, '89.

GRAACH

The combination of deep slate soils and some of the Mittel Mosel's steepest slopes results in naturally sweet Rieslings with a strong blackcurrant aroma, very firm structure and great aging potential.

First growth vineyards Domprobst, Himmelreich, Josephshöf (wholly owned by von KESSELSTATT).
Best producers von KESSELSTATT, LOOSEN, Joh Jos PRÜM, Willi SCHAEFER.
Best years 1999, '98, '97, '96, '95, '94, '93, '90, '88, '83.

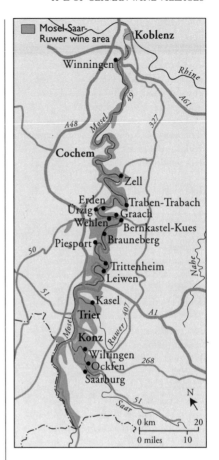

HAARDT

This small suburb of Neustadt is home to some of the finest vineyards in the Pfalz which yield some of the region's most substantial and expressive dry and naturally sweet Riesling wines.

First growth vineyards Bürgergarten, Herrenletten.
Best producers MÜLLER-CATOIR, Weegmüller.
Best years 1999, '98, '97, '96, '93, '92, '90, '89, '88, '85, '83, '79, '76.

HATTENHEIM

This famous Rheingau village with many excellent vineyards gives medium-bodied wines with ample fruit and classical harmony. Owing to vineyard reorganization, the mostly young vines limit the potential at present.

First growth vineyards Nussbrunnen, Pfaffenberg, Wisselbrunnen, also Steinberg (without the village name on the label).

Best producers SCHLOSS REINHARTSHAUSEN, Schloss Schönborn.

Best years 1999, '98, '97, '96, '93, '92, '90, '89.

HOCHHEIM

This village produces the most powerful Rheingau Rieslings – both dry and sweet – with full apricot-citrus fruit, often a pronounced earthiness and great aging potential.

First growth vineyards Domdechaney, Hölle, Kirchenstück, Königin Victoria Berg.

Best producers Franz KÜNSTLER, W J Schäfer, Domdechant WERNER.

Best years 1999, '98, '97, '96, '94, '93, '92, '90.

IHRINGEN

This village in the Kaiserstuhl area of Baden has the region's warmest vineyards. The volcanic soil is ideal for the Pinot family of grapes which give rich, spicy wines with the structure to age.

First growth vineyards Winklerberg.

Best producers Dr HEGER, Stigler.

Best years 1999, '98, '97, '96, '93, '90, '89, '88, '86, '85.

IPHOFEN

The best vineyards in the Steigerwald area of Franken belong to the beautiful town of Iphofen. They give big, earthy dry Rieslings and Silvaners, muscular wines that need 2–3 years to open up.

First growth vineyards Julius-Echter-Berg, Kronsberg.

Best producers JULIUSSPITAL, Johann Ruck, Hans Wirsching.

Best years 1999, '97, '94, '93, '92, '90, '88.

JOHANNISBERG

The Rheingau's most famous wine village produces wines capable of great nobility and extremely long aging but which can often disappoint.

First growth vineyards Goldatzel, Hölle, Schloss Johannisberg.

Best producers JOHANNISHOF, SCHLOSS JOHANNISBERG (since 1996).

Best years 1999, '98, '97, '95, '93, '90, '89, '83, '76, '75, '71.

KALLSTADT

Once a limestone quarry, the Saumagen vineyard's chalky soil makes the most muscular and slow-developing dry Rieslings in the Pfalz, as well as fine dry wines from all the Pinot family.

First growth vineyards Annaberg, Saumagen.

Best producer KOEHLER-RUPRECHT.

FIRST GROWTH VINEYARDS OR *ERSTES GEWÄCHS*

Controversy about vineyard classification still rages in Germany, and reform of the wine law still looks a long way off. The pro-classification lobby on the Rhine have published maps of the 'Grand Cru' vineyards of the Pfalz and Rheingau, and established a framework of rules for the production of wines from them. These have been christened 'Erstes Gewächs' or First Growth vineyards. Historical classification maps for the Nahe and Mosel-Saar-Ruwer have been reprinted, and a hard core of pro-classification winemakers here are already working along principles similar to those of their colleagues on the Rhine, although they do not yet use the 'Erstes Gewächs' name. We shall hear much more about this during the coming years.

Best years 1999, '97, '96, '95, '94, '93, '90.

KASEL

This is the most important wine village in the Ruwer valley. It has 2 superb vineyards which give naturally sweet Rieslings of typical Ruwer steely piquancy enhanced by intense blackberry-blackcurranty aromas and these are some of the longest-lasting Ruwer wines.

First growth vineyards Kehrnagel, Nies'chen.

Best producers KARLSMÜHLE & PATHEIGER, von KESSELSTATT.

Best years 1999, '97, '95, '93, '92, '90, '89, '83.

KIEDRICH

The peachy, yet sleek Rieslings of this historic Rheingau village give them an almost Mosel-like quality, but with more body and richness, in the naturally sweet style, and with great aging potential. The steep Gräfenberg site with its phyllite soil is one of the best in the Rheingau.

First growth vineyards Gräfenberg, Sandgrub, Wasseros.

Best producer Robert WEIL.

Best years 1999, '98, '97, '96, '95, '94, '92, '90.

LEIWEN

This Mittel Mosel village has both mediocre and excellent vineyards and is now home to a handful of ambitious, hard-working young winemakers. The emphasis is on dry Rieslings, but the sweet wines are better.

First growth vineyard Laurentiuslay.

Best producers GRANS-FASSIAN, LOEWEN.

Best years 1999, '98, '97, '96, '95, '93, '90, '88.

MÜNSTER

Though few wines come up to full potential at present, this village in the Lower Nahe has 2 top vineyards capable of

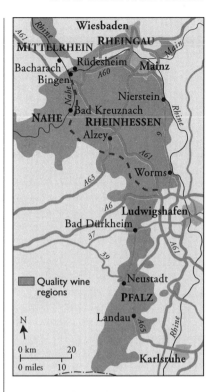

producing substantial, juicy, aromatic wines, especially the drier style of Riesling.

First growth vineyards Dautenpflänzer, Pittersberg.

Best producer Krüger-Rumpf.

Best years 1999, '98, '97, '96, '93, '90, '89.

NACKENHEIM

The soaring slope of the Rothenberg vineyard with its stony, red slate soil right on the bank of the Rhine gives some of the richest dry and sweet Rieslings on the Rhine. They need 2–5 years' aging, but have the potential for much longer.

First growth vineyard Rothenberg.

Best producer GUNDERLOCH.

Best years 1999, '98, '97, '96, '95, '94, '93, '92, '90, '89.

NIEDERHAUSEN

This village has the finest Nahe vineyards. Complex geology results in intensely minerally wines of great aromatic subtlety and raciness. In top vintages the dry wines are good but it is the naturally sweet Rieslings that are world class.

First growth vineyards Hermannsberg, Hermannshöhle, Kerz, Rosenheck, Steinberg.

Best producers CRUSIUS, DÖNNHOFF.

Best years 1999, '98, '97, '96, '95, '93, '90, '89.

NIERSTEIN

On the famous Rheinterrasse where the vineyards rise directly from the Rhine, Nierstein is blessed with a larger area of fine vineyards than any other Rheinhessen wine village, producing rich, supple Rieslings capable of great breeding, unusually for Germany, in both dry and sweet styles.

First growth vineyards Brudersberg, Glöck, Hipping, Oelberg, Orbel, Pettenthal.

Best producers HEYL ZU HERRNSHEIM, ST ANTONY, Dr Alex Senfter.

Best years 1999, '98, '97, '96, '94, '93.

OCKFEN

The Bockstein vineyard can give some of the most charming Saar wines, especially in a sunny year, but few producers currently realize this potential.

First growth vineyard Bockstein.

Best producers Dr WAGNER, ZILLIKEN.

Best years 1999, '97, '95, '93, '90, '89, '88, '83.

PIESPORT

The amphitheatre of the Goldtröpfchen vineyard is one of the greatest sites in the Mittel Mosel, producing Rieslings with baroque fruit aromas and a firm structure that needs natural sweetness to balance.

First growth vineyards Domherr, Goldtröpfchen, Kreuzwingert.

Best producers Reinhold HAART, Kurt Hain, von KESSELSTATT, Weller-Lehnert.

Best years 1999, '98, '97, '95, '94, '93, '92, '90, '89.

RAUENTHAL

In the Rheingau, Rauenthal is blessed with many top sites but few of today's Rieslings have the intense spicy, minerally character for which they were once renowned.

First growth vineyards Baiken, Gehrn, Nonnenberg, Rothenberg, Wülfen.

Best producers J B BECKER, BREUER.

Best years 1999, '98, '97, '96, '95, '94, '93, '92, '90, '89.

RÜDESHEIM

The steep vineyards of the Rüdesheimer Berg lie on the bend of the Rhine in the Rheingau opposite Bingen and produce Rieslings with a silkiness and richness ideal for the dry style. Not to be confused with the Nahe village of the same name.

First class vineyards Berg Roseneck, Berg Rottland, Berg Schlossberg, Bischofsberg.

Best producers BREUER, JOHANNISHOF, Josef LEITZ.

Best years 1998, '97, '96, '94, '93, '92, '90, '89.

SAARBURG

This little known Saar town has the excellent Rausch vineyard which gives minerally wines capable of very long aging.

First growth vineyard Rausch.

Best producers Dr WAGNER, ZILLIKEN.

Best years 1999, '97, '95, '93, '90, '89, '88, '85, '83.

SCHLOSSBÖCKELHEIM

Famous Nahe village producing steely, even austere, Rieslings which need 2–5 years to show at their best but which are also long-living.

First growth vineyards Felsenberg, Kupfergrube.

Best producers CRUSIUS, DÖNNHOFF.

Best years 1999, '98, '97, '96, '95, '94, '93.

ÜRZIG

The red sandstone-slate soil and exceptional mesoclimate of this village, nestling in the crook of a dramatic loop of the Mosel, give intensely spicy, naturally sweet Rieslings, with extraordinary power.
First growth vineyards Goldwingert, Würzgarten.
Best producers J J CHRISTOFFEL, LOOSEN, Mönchhof, Peter Nicolay.
Best years 1999, '98, '97, '96, '95, '94, '93, '92, '90, '88.

WACHENHEIM

An important Pfalz wine town producing medium-bodied, elegant dry and sweet Rieslings, and also great dessert wines.
First growth vineyards Belz, Goldbächel, Rechbächel.
Best producers Josef BIFFAR, BÜRKLIN-WOLF, Karl Schaefer, J L WOLF.
Best years 1999, '98, '97, '96, '94, '93, '92, '90.

WEHLEN

The great steep Sonnenuhr or 'Sundial' vineyard produces the most elegant and finely nuanced Mosel Rieslings. They can be a little facile, but the finest ones are rich and precisely poised.
First growth vineyard Sonnenuhr.
Best producers Pauly Bergweiler, Heribert KERPEN, LOOSEN, Joh Jos PRÜM, S A PRÜM, WEGELER, WEINS-PRÜM.
Best years 1999, '98, '97, '96, '95, '94, '93, '91, '90, '89, '88.

WILTINGEN

An important Saar village with one great vineyard, the south-east-facing Scharzhofberg, whose wines represent the nobility and racy refinement of which Saar Riesling is capable.
First growth vineyards Braune Kupp, Gottesfuss, Scharzhofberg (without the village name on the label).
Best producers von KESSELSTATT, MÜLLER-SCHARZHOF, von Hövel.
Best years 1999, '97, '95, '94, '93, '90, '89, '88.

WINNINGEN

Large Lower Mosel village whose terraced vineyards give unusually full, supple wines for the region, both dry and sweet.
First growth vineyards Röttgen, Uhlen.
Best producer HEYMANN-LÖWENSTEIN.
Best years 1999, '98, '97, '96, '95, '94, '93, '90, '89.

WÜRZBURG

Unofficial wine capital of the Franken region with fine vineyards, including the famous Stein directly overlooking the city, producing the most elegant Franken wines, with good aging potential. Some Rieslings can be great but the real star here is the Silvaner grape.
First growth vineyards Abtsleite, Innere Leiste, Stein.
Best producers Bürgerspital, JULIUSSPITAL, Staatlicher Hofkeller.
Best years 1999, '97, '94, '93, '92, '90.

OAK VERSUS STAINLESS STEEL

For many in Germany's wine industry, new technology has been synonymous with progress. From the 1960s stainless steel tanks began replacing the large traditional barrels of old, neutral wood. Often their arrival was linked to other changes in winemaking and the result was polished wines with little character.

During the early 1980s German winemakers began experimenting with *barriques* or small new oak casks for the maturing of dry white and red wines, at first with disastrous results, in recent years with increasing success. Today a typical German estate's cellar contains stainless steel and old oak casks for Riesling, and barriques for dry wines from the Pinot grapes. Those winemakers who vinify exclusively in wood are no longer regarded as old-fashioned.

A–Z OF GERMAN PRODUCERS

J B BECKER, Walluf, Rheingau   06123 72523/75335

Idiosyncratic estate concentrating on austere dry Rieslings which need long aging, but also making elegant Riesling Spätlese and Auslese and occasional superb dessert wines. A small amount of good Spätburgunder red wine is also made from old vines.

Best wines ★★ Wallufer Walkenberg Riesling TBA ♀, ★Wallufer Walkenberg Riesling Spätlese Trocken ♀ and Rauenthaler Wülfen Riesling Spätlese ♀

Best years 1997, '96, '95, '94, '92, '90, '89, '88, '83, '76, '75, '71

BERCHER, Burkheim, Baden   07662 212/8279

The Bercher brothers, Rainer and Eckhardt, are Baden's most consistent wine producers. Their rich, fleshy Spätburgunder reds are among Germany's best in this style. The powerful, spicy dry Weissburgunder and Grauburgunder whites are also impressive, particularly the new oak-aged 'SE' or Selektion wines.

Best wines ★★ Burkheimer Feuerberg Spätburgunder Spätlese Trocken 'SE' ♥, Burkheimer Feuerberg Weissburgunder Spätlese Trocken 'SE' ♀ and Burkheimer Feuerberg Grauburgunder Spätlese Trocken 'SE' ♀, ★ Burkheimer Feuerberg Chardonnay Spätlese Trocken 'SE' ♀

Best years 1999, '98, '96, '94, '93

BERGDOLT, Duttweiler, Pfalz   06327 5027/1784

Rainer Bergdolt specializes in concentrated dry Weissburgunder vinified in traditional German style and in new oak, which are among the few great dry German wines, and are capable of long aging. Since 1992 he has also made full, silky Spätburgunder reds.

Best wines ★★ Kirrweiler Mandelberg Weissburgunder Spätlese Trocken ♀ and Weissburgunder Spätlese Trocken (oaked) ♀, ★ Chardonnay Spätlese Trocken (oaked) ♀, Riesling Spätlese Trocken and Spätburgunder Spätlese Trocken ♥

Best years 1999, '98, '97, '96, '94, '93, '92, '90

JOSEF BIFFAR, Deidesheim, Pfalz   06326 5028/7697

During the 1990s the Biffars produced some of the finest dry and naturally sweet Rieslings in the Pfalz. Vibrant fruit aromas and crystaline purity of flavour combine with considerable substance. The dry Weissburgunder is good, but not as good as the Riesling. Recently the wines have lacked a little excitement.

Best wines ★★ Deidesheimer Grainhübel Riesling Spätlese trocken ♀ and Wachenheimer Goldbächel Riesling Spätlese ♀, ★ Ruppertsberger Reiterpfad Riesling Spätlese Trocken ♀

Best years 1999, '98, '97, '96, '95, '94, '93, '92, '90

GEORG BREUER, Rüdesheim, Rheingau   06722 1027/4531

During recent years Bernhard Breuer's wines have gained in depth and sophistication by leaps and bounds. Powerful, slow-developing dry Riesling is the focus of production, but the dessert wines now also belong to the Rheingau's top rank. Breuer is a tireless promoter of vineyard class and sells his wines from top sites as 'Erstes Gewächs' (see page 188).

Best wines ★★ Rüdesheimer Berg Schlossberg Riesling 'Erstes Gewächs' Trocken ♀, Rauenthaler Nonnenberg Riesling 'Erstes Gewächs' Trocken ♀ and Rüdesheimer Berg Schlossberg Riesling Auslese ♀, ★ Montosa Riesling Trocken ♀

Best years 1999, '98, '97, '96, '94, '93, '92, '90, '86, '83

DR BÜRKLIN-WOLF, Wachenheim, Pfalz   06322 95330/953330
Since 1993 this large, famous Pfalz estate has shot back towards the top under the
direction of Christian von Guradze. Today the emphasis is on powerful dry Rieslings as
well as Riesling dessert wines which have always been the estate's speciality. Quality is
still on the rise.
Best wines ★★★ Wachenheimer Gerümpel Riesling TBA ♀ and Forster Pechstein Riesling
Auslese ♀, ★★ Forster Kirchenstück Riesling 'Erstes Gewächs' Trocken ♀, ★ Ruppertsberger
Reiterpfad Riesling 'Erstes Gewächs' Trocken ♀
Best years 1999, '98, '97, '96, '95, '94, '93, '90, '89, '76, '71

J J CHRISTOFFEL, Ürzig, Mosel-Saar-Ruwer   06532 2176/1471
Very small estate making extremely elegant, refined wines from the top Würzgarten or
'Spice Garden' site and from the Treppchen site in neighbouring Erden. The prices are
moderate for this quality but limited production means they sell out quickly.
Best wines ★★★ Ürziger Würzgarten Riesling Eiswein ♀, ★★ Ürziger Würzgarten Riesling
Auslese ♀ and Erdener Treppchen Riesling Auslese ♀, ★ Ürziger Würzgarten Riesling Spätlese ♀
Best years 1999, '98, '97, '96, '95, '94, '93, '92, '90

CRUSIUS, Traisen, Nahe   0671 33953/28219
Under Hans Crusius this used to be one of Germany's top estates. Although his son,
Dr Peter, is not yet making wines at this level, his Rieslings with natural sweetness are
impeccably made, clean and racy. They should age well.
Best wines ★ Schlossböckelheimer Felsenberg Riesling Auslese ♀ and Spätlese Halbtrocken ♀
Best years 1999, '98, '96, '95, '94, '93, '88, '85, '83

SCHLOSSGUT DIEL, Burg Layen, Nahe   06721 96950/45047
Armin Diel is the *enfant terrible* of the German wine scene, but since the 1990 vintage
he has concentrated on classic Rieslings with natural sweetness from Dorsheim's top
sites. Today these wines are among the region's most expressive and elegant. Since 1996
the new-style, oak-aged dry Weissburgunder and Grauburgunder have also been good.
Best wines ★★★ Schlossgut Diel Riesling Eiswein ♀, ★★ Dorsheimer Goldloch Riesling
Spätlese ♀, Dorsheimer Pittermännchen Riesling Spätlese ♀ and Dorsheimer Burgberg
Riesling Spätlese ♀
Best years 1999, '98, '97, '96, '95, '93, '90, '89

H. DÖNNHOFF, Oberhausen, Nahe   06755 263/1067
Year in, year out the quiet, winemaking genius Helmut Dönnhoff produces some of
the most complex and minerally naturally sweet Rieslings in Germany. They all
improve with 5-10 years' aging, the best lasting much longer.
Best wines ★★★ Oberhäuser Brücke Riesling Eiswein ♀ and Auslese ♀, Niederhäuser
Hermannshöhle Riesling Auslese ♀ and Spätlese ♀, ★★ Schlossböckelheimer Kupfergrube
Riesling Spätlese ♀, ★ Norheimer Nellchen Riesling Spätlese Trocken ♀
Best years 1999, '98, '97, '96, '95, '94, '93, '90, '89, '83, '79, '76, '71, '69, '66

EMRICH-SCHÖNLEBER, Monzingen, Nahe   06751 2733/4864
Werner Schönleber's wines would be better known if his estate were not situated in the
little-known wine village of Monzingen in the Nahe. This relative obscurity has not
prevented him from making a string of intense, racy dry and naturally sweet Rieslings
during the last decade, however. All improve for 5 years or more.

Best wines ★★ Monzinger Halenberg Riesling Auslese 'Gold Cap' ♀, ★ Monzinger Halenberg Riesling Auslese Trocken ♀ and Monzinger Frühlingsplätzchen Riesling Spätlese ♀

Best years 1999, '98, '97, '95, '94, '93, '92, '90

RUDOLF FÜRST, Bürgstadt, Franken   09371 8642/69230

A rising star in Franken, Paul Fürst makes a string of remarkably elegant wines for a region renowned for rusticity. His full-bodied, dry Rieslings are full of fruit, the new oak-aged Weissburgunder is the most Burgundian white wine produced in Germany and the Spätburgunder red wines are elegant and subtly perfumed.

Best wines ★★ Bürgstadter Centgrafenberg Riesling Spätlese Trocken ♀, Spätburgunder Spätlese Trocken ❗ and Weissburgunder Spätlese Trocken ♀

Best years ❗1999, '97, '96, '94, '90; ♀1999, '98, '97, '96, '94, '93, '92, '90

GRANS-FASSIAN, Leiwen, Mosel-Saar-Ruwer   06507 3170/8167

Recently, Gerhard Grans' Rieslings with natural sweetness have gained considerably in sophistication, and his Trittenheim wines are the best from this famous Mosel village.

Best wines ★★ Trittenheimer Apotheke Riesling Auslese ♀ and Piesporter Goldtröpfchen Riesling Auslese ♀, ★ Trittenheimer Apotheke Riesling Spätlese ♀

Best years 1999, '98, '97, '96, '95, '93, '90

GUNDERLOCH, Nackenheim, Rheinhessen   06135 2341/2431

Husband-and-wife team Fritz and Agnes Hasselbach have been making some of the richest and most noble Rieslings on the entire Rhine at their estate in Nackenheim. The naturally sweet wines are particularly packed with fruit and extract, and need 2–5 years to open up. The monumental dessert wines will live for decades.

Best wines ★★★ Nackenheimer Rothenberg Riesling TBA ♀, BA ♀ and Auslese 'Gold Cap' ♀, ★★ Nackenheimer Rothenberg Riesling Spätlese ♀, ★ 'Jean Baptiste' Riesling Kabinett ♀

Best years 1999, '98, '97, '96, '95, '94, '93, '92, '90, '89

FRITZ HAAG, Brauneberg, Mosel-Saar-Ruwer   06534 410/1347

Wilhelm Haag, one of Germany's greatest winemakers, makes the finest Rieslings from the great Brauneberg vineyards – these are wines of pristine clarity and exceptional elegance. Some Kabinett and Spätlese wines of recent vintages have been a little light, but the dessert wines from Auslese upwards are superb.

Best wines ★★★ Brauneberger Juffer-Sonnenuhr Riesling BA ♀ and Auslese 'Long Gold Cap' ♀, ★★ Brauneberger Juffer-Sonnenuhr Riesling Auslese ♀ and Spätlese (auction bottling) ♀

Best years 1999, '98, '97, '95, '94, '93, '90, '88, '85, '83, '79, '75, '71

WILLI HAAG, Brauneberg, Mosel-Saar-Ruwer   06534 450/689

Since Marcus Haag took charge of the cellar here, this estate's Mosel Rieslings have added some more style and elegance to the abundant body and fruit which they always possessed. The Auslese and Spätlese wines can be impressive.

Best wines ★★ Brauneberger Juffer Riesling Auslese 'Gold Cap' ♀, Auslese ♀ and Spätlese ♀

Best years 1999, '98, '97, '96, '95, '94, '93, '90, '88, '85, '83

REINHOLD HAART, Piesport, Mosel-Saar-Ruwer   06507 2015/5909

Theo Haart's Rieslings from the famous Goldtröpfchen vineyard prove that Piesport's Rieslings marry baroque extravagance with Mosel elegance. His leaner, but no less concentrated wines from the Wintricher Ohligsberg are also capable of long aging.

Best wines ★★★ Piesporter Goldtröpfchen Riesling TBA ♀ and Auslese 'Gold Cap' ♀,
★★ Piesporter Goldtröpfchen Riesling Auslese ♀ and Spätlese ♀
Best years 1999, '98, '97, '96, '95, '94, '93, '92, '90, '89, '88

DR HEGER, Ihringen, Baden   07668 205/9300

This important estate in the Kaiserstuhl area of Baden near the Alsace border makes
powerful, spicy, dry Weissburgunder and Grauburgunder whites and firm, rich
Spätburgunder reds from the precipitously steep volcanic soils of Winklerberg. Some of
the wines are aged in new oak. All can improve with several years' aging.

Best wines ★★ Ihringer Winklerberg Grauburgunder Spätlese Trocken ♀ and Ihringer
Winklerberg Weissburgunder Spätlese Trocken ♀, ★ Ihringer Winklerberg Weissburgunder
Spätlese Trocken ♀ and Spätburgunder ❗
Best years 1999, '98, '97, '96, '94, '93, '92, '90, '89

HEYL ZU HERRNSHEIM, Nierstein, Rheinhessen   06133 5120/58921

This is the only large Nierstein estate still left in the first rank of Rhine wines. Even the
Rieslings with natural sweetness tend to be balanced on the dry side, an unusual and
completely distinctive style for Rheinhessen. There is also impressively spicy dry
Weissburgunder. Marcus Ahr took over direction at the beginning of 1998.

Best wines ★★ Niersteiner Brudersberg Riesling Spätlese ♀, ★ Niersteiner Brudersberg
Riesling 'Erstes Gewächs' Trocken ♀, Niersteiner Pettenthal Riesling Auslese ♀ and Spätlese ♀
and Niersteiner Oelberg Riesling Auslese ♀ and Spätlese ♀
Best years 1999, '98, '97, '96, '93, '92, '90, '89, '88

HEYMANN-LÖWENSTEIN, Winningen, Mosel-Saar-Ruwer   02606 1919/1909

Far and away the leading winemaker in the Terrassen (or Lower) Mosel, Reinhard
Löwenstein makes some of the region's few exciting dry Rieslings and some
magnificent dessert wines. Quality has been particularly impressive since 1995.

Best wines ★★★ Winninger Uhlen Riesling TBA ♀, ★★ Winninger Uhlen Riesling Auslese ♀
and Winninger Uhlen Riesling 'Erstes Gewächs' Trocken ♀, ★ Winninger Röttgen Riesling
'Erstes Gewächs' Trocken ♀
Best years 1999, '98, '97, '96, '95, '94, '93, '92

VON HÖVEL, Oberemmel, Mosel-Saar-Ruwer   06501 15384/18498

Eberhart von Kunow has always made fine Saar Rieslings, but since dramatically
reducing his vineyard yields in 1993 the rise in quality has been spectacular. The
naturally Kabinett and Spätlese wines are rich and aromatic for a region whose wines
are renowned for their austerity. Most wines can be aged for 10 years or more.

Best wines ★★★ Oberemmeler Hütte Riesling Auslese 'Gold Cap' ♀, ★★ Oberemmeler
Hütte Riesling Spätlese ♀ and Scharzhofberger Riesling Spätlese ♀, ★ Oberemmeler Hütte
Riesling Kabinett ♀ and Scharzhofberger Riesling Kabinett ♀
Best years 1999, '97, '96, '95, '94, '93, '90, '89, '88, '85, '83

BERNHARD HUBER, Malterdingen, Baden   07644 1200/8222

Since the early 1990s Bernhard Huber's powerful and concentrated Spätburgunders
have earned him the reputation of being Germany's leading red wine producer. His
new oak-aged Chardonnay and his traditional dry Gewürztraminer are also superb.

Best wines ★★ Spätburgunder 'Reserve' ❗ and Chardonnay 'Reserve' ♀, ★ Spätburgunder ❗
Best years ❗1999, '98, '97, '96, '95, '94, '93, '92, '91

JOHANNISHOF, Johannisberg, Rheingau   06722 8216/6387

Long the local substitute for the under-performing SCHLOSS JOHANNISBERG, this estate has recently added substantial new holdings in Rüdesheim to its vineyards in Johannisberg, Geisenheim and Winkel. The Rieslings are very pure and sleek with discreet sweetness and need several years to open up.

Best wines ★★ Johannisberger Goldatzel Riesling Spätlese ♀, Rüdesheimer Berg Rottland Riesling Spätlese ♀ and Riesling Kabinett 'Charta' ♀

Best years 1999, '98, '97, '95, '94, '93, '92, '90, '89, '86, '83, '76, '75

KARL-HEINZ JOHNER, Bischoffingen, Baden   07662 6041/8380

Created out of nothing in 1985, this estate is the most consistent producer of new oak-aged white and red wines in Germany. Everything here is impeccably made.

Best wines ★★ Chardonnay 'SJ' ♀ and Grauburgunder 'SJ' ♀, ★ Spätburgunder 'SJ' ❢, Spätburgunder ❢ and Weissburgunder & Chardonnay ♀

Best years 1999, '98, '97, '96, '94, '93, '92, '90, '89

TONI JOST, Bacharach, Mittelrhein   06743 1216/1076

The Mittelrhein's leading estate makes Rieslings as elegant as top Mosel wines, but with more body and obvious succulence. Best of all are the naturally sweet wines from the Bacharacher Hahn vineyard, especially occasional exceptional Beerenauslese and Trockenbeerenauslese, which put most Rheingau Rieslings in the shade.

Best wines ★★ Bacharacher Hahn Riesling Auslese ♀ and Spätlese ♀, ★ Bacharacher Hahn Riesling Kabinett ♀

Best years 1999, '98, '97, '96, '95, '94, '93, '92, '90, '89

JULIUSSPITAL, Würzburg, Franken   0931 3931400/3931414

The Juliusspital was Franken's leading estate in the early to mid-1990s and proved that the region could produce great Riesling and Silvaner wines, rich, yet very clean and beautifully balanced. Sadly the 1998 and '97 vintages were not up to the same standard.

Best wines ★★★ Würzburger Stein Riesling TBA ♀, ★★ Würzburger Stein Riesling Spätlese Trocken ♀, Iphöfer Julius-Echter-Berg Riesling Spätlese Trocken ♀ and Silvaner Spätlese Trocken ♀

Best years 1999, '94, '93, '92, '90

KARLSMÜHLE & PATHEIGER, Mertesdorf, Mosel-Saar-Ruwer   0651 5123/52016

Peter Geiben's cellars may look like a Heath Robinson cartoon, but the wines which come out of them are classic Ruwer Rieslings of crystalline clarity. Best are the naturally sweet wines, but everything at Geiben's 2 estates is beautifully made.

Best wines ★★★ Lorenzhöfer Riesling Auslese 'Long Gold Cap' (Karlsmühle) ♀, ★ Kaseler Nies'chen Riesling Spätlese (Karlsmühle) ♀

Best years 1999, '98, '97, '95, '94, '93, '92, '90, '89, '88

KARTHÄUSERHOF, Eitelsbach, Mosel-Saar-Ruwer   0651 5121/53557

This famous Ruwer estate is the sole owner of the Karthäuserhofberg site – the Riesling from here has a natural sweetness, producing wines with a ravishing, racy, aromatic brilliance. It is the only Mosel estate to sell its wines in bottles with neck labels only. The sweetest, most concentrated wines can last for 10 years or more.

Best wines ★★★ Eitelsbacher Karthäuserhofberg Riesling Auslese 'Gold Cap' ♀, ★★ Eitelsbacher Karthäuserhofberg Riesling Spätlese ♀ and Kabinett ♀

Best years 1999, '97, '95, '94, '93, '91, '90, '89, '88, '86

KELLER, Flörsheim-Dalsheim, Rheinhessen   06243 456/6686
During the 1990s Klaus and Hedwig Keller's estate in Flörsheim-Dalsheim attracted a great deal of attention to this little-known corner of Rheinhessen. The excellent naturally sweet Rieslings are particularly remarkable for this region.
Best wines ★★★ Dalsheimer Hubacker Riesling TBA ♀, ★★ Dalsheimer Hubacker Riesling Auslese ♀, ★ Dalsheimer Hubacker Riesling Spätlese ♀
Best years 1999, '98, '97, '95, '94, '93, '92, '90, '89, '88

HERIBERT KERPEN, Wehlen, Mosel-Saar-Ruwer   06531 6868/3464
This estate is rightly best known for its naturally sweet Rieslings from the famous Sonnenuhr or 'Sundial' site. Full of fruit and charm, they only have moderate aging potential except in great vintages.
Best wines ★★ Wehlener Sonnenuhr Riesling Auslese ♀, ★ Wehlener Sonnenuhr Riesling Spätlese ♀ and Graacher Domprobst Riesling Spätlese ♀
Best years 1999, '98, '97, '95, '93, '90, '89, '88, '85, '83

VON KESSELSTATT, Trier, Mosel-Saar-Ruwer   0651 75101/73316
Very large estate by German standards making excellent dry and sweet Rieslings from a string of first class vineyard sites in all 3 areas of the Mosel-Saar-Ruwer. Modern winemaking of the best kind results in wines with effusive fruit and good structure.
Best wines ★★★ Josephshöfer Riesling Auslese 'Gold Cap' ♀, ★★ Scharzhofberger Riesling Auslese ♀, Josephshöfer Riesling Spätlese ♀, Piesporter Goldtröpfchen Riesling Spätlese ♀ and Kaseler Nies'chen Riesling Spätlese ♀
Best years 1999, '97, '96, '95, '94, '93, '91, '90, '89, '88

KOEHLER-RUPRECHT, Kallstadt, Pfalz   06322 1829/8640
Bernd Philippi makes extremely concentrated dry Rieslings with the power and richness of great white Burgundies, which need several years to give their best. Since 1991 he has also made some of the most impressive Burgundian-style Spätburgunder reds. These and his fine new oak-aged Weissburgunder and Grauburgunder are sold under the 'Philippi' name.
Best wines ★★★ Kallstadter Saumagen Riesling Auslese Trocken ♀, ★★ Kallstadter Saumagen Riesling Spätlese Trocken ♀ and Philippi Spätburgunder ♥, ★ Philippi Grauburgunder ♀ and Weissburgunder ♀
Best years 1999, '98, '97, '96, '95, '94, '93, '92, '90, '89, '88, '83

FRANZ KÜNSTLER, Hochheim, Rheingau   06146 82570/5767
Since Gunter Künstler took over the winemaking at his family estate in Hochheim in 1988 it has been one of leading producers of Rheingau Riesling. While his Rieslings with natural sweetness can impress when drunk young, his dry wines need and reward 3–10 years of aging. In 1996 he purchased the vineyards of the run-down Aschrott estate, also in Hochheim, and achieved immediate success with the first wines.
Best wines ★★★ Hochheimer Hölle Riesling Auslese ♀ and Auslese Trocken ♀, ★★ Hochheimer Hölle Riesling Spätlese Trocken ♀ and Hochheimer Domdechaney Riesling Spätlese ♀
Best years 1999, '97, '96, '95, '94, '93, '92, '90, '89, '88

ANDREAS LAIBLE, Durbach, Baden   0781 41238/38339
The star estate of the Ortenau area of Baden produces very elegant, aromatic dry and sweet Riesling, Traminer and Scheurebe wines from the granitic slopes of Durbach.

Best wines ★★ Durbacher Plauelrain Clevner (Traminer) Auslese ♀ and Durbacher Plauelrain Klingelberger (Riesling) Spätlese ♀, ★ Durbacher Plauelrain Scheurebe Spätlese ♀
Best years 1999, '98, '97, '96, '95, '94, '92, '90

JOSEF LEITZ, Rüdesheim, Rheingau   06722 2293/47658
Self-taught Johannes Leitz shot to prominence in the 1992 vintage with his concentrated dry Rieslings from the top vineyards of Rüdesheim. Since then he has also mastered the making of deep, complex wines with natural sweetness.
Best wines ★★ Rüdesheimer Berg Schlossberg Riesling 'Erstes Gewächs' Trocken ♀ and Rüdesheimer Berg Rottland Riesling 'Erstes Gewächs' Trocken ♀, ★ Rüdesheimer Bischofsberg Riesling Kabinett ♀
Best years 1999, '98, '97, '96, '94, '93, '92, '90, '89

CARL LOEWEN, Leiwen, Mosel-Saar-Ruwer   06507 3094/802332
Karl-Josef Loewen is the rising star of the Mittel Mosel, making rich yet beautifully crafted Rieslings in the naturally sweet style. Auslese and Eiswein dessert wines are his speciality and are superb in top vintages.
Best wines ★★★ Leiwener Klostergarten Riesling Eiswein ♀ and Leiwener Laurentiuslay Riesling Auslese ♀, ★★ Leiwener Laurentiuslay Riesling Spätlese ♀, ★ Detzeimer Maximiner Klosterlay Riesling Spätlese ♀
Best years 1999, '98, '97, '96, '95, '94, '93, '92

DR LOOSEN, Bernkastel, Mosel-Saar-Ruwer   06531 3426/4248
Since the 1990 vintage, Ernst Loosen, one of Germany's foremost protaganists of organic methods, has made some of the country's greatest wines. Ungrafted vines up to 100 years old and minimalistic winemaking result in extremely concentrated, naturally sweet Rieslings. The Prälat wines combine aromatic richness with monumental concentration. The estate owns vines in some of the Mittel Mosel's most famous vineyards and all the wines with a vineyard designation will last at least a decade.
Best wines ★★★ Erdener Prälat Riesling Auslese 'Gold Cap' ♀ and Auslese ♀, Ürziger Würzgarten Riesling Spätlese ♀, Auslese 'Gold Cap' ♀ and Auslese ♀, Wehlener Sonnenuhr Riesling Auslese ♀ and Erdener Treppchen Riesling Spätlese ♀, ★★ Wehlener Sonnenuhr Riesling Spätlese ♀
Best years 1999, '98, '97, '96, '95, '94, '93, '92, '90, '89, '88, '85, '76, '71, '69

MAXIMIN GRÜNHAUS/VON SCHUBERT   0651 5111/52122
Mertesdorf, Mosel-Saar-Ruwer
This famous estate makes supremely refined Rieslings from 3 monopoly sites: Brudersberg, Herrenberg and Abtsberg in ascending order of nobility. Winemaking is traditional with minimal handling in the cellar. The Auslese and higher Prädikat dessert wines can age for decades, and even the Kabinetts benefit from 5 years' aging.
Best wines ★★★ Maximin Grünhäuser Abtsberg Riesling Eiswein ♀, Auslese ♀ and Spätlese ♀, ★★ Maximin Grünhäuser Herrenberg Riesling Spätlese ♀ and Maximin Grünhäuser Abtsberg Riesling Kabinett ♀
Best years 1999, '97, '96, '95, '94, '93, '92, '90, '89, '88, '85, '83, '79, '76, '75, '71

MILZ-LAURENTIUSHOF, Trittenheim, Mosel-Saar-Ruwer   06507 2300/5650
This Mosel estate makes light, but characterful Rieslings in traditional style, mainly with some natural sweetness.

Best wines ★ Trittenheimer Leiterchen Riesling Auslese ♀, Trittenheimer Felsenkopf Riesling Spätlese ♀ and Trittenheimer Apotheke Riesling Spätlese ♀

Best years 1999, '98, '97, '96, '95, '90, '89, '85, '79, '76, '71

MÜLLER-CATOIR, Neustadt, Pfalz   06321 2815/480014

Through an uncompromising approach to quality, owner Henrich Catoir and winemaker Hans-Günther Schwarz have made this one of the most renowned estates in all Germany. The explosively rich, aromatic wines combine power, juiciness and racy clarity. The Auslese, BA and TBA have exceptional aging potential.

Best wines ★★★ Mussbacher Eselshaut Rieslaner TBA ♀, BA ♀ and Auslese ♀ and Haardter Herzog Riesling Spätlese ♀, ★★ Haardter Mandelring Scheurebe Kabinett ♀ and Haardter Herrenletten Riesling Spätlese Trocken ♀

Best years 1999, '98, '97, '96, '94, '93, '92, '90, '89, '88, '86, '85, '83

EGON MÜLLER-SCHARZHOF, Wiltingen, Mosel-Saar-Ruwer   06501 17232/150263

A cultural monument as much as a great estate, producing some of the world's greatest dessert wines and Saar Rieslings of classical elegance and refinement at Kabinett and Spätlese level. The top wines have frequently set new, world-record prices for young wines at auction, while the Spätlese and Auslese show their full glory from 10 years of age. The BA, TBA and Eiswein are of sensational quality and deserve long cellaring.

Best wines ★★★ Scharzhofberger Riesling TBA ♀, Eiswein ♀, Auslese 'Gold Cap' ♀ and Auslese ♀, ★★ Scharzhofberger Riesling Spätlese ♀, ★ Scharzhofberger Riesling Kabinett ♀

Best years 1999, '98, '97, '96, '95, '94, '93, '91, '90, '89, '83, '76, '75, '71

PFEFFINGEN, Bad Dürkheim, Pfalz   06322 8607/8603

Run by Doris Eymael, this leading Pfalz estate has been back on form since 1995. Both the dry and naturally sweet Riesling and Scheurebe wines have a Mosel-like sleekness and delicacy. The Scheurebe Beerenausleses are spectacular dessert wines.

Best wines ★★★ Ungsteiner Herrenberg Scheurebe BA ♀, ★★ Ungsteiner Herrenberg Riesling Spätlese ♀, ★ Ungsteiner Herrenberg Riesling Spätlese Trocken ♀ and Scheurebe Spätlese ♀

Best years 1999, '98, '97, '96, '95, '90, '89, '88

JOH JOS PRÜM, Wehlen, Mosel-Saar-Ruwer   06531 3019/6071

This legendary Mittel Mosel estate, with vines in top sites such as Sonnenuhr in Wehlen, makes exceptionally slow-developing and long-lived traditional Rieslings with natural sweetness. Drunk very young, they can still be a little yeasty, but with age they gain great refinement and breeding. The dessert wines are virtually immortal – they should be aged for a minimum of 5 years, but can live for decades.

Best wines ★★★ Wehlener Sonnenuhr Riesling TBA ♀ and Auslese 'Long Gold Cap' ♀, ★★ Wehlener Sonnenuhr Riesling Auslese ♀ and Spätlese ♀ and Graacher Himmelreich Riesling Auslese ♀ and Spätlese ♀

Best years 1999, '98, '97, '96, '95, '94, '93, '91, '90, '89, '88, '86, '85, '83, '79, '76, '75, '71

S A PRÜM, Wehlen, Mosel-Saar-Ruwer   06531 3110/8555

Although his wines have been somewhat erratic in quality recently, in the right vintage Raimund Prüm makes elegant, extremely typical Mosel Rieslings in the sweet style.

Best wines ★★ Wehlener Sonnenuhr Riesling Auslese ♀, ★ Riesling Spätlese ♀

Best years 1999, '98, '97, '95, '93, '90, '88, '86, '85, '83

REBHOLZ, Siebeldingen, Pfalz   06345 3439/7954

The southern Pfalz's top estate has been making first-rate dry and dessert wines since the late 1940s. Hans-Jörg Rebholz has recently added some impressive new oak-aged red wines to the range. All the wines are slow developing and long lived.

Best wines ★★ 'HJR' Spätburgunder ♥, Birrkweiler Kastanienbusch Riesling Spätlese Trocken ♀ and Siebeldinger Im Sonnenchein Weissburgunder Spätlese Trocken ♀

Best years 1999, '98, '97, '96, '94, '93, '92, '90, '89, '86, '85, '79, '76, '71

MAX. FERD. RICHTER, Mülheim, Mosel-Saar-Ruwer   06534 704/933003

Dr Dirk Richter's Rieslings are classic Mosel wines with natural sweetness and lots of character that drink well young or after extended bottle aging. Unusually for Germany he makes successful Eiswein almost every vintage from the Helenenkloster vineyard.

Best wines ★★★ Mülheimer Helenenkloster Riesling Eiswein ♀, ★★ Graacher Domprobst Riesling Auslese ♀ and Brauneberger Juffer-Sonnenuhr Riesling Spätlese ♀

Best years 1999, '97, '96, '95, '94, '93, '90, '89, '88

ST ANTONY, Nierstein, Rheinhessen   06133 5482/59139

The leading estate in Nierstein specializes in rich, minerally dry Rieslings with excellent aging potential. Director Dr Alexander Michalsky is a champion of vineyard classification and sells his best dry wines as 'Erstes Gewächs' (see page 188). In recent years he has also made some impressive Riesling dessert wines.

Best wines ★★ Niersteiner Oelberg Riesling 'Erstes Gewächs' Trocken ♀, Niersteiner Pettental Riesling Spätlese Trocken ♀ and Niersteiner Oelberg Riesling BA ♀, ★ Niersteiner Orbel Riesling Spätlese Trocken ♀

Best years 1999, '98, '97, '96, '94, '93, '92, '90, '89, '86, '85, '83, '76

WILLI SCHAEFER, Graach, Mosel-Saar-Ruwer   06531 8041/1414

This very small Mittel Mosel estate makes the best and most minerally wines from Graach. These are some of the slowest developing German Rieslings and they should either be drunk young or after a decade of bottle-aging. The finest wines are those from the 'First Growth' Domprobst vineyard.

Best wines ★★★ Graacher Domprobst Riesling BA ♀, Auslese 'Gold Cap' ♀ and Auslese ♀, ★★ Graacher Domprobst Riesling Spätlese ♀

Best years 1999, '98, '97, '96, '95, '94, '93, '92, '90, '89, '88, '85, '83, '79, '76, '75

SCHLOSS JOHANNISBERG, Johannisberg, Rheingau   06722 70090/700933

After a long period of under-performance Germany's most famous estate finally looks to be close to top form again. The wines ought to be the epitome of Rheingau elegance – never sweet, never dominated by acidity, nor superficial – and can age for 10 years or more. The star ratings reflect a mixed performance. Since the 1996 vintage quality has improved dramatically.

Best wines ★★ Schloss Johannisberg Riesling Eiswein ♀ and Auslese ♀, ★ Spätlese ♀ and Kabinett ♀

Best years 1999, '98, '97, '96, '90, '89

SCHLOSS LIESER, Lieser, Mosel-Saar-Ruwer   06531 6431/1068

This once-famous estate fell upon hard times before being rescued by Thomas Haag, son of Wilhelm Haag (see Fritz HAAG). His wines have a racy purity similar to his father's, and old vines in the Lieserer Niederberg-Helden site contribute extra power.

Best wines ★★★ Lieserer Niederberg-Helden Riesling Auslese ♀, **★★** Lieserer Niederberg-Helden Riesling Spätlese ♀

Best years 1999, '98, '97, '96, '95, '94, '93

SCHLOSS REINHARTSHAUSEN, Erbach, Rheingau   06123 676333/4222

This large estate, owning several fine vineyard sites including the great Erbacher Marcobrunn, has had an excellent track record since 1989. The classically elegant Rieslings often need 2–5 years to show their best and are capable of long aging.

Best wines ★★★ Hattenheimer Wisselbrunnen Riesling TBA ♀ and Auslese ♀ and Erbacher Siegelsberg Riesling Auslese ♀, **★★** Erbacher Marcobrunn Riesling Spätlese ♀

Best years 1999, '98, '97, '96, '95, '94, '93, '92, '90, '89

SCHLOSS SAARSTEIN, Serrig, Mosel-Saar-Ruwer   06581 2324/6523

These are modern-style Saar Rieslings – they are polished and very clean, but could sometimes be stronger on character. Occasionally, there is spectacularly rich, powerful Eiswein though. Drink the wines young or age for at least 5 years or more.

Best wines ★★★ Serriger Riesling Eiswein ♀ and Auslese 'Gold Cap', **★★** Spätlese ♀

Best years 1999, '97, '95, '94, '93, '90, '89, '88

SELBACH-OSTER, Zeltingen, Mosel-Saar-Ruwer   06532 2081/4014

Very good estate in the Mittel Mosel with excellent vineyards in Zeltingen as well as in Bernkastel, Graach and Wehlen. Johannes Selbach's elegant Mosel Rieslings are of extremely consistent quality, the wines from each site having a distinct personality. Sadly, this is the only top estate in Zeltingen.

Best wines ★★★ Zeltinger Sonnenuhr Riesling TBA ♀, **★★** Zeltinger Sonnenuhr Riesling Auslese ♀ and Spätlese ♀, Graacher Domprobst Riesling Spätlese ♀ and Wehlener Sonnenuhr Riesling Spätlese ♀

Best years 1999, '98, '97, '96, '95, '94, '93, '90, '89, '88, '85, '83

DR WAGNER, Saarburg, Mosel-Saar-Ruwer   06581 2457/6093

Low-profile estate making impressive, traditional Saar Rieslings, both dry and off-dry, which are better with 5 or even 10 years' aging. The rich flavours often mask the steely acidity so typical of the Saar area.

Best wines ★★ Ockfener Bockstein Riesling Auslese ♀ and Spätlese ♀ and Saarburger Rausch Riesling Spätlese ♀ and Kabinett ♀

Best years 1999, '97, '95, '94, '93, '90

J WEGELER ERBEN, Oestrich-Winkel, Rheingau   06723 7031/1453

Until late 1997 this estate was best known as Wegeler-Deinhard. The Wegeler family then sold their majority shareholding in the Deinhard company but retained Deinhard's 3 estates in the Mosel, Pfalz and Rheingau. These estates have long been consistent producers of high-quality, classic German Rieslings, and since the 1980s have also made a selection of good dry wines. During recent years the Mosel estate has improved dramatically, overtaking the Pfalz and Rheingau estates.

Best wines ★★★ Bernkasteler Doctor Riesling Auslese ♀, **★★** Bernkasteler Doctor Riesling Spätlese ♀, Wehlener Sonnenuhr Riesling Spätlese ♀ and Oestricher Lenchen Riesling Auslese ♀, **★** Geisenheimer Rothenberg Riesling Spätlese ♀ and Forster Ungeheuer Riesling Spätlese ♀

Best years Mosel 1999, '98, '97, '96, '95, '94, '93, '90

ROBERT WEIL, Kiedrich, Rheingau   06123 2308/1546

In only a decade director Wilhelm Weil has turned this once under-performing estate in the Rheingau into one of Germany's premier Riesling producers; these are modern wines (both dry and sweet) in the best sense. The auction bottlings of Auslese and higher Prädikats carry a gold capsule. Always drink with at least a little age and the sweet styles will improve for 10 years or much more. Now owned by Suntory, the Japanese drinks giant.

Best wines ★★★ Kiedricher Gräfenberg Riesling TBA ♀, BA ♀, Auslese ♀ and Spätlese ♀, ★★ Riesling Spätlese ♀ and Kabinett ♀

Best years 1999, '98, '97, '96, '95, '94, '93, '92, '90, '89

DR WEINS-PRÜM, Wehlen, Mosel-Saar-Ruwer   06531 2270/3181

This small estate in the Mittel Mosel produces delicate off-dry and naturally sweet Rieslings. The wines possess a natural sweetness and are full of charm, although a little on the light side. Their aging potential is moderate – 5 years or more in top vintages.

Best wines ★★ Wehlener Sonnenuhr Riesling Spätlese ♀, ★ Ürziger Würzgarten Riesling Spätlese ♀ and Erdener Prälat Riesling Auslese ♀

Best years 1999, '98, '97, '95, '94, '93, '90, '89, '88

DOMDECHANT WERNER, Hochheim, Rheingau   06146 835037/835038

Quality is erratic from this estate so choose the vintage carefully. At their best the Rieslings are racy and elegant with a discreet sweetness and can age for 5 years or more.

Best wines ★★ Hochheimer Domdechaney Riesling Spätlese ♀, ★ Hochheimer Kirchenstück Riesling Spätlese ♀ and Hochheimer Hölle Riesling Kabinett ♀

Best years 1999, '98, '97, '96, '94, '92, '90, '88, '85

J L WOLF, Wachenheim, Pfalz   06322 989795/989796

Star Mosel winemaker Ernst LOOSEN rescued this badly run-down estate with holdings in a string of the region's best sites from chaos just before the 1996 vintage. These are powerful wines from old vines which even so have a purity and vibrancy reminiscent of the Mosel. In just 4 vintages the estate has become one of the Pfalz's best.

Best wines ★★ Forster Jesuitengarten Riesling Auslese Trocken ♀, Wachenheimer Gerümpel Riesling Spätlese ♀ and Wachenheimer Belz Riesling Auslese ♀

Best years 1999, '98, '97, '96

ZILLIKEN, Saarburg, Mosel-Saar-Ruwer   06581 2456/6763

These are intensely minerally, steely Rieslings that need 5 or more years of aging to show their best and the sweeter versions are capable of lasting for decades. In the right vintage the wines combine power and delicacy.

Best wines ★★★ Saarburger Rausch Riesling Eiswein ♀ and Auslese 'Gold Cap' ♀, ★★ Saarburger Rausch Riesling Auslese ♀ and Spätlese ♀

Best years 1999, '97, '95, '94, '93, '91, '90, '89, '85, '83, '79, '76, '75, '71

KLAUS ZIMMERLING, Dresden, Sachsen   Tel 0351 2618752

The leading winemaker in former East Germany, Klaus Zimmerling makes surprisingly powerful dry wines for this northerly and continental region. The Riesling can age too.

Best wines ★★ Pillnitzer Königlicher Weinberg Traminer Trocken ♀, ★ Pillnitzer Königlicher Weinberg Riesling Trocken ♀ and Pillnitzer Königlicher Weinberg Grauburgunder Trocken ♀

Best years 1999, '98, '97, '95

Germany's cool climate means substantial variation between vintages in both style and quality. As elsewhere in Europe, improved viticulture and rigorous selection means that, at least for the very top estates, really poor vintages for the Riesling grape are a thing of the past. The Pinot grapes are much more prone to rot, and inclement harvest conditions can still massacre a vintage for them, as happened in most of Germany in 1995.

Aging qualities

A high content of ripe, tartaric acidity and naturally retained sweetness from the grape are essential factors for the long aging potential of German Rieslings. Dry wines, and wines from vintages very low in acidity, tend to age faster. However, other factors such as vine age, yield and vinification style have crucial effects too. The answer is to know the grower. Many people make the mistake of tasting a young Riesling Spätlese still full of youthful vivacity and assuming that because it is so aromatic and fruity now it will not age. Eiswein is much more charming as a young wine than BA/TBA because it has little or no botrytis. However, only the Eisweins from years when conditions were ideal for this style will age positively for decades (e.g. 1996, '93, '91, '90, '83).

As German Rieslings with natural sweetness age, their character changes dramatically. The bright primary fruit aromas of youth slowly recede, being replaced with minerally, waxy and nutty notes. The wines also taste progressively less sweet, so that a fully mature Riesling Spätlese has a balance that is only just off-dry (making it an ideal wine for the dinner table, particularly for fish dishes). The acidity which gives the fruit flavours their vibrancy during the wine's first years of life becomes ever more silky.

Most successful dry German Rieslings taste best at 2–5 years of age. However, exceptional examples (of which ever more are being made) can live much longer. Dry Weissburgunder (Pinot Blanc) and Grauburgunder (Pinot Gris) are generally quicker-maturing, although wines from the top growers will age as long as any dry Rieslings. The first really impressive Spätburgunder reds date from the early 1990s and their aging potential is unknown.

Maturity charts _____

Most fine German Rieslings below BA/TBA level go through a dumb or closed phase, beginning at 2–3 years and lasting until 5–10 years. The higher the acidity content the more extreme this phase will be. BA/TBA wines and top Auslese with intense botrytis character never go through a dumb phase, but take much longer to reach an ideal harmony and for the mature bouquet to fully develop.

1996 Pfalz Riesling Spätlese

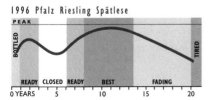

Mosel-Saar-Ruwer Riesling Auslese

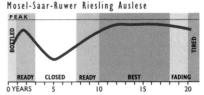

VINTAGE CHART

MOSEL	99	98	97	96	95	94	93	92	90	89	88
QbA, Kabinett, Spätlese	7○	8○	8○	7○	9◐	8◐	8◐	7◐	10○	7●	9◐
Auslese, BA/TBA	7○	7○	9○	8○	9○	8○	9○	7○	10○	8○	9○
RHEINGAU, RHEINHESSEN	**99**	**98**	**97**	**96**	**95**	**94**	**93**	**92**	**90**	**89**	**88**
QbA, Kabinett, Spätlese	7○	8○	7◐	8○	7○	7●	9◐	8◐	10◐	7◐	8◐
Auslese, BA/TBA	8○	8○	8○	9○	8○	9◐	8◐	8◐	9◐	9●	8●
PFALZ	**99**	**98**	**97**	**96**	**95**	**94**	**93**	**92**	**90**	**89**	**88**
Riesling Spätlese	8○	9○	7◐	8◐	5●	7◐	8◐	8●	10●	9●	8●
Grauburgunder, Weissburgunder Auslese	8○	8○	9○	8◐	6●	7●	9●	8●	10●	9●	8◑

KEY ○ = needs more time ◐ = ready but will improve ● = at peak ◑ = fading or tired

Annual vintage reports

1999★★ Harvest rains after a warm September again dashed hopes of a great vintage. Top estates with moderate yields produced richly aromatic wines that will drink well young. Some long-living late-harvest Auslese wines were also made.

1998★★ Riesling grapes survived the torrential harvest rains to produce some of the most classic racy Kabinett and Spätlese wines of recent years. Eiswein looks good and plentiful.

1997★★ The best vintage since 1993 for a number of regions and styles, particularly the Saar and Ruwer and early-ripening Weissburgunder and Grauburgunder.

1996★-★★ The simple quality wines are rather lean (particularly in the Mosel), but at the top estates the wines have enough fruit and extract to balance the high acidity. These wines should be ready in 2-3 years' time. Exciting reds!

1995★-★★ The Pfalz narrowly missed a disaster, its wines often tinged by a hint of rot. In the Mosel this was almost a great vintage, giving wines both rich and racy with extremely long-aging potential.

1994★★ The regular quality wines are a little light, but often already charming. The BA/TBA are rich with botrytis character and the acidity to age for decades.

1993★★ A fine vintage, giving rich, concentrated wines with a silky acidity.

1992★-★★ Much better on the Rhine than the Mosel, where the wines are quite rich and succulent, offering good current drinking. Many Mosels are rather feeble.

1991★ Clearly the weakest vintage of the 1990s, giving rather lean, tart wines.

1990★★★ The last genuinely great vintage. There wasn't a lot of noble rot but a lot of sweet wines were made, nevertheless. Powerful, concentrated Rieslings with ideal acidity for long aging.

1989★★ Hailed as a vintage of the century, but the regular wines are often slightly bitter and have aged quickly. BA/TBA wines are rich, but seldom great.

1988★★ Few blockbusters, but lots of medium-bodied elegant wines. Best Mosel wines now at their peak.

VINTAGES AT A GLANCE

The last decade has seen a string of good vintages in Germany, but only one truly great one, 1990. However, the finest wines from the top growers in other vintages of the 1990s can match them due to reductions in yield and more stringent selection today.

Great Years ★★★	1990, '71, '59, '49, '37, '21, '20, 1893
Good Years ★★	1999, '98, '97, '96, '95, '94, '93, '92 (Rhine), '89, '88, '85, '83, '79, '76, '75, '69
Moderate Years ★	1996 (Mosel), '95 (Pfalz), '92 (Mosel), '91, '87, '81, '77, '73
Poor Years (No Stars)	1984, '82, '80, '78, '74, '72

AUSTRIA

Only recently has the quality of Austria's dry white wines begun to be acknowledged internationally. The best Rieslings and Grüner Veltliners combine the body and concentration found in great white Burgundies with the rich fruit of fine German wines. Austria's great tradition for dessert wines is being revived too, and some exciting reds are starting to be made.

Dry white wines

These have always dominated Austria's wine production. Grüner Veltliner, the principal white grape, gives wines with a bouquet of white pepper, often with green apple or vegetal notes. Most are medium-bodied, crisp wines for everyday drinking, but top sites in Wachau, Kamptal and Kremstal (in Niederösterreich) can give powerful, rich whites with up to 14% natural alcohol. Although Riesling is rare in Austria it is responsible for many of the country's finest dry white wines. They often achieve 12–13% natural alcohol, have a peach/ apricot bouquet and are full and elegant. Like Riesling, Chardonnay arrived in Austria during the 19th century and is primarily grown in Steiermark under the name of Morillon. Sauvignon Blanc is also used there for elegant, aromatic wines. Weissburgunder (Pinot Blanc), Grauburgunder (Pinot Gris) and Neuburger are all important grapes for full dry whites.

Sweet white wines

Burgenland has a long tradition for botrytis wines and the 1990s saw a great revival. Various grapes ares used, from the native Welschriesling (no relative of Riesling and usually very humble) to Chardonnay, from ancient Traminer to the German Scheurebe. Today new oak aging is often used for Ausbruch and BA/TBA wines, but because there is no legal designation for such wines you need to know the grower to be sure of the style.

Red wines

Burgenland also has a red wine tradition. Recently great strides forward have been made, both with indigenous varieties such as Blauer Zweigelt and Blaufränkisch and with imported ones like Cabernet Sauvignon and Pinot Noir.

Classifications

At first glance, the Austrian wine law looks identical to Germany's, but the biggest difference is that the Austrians link some Prädikats to particular wine styles and there are also some maximum alcohol levels.

Qualitätswein Minimum of 9% alcohol, but often much more; usually dry. Maximum yield 60 hectolitres per hectare (also for higher grades). In the Wachau unchaptalized wines of this level are sold as Steinfeder.

Kabinett Minimum of 11% and maximum of 12.7% natural alcohol and always dry. In the Wachau these wines are sold as Federspiel.

Spätlese Minimum of 12.5% potential alcohol, usually dry. In the Wachau wines of this level are sold as Smaragd.

Auslese Usually a light dessert wine, but may also be dry (Trocken).

Beerenauslese (BA) Always a dessert wine, usually with German-style, botrytis character.

Ausbruch Traditionally a dessert wine fermented to Sauternes-like balance (but without new wood). Today often a German-style, botrytized wine, but richer than BA.

Trockenbeerenauslese (TBA) Dessert wines with strong botrytis character, usually in the German style.

GREAT AUSTRIAN WINES

Oz Clarke's selection
Scheurebe TBA ♀
(Kracher) Wonderful, great palateful of pepper, grapefruit and honey.
Langenloiser Steinmassel Riesling ♀ **(Bründlmayer)** Austria can make Rieslings to match Germany's but the style is different – this is beautifully full, almost fat, but scented.
Ruster Ausbruch Cuvée Pinot ♀ **(Feiler-Artinger)** Excellent, syrupy style with an attractive new oak perfume, a savoury tang and a sweet barley-sugar volatility that resembles fine Sauternes.
Tiglat Chardonnay ♀ **(Velich)** World class

Chardonnay, full and ripe, mixing peach and apple fruit with with the spicy hazelnut warmth of good, new oak.
Schilfwein ♀ **(Nekowitsch)** Remarkably intense, exotic sweet wine that swirls spices, peaches and honey together with freshly squeezed lemons and lemon zest.
Steven Spurrier's selection
Sekt Brut Vintage ♀ **(Bründlmayer)** The best estate in Langenlois, producing a fine sparkling wine.
Zöbinger Heiligenstein Riesling 'Alte Reben' ♀ **(Bründlmayer)** One of Austria's very best dry Rieslings.

Spitzer Singerriedel Riesling 'Smaragd' ♀ **(Hirtzberger)** One of the very top Wachau growers, with superb complex Rieslings.
Muskat-Ottonel BA ♀ **(Kracher)** The epitome of what a heady Muskat can be from Austria's greatest sweet winemaker.
Grüner Veltliner BA ♀ **(Opitz)** This spicy, lively varietal is transformed into an extraordinarily luscious wine by Willi Opitz.
Grüner Veltliner 'Smaragd' von den Terrassen ♀ **(Pichler)** One of the finest examples of Austria's local grape, from the Loibner Berg.

Top Austrian producers
Dry Riesling and Grüner Veltliner BRÜNDLMAYER, HIRTZBERGER, Högl, Emmerich KNOLL, Fred Loimer, NIGL, Nikolaihof, PICHLER, Franz PRAGER, Freie Weingärtner WACHAU.
Sauvignon Blanc and Chardonnay/Morillon Gross, Lackner-Tinnacher, POLZ, TEMENT, VELICH.
Sweet wines BRÜNDLMAYER, FEILER-ARTINGER, KRACHER, Nekowitsch, OPITZ, Franz PRAGER, Salomon, VELICH.
Red wines Gesselmann, Gernot Heinrich, Krutzler, Nittnaus, TRIEBAUMER, UMATHUM.

A–Z OF AUSTRIAN PRODUCERS

BRÜNDLMAYER, Langenlois, Kamptal   02734 2172/3748
Top estate in Langenlois, and large by Austrian standards, producing an impeccable range of dry Riesling and Grüner Veltliner wines that combine power and elegance.
Best wines ★★★ Zöbinger Heiligenstein Riesling 'Alte Reben' ♀, Langenloiser Steinmassel Riesling ♀ and Ried Lamm Grüner Veltliner ♀, ★★ Zöbinger Heiligenstein Riesling ♀, Langenloiser Burg Vogelsang Grüner Veltliner ♀ and Sekt Brut Vintage ♀
Best years 1999, '98, '97, '95, '94, '93, '92, '91, '86, '83, '79

FEILER-ARTINGER, Rust, Neusiedlersee-Hügelland   02685 237/6552
Historic estate making spectacular dessert wines in a modern style – with some new oak – since 1993, as well as good dry whites. Since 1997 the reds have been good, too.
Best wines ★★★ Ruster Ausbruch Cuvée Pinot ♀, Ruster Ausbruch ♀ and Cuvée Solitaire ❢
Best years Sweet ♀1999, '98, '97, '96, '95, '93, '91, '89, '81

FRANZ HIRTZBERGER, Spitz, Wachau   02713 2209/220920
Franz Hirtzberger is president of the Wachau winegrowers association and makes the region's most elegant dry whites. Pluris is a Weissburgunder/Grauburgunder blend with a touch of oak. All have excellent aging potential if you have the patience to wait.

Best wines ★★★ Spitzer Singerriedel Riesling 'Smaragd' ♀ and Spitzer Honivogl Grüner Veltliner 'Smaragd' ♀, ★★ Spitzer Hochrain Riesling 'Smaragd' ♀ and Pluris 'Smaragd' ♀
Best years 1999, '98, '97, '95, '94, '93, '92, '90, '88, '86, '83

EMMERICH KNOLL, Loiben, Wachau   02732 79355/793555

Emmerich Knoll's intensely spicy, minerally wines are no charmers when very young, but blossom magnificently with several years in the bottle, and are very long-lasting.
Best wines ★★★ Dürnsteiner Schütt Riesling 'Smaragd' ♀, Loibner Loibenberg Riesling 'Smaragd' ♀ and Loibner Loibenberg Grüner Veltliner 'Smaragd' ♀, ★★ Dürnsteiner Kellerberg Riesling 'Smaragd' ♀
Best years 1999, '98, '97, '96, '95, '94, '93, '92, '91, '90, '89, '88, '86, '85, '83

ALOIS KRACHER, Weinlaubenhof, Burgenland   02175 3377/33774

Kracher not only makes Burgenland's finest dessert wines, he is also an untiring promoter of the wines of his region and nation. 'Zwischen den Seen' denotes wines made in the Germanic style, and 'Nouvelle Vague' those with new oak. Grand Cuvée is a blend of both styles.
Best wines ★★★ Chardonnay-Welschriesling 'Nouvelle Vague' TBA ♀, Scheurebe 'Zwischen den Seen' TBA ♀, Grand Cuvée TBA or BA ♀ and Muskat-Ottonel 'Zwischen den Seen' TBA or BA ♀, ★ Bouvier BA ♀ and Blend No 1 ♥
Best years 1999, '98, '96, '95, '94, '93, '91, '89, '83, '81

FAMILIE NIGL, Senftenberg, Kremstal   02719 2609/26094

When the Nigl family left the local co-operative to go solo in 1986 a new star was born. Their dry white Grüner Veltliners and Rieslings are the most elegant and minerally wines in the Kremstal region and can improve for 5 years or more.
Best wines ★★★ Senftenberger Ried Hochäcker Riesling ♀, ★★ Kremsleiten Riesling ♀, Senftenberger Piri Riesling ♀ and Senftenberger Ried Piri Grüner Veltliner ♀
Best years 1999, '98, '97, '95, '94, '93, '92, '90, '88

WILLI OPITZ, Illmitz, Neusiedlersee   02175 2084/2084

Marketing innovator Willi Opitz is also a winemaking innovator. From only 8ha of vines he makes a remarkable range of dessert wines, including red Eiswein and Schilfwein (made from grapes dried on reeds from the shores of the Neusiedler See).
Best wines ★★ Opitz One TBA ♀, Schilfmandl Weisser Muskat ♀, Blauburger Schilfmandl ♀, and Grüner Veltliner BA ♀
Best years 1999, '98, '96, '95, '94, '91, '89

F X PICHLER, Loiben, Wachau   02732 85375/85375

No Austrian winemaker takes bigger risks in the cause of quality than Franz Xaver Pichler. The result is incredibly concentrated dry Riesling and Grüner Veltliner of majestic proportions, and they are among Austria's finest wines.
Best wines ★★★ Dürnsteiner Kellerberg Riesling 'Smaragd' ♀, Loibner Steinertal Riesling 'Smaragd' ♀, and Dürnsteiner Kellerberg Grüner Veltliner 'Smaragd' ♀, ★★ Loibner Loibenberg Grüner Veltliner 'Smaragd' ♀ and Von den Terrassen ♀, ★ Arachon ♥
Best years 1999, '98, '97, '95, '94, '93, '92, '90, '88, '86

ERICH & WALTER POLZ, Spielfeld, Steiermark   03453 23010/23016

The Polz brothers are Steiermark's most consistent winemakers, producing a wide range of dry varietal white wines with depth and purity. In top years oak-aging is used discreetly for the single-vineyard wines. The regular range is called 'Steirische Klassik'.

Best wines ★★ Sauvignon Blanc Hochgrassnitzberg ♀ and Morillon Hochgrassnitzberg ♀, ★ Sauvignon Blanc 'Steirische Klassik' ♀ and Weissburgunder 'Steirische Klassik' ♀

Best years 1999, '97, '95, '94, '93, '92, '90

FRANZ PRAGER, Weissenkirchen, Wachau   02715 2248/2532

Top Wachau estate making lavishly fruity, aromatic dry Rieslings and Grüner Veltliners that may be drunk young but also age magnificently. Since the early 1990s Prager has pioneered the making of dessert wines in the Wachau.

Best wines ★★★ Weissenkirchener Achleiten Riesling TBA ♀ and Weissenkirchener Achleiten Riesling 'Smaragd' ♀, ★★ Weissenkirchener Klaus Riesling 'Smaragd' ♀

Best years 1999, '97, '96, '95, '94, '93, '92, '90

E & M TEMENT, Berghausen, Steiermark   03453 4101/410130

In higgledy-piggledy cellars Manfred Tement makes the most imposing wines in Steiermark, including some of Austria's top Sauvignon Blanc and Chardonnay (locally called Morillon). The new oak aging for the Zieregg wines has become more restrained.

Best wines ★★ Sauvignon Blanc Zieregg ♀, Morillon Zieregg ♀ and Roter Traminer ♀, ★ Sauvignon Blanc 'Steirische Klassik' ♀

Best years 1999, '98, '97, '95, '94, '93, '92

ERNST TRIEBAUMER, Rust, Neusiedlersee-Hügelland   Tel 02685 528

The leading red wine producer on the western bank of the Neusiedler See specializes in impressive, powerful Blaufränkisch reds with opulent blackberry fruit and good aging potential. There are also increasingly good dry whites, particularly Weissburgunder, and Ausbruch dessert wines.

Best wines ★★ Blaufränkisch Marienthal ♥, ★ Cabernet Sauvignon-Merlot ♥ and Blaufränkisch ♥

Best years 1999, '97, '95, '94, '93, '92, '90

UMATHUM, Frauenkirchen, Neusiedlersee   02172 2173/21734

You could easily mistake Josef Umathum's red wines for Burgundies, such is their elegance. However, in hot years they also have the power and richness typical of Burgenland reds. The top wines are blends of French and native grapes.

Best wines ★★ Hallebühl ♥, ★ Haideboden ♥ and St-Laurent ♥

Best years 1999, '98, '97, '95, '94, '93, '92, '90

VELICH, Apetlon, Neusiedlersee   02175 3187/3187

At this tiny estate casino croupier Roland Velich and his brother Heinz (a full-time winemaker) make far and away Austria's finest Chardonnays, and since 1995 also spectacular dessert wines, especially from Welschriesling.

Best wines ★★★ Tiglat Chardonnay ♀ and Welschriesling TBA ♀, ★★ Muskat Ottonel TBA ♀

Best years Sweet 1999, '98, '96, '95, '94, '91; Dry 1999, '97, '95, '93, '92, '91

FREIE WEINGÄRTNER WACHAU, Dürnstein, Wachau   02711 371/37113

Austria's finest co-operative winery (especially for white wines) has taken a big leap forward since Willi Klinger and Fritz Miesbauer took control with the 1995 vintage.

Best wines ★★ Spitzer Singerriedel Riesling 'Smaragd' ♀, Weissenkirchener Achleiten Riesling 'Smaragd' ♀ and Dürnsteiner Kellerberg Grüner Veltliner 'Smaragd' ♀

Best years 1999, '98, '97, '96, '95, '93, '91, '90, '86, '79, '77

There is no simple rule for identifying a top Austrian vintage, since the conditions that make for fine dessert wines are different from those ideal for dry white and red wines – the former needing moisture for the development of noble rot, the latter dryness for clean ripe fruit.

Aging qualities

High natural alcohol and healthy acidity help give dry Austrian whites great aging potential. A top dry Riesling or Grüner Veltliner can be drunk during the first year after bottling for youthful vivacity, or from 3–5 years when the wine has reached a mature harmony.

Top wines can reach 20–30 years of age in good form, but some modern ones will not achieve this, either because the fermentation has been pushed in order to make a bone-dry wine or because modern viticulture techniques can lead to wines with poor structure.

Austrian dessert wines are appealing to drink at a younger age than top Sauternes and German dessert wines. They can give great pleasure even 1 year after bottling and full maturity is generally reached at 5 years or slightly more. Since wines of comparable quality to today's best wines were very rare 20–30 years ago it is very difficult to assess the long-term aging potential of these modern examples beyond 20 years.

Even less certain is the aging potential of Austrian red wines, since the first impressive ones were made during the top vintages of the early 1990s.

VINTAGE CHART

	99	98	97	96	95	94	93	92	91	90	89
Wachau dry Riesling, Grüner Veltliner	8○	7○	9○	6◐	8○	8●	7●	6●	5◐	9●	7●
	99	98	97	96	95	94	93	92	91	90	89
Neusiedlersee-Hügelland BA and TBA	8○	9○	7○	7○	9◐	7○	6●	6●	8●	7●	8●

KEY ○= needs more time ◐= ready but will improve ●= at peak ◖= fading or tired

VINTAGES AT A GLANCE

Great vintages for all styles of wine are very rare in Austria. The generally dry harvest conditions give top growers the chance to use late and selective picking to compensate for a poor summer. Poor vintages are very rare today.

Great Years ★★★
1998 (dessert wines), '97 (dry wines), '95, '91 (dessert wines), '90 (dry wines), '81 (dessert wines), '77 (dry wines), '71 (dry wines), '69 (dessert wines)
Good Years ★★
1999, '98 (dry wines), '97 (dessert wines), '94, '93, '89, '88, '86, '85, '79, '71 (dessert wines)
Moderate Years ★
1996, '95 (reds), '92, '91, '90 (dessert wines), '83, '82, '76, '75, '73, '70
Poor Years (No Stars)
1987, '84, '80, '78, '74, '72

SWITZERLAND

Most Swiss wine is made as light dry red or white for everyday drinking since the cool climate means that fine wine grapes can be grown only in the most climatically favoured sites. Ambitious producers, however, are using lower yields and oak aging to achieve interesting results.

White wines

Most of Switzerland's vines are in the French-speaking west of the country, where they cling to slopes in the Valais and along the northern shores of Lakes Geneva and Neuchâtel. Here, the Fendant grape gives light, spritzy, dry whites, but in the best communes – Aigle, Dézaley and Yvorne – they can have a nutty-minerally character. The traditional white grapes, Amigne and Arvine, can give fuller-bodied dry whites, the former nutty, the latter peachy and spicy and capable of aging. Experiments with barrel-fermented Chardonnay and Marsanne (usually called Ermitage) have yet to impress.

The Valais has a tradition for sweet wines from Malvoisie (Pinot Gris) and Johannisberg (Silvaner), but only the best can compete internationally.

Red wines

Dôle, a blend of Gamay and Pinot Noir, is the typical red wine of the West. Both here and in the German-speaking East pure Pinot Noir or Blauburgunder wines can be considerably fuller-bodied and more serious. The best ones have black cherry fruit, are medium-bodied with ample tannins and could easily be mistaken for a Côte de Beaune wine. The everyday wine of Italian-speaking Ticino is a light, tart Merlot, but in the 1990s top growers here began to make more powerful, tannic wines. In the Valais experiments with Syrah are still at an early stage. Beware though, as the Swiss are very chauvinistic and even some high-priced reds from 'top' growers can be marred by a vegetal note.

Swiss vintages

For most Swiss wines the best vintage is the latest one, since they simply do not have the potential to age. For the top wines it is often the case that a vintage that is good for one side of the country is mediocre for the other, because the mountains often divide good weather from bad. Lack of ripeness is the most typical problem.

Aging qualities

Most Swiss wines do not age because they are too light in body and structure. Here the high yields which are the norm do not help and ambitious young growers, determined to overcome this problem, often throw too much new oak at their wines. When Swiss wines are good, they impress with bright fruit and a subtle bouquet, rather than body or richness. The Pinot Noir/Blauburgunder reds tend to retain their charm the longest but aging potential is limited to 5–6 years.

Top Swiss producers _____

White wines Badoux, Michel Clavien, Conne, J D Delarze, Fonjallaz, Gantenbein, J Germanier, Gilliard, Grognuz, Caves Imesch, Mathier, du Mont d'Or, Pinget, Raymond, Testuz, Zufferey.
Red wines Gantenbein, Daniel Huber, Werner Stucky, Christian Zündel.

TOKAJI

The hills along the valley of the Bodrog close to Hungary's border with Slovakia give one of the world's great dessert wines: Tokaji, a dense, raisiny, spicy wine of amber-gold colour with slightly less alcohol than Sauternes. At the top level the wines have more acidity and sweetness than Sauternes and can age for a century or more.

Wine styles

Since the fall of Communism in Hungary in 1989 the Tokaji wine industry has undergone a renaissance. This is largely due to the arrival of outside expertise and investment, which has created a string of new wineries. Szamorodni, or 'as it comes', is the simplest quality of wine. It may be dry and steely or slightly sweet and is made from the same trio of grapes responsible for the dessert wines: Furmint, Hárslevelü and Sargamuskotaly (Muscat).

The real glory are the Aszú wines, designated with between 3 and 6 Puttonyos, according to the proportion of shrivelled, nobly rotten grapes in the harvest. The higher the number, the richer, more concentrated and less alcoholic the wine. They all require several years of barrel aging, while the even sweeter 7 Puttonyos Aszú Esszencia, made only in the best years and from completely shrivelled grapes, needs longer still. The ambrosial Esszencia, which has hardly any alcohol and more honey than sugar, is made from the free-run juice of Aszú berries. The leading estates use a certain amount of new oak for aging, and the oxidation which ruined so many wines from the Communist period is a thing of the past.

The main problem today is what to do with the non-botrytized wines. Here experimentation is still under way. So far the results have not been spectacular.

Top Tokaji producers

Bodvin, Disznókö, Hétszölö, Ch. Megyer (5 Puttonyos), Oremus, Ch. Pajzos (5 Puttonyos), Royal Tokaji Wine Co. (5 and 6 Puttonyos Nyula'szó and Szt Tamas, 6 Puttonyos Betsek), Istvan Szepsy (5 Puttonyos).

Tokaji vintages

Sceptism is wise when buying Tokaji wines from the 1960s, '70s and '80s. The standard of vinification during this period was extremely erratic compared with today's professionalism. Pre-war vintages can be magnificent, but they are scarce. Best recent years are 1995 and '93.

GREAT TOKAJI WINES

Oz Clarke's selection

Danczka Essencia ♀ (Szepsy) Leading Tokaji producer creating thrilling wines with concentrated autumn fruits and honey.

Tokaji Aszu 5 Puttonyos Szt Tamas ♀ (Royal Tokaji Wine Co.) Thick exciting wines exhibiting virtually every tropical fruit imaginable, steeped in treacly syrup and topped with lime marmalade.

Tokaji Aszu 5 Puttonyos ♀ (Ch. Megyer) New wave producer creating wines that are uncharacteristically fresh, yet awesomely rich.

Steven Spurrier's selection

Tokaji Aszu 5 Puttonyos ♀ (Ch. Megyer) Classic Tokaji, rich and tangy.

Tokaji Aszu 6 Puttonyos ♀ (Disznókö) A wine of incredible sweetness, yet balanced by a quince-like acidity.

Tokaji Aszu 5 Puttonyos Szt Tamas ♀ (Royal Tokaji Wine Co.) From a historic vineyard classified as 'First Class' in 1700.

ITALY

Not so long ago the words 'Italy' and 'fine wine' were considered by many to be contradictory. At most there would be grudging admission that the odd high-quality wine might occasionally creep out of Tuscany or Piedmont. Things have changed dramatically in the last 20 years and not only is there a plethora of exciting wines, of classic and modern style, from both indigenous and international grapes, issuing from these regions, but other classic zones, like Valpolicella, have seriously pulled up their socks. Meanwhile areas never previously associated with high-quality wine are coming to the fore thanks to modern methods of vinification and improved vineyard techniques. Nor does the fine wine revolution confine itself to the boutique producers, of which there is an ever-growing number: some of the best producers are large private concerns or huge co-operatives.

Classifications

The official quality designation is DOC (Denominazione di Origine Controllata), which guarantees a wine's geographical provenance, its grape mix and certain production details such as length of wood aging. However, only the higher tier, DOCG (the 'G' stands for Garantita) is supposed to guarantee quality (by tasting), and that's not necessarily reliable.

Producers aiming to make top wines in Italy but not wishing to conform to the legal constraints applicable in their zone have in the past 25 years deliberately downgraded their wine to Vino da Tavola in order to upgrade quality; hence the rise of the 'Super-Tuscan' wine and its ilk. The law is now trying to pull these wines back into the official fold by creating new broader DOCs and a higher grade of Vino da Tavola called IGT (Indicazione Geografica Tipica), and the ex-renegades will be incorporated into these categories.

The word 'Riserva' on the label ought to indicate higher quality, certainly extra aging at the winery; the word 'Superiore' may however indicate only a higher alcohol level. So-called 'cru' or vineyard names may have geographical significance in Barolo and Barbaresco, but elsewhere are all too often little more than brand names. The only broadly applicable guarantee of quality is the producer's name.

Top Italian wine zones _____

Red wines Aglianico del Vulture, Alto Adige (Cabernet, Lagrein, Pinot Nero), Barbaresco, Barbera d'Alba, Barbera d'Asti, Barolo, Bolgheri, Breganze, Brindisi, Brunello di Montalcino, Carmignano, Chianti Classico, Chianti Rufina, Cirò, Colli Orientali del Friuli (Cabernet), Collio (Cabernet), Dolcetto d'Alba, Gattinara, Langhe, Montepulciano d'Abruzzo, Roero, Sagrantino di Montefalco, Salice Salentino, Super-Tuscans, Taurasi, Teroldego Rotaliano, Torgiano Riserva, Valpolicella (Classico Superiore, Recioto, Amarone), Valtellina Superiore, Vino Nobile di Montepulciano.

White wines Alto Adige (Chardonnay, Sauvignon), Breganze, Collio and Colli Orientali del Friuli (Chardonnay, Sauvignon, Tocai Friulano), Gavi, Franciacorta, Frascati Superiore, Gavi, Isonzo (Chardonnay, Sauvignon), Langhe, Moscato di Pantelleria, Orvieto, Roero Arneis, Soave (Classico, Recioto), Verdicchio dei Castelli di Jesi, Vermentino di Gallura, Vernaccia di San Gimignano.

Fortified wines Marsala.

Sparkling wines Asti, Franciacorta, Moscato d'Asti, Trento.

Main DOCG / DOC wines

1 Gattinara
2 Barbera d'Asti, Asti, Moscato d'Asti
3 Roero, Roero Arneis, Barbera d'Alba, Langhe
4 Barbaresco, Barbera d'Alba, Barolo, Dolcetto d'Alba, Langhe
5 Gavi
6 Franciacorta
7 Valtellina Superiore
8 Valpolicella Classico, Amarone, Recioto
9 Soave Classico, Recioto
10 Breganze
11 Teroldego Rotaliano
12 Alto Adige
13 Colli Orientali del Friuli, Collio, Isonzo
14 Carmignano
15 Chianti Rufina
16 Vernaccia di San Gimignano
17 Chianti Classico
18 Bolgheri
19 Brunello di Montalcino
20 Vino Nobile di Montepulciano
21 Orvieto
22 Sagrantino di Montefalco
23 Torgiano Rosso Riserva
24 Verdicchio dei Castelli di Jesi, Rosso Conero
25 Montepulciano d'Abruzzo
26 Frascati Superiore
27 Taurasi
28 Aglianico del Vulture
29 Brindisi
30 Salice Salentino
31 Primitivo di Manduria
32 Cirò
33 Marsala
34 Moscato di Pantelleria
35 Vermentino di Gallura

Italian wine areas

0 km   100
0 miles   100

N

MAIN GRAPE VARIETIES

Aglianico
Of Greek origin, it is today found mainly in the uplands of Campania and Basilicata and produces elegant rather than powerful wines of good colour and structure.

Barbera
This prolific red grape is found all over Italy and makes juicy, sappy wines, tending to high acidity but low tannin, combining marvellously with barrique. The best varietals come mainly from Piedmont.

Cabernet Sauvignon
Although covering much less vineyard area than Cabernet Franc, Cabernet Sauvignon has scaled considerably greater heights in various parts of Italy, from Piedmont to Sicily, either varietally or in blend with other grapes, making sophisticated wines to rival the best Bordeaux.

Cannonau
Sardinia's main quality red grape is thought to be related to Grenache and makes full-bodied, spicy reds.

Chardonnay
First planted in the North over 150 years ago, Chardonnay is widely used today both as a varietal and a blender. It is still best in the North, usually when oaked.

Dolcetto
Virtually exclusive to Piedmont, where the best of several DOCs are Alba and Dogliani. Usually fruity and lightweight, the wine can have tremendous concentration and considerable longevity.

Gaglioppo
Calabria's principal red grape tends to light colour and considerable tannin, with a structure not unlike that of Barolo and a similarly sweet-fruit finish.

Garganega
Soave's main white grape can be very neutral when overproduced from vineyards on the plain but subtle and intense from a top producer. It also has good balancing acidity for sweet Recioto di Soave.

Grechetto
An Umbrian speciality of some character, Grechetto is used in blends like Orvieto and also occasionally on its own.

Greco
Of Greek origin, this white grape is found in the South, particularly in Campania where, as Greco di Tufo, it yields wines of definite, faintly citrus fruit character.

Inzolia
Planted mainly in Sicily and also in tiny amounts (as Ansonica) along the Tuscan coast, Inzolia is the secret ingredient in numerous Sicilian whites of character, having good body and plenty of flavour.

Lagrein
An underrated red grape of great character, mainly found in Alto Adige, Lagrein's wines are deeply coloured and richly flavoured with a characteristic bitter twist at the back but not too much tannin.

Malvasia
Various sub-varieties of this ancient Greek vine are grown in Italy, particularly in Friuli, where it's light and aromatic, in Frascati, where it can be rich and nutty, and in Sicily's Lipari islands.

GREAT ITALIAN WINES

Oz Clarke's selection

Barolo Bricco Bussia Vigna Cicala ♥ (Aldo Conterno) From this top producer, a wine that stands out for its power allied to heavenly black cherry and plum blossom perfume.

Langhe Sperss ♥ (Gaja) Gaja is more famous for his Barbaresco, but his Sperss wine is a sensuous and exotic combination of perfume and power.

Ghiaie della Furba ♥ (Capezzana) Another Tuscan mould-breaking red – with marvellous raw-textured blackcurrant and morello cherry fruit wrapped in a gamy cloak.

Cepparello ♥ (Isole e Olena) Austere yet beautiful rendering of Sangiovese emphasizing the bitter-sweet nature of the grape but adding perfume and ripe cherry fruit.

Tassinaia ♥ (Terriccio) From the coast near Livorno, an inspired Cabernet blend of sweet black cherry and blackcurrant scented with sprigs of mint.

Chianti Rufina Riserva Bucerchiale ♥ (Selvapiana) Chianti has never been better and this dark ripe, bitter-sweet red salutes the re-emergence of a great classic wine region.

Capitel San Rocco ♥ (Tedeschi) Thrilling flavours

from the Veneto – pepper, cherry, black chocolate and cedar crunched into unlikely harmony.

Amarone Classico ♥ (Allegrini) Another great original from the Valpolicella hills above Verona – wonderful sweet-sour, black cherry fruit spiced with boudoir scents.

Torcolato ♀ (Maculan) Fabulous treacle-rich white packed with peaches and quince in syrup from a great innovator.

Nemo ♥ (Castello di Monsanto) Monsanto makes elegant, sleek Chianti Classico as well as a range of dark-fruited, beautifully textured, barrique-aged reds – Nemo comes from Cabernet Sauvignon.

Steven Spurrier's selection

Brunello di Montalcino Riserva ♥ (Frescobaldi) Castelgiocondo is the jewel in the crown among the many Frescobaldi vineyards.

Chianti Classico ♥ (Castello di Fonterutoli) The recent decision by the Mazzei family to create a 'château' wine within the DOCG system is an indication of the quality of their Chianti.

Solaia ♥ (Antinori) This stylish blend of Cabernet with 20% Sangiovese is smooth and opulent.

Barolo Vigneto Arborina ♥ (Altare) One of the top modern Barolo producers, Elio Altare makes single-vineyard wines which have immense depth of fruit, thanks to tiny yields.

Barolo Granbussia ♥ (Aldo Conterno) Only produced in the best years, this great Barolo combines the best of modernity and traditionalism.

Barbaresco Sorì Tildin ♥ (Gaja) Piedmont's most famous produces this deeply stylish Barbaresco with a superb use of oak.

Ornellaia ♥ (Tenuta dell'Ornellaia) This superb Cabernet/Merlot blend is a leading Super-Tuscan.

Vino Nobile di Montepulciano ♥ (Avignonesi) The Falvo brothers are making a wine that is a worthy rival to the more famous Brunello di Montalcino.

Franciacorta Brut Dosage Zero ♀ (Ca' del Bosco) From Italy's premium Champagne-method appellation. Only the highest quality sparkling wines can support a zero dosage.

Soave Classico Calvarino ♀ (Pieropan) This elegant, almost minerally, Soave is a benchmark for the region.

Merlot

By far the most widely planted of the French grape varieties in Italy, especially in Friuli, the Veneto and Alto Adige, Merlot had only made mediocre wines for everyday drinking until very recently,

when some spectacularly concentrated, fine-grained wines, such as Masseto (ORNELLAIA), Vigna l'Apparita (CASTELLO DI AMA) and Redigaffi (Tua Rita), began trickling out of Tuscany. It is often blended with Cabernet Sauvignon.

Montepulciano

A red grape grown in great abundance on the East coast, especially in the DOC Montepulciano d'Abruzzo. Usually just a pleasantly fruity drink, of deepish hue, it can be rich, complex and long-lasting as VALENTINI's version demonstrates. GAROFOLI, in the Marche, makes excellent Rosso Conero (Grosso Agontano).

Moscato

Several sub-varieties of this perfumed grape are grown in Italy. Best known is Moscato Bianco or di Canelli, the grape of Asti and Moscato d'Asti, that light, frothing, headily perfumed but low-alcohol wine which finishes the heavy Piedmontese meal so poetically. Moscato Giallo, heavier and more pungent, is the one found in Alto Adige, where it is usually still and may be sweet or dry. Moscato Rosa, pink and redolent of roses, is also used in Alto Adige, but may be found as far south as Rome. On the island of Pantelleria, off Sicily, the grape behind the rich, grapy *passito* wines (DE BARTOLI's Bukkuram is an excellent example) is the table grape Moscato di Alessandria, there called Zibibbo.

Nebbiolo

This red Piedmontese grape is Italy's most exciting but most difficult variety. High in tannins, fairly high in acids, but having the most captivating and complex of aromatic scales ('tar and roses'), Nebbiolo demands the best sites in the vineyard and endless pains in the winery to perform at its best. It is used unblended in Barolo and Barbaresco, and also in Gattinara, Carema and Valtellina Superiore. The wines can be bootleather tough in youth, though the modern style is overcoming that problem; but the best ones age marvellously well.

Negroamaro

The literal translation, 'black and bitter', doesn't quite do this variety justice. It reigns in the southern tip of Puglia, on countless hectares of flat vineyard, often still bush-trained despite the EU's best efforts to stamp out quality in the South, and makes wines (like Salice Salentino or Copertino) of deep colour, ripe, fruity-vegetal aroma and smooth, low tannin.

Nero d'Avola

Sicily's best quality red grape is very deep-coloured, high in fixed acidity but with a wealth of fruit capable of covering the sharpness. Cantina la Elorina turns out a delicious Eloro Rosso which is 100% Nero d'Avola, as is Tasca d'Almerita's famous Rosso del Conte.

Pinot Grigio

Italy's most popular white grape has a coppery colour when ripe. Occasionally this comes through in the wine, but usually it's white and all too often stripped for commercial action. Some Friuli producers, however, know how to give it the weight and creamy texture it can attain in Alsace, and in Alto Adige, where the style is livelier, there are some excellent wines too.

Pinot Nero

The world's most elusive variety has been planted in northern Italy for 150 years or more, finding a home in the Alto Adige on the lower slopes of the eastern side of the valley, around Mazzon. Some fairly convincing trials are going ahead elsewhere too, notably in Tuscany.

Primitivo

Now that it is established that Primitivo and California's Zinfandel are the same variety, we are seeing an explosion of interest in the deep-coloured, high-octane wines of this early-ripening grape. Manduria, in Puglia, is the main DOC (try Pervini's wine called Archidamo).

Sagrantino
Produced in very small amounts almost exclusively around the Umbrian town of Montefalco, this is one of Italy's outstanding red grapes, capable of wines of deep colour, explosive power and tremendous personality.

Sangiovese
Sangiovese is not only the king of central Italy, being the key to famous wines like Chianti, Brunello di Montalcino, Vino Nobile di Montepulciano and many others; it is also Italy's most widely planted variety, and the only native one to have established a convincing quality presence elsewhere in the world. There are many clones and/or sub-varieties, and much research activity is going on into which one does best where. Wine styles range from the light and quaffable to the full, complex, very refined and very long-lived.

Sauvignon Blanc
Sauvignon doesn't have many vineyards in Italy, but the ones that exist, mainly in the North but also in Tuscany and even Puglia, are getting better. Excellent examples are Vieris or Pière from VIE DI ROMANS in Friuli and Sanct Valentin from San Michele Appiano in Alto Adige.

Teroldego
Almost exclusively confined to the Campo Rotaliano in northern Trentino, Teroldego is capable of concentrated wines of considerable finesse and some longevity in the hands of a good producer like FORADORI.

Tocai Friulano
Considered by some to be Sauvignon Vert or Sauvignonasse, this grape, grown mainly in Friuli, is capable of wines of some character, biscuity with a hint of herbaceousness. In Collio, SCHIOPETTO makes an archetypal version.

Trebbiano
Italy's most widely planted white grape variety is found all over the Centre and South, but the best wines are in the North in Lugana (Ca' dei Frati). Trebbiano di Lugana, aka Trebbiano di Soave, the Veneto clone, is nearer to Verdicchio than it is to the prolific Trebbiano di Toscano.

Verdicchio
Often touted these days as Italy's best native white variety, which, some will say, is not saying much. Mainly grown in Le Marche, with 2 DOCs – Castelli di Jesi and Matelica, it can, indeed, turn out white wines of impressive complexity and body, capable of aging well. Try one from Coroncino for a revelation.

Vermentino
Another contender for best Italian white variety, Vermentino is grown in Sardinia and along the Tyrrhenian coast from Liguria's Ponente down to Tuscany's Maremma. In southern Sardinia it can lack substance, but wines from Gallura in the North display much greater body and richness, as do the best of the Tuscans.

Vernaccia di San Gimignano
White associated with one of Tuscany's picture-postcard tourist towns, which is how it became famous. With a few honourable exceptions, the wines have a certain body but not much character. It is no relation to other Vernaccia varieties.

A–Z OF ITALIAN WINE REGIONS

AGLIANICO DEL VULTURE DOC

Some of the South's most distinguished red wines with good aging potential come from vineyards on the slopes of the extinct volcano Monte Vulture.

Best producers Basilium, D'ANGELO, Paternoster.

Best years 1998, '97, '96, '94.

ALTO ADIGE DOC

Enormous umbrella DOC (with over 50 sub-zones and styles) which covers virtually all top-quality wine in the province of Bolzano. High points include Chardonnay, Gewürztraminer, Pinot Grigio, Sauvignon, Moscato Rosa, Cabernet, Merlot, Lagrein and Pinot Nero.

Best producers Casòn Hirschprunn, Dipoli, Haas, Hofstätter, LAGEDER, Muri-Gries, Niedermayr, Tiefenbrunner, Walch; (co-operatives) Caldaro, Colterenzio, Cortaccia, Gries, San Michele Appiano, Santa Maddalena.

Best years 1998, '97, '96, '95.

ASTI/MOSCATO d'ASTI DOCG

Asti is now the name for Asti Spumante (Spumante has been discarded for image reasons). Moscato d'Asti, more perfumed and less alcoholic, is made from better quality grapes. Drink the most recent.

Best producers (Asti) Ascheri, Cinzano, Fontanafredda, Gancia, Martini; (Moscato) Viticoltori dell'Acquese, BRAIDA, Cascina, Caudrina, Icardi, Perrone, Saracco, La Spinetta.

BARBARESCO DOCG

This is one of Italy's great red wines and is made from 100% Nebbiolo, as is Barolo, its famous neighbour on the other side of Alba in Piedmont. Although the area is compact, wine styles can differ greatly between vineyards and producers. A top wine can last for decades.

Best producers PRODUTTORI DEL BARBARESCO, Ceretto, Cigliuti, CISA ASINARI, GAJA, Bruno GIACOSA, Cantina del Glicine, Moccagatta, Paitin, Prunotto (ANTINORI), Albino Rocca, Bruno Rocca, La Spinetta.

Best years 1999, '98, '97, '96, '95, '93, '90, '89, '88, '85.

BARBERA D'ALBA DOC

Some wonderful barrique-aged reds are now appearing from top Albese producers alongside their Barolos, Barbarescos and Roeros. From a good year Barbera can be ripe, soft and succulent, with bags of fruit and a beautifully bright acid backbone.

Best producers ALTARE, Domenico CLERICO, Aldo CONTERNO, Giacomo CONTERNO, CONTERNO FANTINO, Correggia, Elio Grasso, MASCARELLO, Moccagatta, Parusso, Prunotto (ANTINORI), SANDRONE, SCAVINO, Vajra, Viberti, Gianni Voerzio, Roberto VOERZIO.

Best years 1999, '98, '97, '96, '95, '93, '90, '89, '88, '85.

BARBERA D'ASTI DOC

The Astigiano area of Piedmont is the home of Barbera as well as the source of the first and most famous of the moderns, Giacomo Bologna's Bricco dell'Uccellone (BRAIDA). The wines are more rustic than Barbera d'Alba, but have lovely fruit/acid balance nicely offset by oak.

Best producers Viticoltori dell'Acquese, Araldica, La Barbatella, BRAIDA, Cascina Castlet, Chiarlo, Coppo, Il Mangetto, La Tenaglia, C.S. Vinchio e Vaglio.

Best years 1999, '98, '97, '96, '93, '90.

BAROLO DOCG

Italy's greatest red wine, 100% Nebbiolo, comes from south-west of Alba. A century ago it was often sweet, 30 years ago it was

BAROLO COMMUNES AND CRUS
The list below is not exhaustive, and many
sub-divisions exist under other names.
Barolo Bricco delle Viole, Brunate,
Cannubi, Cannubi Muscatel, Cerequio,
Coste di Rose, Fossati, La Villa, Sarmassa.
Castiglione Falletto Bricco Boschis,
Codana, Fiasco, Monprivato, Montanello,
Parussi, Rocche, Scarrone, Villero.
La Morra Arborina, Brunate, Conca dell'
Annunziata, Cerequio, Case Nere, Gattera,
Monfalletto, Rocche, Rocchette, La Serra.
Monforte Bussia, Le Coste, Dardi,
Gavarini, Ginestra, Gremolere, Manzoni
Soprani, Pianpolvere, Pressenda, Santo
Stefano, Visette.
Serralunga Cascina Francia, Cerretta,
Falletto, Gabutti, Gattinera, Lazzarito,
Marenca-Rivette, Ornato, Prapò, Vigna
Rionda.

too often over-tannic and oxidized from
excessive maceration and wood-aging, but
there has been an amazing awakening in
the past couple of decades, with younger
winemakers producing fruit-packed,
powerful wines of intense aromatic
complexity, length and personality.
Another recent development has been the
identification of and vinification by Cru
(see above), to the extent that generic
Barolo has almost been pushed out of
existence, certainly at the top end.
Best producers ALTARE, Azelia, Boglietti,
Bongiovanni, Ceretto, Chiarlo, Domenico
CLERICO, Aldo CONTERNO, Giacomo
CONTERNO, CONTERNO FANTINO,
Corino, Riccardo Fenocchio, GAJA, Bruno
GIACOSA, Elio Grasso, Gromis, Bartolo
Mascarello, Giuseppe MASCARELLO, Pio
Cesare, Principiano, Prunotto (ANTINORI),
Ratti, Rocche dei Manzoni, SANDRONE,
SCAVINO, Vajra, Viberti, VIETTI, Gianni
Voerzio, Roberto VOERZIO.
Best years 1999, '98, '97, '96, '95, '93,
'90, '89, '88, '85, '82, '78, '71, '70, '64,
'55, '47.

BOLGHERI DOC
This arty little village near the Tyrrhenian
coast has become famous primarily
through Italy's greatest Bordeaux Grand
Cru lookalike, Sassicaia, though several
other high-class, high-priced Cabernet-
based wines have now jumped on to the
bandwagon, not to mention the odd star
Merlot wine, and not forgetting
Sangiovese either. Vernaccia, Chardonnay
and Sauvignon make admirable whites.
Best producers ANTINORI, Grattamacco,
Le Macchiole, ORNELLAIA, SAN GUIDO,
Satta.
Best years 1998, '97, '96, '94, '90, '88, '85.

BREGANZE DOC
Dominated by one producer, MACULAN,
this Veneto DOC has earned a name for
top Cabernet and sweet wines (Torcolato).
Best years 1998, '97, '96, '95, '90.

BRINDISI DOC
This port, the 'gateway to Greece', gives its
name to a DOC whose flat vineyards are
dominated by Negroamaro, with the
support of Montepulciano, to give the
wine a bit more class than Salice Salentino.
Best producers Agricole Vallone,
TAURINO.
Best years 1998, '97, '94, '93, '92, '90.

BRUNELLO DI MONTALCINO DOCG
Along with Barolo, this is Italy's most
prestigious wine internationally. Made
from 100% Sangiovese, it must be aged
for 4 years of which 2 are in oak. It can be
incredibly long-lasting, and indeed
BIONDI-SANTI's 1964 wine is still
amazingly youthful. But wines are being
made now for much earlier drinking and
there are scores of small producers doing
an excellent job.
Best producers Altesino, ARGIANO,
BANFI, BIONDI SANTI, Brunelli,
Camigliano, La Campana, Caparzo,
Casanova di Neri, Case Basse,

Castelgiocondo (FRESCOBALDI), La Cerbaiola, Cerbaiona, Ciacci Piccolomini, Col d'Orcia, COSTANTI, Fuligni, Maurizio Lambardi, Lisini, Mastroianni, Silvio Nardi, Siro Pacenti, Pertimali, Pieve Santa Restituta, Poggio Antico, Il Poggiolo, Il Poggione, RUFFINO, Talenti, Val di Suga, Valdicava.
Best years 1998, '97, '95, '93, '90, '88, '85, '82, '75, '71, '64, '55, '45.

CARMIGNANO DOCG
Small zone west of Florence which has included Cabernet and others in the Sangiovese-based blend since the 1970s. The Riserva, made only in top years, can be impressively long lasting for a wine that favours elegance over power.
Best producers Ambra, Artimino, Bacchereto, CAPEZZANA, Il Poggiolo.
Best years 1999, '97, '95, '94, '90, '85.

CHIANTI CLASSICO DOCG
The Classico zone, covering the enchanting Chianti hills extending from just south of Florence to just north of Siena, now has its own DOCG and considers that other wines using the name Chianti are imposters. After many battles white grapes are no longer required in the blend, French grapes are allowed and the wine may even be 100% Sangiovese. The Riserva must now be aged for 2 years.
Best producers Castello di AMA, ANTINORI, Badia a Coltibuono, Castello di Brolio, Castello di Cacchiano, Carobbio, Carpineto, CASTELLARE, Castell'in Villa, Cennatoio, Le Cinciole, Casa Emma, Fattoria di FELSINA, Castello di FONTERUTOLI, FONTODI, ISOLE E OLENA, Lilliano, La Massa, Castello di MONSANTO, Monte Bernardi, MONTEVERTINE, Il Palazzino, Poggerino, Poggiopiano, Castello di Querceto, QUERCIABELLA, Castello di RAMPOLLA, Riecine, Rocca di Montegrossi, RUFFINO,

San Felice, SAN GIUSTO A RENTENNANO, Casa Sola, Terrabianca, Valtellina, Vecchie Terre di Montefili, Vignamaggio, Castello di Vicchiomaggio, Villa Cafaggio, Castello di Volpaia.
Best years 1999, '97, '95, '93, '90, '88, '85.

CHIANTI DOCG
The Chianti zones other than Chianti Classico (Colli Aretini, Colli Fiorentini, Colli Senesi, Colline Pisane, Montalbano, Rufina and just plain Chianti) congregate under this banner. Rufina is the one most likely to deliver excellent wine.
Best producers (Rufina) Basciano, Bossi, Castelli di Trebbio, FRESCOBALDI, Lavacchio, SELVAPIANA, Villa di Vetrice.
Best years 1999, '97, '95, '93, '90, '88, '85.

CIRÒ DOC
This is Calabria's sole quality DOC. The wines, from the Gaglioppo grape, can have a Barolo-like intensity and structure.
Best producers Librandi, San Francesco.
Best years 1998, '97, '94, '93, '91.

COLLI ORIENTALI DEL FRIULI DOC
One of Friuli's 2 principal quality wine zones, with many sub-DOCs, Colli Orientali is more inclined than its neighbour, Collio, to include wines from non-French vines such as Ribolla Gialla and Tocai Friulano, Pignolo and Schioppettino. Even so, Bordeaux and Burgundy varieties still predominate.
Best producers Abbazia di Rosazzo, Dario Coos, Dorigo, Dri, Le Due Terre, Livio Felluga, Miani, Rodaro, Ronchi di Cialla, Ronchi di Manzano, Ronco del Gnemiz, Specogna, Torre Rosazza, La Viarte, Vigna dal Leon, Zamò & Zamò.
Best years 1999, '97, '95, '93, '90.

COLLIO DOC
Collio is probably Friuli's best-known fine wine zone and is where Italy's 'white wine revolution' of the 1970s and 1980s started. An umbrella DOC, it covers wines

from many varieties, mainly white and mainly French, although French reds, especially the Cabernets, are making notable progress today.

Best producers Borgo del Tiglio, La Castellada, Marco Felluga, Gradnik, Gravner, JERMANN, Edi Kante, Edi Keber, Livon, Princic, Puiatti, Russiz Superiore, SCHIOPETTO, Tercic, Venica, Villa Russiz.

Best years 1999, '97, '95, '93, '90.

DOLCETTO D'ALBA DOC

This DOC covers roughly the same area as Barbera d'Alba; here Dolcetto is to some extent leaving behind its old Cinderella image, being made increasingly in the robust, full-coloured, richly fruity but structured style.

Best producers ALTARE, Azelia, Boglietti, Brovia, Cà Viola, Domenico CLERICO, Aldo CONTERNO, CONTERNO FANTINO, Gastaldi, Marcarini, Bartolo Mascarello, Giuseppe MASCARELLO, Nada, Prunotto (ANTINORI), Albino Rocca, SANDRONE, Vajra, Gianni Voerzio, Roberto VOERZIO.

Best years 1999, '98, '97, '96, '93, '90, '88.

FRANCIACORTA DOCG

Italy's most convincing answer to Champagne, made with the same grapes (but riper) and the same method.

Best producers Bellavista, CA' DEL BOSCO, Gatti, Uberti.

Best years 1998, '97, '95, '93, '90.

FRASCATI SUPERIORE DOC

A famous Italian white, often overrated. The best is rich and concentrated.

Best producers Castel de Paolis (Viognier-based Vigna Adriana), Colli di Catone (Colle Gaio), Fontana Candida, Villa Simone.

Best years 1999, '97, '95.

GATTINARA DOCG

Once held in much higher esteem, this Nebbiolo-based red from northern Piedmont sank to a great low in the 1980s but in the 1990s began a comeback.

Best producers Antoniolo, Nervi, Travaglini.

Best years 1998, '97, '95, '93, '90.

GAVI DOCG

Once considered Italy's finest native white, Gavi has been overtaken by Verdicchio, Arneis and even Soave, partly due to too much acidity. Some increasingly well-balanced wines, often barrique-aged, are now emerging. Drink young.

Best producers Nicola Bergaglio, Castellare Bergaglio, La Giustiniana, La Scolca, Villa Sparina.

ISONZO DOC

Some astounding whites and some pretty smart reds are coming out of this less well-known part of Friuli, adjacent to Collio.

Best producers Lis Neris-Pecorari, Pier Paolo Pecorari, Ronco del Gelso, VIE DI ROMANS.

Best years 1999, '97, '95, '93, '90.

LANGHE DOC

Important new DOC covering wines from the Langhe hills around Alba. The range of varietals such as Chardonnay, Barbera and Nebbiolo include several former Vino da Tavola bottlings. Some barrique-aged Chardonnay and Nebbiolo attain first-rate quality while the varietal Arneis is an attractive light white wine.

Best producers ALTARE, Aldo CONTERNO, CONTERNO FANTINO, Domenico CLERICO, GAJA, Giuseppe MASCARELLO, Massolino, Castello di Neive, Pio Cesare, La Spinetta, Vajra.

Best years 1999, '95, '94, '93, '90, '89.

MARSALA DOC

Once the equal of sherry, Marsala was brought low in the 20th century by industrial production. In the past 10–20 years certain producers have worked against enormous opposition to restore its

prestige, mainly through its top wine, the dry, vanilla-fudgy (with acidity) Vergine.
Best producers DE BARTOLI, Florio.

MONTEPULCIANO D'ABRUZZO DOC

That this DOC is capable of top wines, amid a sea of mediocrity, is shown best by a handful of outstanding producers.
Best producers Cornacchia, Illuminati, Masciarelli, Elio Monti, VALENTINI.
Best years 1998, '97, '95, '94, '90.

MOSCATO DI PANTELLERIA DOC

One of Italy's great sweet wines is made from sun-dried Moscato di Alessandria grapes (locally called Zibibbo) grown in the dark soil of this volcanic island.
Best producers DE BARTOLI, Murana.

ORVIETO DOC

This Umbrian white is one of Italy's more interesting food wines if you stick to the Crus. Drink the most recent vintages.
Best producers Barberani, Bigi, Decugnano dei Barbi, Palazzone, Castello della Sala (ANTINORI).

ROERO & ROERO ARNEIS DOCs

This Piedmont wine zone has 2 types of soil: calcareous to suit white grapes (Arneis and Favorita) and clay-sand to suit reds (Nebbiolo and Barbera). The reds are becoming good enough to take on Alba. Roero Arneis is a characterful white (drink the latest vintage).
Best producers ❗ Correggia, Deltetto, Malvirà; (Arneis) Bertini, Malvirà.
Best years ❗1999, '98, '97, '96, '95, '93, '90.

SAGRANTINO DI MONTEFALCO DOCG

Exclusively grown in this small central Umbrian commune, the Sagrantino grape makes rich, powerful reds as well as *passito* wines to knock your socks off.
Best producers Adanti, CAPRAI, Colpetrone.
Best years 1999, '97, '95, '94, '93, '90.

SALICE SALENTINO DOC

From the flatlands of the South, this smooth, dark-chocolaty and damson-fruit red is proving very popular. It is best at 3–5 years of age.
Best producers Candido, Leone de Castris, TAURINO, Vallone.
Best years 1998, '97, '94, '93, '90.

SOAVE CLASSICO DOC

Top Soave from the Classico zone has proved not only that it can be elegant, intense and refined but also that it can last several years, unlike Soave from the plains. There is delicious sweet Recioto also.
Best producers Ca' Rugate, Cantina del Castello, Coffelo, Fattori & Graney, Gini, Inama, MASI, PIEROPAN, Pra, Suavia.
Best years 1998, '97, '95, '93.

TAURASI DOCG

Once considered to be the South's top red, Taurasi has the finesse and structure to improve over 12–20 years and even longer.
Best producers Feudi di San Gregorio, Mastroberardino, Struzziero.
Best years 1998, '97, '96, '94, '91, '90.

TEROLDEGO ROTALIANO DOC

Produced in flat, gravelly vineyards in Trentino, this is potentially one of Italy's finest reds from native grapes.
Best producers Barone de Cles, FORADORI.
Best years 1998, '97, '95, '93, '90.

TORGIANO ROSSO RISERVA DOCG

Lungarotti is the only significant producer of this Sangiovese-based wine, aged for 8 years in barrel and bottle before release.
Best years 1997, '95, '90, '86.

VALPOLICELLA DOC

This historic wine, from the hills north of Verona, is made in 3 styles based on Corvina/Rondinella blends: normal which is light and fruity; full which is alcoholic and rich from dried grapes (sweet Recioto or dry Amarone); or Ripasso, between the

2 styles (the normal is refermented on the lees after racking). Classico is the best zone.

Best producers Accordini, ALLEGRINI, Cecilia Beretta, Bertani, Brigaldara, Brunelli, Bussola, Castellani, DAL FORNO, MASI, Mazzi, Montresor, QUINTARELLI, Le Ragose, Speri, Tedeschi, Viviani.

Best years 1998, '97, '95, '93, '90, '83.

VALTELLINA SUPERIORE DOCG

From Lombardy these Nebbiolo-based wines have less power than Barolo and Barbaresco, except in the *passito* version called Sfursat/Sforzato. The wines have some finesse and medium-aging ability.

Best producers Enologica Valtellinese, Negri, Nera, Rainoldi.

Best years 1999, '97, '95, '93, '90, '88.

VERDICCHIO DEI CASTELLI DI JESI & DI MATELICA DOCs

This white wine, dry and tangy with a slightly oily texture balanced by firm acidity, is rapidly being seen as Italy's finest white wine from native grapes.

Best producers Brunori, Bucci, Coroncino, GAROFOLI, La Monacesca, Monte Schiavo/La Vite, Umani Ronchi.

Best years 1998, '97, '95, '94, '92.

VERNACCIA DI SAN GIMIGNANO DOCG

Tuscany's best native white grape (which isn't saying much) turns out a wine of nutty aroma and reasonable weight on the palate, needing a firm acid backbone which it may lack in hot years. A new San Gimignano DOC is for the local red wines.

Best producers Cesani, Le Colonne, Falchini, Guicciardini Strozzi, Montenidoli, Panizzi, Terruzzi e Puthod.

Best years 1999, '97, '96.

VIN SANTO (VARIOUS DOCs)

Vin Santo (best in Montepulciano), made from dried grapes (Trebbiano, Malvasia, Sangiovese) can come from anywhere in Tuscany, under a variety of DOCs. It may vary from dry and sherry-like to sweet and fruity. The greatest example comes from AVIGNONESI, aged for 11 years in oak, but made only in minuscule quantities.

Best producers AVIGNONESI, CAPEZZANA, Fattoria di FELSINA, ISOLE E OLENA, Castello di MONSANTO, Pieve Santa Restituta, POLIZIANO, Le Pupille, SAN GIUSTO A RENTENNANO.

VINO NOBILE DI MONTEPULCIANO DOCG

Long considered one of Tuscany's classic wines, this Sangiovese-based red wine is making a come-back after a lean period, with wines both more supple and, paradoxically, more capable of long aging (they are less oxidized in the early stages).

Best producers AVIGNONESI, Bindella, BOSCARELLI, La Braccesca (ANTINORI), Le Casalte, Contucci, Dei, POLIZIANO, Salcheto, Trerose, Valdipiatta.

Best years 1998, '97, '95, '93, '90, '88, '85.

SUPER-TUSCANS

These brilliant wines, many of which are barrique-aged, were originally made outside the DOC regulations. Today they are being dragged back within the law via new purpose-built DOCs and IGTs. The top wines include:

Sangiovese and other Tuscan grape varieties Boscarelli, Il Carbonaione, Cepparello, Coltassala, La Corte, Elegia, Flaccianello della Pieve, Fontalloro, La Gioia, Palazzo Altesi, Percarlo, Le Pergole Torte, Sangioveto, I Sodi di San Niccolò.

Sangiovese/Cabernet blends Avvoltore, Balifico, Camartina, Concerto, Grifi, Nardo, Sammarco, Solaia, Tignanello.

Cabernet Collezione de Marchi, Olmaia, Il Pareto, Sassicaia, Le Stanze, La Vigna di Alceo.

Sangiovese/Merlot blends Luce, Siepi.

Merlot Masseto, Redigaffi, Vigna L'Apparita.

Cabernet/Merlot blends Il Fortino, Ghiaie della Furba, Lupicaia, Ornellaia, Federico Primo, Saffredi, Tassinaia.

A–Z OF ITALIAN PRODUCERS

ALLEGRINI, Fumane in Valpolicella, Veneto · 045 7701138/7701774

The next generation of the Allegrini family have adapted their father Giovanni's modernist principles and produce top-quality wines in Valpolicella. Some of the best are from single-named vineyards – La Poja is oak-aged.

Best wines ★★★ La Poja ♥, ★★ La Grola ♥, Amarone Classico ♥ and Recioto Classico Giovanni Allegrini ♥, ★ Palazzo della Torre ♥

Best years 1998, '97, '95, '93, '90, '88, '85

ALTARE, La Morra, Piedmont · 0173 50835

This grower-bottler is guru to a whole new generation of Barolo producers, having declared war on prolonged maceration and protracted aging in large oak. His oak-aged Langhe wines are also showstoppers: Arborina (Nebbiolo) and Larigi (Barbera).

Best wines ★★★ Langhe Arborina ♥ and Langhe Larigi ♥, ★★ Barolo Vigneto Arborina ♥

Best years 1999, '98, '97, '95, '93, '90, '89, '88

CASTELLO DI AMA, Gaiole, Tuscany · 0577 746031/746117

There is a school of thought which holds that Castello di Ama has taken Chianti Classico as far as it can go with its Crus Bellavista (with Malvasia Nera) and La Casuccia (with Merlot) and Merlot yet further with super-Tuscan Vigna l'Apparita.

Best wines ★★★ Vigna l'Apparita ♥, ★★ Chianti Classico La Casuccia ♥, Chianti Classico Bellavista ♥ and Chianti Classico ♥

Best years 1999, '97, '96, '95, '94, '93, '91, '90, '88, '86, '85

ROBERTO ANSELMI, Monteforte d'Alpone, Veneto · 045 7611488/7611490

The man who started the revolution in Soave Classico that so altered people's perception of the wine, bringing in French grapes (Chardonnay), French methods in the vineyard (low training on wires), and French barriques in the winery, has now rocked the establishment by renouncing the Soave DOC.

Best wines ★★★ I Capitelli ♀, ★★ Capitel Foscarino ♀ **Best years** 1998, '97, '95, '93, '90

ANTINORI, Florence, Tuscany · 055 23595/2359877

Piero Antinori deserves more credit perhaps than any other single individual for the transformation of Italian wines in the past 50 years. Top wines include rich, fleshy Chianti Classico Riserva plus superb barrel-aged Cabernet-based Solaia, Sangiovese-based Tignanello, innovative Cabernet/Merlot blend Guado al Tasso and Chardonnay/Grechetto Cervaro della Sala. Antinori also owns Castello della Sala (Orvieto), La Braccesca (Vino Nobile di Montepulciano) and Prunotto (in Piedmont).

Best wines ★★★ Solaia ♥ and Cervaro della Sala ♀, ★★ Tignanello ♥, Chianti Classico Riserva Tenute Marchese Antinori ♥ and Guado al Tasso, Bolgheri ♥

Best years ♥1999, '97, '95, '93, '90, '88, '85

ARGIANO, Montalcino, Tuscany · 0577 864037/864210

Sebastiano Rosa is making relatively ripe, soft, early-drinking yet structured Brunellos from this recently much upgraded property, owned by Noemi Cinzano. Solengo is a dynamic blend of Cabernet, Merlot, Sangiovese and Syrah.

Best wines ★★ Brunello di Montalcino ♥ and Solengo ♥

Best years 1999, '97, '96, '95, '93, '90

ARGIOLAS, Serdiana, Sardinia 070 740606/743264

With the help of enologist Tachis, this is one of the most consistent quality producers in Sardinia for red (Cannonau-based Turriga), white and sweet (Angialis) wines.

Best wines ★★ Turriga ♚ and Angialis ♀   **Best years** ♚1999, '97, '96, '95, '91, '90

AVIGNONESI, Montepulciano, Tuscany 0578 757872/757847

Ettore and Alberto Falvo have raised this estate in 20 years to be one of the stars of Italian wine. Outstanding not only for classic Montepulciano but also for Il Marzocco (Chardonnay), Grifi (Sangiovese/Cabernet) as well as numerous experimental wines.

Best wines ★★★ Vin Santo ♚♀, ★★ Vino Nobile di Montepulciano ♚ and Il Marzocco ♀

Best years 1999, '97, '95, '93, '90, '88, '85

BANFI, Montalcino, Tuscany 0577 840111/840444

With over 800ha under vine, around half Sangiovese, this is the largest single estate in Italy. Ezio Rivella's challenge was to produce high-quality wine in quantity. There have been problems, but the peaks are high. Excelsus is a Cabernet/Merlot blend.

Best wines ★★ Brunello di Montalcino Riserva ♚ and Excelsus ♚, ★ Brunello di Montalcino ♚

Best years 1999, '97, '95, '93, '90, '88

PRODUTTORI DEL BARBARESCO, Barbaresco, Piedmont 0173 635139/835130

One of Italy's top co-operatives grouping 60 growers whose vineyards include some of Barbaresco's most vaunted Crus, specializes in Nebbiolo, turning out an impressive array of different wines. Its production of Barbaresco represents one-quarter of the total produced.

Best wines ★★ Barbaresco Riserva Asili ♚, Barbaresco Riserva Montestefano ♚ and Barbaresco Riserva Rio Sordo ♚, ★ Barbaresco ♚

Best years 1999, '98, '97, '95, '90, '88, '85

BIONDI-SANTI, Montalcino, Tuscany 0577 848087/849396

The Biondi-Santi family helped forge Montalcino's international reputation. The past 20 years have seen uneven quality but the best Riservas still repay a minimum of 10 years' keeping. Jacopo Biondi-Santi, the new generation, is now making more modern-style wines (Sangiovese Sassoalloro and super-Tuscan Schidione).

Best wines ★★★ Brunello di Montalcino Riserva ♚, ★★ Brunello di Montalcino ♚

Best years 1999, '98, '97, '96, '95, '93, '90, '88, '85, '82, '75, '71, '64, '55, '25

BOSCARELLI, Montepulciano, Tuscany 0578 767277

Paola de Ferrari and sons make some of Montepulciano's richest and most stylish reds. Their energy and hard work is complemented by advice from Maurizio Castelli, one of the best of Italy's high-profile enologists.

Best wines ★★★ Boscarelli ♚, ★★ Vino Nobile di Montepulciano ♚ and Vino Nobile di Montepulciano Riserva del Nocio ♚

Best years 1999, '97, '96, '95, '94, '93, '91, '90, '88, '85

BRAIDA, Rocchetta Tanaro, Piedmont 0141 644113/644584

The late Giacomo Bologna was one of the movers and shakers of Italy's wine renaissance, in particular with his barriqued Bricco dell'Uccellone which, under his heirs, continues to be a leading Barbera wine. Il Bacialé is a Pinot Nero/Barbera blend.

Best wines ★★ Bricco dell'Uccellone ♚ and Barbera d'Asti Ai Suma ♚, ★ Dolcetto d'Alba Serra dei Fiori ♚ and Monferrato Rosso Il Bacialé ♚

Best years 1999, '98, '97, '96, '95, '93, '90

CA' DEL BOSCO, Erbusco, Lombardy ⠀⠀⠀⠀⠀⠀⠀⠀⠀⠀⠀⠀ 030 7760600/7268425
Under the Franciacorta DOC, Ca' del Bosco is the leading producer of Champagne-
method sparklers in Italy. It also successfully turns out other French-style wines,
especially Bordeaux (called Maurizio Zanella after the former owner of the company
and now director) and Burgundy (Pinero and Chardonnay) lookalikes.
Best wines ★★★ Franciacorta Cuvée Annamaria Clementi ♀, ★★ Terre di Franciacorta
Chardonnay ♀, Maurizio Zanella ❗ and Franciacorta Brut Dosage Zero, ★ Pinero ❗
Best years Maurizio Zanella 1998, '97, '96, '95, '93, '91, '90, '88

TENUTA DI CAPEZZANA, Carmignano, Tuscany ⠀⠀⠀⠀⠀ 055 8706005/8706673
Conte Ugo Contini Bonacossi is one of the pioneers of the Tuscan wine revolution,
though unlike others he has remained within the DOC laws. Sangiovese blended with
one or several of the Bordeaux grapes is Capezzana's principal style. Ghiaie della Furba
is a Bordeaux-style red from Cabernet Sauvignon, Merlot and Cabernet Franc. The
Riserva, capable of considerable aging, is produced only in the best years.
Best wines ★★ Carmignano Riserva ❗, Carmignano Vin Santo ♀ and Ghiaie della Furba ❗
Best years ❗ 1998, '97, '95, '94, '90, '88, '85

ARNALDO CAPRAI, Montefalco, Umbria ⠀⠀⠀⠀⠀⠀⠀⠀⠀ 0742 378802/378422
Marco Caprai takes an intelligent and experimentalist approach both to his splendid
Sagrantinos and to his field trials with numerous Italian and French varieties. The 1993
Sagrantino Riserva 25 Anni caused quite a stir on its release with its awesome depth
and complexity and it requires at least 10 years' aging.
Best wines ★★★ Sagrantino di Montefalco Riserva 25 Anni ❗, ★★ Sagrantino di Montefalco ❗
and Sagrantino di Montefalco Passito ❗
Best years 1998, '97, '95, '94, '93, '90

CASTELLARE, Castellina-in-Chianti, Tuscany ⠀⠀⠀⠀⠀ 0577 740490/0577 742814
Castellare has a fine track record, likely to be maintained following recent investment.
Consultancy from top enologist Maurizio Castelli and good raw materials – grapes
from vines grown in stony soils on high slopes – are also part of the equation. It is well-
known, too, for I Sodi di San Niccolò (unusual in adding 10% Malvasia Nera to
Sangiovese) and its varietal wines, including Canonico (Chardonnay).
Best wines ★★ Chianti Classico Riserva ❗, Canonico ♀ and I Sodi di San Niccolò ❗
Best years ❗1999, '97, '96, '95, '94, '93, '91, '90, '88, '86, '85

CISA ASINARI, Barbaresco, Piedmont ⠀⠀⠀⠀⠀⠀⠀⠀⠀⠀ 0173 635222/635187
The Marchesi di Gresy are the most prominent presence in this commune after GAJA,
making consistently good wines with the local Albese grapes, especially Nebbiolo.
Best wines ★★ Barbaresco Camp Gros ❗, ★ Barbaresco Martinenga ❗ and Barbaresco Gaiun ❗
Best years 1999, '98, '97, '95, '93, '90, '89, '88

DOMENICO CLERICO, Barolo, Piedmont ⠀⠀⠀⠀⠀⠀⠀⠀⠀⠀⠀ Tel 0173 78171
One of the best of the younger generation of Barolo producers, Clerico produces
impressive Barolo, and fine Dolcetto and Barbera; all are wonderfully balanced. Arte is
Nebbiolo blended with a little Barbera and then barrique-aged.
Best wines ★★★ Barolo Ciabot Mentin Ginestra ❗, ★★ Barolo Pajana ❗ and Langhe Arte ❗,
★ Barbera d'Alba Clerico ❗
Best years 1999, '98, '97, '96, '95, '93, '92, '91, '90, '89, '88, '85

ALDO CONTERNO, Monforte d'Alba, Piedmont   0173 78150/787240

Perhaps the most revered and well-loved figure on the Alba wine scene is the congenial Aldo Conterno, rightly hailed as a grand master of the art of producing Barolo (with a tendency towards the traditional) as well as other more modern wines including Bussiador, a Chardonnay fermented and aged in new wood.

Best wines ★★★ Barolo Granbussia ❦, Barolo Vigna Colonello ❦ and Barolo Vigna Cicala ❦, ★★ Barbera d'Alba Conca Tre Pile ❦, ★ Bussiador ♀

Best years 1999, '98, '97, '96, '95, '93, '90, '89, '88, '85, '82

GIACOMO CONTERNO, Monforte d'Alba, Piedmont   0173 78221/787190

Giovanni Conterno (Giacomo was his father, and Aldo's) makes arguably the greatest, longest-lived Barolos of all, certainly among those of the 'traditional' style (long maceration and years in barrel). Son Roberto is following seamlessly in his path.

Best wines ★★★ Barolo Riserva Monfortino ❦, ★★ Barolo Cascina Francia ❦

Best years 1999, '98, '97, '96, '95, '93, '90, '88, '85, '82, '71, '70

CONTERNO FANTINO, Monforte d'Alba, Piedmont   0173 78204/787326

Guido Fantino is of the 'modernist' school: his wines, in which barrique-aging plays a significant role, tend to emphasize the fruit and are relatively early drinking. Monprà is a Nebbiolo/Barbera blend.

Best wines ★★ Monprà ❦, Barolo Sorì Ginestra ❦, Barolo Vigna del Gris ❦, Barbera d'Alba Vignota ❦ and Dolcetto d'Alba Bricco Bastia ❦

Best years 1999, '98, '97, '96, '95, '90, '89

COSTANTI, Montalcino, Tuscany   0577 848195/849349

This estate on a high ridge east of Montalcino town is one of the great perennials of the Brunello DOC and Andrea Costanti, with the help of enologist Vittorio Fiore, draws the essence of every vintage from his grapes.

Best wines ★★★ Brunello di Montalcino Riserva ❦, ★★ Brunello di Montalcino ❦

Best years 1999, '97, '95, '90, '88, '85, '83

DAL FORNO, Illasi, Veneto   045 7834923

On his small estate outside Illasi, outside the Valpolicella Classico area, Romano Dal Forno makes, arguably, the most impressive wines of the appellation.

Best wines ★★★ Amarone della Valpolicella Vigneto di Monte Lodoletta ❦, ★★ Recioto della Valpolicella Monte Lodoletta ❦ and Valpolicella Superiore Monte Lodoletta ❦

Best years 1997, '95, '93, '91, '90, '88, '86, '85

D'ANGELO, Rionero, Basilicata   0972 721517/723495

Basilicata's leading winery gained its reputation for Aglianico del Vulture. Canneto, the barrique-aged Aglianico, is of similar quality and depth, but more forward and oaky.

Best wines ★★ Aglianico del Vulture Riserva Vigna Caselle ❦ and Canneto ❦

Best years 1998, '97, '93, '90, '88, '85

DE BARTOLI, Marsala, Sicily   0923 962093/962910

The resurgence of fine Marsala owes a great deal to the courageous Marco De Bartoli. His best wines, of the dry Vergine style, are not DOC because they're unfortified. But they're better than any official Marsalas.

Best wines ★★ Vecchio Samperi Riserva – 10 years, 20 years, 30 years ♀ and Marsala Superiore Riserva 20 years ♀, ★ Moscato Passito di Pantelleria Bukkuram ♀

FATTORIA DI FELSINA, Castelnuovo Berardenga, Tuscany   0577 355117/355651
Giuseppe Mazzocolin, with enologist Franco Bernabei, has succeeded in placing the
deep, chewy Sangioveses of this sizeable estate on the southern outskirts of Chianti
Classico among the world leaders, achieving almost as much with Cabernet Sauvignon.
Fontalloro is the leading Sangiovese, Maestro Raro the top Cabernet Sauvignon.
Best wines ★★★ Chianti Classico Riserva Rancia ❢ and Fontalloro ❢, ★★ Maestro Raro ❢
Best years 1999, '97, '95, '93, '90, '88, '85

CASTELLO DI FONTERUTOLI, Castellina-in-Chianti, Tuscany   0577 740476/741070
The Mazzei family, who have lived here for centuries, have recently made the radical
decision to sacrifice their top wines – Concerto (Sangiovese/Cabernet) and Ser Lapo
(Chianti Classico) – in order to create a new 'super-Chianti' called, simply, Castello di
Fonterutoli Chianti Classico Riserva. Siepi is an elegant Sangiovese/Merlot blend.
Best wines ★★ Castello di Fonterutoli Chianti Classico Riserva ❢ and Siepi ❢
Best years 1999, '97, '95, '93, '90, '88, '85

FONTODI, Panzano, Tuscany   055 852005/852537
At this estate, on a commanding hill in the very heart of Chianti Classico, Franco
Bernabei helps Giovanni Manetti in the making of some very elegant, yet concentrated
wines from Sangiovese, Cabernet Sauvignon, Pinot Nero and Syrah. Flaccianello della
Pieve is an exemplary Sangiovese from a single vineyard of old vines.
Best wines ★★★ Flaccianello della Pieve ❢, ★★ Chianti Classico Vigna del Sorbo Riserva ❢,
★ Pinot Nero Case Via ❢   **Best years** 1999, '97, '95, '93, '90, '88, '85

FORADORI, Mezzolombardo, Trentino   0461 601046/603447
Elisabetta Foradori is a gutsy lady who, following her father's death, took the
Teroldegos of this small estate to the greatest heights achieved by that grape (Sgarzon
and Granato). She was one of the first to experiment with Syrah here (Ailanpa).
Best wines ★★ Teroldego Rotaliano Vigneto Sgarzon ❢ and Granato ❢, ★ Ailanpa ❢
Best years 1998, '97, '95, '94, '93, '91

FRESCOBALDI, Florence, Tuscany   055 27141/211527
A company best known internationally for inexpensive blended Chianti, Frescobaldi
also owns vineyards in Chianti Rufina, making excellent Riserva wines, and the noted
estate Castelgiocondo, which is the source of some impressive Brunello, a highly-rated
Merlot called Lamaione and the Sangiovese/Merlot blend known as Luce, the result of
an exciting joint venture with California's Robert MONDAVI.
Best wines ★★ Brunello di Montalcino Riserva ❢, Luce ❢, Lamaione ❢, Chianti Rufina
Riserva Castello di Nipozzano, ❢ and Chianti Rufina Montesodi ❢
Best years 1999, '97, '96, '95, '94, '93, '91, '90, '88, '85

ANGELO GAJA, Barbaresco, Piedmont   0173 635255/635256
Dynamism oozes from every pore of this extraordinary man, recognized as being
among the master vintners of the world, with his base in Barbaresco. Into this fiercely
conservative area he was responsible for introducing the great French grape varieties
such as Cabernet Sauvignon (Darmagi) and Chardonnay (Gaia e Rey). In a surprising
move he has decided that except for a single, premium bottling of Barbaresco his
single-vineyard Barolo and Barbaresco wines will soon appear under the Langhe DOC.
Outside Piedmont, Gaja has invested heavily in Brunello di Montalcino and Bolgheri.

Best wines ★★★ Barbaresco Sorì Tildin ♟, Barbaresco Costa Russi ♟, Barbaresco Sorì San Lorenzo ♟ and Langhe Sperss ♟, ★★ Langhe Darmagi ♟, Gaia e Rey ♀
Best years 1999, '98, '97, '95, '93, '90, '89, '88, '85, '82, '78

GAROFOLI, Loreto, Le Marche   071 7820162/7821437
Quality leaders in the Marche with Verdicchio dei Castelli di Jesi – notably the single-vineyard Macrina and barrel-aged Serra Fiorese wines – and Rosso Conero.
Best wines ★★ Rosso Conero Grosso Agontano ♟ and Verdicchio dei Castelli di Jesi Classico Serra Fiorese ♀, ★ Verdicchio dei Castelli di Jesi Classico Macrina ♀
Best years Grosso Agontano 1998, '97, '95, '94, '93, '92, '90, '88

BRUNO GIACOSA, Neive, Piedmont   0173 67027/677477
Though owning few vineyards until recently, this producer has earned a reputation as a Nebbiolo wizard. Always reliable, his Barbarescos and Barolos can be quite magical, the best expression of why Nebbiolo is rated among the world's leading grape varieties.
Best wines ★★★ Barbaresco Santo Stefano di Neive ♟ and Barolo Collina Rionda Riserva ♟, ★★ Barbaresco Gallina di Neive ♟ and Barolo Falletto ♟
Best years 1999, '98, '97, '96, '95, '93, '90, '89, '88, '85, '82, '78, '71

ISOLE E OLENA, Barberino Val d'Elsa, Tuscany   055 8072763/8072236
Paolo de Marchi, in his quiet way, is one of the moving forces of the Tuscan wine revolution. Constantly experimenting in vineyard (he introduced Syrah to Tuscany, with L'Eremo) and *cantina*, he shows his perfectionism in consistently well-bred wines. His top wine, Cepparello, is made from 100% Sangiovese.
Best wines ★★★ Cepparello ♟ and Vin Santo ♀, ★★ Chianti Classico ♟, Cabernet Sauvignon Collezione de Marchi ♟, L'Eremo ♟ and Chardonnay Collezione de Marchi ♀
Best years ♟1999, '97, '96, '95, '94, '93, '90, '88

JERMANN, Farra d'Isonzo, Friuli   0481 888080/888512
Silvio Jermann is one of several producers who brought a whole new image to Friulian wine, in particular, and Italian whites in general. He makes several wines – the best are the Chardonnay-based blend, Vintage Tunina, the oddly named Chardonnay, Were Dreams, now it is Just Wine!, and the Pinot Bianco blend, Capo Martino.
Best wines ★★ Vintage Tunina ♀ and Were Dreams… ♀, ★ Capo Martino ♀
Best years 1999, '97, '96, '95, '94, '93

ALOIS LAGEDER, Magrè, Alto Adige   0471 809500/809500
Probably the leading private producer in Alto Adige, Lageder maintains a typically wide range with some very high notes, among both whites and reds.
Best wines ★★ Alto Adige Cabernet Sauvignon Cor Romigberg ♟, Alto Adige Cabernet Sauvignon Löwengang ♟, Alto Adige Chardonnay Löwengang ♀ and Alto Adige Pinot Grigio Benefizium Porer ♀   **Best years** ♟1998, '97, '96, '95, '93, '90

MACULAN, Breganze, Veneto   0445 873733/300149
One of the leading Francophiles of Italy's wine renaissance, with vineyards planted to French grapes in the French manner, Fausto Maculan achieves his highest peak with sweet wines such as Acininobili and Torcolato from local grapes.
Best wines ★★★ Acininobili ♀, ★★ Breganze Cabernet Sauvignon Ferrata ♟, Breganze Cabernet Fratta ♟ and Torcolato ♀, ★ Breganze Merlot Marchesante ♟
Best years ♟1998, '97, '95, '94, '91, '90; ♀1999, '97, '95, '93, '92, '91, '90

FATTORIA DI MANZANO, Cortona, Tuscany   0575 618667/618411

Relatively low-lying vineyards not far from Cortona in eastern Tuscany certainly do not sound like the ideal setting for a fine wine estate. Yet massive investment, the best winemaking advice on offer and, equally importantly, the freedom to plant and replant with a New World abandon has resulted in the world clamouring for Tuscan Syrah (Podere Il Bosco), Viognier and even Gamay (Podere Il Vescovo), as well as Chardonnay (Podere Fontarca) and Sauvignon blend Podere Le Terrazze.

Best wines ★★ Podere Fontarca ♀ and Podere Il Bosco ♥, **★** Podere Le Terrazze ♀

Best years ♀1999, '97, '96, '95, '94

GIUSEPPE MASCARELLO, Castiglione Falletto, Piedmont   0173 792126/792124

Mauro Mascarello, aided by his son Giuseppe, produces superb, intense Barolo from the Monprivato vineyard and a rich cherry- and bramble-flavoured Dolcetto.

Best wines ★★★ Barolo Monprivato ♥, **★★** Dolcetto d'Alba Bricco ♥

Best years Monprivato 1999, '97, '96, '95, '93, '91, '90, '89, '88, '85, '82

MASI, Sant'Ambrogio, Veneto   045 6800588/6800608

Led by Sandro Boscaini, Masi has been turning out classic Amarone and Valpolicella as well as trail-blazing wines like the *ripasso* Campofiorin and the local grape blend called Toar for over 30 years. Masi also makes the wines of the Serègo Alighieri estate.

Best wines ★★ Amarone Mazzano ♥, Serègo Alighieri Amarone Vajo Armaron ♥ and Serègo Alighieri Recioto Casal dei Ronchi ♥, **★** Campiofiorin ♥ and Toar ♥

Best years 1999, '97, '95, '93, '90, '88

CASTELLO DI MONSANTO, Barberino Val d'Elsa, Tuscany   055 8059000/8059049

Fabrizio Bianchi has been producing some of the most esteemed Chianti Classico over 3 decades. There is also fine Vin Santo, La Chimera, and a range of premium barrique-aged reds, including Fabrizio Bianchi (Sangiovese) and Nemo (Cabernet Sauvignon).

Best wines ★★ Chianti Classico Riserva Il Poggio ♥ and Fabrizio Bianchi ♥ **★** Nemo ♥

Best years 1999, '97, '95, '93, '90, '88, '86, '85

MONTEVERTINE, Radda in Chianti, Tuscany   0577 38009/738265

Although this estate is in the heart of the Chianti Classico region, it is famous for non-DOC wines, especially the elegantly-labelled Le Pergole Torte, one of the first super-Tuscans to be produced solely from Sangiovese, and still one of the best. Il Sodaccio is a judicious blend of Sangiovese and Canaiolo, as is the Montevertine Riserva.

Best wines ★★★ Le Pergole Torte ♥, **★★** Il Sodaccio ♥ and Montevertine Riserva ♥

Best years 1999, '97, '95, '93, '90, '89, '88, '86, '85, '83

ORNELLAIA, Bolgheri, Tuscany   0565 762140/762144

Piero ANTINORI's younger brother Lodovico owns this large estate in Italy's 'California'. Ornellaia (Cabernet/Merlot) is a true rival to the legendary Sassicaia (see Tenuta SAN GUIDO); Merlot-based Masseto is Pomerol-like with great fruit depth and structure and Poggio is an intense Sauvignon Blanc.

Best wines ★★★ Masseto ♥ and Ornellaia ♥, **★★** Poggio alle Gazze ♀

Best years ♥1999, '97, '94, '93, '92, '90, '88

PIEROPAN, Soave, Veneto   045 6190171/6190040

Leonildo Pieropan and his father before him kept the flag of quality flying through those years when the industrialists of Verona were rubbishing the Soave name. His wines are subtle and penetrating, and his Cru La Rocca shows that Soave has the power to last for 10 years or more in bottle. His sweet wines are beautifully balanced.

Best wines ★★★ Soave Classico La Rocca ♀, ★★ Soave Classico Calvarino ♀, Recioto di Soave Le Colombare ♀ and Passito della Rocca ♀

Best years 1998, '97, '95, '93, '90, '88

POLIZIANO, Montepulciano, Tuscany   0578 738171/738171

Federico Carletti, with the help of enologist Carlo Ferrini, has turned this property over a 25-year period into one of the jewels of Montepulciano with classic Sangioveses, including Elegia, and an excellent Cabernet Sauvignon, Le Stanze.

Best wines ★★ Vino Nobile di Montepulciano Vigna Asinone ♥, Elegia ♥ and Le Stanze ♥

Best years 1999, '97, '95, '94, '93, '90, '88

QUERCIABELLA, Greve-in-Chianti, Tuscany   055 853834/8544657

This superbly converted estate turns out Sangioveses of a high level of craftsmanship, made by Guido de Santi, although perhaps his most surprising success is a barriqued white from (mainly) Pinot Bianco, called Batàr.

Best wines ★★★ Camartina ♥, ★★ Batàr ♀, Chianti Classico Riserva ♥ and Chianti Classico ♥

Best years ♥1999, '97, '95, '94, '93, '90

QUINTARELLI, Negrar, Veneto   045 7500016/7500016

Giuseppe Quintarelli is by now an institution in Valpolicella, a man who uses the best quality grapes and then intervenes as little as possible in the winemaking process, leaving Nature to do the work.

Best wines ★★★ Amarone della Valpolicella Monte Cà Paletta ♥, ★★ Alzero Passito ♥, Recioto della Valpolicella Monte Cà Paletta ♥ and Valpolicella Classico Superiore Monte Cà Paletta ♥   **Best years** 1997, '95, '90, '86, '85, '83

CASTELLO DEI RAMPOLLA, Panzano, Tuscany   055 852001/852533

Superbly located Chianti estate for stylish Classico and the fine super-Tuscan Sammarco (Cabernet Sauvignon with some Sangiovese). Top wine today is the Cabernet La Vigna di Alceo.

Best wines ★★★ La Vigna di Alceo ♥ and Sammarco ♥, ★★ Chianti Classico ♥

Best years 1999, '97, '96, '95, '94, '93, '90, '89, '86

REGALEALI, Vallelunga Pratameno, Sicily   0921 542522/542783

For decades Sicily's finest winery, Regaleali has added blockbuster versions of international grape varieties (Cabernet Sauvignon and Chardonnay) to the excellent range based on native grapes Nero d'Avola (the basis of Rosso del Conte) and Inzolia.

Best wines ★★ Rosso del Conte ♥, Cabernet Sauvignon ♥ and Chardonnay ♀

Best years 1998, '95, '94, '93, '92, '90, '89

RUFFINO, Pontassieve, Tuscany   055 83605/8313677

The Folonari family have interests in various areas of the Italian wine industry, principally in Tuscany. Their Chiantis can be superb and some fine super-Tuscans include Il Pareto, an intense, full-bodied pure Cabernet Sauvignon; Cabreo Il Borgo, a spicy Sangiovese/Cabernet blend, and Nero del Tondo, an oak-aged Pinot Noir.

Best wines ★★ Il Pareto (Fattoria di Nozzole) ♥, Cabreo Il Borgo ♥ and Chianti Classico Riserva Ducale Oro ♥, ★ Nero del Tondo ♥, Brunello di Montalcino Greppone Mazzi ♥

Best years 1999, '97, '95, '93, '90, '88

SANDRONE, Barolo, Piedmont   0173 56239/56239

Hailed as a star of the new generation, Luciano Sandrone nevertheless makes classic wines – capable of lasting for decades, with chewy, ripe tannins.

Best wines ★★★ Barolo Cannubi Boschis ❢ and Barolo le Vigne ❢, ★★ Dolcetto d'Alba ❢

Best years 1999, '98, '97, '96, '95, '90, '89, '86, '85

SAN GIUSTO A RENTENNANO, Gaiole-in-Chianti, Tuscany   0577 747121/747109

Francesco Martini di Cigala and family at their small estate in Chianti make wines of unequalled power, exemplified by the pure Sangiovese super-Tuscan Percarlo. Even the normal Chianti Classico has unusual strength and stamina, surpassed by a Riserva that needs a decade to reach its peak. The Vin Santo ranks with Tuscany's finest.

Best wines ★★★ Percarlo ❢ and Vin Santo Toscana ♀, ★★ Chianti Classico Riserva ❢

Best years ❢1999, '97, '95, '94, '93, '92, '91, '90, '88, '86, '85

TENUTA SAN GUIDO, Bolgheri, Tuscany   0565 762003/762017

This is the home of the legendary Sassicaia, the Bordeaux Grand Cru Classé lookalike that took the wine-world by storm in the 1970s. It was devised by present Marchese Niccolo's father Mario with Giacomo Tachis and Bordeaux's Professor Émile Peynaud, and the dominant grape is Cabernet Sauvignon with a hint of Cabernet Franc. Sassicaia has now been honoured with its own DOC of Bolgheri-Sassicaia.

Best wine ★★★ Sassicaia ❢

Best years 1996, '95, '93, '92, '90, '88, '85, '84, '83, '71

PAOLO SCAVINO, Barolo, Piedmont   0173 62850

Enrico Scavino makes some of the sexiest wine in the Albese, combining lip-smacking fruit and soft tannins with a level of oak pleasing to the international palate, if not always to the purist. His Barbera, in a good year, can be utterly enticing.

Best wines ★★★ Barolo Cannubi ❢ and Barolo Bric del Fiasc ❢, ★★ Barbera d'Alba Affinato in Carati ❢

Best years 1999, '98, '97, '96, '95, '93, '91, '90, '89, '88, '86, '85, '82

SCHIOPETTO, Capriva del Friuli, Friuli-Venezia Giulia   0481 80332/808073

Mario Schiopetto was one of the pioneers of fine wine in Friuli. All his unoaked varietal whites last for an unusually long time. Amrità is a Pinot Bianco varietal, Blanc des Rosis is a Pinot Bianco blend and Rivarossa a good Bordeaux-style red.

Best wines ★★★ Amrità ♀, Collio Pinot Bianco ♀, Collio Tocai ♀ and Blanc des Rosis ♀, ★ Rivarossa ❢

Best years 1998, '97, '95, '93, '90

FATTORIA SELVAPIANA, Rufina, Tuscany   055 8639848/8316840

Francesco Giuntini is one of the greats of Tuscany, a gentleman of unique wit and wisdom. Together with adopted son Federico Giuntini and consultant Franco Bernabei he produces wines of uncompromising purity and great character, capable of lasting up to 50 years and more (he will sell you an old bottle as proof).

Best wines ★★★ Chianti Rufina Riserva Bucerchiale ❢, ★★ Chianti Rufina Riserva Fornace ❢, ★ Chianti Rufina ❢

Best years 1999, '98, '97, '95, '93, '90, '88, '85, '70, '68

TAURINO, Guagnano, Puglia   0832 706490/706242

The late Cosimo Taurino represented the club of rising-star grower-producers in

southern Puglia, all of whom are indebted to enologist Severino Garofano. The specialities here are the beefy, long-aged, and increasingly famous Patriglione from Negroamaro and Malvasia Nera, and Notarpanaro from the same grapes.
Best wines ★★ Brindisi Rosso Patriglione ¶, ★ Rosso del Salento Notarpanaro ¶
Best years 1998, '97, '93, '90, '88, '85

TENUTA DEL TERRICCIO, Castellina Marittima, Tuscany   050 699709/699789
Tuscan superstar estate producing international-style reds and dry whites, most notably an expensive eucalyptus-scented red called Lupicaia from Cabernet and Merlot. Tassinaia is also a blend of Bordeaux grapes but ready to drink a little sooner.
Best wines ★★ Lupicaia ¶ and Tassinaia ¶   **Best years** 1998, '97, '95, '94, '93

VALENTINI, Loreto Aprutino, Abruzzo   085 8291138/8291138
Edoardo Valentini is a gentleman farmer with a large estate which includes some 130ha of grapes. The best 5% (or so) of these go into his own bottled wines, which, for richness of fruit, complexity of aroma and longevity, are a revelation for anyone acquainted with the rivers of basic wine that flow from Abruzzo.
Best wines ★★★ Montepulciano d'Abruzzo ¶ and Trebbiano d'Abruzzo ♀
Best years ¶1998, '97, '92, '90, '88, '85, '77

VIE DI ROMANS, Mariano del Friuli, Friuli-Venezia Giulia   0481 69600/69600
Gianfranco Gallo typifies the serious search for ultimate quality of the so-called 'Isonzo boys'. He ages his wines longer than most and his varietals are unrivalled for depth of flavour and creamy texture. Flors di Uis is a Malvasia/Riesling/Chardonnay blend.
Best wines ★★★ Isonzo Sauvignon Vieris ♀, ★★ Isonzo Sauvignon Pière ♀, Isonzo Chardonnay ♀ and Flors di Uis ♀
Best years 1999, '97, '95, '93, '92, '91, '90

VIETTI, Castiglione Falletto, Piedmont   0173 62825/62941
Alfredo Currado and family select from choice plots in the Alba area to make wines of unerring class. The wines that best express Vietti's enlightened traditional style come from vineyards closest to home.
Best wines ★★★ Barolo Riserva Villero ¶, ★★ Barbera d'Alba Scarrone Vigna Vecchia ¶ and Dolcetto d'Alba Lazzarito ¶
Best years 1999, '98, '97, '96, '95, '93, '90, '89, '88, '86, '85, '82

ROBERTO VOERZIO, La Morra, Piedmont   0173 509196/509196
The key to this eternally youthful grower's undoubted success is his meticulous care to produce the highest quality fruit. At heart a modernist, he just wants to get on with doing his thing, which is to make perfect Barolo.
Best wines ★★★ Barolo Cerequio ¶, ★★ Barolo Brunate ¶ and Barolo La Serra ¶
Best years 1999, '98, '97, '96, '95, '93, '90, '89, '88

ZERBINA, Marzeno, Romagna   0546 40022/40275
There are many 'Donne del Vino' in Italy, but few as attentive as Cristina Geminiani. This corner of south-east Romagna will doubtless receive greater attention as the fame of her excellent wines, mainly Sangiovese-based, spreads.
Best wines ★★ Sangiovese di Romagna Riserva Pietramora ¶, Sangiovese di Romagna Superiore Torre di Ceparano ¶, Marzieno ¶ and Albana di Romagna Passito Scacco Matto ♀
Best years ¶1999, '98, '97, '95, '94, '93, '91, '90

ITALIAN VINTAGES

Italian wines, both classics and new classics, are increasingly catching on as investment wines in auction rooms and on fine wine lists. Starting with Barolo, Barbaresco, Brunello and the like, the provenance of 'super-Italian' wines for laying down is widening and deepening year by year. Italians today are even beginning to accept the concept of white wines for bottle-aging.

Aging qualities

The chemical components that enable wines to age well are tannin, acidity, alcohol and sugar. Correct storage is also important. The Nebbiolo grape, and therefore Barolo and Barbaresco, has intense tannins and for winemakers the struggle has been to render these potentially aggressive tannins acceptable if not agreeable. This has been achieved by certain modernist producers with, as yet, uncertain effects on longevity; they claim that the aging potential of the new softer-tannin style will be just as good if not better because there will be less oxidation. Nebbiolo is not short of acids or alcohol

Maturity charts _____

1997 was an outstanding year throughout Italy, the best since the great 1990. Superb ripe fruit will make many Barolos accessible within 5 years though the best will keep longer, the Amarone are rich, powerful and ageworthy and in Tuscany the premium reds should be kept for at least 10 years.

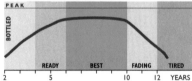

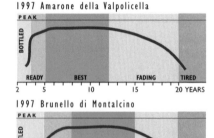

VINTAGE CHART

	99	98	97	96	95	94	93	92	91	90	89	88
Barolo, Barbaresco	8○	9○	10○	10○	8○	6◑	7◑	4◑	6○	10○	9◑	8●
Barbera	8○	9○	10○	7●	8○	6●	7●	4●	7●	10●	9●	8○
Amarone, Recioto, Ripasso	6○	8○	10○	7○	9○	7○	8○	5○	6○	10○	6●	9○
Chianti Riserva (Classico, Rufina), Carmignano Riserva	9○	7○	10○	7○	9○	6●	8●	4●	7●	10○	6●	9◑
Vino Nobile di Montepulciano	9○	7○	10○	8○	9◑	6○	7◑	4●	7●	10●	6●	9○
Brunello di Montalcino	9○	8○	10○	8○	9○	8◑	8◑	5●	8◑	10○	6●	9●

KEY ○= needs more time ◑= ready but will improve ●= at peak ◐= fading or tired

either. A top Barolo or Barbaresco from a great vintage can therefore be expected to last for several decades, provided it is stored correctly.

Recioto and Amarone are styles of wine chock-a-block with alcohol and have good tannins and acids, as well as residual sugar in the case of Recioto, so the potential for long aging is excellent, the only snag being a tendency to oxidation.

There is Sangiovese and Sangiovese, of course, but at its best – from a top site in Montalcino, Montepulciano or Chianti Classico or Rufina – the wines can have excellent structure and age in a most interesting way in respect of tertiary aromas. Other reds capable of good to excellent aging include Sagrantino di Montefalco, Taurasi, Montepulciano d'Abruzzo, as well as top Cabernets and/or Merlots from Tuscany and the North.

Dry Italian whites for long aging have been rare for lack of a home market. Today, however, producers like Pieropan (Soave) have shown that 10-year-old Italian white can be delicious, as have Gravner (Friuli), Bucci (Le Marche), Biondi-Santi (Montalcino) and others. Sweet or apéritif styles with potential for aging include Moscato Passito di Pantelleria, Brachetto d'Acqui Passito and Marsala Vergine.

VINTAGES AT A GLANCE

Barolo/Barbaresco/Barbera d'Alba
Albese producers have never seen the like of it – 5 consecutive good to great vintages, 1995–1999 inclusive. The previous record, held by 1988–1990, was 3 years. Compensation for the lean years of the early 1990s or the effects of global warming?

Great Years ★★★	1998, '97, '96, '90, '89, '88, '85, '82, '78, '74, '71, '70, '67, '64, '61, '55, '47
Good Years ★★	1999, '95, '93, '86, '83, '79
Moderate Years ★	1994, '91, '87, '81, '80
Poor Years (No Stars)	1992

Amarone/Recioto/Valpolicella Superiore
For wines such as these made from dried grapes there are 2 vintage factors: the weather up to and including picking and the weather during the drying process. The artificial drying or *appassimento* of the first 10% of moisture is now reducing the importance of the latter.

Great Years ★★★	1998, '97, '95, '90, '88, '85, '81
Good Years ★★	1993, '86, '83
Moderate Years ★	1999, '96, '94, '91, '89
Poor Years (No Stars)	1992, '87, '84 (for Valpolicella Superiore), '82 (for Amarone)

Chianti Classico and Rufina
In general the 1990s have been pretty reasonable. Perhaps this is one of the factors behind the recent dramatic price rises of Tuscan wines, now fortunately levelling out.

Great Years ★★★	1997, '95, '90, '88, '85, '75, '71, '58
Good Years ★★	1999, '98, '96, '93, '86, '83, '82, '79, '70, '68
Moderate Years ★	1994, '91
Poor Years (No Stars)	1992, '89

Brunello di Montalcino
Italy's supposedly longest-lived wine depends on certain conditions to enable it to pull off its longevity feat, and it got them in 1997, '95 and '90 – and in many cases in 1999.

Great Years ★★★	1997, '95, '90, '88, '85, '75, '64, '55, '45
Good Years ★★	1999, '98, '96, '93, '86, '83, '82
Moderate Years ★	1994, '91
Poor Years (No Stars)	1992, '89

Annual vintage reports
Barolo/Barbaresco/Barbera d'Alba
1999★★ In sharp contrast to 1998, the summer was on the cool side with regular but not excessive rain. Early September rain caused a few headaches, but late pickers enjoyed a fine harvest end.

1998★★★ A hot summer and little rain caused growers to worry about imbalance in the vine, but timely rain saved the situation and early pickers were rewarded with wines of great depth and richness.

1997★★★ A summer and autumn of little but enough rain, combined with brilliant weather at harvest time which was early. Wines of great colour and concentration.

1996★★ Cool temperatures and some substantial downpours in late September/early October made life tricky for growers. On the whole, vines remained rot-free. The winners either got it over with early or waited until late in October.

1995★★★ A good-looking harvest seemed compromised by a lot of rain in early September, but from then on the sun shone and shone. Late pickers got beautifully ripe, balanced grapes, so excellent Nebbiolo, good Barbera and poor Dolcetto.

1994★ Maddeningly rainy from late September through most of October, so good for the early ripeners – whites and Dolcetto – but a write-off for classic Nebbiolo and Barbera.

1993★★ After 1991 and '92 growers were beginning to wonder whether decent harvest weather was gone forever, so they grabbed at the small mercy of mere showers. Grapes on the whole were ripe, giving wines of colour and body.

1992 Only berry-by-berry picking could overcome the particularly adverse cold-and-wet conditions at vintage time. Wines were generally but not universally feeble.

1991★ A better year than has been broadcast. After 3 top years, producers were becoming a bit cocky, but the serious ones made some decent Barbera and Nebbiolo wines.

1990★★★ The third outstanding vintage in a row, all conditions perfect, one of those years of which it is said that only a fool could mess it up. A few fools managed, the best excelled.

1989★★★ A beautiful summer was crowned by a harvest during which the rains that washed everyone else in Italy down the drain miraculously withheld their worst. In some cases wines are superior to the 1990s.

1988★★★ Early ripeners did well, though October rains threatened to mar the promising Nebbiolos, which in the end came through reasonably unscathed. Wines of elegance rather than power.

1985★★★ Excellent conditions and harvest. Powerful wines, some still developing.

Other good years 1982, '78, '74, '71, '70, '67, '64, '61. These all had their top examples, although the chances of finding some of them today are low, let alone finding them in mint condition.

Amarone, Recioto and Valpolicella Superiore
1999★ A rainy growing season and September caused some rot and a lot of problems in vinification, but there are some very good wines amid the rubbish.

1998★★ Drought was the problem and where the vines suffered excessive stress results were not impressive. Where the vines held their own, the wines are of excellent concentration and structure.

1997★★★ Outstanding year although there were fears regarding drought damage. High sugar levels should yield big Superiore and monster Amarone wines, capable of aging for decades.

1996★ A wet vintage achieved high acid levels but dampened high expectations. Some good wines from growers willing to spend time sorting out the ripe berries.

1995★★★ Early September rains threw a cloud over growers' hopes, but a glorious 6 weeks from mid-September ensured conditions ideal for both harvest and *appassimento*. Rich, well-balanced wines.

1994★ One of the several promising vintages of the 1990s compromised by harvest rain. Some good, if dilute, wines.

1993★★ October rains meant that early pickers prospered provided they managed to control rot in the early stages of *appassimento*. Some excellent *ripasso* wines.

1992 Another rain-spoilt vintage, though a number of exceptions to the rumour that 1992 was terrible do exist.

1991★ Yet another vintage in which harvest rain took its toll.

1990★★★ A rare year, outstanding for table wines and dried-grape wines alike. The best will be long-lived.

1989★ A lesser year, now fading.

1988★★★ Wines of considerable power and excellent equilibrium, from top growers opening out around now.

1985★★★ Big, full, rich wines and Amarones of great potency and longevity. The very best still have a long way to go.

Other good years The best wines from 1983 and '81 are still going strong.

Chianti Classico, Chianti Rufina, Brunello di Montalcino and Vino Nobile di Montepulciano

1999★★ Patchy weather, with scattered but not excessive showers, and even temperatures made for good conditions for quantity (up 10%) and quality. Some excellent, nicely balanced wines.

1998★★ Drought and great heat caused some stress to the vines, but many growers were delighted with one of the earliest harvests on record. Better for Brunello than Chianti Classico.

1997★★★ This potentially marvellous year was marred for many by a devastating spring frost. Otherwise, near-drought conditions resulted in wines with tremendous colour and high alcohol.

1996★★ Despite scattered rain at vintage time most of the grapes were ripe and healthy. The wines have good colour, lots of fruit and are relatively forward.

1995★★★ A great vintage only for late pickers and the wines from genuinely late-picked grapes are for the long haul.

1994★ Vintage rains were not sufficient to knock this year out, though it did knock it back from potentially excellent to merely fairly good. Better in Montalcino and Montepulciano than in Chianti.

1993★★ October rains meant that early pickers did best. The wines are medium-weight and have medium-aging potential, good for early drinking.

1992 Something of a washout, though with the best grapes going into the basic *normale* wines rather than the Riserva there were some modest achievements; for drinking now.

1991★ Chiantis were generally moderate, Brunello and Vino Nobile considerably better than rated by the pundits.

1990★★★ The so-called 'vintage of the century', when new techniques in vineyard and winery were met by glorious weather. Some big, complex wines for long aging.

1989 A year to forget.

1988★★★ Some splendid modern-style Crus burst upon the scene this year. Firm tannins should ensure long life among those with sufficient fruit to merit aging.

Other good years (Brunello) 1985, '75, '64, '55, '45; (Chianti) 1985, '79, '71, '70, '68, '58.

SPAIN

First there was sherry, but it faded from fashion despite its dryness and elegance, which should have made it a successful modern wine. Then along came Rioja, but success went to the heads of many producers and excessive yields diluted the wines in the 1970s. So Spain, with the world's largest vineyard surface and a rich diversity of terroirs, became a sideshow in the realm of fine wine. The fabled Vega Sicilia held the fort, but few in Spain and even fewer abroad had ever tasted it. However, the end of the jug wine era and the drive to better quality shook vinous Spain down to its roots in the 1980s and, even more, in the 1990s. From verdant Galicia to warm southern Cataluña, whole regions producing fine wine were born or reborn.

Main Spanish wine areas

Main DOC/DO wines	5 Toro	10 Somontano	15 Alicante
1 Rías Baixas	6 Rueda	11 Costers del Segre	16 Valdepeñas
2 Ribeiro	7 Ribera del Duero	12 Conca de Barberá	17 Montilla-Moriles
3 Ribeira Sacra	8 Rioja	13 Penedès	18 Málaga
4 Valdeorras	9 Navarra	14 Priorat	19 Jerez-Xérès-Sherry

GREAT SPANISH WINES

Oz Clarke's selection
Ribera del Duero ❢ (Briego) An amazing marriage of sweet blackcurrant and strawberry with the savoury spice of dill, coriander and melting butter.
Fleur de Pingus ❢ (Dominio de Pingus) New style Ribera del Duero at its best with rich loganberry fruit scented with violets.
Priorat ❢ (Finca La Planeta) Powerful, disturbing dark wine laden with black fruit and cream and held inside a fortress of tannin.
Monastrell Dulce ❢ (Olivares) Remarkable, Port-like, intensely sweet red oozing black treacle, blackberry juices, tobacco leaf and pepper spice.
Priorat Dolç de l'Obac ❢ (Costers del Siurana) Amazing superripe red, thick Port-like dark fruit mingling with myrtle and eucalyptus.
Conca de Barberá Milmanda Chardonnay ♀ (Torres) Spain's first world class, coolish-climate Chardonnay and still her best.
Inocente Fino ♀ (Valdespino) Quite simply,

this dry Fino is the greatest example of one of the world's great wine styles.
Coliseo ♀ (Valdespino) Incomparable, complex, thrilling old Oloroso.
Solera India ♀ (Osborne) Another great Oloroso that has a perceptible sweetness matched by acidity.

Steven Spurrier's selection
Priorat L'Ermita ❢ (Alvaro Palacios) Ultra-concentrated wines from very low-yielding old vines.
Pesquera Reserva Ribera del Duero ❢ (Alejandro Fernández) Richly coloured, firm, fragrant wine from 100% Tempranillo with a judicious use of oak.
Penedès Chardonnay ♀ (Jean León/Torres) A well-

structured, not over-oaky Chardonnay that benefits from aging.
Rioja Reserva Barón de Chirel ❢ (Marqués de Riscal) The oldest bodega in Rioja has produced a modern wine, based on Cabernet Sauvignon.
Ribera del Duero Viña Pedrosa Gran Reserva ❢ (Hermanos Pérez Pascuas) Elegant wine, with sophisticated oak and fruit and good depth.
Penedès Mas La Plana ❢ (Torres) Miguel Torres's award-winning, concentrated Cabernet Sauvignon wine.
Manzanilla La Gitana ♀ (Hidalgo) The most refreshing, most typical and bestselling Manzanilla Sherry in Spain.
Don Gonzalo Old Dry Oloroso ♀ (Valdespino) From a solera approaching 100 years old, this is one of the marvels of Sherry.
Matusalem ♀ (González Byass) Rich, ripe, concentrated Oloroso, with deep, nutty flavours and endless warmth and length.

Appellations and classifications

Spain's version of the appellation system is the *denominación de origen* (DO), with a growing number (now more than 50) of these areas of origin. Only Rioja has been promoted to the higher, newer *denominación de origen calificada* (DOC) status, which theoretically entails stricter quality controls.

The large size of most DOs minimizes the stylistic meaning of many of the appellations. Instead of smaller sub-appellations, the Spanish system relies on a classification according to a wine's aging,

which originated in Rioja: *joven, crianza, reserva, gran reserva.* This system, in which more time spent in cask and bottle equates with greater quality, is fading fast.

Top Spanish wine regions _____
Red wines Alicante, Costers del Segre, Navarra, Penedès, Priorat, Ribera del Duero, Rioja, Somontano, Toro.
White wines Conca de Barberá, Costers del Segre, Navarra, Penedès, Rías Baixas, Ribeiro, Rioja, Rueda, Somontano, Valdeorras.
Fortified wines Jerez-Xérès-Sherry y Manzanilla de Sanlúcar, Montilla-Moriles, Fondillón (Alicante), Ranci (Priorat).

A–Z OF SPANISH WINE REGIONS

ALICANTE DO

This DO covers 2 disparate areas – the coastal Marina Alta produces fragrant Muscat grapes and the southern, inland zone is covered with the native Monastrell (Mourvèdre), producing powerful red wines and the rare, fortified Fondillón.
Best producers Bocopa co-op, GUTIÉRREZ DE LA VEGA, Enrique Mendoza.
Best years 1999, '98, '97.

CONCA DE BARBERÁ DO

Most of the grapes from this cool valley west of Tarragona go into Cava, Spain's Champagne-method sparkling wine (which has a separate DO). The slopes here are some of Spain's best for Chardonnay.
Best producers Concavins, Sanstravé.
Best years 1998, '96, '95.

COSTERS DEL SEGRE DO

Created around the huge Raïmat estate, owned by fizz giant CODORNÍU, this area in arid western Cataluña covers 5 sub-zones. Foreign grape varieties play a leading role and in general the wines are good.
Best producers Raïmat, Castell del Remei.
Best years ❗1999, '98, '96, '95, '93.

JEREZ-XÉRÈS-SHERRY Y MANZANILLA DE SANLÚCAR DO

The chalky *albariza* soil and the humid, cooling Atlantic breezes are the keys to this historic region, in which the neutral Palomino grape is made into the world's greatest dry fortified wines. Despite sherry's lightness and tanginess, its popularity has suffered setbacks recently, leading to the merger of wineries and to a sharp reduction in the land devoted to vineyards. The cooler, coastal Sanlúcar sub-area produces the highly individual, somewhat salty Manzanilla wines.
Best producers Herederos de Argüeso, BARBADILLO, Delgado Zuleta, Díez

Mérito, DOMECQ, Garvey, GONZÁLEZ BYASS, Hidalgo, LUSTAU, Jesús Ferris Marhuenda, OSBORNE, Sánchez Romate, Sandeman, José de Soto, Valdespino, Williams & Humbert.

MONTILLA-MORILES DO

This large area is home to the Pedro Ximénez grape. Vineyards are losing the battle against olive trees, but a number of outstanding sherry-like wines, which usually don't need fortifying, are still made.
Best producers Alvear, Pérez Barquero, Tomás García, TORO ALBALÁ.

NAVARRA DO

This is a 'political' DO covering a whole autonomous region; it has enjoyed a boom since foreign grape varieties and new techniques were introduced, and native varieties (Garnacha and Moscatel de Grano Menudo) were re-launched. A 'loss of personality' has been criticized, but the well-made, usually good-value wines have had great commercial success.
Best producers Camilo Castilla, CHIVITE, GUELBENZU, Magaña, Alvaro Marino, Castillo de Monjardín, Vinícola Navarra, Nekeas, Ochoa, Palacio de la Vega, Piedemonte Olite co-op, Príncipe de Viana, Señorío de Sarría.
Best years 1999, '98, '97, '96, '95, '94, '93, '92, '91, '90.

PENEDÈS DO

Cataluña's largest appellation shares its vineyard surface with the Cava DO (a non-geographical appellation, most of whose production is in Penedès.) There are 3 sub-areas, from the Tarragona coast to the high, cooler inland hills of the Alt Penedès. The region produces still wine, and after a ballyhooed start it seems to have settled on good-but-not-great wines. Most reds can't shake off some herbaceousness, while white wines show the most distinction and promise.

Best producers Albet i Noya, CAN FEIXES, CAN RÀFOLS DELS CAUS, Chandon, CODORNÍU, Ferret, Freixenet, Gramona, Masía Bach, Parxet, Puig & Roca, Josep Maria Raventós i Blanc, Joan Raventós Rosell, Rovellats, Olivella Sadurní, Signat, Agustí Torelló, TORRES, Vallformosa, Jané Ventura.

Best years 1998, '97, '96, '95, '94, '91.

PRIORAT DO

Forgotten since its highly alcoholic fortified Garnacha reds went out of fashion, the beautiful, mountainous area in southern Cataluña was revived in the 1980s by a group of young growers who changed the style by introducing foreign grape varieties to buttress the native Garnacha and Cariñena. The highly personal, minerally, powerful reds began attracting attention in the late 1990s.

Best producers Clos Erasmus, CLOS MOGADOR, Clos i Terrasses, COSTERS DEL SIURANA, Finca La Planeta, MAS MARTINET, Alvaro PALACIOS, Rotllan Torra, Scala Dei.

Best years 1998, '97, '95, '94, '93, '90, '89, '87.

RÍAS BAIXAS DO

This verdant area is home to Spain's most distinctive and aromatic white variety, Albariño. Excesses notwithstanding (high yields and unfettered technology), it can produce hugely fragrant wines to be drunk young, in the Viognier mould. Beware of significant vintage variation.

Best producers Adegas Galegas, Agro de Bazán, Aldea de Abaixo, Castro Martín, Quinta de Couselo, Granxa Fillaboa, Lagar de Fornelos, LUSCO DO MIÑO, Morgadío, Palacio de Fefiñanes, Pazo de Barrantes, Pazo San Mauro, Pazo de Señorans, Salnesur, Santiago Ruiz, TERRAS GAUDA, Vilariño-Cambados.

RIBEIRO DO

Traditionally the most prestigious Galician wine region, this area making lightweight wines was slow to return to finer indigenous varieties, led by Torrontés and Treixadura. Now it's following Rías Baixas' lead and the quality of the white wines has improved markedly. Drink young.

Best producers Viña Meín, Ribeiro co-op, Emilio Rojo, Vilerma.

RIBERA DEL DUERO DO

A renowned vineyard area along the upper Duero/Douro river, this region lacked a name and winemaking skills: most of the wine was made primitively and sold locally. The skills came from imitating the legendary VEGA SICILIA estate and following its example of quality, oak-aged wines. The name was settled on in 1982, when Ribera del Duero reached DO status and there are more than 70 wineries now. The depth and pungency attained by red wines from the Tinto Fino (alias

---

A NEW BREED OF 'SUPER-SPANISH' WINES

As well as exciting new estates within existing DOs, a number of new bodegas outside recognized DO boundaries have sprouted up throughout Spain in recent years, often with innovative viticultural practices: Richard Smart's canopy vine-training system was first used in Europe at the Marqués de Griñón's Valdepusa estate near Toledo. With freedom from DO restrictions and winemaking help from the likes of Pascal Delbeck and Michel Rolland, the 'super-Spanish' wines have quickly reached the top of the hierarchy. The best are: (Castilla y León) Abadía Retuerta, Alta Pavina, Duratón, Mauro; (Castilla-La Mancha) Dehesa del Carrizal, Dominio de Valdepusa, Manuel Manzaneque; (Cataluña) Celler Mas Gil; (Andalucía) Las Monjas-Principe Alfonso; (Mallorca) Miguel Oliver.

Tempranillo) grape in the extreme climatic conditions of the narrow Duero valley was the reason for this unprecedented boom.

Best producers Alión, ARROYO, Balbás, Briego, Félix Callejo, Condado de Haza, Dehesa de los Canónigos, Emina, Alejandro FERNÁNDEZ, Finca Villacreces, Navarro, Pago de Carraovejas, Peñalba López, Hermanos PÉREZ PASCUAS, Dominio de PINGUS, Protos, Teófilo REYES, Emilio Rojo, Hermanos Sastre, Señorío de Nava, Tionio, Valduero, Valtravieso, VEGA SICILIA, Viñedos y Bodegas, Winner Wines.

Best years 1999, '98, '96, '95, '94, '91, '90, '89.

RIOJA DOC

Spain's foremost table wine region since the mid-19th century is actually several quite different wine regions under a single appellation. The cooler, limestone-rich terroirs of Rioja Alta and Rioja Alavesa are more conducive to quality wine than the warm Rioja Baja and its clay soils. Widespread uprooting of old vineyards since the 1970s and skyrocketing yields are other reasons why, when determining quality today, the name of a bodega is more important than the Rioja name on the label. The emergence of smaller, ambitious estates and a change in attitude of some large companies started a revolution in the 1990s, with a return to almost forgotten levels of power and concentration in the red wines. The gap between these 'new' Riojas and routine commercial products has grown markedly.

Best producers Amézola de la Mora, ARTADI, Beronia, Bretón, Campillo, Contino, CVNE, Domecq, Faustino Martinéz, FINCA ALLENDE, Viña IJALBA, Herencia Lasanta, Marqués de Cáceres, Marqués de Griñon, Marqués de Murrieta, MARQUÉS DE RISCAL, Marqués de Vargas, MARTÍNEZ BUJANDA, Montecillo, MUGA, Ondarre, PALACIO, REMELLURI, Remírez de Ganuza, La RIOJA ALTA, Riojanas, RODA, SAN VICENTE, Sierra Cantabria, Torre de Oña.

Best years 1999, '98, '96, '95, '94, '91, '89, '88, '87.

RUEDA DO

This high-altitude, dry region is enjoying the rediscovery of native grape varieties – in this case, the distinctive white Verdejo – that were almost lost after the onset of phylloxera. Sauvignon Blanc has also adapted well and modern, appley wines now dominate. Drink young.

Best producers Alvarez y Díez, ANTAÑO, BELONDRADE Y LURTON, Angél Lorenzo Cachazo, Castilla la Vieja, Hermanos Lurton, Marqués de Irún, MARQUÉS DE RISCAL, Nieva co-op, Sanz, Vega de la Reina, Ángel Rodríguez Vidal.

SOMONTANO DO

Largely relying on new plantings of foreign grape varieties, 3 large wineries have led the wine revolution in Aragón's coolest wine region in the Pyrenean foothills.

Best producers ENATE, Pirineos, VIÑAS DEL VERO.

Best years 1998, '97, '96, '95, '94.

TORO DO

Forgotten between its two famed neighbours (Port and Ribera del Duero), this region shows potential for structured reds made from the Tinta de Toro grape.

Best producers Fariña, Frutos Villar, Vega Saúco.

Best years 1999, '98, '96, '95, '94, '91, '90.

VALDEORRAS DO

Relatively warm and dry, this area gained prominence as the native grape varieties, the white Godello and the red Mencía, were recovered from near extinction. Drink the wines young.

Best producers Godeval, Joaquín REBOLLEDO, La TAPADA.

ABADÍA RETUERTA, Sardón de Duero   983 68 03 14/68 02 86
A new vineyard on an historic site, a state-of-the-art winery designed by winemaker
Pascal Delbeck, and $20 million invested by Swiss company Novartis: instant fame!
Best wines ★★★ Cuvée El Palomar ! and Cuvée El Campanario !, ★★ Pago Negralada !,
Pago Valdebellón ! and Abadía Retuerta PV !, ★ Abadía Retuerta ! and Rívola !
Best years 1998, '97, '96

ANTAÑO, Rueda DO   983 86 85 33/86 85 14
Atop the most amazing, centuries-old cellar in Rueda (4km of rebuilt galleries), José
Luís Ruiz-Solaguren produces uninhibited, full-throttle Verdejo whites. Drink young.
Best wine ★★ Viña Mocen Rueda Superior ♀   **Best years** 1999, '98, '96, '95

ISMAEL ARROYO, Ribera del Duero DO   947 53 23 09/53 24 87
The coolest aging cellars in Ribera del Duero are one of the keys to the huge success
encountered by the tiny winery run by the Arroyo family, renowned for their
powerfully structured, tannic wines that blossom into refined, long-lasting reds for
drinking between 5 and 12 years.
Best wines ★★★ Val Sotillo Gran Reserva !, ★★ Val Sotillo Reserva !, ★ Val Sotillo Crianza !
Best years 1999, '98, '96, '95, '94, '91, '90, '89, '86

ARTADI, Rioja DOC   941 60 01 19/60 08 50
Cosecheros Alareses has moved from being an obscure co-operative to a Rioja quality
leader within 5 years under the Artadi brand name. Juan Carlos López de la Calle is a
champion of dense, long-maceration wines.
Best wines ★★★ Grandes Añadas !, ★★ Viñas de Gain Fermentado en Barrica ♀, Viña El
Pisón ! and Pagos Viejos Reserva !, ★ Viñas de Gain !
Best years 1999, '98, '97, '95, '94, '92, '91

ANTONIO BARBADILLO, Jerez DO   956 36 02 41/36 51 03
This is the largest sherry bodega in the coastal town of Sanlúcar de Barrameda, and one
of the best, with a superb range of good to excellent wines, particularly salty, dry
Manzanillas and nutty but dry Amontillados and Olorosos.
Best wines ★★★ Amontillado Príncipe ♀, ★★ Manzanilla Pasada Solear ♀, Manzanilla Fina
Eva ♀ and Dry Oloroso Cuco ♀

BELONDRADE Y LURTON, Rueda DO   983 85 01 25/85 01 25
Brigitte Lurton commutes between Paris, Sauternes (Ch. CLIMENS) and Rueda, and
finds time to make a Burgundian-style white wine in Spain with her husband Didier
Belondrade and winemaker cousin Jacques Lurton.
Best wine ★★ Rueda Belondrade y Lurton ♀
Best years 1999, '98, '97, '96, '95

CAN FEIXES, Penedès DO, Cava DO   93 771 82 27/771 80 31
Josep-Maria Huguet's well-run estate makes Cava sparkling wine and fine still wines,
led by a delicate white, made from Parellada, Macabeo and Chardonnay.
Best wines ★★ Can Feixes Blanc Selecció ♀, ★ Can Feixes Negre Selecció !, Cava Huguet
Brut Nature Vintage ♀ and Can Feixes Chardonnay ♀
Best years !1998, '97, '96, '95, '94, '93, '91

CAN RÁFOLS DELS CAUS, Penedès DO   93 897 00 13/897 03 70

Carles Esteva makes good extra virgin olive oil as well as very original wines under the Gran Caus label on his bucolic Penedès estate. The reds drink well with 5-10 years of age.

Best wines ★★ Caus Lubis ❢, ★ Gran Caus ❢   **Best years** 1998, '96, '94, '91, '90

JULIÁN CHIVITE, Navarra DO   948 81 11 00/81 14 07

Wine merchants for over 300 years and the longtime leaders in exporting Navarra wine, the Chivite family has dramatically upgraded its operation with its own, new Arínzano vineyards in western Navarra. The Colección wines are the top range.

Best wines ★★ Colección 125 Reserva ❢, Colección 125 Chardonnay ♀, Colección 125 Vendimia Tardía ♀

Best years ❢1999, '98, '97, '95, '94, '92, '90, '88; ♀1999, '98, '97, '96, '95

CLOS MOGADOR, Priorat DO   977 83 91 71/83 94 26

René Barbier tills his vineyard with only the help of his son and makes a captivating new-age Priorat red. Note that this estate is not connected with the widely seen, inexpensive wines labelled René Barbier.

Best wine ★★★ Clos Mogador ❢

Best years 1998, '97, '96, '95, '94, '93, '92, '91, '90

CODORNÍU, Cava DO, Costers del Segre DO   93 818 32 32/317 48 88

Both the huge, quality-driven Cava winery (the biggest Champagne-method sparkling wine company in the world) and the huge, top-quality Raïmat estate in Costers del Segre deserve equal attention. All the sparkling wines are better than the average Cava.

Best wines ★★ Cava Jaume Codorníu Brut ♀, ★ Cava Anna de Codorníu Brut ♀ and Raïmat Cabernet Sauvignon Mas Castell ❢   **Best years** ❢1994, '91, '90

COSTERS DEL SIURANA, Priorat DO   977 83 92 76/83 93 71

The idiosyncratic Carles Pastrana continues to go his own way in Priorat, making stylish, structured reds and a sweet red vintage Port-style wine called Dolç de l'Obac.

Best wines ★★★ Dolç de l'Obac ❢ and Clos de l'Obac ❢, ★★ Miserere ❢, ★ Usatges ♀

Best years ❢1998, '97, '95, '94, '92, '91

CVNE, Rioja DOC   941 31 06 50/31 28 19

Compañía Vinícola del Norte de España, better known as CVNE or 'coonay', is old-time Rioja, but it has never been averse to innovation. Imperial Gran Reserva is rich and meaty. The Contino estate, jointly owned by CVNE, is making a comeback.

Best wines ★★ Imperial Gran Reserva ❢ and Viña Real Fermentado en Barrica ♀, ★ Viña Real Gran Reserva ❢, Contino Graciano ❢ and Contino ❢

Best years ❢1999, '98, '96, '95, '94, '91, '90, '89, '87, '85, '82; ♀1999, '98, '97, '96, '94, '93

PEDRO DOMECQ, Jerez DO   956 36 07 36/36 10 27

Now part of the huge Allied Domecq conglomerate, the Jerez bodega still maintains some prestigious soleras. It is also the world's biggest brandy producer and makes light, elegant Rioja from its own vineyards under the Marqués de Arienzo label.

Best wines ★★★ Amontillado 51-1A ♀ and Palo Cortado Sibarita ♀, ★★ Fino La Ina ♀, ★ Pedro Ximénez Venerable ♀

ENATE, Somontano DO   974 30 23 23/30 00 46

One of the New World-style estates in the reborn Somontano region near the Pyrenees, led by clever winemaker Jesús Artajona.

Best wines ★★ Enate Reserva ❗ and Enate Reserva Especial ❗ ★ Enate Chardonnay
Fermentado en Barrica de Roble ♀
Best years ❗1998, '97, '96, '95, '94, '92; ♀1997, '96, '95, '94

ALEJANDRO FERNÁNDEZ, Ribera del Duero DO   983 87 00 37/87 00 88
The wily Alejandro Fernández was the first real challenger to VEGA SICILIA in the Ribera
del Duero region. His formula of using 100% Tempranillo for his deeply concentrated
wines took Spain by storm in the 1980s and the top wines are now among the country's
most expensive – but also the best. The Crianzas are surprisingly affordable.
Best wines ★★★ Pesquera Gran Reserva ❗ and Pesquera Janus ❗, ★★ Pesquera Crianza ❗,
Pesquera Reserva ❗ and Condado de Haza Crianza ❗
Best years 1999, '98, '97, '96, '95, '94, '92, '91, '90, '89, '86, '85

FINCA ALLENDE, Rioja DOC   941 45 75 64/45 75 64
Miguel Angel de Gregorio left Bodegas Bretón to launch his own winery at Briones, a
top Rioja Alta site. Old vines and an updating of a Rioja tradition (carbonic
maceration followed by oak aging) has resulted in tannic, concentrated wines.
Best wine ★★ Rioja Aurus ❗ and Allende ❗   **Best years** 1997, '96 '95

GONZÁLEZ BYASS, Jerez DO   956 34 00 00/33 20 89
This family-owned bodega has revived the practice of making single-vintage or non-
solera sherries (Viejo de Añada) which were commonly made in the 19th century. It
offers an unequalled range of top-drawer dry and sweet wines.
Best wines ★★★ Oloroso Viejo de Añada ♀, Amontillado del Duque ♀, Oloroso Matusalem ♀
and Pedro Ximénez Noé ♀, ★★ Fino Tío Pepe ♀ and Oloroso Apóstoles ♀
Best years Vintage-dated sherries 1970, '66, '64, '63

GUELBENZU, Navarra DO   948 85 00 55/85 00 97
This rebuilt southern Navarra estate is well run by the many Guelbenzu brothers and
makes top-notch, oak-aged blends and nicely structured, unoaked Garnachas.
Best wines ★★ Evo ❗ and Lautus ❗ ★ Guelbenzu Tinto ❗ and Jardín Garnacha ❗
Best years 1999, '98, '97, '96, '95, '94, '92, '91, '89

GUTIÉRREZ DE LA VEGA, Alicante DO   96 640 52 66/640 52 27
In orange-grove country on the coast, Felipe Gutiérrez de la Vega makes several
respectable red and white wines and one gorgeous sweet old-wine Muscat.
Best wine ★★ Moscatel Casta Diva ♀   **Best years** 1999, '98, '97

VIÑA IJALBA, Rioja DOC   941 26 11 00/26 11 28
One of the most innovative new wineries in Rioja has devoted itself to the rediscovery
of the native Graciano grape, which traditionally added structure to blended wines.
Best wines ★★ Viña Ijalba Reserva Especial ❗, ★ Viña Ijalba Graciano ❗
Best years 1998, '96, '95, '94, '91, '90

LUSCO DO MIÑO, Rías Baixas DO   Tel 986 65 85 19
A most original Albariño white, more concentrated and with far less residual sugar than
usual, is made by José Antonio López from the Pazo Piñeiro vineyard. Age for 2–3 years.
Best wine ★★ Lusco ♀   **Best years** 1999, '98, '97, '96

EMILIO LUSTAU, Jerez DO   956 34 15 97/34 77 89
Becoming part of the large Caballero conglomerate in 1990 has not overtly affected
this detail-obsessed bodega, particularly renowned for its Almacenista range of single-

batch sherries, very individual dry sherries from small, private producers.

Best wines ★★★ Almacenista range ♀, **★★** Oloroso Emperatriz Eugenia ♀

MARQUÉS DE RISCAL, Rioja DOC, Rueda DO   941 60 60 00/60 60 23

A pioneering firm in Rioja in the 1860s and in Rueda in the 1970s, it retains a unique cache of bottles from old vintages and shows a renewed commitment to quality.

Best wines ★★ Barón de Chirel Reserva ♥ and Marqués de Riscal Gran Reserva ♥, **★** Marqués de Riscal Sauvignon ♀, Marqués de Riscal Reserva ♥ and Marqués de Riscal Limousin Barrel Fermented ♀

Best years ♥1999, '98, '96, '95, '94, '91, '88, '86; ♀1997, '95, '94

MARTÍNEZ BUJANDA, Rioja DOC   941 12 21 88/12 21 11

The Martínez Bujanda brothers produced the first single-vineyard white in modern Rioja (and now a single-estate red), plus original Garnacha and Cabernet Sauvignon wines.

Best wines ★★ Finca Valpiedra ♥, **★** Garnacha Reserva ♥, Conde de Valdemar Gran Reserva ♥, Vendimia Seleccionada Gran Reserva ♥ and Conde de Valdemar Fermentado en Barrica ♀

Best years ♥1999, '98, '96, '95, '94, '92, '89; ♀1998, '97, '96

MAS MARTINET, Priorat DO   977 83 05 77/83 05 77

Josep-Lluís Pérez í Verdú is the foremost viticultural innovator in the reconquered and relaunched Priorat region. His wines are also among the most consistent in the area.

Best wines ★★★ Mas Martinet ♥ and Cims de Porrera Classic ♥, **★★** Martinet Bru ♥

Best years 1998, '97, '96, '95, '94, '93, '92, '90

MAURO, Tudela de Duero   983 68 02 65/68 10 72

A small venture just outside the Ribera del Duero DO, with former VEGA SICILIA winemaker Mariano García as partner and winemaker, makes lush, concentrated reds.

Best wines ★★ Mauro ♥, Térreus ♥ and Mauro Selección Especial ♥

Best years 1998, '97, '96, '95, '94

MUGA, Rioja DOC   941 31 18 25/31 28 67

Every single container in this winery is made with oak, and the Muga brothers are just as traditional in everything else too. The fruitier Torre Muga marks a change in style.

Best wines ★★ Prado Enea Gran Reserva ♥, **★** Torre Muga Reserva ♥ and Muga Fermentado en Barrica ♀   **Best years** ♥1999, '98, '95, '94, '93, '91, '89; ♀1998, '96, '95

OSBORNE, Jerez DO   956 85 52 11/85 21 83

The biggest drinks company in Spain is better known for brandy and other spirits than for sherries, but its new Rare Sherry range ranks right at the top.

Best wines ★★★ Palo Cortado PP ♀ and Oloroso Bailén ♀, **★★** Oloroso Solera India ♀ and Amontillado AOS ♀, **★** Fino Quinta ♀ and Amontillado Coquinero ♀

BODEGAS PALACIO, Rioja DOC   941 60 00 57/60 02 97

Over 100 years old but renovated in the late 1980s by then-owner Jean Gervais and Pomerol winemaker Michel Rolland, this winery buys grapes from top growers around Laguardia. Cosme Palacio, a fruitier style of Crianza Rioja, has become a cult wine.

Best wines ★★ Cosme Palacio ♥, **★** Glorioso Reserva ♥ and Cosme Palacio Fermentado en Barrica ♀

Best years 1999, '98, '96, '95, '94, '92, '91

ALVARO PALACIOS, Priorat DO   977 83 91 95/83 91 97

This young man from Rioja has risen to the top in Priorat, with meticulous winemaking from a great mountain vineyard called L'Ermita planted with 70-year-old vines.

Best wines ★★★ L'Ermita ❢ and Finca Dofí ❢, ★★ Les Terrasses ❢

Best years 1998, '97, '96, '95, '94, '93, '92, '90

HERMANOS PÉREZ PASCUAS, Ribera del Duero DO   947 53 01 00/53 00 02

This is one of a handful of Ribera del Duero wineries to have found a truly age-worthy style for their well-structured reds.

Best wines ★★ Pérez Pascuas Reserva Especial ❢, Viña Pedrosa Gran Reserva ❢ and Viña Pedrosa Reserva ❢, ★ Viña Pedrosa Crianza ❢

Best years 1999, '98, '96, '95, '94, '92, '91, '90, '89

DOMINIO DE PINGUS, Ribera del Duero DO   939 83 38 54/938 48 40 20

The microwinery created by young Danish winemaker Peter Sisseck is basically just a converted shed. The secret is in the ultra-concentrated juice of grapes from very old vines which is then slowly aged for 20 months in new French oak barrels.

Best wines ★★★ Pingus ❢, ★★ Fleur de Pingus ❢   **Best years** 1997, '95

JOAQUÍN REBOLLEDO, Valdeorras DO   988 37 23 07/37 14 27

A lawyer-grower who introduced Merlot to southern Galicia, Joaquín Rebolledo has also been a driving force behind the rebirth of the almost extinct native Godello grape.

Best wines ★★ Rebolledo Godello ♀, ★ Rebolledo Mencía ❢ and Rebolledo Reserva ❢

Best years ❢1999, '97, '96, '95, '92, '90; ♀1999, '98, '97, '96, '95

REMELLURI, Rioja DOC   941 33 12 74/33 14 41

Telmo Rodríguez, a rebel winemaker and a very active viticulturist, is the heart and soul of Rioja's highest and coolest estate near Laguardia, which is farmed organically.

Best wines ★★ Remelluri Gran Reserva ❢, Remelluri Reserva ❢ and Remelluri Crianza ❢

Best years 1999, '98, '96, '95, '94, '92, '91, '90, '89

TEÓFILO REYES, Ribera del Duero DO   983 48 40 19

In his seventies, the former winemaker for Protos and Alejandro FERNÁNDEZ has created his own winery with his children. The first vintage was 1994 and his concentrated, aromatic wines won immediate worldwide acclaim.

Best wine ★★ Teófilo Reyes ❢   **Best years** 1999, '98, '96, '95, '94

LA RIOJA ALTA, Rioja DOC   941 31 03 46/31 28 54

From a bevy of classic Rioja bodegas, La Rioja Alta has progressively detached itself as the leading upholder of tradition, specializing in Reservas and Gran Reservas. Gran Reservas keep for 10 years or more; Reservas for at least 5 years.

Best wines ★★★ Gran Reserva 890 ❢, ★★ Gran Reserva 904 ❢ and Viña Ardanza Reserva ❢, ★ Viña Arana Reserva ❢ and Viña Ardanza Reserva Blanco ♀

Best years 1999, '98, '96, '95, '94, '93, '91, '90, '89, '87, '85, '82, '81, '78

RODA, Rioja DOC   941 30 30 01/31 27 03

Roda is another revolutionary Rioja firm, this time Catalan-owned, which is shaking the old hierarchy to its roots with its red wines made from old vines.

Best wines ★★ Roda I Reserva ❢ and Círsion Reserva ❢, ★ Roda II ❢

Best years 1999, '98, '96, '95, '94, '92

SEÑORIO DE SAN VICENTE, Rioja DOC   941 30 80 40/33 43 71

The Eguren family was very successful with its Sierra Cantabria winery and has now gone one better with this single-vineyard estate, planted to a particular clone of Tempranillo.

Best wine ★★ San Vicente ❢   **Best years** 1999, '98, '96, '95, '94, '91

LA TAPADA, Valdeorras DO   988 32 41 95/32 41 97

An exceptional vineyard site and José Hidalgo's winemaking skills are the keys to the discovery of an exciting, barrel-fermented white from this area of Galicia.

Best wines ★★ Guitián Godello Fermentado en Barrica ♀, ★ Guitián Godello ♀

Best years 1998, '97, '96, '95

TERRAS GAUDA, Rías Baixas DO   986 62 10 01/62 10 84

A large producer specializing in a very original, concentrated white that is a blend of classic indigenous grapes rather than a varietal Albariño. Drink within 3–4 years.

Best wines ★★ Terras Gauda White Label ♀, ★ Terras Gauda Black Label Barrel-fermented ♀

Best years 1999, '98, '97

TORO ALBALA, Montilla-Moriles DO   957 66 00 46/66 14 94

Antonio Sánchez is easily the most creative winemaker in a tradition-bound region in central Andalucía. His old, single-vintage Pedro Ximénez can be extraordinary.

Best wines ★★★ Pedro Ximénez Marqués de Poley ♀, ★★ Pedro Ximénez Eléctrico ♀

MIGUEL TORRES, Penedès DO   93 817 74 00/817 74 44

The giant, pioneering Penedès house maintains several high-quality ranges, both from local grapes like Parellada and Tempranillo, and French varieties. Top of the range are the relatively rich, red Mas La Plana (Cabernet Sauvignon) and the grassy Fransola (Sauvignon Blanc/Parellada). Keep Mas La Plana for 10 years or so, Gran Coronas (Tempranillo/Cabernet) for 5 or 6 years. Torres has recently assumed production of the Jean León wines, including an oak-aged Chardonnay and Reserva Cabernet Sauvignon.

Best wines ★★ Penedès Mas La Plana Cabernet Sauvignon ♥, Conca de Barberá Milmanda Chardonnay ♀ and Penedès Fransola ♀, ★ Penedès Gran Sangre de Toro ♥, Penedès Mas Borrás Pinot Noir ♥, Penedès Torres Atrium Merlot ♥ and Penedès Gran Coronas ♥

Best years ♥1998, '97, '96, '94, '91, '90, '89, '88, '87, '83, '81, '79, '76; ♀1999, '98, '97, '96

VEGA SICILIA, Ribera del Duero DO   983 68 01 47/68 02 63

Since the Alvarez family acquired Vega Sicilia, Spain's most hallowed winery making its most expensive red wines, it has modernized the techniques ever so slightly but without any loss of quality. Vega Sicilia Unico, the top wine, has traditionally had about 10 years' wood aging but this has now been reduced. Its new winery, Bodegas Alión, makes more modern-style, 100% Tempranillo wine from different vineyards for drinking earlier.

Best wines ★★★ Vega Sicilia Unico Reserva Especial NV ♥ and Vega Sicilia Unico ♥, ★★ Valbuena ♥ and Alión ♥

Best years Unico 1990, '86, '85, '83, '82, '81, '80, '79, '76, '75, '74, '70, '68, '64, '62

DOMINIO DE VALDEPUSA, Malpica de Tajo   925 87 72 92/87 71 11

In the sunny, dry Toledo plateau, the Marqués de Griñón has teamed up with Australian viticulturist Richard Smart and French winemaker Michel Rolland to create a New World-style estate.

Best wines ★★ Petit Verdot ♥ and Syrah ♥, ★ Cabernet Sauvignon ♥ and Chardonnay ♀

Best years 1998, '96, '95, '94, '92, '91, '86

VIÑAS DEL VERO, Somontano DO   974 30 22 16/30 20 98

The largest new venture in Somontano is now aiming at the top end of the market.

Best wines ★ Viñas del Vero Chardonnay Fermentado en Barrica ♀, Gran Vos ♥ and Val de Vos ♥

Best years ♥1998, '97, '96, '95, '94, '92, '91; ♀1999, '98, '97, '96, '95

SPANISH VINTAGES

The myth that vintage variation in Spain is less marked than in northern Europe owes much to the decades-old habit of blending wines from very different areas within one DO region and sometimes from different vintages. But better controls and increasing reliance on the wineries' own vineyards make variations quite apparent. So now the gulf between, for example, a 1993 and a '94 Ribera del Duero wine is very obvious.

Aging qualities

Apart from the fortified wines of Jerez and Montilla (in which freshness is a necessity for Finos and Manzanillas, while other types can keep almost forever), age-worthy Spanish wine usually equates with oak-aged Rioja and Ribera del Duero wines and with some Cabernet Sauvignons from Cataluña and Navarra.

Tradition in Rioja means that Reserva and Gran Reserva reds last the longest, but this is often due to the selection of the very best grapes which is made to produce those classic styles rather than to the protracted periods spent in barrel that official regulations demand for these wines. In reality, in Spain as elsewhere, aging potential is born in the vineyard and derives from a proper balance in acidity, tannins, alcohol and concentration.

Many producers in Ribera del Duero still struggle with low acidity in their grapes, which hinders the wines' aging capability. Rioja Alta and Rioja Alavesa offer better conditions for balanced wines that can often keep as long as top Bordeaux. Newer regions, including Priorat, still lack much of a track record.

Maturity charts _____

Two classic types of Spanish red wine are Rioja Reserva (a wine that must be aged for at least one year in barrel and two in bottle) and Crianza from Ribera del Duero (one year in barrel, one in bottle). Ribera wines generally mature faster than Riojas, particularly in a hot year like 1994, which produced powerful wines with low acidity. 1994 was a classic Rioja vintage.

1994 Rioja Reserva

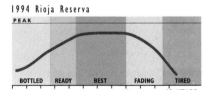

1994 Ribera del Duero Crianza

VINTAGE CHART

	99	98	97	96	95	94	93	92	91	90	89	88
Rioja reds	7○	8○	6◐	8○	8◐	9●	5●	6●	8◐	7●	7●	4◑
Ribera del Duero	7○	7○	6○	9○	8○	9○	4●	6●	8●	8●	8●	6◑
Penedès, Conca de Barberá whites	8○	7◐	7○	8◐	7○	7◐						

KEY ○= needs more time   ◑= ready but will improve   ●= at peak   ◑= fading or tired

249

PORTUGAL

Port is one of the world's great classic wine styles but Portugal is also famous for Madeira, another historic fortified wine, as well as having a growing reputation for fine table wines. The 1990s witnessed a quality revolution, triggered by Portugal's membership of the EU in 1986, and long under-performing areas such as the Dão in northern Portugal are being revived. For historical reasons the wines of the Douro have long been fortified into Port; even though the best grapes are still reserved for making Port, excellent Douro table wines are on the increase.

GREAT PORTUGUESE WINES

Oz Clarke's selection

Douro (Quinta do Portal) ❗ This Douro quinta makes scented, seductive reds from single grape varieties that are simply irresistible.

Bairrada Vinha Pan ❗ **(Luis Pato)** Bairrada wines can be pretty rough but Luis Pato is a brilliant winemaker who crafts superb reds, rich yet austere, aggressive yet seductive – all in the same glass.

Riserva ❗ **(Esporão)** Marvellous, single varietal, succulent reds from the Trincadeira grape.

Pegos Claros ❗ **(Sociedade Agrícola de Pegos Claros)** Excellent example of the native Periquita grape.

Taylor's Vintage ❗ All top Vintage Ports have power and head-spinning richness, but Taylor's has an extra dimension of exotic spice and turbulent sweet loganberry and blackberry fruit.

Warre's Vintage ❗ Quite different from Taylor's – more muscular, less seductive, yet despite its aggressive, peppery, exterior, Warre's has a heart of black sweet fruit.

Fonseca Guimaraens ❗ In non-declared years Fonseca still releases a Vintage Port under this label, and, while not quite so rich and scented as

declared Fonseca vintages, is still a triumph of silky sweet black fruit and cedar perfume.

Quinta de Vargellas ❗ Taylor's best property produces a marvellous rich wine, ready to drink at 10 years, only lacking the extra flesh and sensuality of a true Taylor's Vintage Port.

Niepoort Colheita ❗ Niepoort is the master at this style of vintage-dated Tawny Port, combining the tawny richness of demerara sugar and hazelnut with a deeper fresher dark red fruit.

Fonseca 20-year-old Tawny ❗ Tawny Ports can be younger or older than this but I think 20-year-old ones generally have the best balance between sweet fruit and the mellow comfort of maturity.

TAYLOR'S
1985
Vintage Port
TAYLOR, FLADGATE & YEATMAN

Steven Spurrier's selection

Bairrada Vinha Pan ❗ **(Luis Pato)** The most innovative producer of Bairrada, Luis Pato is convinced of the quality of the local Baga grape.

Douro Grande Escolha ❗ **(Quinta do Côtto)** A new

classic table wine from the Port region – oaky and powerful when young, rich and cedary when mature.

Periquita ❗ **(J M da Fonseca)** Robust and long-lived, this is one of Portugal's most reliable wines.

Cossart Gordon 15-year-old Bual ♀ **(Madeira Wine Co)** Rich and warm, with a touch of 'rancio' after 15 years in cask.

Moscatel de Setúbal 20-year-old ♀ **(J M da Fonseca)** A magnificent light tawny colour precedes an explosion of richness on the palate.

Churchill's Crusted ❗ One of the rare Port houses to continue to produce this full-bodied, bottle-aged Ruby style of Port.

Quinta de Vargellas ❗ **(Taylor)** The base of Taylor's superb Vintage Ports, made only in non-declared years.

Fonseca Vintage ❗ Huge depth of colour and sweetness of fruit typify this long-lived Port.

Dow Vintage ❗ Firm and classic Port, looking for elegance above power.

Cockburn's 20-year-old Tawny ❗ Tawny Port almost fading to orange colour, with a wonderful sweet taste and dryish finish.

Nearly all Portugal's fine wines fall within the DOC level. However, an increasing number fall outside the constraints of the specific DOC, as the wine may be blended from grapes grown over a much wider area or from unauthorized varieties (especially international ones). For this reason the Vinho Regional category is of growing importance.

Denominação de Origem Controlada (DOC)

Since 1990 this has been Portugal's top regional wine classification. It includes the established regions formerly known as Região Demarcada (RD) as well as new emerging quality regions.

Indicação de Proveniência Regulamentada (IPR) or Vinho de Qualidade Produzido em Região Determinada (VQPRD)

The second tier, but as for DOCs there are controls and restrictions over grape varieties, yields and aging requirements. Many were promoted to DOC in 1999.

Vinho Regional

Grapes may come from a wide area and there is considerable latitude in permitted grape varieties and aging requirements. Wines may be varietally labelled.

Top Portuguese table wine producers _____
Red wines Boas Quintas (Fonte do Ouro), Quinta do CARMO,Quinta do Côtto (Grande Escolha), Quinta do CRASTO (Douro Reserva and Touriga Nacional), FERREIRA (Barca Velha), J M da FONSECA, Quinta da Foz do Arouce, Fundação Eugénio de Almeida (Pera Manca), Quinta da GAIVOSA, Gonçalves Faria, Luis PATO (Vinha Pan, Vinha Barrosa, Quinta do Ribeirinho), J

Main DOC wine regions
1 Vinho Verde	5 Bucelas	9 Ribatejo
2 Porto/Douro	6 Colares	10 Alentejo
3 Dão	7 Carcavelos	11 Madeira
4 Bairrada	8 Setúbal	

Portuguese wine areas
BEIRAS = Vinho Regional

Portugal Ramos (Trincadeira, Vila Santa), RAMOS PINTO (Duas Quintas Reserva, Quinta dos Bons Ares Reserva), Quinta dos Roques (Alfrocheiro Preto, Touriga Nacional), Sogrape.
White wines J M da FONSECA (Quinta de Camarate and Primum), Quinta da Foz do Arouce, Sogrape, Quinta do Valdoeiro.
Port and Madeira See pages 252–3.

A–Z OF PORTUGUESE WINE REGIONS

ALENTEJO DOC

This large region, recently promoted to DOC, encompasses a number of subregions and is already the source of Portugal's top reds. Rich and spicy, the wines come from Aragonês (Tinta Roriz) or Trincadeira, both indigenous varieties, and Cabernet Sauvignon. There are also a few classy whites emerging.

Best producers Quinta do CARMO, Esporão, J M da FONSECA, Fundação Eugénio de Almeida, J Portugal Ramos.
Best years ❗1999, '97, '95, '94, '91, '90, '89.

BAIRRADA DOC

The combination of clay soils with the amazingly tannic native Baga grape requires sophisticated winemaking and, while producers are a step ahead of neighbouring Dão, menacingly tannic wines still remain. However, Luis PATO leads the way with complete destemming, lower yields, more gentle winemaking techniques and, in some instances, blending with a proportion of Touriga Nacional. Rich, spicy, structured, wild blackberry-fruited wines with excellent aging potential are now appearing.

Best producers Quinta das Bágeiras, Quinta do CARMO, Gonçalves Faria, Luis PATO, Casa de Saima, Caves São João.
Best years ❗1999, '97, '96, '95, '94, '92, '91, '90.

DÃO DOC

New investment and expertise is producing a remarkable transformation in the wines after years in the doldrums. Most exciting are the results from recent plantings of Touriga Nacional and the increasing use of French oak.

Best producers Boas Quintas, Quinta da Pellada, Quinta dos Roques, Quinta de Saes, Sogrape (Quinta dos Carvalhais).
Best years ❗1999, '98, '97, '96, '95, '94, '92.

DOURO DOC

A small number of producers are making red wines that are among the best in Portugal. Given that the very best sites still provide grapes for the great Ports, the potential for even higher quality exists, though as yet the Port producers still have first refusal on the ripest grapes.

Best producers Quinta do Côtto, Quinta do CRASTO, FERREIRA (Barca Velha), Quinta da GAIVOSA, NIEPOORT, Quinta do NOVAL, Quinta do Portal, RAMOS PINTO, Quinta de la ROSA, Sogrape.
Best years ❗1999, '97, '96, '95, '94, '92, '91, '90.

MADEIRA DOC

Phylloxera devasted Madeira's vineyards during the 19th century. Unfortunately, farmers mostly replanted with inferior hybrids rather than the traditional noble varieties (Malvasia, Bual, Verdelho and Sercial) and consequently for most of the 20th century the greater part of Madeira's production was of cheap and relatively nasty stuff that quite correctly ended up in Sauce Madère rather than in wine connoisseurs' glasses at the end of a civilized dinner.

The tiny percentage of vineyards that remained planted to noble varieties has now increased substantially and there's no doubt that the basic quality of Madeira is rapidly improving. Tiny quantities of single-vintage or solera wines represent the quality peak, but some excellent 10- and 15-year-old Sercial, Verdelho, Bual and Malmsey is now being produced.

Best producers Barbeito, HENRIQUES & HENRIQUES, MADEIRA WINE COMPANY (Blandy, Cossart Gordon, Leacock, Rutherford & Miles), Pereira d'Oliveira.

PORT DOC

Portugal's most famous wine comes from the upper Douro Valley inland from Oporto. It can be made in both red and white styles and from up to 80 different grape varieties. Vintage Port is the premium style, made from grapes from the best vineyards and made only in exceptional or 'declared' years. Usually there are 3–4 declarations per decade. Vintage Port should be superior to any Port from a generally non-declared year but since declarations are rarely made in consecutive years regardless of the quality, some excellent wines are made in non-declared years, in particular when the wines of the best *quintas* or farms are kept unblended.

Such single-quinta wines are made by the estates themselves, or by the major shipping houses, and are available in most 'non-declared' years. The quality is generally excellent and the price appreciably lower than for Vintage Port.

A few houses also produce Traditional Late-Bottled and Crusted styles which are delicious and, though ready to drink on release, they can develop delightful mellow complexity with a few years' extra aging in bottle. Colheitas and aged Tawnies undergo long maturity in barrel rather than the bottle and, though lighter than vintage-style Ports, the best can offer real refinement and elegance combined with a smooth nutty complexity. But all styles of Port are changing – much as Burgundy and red Bordeaux have done in recent years – and many wines are now accessible from a much younger age, with more forward fruit and riper tannins.

Best producers

Vintage Burmester, Cálem, CHURCHILL, COCKBURN, Quinta do Côtto, Quinta do CRASTO, CROFT, Delaforce, DOW, FERREIRA, FONSECA, Gould Campbell, GRAHAM, Quinta do Infantado, Martinez, NIEPOORT, Quinta do NOVAL (including Nacional), Quarles Harris, Quinta de la ROSA, RAMOS PINTO, SMITH WOODHOUSE, TAYLOR, Quinta do VESÚVIO, WARRE.

Single-quinta (or off-vintage) Vintage CHURCHILL (Quinta da Agua Alta), COCKBURN (Quinta dos Canais), CROFT (Quinta da Roêda), Delaforce (Quinta da Corte), DOW (Quinta do Bomfim), FONSECA (Guimaraens, Quinta do Panascal), GRAHAM (Malvedos), Martinez (Quinta da Eira Velha), NIEPOORT (Quinta do Passadouro), Quinta do NOVAL (Quinta do Silval, Quinta do Roriz), RAMOS PINTO (Quinta da Ervamoira), TAYLOR (Quinta de Vargellas), WARRE (Quinta da Cavadinha).

Aged Tawny/Colheita Cálem, COCKBURN, DOW, FERREIRA, FONSECA, NIEPOORT, RAMOS PINTO, Sandeman, TAYLOR.

Late-Bottled Vintage CHURCHILL, FERREIRA, NIEPOORT, Quinta do CRASTO, Quinta de la ROSA, RAMOS PINTO, SMITH WOODHOUSE, WARRE.

Crusted CHURCHILL, COCKBURN, DOW, SMITH WOODHOUSE, WARRE.

Best years (Vintage Port) 1997, '94, '92, '91, '85, '83, '80, '77, '70, '66, '63, '60, '55, '48, '45, '35, '34, '27, '12, '08, '04, 1900.

TERRAS DO SADO

Best known for its fortified Muscat wines, this region is also producing an increasing number of good red and white table wines. Star producer is the large firm of José Maria da FONSECA whose production includes excellent fortified Moscatel de Setúbal (both vintage and 20-year-old versions) but who is also blending this grape variety into increasingly stylish dry whites.

Best producers J M da FONSECA, J P Vinhos, Pegos Claros.

A–Z OF PORTUGUESE PRODUCERS

QUINTA DO CARMO, Alentejo DOC   026 833 2024/833 2025

Co-owned by Julio Bastos and Domaines Rothschild (of LAFITE), this estate is one of the stars of southern Portugal. Change of direction in recent vintages has resulted in the wine becoming more refined – but the inevitable consequence is a style more international and less characterful. Dom Martinho is a sound second label.

Best wines and years ★★ Quinta do Carmo ❢ (1998, '97, '95, '94, '93, '92, '90, '89, '87, '86)

CHURCHILL, Port DOC, Douro DOC   022 370 3641/370 3642

Established only in 1981 by Johnny Graham, who named the company after his wife Caroline Churchill. The range is excellent across the board.

Best wines and years ★★ Vintage Port ❢ (1997, '94, '91, '85) and Quinta da Agua Alta ❢ (1996, '95, '92, '87), ★ 10-year-old Tawny Port ❢ and Crusted Port ❢

COCKBURN, Port DOC, Douro DOC   022 379 4031/375 0550

An important producer commercially with the modest but very successful Special Reserve. After a dull patch the vintage Ports are coming back into form with the most recent vintages recalling some stupendous past efforts.

Best wines and years ★★ Vintage Port ❢ (1997, '94, '91, '70, '67, '63, '55, '47, '35, '27, '12, '08) and 20-year-old Tawny Port ❢, ★ Quinta dos Canais ❢ (1995, '92)

QUINTA DO CRASTO, Port DOC, Douro DOC   022 610 8322/610 7845

The Roquette family estate – perched on the site of an old Roman fort, and with one of the most breathtaking views in the Douro Valley – is a powerhouse of investment and innovation. Australian David Baverstock is the inspired winemaker producing excellent vintage Port and leading the way in creating scented, fruit-drenched red table wine.

Best wines and years ★★ Vintage Port ❢ (1997, '95, '94), Douro Reserva ❢ (1997, '96, '95, '94) and Touriga Nacional ❢ (1997, '95), ★ Late Bottled Vintage ❢ (1994, '92, '91)

CROFT, Port DOC, Douro DOC   022 377 2950/370 7166

Over 300 years old, Croft has it all: extensive lodges in Vila Nova de Gaia, a showpiece estate in Quinta da Roêda and excellent vineyards. The sleek vintage Ports are fine medium-term Ports just lacking the extra depth and structure of the very best.

Best wines and years ★★ Vintage Port ❢ (1994, '91, '77, '70, '66, '63, '60, '45, '35, '27), 20-year-old Tawny ❢ and Quinta da Roêda Vintage Port ❢ (1997, '95)

DOW, Port DOC, Douro DOC   022 377 6300/377 6301

Celebrating its bicentenary in 1998 this is one of the most famous Port houses and is now part of the large Symington group. Dow produces a noticeably drier style of vintage Port that often really comes into its own with 30 years age or more.

Best wines and years ★★★ Vintage Port ❢ (1997, '94, '91, '85, '83, '80, '77, '70, '66, '63, '60, '55, '45), ★★ Quinta do Bomfim ❢ (1995, '92, '90, '87, '86, '84) and 30-year-old Tawny ❢

FERREIRA, Port DOC, Douro DOC   02 370 0010/309 732

If not quite among the elite of Port producers the Casa Ferreirinha has long produced some of Portugal's most outstanding table wines. Barca Velha (first produced in the 1950s) was until the 1980s the only outstanding Douro red. It is made only in exceptional vintages and released when mature. Ferreira's vintage Port is increasingly fine and the 20-year-old Tawny has long been excellent.

Best wines and years ★★★ Barca Velha ▐ (1991, '85, '83, '82, '81, '78), ★★ Vintage Port ▐ (1997, '95, '94, '91, '87, '85, '83, '78, '77, '70, '66, '63), Reserva Especial ▐ (1990, '89, '86, '80) and Duque de Bragança 20-year-old Tawny ▐

FONSECA, Port DOC, Douro DOC   022 371 9999/379 5570
Under the same ownership as TAYLOR's and the wines are similarly sought after. Fonseca Ports are richer and more robust than the more elegant Taylor's. Quinta do Panascal has recently been developed as the showpiece estate. Guimaraens is the name of the Vintage Port made in the best non-declared years.
Best wines and years ★★★ Vintage Port ▐ (1997, '94, '92, '85, '83, '77, '75, '70, '66, '63, '60, '55, '48, '45, '34, '27), ★★ Guimaraens ▐ (1996, '95, '91, '88, '87, '84, '78, '76, '72, '67, '65, '62, '61, 57) and 20-year-old Tawny ▐

JOSÉ MARIA DA FONSECA SUCCESSORES, Terras do Sado   0212 198940/198942
Famous for its Moscatel de Setúbal in both 20-year-old and vintage-dated versions, J M da Fonseca is also creating ever better dry reds and white. D'Avillez and Periquita reds and Quinta de Camarate and Primum whites are quality trailblazers.
Best wines and years ★★ Moscatel de Setúbal vintage ♀ (1966, '65), Moscatel de Setúbal 20-year-old ♀ and Moscatel de Setúbal Roxo 20-year-old ♀

QUINTA DA GAIVOSA, Douro DOC   059 72440
The Douro wines of Domingos Guilhermino Alves de Sousa include Quinta da Estação, Quinta do Vale da Raposa (Tinto, Tinta Cão, Tinta Roriz and Touriga Nacional) and flagship red Quinta da Gaivosa. Great strides have been made recently.
Best wines and years ★★ Quinta da Gaivosa ▐ (1997, '95, '94)

GRAHAM, Port DOC, Douro DOC   022 377 6300/377 6301
The most sumptuous Vintage Port in the Symington stable (acquired in 1970), Graham's is both richer and sweeter than DOW's or WARRE's. New plantings made in the 1980s are only now coming on stream, raising the prospect of still better wines.
Best wines and years ★★★ Vintage Port ▐ (1997, '94, '91, '85, '83, '80, '77, '75, '70, '66, '63, '60), ★★ Malvedos ▐ (1995, '92, '90, '87, '86, '84, '82)

HENRIQUES & HENRIQUES, Madeira DOC   091 941551/941590
Next in importance in Madeira after the Madeira Wine Company, Henriques makes some fabulous rich Madeiras under its own name, including widely available 10-year-old and 15-year-old styles that are unequalled.
Best wines ★★ Sercial 10-year-old ♀, Verdelho 10-year-old ♀, Bual 10-year-old ♀, Malmsey 10-year-old ♀, Bual 15-year-old ♀, Sercial 15-year-old ♀ and Verdelho 15-year-old ♀

MADEIRA WINE COMPANY, Madeira DOC   02 377 6300/377 6301
Owned by the Symington family of Port fame, and includes Blandy, Cossart Gordon, Leacock and Rutherford & Miles. Much is being done to improve viticultural practices and increase plantings of the 4 noble varieties (Sercial, Verdelho, Bual and Malvasia). Rare and expensive, but outstanding vintage wines include examples of a fifth noble variety, Terrantez.
Best wines ★★★ Blandy vintage ♀ (Bual, Malmsey and Terrantez), Cossart Gordon vintage ♀ (Sercial, Verdelho, Bual, Malmsey and Terrantez) and Rutherford & Miles vintage ♀ (Sercial and Malvasia), ★★ Blandy 15-year-old Malmsey ♀, Blandy 10-year-old Malmsey ♀, Cossart Gordon 15-year-old Bual ♀ and Cossart Gordon 10-year-old Bual ♀

NIEPOORT, Port DOC, Douro DOC   022 200 1028/332 0209

Source of some of the finest, most elegant Port made – whether Vintage, single-quinta, Tawny or Colheita. Dirk van der Niepoort also makes good red and white Douro table wines under the Redoma and Passadouro labels.

Best wines and years ★★★ Vintage Port ❗ (1997, '94, '92, '91, '87, '85, '83, '82, '80, '77, '70, '66, '63, '55, '45, '42, '27), **★★** Quinta do Passadouro ❗ (1997, '95, '94, '92), Colheita ❗ (1988, '87, '85, '83, '78, '76, '70, '67, '63, '62, '60, '57, '37, '34) and 10-year-old Tawny ❗

LUIS PATO, Bairrada DOC   0231 596432/528426

Luis Pato has moved quality up several notches since 1995. With lower yields and complete destemming the wines have become richer and more scented but mercifully less tannic. Now Bairrada's leader with a splendid range of ageworthy wines.

Best wines and years ★★ Vinha Pan ❗ (1997, '96, '95), Vinha Barrosa ❗ (1997, '96, '95) and Quinta do Ribeirinho ❗ (1997, '96, '95), ★ Vinhas Velhas ❗ (1996, '95) and Quinta do Ribeirinho Primeira Escolha ❗ (1996, '95)

QUINTA DO NOVAL, Port DOC, Douro DOC   022 377 0270/375 0365

Owned by the giant AXA insurance group this shipper has recently upped quality across the range. Besides the majestic Nacional, made from ungrafted vines, and much improved Vintage Port, this is also the source of some good Colheitas and single-quintas Quinta do Silval and Quinta do Roriz.

Best wines and years ★★★ Nacional Vintage Port ❗ (1997, '94, '87, '85, '70, '66, '63, '62, '31), **★★** Vintage Port ❗ (1997, '95, '94, '91, '87, '85, '75, '70, '66, '63, '60, '55, '47, '45, '34, '31, '27)

RAMOS PINTO, Port DOC, Douro DOC   022 370 7000/379 3121

Owned since 1990 by the Champagne house of ROEDERER. Winemaker João Nicolau de Almeida, whose father created Barca Velha (see FERREIRA), has developed some impressive reds to complement the range of Ports, which includes excellent Tawnies and much improved Vintage Port.

Best wines and years ★★ Duas Quintas Reserva ❗ (1995, '94, '92, '91), Quinta dos Bons Ares Reserva ❗ (1995, '94), Vintage Port ❗ (1997, '95, '94, '83) and Quinta do Bom Retiro 20-year-old Tawny Port ❗, ★ Quinta da Ervamoira 10-year-old Tawny Port ❗

QUINTA DE LA ROSA, Port DOC, Douro DOC   0254 732254/732346

The Bergqvist family once supplied some of the Douro's biggest Port houses but since 1986 have established a genuine single *quinta* producing fine Ports, beautifully scented red and white table wines and very tasty olive oil. The whole operation, including production, maturation and bottling, takes place in cellars just south of Pinhão.

Best wines and years ★★ Vintage Port ❗ (1997, '95, '94, '92, '91) ★ Douro Reserva ❗ (1997, '96, '95, '94) and Finest Reserve ❗

SMITH WOODHOUSE, Port DOC, Douro DOC   022 377 6300/377 6301

Owned by the Symington family, this shipper makes intensely fruity yet strangely underrated traditional Ports. The structured but rich Vintage Port ages very well and the fine traditional Late Bottled Vintage also improves beyond its delayed release. Both are particularly noted for their consistency.

Best wines and years ★★ Vintage Port ❗ (1997, '94, '92, '85, '83, '80, '77, '70, '63), ★ Late Bottled Vintage ❗ (1986, '84, '82)

TAYLOR, Port DOC, Douro DOC   022 371 9999/370 7321

The aristocrat of Vintage Port styles. Produced from the estates of Terra Feita and the fabled isolated Vargellas, it is the most prized regular bottling of Vintage Port. Sold as Vargellas in non-declared years it is more affordable but still often remarkably good.
Best wines and years ★★★ Vintage Port ! (1997, '94, '92, '85, '83, '80, '77, '75, '70, '66, '63, '60, '55, '48, '45, '27), ★★ Quinta de Vargellas ! (1996, '95, '91, '88, '87, '86, '82, '78, '67, '64, '61, '52, '47)

QUINTA DO VESÙVIO, Port DOC, Douro DOC   022 377 6300/377 6301

The Symington group have resurrected this famous 19th-century estate. Though many of the vines are still young, a string of fine vintages has already appeared.
Best wines and years ★★Vintage Port ! (1997, '96, '95, '94, '92, '91, '90)

WARRE, Port DOC, Douro DOC   022 377 6300/377 6301

Established in 1670 and the first British Port house, Warre is another in the Symington empire. The aromatic figgy Vintage Port is consistently one of the best and the traditional-style Late Bottled Vintage is one of the few characterful, concentrated LBVs.
Best wines and years ★★★ Vintage Port ! (1997, '94, '91, '85, '83, '80, '77, '70, '66, '63, '55, '47, '45, '34, '27), ★★ Quinta da Cavadinha ! (1995, '92, '90, '88, '87, '86, '82)

PORTUGUESE VINTAGES

With the exception of Ferreira's Barca Velha and Quinta do Côtto's Grande Escolha and a mere handful of others, Portugal's great red table wines have yet to establish a proven track record, though there is no doubt the situation in 10 or 20 years will be very different. Portugal has, however, a fantastic vintage record with Vintage Port and Madeira. Both experience considerable vintage variation, though viticultural improvements and greater certainty in winemaking have meant more hits than misses over the past decade or so.

Aging qualities

Modern, serious Portuguese reds should be ready at 2–3 years, although more structured Reservas are likely to benefit from 3–5 years. Much depends on the individual wine, but top ones should still drink well with 5–10 years' age. The more traditional Barca Velha needs at least 10 years and will often benefit from 15–20.

Traditional Late Bottled Vintage and fine single-quinta and off-vintage Ports will typically be at or near their best with 10–15 years of aging, though some can be ready sooner (if available) and the most outstanding examples can be expected to improve for much longer. Vintage Port is now increasingly being made with riper, finer tannins and medium-weight examples might be drunk with as little as 5–10 years' aging, even from a great year. However the finest, rich versions can repay keeping for 30 years or more and are likely to need at least half this time to be fully appreciated. It is also not uncommon for a particular year to go through a dumb period and be unjustly downgraded. Often a little more patience pays dividends.

Both Port and Madeira with a designated age such as '10-years-old' will be ready to drink. Vintage Madeira is quite rare and is only bottled when ready to drink (after about 20 years in cask) but thereafter is likely to remain in excellent condition for a very long time.

Maturity chart _____

1994 was unquestionably a great year for Vintage Port and all the major houses have declared a 1994 vintage. Such is the fruit quality they will be accessible with just a few years of bottle age but the best wines will age for decades and are much in demand.

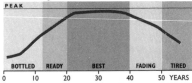

1994 Vintage Port

VINTAGE CHART													
VINTAGE PORT	97	95	94	92	91	87	85	83	80	77	70	66	63
	8◯	8◯	10◯	9◯	8◯	7◑	9◯	8◑	7◑	9●	9●	9●	10●
RED WINES	99	98	97	96	95	94	92	91	90	89	87		
Douro	7◯	6◯	8◑	7◑	8◑	9◑	8●	7◑	7●	7●	7◑		
Dão	7◯	6◯	8◑	8◑	7◑	7◑	7●	7◑	6◑	6●	7◑		
Alentejo	7◯	6◯	8◑	6◑	8◑	7◑	6●	7●	9●	8●	7●		

KEY ◯= needs more time   ◑= ready but will improve   ●= at peak   ◐= fading or tired

PORT AND MADEIRA VINTAGES AT A GLANCE

Port Really poor vintages now come no more than perhaps once in a decade. Greater care in the vineyard resulting in better fruit even in adverse conditions; lower yields; tighter selection; and winemaking advances allowing winemakers to make something palatable from poorer material; all contribute to better wines. Riper tannins and richer, riper fruit in wines from more progressive estates are ensuring an earlier drinkability. The current fashion in some markets for drinking Vintage Port with as little as 5 years' age is therefore not perhaps the lunacy it might once have been. However, it remains true that for the wonderful mellow complexity of mature Port to be realized, 10 or sometimes 20–30 years or more is required.

Madeira Vintage Madeira will be ready to drink, once bottled, after 20 years or so but exceptional examples are virtually immortal.

Great Years ★★★
Vintage Port 1994, '92, '85, '77, '70, '66, '63, '55, '48, '45, '35, '31, '27, '12, '08, '04, 1900
Vintage Madeira 1997, '96, '95, '94, '90, '83, '36, '34, '20, '10, 1900
Good Years ★★
Vintage Port 1997, '95, '91, '87, '83, '80, '60, '47, '44, '34, '24, '22, '20, '17
Vintage Madeira 1992, '91, '88, '87, '68, '67, '57, '54, '52, '41, '40, '39, '27, '16, '15, '13
Moderate Years ★
Vintage Port 1999, '98, '96, '90, '89, '88, '86, '84, '78, '75, '68, '67, '62, '61, '58, '42
Vintage Madeira 1993, '89, '86, '82, '81, '64, '60, '50, '33, '32
Poor Years (No Stars)
Vintage Port 1993, '82, '81, '79, '76, '74, '73, '72, '71, '69, '65, '64

Annual vintage reports for Port

1999★ A damp end to the growing season means a wide declaration looks unlikely.
1998★ Quality is likely to be variable at best although the yield is very low.

1997★★ An almost unanimous declaration. Late, hot, dry conditions yielded ripe, concentrated fruit and hopes are high. The top examples are likely to be particularly age-worthy.

1996★ A huge crop with mixed opinions about quality. Those who picked late are quite bullish.

1995★★ Generally not declared (FERRIERA and Quinta do NOVAL are exceptions) but this has as much to do with following 1994 as anything else. Some excellent single-quinta wines from a very good year.

1994★★★ An extremely high quality year, surpassing both 1992 and '91, though quantities were down. All major houses have declared a 1994 vintage. Some outstanding wines have already drawn comparison with the older classics and are in much demand.

1992★★★ A much smaller declaration than 1991 (Burmester, FONSECA, NIEPOORT and TAYLOR's), but the quality is even higher. Many outstanding wines, both vintage and single-quinta.

1991★★ Most Port houses declared a vintage, but the recession meant that they only declared relatively small quantities. The quality is very good to excellent.

1987★★ Declared by 4 houses only (FERREIRA, Martinez, NIEPOORT and Offley). It's a good but small vintage. Most shippers opted to declare the 1985s instead. There are some excellent single-quinta wines.

1985★★★ An excellent vintage that was almost unanimously declared. The best wines have tremendous lush fruit and good structure.

1983★★ Big, sturdy wines thought to need 20 years to mature but only a handful look like fulfilling their early potential.

1982 This has turned out to be far less exciting than was first thought. Most Ports should have been drunk already. Sandeman is a notable exception.

1980★★ A generally declared year of delicious, fairly dry wines. Still underrated, they're just coming up to their peak now, but they'll go on happily for the next 5 years. DOW, Gould Campbell, GRAHAM and WARRE are the best.

1977★★★ An outstanding year. These are powerful, deep, spicy wines, many of which are drinking well now though some will keep well into the 21st century.

1975★ Only the best can still make attractive drinking now, for this is one of those years that promised well in youth, but failed to deliver. Many are just too light, although TAYLOR's is super.

1970★★★ A lovely, balanced, ripe vintage that is drinking beautifully now. It will last, though.

1966★★★ This was underrated at first, but now is considered a classic. The wines are really coming into their own at the start of the new millennium. Expect muscle and weight but not the elegance of the '63s.

1963★★★ A classic year and the best of the last few decades, being considered the equal of the great 1945 vintage. There are wines of remarkable structure with tremendous finesse and harmony which are wonderful now, but there is absolutely no hurry to drink them. COCKBURN, DOW, FONSECA, GRAHAM and TAYLOR's are excellent.

Other good years 1960 was widely declared and good, but most wines are beginning to tire. The '55s are also very good, as are the '48s, though the latter vintage was only declared by 9 shippers. 1945 was a great year, though quantity was well down, '35 was a good, small vintage and while '31 was not generally declared, the wonderful Quinta do NOVAL Nacional 1931 has made the year famous. 1927 was classic and '12 was rich. Other great years include 1908, '04 and 1900. Bottles from the oldest years may now be fading, but can still be marvellous.

USA

California is by far and away the most important state for wine production, producing many exciting wines. Washington, Oregon and New York State are also now making superb red and white wines.

Classification

The appellation concept is very new in the US and it was only during the 1970s that a rudimentary system was established. An American Viticultural Area (AVA) merely defines the boundaries of an area and decrees that at least 85% of the wine's volume must come from grapes grown within that AVA. Many of the initial AVAs were whole valleys or mountain slopes but the focus is now on smaller areas around specific towns and villages. When a wine has a specific vineyard name it has to be made 100% from that vineyard.

GREAT AMERICAN RED WINES

Oz Clarke's selection

Cabernet Sauvignon Monte Bello (Ridge) Regularly the greatest California Cabernet, combining prodigious depth with heart-stopping fruit and perfume.

Syrah Bien Nacido Reserve (Qupé) Thrilling wild-eyed Syrah in the classic French Rhône style, but riper.

Merlot (Leonetti) Inspired, lush-textured Merlot from Washington's top producer.

Cabernet Sauvignon (Laurel Glen) Dark, serious mountain red, rich and ripe, but brooding and dark and capable of long aging.

Cabernet Sauvignon (Quilceda Creek) Stupendous marriage of dark, deep plum fruit and spicy oak perfume from another of Washington's top wineries.

Cabernet Sauvignon (Spottswoode) Impressive red that manages to combine Napa power with sweet cassis fruit and mint perfume.

Cain Five (Cain) Dark, exciting blend of all 5 Bordeaux red grape varieties, packed with fruit, but also great balance for aging.

Pinot Noir Laurène (Domaine Drouhin) Beautiful scented Oregon Pinot Noir capable of surpassing many of Drouhin's top Burgundies.

Harlan Estate (Harlan Estate) Intensely concentrated but rich and delicious red from a new wave superstar.

JADE MOUNTAIN

SYRAH
HUDSON VINEYARD • NAPA VALLEY

Steven Spurrier's selection

Pinot Noir Jensen Vineyard (Calera) A Pinot Noir with true Burgundian depth and aging qualities from low-yielding vines on a rare limestone-based soil.

Cabernet Sauvignon (Diamond Creek) With unwavering dedication the great Al Brounstein produces California's most perfectly concentrated Cabernets .

Pinot Noir (Domaine Drouhin) Véronique Drouhin, from Burgundy, produces the finest Pinot Noir in Oregon.

Syrah (Jade Mountain) From the same Mount Veeder Paras vineyard as their Viognier, this is a great Syrah by any standards.

Cabernet Sauvignon Reserve (Robert Mondavi) A wine famous for its depth and power and year in, year out one of the finest Napa Valley Cabernets.

Opus One Superb wine from the 20-year-old joint venture between Mouton-Rothschild and Robert Mondavi.

Insignia (Joseph Phelps) An excellent blend of Cabernet Sauvignon, Merlot and Cabernet Franc of immense quality and flavour.

Zinfandel Lytton Springs (Ridge) From very old, low-yielding vines, this intensely flavoured, robust Zinfandel is a California classic.

SLV Reserve (Stag's Leap Wine Cellars) The Stag's Leap Vineyard and adjoining Fay Vineyard are the jewels in the crown of Warren Winiarski's estate, producing very polished, elegant wines.

GREAT AMERICAN WHITE WINES

Oz Clarke's selection

Viognier (Calera) Brilliant example of one of the world's rarest and most capricious grape varieties – all apricots and orange peel and *crème fraîche*.

Unfiltered Chardonnay (Newton) The original unfiltered California Chardonnay – rich, toasty and oozing apricot fruit.

Talley Vineyard Chardonnay (Au Bon Climat) Ripe, nutty, beautifully balanced Chardonnay with just a suggestion of wildness at its core.

Chardonnay (Ridge) Powerful, almost savage, Chardonnay but with a marvellous cream and hazelnut heart.

Chardonnay Reserve (Saintsbury) Exceptional Carneros Chardonnay that is always heavily oaked but still keeps its rich peach fruit and bright lemon acid.

Chardonnay (Pellegrini) Deliciously balanced Long Island Chardonnay marrying full apricot fruit, toasty oak and gentle acidity.

Steven Spurrier's selection

Pinot Blanc (Chalone) The first good Pinot Blanc in California and still the best.

Dolce (Far Niente) Highly aromatic and richly sweet dessert wine.

Dutton Ranch Chardonnay (Kistler) Each of Kistler's Chardonnays from 4 different vineyards is a marvel of ripe fruit, intense complexity and balanced oak.

Chardonnay Reserve (Mondavi) The classic California Chardonnay, a worthy rival to the best white Burgundy.

Don Miguel Chardonnay (Torres) This recently planted vineyard produces some of California's most sophisticated Chardonnay.

Brut Quartet (Roederer Estate) This brilliant sparkling wine, with a zesty creaminess, is a triumph of blending and aging.

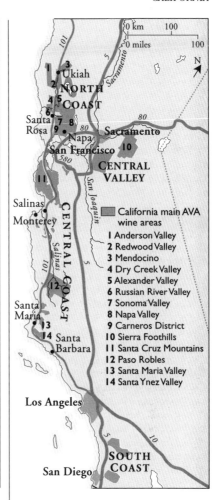

California main AVA wine areas

1 Anderson Valley
2 Redwood Valley
3 Mendocino
4 Dry Creek Valley
5 Alexander Valley
6 Russian River Valley
7 Sonoma Valley
8 Napa Valley
9 Carneros District
10 Sierra Foothills
11 Santa Cruz Mountains
12 Paso Robles
13 Santa Maria Valley
14 Santa Ynez Valley

CALIFORNIA

California's fine wine regions are found within several coastal valleys north and south of San Francisco where abundant sunshine is tempered by periodic fog or cool marine air allowing grapes to mature slowly. Similarly, there are mountainous sites where the otherwise warm, sunny climate is moderated by a combination of elevation and exposure.

Wine styles

Pioneered by small-scale artisan producers, Napa Valley emerged early on as the leading region, but as quality-minded winemakers elsewhere have matched grape variety to their own mesoclimate, California's fine wine roster has been expanding. While Napa's strength is still Cabernet Sauvignon, Sonoma County and other coastal valleys have proved equally adept with Chardonnay and other noble varieties. Assertive and fruit-driven, California wines have until recently been expressions of the grape variety, but the current trend is to allow the specific site a voice. With a diversity of sites on hillsides and along river benches, Napa Valley offers Cabernet, Chardonnay and Merlot, ranging from subtle and supple to rugged and concentrated while Sonoma County is capable of fine Cabernet, Merlot and Zinfandel. Recently Russian River Valley and Carneros have been running neck and neck with Napa for Chardonnay honours as well as securing a stronghold for lush, silky Pinot Noir. Rave notices for Chardonnay also go to Santa Barbara and Monterey counties.

CALIFORNIAN GRAPES AND WINES

Bordeaux-style blends (red Meritage)
Typically made from Cabernet Sauvignon, Merlot and Cabernet Franc with a splash of Malbec, Bordeaux-style reds are often aged in the finest and newest oak barrels. The general style is a no-holds barred, fruit-driven one with rich, high-extract flavours and meant to age a decade or more.

Cabernet Sauvignon
California's finest wine, Cabernet Sauvignon ranges in aroma from sweet red fruits (plums, cherries) to slightly herbal, spicy and floral. Usually full-bodied and powerful with mouthfilling flavours, Cabernets from low-yielding sites can be very concentrated and heady, with cooler climates yielding a more supple, soft tannin style. The best can age for a decade.

Chardonnay
Now outselling White Zinfandel, the overwhelming majority of Chardonnay has become a generic white wine. The exceptions, however, can be world-class. Almost always tending towards the lush, fruity style (ripe apple, peach and pear), California Chardonnay can also offer an exotic tropical fruit melange. With most top wines now fermented and aged in small barrels and left aging *sur lie* for several months, fine Chardonnay often picks up a roasted grain flavour and buttery, creamy texture.

Gewürztraminer
Winemakers have experimented with every style from barrel-fermented to late harvest. Today, the finest are grown in cool climates or low-yielding sites. Almost always finished on the dry side, the best possess an exotic aroma of oriental spice and flowers.

Merlot
This is rapidly becoming a commodity wine for its soft, full-flavoured appeal, but in some winemakers' hands Merlot is a serious wine indeed. The best, usually from the North Coast, offer a lush, mouth-coating texture and dense flavours of spice, plum, and black cherries. At their finest, Merlots are multifaceted with layers of flavours and are inviting when young, but better with 3–5 years of bottle-aging. The worst are insipid and diluted or too herbal.

Pinot Noir

Now concentrated in cooler locations, Pinot Noir ranges from the relatively early-bottled, unoaked style to one that has an eye on Burgundy in the way it displays toasty oak and a concentrated riper character. The finest wines come from Carneros, Russian River and Santa Maria Valley.

Rhône-style blends

Winemakers are experimenting with different combinations of Syrah, Grenache and Mourvèdre with exciting results so far. The wines are usually medium-bodied and intended for early drinking.

Sangiovese

The styles range all over the board because it is new to winemakers and also because there is a wide variety of clones being used. Some winemakers insist on 100% Sangiovese while others think it needs a boost from Cabernet Sauvignon, Syrah or even Zinfandel. On its own, Sangiovese is streamlined with bright, berry cherry fruit, spicy flavours and a finish of racy tartness and chalky tannins. Fleshed out by skilful blending, it becomes a polished wine with the depth of a super-Tuscan.

Sauvignon Blanc/Fumé Blanc

Once winemakers decided to veer away from the herbaceous and grassy side to capture more of a fresh melon, pear and spicy-floral character, Sauvignon Blanc was upgraded to first class. However, with a wider use of oak, the finer wines today have less varietal character. Among serious Sauvignon winemakers, the trend is to barrel ferment the Sauvignon and add a splash of Sémillon or Viognier for more flavour and roundness. The term Fumé Blanc is generally used for the oaked styles.

Sparkling wine

California bubbly is no longer simple fizzy fruity stuff. With several Champagne houses setting up here, Californians can duplicate the classic style faithfully. Based on Chardonnay and Pinot Noir, the best examples are highly enjoyable.

Syrah

After a slow start in California, Syrah is making up for lost time. It is capable of being a very powerful wine, full on the palate with enormous, almost chewy flavours. From cooler coastal sites it develops an aroma of raspberry and blueberry fruit with a hint of licorice. In warmer regions it takes on an intense ripe fruit style with loads of spice and peppery notes, along with hints of smoked meat, leather and game in its flavours.

Viognier

Another new variety on the West Coast, Viognier ranges widely in style as producers explore what it can do. The popular styles feature full-frontal fruitiness reminiscent of a fruit salad, but the more serious versions display apricot and peach aromas with a subtle but wonderful wildflower meadow character.

Zinfandel

A local favourite, Zinfandel improved tremendously once winemakers began treating it as a first-class variety. Usually aged in American oak or a combination of American and French barrels, Zinfandel ranges from effusively fruity with heaps of jammy blackberry and strawberry fruit to a streamlined, focused, berry-spicy wine with a touch of pepper, or a wine in between these 2 extremes. With 5 years or more aging, these Zinfandels can evolve into a Bordeaux-style wine.

A–Z OF CALIFORNIAN WINE REGIONS

ALEXANDER VALLEY AVA

A large, sprawling inland valley. Warmer than its Sonoma County neighbours, it contains hillside and river benchland vineyards growing first-rate Cabernet Sauvignon, Merlot and Chardonnay. The expected successes with Zinfandel are along the warmer valley floor and old vineyards on benchland areas. Although sharing a tendency towards power and high alcohol, wines such as the Cabernets are soft, round and mouthfilling. The Chardonnays have fruit intensity and viscosity to balance the power and a few exceptional, big-style Sauvignon Blancs are grown here too.

Best producers Alexander Valley Vineyards, Chateau Souverain, Clos du Bois, Estancia, FERRARI-CARANO, Field Stone, GALLO SONOMA, GEYSER PEAK, JORDAN, Murphy-Goode, Optima, Seghesio, SILVER OAK, SIMI, STONESTREET.

Best years ▼1999, '98, '97, '95, '94, '93, '92, '91, '90, '88; ♀1999, '98, '97, '96, '95.

ANDERSON VALLEY AVA

With the majority of vineyards established in the cooler western sector, Mendocino's Anderson Valley is known for Pinot Noir, sparkling wines and Gewürztraminer. Chardonnay can be fine here, but is inconsistent. Along several ridgetops, a few century-old vineyards grow Zinfandel, which is made into dense, exotic wine, and Cabernet Sauvignon. The valley is also home to top-class California sparkling wines (ROEDERER, Handley and Pacific Echo).

Best producers Edmeades, Greenwood Ridge, Handley, Lazy Creek, Navarro, Pacific Echo, ROEDERER.

Best years ▼1999, '98, '97, '96, '95, '94, '92, '91, '90; ♀1999, '98, '97, '96, '95; **sparkling wine** 1994, '93, '92, '91, '90.

CARNEROS DISTRICT AVA

Hugging the north shores of San Francisco Bay and benefiting from natural summertime cooling, Carneros includes parts of both Napa and Sonoma counties. As one of California's top cool-climate areas, it is highly suitable for both Chardonnay and Pinot Noir. Of these two proven stars, Pinot Noir has displayed more regional identity – a perfumed black cherry fruitiness and a fleshy, supple texture, but Chardonnay, a close second, has proved to be a good ager. Carneros has emerged as a major player in California's fine sparkling wine. Vineyard replanting in the 1990s saw Merlot and Syrah being planted in warmer sites.

Best producers ACACIA, BEAULIEU, Buena Vista, CARNEROS CREEK, ETUDE, Havens, KISTLER (Chardonnay), Robert MONDAVI (Chardonnay, Pinot Noir), PINE RIDGE, SAINTSBURY, Truchard, ZD.

Best years ▼1999, '98, '97, '96, '95, '94, '92, '91, '90; ♀1999, '98, '97, '96, '95, '94.

DRY CREEK VALLEY AVA

Due west of Alexander Valley, this valley is quintessential Zinfandel country. Its Zins display the classic berry, spicy, peppery regional characteristics in spades. Now a distant second in plantings, Sauvignon Blanc still yields impressive wines here with a decided, but mild enough, herbaceous streak and lively flavours. Cabernet Sauvignon and Merlot are improving and a few wineries are into Syrah in a big way.

Best producers DRY CREEK VINEYARDS, FERRARI-CARANO, GALLO SONOMA, Lambert Bridge, Meeker, NALLE, Pezzi King, Preston, QUIVIRA, RAFANELLI, Michel Schlumberger.

Best years ▼1999, '98, '97, '96, '95, '94, '92, '91; ♀1999, '98, '97, '96, '95.

HOWELL MOUNTAIN AVA

Located above the fog and frost lines in Napa's north-east corner, Howell Mountain has become almost synonymous with rugged and slow-to-mature wines. However, winemakers are learning how to soften the tannins without sacrificing regional individuality. Recent Cabernets, Merlots and Zinfandels are better than ever. The finest still need 5–10 years to show their best. Chardonnay and Viognier are the only significant whites.

Best producers BERINGER (Merlot), Chateau Woltner, Robert Craig, DUCKHORN, DUNN, La Jota, Lamborn Family, Liparita, PINE RIDGE, ST CLEMENT, TURLEY, VIADER.

Best years ▌1999, '98, '97, '96, '95, '94, '93, '92, '91, '90, '89, '87, '86; ♀1999, '98, '97, '96, '95, '94, '93.

MENDOCINO AVA

The Mendocino AVA is frequently used because some of the smaller ones within it are too obscure or because the wine is made from more than one region within Mendocino County. Wines from the cool Anderson Valley are often blended with ones from the warmer inland regions to achieve better balance.

Best producers Fetter, Husch, Jepson, Navarro, Parducci.

Best years ▌1999, '98, '97, '96, '95, '94, '93, '92, '91.

MONTEREY AVA

The largest Central Coast region, Monterey is cooled by strong winds in the north and becomes progressively calmer and warmer in the southern half. Chardonnay dominates the top-quality wines here, but a few winemakers craft impressive Pinot Blancs and Pinot Noirs. Several small sub-regions – Arroyo Seco, Santa Lucia Highlands and Chalone – fall within the Monterey appellation.

Best producers Bernardus (Chardonnay), CHALONE, Estancia, Lockwood, Mer & Soleil, Morgan, Talbott.

Best years ▌1999, '98, '97, '95, '94, '92; ♀1999, '98, '97, '95, '94.

MOUNT VEEDER AVA

Rugged hilly terrain in Napa's south-western mountain range, Mount Veeder now seems to have sorted itself out and is red wine country. Its history with Cabernet and Zinfandel is long and impressive. Some of California's longest-lived Cabernets (Mayacamas, HESS COLLECTION, Mount Veeder) have originated here. Merlot has found a home in some vineyards, and small-scale experiments with Syrah are underway.

Best producers Chateau Potelle, Robert Craig, HESS, JADE MOUNTAIN, Lokoya, Mount Veeder Vineyards.

Best years ▌1999, '98, '97, '95, '94, '92, '91, '90; ♀1998, '97, '95, '94, '93.

OLD VINE WINE

Many vineyards in California were developed from 1890–1920, between the first phylloxera epidemic and the beginning of Prohibition. Most often Zinfandel and other red varieties, these early vines were grafted onto resistant rootstocks, were non-irrigated and head- or gobelet-pruned for low yields. Some of these vines now approach or exceed 100 years of age. Recognizing the special attributes of these old vineyards, winemakers began making individual bottlings from old vines. By the 1990s, with dozens of old vineyards in the North Coast, the Sierra Foothills, Paso Robles and other regions identified and much in demand by winemakers, a new category of wines – Old Vines – came into being. Whether Zinfandel or Petite Sirah, Old Vine wines share rich body, high alcohol, concentrated flavours and velvety texture – factors of both their age and low yields.

NAPA VALLEY AVA

Flanked on the west by the Mayacamas mountains and on the east by the Coast Range, Napa Valley has over 35,000 acres of vineyards and is a leading region for Cabernet Sauvignon, Chardonnay, Merlot and Pinot Noir. Hit hard by phylloxera, Napa has replanted almost half its vineyards since 1989 and with this has come a better matching of variety to site. Also new are many viticultural practices such as dense vine-planting, diversity of clones and rootstocks, and vertical vine-training to maximize sunlight and improve air circulation. There are now over 300 wineries lining the valley or overlooking it from slopes or mountain perches.

Napa Valley contains many important sub-regions: Atlas Peak, Carneros, Diamond Mountain, Howell Mountain, Mount Veeder, Oakville, Rutherford, St Helena, Spring Mountain, Stags Leap District, Yountville.

Best producers ARAUJO, ATLAS PEAK, BEAULIEU, BERINGER, Burgess, CAFARO, CAIN, CAKEBREAD, CAYMUS, CHAPPELLET, CHATEAU MONTELENA, CLOS PEGASE, COLGIN, DALLA VALLE, DIAMOND CREEK, DOMINUS, DUCKHORN, DUNN, ETUDE WINES, FAR NIENTE, FLORA SPRINGS, FORMAN, Frogs Leap, GRACE FAMILY, GRGICH HILLS, HEITZ, HESS COLLECTION, Charles Krug, LEWIS CELLARS, Markham, Mayacamas, MERRYVALE, MONDAVI, Mumm Napa Valley, NEWTON, PAHLMEYER, PARADIGM, Joseph PHELPS, ST CLEMENT, St Supery, SCHRAMSBERG, SILVERADO, SILVER OAK, Spottswoode, STERLING, Stony Hill, SWANSON, Trefethen, TURLEY, Whitehall Lane, ZD.
Best years ❢1999, '98, '97, '96, '95, '94, '92, '90, '91, '87, '86, '85; ♀1998, '97, '96, '95, '94, '92, '90.

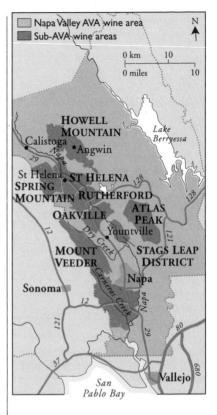

Napa Valley AVA wine area
Sub-AVA wine areas

OAKVILLE AVA

Oakville is much like its neighbour, Rutherford, in its emphasis upon Cabernet, but its wines have yet to reveal a consistent personality. Even its most famous vineyards – HEITZ Martha's, MONDAVI'S To-Kalon and OPUS ONE – fail to offer a common theme, except for high-quality, long-lived Cabernet wines.

Best producers DALLA VALLE, FAR NIENTE, GROTH, HARLAN, HEITZ, LEWIS CELLARS, Lokoya, MONDAVI, OPUS ONE, PARADIGM, SCREAMING EAGLE.
Best years ❢1999, '98, '97, '95, '94, '93, '92, '91, '90, '87, '86, '85, '84.

PASO ROBLES AVA

Old region coming back to life on the strength of impressive reds such as Zinfandel, Cabernet and Syrah, Paso Robles brings out intense flavours in the grapes which are now being controlled by prudent viticultural practices. Several new vineyards, including Tablas Creek owned by Châteauneuf-du-Pape's Ch. BEAUCASTEL, see a great future for Syrah here.

Best producers Adelaida, Eberle, Justin, Meridian, Tobin James, WILD HORSE.

Best years ❢1999, '98, '97, '96, '95, '94, '93, '92; ♀1999, '98, '97, '96.

REDWOOD VALLEY CALIFORNIA AVA

This Mendocino region is going through a period of transition as more of its grapes are used by local winemakers rather than being sent elsewhere. It has long been known for Zinfandel, much of it planted in old, non-irrigated vineyards. Syrah and Sangiovese are also looking promising.

Best producers Fetzer Vineyards, Fife, Gabrielli, Hidden Cellars.

Best years ❢1999, '98, '97, '95, '94, '92; ♀1999, '98, '97, '95, '94.

RUSSIAN RIVER VALLEY AVA

Arguably the finest region in California for Pinot Noir because its cool climate is marginal and vines have to struggle against windy, often foggy conditions, Russian River Valley is also capable of exquisite Chardonnay with great concentration. The Pinot Noirs show deep, black cherry fruit and are full, supple and earthy. It also has dozens of the best old Zinfandel vineyards in the North Coast.

Best producers DEHLINGER, FARRELL, IRON HORSE, KISTLER, ROCHIOLI, Rutz, Sonoma-Cutrer, Marimar TORRES, WILLIAMS SELYEM.

Best years ❢1999, '98, '97, '95, '94, '92, '91, '90, '87; ♀1999, '98, '97, '96, '95, '94.

RUTHERFORD AVA

New AVA in mid-Napa Valley with a long record for fine Cabernet Sauvignon which displays a combination of black, ripe fruit with a slightly tannic character that came to be known as 'Rutherford dust'. Several of California's finest vineyards (Bosche, Bella Oaks) are here.

Best producers BEAULIEU, CAKEBREAD, CAYMUS, FLORA SPRINGS, Freemark Abbey (Bosche), HEITZ (Bella Oaks), Lokoya, NIEBAUM-COPPOLA.

Best years ❢1999, '98, '97, '96, '95, '94, '93, '92, '91, '90, '87, '86, '85, '84.

SANTA CRUZ MOUNTAINS AVA

South of San Francisco Bay, this large area contains a modest number of vineyards, including the great Monte Bello, and several iconoclastic winemakers. Depending upon elevation, exposure and vineyard practices, winemakers have had great success with a wide range of wine styles. Santa Cruz Pinot Noir and Cabernet Sauvignon reflect the concentration and power associated with mountain vineyards.

Best producers BONNY DOON, David BRUCE, Cinnabar, Cronin, MOUNT EDEN, RIDGE, Santa Cruz Mountain Vineyard.

Best years ❢1999, '98, '97, '96, '95, '94, '92, '91, '90; ♀1999, '98, '97, '96, '95, '94, '93.

SANTA MARIA VALLEY AVA

The only California wine valley running east to west, Santa Maria has emerged as a special site for Pinot Noir and Chardonnay. Though almost all of the finest Pinots are from the large 700-acre Bien Nacido Vineyard, all Santa Maria Valley Pinot shows black cherry fruit with elements of woody and gamy character as its hallmarks. As expansion of the area under vine continues, slightly warmer sites are being developed to Syrah and other Rhône varieties which are beginning to acquire a fine track record.

Best producers AU BON CLIMAT, BYRON, Foxen, QUPÉ, Lane TANNER.
Best years ▌1999, '98, '97, '95, '94, '92; ♀1998, '97, '96, '95, '94, '93.

SANTA YNEZ VALLEY AVA

The warmer part of Santa Barbara County, Santa Ynez fares well with Cabernet Franc, Sauvignon Blanc and Syrah as well as with Pinot Noir and Chardonnay. More powerful than their Santa Maria neighbours, the Santa Ynez Chardonnays age quite well.
Best producers BABCOCK, Firestone, SANFORD.
Best years Pinot Noir 1999, '98, '97, '95, '94, '92, '91, '90; ♀1999, '98, '97, '95.

SIERRA FOOTHILLS AVA

South-east of Sacramento is the old gold-mining district which includes the counties of Amador, El Dorado and Calaveras. Amador's producers have a long, solid history with Zinfandel, often in a rustic style, but are now adding some flair as they work with Barbera, Sangiovese and Syrah. With vineyards situated at extremely high elevations, El Dorado has been more versatile, and in the long run has great potential for Rhône varieties, Syrah, Viognier and Roussanne.
Best producers Boeger, Lava Cap, Montevina, Shenandoah Vineyards, Sierra Vista, Terre Rouge.
Best years ▌1999, '98, '97, '96, '95; ♀1999, '98, '97.

SONOMA COUNTY

Unlike its compact neighbour, Napa, Sonoma is a big, sprawling area with dozens of different mesoclimates and has potential for further vineyard growth. The main sub-regions are Alexander Valley, Carneros, Chalk Hill, Dry Creek Valley, Green Valley, Knights Valley, Russian River Valley, Sonoma Coast, Sonoma Mountain and Sonoma Valley. Because

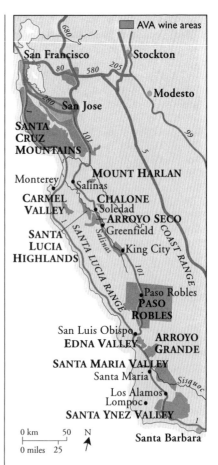

many producers have vineyards in several of these sub-regions, they often use the term Sonoma County on their labels even though it lacks real precision and AVA status.
Best years ▌1999, '98, '97, '95, '94, '93, '92, '91, '90, '87; ♀1999, '98, '97, '95.

SONOMA MOUNTAIN AVA

Falling within the Sonoma Valley AVA, Sonoma Mountain includes the slopes and mountainsides to the west of the town of

Glen Ellen. One of the first mountain AVAs defined, Sonoma Mountain incorporates east-facing and west-facing slopes known to be above the fog line and also sharing a uniform type of soil. It is further distinguished by temperatures that do not fluctuate widely during the growing season. The climate found here is ideal for varieties like Cabernet Sauvignon and Zinfandel that enjoy warm days and cool evenings.

Best producers Benziger Family Winery, CARMENET, Paul Hobbs (Dinner Vineyard), Landmark, LAUREL GLEN, Louis Martini, RAVENSWOOD (Pickberry).

Best years 1999, '98, '97, '96, '95, '94, '92, '91, '87, '85.

SONOMA VALLEY AVA

Located on the flip-side of Napa, this valley is a smaller mirror image of Napa Valley. Chardonnay and Pinot Noir are in the cool southern end of Carneros and Sonoma town. The slopes and hillsides further north cultivate Cabernet and Zinfandel, with many old Zinfandel vineyards still well-preserved.

Best producers ARROWOOD, CARMENET, CHATEAU ST JEAN, HANZELL, Kunde, LAUREL GLEN, MATANZAS CREEK, RAVENSWOOD, ST FRANCIS.

Best years 1999, '98, '97, '95, '94, '93, '92, '91, '90, '87; 1999, '98, '97, '95.

SPRING MOUNTAIN DISTRICT AVA

Historic region in Napa's western hills is now on the upswing after a roller-coaster history. Its vineyards are hidden away at varying elevations and enjoy a wide range of exposures, making it possible to grow a range of grapes. Cabernet Sauvignon and Meritage blends are far and away the consistent successes, but Sauvignon Blanc, Viognier, Riesling, Chardonnay and Gewürztraminer also do well.

Best producers Barnett, CAIN CELLARS, Robert Keenan, NEWTON, Pride Mountain, Spring Mountain Vineyard, Stony Hill, Philip Togni.

Best years 1999, '98, '97, '96, '95, '94, '92.

STAGS LEAP DISTRICT AVA

This small area in Napa Valley with red soils is known for its supple, elegant red wines, particularly Cabernet Sauvignon and Merlot. It is one of California's more meaningful AVAs, with a growing season reckoned to be longer than in the Napa Valley proper to the west. With well-integrated soft tannins, the reds here age surprisingly well. Recent interest in Sangiovese is also yielding good results.

Best producers ANDERSON, CHIMNEY ROCK, CLOS DU VAL, PINE RIDGE, SHAFER, SILVERADO, STAG'S LEAP WINE CELLARS, Stags' Leap Winery.

Best years 1999, '98, '97, '95, '94, '92, '90, '87, '86, '85; 1998, '97, '95, '94, '93.

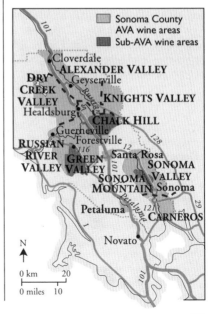

A–Z OF CALIFORNIAN PRODUCERS

ACACIA, Carneros AVA   707 226 9991/226 1685

Acacia was an early leader exploring vineyard-specific Pinot Noirs and Chardonnays from Carneros. Part of the CHALONE Group since 1986, it has trimmed the roster of vineyard-designated wines to a St Clair Vineyard Pinot and Beckstoffer Vineyard Pinot, but the Reserve wines are now absolutely first-rate.

Best wines ★★★ Pinot Noir Reserve ♥, ★★ Chardonnay Reserve ♀, ★ Pinot Noir Carneros ♥

Best years ♥1998, '97, '96, '95, '94, '93, '92, '91, '90; ♀1999, '97, '96, '95, '94, '93, '92

S ANDERSON VINEYARDS, Stags Leap District AVA   707 944 8642/944 8020

The Anderson family now produce excellent sparkling wine and limited amounts of high-quality varietal wines. The family vineyard in Carneros supplies fruit for the sparkling wines, which include a stunning Blanc de Noirs.

Best wines ★★ Blanc de Noirs sparkling wine ♀ and Cabernet Sauvignon ♥, ★ Brut sparkling wine ♀, Cabernet Sauvignon ♥ and Chardonnay ♀

Best years ♥1997, '96, '95, '94, '92; ♀1998, '97, '96, '95, '94, '93; **Sparkling wine** 1997, '95, '93, '92, '90

ARAUJO ESTATE, Napa Valley AVA   707 942 6061/942 6471

With Tony Soter of ETUDE overseeing production, Araujo Estate is now much in demand for its Cabernet Sauvignon. The winery has added a splendid Sauvignon Blanc blended with a splash of Viognier and also makes a limited production of Syrah.

Best wines ★★ Cabernet Sauvignon ♥, ★ Sauvignon Blanc ♀

Best years ♥1998, '97, '96, '95, '94, '92, '91; ♀1999, '98, '97, '96, '95

ARROWOOD VINEYARDS & WINERY, Sonoma Valley AVA   707 938 5170/938 5195

Winemaker Dick Arrowood's Cabernets and Merlots have been sensational, and with a shift to using Carneros grapes for Chardonnay, both Sonoma County Chardonnay and Reserve Chardonnay have reached high quality levels. Limited-volume Viognier, Pinot Blanc and Syrah from Saralee's Vineyard in Russian River Valley are also good.

Best wines ★★ Cabernet Sauvignon ♥, Chardonnay ♀ and Merlot ♥, ★ Viognier ♀ and Pinot Blanc ♀

Best years ♥1998, '97, '96, '95, '94, '92, '91, '90; ♀1999, '98, '97, '96, '95, '94

ATLAS PEAK VINEYARDS, Atlas Peak AVA   707 252 7971/252 7974

After several years of drifting, Atlas Peak was put back on course when ANTINORI of Italy gained complete ownership. Its hillside vineyard represents the biggest planting of Sangiovese in California. It offers 3 Sangiovese wines: a regular varietal, a Reserve bottling, and Consenso, a special Cabernet Sauvignon blended with Sangiovese.

Best wines ★★ Sangiovese Reserve ♥, ★ Sangiovese ♥ and Consenso ♥

Best years ♥1999, '98, '97, '96, '95

AU BON CLIMAT, Santa Maria Valley AVA   805 688 8630/937 2539

Pace-setting winery ABC, as it is known, is run by the highly talented Jim Clendenen who spends much time in the cellars of Burgundy and Piedmont. Lush, compact Chardonnays and intense Pinot Noirs (especially the Isabelle bottling) are the top wines. For Bordeaux-inspired wines, Clendenen uses the Vita Nova label, and for a wide range of often dazzling Italian varietals, he uses the Il Podere dell'Olivos label.

Best wines ★★★ Pinot Noir Sanford & Benedict Vineyard ❢, ★★ Chardonnay ♀,
Chardonnay Le Bouge d'à Côté ♀, Chardonnay Talley Vineyard ♀ and Pinot Noir La Bauge
au Dessus ❢

Best years ❢1998, '97, '96, '95, '94, '91, '90, '89, '87, '86; ♀1999, '98, '97, '95, '92

BABCOCK VINEYARDS, Santa Ynez Valley AVA   805 736 1455/736 3886

Stunning wines have come from this no-frills winery. Winemaker Bryan Babcock does
not like to hold back much and his Chardonnay Grande Cuvée and Eleven Oaks
Sauvignon Blanc both testify to that. The Pinot Noirs show a lighter touch, but remain
relatively intense. A Burgundian at heart, Babcock has also proved adept with Syrah.

Best wines ★★ Chardonnay Grande Cuvée ♀ and Sauvignon Blanc Eleven Oaks ♀,
★ Riesling Dry ♀ and Pinot Noir Santa Barbera ❢

Best years ❢ 1998, '97, '96, '95, '94; ♀1999, '98, '97, '96, '95

BEAULIEU, Napa Valley AVA   707 967 5200/963 5920

As winemaker from the 1930s to the early 1970s, the late André Tchelistcheff created
the icon for Napa Valley Cabernet Sauvignon in general and for Cabernet from the
Rutherford–Oakville region in particular. After he departed to pursue a busy
consulting career, Beaulieu missed a few beats and was living on its reputation until
Tchelistcheff returned for a few years in the early 1990s. Its flagship Cabernet, Private
Reserve, is back on form and Beaulieu has enjoyed smoother sailing for all wines.

Best wines ★★ Cabernet Sauvignon Private Reserve ❢, ★ Chardonnay Carneros Reserve ♀,
Pinot Noir Carneros Reserve ❢ and Tapestry ❢

Best years Private Reserve Cabernet 1997, '96, '95, '94, '92, '91, '90, '85, '78, '70; ❢1997,
'96, '95, '94, '92, '91, '90; ♀1999, '98, '97, '96, '95, '94, '93

BERINGER VINEYARDS, Napa Valley AVA   707 963 7115/259 4510

If Beringer made only Private Reserve Cabernet Sauvignon, it would still be a star
performer. The Reserve Cabernets, blended from 4–5 outstanding vineyards, have
proved to be among the very best when new and still among the best after a decade or
more of aging. But Beringer, with vast vineyard holdings, also offers many other fine
wines, especially Chardonnay, Merlot, Pinot Noir, Syrah and Viognier.

Best wines ★★★ Cabernet Sauvignon Private Reserve ❢, Cabernet Sauvignon Chabot
Vineyard ❢ and Chardonnay Sbragia Limited Release ♀, ★★ Chardonnay Private Reserve ♀
and Merlot Bancroft Vineyard, Howell Mountain ❢, ★ Cabernet Sauvignon Knights Valley ❢

Best years Private Reserve Cabernet 1998, '97, '96, '95, '94, '93, '92, '91, '90, '87, '86,
'85, '84, '81; ❢1998, '97, '96, '95, '94, '93, '92, '91, '90; ♀1998, '97, '96, '95, '94, '93, '91

BONNY DOON, Santa Cruz Mountains AVA   831 425 3625/425 3528

Part-philosopher, part-poet, and full-time iconoclast, Randall Grahm revels in the
unexpected. His two main interests are Rhône-inspired wines and Italian varietals, but
he often strays off to make Zinfandel, Riesling and Pinot Noir. His finest Italian wines
appear under the Ca' del Solo label; the Rhônes under Bonny Doon and often with
special names – his red Châteauneuf-du-Pape-style blend is called Le Cigare Volant and
his white, Le Sophiste. Mourvèdre is labelled Old Telegram and Syrah is labelled Syrah.

Best wines ★★ Le Sophiste ♀, Old Telegram ❢ and Ca' del Solo Muscat Canelli ♀, ★ Le
Cigare Volant ❢, Syrah ❢, Ca' del Solo Barbera ❢ and Ca' del Solo Malvasia Bianca ♀

Best years ❢1998, '97, '96, '95, '94, '92, '91, '90; ♀1998, '97, '96, '95, '94, '93

DAVID BRUCE WINERY, Santa Cruz Mountains AVA   408 354 4214/395 5478
Pioneering Santa Cruz winemaker David Bruce made behemoth Chardonnays in the late 1960s and '70s that became the stuff of legends. In the 1990s he resurfaced with a variety of Pinot Noirs, placing him back in centre stage. The Santa Cruz Mountains Reserve is sometimes his best wine, but the Pinot Noirs from the Russian River Valley, Chalone Vineyard and the Anderson Valley are sometimes as good.
Best wines ★★ Pinot Noir Santa Cruz Mountains Reserve ❗ and Pinot Noir Russian River Valley ❗
Best years ❗1997, '96, '95, '94, '93, '92, '91, '90; ♀1999, '98, '96, '95, '94

BYRON VINEYARD, Santa Maria Valley AVA   805 937 7288/937 1246
Owned by Robert MONDAVI, Byron has a new winery to work in and a new vineyard, the esteemed Sierra Madre Vineyard. Both changes should help it continue its fine performances with Pinot Noir Reserve (deep black cherry fruit and spice) and Chardonnay Reserve (rich, with earthy-mineral notes). Each invites early drinking, but will age well for several years. New Rhône blends look promising.
Best wines ★★ Chardonnay Reserve ♀ and Pinot Noir Reserve ❗
Best years ❗1999, '98, '97, '96, '95, '94, '92; ♀1998, '97, '96, '95, '94, '93, '92

CAFARO, Napa Valley AVA   707 963 7181/963 8458
Typically blending grapes from 5–6 vineyards in 3 or 4 mesoclimates, Joe Cafaro builds Cabernets to evolve slowly with aging. His Merlots fulfil their youthful promise 4–5 years after the vintage. Both wines are known for their depth of flavour and structure.
Best wines ★★ Cabernet Sauvignon ❗ and Merlot ❗
Best years 1997, '96, '95, '94, '92, '91, '90

CAIN CELLARS, Spring Mountain AVA   707 963 1616/963 7952
Created to produce a Bordeaux-style wine, this estate has wandered off course a few times, but is now back on track. Its flagship blend, Cain Five, starts slowly but is well worth waiting for, and its stablemate, Cain Cuvée, is far more accessible.
Best wines ★★ Cain Five ❗, ★ Cain Cuvée ❗
Best years 1997, '96, '95, '94, '93, '92, '91, '90, '87, '86

CAKEBREAD CELLARS, Rutherford AVA   707 963 5221/963 1067
Cakebread was one of the first phylloxera victims to totally remove and replant vineyards in the 1990s. Throughout the changes, it has continued its winning ways with a full-flavoured, moderately oaked Sauvignon Blanc and a well-defined Chardonnay that takes well to 2–3 years of aging. Relatively new Cabernet Sauvignon Reserve seems destined to become the flagship wine.
Best wines ★★ Sauvignon Blanc ♀, ★ Chardonnay ♀ and Cabernet Sauvignon Reserve ❗
Best years ❗1997, '96, '95, '94, '92, '91; ♀1999, '98, '97, '96, '95, '94

CALERA, Mount Harlan AVA   408 637 9170/637 9070
Josh Jensen made Calera a pace-setter for Pinot Noir in the 1980s and for Viognier in the 1990s. His complex Pinot Noirs from 4 vineyard sites – Selleck, Reed, Jensen and Mills – display power, balance and the individuality of place. With succulent, sensuous fruit, Calera Viognier is also rich and powerful enough to rank as California's finest.
Best wines ★★★ Pinot Noir Selleck Vineyard ❗, Pinot Noir Jensen Vineyard ❗ and Viognier ♀, **★★** Pinot Noir Reed Vineyard ❗ and Chardonnay Mount Harlan ♀
Best years ❗1997, '96, '95, '94, '92, '91, '90, '88; ♀1998, '97, '96, '95, '94, '92

CARMENET, Sonoma Valley AVA   707 996 5870/996 5302
Planned as the CHALONE group's Bordeaux-style winery, Carmenet has been a
frontrunner with 2 Meritage blends, a red and barrel-aged white, called simply
Meritage. Moon Mountain, the special red Meritage, is made from low-yielding
mountain vineyards and demands aging. The longest-lived wine is a Cabernet
Sauvignon, appropriately dubbed Vin de Garde Reserve.
Best wines ★★ Moon Mountain Reserve ❢, Vin de Garde Reserve ❢, Meritage ♀ and
Chardonnay Sangiacomo ♀
Best years ❢1998, '97, '96, '95, '94, '92, '91, '90, '88, '87, '86; ♀1999, '98, '97, '95, '94, '93
CARNEROS CREEK, Carneros AVA   707 253 9463/253 9465
An active player in the evolution of Carneros as a prime Pinot Noir region, Carneros
Creek has been a marvel of consistency with Pinot Noir since the early 1970s, the
Signature Reserve wine showing great depth, lush texture and aging ability. Fleur de
Carneros is lighter bodied.
Best wines ★★ Pinot Noir Signature Reserve ❢, ★ Pinot Noir, Fleur de Carneros ❢
Best years 1998, '97, '96, '95, '94, '93, '92
CAYMUS VINEYARDS, Napa Valley AVA   707 963 4204/963 5958
A Cabernet Sauvignon star for over 20 years, Caymus emphasizes a deep, ripe, intense
and generally well-oaked tannic style. The deluxe Special Selection is often outstanding
and Conundrum, an exotic melange of Sauvignon, Viognier and other grapes, is an
opulent, delicious white.
Best wines ★★ Cabernet Sauvignon Special Selection ❢, ★ Cabernet Sauvignon Napa Valley ❢
and Conundrum ♀
Best years ❢1997, '96, '95, '94, '92, '91, '90, '87, '86, '85, '84, '80; ♀1999, '98, '97, '96,
'95, '94, '93
CHALONE VINEYARD, Monterey AVA   707 254 4200/254 4201
From low-yielding vineyards in a remote arid site above the fog line in eastern
Monterey County, Chalone developed a reputation for intense, slow-developing
Chardonnay and concentrated Pinot Noir. Limited output of very good Chenin Blanc
and Pinot Blanc enjoy a cult following. These are strongly individualistic wines and all
benefit from a few years' aging.
Best wines ★★★ Chardonnay Reserve ♀, ★★ Pinot Noir Reserve ❢ and Pinot Noir ❢, ★ Pinot
Blanc ♀ and Chenin Blanc ♀
Best years ❢1997, '96, '95, '94, '92, '91, '90, '88, '86, '83; ♀1998, '97, '96, '95, '94, '93,
'91, '90, '89, '85
CHAPPELLET VINEYARD, Napa Valley AVA   707 963 7136/963 7445
From beautiful mature hillside vineyards to the east of St Helena, this winery is again a
Cabernet force with a ripe, somewhat austere style that takes well to 5–7 years of aging.
Only wines from the best vintages have enough fruit richness to match the firm
tannins. Intense old-vine Chenin Blanc from a single vineyard is a wonderful gem.
Best wines ★★ Chenin Blanc Old Vines ♀, ★ Cabernet Sauvignon ❢
Best years ❢1997, '96, '95, '94, '93, '92, '91, '90, '87; ♀1999, '98, '97, '96, '95, '94
CHATEAU MONTELENA, Napa Valley AVA   707 942 5105/942 4221
Better known early in its history for balanced, age-worthy Chardonnay, Montelena has

come on strong for Cabernet Sauvignon in a sturdy, slow-maturing style. Its Calistoga Cuvée, made from Cabernet not used in the estate bottling, is also rich and tasty.
Best wines ★★ Cabernet Sauvignon Estate ▮ and Calistoga Cuvée ▮, ★ Chardonnay ♀
Best years ▮1997, '96, '95, '94, '93, '92, '91, '90, '87, '86; ♀1998, '97, '96, '95, '94, '93, '92

CHATEAU ST JEAN, Sonoma Valley AVA   707 833 4134/833 4200

A white wine house noted for often superb Chardonnay, St Jean developed an impressive range of red wines in the late 1980s, including Reserve Cabernet and Merlot and a red Meritage named Cinq Cepages which all enjoy a delicious fruit-driven style.
Best wines ★★ Cabernet Sauvignon Reserve ▮ and Chardonnay Robert Young Vineyard ♀,
★ Chardonnay Sonoma County ♀, Fumé Blanc ♀, Cinq Cepages ▮ and Merlot ▮
Best years ▮1998, '97, '96, '95, '94, '93, '92, '91, '90, '89; ♀1999, '98, '97, '96, '95, '94, '92, '91, '90

CHIMNEY ROCK, Stags Leap District AVA   707 257 2641/257 2036

With its redeveloped estate vineyard now devoted entirely to red Bordeaux varieties, this always solid winery is coming on strong. Both its Reserve and red Meritage, called Elevage, display juicy black cherry fruit and lush, distinctive Stags Leap flavours.
Best wines ★★ Cabernet Sauvignon Reserve ▮, ★ Elevage ▮ and Cabernet Sauvignon ▮
Best years ▮1998, '97, '96, '95, '94, '92, '91, '90, '87, '86; ♀1999, '98, '97, '95

CLOS PEGASE, Napa Valley AVA   707 942 4981/942 4993

Once its Carneros vineyard reached maturity, Clos Pegase began to live up to the early publicity surrounding its owner, art collector Jan Schram. The finest reds are the Merlot (rich but well-structured) and a Meritage, Hommage, a wine to age for 3–5 years. With elegant fruit and excellent balance the Chardonnay is also charming.
Best wines ★★ Merlot ▮, ★ Hommage ▮   **Best years** ▮1998, '97, '96, '95, '94, '92, '91, '90

CLOS DU VAL, Stags Leap District AVA   707 259 2255/252 6125

This first-class producer is so well established it is sometimes overlooked. But its elegant Cabernet Sauvignon and ultra-rich, long-lived Reserve Cabernet are always noteworthy. The house style of balance and elegance is nicely typified by its Zinfandel.
Best wines ★★ Cabernet Sauvignon Reserve ▮, ★ Cabernet Sauvignon ▮ and Zinfandel ▮
Best years ▮1997, '96, '95, '94, '92, '91, '90, '87, '86, '85, '84; ♀1999, '98, '97, '96, '95, '94, '93, '92

COLGIN, Napa Valley AVA   707 963 0999/310 274 0899

Achieving success practically overnight, Colgin makes only Cabernet Sauvignon in the range of 500–700 cases a year. A top California collectable since its first 1992 vintage was released, the wine is now made by Mark Aubert of PETER MICHAEL WINERY. It is an intensely flavoured but approachable kind of Cabernet.
Best wines ★★ Cabernet Sauvignon ▮   **Best years** 1998, '97, '96, '95, '94, '93, '92

DALLA VALLE, Napa Valley AVA   707 944 2676/944 8411

It took a few years, but once Dalla Valle put everything together its record has been spotless. Maya, a gorgeous, rich blend of Cabernet Sauvignon and Cabernet Franc, is the star here. The fine hillside vineyard also yields brilliant Cabernet Sauvignon and a good 100% Sangiovese called Pietre Rosse.
Best wines ★★★ Maya ▮, ★★ Cabernet Sauvignon ▮, ★ Sangiovese Pietre Rosse ▮
Best years 1998, '97, '96, '95, '94, '93, '92, '91, '90

DEHLINGER WINERY, Russian River Valley AVA   Tel 707 823 2378
Full-bodied and beautifully crafted Pinot Noir in several guises (Goldridge Vineyard,
Octagon Vineyard, Russian River Valley and Reserve) are the Dehlinger specialities,
but the Chardonnays can also rank near the top of the competition. Syrah, in a rich
Hermitage-like style, was first made in 1992 and is already considered among the best.
Best wines ★★★ Pinot Noir Reserve ❢, ★★ Pinot Noir Goldridge Vineyard ❢, Chardonnay
Russian River Valley ♀ and Syrah Russian River Valley ❢
Best years ❢1998, '97, '96, '95, '94, '93, '92, '91, '90; ♀1999, '98, '97, '96, '95, '94

DIAMOND CREEK VINEYARDS, Diamond Mountain AVA   707 942 6926/942 6936
A producer of 3 distinct Cabernet Sauvignons – Red Rock Terrace, Gravelly Meadow
and Volcanic Hill – Diamond Creek preserves the special character of each vineyard
while also making blockbuster wines. Give them plenty of time (a decade or more) to
come round. Made only in certain years, Lake Cabernet is the rarest and priciest.
Best wines ★★★ Cabernet Sauvignon Volcanic Hill ❢, Cabernet Sauvignon Gravelly
Meadow ❢ and Cabernet Sauvignon Red Rock Terrace ❢
Best years 1998, '97, '96, '95, '94, '92, '91, '90, '87, '86, '85, '84, '80, '75

DOMINUS, Napa Valley AVA   707 944 8954/944 0547
Owned by Christian Moueix of Ch. PÉTRUS, Dominus is a red wine made from a
vineyard once part of Inglenook's legendary holdings. The early vintages were tannic
and controversial, but quality began to stabilize by 1990. Since then Moueix has held
the brand together amid frequent changes of winemaker.
Best wine ★★★ Dominus   **Best years** 1998, '97, '96, '95, '94, '92, '91, '90

DRY CREEK VINEYARDS, Dry Creek Valley AVA   707 433 1000/433 5329
Prime mover in the formative years of Dry Creek Valley, owner David Stare was also an
advocate of brisk, racy Fumé Blanc. Today's wine is still crisp and true to the original,
but what the winery does best today is red wines, particularly Old Vine Zinfandel.
Best wine ★★ Merlot Reserve ❢ and Zinfandel Old Vine ❢, ★ Cabernet Sauvignon ❢ and
Fumé Blanc ♀
Best years ❢1998, '97, '96, '95, '94, '92, '91; ♀1999, '98, '97, '96, '95

DUCKHORN, Napa Valley AVA   707 963 7108/963 7595
For many years Duckhorn produced California's most highly regarded Merlot. Though
competition has increased, its chunky, tannic Three Palms Merlot has its followers.
Insiders have often preferred the well-rendered Cabernet Sauvignon. New wines include
an intense Howell Mountain Merlot and Paraduxx, a Cabernet/Zinfandel blend.
Best wines ★★ Merlot Howell Mountain ❢, ★ Merlot Three Palms Vineyard ❢ and Cabernet
Sauvignon Napa Valley ❢
Best years 1997, '96, '95, '94, '92, '91, '90, '87, '86, '85

DUNN VINEYARDS, Howell Mountain AVA   707 965 3642/965 3805
Massive, intense, compact and slow-to-age Howell Mountain Cabernet is Randy
Dunn's trademark. The Napa Valley Cabernet Sauvignon is tamer and prettier when
young, but less memorable.
Best wines ★★★ Cabernet Sauvignon Howell Mountain ❢, ★ Cabernet Sauvignon Napa
Valley ❢
Best years 1998, '97, '96, '95, '94, '92, '91, '90, '87, '86, '85, '84, '82

EDMUNDS ST JOHN, Contra Costa   Tel 510 981 1510

A major figure in California's revival of Rhône-style wines, Steve Edmunds sources grapes from many vineyards, but has settled on Durell in Carneros for his weighty, intense and impressive Syrah. He has also shown great skill with Zinfandel.

Best wines ★★★ Syrah Durell Vineyard ❢, ★★ Zinfandel ❢

Best years 1998, '97, '96, '95, '94, '93, '92, '91

ETUDE WINES, Napa Valley AVA   707 257 5300/257 6022

The highly-regarded wine consultant Tony Soter oversees production at DALLA VALLE and NIEBAUM-COPPOLA among others, but he also puts considerable effort into Etude, his own label. His Carneros Pinot Noirs are skillfully packed with vigorous ripe fruit and his Cabernets are classic Napa Valley fare. Soter's wines usually rise above vintage weaknesses.

Best wines ★★ Cabernet Sauvignon ❢ and Pinot Noir ❢

Best years 1997, '96, '95, '94, '93, '92, '91

FAR NIENTE WINERY, Napa Valley AVA   707 944 2861/944 2312

A spare-no-expense attitude is evident everywhere in this beautifully restored winery. It turned the quality corner in 1990, and the Cabernets have been better balanced, less tannic, but still age-worthy ever since. The Chardonnays, with 2–3 years of aging, acquire smoothness and complexity. Dolce is a successful Sauternes-style beauty.

Best wines ★★ Cabernet Sauvignon ❢ and Dolce ♀, ★ Chardonnay ♀

Best years ❢1997, '96, '95, '94, '93, '92, '91, '90; ♀1998, '97, '96, '95, '93, '91, '90

GARY FARRELL WINES, Russian River Valley AVA   707 433 6616/433 9060

Farrell focuses on small-batch, single-vineyard wines. As well as lovely soft Ladi's Vineyard Merlot and good Zinfandel, there are excellent Russian River Valley Pinot Noirs which show he is a Burgundian at heart.

Best wines ★★ Pinot Noir Allen Vineyard ❢, Pinot Noir Rochioli Vineyard ❢ and Merlot Ladi's Vineyard ❢, ★ Zinfandel ❢

Best years 1998, '97, '96, '95, '94, '92, '91

FERRARI-CARANO WINERY, Dry Creek Valley AVA   707 433 6700/431 1742

This dynamic winery with considerable vineyard holdings in choice Sonoma sites has offered exciting, seductively rich Chardonnay from its very first vintage. The lush Merlot has also earned high marks, but the wine to watch is the super-Tuscan-style red, Siena.

Best wines ★★ Chardonnay ♀, Merlot ❢ and Siena ❢

Best years ❢1998, '97, '96, '95, '94, '92, '91; ♀1998, '97, '96, '95, '94, '93, '92

FLORA SPRINGS, Napa Valley AVA   707 963 5711/963 7518

This former white wine house has been reborn after considerable vineyard redevelopment as a red wine producer, but its Chardonnay Reserve remains top-drawer, and Soliloquy, a special racy Sauvignon Blanc, is as good as ever. Its new arsenal of red wines is led by Trilogy, a Bordeaux blend, and by a Rutherford Cabernet Sauvignon Reserve, a concentrated, layered, knock-out punch of a wine.

Best wines ★★★ Cabernet Sauvignon Reserve ❢, ★★ Chardonnay Reserve ♀ and Trilogy ❢

Best years ❢1997, '96, '95, '94, '92, '91; ♀1999, '98, '97, '96, '95, '94, '92

FORMAN, Napa Valley AVA   707 963 0234/963 5384

As a brilliant young winemaker, Ric Forman helped establish STERLING and later NEWTON before beginning his own label. His Chardonnays are among the richest, but

always nicely restrained. Relying on a dollop of Merlot and Cabernet Franc, Forman's Cabernets are intense but balance oak and ripe fruit. They peak at about 10 years.
Best wines ★★ Cabernet Sauvignon ❢ and Chardonnay ♀
Best years ❢1997, '96, '95, '94, '93, '92, '91, '90, '88, '87, '86, '85, '84; ♀1998, '97, '96, '95, '94, '92, '91, '90

GALLO SONOMA, Dry Creek Valley AVA   707 431 5500/431 5515
Fine wines from the world's largest winery? Better believe it, because Gallo has developed over 2000 acres in several of Sonoma County's finest sub-regions. Topping the list is the estate-bottled Cabernet Sauvignon. Other noteworthy wines are lower-priced but shockingly good, including Dry Creek Zinfandel, Laguna Vineyard Chardonnay, with great flavours and a touch of oak, and Alexander Valley Cabernet Sauvignon, called Barelli Ranch. Pinot Noir from Russian River is in the works.
Best wines ★★ Cabernet Sauvignon Northern Sonoma ❢ and Chardonnay Laguna Vineyard ♀, ★ Cabernet Sauvignon Alexander Valley Barelli Ranch ❢ and Chardonnay Sonoma County ♀
Best years ❢1998, '97, '96, '95, '94, '92; ♀1999, '98, '97, '96, '95

GEYSER PEAK VINEYARDS, Alexander Valley AVA   707 857 9463/857 3545
The new and improved Geyser Peak makes incredible Syrah which it labels Shiraz, along with some of the finest Alexander Valley Cabernet Sauvignon. Experimental Sangiovese and single-vineyard Cabernet Sauvignon under the Venezia label also merit seeking out. The Geyser Peak Chardonnay Reserve is coming on strong.
Best wines ★★ Cabernet Sauvignon Estate Reserve ❢, Reserve Alexandre ❢ and Shiraz Reserve ❢, ★ Chardonnay Reserve ♀ and Venezia Sangiovese ❢
Best years ❢1998, '97, '96, '95, '94, '93, '92, '91, '90; ♀1999, '98, '97

GRACE FAMILY VINEYARD, Napa Valley AVA   707 963 0808/963 5271
With a tiny winery and 2 acres of manicured vineyards surrounding the home, Grace Family Vineyard is anything but typical. A major portion of its extremely limited production is donated to charities. At best, Dick and Ann Grace produce 200 cases a year of intense, voluptuous Cabernet Sauvignon aged entirely in new French oak.
Best wine ★★ Cabernet Sauvignon ❢
Best years 1997, '96, '95, '94, '91, '90, '87, '86, '85, '84, '83, '80

GRGICH HILLS CELLAR, Napa Valley AVA   707 963 2784/963 8725
Mike Grgich has winning ways with Chardonnay in a firm, well-oaked style, but equally prominent is his brawny, slightly rustic Sonoma County Zinfandel. An under-appreciated wine that evolves beautifully with age, Napa Valley Cabernet Sauvignon has plenty of ripe fruit and tannin to last a decade or more.
Best wines ★★ Chardonnay ♀, Zinfandel ❢ and Cabernet Sauvignon ❢
Best years ❢1997, '96, '95, '94, '93, '91, '87, '86, '85, '84; ♀1998, '97, '96, '95, '94, '92

GROTH VINEYARDS, Oakville AVA   707 944 0290/944 8932
Cabernet Sauvignon is Groth's strong suit, and while the record is erratic, the big, brash Reserve Cabernet has on occasion soared off the charts. When not over-oaked, the Napa Valley Cabernet can be good, especially in favourable vintages.
Best wines ★★★ Cabernet Sauvignon Reserve ❢, ★ Cabernet Sauvignon Napa Valley ❢ and Chardonnay ♀
Best years ❢1996, '95, '94, '92, '91, '90, '86, '85, '84; ♀1999, '98, '97, '96, '95, '93, '92, '91

HANZELL VINEYARDS, Sonoma Valley AVA   707 966 3860/996 3862

One of the early advocates of small French oak barrels for aging, Hanzell was also a proponent of small-batch methods for Pinot Noir. The winery has hit a few bad patches over 4 decades, but the Pinot Noir is back on track and as big and full-flavoured as can be. Chardonnays, reticent when young, have also proved to be long-agers.
Best wines ★★ Chardonnay ♀ and Pinot Noir ♥
Best years ♥1997, '96, '95, '94, '92, '91, '90, '88, '85; ♀1997, '96, '95, '94, '92, '91, '90

HARLAN ESTATE, Oakville AVA   707 944 1441/944 1444

Co-founder of MERRYVALE, Bill Harlan's red is a Bordeaux blend of Cabernet Sauvignon, Cabernet Franc and Merlot, built to last. Displaying depth and concentration indicative of a rigorous selection of fruit, classic winemaking and heaps of new French oak, the first few vintages gained overnight critical fame. High-priced when first released, the wines have also stirred up bidding frenzy on the auction circuit.
Best wine ★★★ Harlan Estate ♥   **Best years** 1998, '97, '96, '95, '94, '93, '92, '91, '90

HEITZ WINE CELLARS, Napa Valley AVA, California   707 963 3542/963 7454

Heitz Cabernet from Martha's Vineyard was the rage in the 1960s and '70s as collectors lined up to buy this polished, long-lived wine with its distinctive minty-eucalyptus overtones. Controversy over off-aromas surfaced in the '80s, but Heitz survived. The winery makes Cabernet Sauvignon from Bella Oaks Vineyard, Napa Valley Trailside, and except for 1993–96 when the vineyard was replanted, from Martha's Vineyard.
Best wines ★★ Cabernet Sauvignon Martha's Vineyard ♥, ★ Cabernet Sauvignon Bella Oaks ♥ and Cabernet Sauvignon Napa Valley ♥
Best years Martha's Vineyard 1992, '91, '86, '85, '75, '74, '70, '69, '68;
other Cabernets 1997, '95, '94, '92, '91, '87, '86

HESS COLLECTION WINERY, Mount Veeder AVA   707 255 1144/253 1682

Intensely ripe mountain-grown fruit along with distinctive lime and black cherry overtones are hallmarks of the Cabernet Sauvignon. The Reserve Cabernet offers incredible mouth-filling cassis and cherry flavours. With a shift to cooler sites, Hess Chardonnay is much improved in a bright crisp style.
Best wines ★★ Cabernet Sauvignon Reserve ♥, Cabernet Sauvignon Napa Valley ♥ and Chardonnay ♀
Best years ♥1997, '96, '95, '94, '92, '91, '90, '89; ♀1999, '98, '97, '96, '95, '94, '93, '91

IRON HORSE VINEYARDS, Russian River Valley AVA   707 887 1507/887 1337

Dividing its time equally between sparkling and table wines, Iron Horse manages to be equally and uncommonly adept with both types. Its outstanding sparkling wines are a sophisticated, citrus-edged Blanc de Blancs and a long-aged, fruit-tinged vintage Vrais Amis. Among the table wines, the delicate, finely scented Pinot Noir is a rising star and the wonderfully brisk Chardonnay, when aged 3–4 years, is a delight.
Best wines ★★ Blanc de Blancs ♀ and Vrais Amis ♀, ★ Chardonnay ♀ and Pinot Noir ♥
Best years ♥1997, '96, '95, '94, '93, '92, '91, '90; ♀1998, '97, '96, '95, '93, '92, '91, '90;
Sparkling 1995, '94, '93, '91, '89, '87

JADE MOUNTAIN, Mount Veeder AVA   707 965 3048/257 7922

Specializing in Rhône wines from Carneros vineyards, Mount Veeder and other parts of the North Coast, Jade Mountain has quietly become a leader. Its Rhône-style blends

– La Provençale and Les Jumeaux – are superb. Mourvèdre regularly ranks as one of the best and the Syrah is made in a big, ripe, gamy style.

Best wines ★★★ Syrah ❢, ★★ Les Jumeaux ❢ and La Provençale ❢, ★ Merlot ❢ and Mourvèdre ❢

Best years 1998, '97, '96, '95, '94, '93, '92, '91, '90

JORDAN WINERY, Alexander Valley AVA   707 431 5250/431 5259

Oilman Tom Jordan set out to produce world-class Cabernet, and to date his winery has offered consistently good, sometimes very good Cabernet in a spicy, cedary, polished style. The world-beater in the family may ultimately end up being daughter Judy whose 'J' sparkling wine has progressed quickly since 1990. Made from Russian River Valley grapes, 'J' combines some of the best traits of Champagne with California's fruity profile.

Best wines ★★ Cabernet Sauvignon ❢ and 'J' ♀

Best years ❢1997, '96, '95, '94, '91, '90, '87, '86; **Sparkling** 1996, '95, '94, '93, '92, '91

KISTLER VINEYARDS, Russian River Valley AVA   707 823 5603/823 6709

Arguably the finest US Chardonnay producer, Kistler discovered long before anyone else where the best vineyards are located and also how to bring out great complexity and aging ability from each one. Success has been consistently achieved with single-vineyard Chardonnay from sites including Dutton Ranch, Durell Vineyard, McCrea Vineyard, Kistler Estate and Vine Hill Road Vineyard. Now focusing attention on Pinot Noir instead of Cabernet Sauvignon, Kistler is working its wonders with Pinots from Vine Hill Road Vineyard and new sites in the Russian River Valley.

Best wines ★★★ Chardonnay Kistler Vineyard ♀, Chardonnay Dutton Ranch ♀ and Pinot Noir Cuvée Catherine ❢, ★★ Chardonnay Durell Vineyard ♀, Chardonnay McCrea Vineyard ♀, Chardonnay Vine Hill Road Vineyard ♀ and Pinot Noir Vine Hill Road Vineyard ❢

Best years ❢1997, '96, '95, '94, '93, '92, '91; ♀1998, '97, '96, '95, '94, '93, '92, '91, '90, '88, '87

LAUREL GLEN VINEYARDS, Sonoma Mountain AVA   707 526 3914/526 9801

Only Cabernet Sauvignon is produced by winemaker/owner Patrick Campbell. The top wine is from the estate hillside vineyard. Blended with Merlot and Cabernet Franc, it is rich with great concentration and, with extended aging, it develops a Bordeaux-like character. Counterpoint is the good-value second wine.

Best wines ★★ Cabernet Sauvignon Estate ❢, ★ Cabernet Sauvignon Counterpoint ❢

Best years 1997, '96, '95, '94, '93, '92, '91, '90, '87, '86, '85

LEWIS CELLARS, Oakville AVA   650 342 8017/342 8018

Randy Lewis, a former Indy 500 race driver and partner in the Oakville Ranch Vineyard, is behind the wheel of Lewis Cellars. Making Napa Valley Cabernet Sauvignon, Merlot and Chardonnay, Lewis packs plenty of ripe fruit and concentrated flavours into his wines, and will probably take the same approach with Syrah when it joins the line-up. The Cabernet is capable of 7–10 years' aging or more.

Best wine ★★ Chardonnay Reserve ♀

Best years ❢1997, '96, '95, '94; ♀1998, '97, '96, '95, '94

MARCASSIN VINEYARD, Sonoma County   707 258 3608/942 5633

Consultant winemaker Helen Turley now has her own vineyard in the cool part of Sonoma County concentrating on Chardonnay and Pinot Noir. She favours big powerful flavours that sometimes go over the top. The outstanding single-vineyard Chardonnays are Alexander Mountain, Lorenzo, Hudson and Marcassin.

Best wines ★★★ Chardonnay Alexander Mountain ♀, **★★** Chardonnay Hudson ♀, Chardonnay Lorenzo ♀ and Chardonnay Marcassin ♀

Best years ❢1998, '97, '95; ♀1998, '97, '96, '95, '94, '93

MATANZAS CREEK VINEYARDS, Sonoma Valley AVA   707 528 6464/571 0156

Perennial high-ranking Sauvignon Blanc (barrel-fermented and fleshed out with Sémillon) goes back many years, but the 1990s saw the rise to prominence of Merlot too. Journey, a label for limited edition, very expensive wines, now includes Chardonnay and Merlot, each wine opulent, seductive and hedonistic.

Best wines ★★★ Merlot ❢ and Sauvignon Blanc ♀, **★★** Chardonnay Journey ♀ and Chardonnay Sonoma Valley ♀

Best years ❢1997, '96, '95, '94, '93, '92, '91, '90, '88; ♀1998, '97, '96, '95, '94, '93, '92

MERRYVALE, Napa Valley AVA   707 963 7777/963 1949

After an opening decade of quiet competency, Merryvale redeveloped its vineyards, adjusted its thinking and aimed higher. Its Chardonnays regularly hit the bull's eye these days. Starmont Chardonnay is poised and balanced, and the limited edition, Silhouette is an incredibly rich, shoot-for-the-moon style of Chardonnay. Merlot is also improving, but the best red is the Meritage named Profile which could be mistaken for a fine Pauillac. Recent vintages of Cabernet Sauvignon are also impressive.

Best wines ★★ Chardonnay Silhouette ♀ and Profile ❢, **★** Chardonnay Starmont ♀

Best years ❢1998, '97, '96, '95, '94, '92, '91; ♀1998, '97, '96, '95, '94, '92

PETER MICHAEL WINERY, Knights Valley AVA   707 942 4459/942 0209

British-born Sir Peter Michael expanded a vacation home in Sonoma County into a small vineyard and winery and before long was making headlines with spectacular Chardonnay. The winery now offers an estate-grown Cabernet/Merlot blend, Les Pavots, a sensational, intense Chardonnay, Mon Plaisir, and Sauvignon Blanc with more flavours than most. The rare Cuvée Indigène and Pinot Rouge Chardonnays are exquisite.

Best wines ★★ Chardonnay Mon Plaisir ♀ and Les Pavots ❢

Best years ❢1997, '96, '95, '94, '93, '92, '91, '90; ♀1999, '98, '97, '96, '95, '94, '93, '92

ROBERT MONDAVI WINERY, Napa Valley AVA   707 259 9463/963 1007

As innovator, publicist and winemaker, Bob Mondavi put California on the quality wine map. From its first vintage in 1966, the winery was linked to Cabernet Sauvignon. Today's Cabernets include a remarkable Reserve from the To-Kalon Vineyard. Mondavi also reinvented Sauvignon Blanc as Fumé Blanc, and today's versions, Napa Valley and Reserve (deep fruit and bright oak), are better than ever. From its Carneros winery, Mondavi's Chardonnay Reserve might well be mistaken for a big Bâtard-Montrachet, and the Pinot Noir Reserve is as good as it gets in California. High-profile joint ventures include OPUS ONE and Luce with FRESCOBALDI in Italy.

Best wines ★★★ Cabernet Sauvignon Reserve ❢ and Chardonnay Reserve ♀, **★★** Pinot Noir Reserve ❢, **★** Fumé Blanc ♀

Best years Cabernet Sauvignon Reserve 1997, '96, '95, '94, '93, '92, '91, '90, '87, '86, '85, '84, '82, '78, '74, '71; **Pinot Noir Reserve** 1998, '97, '96, '95, '94, '93, '92, '91, '90, '88, '87, '85; **Chardonnay Reserve** 1997, '96, '95, '94, '93, '92, '91, '90, '87

MOUNT EDEN VINEYARDS, Santa Cruz Mountains AVA   408 867 5832/867 4329
One of the early and great pioneering names, Mount Eden bounced back in the mid-1980s. The big, richly fruited Pinot Noir is good, and the estate Cabernet Sauvignon, though a slow starter, comes around after 8–10 years of aging to show an attractive, deep brambly flavour. Both Chardonnays – Estate and MacGregor – age well.
Best wines ★★ Cabernet Sauvignon Estate ❢, Chardonnay MacGregor ♀ and Pinot Noir Estate ❢, **★** Chardonnay Estate ♀
Best years ❢1997, '96, '95, '93, '94, '91,'90, '88, '86, '85; ♀1998, '97, '96, '95, '94, '93, '92

NALLE WINERY, Dry Creek Valley AVA   707 433 1040/433 6062
In the 1980s owner-winemaker Doug Nalle helped define the style of Dry Creek Zinfandel now in vogue. Using older vineyards and aging in American oak, Nalle produces a textbook Zinfandel with blackberry fruit, spice and mouthfilling flavours.
Best wines ★★ Zinfandel ❢   **Best years** 1999, '98, '97, '96, '95, '94, '91

NEWTON VINEYARDS, Spring Mountain District AVA   707 963 9000/963 5408
A magnificent mountainside winery, Newton has long had a fine touch for rich, opulent, but balanced estate Cabernet Sauvignon, Merlot and Claret, a Bordeaux-inspired red. More recent Chardonnays follow the same quality path with succulent fruit but structured to last. Newtonian is an export label for classy Cabernet and Chardonnay. Quality remains better than ever despite recent winemaker changes.
Best wines ★★★ Cabernet Sauvignon ❢, Unfiltered Chardonnay ♀ and Merlot ❢, **★★** Cabernet Sauvignon Newtonian ❢ and Chardonnay Newtonian ♀
Best years ❢1997, '96, '95, '94, '92, '91, '90; ♀1998, '97, '96, '95, '94, '93, '92

NIEBAUM-COPPOLA ESTATE, Rutherford AVA   707 963 9099/963 9084
Niebaum-Coppola's main wine is a red Meritage blend, Rubicon, which was always rich and firm, but early vintages were rough and tannic. Recent vintages show fine depth, with greater finesse to place them among today's collectable wines. A Zinfandel called Edizione Pennino is a big, hardy wine with good solid fruit.
Best wines ★ Rubicon ❢ and Zinfandel ❢
Best years Rubicon 1997, '96, '95, '94, '93, '91, '87, '86

OPUS ONE, Oakville AVA   707 944 9442/944 2753
The first of several joint ventures involving MONDAVI, Opus One is a Napa Valley wine made in partnership with Bordeaux's Ch. MOUTON-ROTHSCHILD. It is a blend of Cabernet Sauvignon, Cabernet Franc and Merlot that receives extensive aging in new French oak. No longer the most expensive, Opus One is a consistent high-quality wine, but perhaps not quite on a par with Mondavi's Reserve Cabernet.
Best wine ★★ Opus One ❢
Best years 1997, '96, '95, '94, '93, '92, '91, '90, '88, '87, '86, '85, '84

PAHLMEYER, Napa Valley AVA   707 255 2321/255 6786
Jason Pahlmeyer's red Meritage is a massive, formidable wine, but the tannins are well integrated to ensure good aging. The unfiltered Chardonnay displays loads of concentration and the new Merlot is a fruit-filled, spice and oak powerhouse that completes a remarkable trio of wines.
Best wines ★★ Chardonnay ♀, Merlot ❢ and Pahlmeyer Meritage ❢
Best years ❢1997, '96, '95, '94, '93, '92; ♀ 1998, '97, '96, '95, '94

PARADIGM WINERY, Napa Valley AVA   707 944 1683/944 9328
Ren & Marilyn Harris produce modest amounts of wine from their much-esteemed vineyard in the heart of Oakville. Cabernet Sauvignon is the star attraction and ages for a decade or more. Tiny quantities of rich Merlot and potent Zinfandel disappear quickly.
Best wines ★★ Cabernet Sauvignon ❢, ★ Merlot ❢ and Zinfandel ❢
Best years 1998, '97, '96, '95, '94, '93, '92

JOSEPH PHELPS VINEYARDS, Napa Valley AVA   707 963 2745/963 4831
Insignia, a red Meritage, has consistently ranked at the top of California's finest wines. Two other Cabernets are also quite good. The medium-weight Napa Valley shows lovely fruit and the Backus Vineyard is more intense. Ovation is the name of the deluxe toasty Chardonnay and, working with Rhône wines as long as anyone in California, Phelps has been making headway with its Vin du Mistral wines, including Syrah.
Best wines ★★★ Insignia ❢, ★★ Cabernet Sauvignon Backus Vineyard ❢, ★ Cabernet Sauvignon Napa Valley ❢, Chardonnay Ovation ♀ and Syrah Vin du Mistral ❢
Best years Insignia and Cabernets 1997, '96, '95, '94, '93, '92, '91, '90, '88, '87, '85, '84, '80

PINE RIDGE WINERY, Stags Leap District AVA   707 253 7500/253 1493
Though Stags Leap is its home, Pine Ridge has a strong presence in several other AVAs. Two nicely structured Cabernet Sauvignons are from Stags Leap and Rutherford, and a ripe Cabernet from Howell Mountain is awesome. Chardonnays from Stags Leap (succulent fruit, good balance) and Carneros (mineral and citrus notes) are well-knit.
Best wines ★★ Cabernet Sauvignon Stags Leap ❢, Cabernet Howell Mountain ❢, Chardonnay Stags Leap ♀ and Merlot Selected Cuvée ❢, ★ Chenin Blanc ♀
Best years ❢1998, '97, '96, '95, '94, '92, '91

QUIVIRA VINEYARDS, Dry Creek Valley AVA   707 431 8333/431 1664
Ultra-smooth Zinfandel loaded with bright Dry Creek fruitiness and a serious Sauvignon Blanc have been consistently coming out of this compact estate. Enjoy the Zinfandel early, but it will also last for 5–6 years.
Best wines ★★ Zinfandel ❢, ★ Sauvignon Blanc Reserve ♀
Best years ❢1999, '98, '97, '96, '95, '94; ♀1999, '98, '97

QUPÉ, Santa Maria Valley AVA   805 688 8630/937 2519
Winemaker Bob Lindquist has been setting the California standard for Syrah and other Rhône-style wines. His opulent Reserve Syrah and his fruit-filled Syrah/Mourvèdre blend (Los Olivos) win high praise. The Santa Maria Chardonnay, packed with spice, apple and lime flavours, also earns rave reviews.
Best wines ★★★ Chardonnay Santa Maria Valley ♀ and Syrah Bien Nacido Reserve ❢, ★ Los Olivos Cuvée ❢
Best years ❢1998, '97, '96, '95, '94; ♀1999, '98, '97, '96, '95, '94

A RAFANELLI WINERY, Dry Creek Valley AVA   Tel 707 433 1385
Classic Dry Creek Valley Zinfandel from old vines has customers lining up as each new vintage is released. Almost as good is the Cabernet Sauvignon which shares a similar core of ripe fruit, solid structure and judicious use of oak for balance. Both wines can age, but the Zinfandel is best at 3–5 years, the Cabernet at twice the age.
Best wines ★★★ Zinfandel ❢, ★★ Cabernet Sauvignon ❢
Best years 1999, '98, '97, '96, '95, '94, '93, '92, '91, '87

RAVENSWOOD WINERY, Sonoma Valley AVA · · · · · 707 938 1960/938 9459
Zinfandel in 15 different guises represents a typical vintage for Zin-fanatic Joel Peterson who began making full-flavoured Zinfandel when the public was drinking White Zinfandel. Sourcing the finest, usually low-yielding old Zinfandel vineyards in Napa, Sonoma and the Sierra Foothills, Peterson is known for ripe, concentrated wines. Whether single-vineyard wines or blends, his finest Zinfandels are bold and beautiful. Ravenswood also makes good Merlot and red Meritage, Pickberry.
Best wines ★★★ Zinfandel Old Vines ♥, ★★ Zinfandel Dickerson Vineyard ♥, Zinfandel Old Hill Vineyard ♥, Zinfandel Cooke Vineyard ♥ and Pickberry ♥, ★ Merlot North Coast ♥ and Zinfandel Vintners Blend ♥
Best years Zinfandel 1998, '97, '96, '95, '94, '92, '91, '90, '87, '86, '85

RIDGE VINEYARDS, Santa Cruz Mountains AVA · · · · · 408 867 3233/867 2986
Long before it was trendy, winemaker Paul Draper was lining up outstanding old Zinfandel vineyards. Later, using traditional methods, he refined what is a most formidable, distinctive Cabernet, Monte Bello, made from an old hillside vineyard. Beginning in 1970, Monte Bello Cabernets have been on a terrific run, and many of these wines have reached their 20th or 25th year with life and grace. The most prized Zinfandels today are those labelled Geyserville, Lytton Springs and Dusi from Paso Robles. York Creek is Draper's favourite Petite Sirah.
Best wines ★★★ Cabernet Sauvignon Monte Bello ♥, Zinfandel Geyserville ♥, ★★ Zinfandel Lytton Springs ♥, Zinfandel Dusi Ranch ♥, Zinfandel Pagani Ranch ♥ and Chardonnay ♀ ★ Merlot Bradford Mountain ♥ and Petite Sirah York Creek ♥
Best years Monte Bello 1997, '96, '94, '93, '92, '91, '90, '89, '87, '85, '84, '81, '78, '77, '75, '74, '70, '69, '64; **Zinfandel** 1998, '96, '95, '94, '93, '92, '91, '90, '87, '85, '84

J ROCHIOLI VINEYARDS, Russian River Valley AVA · · · · · 707 433 2305/433 2658
From their meticulously maintained vineyard, the Rochioli family produces highly distinctive Pinot Noir, Chardonnay and Sauvignon Blanc. The regular Pinot Noir highlights gorgeous black cherry fruit and a silky texture. The Reserve is richer and more intense, while the West Block Reserve is superb. Chardonnay Reserve shows complexity and good aging ability and the Sauvignon Blanc is bursting with flavours.
Best wines ★★★ Pinot Noir West Block Reserve ♥, ★★ Pinot Noir Estate ♥ and Chardonnay Reserve ♀, ★ Sauvignon Blanc ♀
Best years ♥1999, '98, '97, '96, '95, '94, '93, '92, '91, '90; ♀1999, '98, '97, '96, '95, '94

ROEDERER ESTATE, Anderson Valley AVA · · · · · 707 895 2288/895 2120
The California off-shoot of the Champagne house ROEDERER first made a serious statement with its sophisticated, somewhat austere Brut (exported under the Quartet label) that retains just a hint of California fruit personality. Its deluxe cuvée, L'Ermitage, aged for over 4 years and made in small quantities, is a rich, stunning bottle of bubbly that may be the New World's best.
Best wines ★★ L'Ermitage ♀ and Estate Rosé ♀, ★ Brut Quartet ♀
Best years L'Ermitage 1994, '93, '92, '91

ST CLEMENT, Napa Valley AVA · · · · · 707 963 7221/963 1412
Noted for balanced, beautifully defined wines, St Clement has a lengthy track record for Chardonnay and Merlot, each emphasizing fruit, but its top style is Cabernet

Sauvignon. Napa Valley Cabernet is elegant, while the Oroppas blend is more concentrated and capable of aging for 5 years or more. Howell Mountain Cabernet is even bigger. Seamless Chardonnay (Abbotts Vineyard) ages well for 3–5 years.

Best wines ★★ Cabernet Sauvignon Napa Valley ▼ and Cabernet Sauvignon Howell Mountain ▼, ★★ Oroppas ▼, ★ Merlot ▼

Best years ▼1998, '97, '96, '95, '94, '93, '92, '91, '90; ▽1998, '97, '95, '94, '93, '92

ST FRANCIS VINEYARDS, Sonoma Valley AVA   707 833 4666/833 6534

Red wines of power and concentration in an approachable style are what St Francis does best. Merlot is full-flavoured, concentrated yet supple, and the Reserve ages better than most. Cabernets follow a similar pattern with the Reserve improving for a decade. With great old vineyards in the vicinity, St Francis usually comes up with a formidable Old Vine Zinfandel needing at least 3 years of aging.

Best wines ★★ Cabernet Sauvignon Reserve ▼ and Merlot Reserve ▼, ★ Cabernet Sauvignon Sonoma Valley ▼ and Chardonnay ▽

Best years ▼1998, '97, '96, '95, '94, '93, '92, '91, '89, '85; ▽1998, '97, '96, '95, '94, '93, '92

SAINTSBURY, Carneros AVA   707 252 0592/252 0595

Saintsbury's Pinot Noirs are brilliant examples of the perfume and refined fruit quality of Carneros. Ranging from the light, picnic-perfect Garnet to the intense, oak-aged Reserve, the Pinots are satiny smooth and well balanced. The Chardonnay Reserve has recently blossomed into one of the best.

Best wines ★★★ Chardonnay Reserve ▽ and Pinot Noir Reserve ▼, ★★ Pinot Noir Carneros ▼, ★ Chardonnay ▽ and Pinot Noir Garnet ▼

Best years ▼1998, '97, '96, '95, '94, '93, '92, '91; ▽1999, '98, '97, '96, '95, '94, '93, '91, '90

SANFORD WINERY, Santa Ynez Valley AVA   805 688 3300/688 7381

In 1971 Sanford helped develop the Benedict Vineyard, which proved to be a special site for Pinot Noir; Sanford's early vintages from that vineyard helped establish Santa Barbara as a prime region. Today, its Pinot Noirs are rich and satiny with an intriguing earthiness in their flavours. Reserve-style Chardonnay, labelled Barrel Select, ages well. Intensely flavoured, the Sauvignon Blanc is often a winner.

Best wines ★★★ Chardonnay Reserve ▽ and Pinot Noir Reserve ▼, ★★ Pinot Noir Carneros ▼, ★ Chardonnay ▽ and Pinot Noir Garnet ▼

Best years ▼1998, '97, '96, '95, '94, '93, '92, '91, '90; ▽1999, '98, '97, '96, '95, '94, '93, '92

SCHRAMSBERG, Napa Valley AVA   707 942 4558/942 5943

The first California winery to make Champagne-method sparklers wine using classic grapes, Schramsberg has hit many high notes over the ensuing 30 years. Today, despite stiffer competition, its Blanc de Noirs and Blanc de Blancs still often lead the way. The Reserve Brut, its deluxe Cuvée, can reach world class status and J Schram, rich and flavoursome, is increasingly good. There is also a sweetish, dessert style called Crémant.

Best wines ★★ Reserve Brut ▽ and J Schram ▽, ★ Blanc de Blancs ▽, Blanc de Noirs ▽ and Crémant ▽

Best years 1994, '93, '92, '91, '90, '89, '87, '85, '84, '82

SCREAMING EAGLE WINERY, Oakville AVA   707 944 0749/944 9271

Jean Phillips owns 50 acres in Oakville and sells most of her grapes. However, she retains enough to produce around 500 cases a year of Cabernet Sauvignon. Made by well-known Cabernet specialist, Heidi Peterson-Barrett, the Screaming Eagle 100% Cabernet is highly concentrated and structured to age for a decade or longer. If you can overlook its high price and the hysteria surrounding it in collectors' circles, it is an impressive, heavyweight Cabernet. Every bottle is sold practically overnight to mailing list customers.

Best wine ★★ Cabernet Sauvignon **♥**   **Best years** 1998, '97, '96, '95, '94, '93, '92

SHAFER VINEYARDS, Stags Leap District AVA   707 944 2877/944 9454

A rising star, Shafer makes unusual, intensely fruity Stags Leap Cabernet Sauvignon and a dramatic, Reserve-style Hillside Select Cabernet. The latest mould-breaking wines are Merlot and a super-Tuscan-style Sangiovese called Firebreak. A new Carneros vineyard, Red Shoulder, has improved the quality of the Chardonnays.

Best wines ★★★ Cabernet Sauvignon Hillside Select **♥, ★★** Chardonnay Red Shoulder **♀** and Merlot **♥, ★** Cabernet Sauvignon Stags Leap **♥** and Firebreak **♥**

Best years ♥1997, '96, '95, '94, '93, '92, '91, '90, '87, '86, '85, '84; **♀**1999, '98, '97, '96, '95, '94

SILVER OAK CELLARS, Napa Valley AVA   707 944 8808/944 2817

Veteran winemaker Justin Meyer specializes in Cabernet Sauvignon. Both the Alexander Valley and Napa Cabernet benefit from over 3 years of oak aging and are accessible and polished on release. The Alexander Valley shows more forward fruit; the Napa displays firm structure. Both age well, with 10 years the norm and many vintages reaching 20 years.

Best wines ★★★ Cabernet Sauvignon Napa Valley **♥, ★★** Cabernet Sauvignon Alexander Valley **♥**

Best years 1998, '97, '96, '95, '94, '93, '92, '91, '90, '88, '87, '86, '85, '81, '78

SILVERADO VINEYARDS, Stags Leap District AVA   707 257 1770/257 1538

Owned by a branch of the Disney family, Silverado is well-known for its friendly style of juicy-fruity wines. Estate Chardonnay and Cabernet are soft yet splendid in their easy-going way. Reserve Cabernet Sauvignon is bigger and built for the long haul, and the super-Tuscan-style Sangiovese is now flexing its muscles. Merlot remains popular.

Best wines ★★ Cabernet Sauvignon Reserve **♥** and Chardonnay **♀**

Best years ♥1997, '96, '95, '93, '92, '91, '90; **♀**1998, '97, '96, '95, '94

SIMI WINERY, Sonoma County   707 433 6981/433 6253

When Zelma Long arrived from MONDAVI as winemaker in 1979, she introduced high standards and a sense of direction and style to this historic winery. Sendal is a Bordeaux blend of Sauvignon Blanc and Sémillon.

Best wines ★★ Cabernet Sauvignon Reserve **♥**, Chardonnay Reserve **♀** and Sendal **♀, ★** Cabernet Sauvignon **♥**, Chardonnay **♀** and Sauvignon Blanc **♀**

Best years ♥1997, '96, '95, '94, '93, '92, '91, '90, '87, '86; **♀**1998, '97, '96, '95, '94, '93

STAG'S LEAP WINE CELLARS, Stags Leap District AVA   707 944 2020/257 7501

With its reputation built upon Cabernet Sauvignon from the 1970s, this winery is still capable of making stunning Cabernet. The SLV Cabernet Reserve is more consistently fine than the Cask 23, which is more expensive. Over the last decade Chardonnay has shown the greatest improvement, and the Chardonnay Reserve responds well to aging.

Best wines ★★★ Cabernet Sauvignon Cask 23 **♥** and Cabernet Sauvignon SLV Reserve **♥, ★★** Chardonnay Reserve **♀** and Chardonnay Napa Valley **♀, ★** Merlot **♥**

Best years Cabernet SLV Reserve 1997, '96, '95, '94, '93, '92, '91, '90, '87, '86, '85, '84, '81, '78; **Cask 23** 1995, '94, '92, '91, '90, '85, '84, '79, '78; ♀1998, '97, '96, '95, '94, '93, '91

STEELE WINES, Lake County   707 279 9475/279 9633

Well-known winemaker and consultant Jed Steele focuses on single-vineyard Zinfandel, Chardonnay and Pinot Noir. His experience with Zinfandel comes through in the deep, ripe DuPratt Vineyard, Pacini Vineyard and Catfish Vineyard wines.

Best wines ★★ Zinfandel Catfish Vineyard ♥ and Zinfandel DuPratt Vineyard ♥, ★ Chardonnay Lolonis ♀, Chardonnay Carneros ♀ and Chardonnay Sangiacomo♀

Best years ♥1998, '97, '96, '95, '94, '93; ♀1998, '97, '96, '95, '94, '93

STERLING VINEYARDS, Napa Valley AVA   707 942 3300/942 3466

Over the years Sterling has taken a few knocks for some of its wines. Throughout it all, Reserve Cabernet Sauvignon remained its best wine and, like the Napa Valley Cabernet Sauvignon, is improving. Two good single-vineyard wines are the Winery Lake Pinot Noir and the slow-aging Diamond Mountain Chardonnay. The once-superb Merlot from the Three Palms Vineyard appears back on track.

Best wines ★★ Cabernet Sauvignon Reserve ♥, ★ Chardonnay Diamond Mountain ♀ and Pinot Noir Winery Lake ♥

Best years ♥1997, '96, '95, '94, '93, '92, '91, '90, '87, '86, '85; ♀1998, '97, '96, '95, '92

STONESTREET, Alexander Valley AVA   707 433 9463/544 1056

The jewel in the Kendall-Jackson crown, Stonestreet has access to many outstanding Sonoma County vineyards owned by the parent company. Its strong suit is powerful Bordeaux reds, which include Cabernet Sauvignon, Merlot and Legacy, a splendid, almost-over-the-top Meritage red. Legacy should age for a decade or two.

Best wines ★★ Cabernet Sauvignon ♥, Legacy ♥ and Merlot ♥

Best years 1997, '96, '95, '94, '93, '92, '91

SWANSON, Napa Valley AVA   707 944 0905/944 0955

Swanson has consistently shown a deft touch with Merlot that is deep and capable of complexity. It has also become a leader with Sangiovese (cherry fruit, with supple flavours) and Syrah that looks to Hermitage for its model. When avoiding over-oaking, the Reserve Chardonnay is rich enough to age well for 5 years or so. Alexis combines Cabernet Sauvignon and Syrah in the best Australian tradition.

Best wines ★★ Alexis ♥, Chardonnay Reserve ♀, Merlot ♥ and Sangiovese ♥, ★ Syrah ♥

Best years ♥1998, '97, '96, '95, '94, '92, '91; ♀1998, '97, '96, '95, '94, '93, '92, '90

TALLEY VINEYARDS, Arroyo Grande Valley AVA   805 489 0446/489 0996

As outstanding growers, the Talleys sell their prized grapes to the likes of AU BON CLIMAT, and as winemakers they are also on top of their game. With rich flavours, the Chardonnay is balanced by crisp acidity that enables long aging. The Pinot Noir from Rosemary's Vineyard is almost Rhône-like in its depth, but has the velvety texture and ripe cherry qualities typical of fine Pinot.

Best wines ★★ Chardonnay ♀ and Pinot Noir Rosemary's Vineyard ♥, ★ Pinot Noir ♥

Best years ♥1998, '97, '96, '95, '94, '93; ♀1999, '98, '97, '96, '95, '94, '93

LANE TANNER WINERY, Santa Barbara   805 929 1826/929 1826

One of California's most accomplished winemakers, Lane Tanner focuses on subtle, elegant Pinot Noirs. Several single-vineyard wines have been whittled down to one

from Bien Nacido Vineyard and an occasional one from Sanford & Benedict Vineyard.
Best wine ★★ Pinot Noir Bien Nacido ❢
Best years 1998, '97, '96, '95, '93

MARIMAR TORRES ESTATE, Russian River Valley AVA   707 823 4365/823 4496
Part of the TORRES wine dynasty of Spain and Chile, Marimar Torres decided to settle
in the cool Green Valley sub-district of Sonoma County where she specializes in
Chardonnay and Pinot Noir. Adhering to traditional production methods, she has
made great strides with a rich, perfumed Pinot Noir and a solid, if heavy on the oak,
style of Chardonnay. ·
Best wines ★★ Chardonnay Don Miguel Vineyard ♀, ★ Pinot Noir ❢
Best years ❢1998, '97, '96, '95, '94, '93, '92; ♀1998, '97, '96, '95, '94, '93, '92, '91, '90

TURLEY, Napa Valley AVA   707 963 0940/963 8683
Larry Turley's obsession is with Zinfandel and Petite Sirah made from old and some
extremely old vines. Most wines are big, and a few are gargantuan, closer to Port in style.
Best wines ★★★ Zinfandel Hayne Vineyard ❢ and Zinfandel Moore Vineyard ❢
Best years 1997, '96, '95, '94

VIADER, Howell Mountain AVA   707 963 3816/963 3817
With Tony Soter of ETUDE overseeing winemaking, owner Dahlia Viader focuses on
one wine, a polished, elegant blend of Cabernet Sauvignon and Cabernet Franc.
Though possessing great depth, the wine still has impressive, supple and engaging
flavours and rewards 4–5 years of aging. The first vintage was in 1989.
Best wine ★★ Viader Estate ❢
Best years 1997, '95, '94, '93, '92, '91

WILD HORSE VINEYARD, Paso Robles AVA   805 434 2541/434 3516
Making a reputation for himself with a series of fine Pinot Noirs from Santa Barbera in
the 1980s, winemaker Ken Volk branched out to offer a variety of wines, all of them
more than good. But Pinot Noir remains his obsession.
Best wines ★★ Pinot Noir Cheval Sauvage ❢, ★ Chardonnay ♀
Best years ❢1998, '97, '96, '95, '94, '93, '92, '91

WILLIAMS SELYEM WINERY, Russian River Valley AVA   Tel 707 433 6425
Enjoying a cult following for Pinot Noir, Williams Selyem has also done well with
Chardonnay and Zinfandel. With plenty of toasty oak and black cherry fruit, the finest
Pinots have been the Rochioli Vineyard and Allen Vineyard. See also MILLBROOK.
Best wines ★★★ Pinot Noir Rochioli Vineyard ❢, ★★ Pinot Noir Allen Vineyard ❢, Pinot
Noir Russian River Valley ❢ and Zinfandel ❢
Best years 1998, '97, '96, '95, '94, '92, '91

ZD, Napa Valley AVA   707 963 5188/963 2640
For over 2 decades ZD has enjoyed a strong following for ripe-fruited, well-oaked
Chardonnay made from the Central Coast. Cabernet Sauvignon, both Napa Valley and
Reserve, are classic wines that show at their best only after at least 5 years. Pinot Noir
from Carneros has a compressed, cherry-spice style and needs 1–2 years' aging.
Best wines ★★ Chardonnay ♀, Cabernet Sauvignon Reserve ❢ and Cabernet Sauvignon
Napa Valley ❢, ★ Pinot Noir ❢
Best years ❢1997, '96, '95, '94, '92, '91, '90, '87, '86; ♀1998, '97, '96, '95, '93, '92, '91, '90

CALIFORNIAN VINTAGES

Vintages in California vary enough to make vintage generalizations useful pieces of information. Those grapes that ripen early in the season such as Chardonnay and Pinot Noir are normally subject to different conditions from those that ripen late, primarily Cabernet Sauvignon and Zinfandel. The quality of the grapes at the harvest is influenced by weather conditions, and weather patterns in the North Coast normally vary to some degree from those in the South Coast.

Aging qualities

With a home market demanding instant gratification, most Californian wines are made in a fruit-filled, soft style. The exception among whites is Chardonnay from low-yielding sites, which improves with 3–5 years' aging. Among reds, Merlot and Pinot Noir are best after 3–4 years, with Zinfandel peaking at 5–7 years. Concentrated Cabernets from Napa Valley and Sonoma are worth keeping beyond a decade, but most are best at 4–6 years.

Maturity charts _____

1999 produced some excellent Cabernet Sauvignon in the Napa Valley. Elegant Carneros Pinots will be at their best within 2–4 years, with Santa Barbara's more intense version peaking at 5–7 years.

1999 Napa Cabernet Sauvignon (premium)

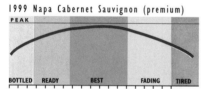

1999 Santa Barbara/Carneros Pinot Noir

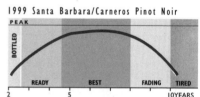

VINTAGE CHART

	99	98	97	96	95	94	93	92	91	90	89
NAPA VALLEY											
Cabernet/Merlot	9○	8○	8○	7○	9○	8○	7◐	8●	8◑	9●	6●
Zinfandel	8○	7○	8○	7◑	8○	9◑	7●	8●	9●	9●	7◑
SONOMA COUNTY											
Cabernet/Merlot	7○	8○	8○	6○	9○	8◑	7◑	8●	8◑	9●	7●
Zinfandel	8○	7○	9○	7◑	7○	9◑	7●	8●	8●	9●	7●
NAPA/SONOMA											
Chardonnay	8○	6○	7◑	8●	8●	9●	7◑	8◑			
CARNEROS/RUSSIAN RIVER											
Pinot Noir	9○	8○	8○	7◑	8◑	9●	6◑	8●	9●	8◑	7◑
CENTRAL COAST											
Pinot Noir	7○	8○	8◑	7◑	8○	9●	7●	8●	9●	9◑	7◑
Chardonnay	7○	7○	7◑	8●	8●	9●	7◑	8◑			

KEY ○ = needs more time   ◐ = ready but will improve   ● = at peak   ◑ = fading or tired

---

VINTAGES AT A GLANCE

This chart takes a varietal approach and should be viewed together with the vintage chart on page 288.

Cabernet Sauvignon, Merlot and Zinfandel

Great Years ★★★	1995, '94, '90, '86, '85, '81, '78, '74, '70, '68, '59
Good Years ★★	1999, '97, '92, '91, '87, '84, '79, '75, '71, '69, '66, '64, '58
Moderate Years ★	1998, '96, '93, '88, '77, '73, '67, '65
Poor Years (No Stars)	1989, '83, '76, '72

Carneros, Central Coast – Pinot Noir and Chardonnay

Great Years ★★★	1995, '94, '91, '85
Good Years ★★	1997, '92, '90, '89, '86
Moderate Years ★	1999, '98, '96, '93, '88, '87, '84
Poor Years (No Stars)	1983

Annual vintage reports

1999★★ Cool, late-ripening year produced uneven quality in Chardonnay and Sauvignon Blanc. Pinot Noir looks fine overall, whereas Cabernet Sauvignon and Zinfandel vary widely, with those who selectively picked doing best.

1998★ A difficult, late-ripening crop of highly variable quality. Cabernet Sauvignon is likely to be the most consistent and some Pinot Noir could be exciting. Average quality Chardonnay.

1997★★ Abundant, record-setting crop resulted from a warm spring, mild summer, and new vineyards. Occasional rains around harvest time caused problems with over-cropped Chardonnay and some Zinfandel. Overall quality should be fine, with Cabernet Sauvignon and Zinfandel verging on outstanding.

1996★ More variable than recent vintages. Only the best producers are likely to be really successful. In general, Cabernet Sauvignon is likely to be somewhat austere but Pinot Noir and Chardonnay from Carneros and Central Coast are very good.

1995★★★ Good to very good. In spite of poor spring weather, which substantially reduced yields by causing poor flowering, a long cool season continued right to November, allowing slow but full ripening.

Cabernet Sauvignon looks like the shining star of this vintage, with Pinot Noir not far behind. Chardonnay is best from Central Coast.

1994★★★ Zinfandel and Cabernet Sauvignon are excellent. Quantities overall were down, but this is undoubtedly another fine vintage. Chardonnay and Pinot Noir are outstanding from top producers. More Chardonnays than usual could age for 5–7 years.

1993★ Not a bad vintage in spite of poor weather. The whites were elegant and stylish and the reds have good potential. Even the Zinfandels seem to have defied the odds. Pinot Noir is good from the southern Central Coast but those from Carneros and the Russian River Valley are only fair. Napa and Sonoma Cabernets at their best show elegance and pretty fruit.

1992★★ A big, but high-quality vintage. The Cabernets were somewhat precocious and showy but many have kept well. The best-aging Cabernets are from vineyards within mountain AVAs.

1991★★-★★★ Stylish, well-structured wines, many of which are extremely good. The best Cabernets should be aged.

1990★★-★★★ A generally superb vintage. There are rich, concentrated Cabernets and Zinfandels and rich Chardonnays, too.

1989 0-★★ A damp harvest spoiled what should have been a fine year. Those producers in regions that escaped the bad weather (such as Santa Barbara) made very good wines, as did most of the committed producers elsewhere in California.

1988★ All but the top reds are light and past their best. Sonoma Cabernets had more depth and have lasted longer.

1987★-★★ Excellent Zinfandel. Cabernet was more irregular but was seldom less than good – the result of a hot and especially dry growing region.

1986★★-★★★ A year of full-bodied, tannic reds. Chardonnay was rich and opulent and the wines should have been drunk by now. Most Cabernets are close to their peak now.

1985★★★ A nearly perfect Cabernet vintage, producing big wines that have kept well and many are at their best now.

1984★-★★ The first of 3 excellent mid-'80s vintages. Only the very best are still good.

1980 Originally thought to be a great year, this has been gradually downgraded. However, some very good wines still exist.

Other good years 1978, '74 and '70 were outstanding, particularly for Cabernet Sauvignon. It is possible to find great bottles from 1975, '73 and '71. Older classics may come from 1969, '68, '66, '59, '58, '54, '51, '47 and '46.

PACIFIC NORTHWEST

Success has come quickly for Washington and Oregon since their oldest growing regions actively began producing varietal table wines as recently as the mid-1960s. Both states are now producing red and white wines that rank with the best in the world.

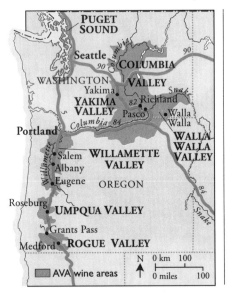

Oregon's wine styles

The Willamette Valley is the largest and most important wine area in Oregon and boasts an increasing number of high-quality producers. The climate is warm enough to ripen grapes fully yet cool enough to produce stunning Pinot Noir and Gewürztraminer. In great vintages, the Pinot Noirs from here embody all the complexity and depth of flavour of fine red Burgundy. New clones of Chardonnay and Pinot Noir are helping even out the vintage variation of the often wet harvest conditions.

The Umpqua Valley has found a niche selling local wine to tourists and some remarkable bottles may be found. The conditions are fertile and future experimentation may identify specific grape/soil combinations that excel. The

Rogue Valley has several different growing areas that allow for both cool-climate varietals and warmer-climate Cabernet and Merlot to be grown.

Washington's wine styles

The desert conditions of Washington's Columbia Valley, Yakima Valley and Walla Walla Valley lack the romantic appeal of Oregon's Willamette Valley or California's Napa Valley and most of the new vineyards have been planted by entrepreneurs, not romantics. Columbia Valley is the most commonly used AVA as it encompasses all but western Washington. The important sub-region Yakima Valley is known for well-structured Merlot and Cabernet Sauvignon in contrast to the more fruit-forward reds of the Walla Walla Valley. Crisp, high-acid whites, from Chardonnay, Riesling and Sauvignon Blanc, are the standard styles across the state.

GRAPES AND WINES

Bordeaux-style blended reds

Bordeaux-style blends from Washington are in vogue. The intense varietal character of Columbia Valley Merlot and Cabernet Sauvignon can be tamed through blending.

Botrytized and late-harvest wines

Excellent late-harvest wines are made in Washington and Oregon. Exceptional acidity balances intense sugar levels. The cold late autumn weather in eastern Washington frequently allows for the production of Icewine from grapes frozen on the vine.

Cabernet Sauvignon

Washington Cabernet Sauvignon possesses the plumpness of California Cabernet fruit with the firm acidity and structure of fine Bordeaux. Oregon Cabernet Sauvignon has more earthy and stemmy qualities but has been improving with better vineyard site selection and viticultural practices.

Chardonnay

New clones are dramatically improving the quality of Chardonnay in Oregon and rich, full-bodied wines are now being made. In Washington, Chardonnay has steadily improved as fermentation in small oak barrels and better grape selection have been employed.

Gewürztraminer

Excellent Gewürztraminer is made in both Washington and Oregon. However, much of it goes into inexpensive fresh-and-fruity wines that show minimal character.

Merlot

Washington Merlot has flourished with renewed health-conscious interest in red wine. The variety develops fullness and complexity in the arid Columbia Valley. A small quantity of fruity, appealing Merlot is made in southern Oregon.

Pinot Gris

Pinot Gris is the darling of the Oregon wine industry – it is best young, doesn't require oak aging and sells quickly. Crisp and refreshing, it is a food-friendly wine. A tiny amount is grown in Washington.

Pinot Noir

Pinot Noir is arguably the Pacific Northwest's most successful grape variety, with an international reputation for wines from Oregon's Willamette Valley. It is also the most fickle variety to grow and only a few sites in Washington are suitable, mainly in western Washington.

Riesling

Riesling was the variety that made Washington's reputation. Today, it is still popular but has faded from its high level. Both in Oregon and Washington, the majority of Riesling is used to make inexpensive, early-drinking wines.

Sauvignon Blanc

Sauvignon Blanc succeeds in both Oregon and Washington where the crisp, refreshing wine attains full maturity while its acidity is still high.

Sémillon

Only a few producers choose to make Sémillon despite its very attractive style. Washington Sémillon, when ripe, has hints of melon and fig, and crisp refreshing acidity.

Syrah

Washington wineries are planting many acres of Syrah and their early wines are achieving popular success. The smoky, peppery aromas are reminiscent of flavours from France's Rhône Valley.

A–Z OF PACIFIC NORTHWEST WINE REGIONS

COLUMBIA VALLEY AVA

Columbia Valley is the largest AVA in Washington, encompassing more than 12,000 square miles, including the Yakima Valley and Walla Walla sub-regions and many different mesoclimates.

The presence of the Cascade Mountains to the west means that rainfall is very low but irrigation is made possible by extracting water from the Columbia River. The hot days and cool nights of the desert-like conditions are well suited to grape-growing. Many excellent Cabernet Sauvignon, Merlot and Syrah wines use the Columbia Valley designation.
Best producers ANDREW WILL, CHATEAU STE MICHELLE, COLUMBIA, HEDGES, McCREA, QUILCEDA CREEK.
Best years ●1999, '98, '97, '96, '95, '94.

PUGET SOUND AVA

New, large regional AVA with only a few producers making wine from within its boundaries as the climate is wet and cool. Pinot Gris and Pinot Noir make the most interesting wines. Most of the leading wineries here use Columbia Valley grapes.
Best producers Bainbridge Island Winery, Mount Baker Vineyards.

ROGUE VALLEY AVA

The southernmost viticultural region in Oregon, stretching from the California border north to Grants Pass, benefits from a higher altitude than Oregon's other wine regions. Three sub-appellations provide a broad range of mesoclimates for both cool-climate varietals and Bordeaux grapes – the Illinois Valley to the west (cooler-climate varietals), the Applegate Valley in the centre (much warmer) and the Rogue River sub-appellation, the eastern border of the AVA (warm and very dry).
Best producers Bridgeview, Foris, Valley View, Weisinger's of Ashland.
Best years ●1999, '98, '96, '94, '92.

UMPQUA VALLEY AVA

Nestling between the Coast Mountains to the west and the Cascade Mountains to the east, the valley follows the Umpqua River to the Pacific Ocean. Coastal breezes come upriver, moderating the daytime heat and allowing high levels of acidity to develop in grapes grown in the hot day/cool evening sites.
Best producers Callahan Ridge, Henry Estate, La Garza Cellars.
Best years ●1999, '98, '96, '94.

WALLA WALLA VALLEY AVA

This tiny AVA extends from eastern Washington across the border into Oregon. Long hot days and very cool nights provide excellent growing conditions for Merlot, Syrah and Cabernet Sauvignon and some of Washington's best-known wineries are located here.

Best producers Canoe Ridge Vineyard, L'ÉCOLE #41, LEONETTI CELLAR, Waterbrook, WOODWARD CANYON.

Best years ❢1999, '98, '97, '96, '95, '94, '93, '92, '91, '90.

WILLAMETTE VALLEY AVA

The largest and most successful AVA in Oregon, Willamette Valley is home to many of the state's best wineries. Though an enormous valley, the greatest concentration of producers is in a short stretch of low rolling hills west of the Willamette river from between Portland to just south of Salem. The climate is warm enough to ripen grapes fully yet cool enough to produce stunning Pinot Noir, Gewürztraminer and Pinot Gris.

Best producers ADELSHEIM VINEYARD, ARCHERY SUMMIT, ARGYLE, BEAUX FRÈRES, CAMERON, DOMAINE DROUHIN, The EYRIE VINEYARDS, PONZI VINEYARDS, REX HILL VINEYARDS, WILLAKENZIE ESTATE, Ken WRIGHT.

Best years ❢1999, '98, '96, '94, '93, '92, '91, '90.

YAKIMA VALLEY AVA

Although many vineyards thrive here, only a few producers use this AVA on their labels, preferring to use the broader Columbia Valley AVA name instead. Older vineyards are planted with a wide range of varietals. Sauvignon Blanc, Chardonnay, Merlot and Cabernet Sauvignon do well here and wines with real personality continue to emerge.

Best producers CHINOOK, DELILLE CELLARS, Staton Hills.

Best years ❢1999, '98, '97, '96, '95, '94, 92.

A–Z OF PACIFIC NORTHWEST PRODUCERS

ADELSHEIM VINEYARD, Willamette Valley AVA, Oregon   503 538 3652/538 2248
David Adelsheim was one of the pioneers of Pinot Noir in Oregon, planting a vineyard in 1971. Winemaker Don Kautzner and business partner Michael Adelsheim round out the team. The Reserve Chardonnay is always rich and very nutty. The Pinot Noir Seven Springs Vineyard and Elizabeth's Reserve are some of the best Pinots in Oregon.
Best wines ★★ Chardonnay Reserve ♀, Pinot Noir Seven Springs Vineyard ❢ and Pinot Noir Elizabeth's Reserve ❢
Best years ❢1998, '97, '96, '94, '91, '90; ♀1998, '97, '96, '95

ANDREW WILL WINERY, Washington   Tel 206 463 3290
Chris Camarda makes complex and textured reds that rank with the finest in the United States. His Bordeaux-style blend Sorella reveals the deftness of his winemaking, balancing ripe berry fruit, oak, and glycerin in perfect proportions. The Merlot 'R' is a Reserve version of the varietal crafted with plenty of new oak.
Best wines ★★★ Sorella ❢, ★★ Merlot 'R' ❢ and Cabernet Sauvignon ❢
Best years 1998, '97, '96, '95, '94

ARCHERY SUMMIT WINERY, Willamette Valley AVA, Oregon   505 864 4300/864 4038
Production is increasing at this relatively new winery in the Dundee Hills owned by the Andrus family of Napa Valley's PINE RIDGE, which concentrates on Pinot Noir.

Best wines ★★ Pinot Noir Arcus Estate ♀, Pinot Noir Red Hills Estate ♀ and Vireton ♀
Best years ♀1998, '97, '96, '94; ♀1999, '98, '97

ARGYLE /DUNDEE WINE COMPANY   503 538 8520/538 2055
Willamette Valley AVA, Oregon
Argyle makes a relatively large quantity of excellent sparkling wine – nearly 16,000 cases a year. Oregon's cool climate is perfect for harvesting high-acid Pinot Noir and Chardonnay. Working with yeast strains from the Champagne firm of BOLLINGER, winemaker Rollin Soles crafts crisp, yeasty vintage Brut.
Best wine ★★ Vintage Brut ♀   Best years 1996, '95, '94, '93

BEAUX FRÈRES, Willamette Valley AVA, Oregon   503 537 1137/537 2613
Noted wine authority Robert M. Parker, Jr is a partner in this small Willamette Valley winery, a controversial issue early on that quickly faded after a few intense, full-bodied Pinot Noirs were released. The unfiltered Pinot Noir shows tremendous blackberry fruit and new oak flavours.
Best wine ★★ Pinot Noir ♀   Best years 1998, '97, '96, '94, '93

CAMERON WINERY, Willamette Valley AVA, Oregon   503 538 0336
Cameron's jovial winemaker John Paul likes to act crazy but takes his winemaking seriously. He uses lots of new oak to embellish his Chardonnay and Pinot Noir. The Pinot Noir Clos Electrique, named after the electric fence that surrounds the vineyard, is a complex and layered wine that ages nicely.
Best wine ★★ Pinot Noir Clos Electrique ♀   Best years ♀1998, '97, '96, '95, '94

CHATEAU STE MICHELLE, Columbia Valley AVA, Washington   425 488 1133/488 4657
The international acclaim achieved by this large winery has created a market for Washington State wines. Under the direction of winemaker Mike Januik, individual vineyard wines that express the region's terroir are the speciality.
Best wines ★★ Chardonnay Reserve ♀, Cabernet Sauvignon Cold Creek Vineyard ♀, Chardonnay Cold Creek Vineyard ♀ and White Riesling Icewine ♀, ★ Merlot Indian Wells Vineyard ♀
Best years ♀1998, '97, '96, '95, '94; ♀1999, '98, '97, '96

CHINOOK WINES, Yakima Valley AVA, Washington   509 786 2725/786 2777
The team of Kay Simon and Clay Mackay combines the viticultural and winemaking talents of 2 of the state's early specialists. Chardonnay and Sauvignon Blanc are technically correct and consistently good. The Cabernet Sauvignon is given additional bottle age before release and is one of Washington's best reds.
Best wines ★★ Cabernet Sauvignon ♀, ★ Chardonnay ♀
Best years ♀ 1997, '95, '94, '93, '91; ♀1999, '98, '97, '96

COLUMBIA WINERY, Columbia Valley AVA, Washington   425 488 2776/488 3460
Under the direction of David Lake MW, Columbia Winery makes a complete line of well-priced varietals. Syrah Red Willow Vineyard exhibits a smoky character reminiscent of northern Rhône reds but the Cabernet Sauvignon Red Willow Vineyard is the outstanding wine – a dense and complex expression of the variety.
Best wines ★★★ Cabernet Sauvignon Red Willow Vineyard ♀, ★ Syrah Red Willow Vineyard ♀ and Sauvignon Blanc ♀
Best years ♀1999, '98, '97, '95, '94; ♀1999, '98, '97

DELILLE CELLARS, Yakima Valley AVA, Washington   425 489 0544/402 9295
Winemaker Chris Upchurch crafts heady, oaky, cherry-filled reds that appeal to many palates. Using fruit from a variety of top Yakima Valley vineyards, he selects his best lots for a Bordeaux-style blend called Chaleur Estate. The second wine, D2, is made predominantly from Merlot.
Best wines ★ Chaleur Estate ❦ and D2 ❦   **Best years** 1998, '97, '96, '95, '94

DOMAINE DROUHIN, Willamette Valley AVA, Oregon   503 864 2700/864 3377
In 1987, French *négociant* Robert DROUHIN surprised the wine world by purchasing 180 acres of Yamhill farmland and planting Pinot Noir and Chardonnay with the aim of making Oregon versions of top-quality red and white Burgundy. Today Domaine Drouhin wines, made by his daughter Véronique, are outstanding. Her Pinot Noir is one of the most supple made in Oregon and the Pinot Noir Laurène ranks with the Côte d'Or's finest. An excellent Chardonnay has been produced since 1996.
Best wines ★★★ Pinot Noir Laurène ❦, ★★ Pinot Noir ❦ and Chardonnay ♀
Best years 1998, '97, '96, '95, '94, '93, '92; ♀1998, '97, '96

THE EYRIE VINEYARDS, Willamette Valley AVA, Oregon   503 472 6315/472 5124
David Lett is a visionary who many feel is the architect of Oregon's wine industry. In 1966, he found a vineyard site to plant Pinot Noir in the cool hills near Dundee and in doing so, founded an industry. His successful experiments with Pinot Gris and Pinot Noir have set the style for Oregon wine. His Chardonnay Reserve is delicious.
Best wines ★★ Pinot Gris ♀ and Pinot Noir Reserve ❦, ★ Chardonnay Reserve ♀
Best years ❦1998, '97, '96, '95, '94, '93, '90; ♀1997, '96, '95

HEDGES CELLARS, Columbia Valley AVA, Washington   425 391 6056/391 3827
Hedges gained a reputation with an inexpensive Cabernet/Merlot blend that was an international success. The barrel-aged version, Red Mountain Reserve, is a step up in quality and price and one of the state's best.
Best wine ★ Red Mountain Reserve ❦   **Best years** 1998, '97, '96, '95, '94

L'ÉCOLE #41, Walla Walla Valley AVA, Washington   509 525 0940/525 2775
An odd name (French for the former Walla Walla schoolhouse where the winery is located) and a curious label (artwork done by a schoolchild) have done nothing to deter the efforts at this winery. Fine Merlot has always been produced here and single-vineyard Merlot and Cabernet Sauvignon from the Seven Hills Vineyard are worth seeking out. An oaky, herbal, pushed-to-the-limit Sémillon is exceptionally popular. Apogee is a new Meritage red from Merlot and Cabernet Sauvignon.
Best wines ★★ Merlot Seven Hills Vineyard ❦ and Apogee ❦, ★ Sémillon ♀, Merlot ❦ and Cabernet Sauvignon Seven Hills Vineyard ❦
Best years ❦1998, '97, '96, '95, '94; ♀1999, '98, '97

LEONETTI CELLAR, Walla Walla Valley AVA, Washington   509 525 1428/525 4006
Leonetti Cellar is legendary for its toasty Merlot, sought after by collectors around the world. Winemaker Gary Figgins uses plenty of spicy new oak to enhance Walla Walla and Yakima fruit. Chocolaty reds that are easy to enjoy are the hallmark. The Cabernet Sauvignon ages nicely for 3–5 years.
Best wines ★★★ Merlot ❦, ★★ Cabernet Sauvignon ❦
Best years 1998, '97, '96, '95, '94, '93, '92, '91, '90

McCREA CELLARS, Columbia Valley AVA, Washington   360 458 9463/458 8559
Working with Chardonnay and Rhône varietals exclusively, Doug McCrea produces full-flavoured wines. His excellent, buttery, apple-scented Chardonnay is one of the top produced in Washington. Syrah, made only in the best years, is a most impressive red.
Best wines ★★ Syrah ❢, ★ Chardonnay Elerding Vineyard ♀
Best years ❢1999, '98, '97, '96, '94; ♀1999, '98, '97, '96, '95

PONZI VINEYARDS, Willamette Valley AVA, Oregon   503 628 1227/628 0354
The first vineyard at Ponzi was planted in 1970 and the winery gained an early reputation for Pinot Gris and Pinot Noir. Today these remain the best wines and when available, the Pinot Noir Reserve is always worth tracking down.
Best wine ★★ Pinot Noir Reserve ❢   **Best years** ❢1998, '97, '96, '95, '94, '91, '90

QUILCEDA CREEK, Washington   360 568 2389/568 2389
World-class Cabernet Sauvignon is made at this tiny western Washington winery. Skillfully blending fruit from various Washington vineyards, the winemaking team of Alex and Paul Golitzen creates a chewy, dense, well-balanced wine that ages gracefully.
Best wine ★★★ Cabernet Sauvignon ❢   **Best years** 1998, '97, '96, '95, '94

REX HILL VINEYARDS, Willamette Valley AVA, Oregon   503 538 0666/538 1409
Many wines are produced at Rex Hill Vineyards, but the best ones are the Pinot Gris and the Pinot Noir Reserve. Winemaker Lynn Penner-Ash has a skilled hand and selects fruit from the more than 250 acres managed by the winery.
Best wines ★★ Pinot Noir Reserve ❢, ★ Pinot Gris ♀
Best years ❢1998, '97, '96, '95; ♀1999, '98, '97

WILLAKENZIE ESTATE, Willamette Valley AVA, Oregon   503 662 3280/662 4829
WillaKenzie Estate is an ultra-modern, gravity-flow winery. The vineyards are densely planted with traditional varietal clones and newer, early-ripening ones. The results are fine Pinots vinified by Laurent Monthelieu, including a rare, delicately scented red Pinot Meunier. The Pinot Gris is very viscous and intense and the Pinot Blanc is one of the best in Oregon. All the wines should be drunk young with only a little aging.
Best wines ★★ Pinot Blanc ♀ and Pinot Meunier ❢ ★ Pinot Gris ♀
Best years ❢1998, '97, '96, '95; ♀1999, '98, '97

WOODWARD CANYON WINERY   ·   509 525 4129/522 0927
Walla Walla Valley AVA, Washington
Chardonnay is the leading varietal for this renowned Washington winery and the Celilo Vineyard blend, from grapes grown at 1000ft above sea level, is the best wine.
Best wines ★★ Chardonnay Celilo Vineyard ♀, Cabernet Sauvignon Artist Series ❢
Cabernet Sauvignon Dedication Series ❢ and Chardonnay ♀
Best years ❢1998, '97, '96, '95; ♀1999, '98, '97, '96, '95

KEN WRIGHT CELLARS, Willamette Valley AVA, Oregon   503 852 7070/852 7111
Ken Wright makes a broad range of varietal and single-vineyard wines in small quantities that can be difficult to find. Many wines are sold to clients as futures while they are still in barrel. His Chardonnay Celilo Vineyard (from Washington State fruit) is always first-rate. Pinot Noir Carter Vineyard is consistently good.
Best wines ★★ Chardonnay Celilo Vineyard ♀ and Pinot Noir Carter Vineyard ❢
Best years ❢1999, '98, '97, '96, '95; ♀1999, '98, '97

PACIFIC NORTHWEST VINTAGES

Washington and Oregon vineyards experience very different vintage conditions. Washington State has only modest weather fluctuations, whereas Oregon experiences severe swings in rainfall levels from year to year. Even in years when rain falls prior to harvest, Washington growers can usually wait a few days and let it pass. Oregon winemakers are learning to adapt to wet conditions and new viticultural practices and clonal selections are moderating the effects of wet weather.

Aging qualities

Crisp Northwest whites made from Riesling and Sauvignon Blanc are at their best young. Few, other than dessert-styles, age for more than 3 years. Washington and Oregon Chardonnays soften for 3–5 years but few have the balance to develop longer. Pinot Noir from Oregon comes in many varying styles. The fruit-driven, oaky, ripe styles are at their best within 5–7 years from vintage while the more delicate, balanced styles can often age gracefully for more than 10 years. Washington reds, particularly Cabernet Sauvignon, also vary but most improve for 8–10 years. To soften the new oak flavours, they should be held for 2–3 years before consumption.

Maturity charts _____
1998 was an excellent year in the Pacific Northwest. Washington enjoyed a long, hot summer followed by a long, warm harvest. Oregon also enjoyed a warm summer and mild harvest conditions. Many dark-coloured wines with opulent fruit were made.

1998 Washington State Cabernet Sauvignon

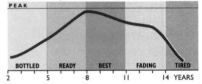

1998 Washington State/Oregon Chardonnay

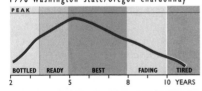

1998 Oregon Pinot Noir

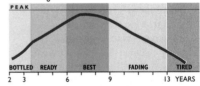

VINTAGE CHART

	99	98	97	96	95	94	93	92	91	90	89
OREGON											
Pinot Noir	9○	9○	5◐	7○	5●	9●	7●	9○	8◐	9●	8◐
Chardonnay	8○	8◐	5●	7◐	7◐	8●	7●	8◐	7◐	8◐	8◐
WASHINGTON STATE											
Cabernet (or Merlot)	8○	8○	8◐	8◐	7◐	9●	7◐	9●	8◐	7●	9◐
Chardonnay	8○	7◐	8◐	8◐	8●	8●	7◐	8◐	7◐	6◐	9◐

KEY ○ = needs more time ◐ = ready but will improve ● = at peak ◐ = fading or tired

VINTAGES AT A GLANCE

New clones and better site selection are enhancing the quality of the grapes in Oregon and Washington and as the weather patterns and conditions have become easier to predict, winemakers have learned to respond properly to conditions.

Great Years ★★★
Washington 1994, '89   Oregon 1999, '98, '94, '91
Good Years ★★
Washington 1999, '98, '97, '96, '95, '92, '91   Oregon 1996, '92, '89
Moderate Years ★
Washington 1993, '90   Oregon 1997, '95, '93, '90
Poor Years (No Stars)
1987 was the last really poor year.

Annual vintage reports

1999 Washington★★ Oregon★★★ Hot weather in the second half of the summer led to a record crop of well-ripened fruit in Washington and it was another excellent year in Oregon.

1998 Washington★★ Oregon★★★ In Washington El Niño was kind, giving good quality and a record crop size. Oregon had a tiny crop but potentially some really excellent Pinot Noir.

1997 Washington★★ Oregon★ The harvest was long and late in Washington, and overall the quality is promising. In Oregon only grapes grown in newer vineyards from early-ripening clones escaped the rain.

1996★★ A bitter freeze in early winter reduced crop levels severely in Washington. The resulting wines are intensely coloured and quite tannic. In Oregon, the harvest was marred by rain but many fine wines were made.

1995 Washington★★ Oregon★ Washington had a cool, wet summer but the autumn was sunny and warm. Merlot and Cabernet Sauvignon are well-balanced and complex. Oregon had a wet, difficult harvest and the Pinot Noirs are delicate and early maturing.

1994★★★ Both states had lower yields due to rain during flowering. Warm weather lasted from early summer through to harvest. Ripe, very extracted reds were made in Washington. Dark, opulent, blackberry-filled Pinot Noirs are the rule in Oregon. Many of the Chardonnays are age-worthy and both are at their peak.

1993★ Washington fared better than Oregon. The cool spring made for a long protracted harvest. Warm weather saved a difficult year. In Oregon, rain made conditions laborious. Talented winemakers made fine wines but many are tannic without the acidity for long aging.

1992★★ Early vintages in both Washington and Oregon. Dry, warm weather with intermittent rain made for large crops. Washington reds are fruit-forward and early maturing. Oregon Pinot Noirs were ripe, fruity wines that have lots of colour but will develop early.

1991 Washington★★ Oregon★★★ In Washington, the severely reduced crops from frozen winter conditions gave attractive wines. Oregon Pinots have fared well with aging, somewhat unexpectedly.

1990★★ The wines are round and soft but lack vibrant acidity for further aging.

1989 Washington★★★ Oregon★★ Low yields and extended, dry harvesting meant excellent wines. Washington reds have aged gracefully and will keep further. Oregon Pinot Noirs are at their prime.

NEW YORK STATE

New York State contains 3 fine wine regions – the fast-growing Long Island area, the large Finger Lakes and the historic Hudson River Valley. Bordeaux varieties fare well in the moderate climate of Long Island's North Fork and the Hamptons where Merlot and Cabernet Franc share top honours. The best vineyards of the cool-climate Finger Lakes region are clustered near Seneca, Keuka and Cayuga. Rieslings, Chardonnays, sparkling wines and hybrids are the specialities here, but Pinot Noir and Cabernet Franc have been coming on strong recently. Hudson River Valley, long noted for Seyval Blanc and Baco Noir, is now making impressive Cabernet Franc and Chardonnay.

WINE STYLES AND VINTAGES

Because New York's wine regions are so far apart they range widely in climate and therefore vintage generalizations are difficult to make. The erratic weather patterns of the East Coast can also pose ripeness problems. Low winter temperatures and slow growing seasons can ruin everything for growers in the Finger Lakes, whereas their colleagues in Long Island and Hudson River Valley worry about excessive humidity or heatwaves in the growing season. Hurricanes have ruined some vintages on Long Island, something few other premium wine regions have to face.

Vintage reports

The best recent vintages are 1999, '97 and '95. Made glorious by balmy September weather, 1997 is said to be the finest in 20 years. Though an undersized, slow-developing year, it produced superb, crisp white wines from the Finger Lakes and rich reds from Long Island.

Chardonnay

The style ranges from full-bodied, usually buttery and oaked flavours from the North Fork, to the crisp and medium-bodied Finger Lakes' version.

Best producers Bedell, Fox Run, GLENORA, HARGRAVE, Heron Hill, Knapp, LAMOREAUX LANDING, MILLBROOK, PALMER, Peconic Bay, Pellegrini, Pindar.
Best years 1999, '97, '95.

Merlot

It was a string of successful Long Island North Fork Merlot wines in the 1980s that made the world take notice of New York State. Red grapes benefit from Long Island's long growing season and the best Merlots from here, full of spice and blueberry, black cherry flavours, need no apology in the world of fine wine.
Best producers Bedell, HARGRAVE, LAMOREAUX LANDING, Lenz, PALMER, Pamanok, Peconic Bay, Pellegrini, Pindar.
Best years 1999, '97, '95.

Riesling

Riesling from the Finger Lakes, especially those wines finished on the dry side, can be superb. Lean and racy, they improve with 2–3 years, but are tempting to drink when first released.
Best producers Chateau LaFayette Reneau, Dr Konstantin Frank, GLENORA, Heron Hill, LAMOREAUX LANDING, Peconic Bay, Hermann J Wiemer.
Best years 1999, '97, '95.

A–Z OF NEW YORK STATE PRODUCERS

GLENORA WINE CELLARS, Finger Lakes District AVA   607 243 5511/243 5514
One of the largest and best producers of wines in the eastern US, Glenora established
vineyards along the steep slopes off Lake Seneca. Chardonnay, Riesling and Seyval
Blanc are annual successes. Using the Champagne method, Glenora has been turning
out a yeasty complex Brut Reserve that often ranks among the best in the New World.
Its opulent, beautifully balanced Riesling is hard to beat, and the Cayuga, a white
hybrid developed in New York, is excellent too.
Best wines ★ Pinot Gris ♀, Seyval Blanc ♀ and Brut Reserve ♀
Best years 1998, '97

HARGRAVE VINEYARD, North Fork AVA   516 734 5111/734 5485
The pioneering name in Long Island's fine wines, Hargrave planted vineyards in the
1970s. Some varieties felt more at home here than others. Today, Hargrave still offers
an exceptional Chardonnay in most vintages, along with Merlot and Cabernet Franc.
Alex Hargrave is now concentrating on Pinot Noir that should not be overlooked.
Best wines ★ Chardonnay ♀, Merlot ❢ Cabernet Franc ❢ and Pinot Noir ❢
Best years ❢1997, '96, '95, '94; ♀1998, '97, '96

LAMOREAUX LANDING, Finger Lakes District AVA   607 582 6011/582 6010
Working within a magnificent winery designed as a Greek revival building, owner
Mark Wagner grew up in a winemaking family and is now applying his expertise to a
fascinating array of often first-class wines. To date he has developed some 135 acres of
vineyards and though production is still in its infancy, it has quickly become one of the
most important East Coast wineries. The range of wines features a bold, oak-laced
Chardonnay Reserve, a firm but lovely Dry Riesling, steadily improving Pinot Noir
and Cabernet Franc and a limited amount of sparkling Blanc de Blancs.
Best wines ★★ Chardonnay Reserve ♀, ★ Dry Riesling ♀, Pinot Noir ❢ and Blanc de Blancs ♀
Best years ❢1998, '97, '96; ♀1998, '97, '96, '95

MILLBROOK VINEYARDS Hudson River Valley AVA   914 677 8383/677 6186
Millbrook is the Hudson Valley's flagship winery. Half its 50-acre vineyard is planted to
Chardonnay and there is also silky smooth Cabernet Franc and well-focussed Cabernet
Sauvignon. As half of the name behind the Smart-Dyson trellis system, part-owner
John Dyson knows something about grape-growing. Owning vineyards also in
California, he bought the WILLIAMS SELYEM winery in Sonoma County in 1998.
Best wines ★ Cabernet Franc ❢ and Cabernet Sauvignon ❢
Best years ❢1998, '97, '96; ♀1998, '97, '96, '95

PALMER VINEYARDS North Fork AVA   631 722 9463/631 5364
Relatively modern, high-tech and big by Long Island standards, Palmer has 90 acres of
vines located on an old country estate. It was among the first to offer eye-catching
Cabernet Sauvignon and Merlot, but more recently it has turned its attention to
Cabernet Franc, another success story in the making.
Best wines ★ Merlot Reserve ❢, Cabernet Franc ❢, Cabernet Sauvignon ❢ and Chardonnay
Reserve ♀
Best years ❢1999, '98, '97; ♀1998, '97, '96, '95

CANADA

Contrary to popular belief Canada's snow-covered, windswept landscape does thaw out annually and in 2 well-defined regions, separated by nearly 2000 miles, growing grapes for wine is a viable and increasingly thriving industry. In the west, British Columbia's main vineyard area is the Okanagan Valley, located approximately 180 miles inland from the coast. In central Canada Ontario's Niagara Peninsula clings to the southern edge of Lake Ontario, some 31 miles as the crow flies south of Toronto.

WINE STYLES

Both the Okanagan Valley and the Niagara Peninsula can lay claim to a range of different mesoclimates. Icewine is Canada's speciality and, unlike Germany, the other specialist producer of Icewine or Eiswein, the climate means that these intense concentrated dessert wines can be made every year.

White wines
British Columbia Pinot Blanc, Chardonnay, Riesling, Pinot Gris.
Best years 1999, '96, '95.
Ontario Chardonnay, Riesling (both sweet and dry) and Vidal for Icewine.
Best years 1999, '98, '97, '95, '93.

Red wines
British Columbia Pinot Noir, Merlot, Cabernet Sauvignon, Cabernet Franc.
Best years 1999, '98, '95.
Ontario Cabernet Franc, Merlot, Cabernet Sauvignon, Pinot Noir.
Best years 1999, '98, '97, '95, '93.

Top Canadian producers —————
BLUE MOUNTAIN, BURROWING OWL VINEYARDS, CAVE SPRING CELLARS, CedarCreek, CHATEAU DES CHARMES, Cilento Wines, Colio Estates Wines, Domaine de Chaberton, Domaine Combret, Gehringer Brothers, Gray Monk, Hainle Vineyards, HENRY OF PELHAM, Hillebrand (Andrès Wines), INNISKILLIN OKANAGAN, INNISKILLIN WINES, Jackson-Triggs Estate Winery, Kettle Valley, Konzelmann, Lakeview Cellars, Marynissen, MISSION HILL, Pillitteri, QUAILS' GATE, Pelee Island, Reif, Southbrook Farm, Stoney Ridge Cellars, Strewn Estate Winery, SUMAC RIDGE ESTATE WINERY, Summerhill Estate Winery, THIRTY BENCH WINERY, Tinhorn Creek Vineyards, Venturi-Schulze, Vineland Estates, Willow Heights.

GREAT CANADIAN WINES

Oz Clarke's selection
Chardonnay ♀ (Mission Hill) Canada's first world class Chardonnay, from the fast improving Okanagan Valley.
Late Harvest Riesling ♀ (Chateau des Charmes) Canada has quickly created a considerable reputation for sweet wines: this is excellent rich wine with a beguiling scent of white peaches.

Framboise ♀ (Southbrook Farm) Stunning sweet wine tasting of the purest essence of ripe raspberries. Not surprisingly as that's what it's made of!
Steven Spurrier's selection
Dry Riesling ♀ (Hainle Vineyards) An outstanding example of the vibrant, petrolly style of Riesling, from a tiny vineyard in Okanagan.

Vidal Icewine ♀ (Inniskillin Wines) This groundbreaking unctuous Icewine put Inniskillin, and Canada, on the international wine map in the late 1980s.
Gewürztraminer Reserve ♀ (Sumac Ridge) One of the very best Gewürztraminer wines made outside Alsace – this example is intensely aromatic, spicy and floral.

A–Z OF CANADIAN PRODUCERS

BLUE MOUNTAIN, Okanagan Valley, British Columbia   250 497 8244/497 6160

In just a few short years, owners Ian and Jane Mavety have established a reputation at Blue Mountain that places it among Canada's leading wine producers. The best efforts of Blue Mountain are concentrated on a handful of grapes led by Pinot Blanc, Pinot Gris and Pinot Noir.

Best wines ★★ Pinot Blanc ♀ and Pinot Noir Reserve ❢, ★ Pinot Gris ♀
Best years ❢1999, '98, '95; ♀1999, '98

BURROWING OWL VINEYARDS, Oliver, British Columbia   250 498 0620/498 0621

A new 28-acre winery, owned by a small number of partners in concert with Calona Wines, concentrates on Pinot Gris, Chardonnay, Merlot and Cabernet Sauvignon. Consulting winemaker Bill Dyer, formerly of Napa Valley's STERLING VINEYARDS, has done a masterful job with his first vintages and in particular with Pinot Gris.

Best wines ★★★ Pinot Gris ♀, ★★ Chardonnay ♀, ★ Merlot ❢
Best years 1999, '98, '97

CAVE SPRING CELLARS, Niagara Peninsula, Ontario   905 562 3581/562 3232

Founder and president Leonard Pennachetti, along with winemaker Angelo Pavari, are making first-rate Riesling, Chardonnay and late-harvest wines, including one of the region's best Riesling Icewines.

Best wines ★★ Late Harvest Chardonnay Musqué ♀, Late Harvest Riesling Indian Summer ♀ and Riesling Icewine ♀, ★ Chardonnay Reserve ♀
Best years 1999, '98, '96, '95, '94

CHATEAU DES CHARMES, Niagara Peninsula, Ontario   905 262 4219/262 5548

Owner Paul Bosc is one of the fathers of the modern-day Ontario wine industry. Chateau des Charmes' two key vineyards, Paul Bosc Estate and St David's Bench, are responsible for many outstanding wines.

Best wines ★★★ St David's Bench Vineyard Cabernet Franc ❢ and St David's Bench Vineyard Chardonnnay ♀, ★★ Paul Bosc Vineyard Cabernet Franc ❢, Paul Bosc Vineyard Chardonnay ♀ and Riesling Icewine ♀, ★ Merlot ❢ and Late Harvest Riesling ♀
Best years ❢1999, '98, '97, '95; ♀1998, '97, '96, '95, '94

HENRY OF PELHAM FAMILY ESTATE WINERY   905 684 8423/684 8444

Niagara Peninsula, Ontario

Winemaker Ron Giesbrecht is a fan of concentrated wines from low-yielding vines. Among the whites Chardonnay and Riesling shine, as does his Cabernet/Merlot blend.

Best wines ★★★ Riesling Icewine ♀, ★★ Proprietor's Reserve Chardonnay ♀ and Cabernet/ Merlot ❢, ★ Barrel-Fermented Chardonnay ♀ and Select Late Harvest Riesling ♀
Best years ❢1999, '98, '97, '95; ♀1999, '98, '97, '95

INNISKILLIN OKANAGAN, Oliver, British Columbia   250 498 6663/498 4566

Ontario vintners Donald Ziraldo and Karl Kaiser set up Inniskillin Okanagan in 1994. Their 22-acre Dark Horse Vineyard is the source for fine red and white Meritage blend, Chardonnay, Pinot Blanc, Gewürztraminer and some terrific Icewine.

Best wines ★★ Dark Horse Vineyard Meritage Red ❢ and Pinot Blanc ♀, ★ Chardonnay ♀
Best years ❢1999, '98, '97, '95; ♀1999, '98, '97, '95

INNISKILLIN WINES, Niagara-on-the-Lake, Ontario   416 468 2187/468 5355
Inniskillin co-founders Donald Ziraldo and Karl Kaiser established Canada's first estate winery in 1975. Winemaker Karl Kaiser concentrates on Pinot Noir, Chardonnay and an outstanding Icewine that caused the world to sit up and take note of Ontario wines for the first time. All the grapes come from the estate's own 120 acres of vineyards or from a handful of specially selected growers on the Niagara Peninsula. A pair of wines that have met with great success are Alliance Chardonnay and Alliance Pinot Noir.
Best wines ★★★ Vidal Icewine, ★★ Alliance Chardonnay ♀, ★ Pinot Noir Reserve ▮ and Alliance Pinot Noir ▮
Best years ▮1998, '97, '95, '94; ♀1999, '98, '97, '95, '94; **Icewine** 1999, '98, '97, '95, '94, '92, '89

MISSION HILL WINERY, Okanagan Valley, British Columbia   250 768 7611/768 2044
The arrival of Kiwi winemaker John Simes coincides with the dramatic rise in quality at Mission Hill. Simes has developed a series of intense, highly flavoured varietal wines that include excellent Chardonnay, Merlot/Cabernet and Pinot Noir.
Best wines ★★ Grand Reserve Chardonnay ♀ and Grand Reserve Merlot/Cabernet ▮, ★ Grand Reserve Pinot Noir ▮
Best years 1998, '97, '96, '95; ♀1999, '98, '97, '95, '94

QUAILS' GATE ESTATE WINERY   250 769 4451/769 3451
Okanagan Valley, British Columbia
Two Australian winemakers, Jeff Martin and Peter Draper, are the force behind this respected central Okanagan winery. As well as Burgundian-style Pinot Noir and Chardonnay, under a Limited Release label and in tiny quantities under the new Family Reserve designation, there is also a good Shiraz-style blockbuster, called Old Vines Foch.
Best wines ★★ Family Reserve Chardonnay ♀ and Family Pinot Noir ▮, ★ Limited Release Chardonnay ♀ and Old Vines Foch ▮
Best years ▮1998, '97, '96, '95, '94; ♀1999, '98, '97

SUMAC RIDGE ESTATE WINERY,   250 494 0451/494 3456
Summerland, British Columbia
Sumac Ridge is known for its mostly varietal wines, led by one of the valley's finest Gewürztraminer Reserves, and one of the country's best Champagne-method sparklers, Steller's Jay Brut, with crisp, apple/lemon fruit. Recent expansion in the warmer south Okanagan Valley has produced a promising red and white Meritage blend and a very fine Merlot.
Best wines ★★★ Merlot ▮, ★★ Meritage Red ▮, Meritage White ♀ and Steller's Jay Brut, ★ Gewürztraminer Reserve ♀
Best years ▮1998, '97, '96, '95; ♀1999, '98, '96, '95, '94

THIRTY BENCH WINERY, Niagara Peninsula, Ontario   905 563 1698/563 3921
Thirty Bench is a relative newcomer in Ontario but tiny amounts of serious Bordeaux-style reds have placed it firmly among the region's finest producers. Low yields and deft use of new oak makes this a winery to watch. 80% of the production is Riesling based.
Best wines ★★★ Cabernet Franc ▮, ★★ Merlot ▮ and Reserve Blend ▮
Best years ▮1998, '97, '95; ♀1999, '98, '97, '96

SOUTH AMERICA

While both Chile and Argentina have produced a number of wines of exceptional value for some time, premium wines of international standing are only just beginning to emerge. With greater political stability, both countries are successfully luring both investors and expertise from leading wine countries, particularly France and the USA.

Chile

Chile's geographical isolation and phylloxera-free conditions are often cited as reasons for her exciting potential. Yet this potential remained unrealized until relatively recently. Major improvements in both vinification and viticulture have now taken place at numerous estates.

Argentina

As the world's fifth-largest producer Argentina's wine production is on a considerably larger scale than Chile's. Many of the wine companies are large and their reputations rest on simple, everyday wines. Like Chile, Argentina is dependent on irrigation from the snow-melt of the Andes. As in Chile, most vineyard yields remain too high for exceptional flavours, though fine for good, juicy everyday stuff.

Wine styles

Chile has transformed a considerable portion of its area under vine to Cabernet Sauvignon, Merlot, Chardonnay or Sauvignon Blanc with nearly all its fine wines produced from these international varieties. In contrast, Argentina has the

GREAT SOUTH AMERICAN WINES

Oz Clarke's selection

Gold Reserve Cabernet Sauvignon ❢ (Carmen) Outstanding example of juicy, sweet blackcurrant and Cabernet fruit made complex and exciting with chocolate, herbs and tannin.

Cadus Malbec ❢ (Nieto y Senetiner) Outstanding red from Argentina's top grape, bursting with black cherry and black plum fruit yet holding on to a divine perfume.

Fabre Montmayou Grand Vin ❢ (Dom. Vistalba) French-inspired red of tremendous power but succulent fruit and delightful mint and cedar perfume.

Triple 'C' ❢ (Santa Rita) Based on Cabernet Franc but with some Cabernet Sauvignon and Carmenère

this is powerful, intense and wonderfully ripe.

20 Barrels Merlot ❢ (Cono Sur) Merlot is supposed to be soft, ripe and desperately approachable. This top example fills the role perfectly.

Santa Isabel Barrel-Fermented Chardonnay ♀ (Viña Casablanca) Excellent Chardonnay from Chile's Casablanca Valley, with syrupy richness, toasty oak and refreshing acidity.

Steven Spurrier's selection

Alpha Chardonnay ♀ (Montes) A barrel-fermented wine from a single estate with some 50-year-old vines.

Santa Isabel Estate Sauvignon Blanc ♀ (Viña Casablanca) Chile's first Sauvignon Blanc to combine ripe fruit with lively acidity.

Merlot Cuvée Alexandre ❢ (Casa Lapostolle) With old vines and Pomerol's Michel Rolland as consultant, this dark, luscious wine is Chile's best Merlot.

Don Melchor Private Reserve Cabernet Sauvignon ❢ (Concha y Toro) A dense Cabernet, packed with ripe fruit and with fine aging potential.

Casa Real Cabernet Sauvignon ❢ (Santa Rita) Behind the elegant label lies a deep-flavoured Cabernet, with minty overtones and fine use of new oak.

Cabernet Sauvignon ❢ (Weinert) Established over a century ago, this winery still produces the most dense, longest-lived Argentinian Cabernet Sauvignon.

capacity to produce a wider range of wines from long-established varieties which include Malbec, Sangiovese, Tempranillo and Syrah as well as Cabernet Sauvignon, Chardonnay, Chenin and Torrontes.

Cabernet Sauvignon

Undoubtedly Cabernet makes the greatest number of top wines in Chile, partly because of its inherent classiness and partly because of its great adaptability. At the top level the wines display a rich pure blackcurrant fruit, now with additional depth and complexity.

Chardonnay

The best Chardonnay now has greater complexity, concentration and structure than early, tropical-fruited examples.

Malbec

This variety is more associated with Argentina than Chile but some outstanding reds with a spicy black fruit depth are produced in both.

Merlot

Though many wines sold as Merlot are in fact from Carmenère, the number of rich, ripe plummy Merlot wines is increasing.

Pinot Noir

A few wines have already illustrated Chile's true potential with this variety and others are sure to emerge from new plantings in cooler areas like the Casablanca Valley.

Sauvignon Blanc

For a long time Chilean Sauvignon Blanc was lousy – the vineyards were actually planted with Sauvignonasse. However, new true Sauvignon Blanc from Casablanca delivers a range of intense ripe flavours underpinned by a zingy acidity.

Main wine areas

CHILE

1 Aconcagua Valley	5 Curicó Valley
2 Casablanca Valley	6 Maule Valley
3 Maipo Valley	7 Itata Valley
4 Rapel Valley	8 Bio-Bio Valley

Top South American producers _____

Cabernet Sauvignon and Bordeaux blends
Caliterra, Canepa, CARMEN, CASA LAPOSTOLLE, CATENA (Alta), CONCHA Y TORO (Almaviva), Cousiño Macul, Dom. Paul Bruno, Echeverría, ERRÁZURIZ, Montes (Alpha), Norton (Privada), La Rosa, Santa Rita (Casa Real), Tarapacá, WEINERT.

Other red blends Tarapacá (Milenium), VALDIVIESO (Caballo Loco).

Chardonnay CASA LAPOSTOLLE, CATENA (Alta), CONCHA Y TORO, ERRÁZURIZ, Montes (Montes Alpha), VILLARD, VIÑA CASABLANCA.

Malbec CATENA (Alta), Nieto y Senetiner (Cadus), VALDIVIESO, Fabre Montmayou (Grand Vin), WEINERT.

Merlot CARMEN, CASA LAPOSTOLLE, CONCHA Y TORO, ERRÁZURIZ, Tarapacá, VALDIVIESO.

Pinot Noir CONO SUR, VALDIVIESO.

Sauvignon Blanc CASA LAPOSTOLLE, VILLARD, VIÑA CASABLANCA.

South American vintages

A number of premium wines are now being made from grapes grown in more marginal areas with greater climate variation. These wines increasingly reflect the differences between vintages.

However, modern winemaking techniques and greater certainty about weather conditions during the growing season than in many European wine regions mean that the reputation of the producer is generally more important than the vintage.

In general, Sauvignon Blanc and Torrontes should be drunk within a year of the vintage but Chardonnay will take 2–4 years' aging. Merlot and Malbec are best with 2–6 years, while the top Cabernet Sauvignon or Cabernet-based wines do develop over 3–5 years and can keep for a decade despite generally being extremely attractive at only a year or so old.

A–Z OF SOUTH AMERICAN PRODUCERS

CARMEN, Maipo Valley, Chile   02 331 5322/331 5324

A subsidiary of the large Santa Rita, this streamlined operation has maintained a consistently higher standard than its parent company. The reds are best (especially the Medalla Real or Gold label range) but the white wines have always been well made.
Best wines ★ Reserve Merlot ♀ and Gold Reserve Cabernet Sauvignon ♀
Best years 1998, '97, '96

CASA LAPOSTOLLE, Rapel Valley, Chile   02 242 9774/234 4536

A relatively new undertaking between two wine families – one French, the other Chilean. International winemaking star Michel Rolland has helped in the production of the intense, structured Cuvée Alexandre wines which have further raised expectations of quality in Chilean wine. Clos Apalta is a new premium red wine.
Best wines ★★ Merlot Cuvée Alexandre ♀, Chardonnay Cuvée Alexandre ♀ and Sauvignon Blanc ♀, ★ Merlot ♀ and Chardonnay ♀
Best years ♀1999, '98, '97, '96, '95

CATENA, Mendoza, Argentina   01 723 0867/723 0869

Dr Nicolas Catena has invested hugely in his top-of-the-range wines, though his cheaper offerings are less reliable. All 3 flagship wines are fabulously concentrated.
Best wines ★★ Catena Alta Chardonnay (from 1995) ♀, Catena Alta Malbec (from 1996) ♀ and Catena Alta Cabernet Sauvignon (from 1994) ♀
Best years 1999, '97, '96, '95

CONCHA Y TORO, Maipo Valley, Chile   02 556 7882/551 1961

One of the giants of the Chilean wine industry and now probably its leader – such is the high quality found in its premium wines: the good-value Trio range (Chardonnay, Cabernet Sauvignon and Merlot), the Explorer range (smoky Cabernet/ Syrah, lush Pinot Noir and rustic Malbec) and the Toro Terrunyo range which places more emphasis on specific vineyard origins. Almaviva is the new super-premium Bordeaux-style red jointly made with Ch. MOUTON-ROTHSCHILD. Don Melchor Cabernet Sauvignon shows a depth and richness we should see more often in Chilean reds.
Best wines ★★ Don Melchor Private Reserve Cabernet Sauvignon ♀ and Almaviva ♀
Best years 1998, '97, '96, '95, '93, '92, '91

CONO SUR, Rapel Valley, Chile   02 203 6100/203 6732
Owned by CONCHA Y TORO, this name is synonymous with good Chilean Pinot
Noir. While the standard example is more a high-quality quaffer, the Reserve and 20
Barrels wines add more structure, complexity and perfume.
Best wines ★ Pinot Noir Casablanca Reserve ❢ and Cabernet Sauvignon Special Selection ❢
Best years Pinot Noir 1999, '98, '97, '96; **Cabernet Sauvignon** 1999, '98, '97, '96, '95
ERRÁZURIZ, Aconcagua Valley, Chile   02 203 6688/02 203 6689
A winery that built a reputation in the 1990s under New Zealander Brian Bicknell is
now in the hands of talented Californian Ed Flaherty (ex-CONO SUR). Though one of
the leading Chilean Merlot producers, Errázuriz's best red is the Don Maximiano
Cabernet Sauvignon. New and overpriced Seña, a ripe, supple, Cabernet-based
Bordeaux blend, is the result of a joint venture with MONDAVI of California.
Best wines ★★ Don Maximiano Cabernet Sauvignon ❢ and Merlot Reserve ❢, ★ Chardonnay
Reserve la Escultura ♀
Best years Cabernet 1998, '97, '96, '95, '94, '93, '92; **Merlot** 1999, '97, '96, '95; **Chardonnay**
1998, '97
VALDIVIESO, Curicó Valley, Chile   02 238 2511/238 2383
A rising star in Chile for succulent juicy reds from Cabernet Sauvignon, Merlot,
Malbec and Cabernet Franc. Reserve versions can seem over-oaked but the intensity of
fruit should win the day in most cases. Exciting new wines include Caballo Loco, a non-
vintage, multi-varietal blend. Wines are sold in the USA under the Stonelake label.
Best wines ★ Malbec Reserva ❢, Merlot Reserva ❢, Cabernet Franc Reserva ❢, Pinot Noir
Reserva and Caballo Loco ❢
Best years 1999, '98, '97, '96
VILLARD, Casablanca Valley, Chile   02 220 2120/229 4459
Frenchman Thierry Villard's operation is one of Chile's exciting new white-wine
producers. Based in Casablanca Valley, he also produces good Pinot Noir and Merlot
from the Cachapoal Valley in the Maipo.
Best wines ★ Sauvignon Blanc ♀ and Chardonnay Reserve ♀
Best years 1999, '98, '97, '96
VIÑA CASABLANCA, Casablanca Valley, Chile   02 238 2855/238 0307
This winery has come to epitomize the quality and further potential of the Casablanca
Valley thanks at least in part to the winemaker, Ignacio Recabarren. Besides fine
examples of the usual Chilean styles, especially complex, grassy Sauvignon, there is also
the country's best Gewürztraminer.
Best wines ★ Sauvignon Blanc Santa Isabel Estate ♀, Cabernet Sauvignon El Bosque Estate ❢
and Barrel-Fermented Chardonnay Santa Isabel Estate ♀
Best years 1999, '98, '97, '96
WEINERT, Mendoza, Argentina   061 96 0409/01 812 1255
Now part-owned by Nicolas CATENA, this winery has long produced Argentina's most
renowned reds. These powerful, slightly old-fashioned (aged for long periods in old
oak) but extremely age-worthy reds are well worth seeking out from older vintages.
Best wines ★★ Malbec ❢, Cabernet Sauvignon ❢ and Cavas de Weinert ❢
Best years ❢1999, '97, '95, '94, '93, '91, '90, '89, '88, '85, '83, '79, '77

AUSTRALIA

Australia's initial venture into international markets featured ripe, fruity varietal wines with distinctive mouthfilling sweetness and the aroma of new oak. Where companies like Rosemount led the way, others soon followed and recently there has been a definite consumer shift towards finer wines. Technical innovation has gone hand in hand with superior winemaking techniques, yielding wines which can challenge some of the great classics of the Old World. Where Penfolds Grange Hermitage was once the only Australian wine sought by collectors, today there is a whole galaxy of stars.

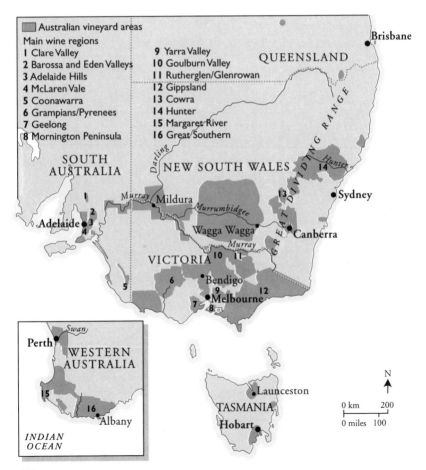

Australian vineyard areas

Main wine regions
1 Clare Valley
2 Barossa and Eden Valleys
3 Adelaide Hills
4 McLaren Vale
5 Coonawarra
6 Grampians/Pyrenees
7 Geelong
8 Mornington Peninsula
9 Yarra Valley
10 Goulburn Valley
11 Rutherglen/Glenrowan
12 Gippsland
13 Cowra
14 Hunter
15 Margaret River
16 Great Southern

GREAT AUSTRALIAN WINES

Oz Clarke's selection

Grange ! (Penfolds) The stupendously complex, thrillingly rich red wine that not only led the way for the Australian wine industry, but for most of the New World.

Aberfeldy Shiraz ! (Tim Adams) Massive Shiraz from 100-year-old vines in the Clare Valley.

Mount Edelstone ! (Henschke) The Henschke family have some of the oldest vines in Australia; Mount Edelstone Shiraz vines yield sumptuous perfumed reds.

Piccadilly Chardonnay ! (Grosset) Jeffrey Grosset is a brilliant creator of top Riesling but his touch with Chardonnay is, if possible, even better.

Stonewell ! (Peter Lehmann) Supercharged Shiraz, created from some of Barossa's finest old vineyards.

Noble One ♀ (de Bortoli) Brilliant noble-rot Semillon that can equal any of the great sweet wines of the world.

Pirie ♀ (Piper's Brook) New and thrilling addition to the Aussie fizz portfolio from Tasmania's top producer.

Vat One Semillon ♀ (Tyrrell's) A true Hunter Valley original; lean and reserved at first, the wine builds up to a parade of quince, nuts and cream after 10 years' aging.

Hill of Gold ! (Rosemount) Mudgee has long been touted as a top vineyard region but has lacked star winemakers. Hill of Gold Shiraz and Cabernet are proof that Rosemount can fill the gap.

The Patriarch ! (David Wynn) Consistently superb Shiraz from cool Eden Valley vineyards, rich hot pepper and perfectly balanced.

Semillon ♀ (Mount Horrocks) Wonderfully scented version of Semillon from one of Clare Valley's top young talents.

Steven Spurrier's selection

Semillon-Sauvignon ♀ (Cape Mentelle) A superb blend of liveliness and ripeness, with a good potential for aging.

Chardonnay ♀ (Leeuwin Estate) A magnificently richly fruity, complex wine, from an estate dedicated to the absolute peak of quality.

Chardonnay ♀ (Petaluma) Brian Croser (with Len Evans) is Australia's best ambassador for fine wine, making his own

brilliant Chardonnay from Distinguished Vineyard Sites.

Riesling ♀ (Petaluma) Dry but packed with fruit and possessing wonderful length, this wine has inspired a Riesling renaissance.

Old Liqueur Muscat ♀ (Chambers) Perhaps the greatest fortified Muscat in the world, a nectar based on very old wood-matured stocks.

Shiraz ! (Cape Mentelle) A superbly concentrated wine, backed by the elegance found in all David Hohnen's wines.

Reserve Pinot Noir ! (Coldstream Hills) The Burgundian influence is clear in James Halliday's polished and complex Pinot Noir.

Eileen Hardy's Shiraz ! (Hardy) A very intense Shiraz, built for long aging.

Cabernet Sauvignon ! (Leeuwin Estate) A powerful, fruity Cabernet, possessing all the elegance and class expected from this superb estate.

Basket Press Shiraz ! (Rockford) Superbly intense Shiraz made from 100-year-old vines and made in the same way as it would have been a century ago.

Dry Red No 1 ! (Yarra Yering) This idiosyncratic, Cabernet-based wine comes from the exceptional vineyard owned by Dr Bailey Carrodus.

Appellations and classifications

In a country so keen on inter-regional blending, appellation control is unknown except in Mudgee and Tasmania and there it is more a guarantee of authenticy than a guide to quality. The Label Integrity Program (LIP) guarantees all claims made on labels. The Geographical Indications (GIs) committee is finally clarifying zones, regions and sub-regions – albeit with plenty of lively debate. One useful development has been the concept of 'Distinguished Vineyard Sites', along the lines of the Bordeaux classifications, which should help to establish the Australian equivalent of French terroir.

LANGTON'S CLASSIFICATION

This Classification of Australia's most distinguished wines is widely accepted in the trade as a useful and authoritative guide. It was first conceived in 1990 to assist wine auctioneers. Wines must have been produced over a period of at least 10 years with a record of quality and reliability during that time.

Exceptional Penfolds Bin 95 Grange Shiraz 🍷; Henschke 'Hill of Grace' Shiraz 🍷; Mount Mary 'Quintet' Cabernets 🍷; Leeuwin Estate 'Art Series' Chardonnay ♀; Moss Wood Cabernet Sauvignon 🍷; Penfolds Bin 707 Cabernet Sauvignon 🍷; Wendouree Shiraz 🍷.

Outstanding Bannockburn Pinot Noir 🍷; Jim Barry 'The Armagh' Shiraz 🍷; Bass Phillip 'Premium' Pinot Noir 🍷; Brokenwood 'Graveyard Vineyard' Shiraz 🍷; Cape Mentelle Cabernet Sauvignon 🍷; Cullen Cabernet/Merlot 🍷; Dalwhinnie Shiraz 🍷; Giaconda Chardonnay ♀; Giaconda Pinot Noir 🍷; Grosset 'Polish Hill' Riesling ♀; Henschke 'Cyril Henschke' Cabernet Sauvignon 🍷 and 'Mount Edelstone' Shiraz 🍷; Jasper Hill 'Emily's Paddock' Shiraz/Cabernet Franc 🍷 and 'Georgia's Paddock' Shiraz 🍷; Mount Mary Pinot Noir 🍷; Pierro Chardonnay ♀; Rockford 'Basket Press' Shiraz 🍷; Tahbilk '1860 Vines' Shiraz 🍷; Wendouree Cabernet/Malbec 🍷; Wendouree Cabernet Sauvignon 🍷, Shiraz/Malbec 🍷 and Wendouree Shiraz/Mataro 🍷; Yarra Yering 'Dry Red No.1' Cabernet 🍷; Yeringberg Cabernet Blend 🍷.

Excellent Bannockburn Chardonnay ♀; Barossa Valley Estate 'E & E' Black Pepper Shiraz 🍷; Coriole 'Lloyd Reserve' Shiraz 🍷; Craiglee Shiraz 🍷; Dalwhinnie Cabernet 🍷; De Bortoli 'Noble One' Botrytis Semillon ♀; Elderton Command Shiraz 🍷; Grosset 'Watervale' Riesling ♀; Hardy's 'Eileen Hardy' Shiraz 🍷; Howard Park Cabernet/Merlot 🍷; Irvine Grand Merlot 🍷; Joseph 'Moda Amarone' Cabernet/Merlot 🍷; Lake's Folly 'White Label' Cabernet 🍷; Peter

Lehmann 'Stonewell' Shiraz 🍷; Charles Melton 'Nine Popes' Shiraz/ Grenache/ Mourvèdre 🍷; Mount Langi Ghiran Langi Shiraz 🍷; Mount Mary Chardonnay ♀; Penfolds Bin 389 Cabernet/Shiraz 🍷; Penfolds St Henri 🍷; Petaluma Chardonnay ♀, Coonawarra 🍷 and Riesling ♀; Redbank 'Sally's Paddock' Cabernet/ Shiraz/Cabernet Franc/Merlot 🍷; St Hallett 'Old Block' Shiraz 🍷; Tyrrell's Vat 47 Pinot Chardonnay ♀ and Vat 1 Semillon ♀; Wolf Blass 'Black Label' Cabernet Blend 🍷; Wynn's Coonawarra Estate 'John Riddoch' Cabernet Sauvignon 🍷; Yarra Yering 'Dry Red No.2' Shiraz 🍷.

Distinguished Bowen Estate Cabernet Sauvignon 🍷 and Shiraz 🍷; Cape Mentelle Chardonnay ♀; Cape Mentelle Shiraz 🍷; Coldstream Hills Reserve Chardonnay ♀ and Reserve Pinot Noir 🍷; Cullen Chardonnay ♀; Katnook Estate Cabernet Sauvignon 🍷; Lake's Folly 'Yellow Label' Chardonnay ♀; Leconfield Cabernet Sauvignon 🍷; Leeuwin Estate 'Art Series' Cabernet Sauvignon 🍷;Lindemans 'Limestone Ridge Vineyard' Shiraz/Cabernet 🍷, 'Pyrus' Cabernet 🍷 and 'St. George' Cabernet Sauvignon 🍷; Mountadam Chardonnay ♀; Orlando 'Lawsons' Shiraz 🍷 and 'St Hugo' Cabernet Sauvignon 🍷; Penfolds 'Magill Estate' Shiraz 🍷; Piper's Brook Vineyard Riesling ♀; Plantagenet Cabernet Sauvignon 🍷; Seppelt 'Dorrien' Cabernet Sauvignon 🍷; Seppelt 'Great Western Vineyard' Shiraz 🍷; Taltarni Cabernet Sauvignon 🍷; Tyrrell's Vat 9 Shiraz 🍷; Vasse Felix Cabernet Sauvignon 🍷; Virgin Hills Cabernet-Shiraz 🍷; Wynn's Coonawarra Estate Cabernet Sauvignon 🍷; Xanadu Cabernet Reserve 🍷; Yarra Yering Pinot Noir 🍷.

The distance between vineyards in the Hunter Valley in New South Wales and those in the Margaret River in Western Australia is approximately 3900km and there is now a very clear movement towards regionality and the concept of 'Distinguished Vineyard Sites'.

New South Wales

HUNTER VALLEY SEMILLON

These are some of the lower-alcohol wines produced in Australia; the best are invariably unoaked. When young, they show herbaceous, tropical fruit aromas, quite lean palates and good acid back bone. The aging process sees these wines develop remarkably. The primary aromas give way to a complex, honeyed, straw-like bouquet. The palate fleshes out with concentrated flavours, apparent custard and pastry sweetness, cutting acid and great length. This is a much misunderstood wine favoured by passionate wine enthusiasts.

Best producers Brokenwood, LINDEMANS, MCWILLIAMS, ROTHBURY ESTATE, TYRRELL'S.

Best years 1999, '98, '95, '91, '89, '87, '86.

HUNTER VALLEY SHIRAZ

Hunter Valley Shiraz used to be seen as the great classic wine of Australia but its reputation has been somewhat tarnished over the years as the region has become more commercialized. Brokenwood, TYRRELL'S, Tamburlaine, ROTHBURY ESTATE and other producers are doing much to win back the confidence of fine wine buyers. The early leaders, LINDEMANS and MCWILLIAMS, after a rather dull performance in the last decade, are making a comeback too. Classic Hunter Valley Shiraz shows a complex plummy earthy-leathery bouquet with concentrated flavours, plenty of fruit sweetness, ripe tannins and length. The term 'sweaty saddle' has often been used to describe old Hunter Shirazes. Recent classics are the 1986 Brokenwood Graveyard Shiraz and the 1987 and 1991 Tyrrell's Vat 9.

Best producers Brokenwood, LINDEMANS, MCWILLIAMS, ROTHBURY ESTATE, Tamburlaine, Tullochs, TYRRELL'S.

Best years 1998, '96, '95, '93, '91, '89, '87.

HUNTER VALLEY CHARDONNAY

A plethora of styles from the innocuous to the refined; from the rich and unctuous, deep yellow, oaky styles to the tightly structured and beautifully defined TYRRELL'S Vat 47. ROSEMOUNT Show Reserve is a fine wine with excellent varietal definition, fruit sweetness and balance. LAKE'S FOLLY can be Burgundian and excellent. Cork taint problems in the early 1990s have been no help to this producer.

Best producers Brokenwood, LAKE'S FOLLY, LINDEMANS, Peterson's, ROSEMOUNT, Scarborough, Tamburlaine, TYRRELL'S.

Best years 1999, '97, '96, '95, '94, '91.

Victoria

GRAMPIANS/
PYRENEES SHIRAZ

These Shiraz wines show immense pepper and spice aromas and massive fruit concentration with quite finely structured tannins. They often develop meaty/gamy bouquets and silken palates. There are, however, various styles. In the Pyrenees

District the philosophy is for more restrained, structured wines. The Taltarni Shiraz is quite Rhône-like with very intense ripe blackberry and raspberry aromas, indelible acidity and pronounced tannins. Over time, the wine will develop quite a prune, licorice and earth bouquet and the palate will soften out. Trevor Mast at MOUNT LANGI GHIRAN is producing quintessential Australian cool-climate Shiraz with intense peppery/spice aromas, fine tannins, concentration and pure plum fruit.

Best producers Dalwhinnie, Mount Ida, MOUNT LANGI GHIRAN, SEPPELT, Summerfield, Taltarni.

Best years 1998, '97, '95, '94, '93, '92.

HEATHCOTE/GOULBURN VALLEY SHIRAZ

Jasper Hill, at Heathcote, produces a Shiraz that is concentrated and oak-driven. These are very complex ripe plummy, meaty wines with abundant fruit, ripe tannins and concentration. Chateau Tahbilk's 1820 Old Vines is produced in limited quantities but shows extraordinary earthy mulberry aromas, structured tannins and pronounced acid. Both of these wines benefit from age. The Jasper Hill wines, because of their ripe fruit expression, are appealing when young, whereas Tahbilk 1820 wines are hard and tannic when young, but soften out over a period of time.

Best producers Chateau Tahbilk, Jasper Hill, Mitchelton.

Best years 1998, '97, '95, '94, '93, '92.

RUTHERGLEN MUSCAT AND TOKAY (MUSCADELLE)

These opulent and sensuous fortified wines or 'stickies' come from North-East Victoria where there are no maritime breezes and the grapes really do bake in the heat, often reaching 20°–22° of potential alcohol. They are blended from several vintages and often some of the base wine will be as old as 50 or 60 years. These are phenomenal wines which will bring joy to any serious wine lover with their rich 'rancio' aromas and decadently luscious flavours.

Best producers All Saints, Bailey's, Brown Brothers, Buller and Son, Campbells, CHAMBERS, MORRIS, Rosewood.

YARRA VALLEY CABERNET

The beautiful Yarra Valley, with its rolling hills and splendid vistas, is a landscape that delights the painter's eye. It is a very old wine region, first developed in the 1850s and after many years of decline, it has emerged as an important producer of Cabernet Sauvignon. The idiosyncratic trio of Dr John Middleton from MOUNT MARY, Dr Bailey Carrodus from Yarra Yering and a more recent arrival in the form of James Halliday at COLDSTREAM HILLS reflect the range of Cabernet styles in the region today.

Best producers COLDSTREAM HILLS, DE BORTOLI, MOUNT MARY, Oakridge, Yarra Yering, Yeringberg.

Best years 1998, '97, '94, '91, '90, '88.

YARRA VALLEY PINOT NOIR

Not at all hot by Australian standards, the Yarra Valley is emerging as a new classic region for the finicky, cool-climate Pinot Noir. MOUNT MARY and Yarra Yering have been making Pinot Noir for years and the wines are quite individual – the Mount Mary is more mainstream, showing good fruit definition and purity, whereas Yarra Yering is a highly concentrated style. COLDSTREAM HILLS, DE BORTOLI, Yarra Ridge, and Tarrawarra all make Pinot Noir wines that have an enthralling Burgundian quality.

Best producers COLDSTREAM HILLS, DE BORTOLI, Diamond Valley, MOUNT

MARY, Tarrawarra, Yarra Ridge, Yarra Yering.

Best years 1998, '97, '96, '94.

MELBOURNE DRESS CIRCLE CHARDONNAY

Without question, some of the most seductive and beautifully made Chardonnays in Australia come from around Melbourne, in the Yarra Valley, Geelong and the Mornington Peninsula. Comparisons with the great white wines of Burgundy would not be out of place. The best producers make classically proportioned Chardonnay with complex cashew nut, tropical fruit aromas and plenty of vanillin (new oak). The palate is richly textured with layer upon layer of flavour. The kings of Chardonnay are Bannockburn in Geelong and COLDSTREAM HILLS (particularly the Reserve wine) in the Yarra Valley. MOUNT MARY makes a controversial style that is less fruit-oriented, but with an important following. Mornington Peninsula, on the easternside of Port Phillip Bay, is one of Australia's coolest wine regions and the climate is about as reliable as Burgundy's – often failing to ripen the fruit adequately. Sugaring is not an option in Australia, so producers frequently struggle.

Best producers (Geelong) Bannockburn , Clyde Park, Scotchman's Hill; (Mornington Peninsula) Mooruduc, Massoni, Main Ridge; (Yarra Valley) COLDSTREAM HILLS, DE BORTOLI, MOUNT MARY, Tarrawarra, Yeringberg.

Best years 1998, '97, '94, '93, '91.

South Australia

COONAWARRA CABERNET SAUVIGNON

Coonawarra is one of the classic Cabernet regions and has been described as the Médoc of the Southern Hemisphere – a good description as these wines can taste disarmingly like red Bordeaux when young – highly perfumed with striking blackcurrant/licorice, cedary fruit characters, beautifully structured palates and finely grained tannins. BOWEN ESTATE, HOLLICK, Katnook, Leconfield, LINDEMANS, PENLEY ESTATE and PETALUMA fall more or less within this category. The super-concentrated style of WYNNS 'John Riddoch' is almost an essence of Cabernet.

Best producers BOWEN ESTATE, HOLLICK, Katnook, Leconfield, LINDEMANS, Mildara, ORLANDO, PARKER ESTATE, PENLEY ESTATE, PETALUMA, WYNNS, Zema Estate.

Best years 1999, '98, '97, '96, '94, '93, '90.

COONAWARRA SHIRAZ

WYNNS Coonawarra Estate 'Michael' is the alter ego of 'John Riddoch'; a richly concentrated wine with pronounced spicy, blackberry-licorice aromas and substantial oak. Most Coonawarra Shirazes are more elegant and refined. They can be mistaken for Cabernet, as they often show blackcurrant-like fruit. The palate is the giveaway with much riper and less structured tannins.

Best producers BOWEN ESTATE, Leconfield, WYNNS Coonawarra Estate, Zema Estate.

Best years 1999, '98, '97, '96, '94, '91, '90.

BAROSSA SHIRAZ

Barossa Shiraz is the classic wine style of Australia. PENFOLDS Grange and HENSCHKE Hill of Grace (from the Barossa Ranges) perhaps exemplify the extraordinary vibrancy, intensity and density of fruit that the finest Barossa Shirazes bring. Often combined with American oak, seasoned and coopered in Australia, classic Barossa Shiraz has a complex and lush aroma of plums, licorice, chocolate and vanillin, a palate packed with fruit sweetness, massive concentration, ripe tannins and exceptional length. They age beautifully. Mature Barossa Shiraz can often show a meaty, Christmas cake-like character and spectacular richness on the palate. PENFOLDS is the leading large company, but there are also many excellent smaller producers, led by HENSCHKE (Hill of Grace and Mount Edesltone).

Best producers Barossa Valley Estate, Bethany, GRANT BURGE, HENSCHKE, Peter Lehmann, CHARLES MELTON, PENFOLDS, ROCKFORD, ST HALLETT, Torbreck, Turkey Flat, YALUMBA.

Best years 1998, '97, '96, '95, '94, '91, '90.

ADELAIDE HILLS CHARDONNAY

Adelaide Hills was pioneered by PETALUMA's search for cooler climate sites and is now emerging as one of Australia's classic wine regions. Many of the Chardonnays from here have tropical fruit/grapefruit-like aromas with a complex grilled nut bouquet and a creamy flavoursome palate with fine acidity.

Best producers HENSCHKE, Knappstein, PENFOLDS, PETALUMA, SHAW & SMITH, Geoff WEAVER.

Best years 1998, '97, '97, '95, '94, '90.

MCLAREN VALE SHIRAZ

This region is often called the middle palate of Australia because McLaren Vale Shiraz has such mouthfilling quality. The best have immense blackberry-licorice aromas, often modified a little by American oak. The palate is fleshy with ripe tannins. D'ARENBERG and CHAPEL HILL are beacons of quality. CLARENDON HILLS Shiraz is a controversial, palate-filling wine. Hardy's Eileen Hardy Shiraz has some super-ripe McLaren Vale fruit. ROSEMOUNT Balmoral impresses with lush fruit, American oak and ripe tannins.

Best producers CHAPEL HILL, CHATEAU REYNELLA, CLARENDON HILLS, Coriole, D'ARENBERG, Fox Creek, Hardy's, ROSEMOUNT.

Best years 1999, '98, '97, '96, '95, '94, '91, '90.

CLARE VALLEY SHIRAZ

Clare Valley Shiraz is rarely as opulent as Barossa Shiraz. Concentrated, yes, but with more spicy pepper-anis aromas over ripe prune-like fruit. The palate is slightly more structured with more finely focussed tannins. Jim Barry's The Armagh is a fine combination of intensity and depth. WENDOUREE and TIM ADAMS produce succulent blockbusters from ancient vines.

Best producers TIM ADAMS, Jim Barry, Leasingham, MITCHELL, Pike's, WENDOUREE.

Best years 1998, '97, '96, '95, '94, '91, '90.

CLARE VALLEY RIESLING

After Hunter Valley Semillon, Clare Valley Rieslings are some of the most recognizable wines of Australia. When young they have a very strong lime/citrus, floral aroma, moderate to high alcohol, incredible fruit purity and an indelible mineral-like acid cut. Over time, the palate fleshes out and the lime-zest freshness deepens to a memorable buttered toast and honey richness.

Best producers TIM ADAMS, GROSSET, Mount Horrocks, MITCHELL, Wilson Vineyard, PETALUMA, Skillogalee.

Best years 1999, '98, '97, '96, '95, '94, '91, '90.

EDEN VALLEY RIESLING

Initially famous as a source for the fabled Leo BURING Rieslings, but now several producers are making good zesty wines.

Best producers HENSCHKE, Peter Lehmann, MOUNTADAM.

Best years 1999, '98, '97, '96, '95, '94, '91, '90.

Western Australia
MARGARET RIVER CABERNET

Scientists advised planting Cabernet Sauvignon here back in the l960s and the best wines can claim to rival Bordeaux Classed Growths. The Cabernets from Margaret River are less opulent but more structured than those of Coonawarra. Cedar/cassis-like aromas, wonderful purity of fruit, pronounced but fine minerally tannins with acidity and superb length are all hallmarks.

Unlike Coonawarra with its wide range of Cabernet styles and quality, the Margaret River producers seem to have a very definite view of what their Cabernet should be and new oak is used sparingly. The idea that a particular vineyard site brings uniqueness to each individual wine is enthusiastically embraced. There is a strong belief that Cabernet from the area around Cowaramup has a riper style.

Best producers CAPE MENTELLE, CULLEN, Chateau Xanadu, DEVIL'S LAIR, LEEUWIN ESTATE, MOSS WOOD, PIERRO, VASSE FELIX.
Best years 1999, '97, '96, '95, '94, '93, '91.
GREAT SOUTHERN CABERNET

Mount Barker is one of Australia's first sub-regions and Cabernet from here is showing great promise. PLANTAGENET is leading the way with wines showing strong cassis-like aromas and a fruity but well-structured palate. HOWARD PARK is probably the most exciting winery, although its philosophy runs along similar lines to PENFOLDS (see below). Howard Park's excellent 'Cabernets' has a major Great Southern component but sources grapes from all over Western Australia, lending complexity and depth.

Best producers HOWARD PARK, PLANTAGENET.
Best years 1999, '97, '96, '95, '94, '93, '91.
MARGARET RIVER CHARDONNAY

Margaret River Chardonnay has an immense following. LEEUWIN ESTATE, with their benchmark Art Series Chardonnay, has led the way. Its creamy tropical fruit, lime zest and green melon acidity with hints of cashew nut and warm toast have given the wine an enviable reputation. CULLEN and MOSS WOOD are making equally seductive wines, while PIERRO's are a little fleshier and more alcoholic. CAPE MENTELLE has also been making some beautifully defined Chardonnay recently.

Best producers Brookland Valley, CAPE MENTELLE, CULLEN, DEVIL'S LAIR, LEEUWIN ESTATE, MOSS WOOD, PIERRO, VASSE FELIX.
Best years 1998, '96, '95, '93.

RED WINES FROM PENFOLDS

Penfolds, part of the giant Southcorp group, has had a huge impact on the development of a connoisseur's market for Australian wine and has proved that quality can go hand in hand with quantity. Its philosophy of multiregional blends flies in the face of the move in Australia towards regionality. The Penfolds house style, with its ripe fruit, barrel-fermented meaty nuances, ripe tannins and immense fruit sweetness, has been so revered by the consumer that some collectors would only buy Penfolds wine. Grange, Bin 707 Cabernet, St Henri, Bin 389 Cabernet Shiraz, Magill Estate and even the lower end of the Penfolds range have all shown incredible reliability despite the differing styles and winemaking philosophies. Every 2 years Penfolds offers collectors a chance to have their bottles from older vintages recorked. **Best wines** Grange, Bin 707 Cabernet Sauvignon, Magill Estate Shiraz, St Henri Shiraz, Bin 407 Cabernet Sauvignon, Bin 389 Cabernet/Shiraz, Bin 28 Kalimna Shiraz and Bin 128 Coonawarra Shiraz. See also page 321.

A–Z OF AUSTRALIAN PRODUCERS

TIM ADAMS, Clare Valley, SA   08 8842 2429/8842 3550

Small but energetic producer immersed in Shiraz production, but also making excellent Riesling and Semillon. The Aberfeldy is a very perfumed wine with immense concentration and fruit definition will benefit from up to 10 years' aging. The Shiraz is more generous and more loosely knitted but still packed with fruit.

Best wines ★★ Aberfeldy Shiraz ♥, ★ Shiraz ♥

Best years ♥1998, '97, '96, '95, '92, '91, '90; ♀1999, '98, '97, '96, '94, '92, '91, '90, '88

BASS PHILLIP, Gippsland, Victoria   03 5664 3341/5664 3209

Idiosyncratic Pinot Noir specialist with a cult following. The wines are produced in minute quantities and every bottle is bought within days of release. The Reserve Pinot Noir with its microdot label is a true collector's item – very expensive.

Best wines ★★★ Reserve Pinot Noir ♥, ★★ Premium Pinot Noir ♥

Best years 1998, '97, '96, '95, '94, '93, '92, '91, '89

BOWEN ESTATE, Coonawarra, SA   08 8737 2229/8737 2173

Bowen Cabernet is a reliable and well-priced wine. Its Shiraz is a really good Coonawarra example, with opulent blackberry aromas and ripeness on the palate.

Best wines ★★ Cabernet Sauvignon ♥ and Shiraz ♥

Best years 1999, '98, '97, '96, '94, '93, '92, '91, '90, '86

GRANT BURGE, Barossa Valley, SA   08 8563 3700/8563 2807

With superb vineyards, an interesting family history and a bit of show business, Grant Burge has steered Meshach in the same direction as HENSCHKE Mount Edelstone or Jim Barry's The Armagh. The wine is hugely concentrated with sweet American oak, ripe tannins and length, a fine example of quality Barossa Shiraz.

Best wine ★★★ Meshach ♥   **Best years** 1996, '95, '94, '92, '91, '90, '88

LEO BURING, Clare Valley and Eden Valley, SA   08 8563 2184/8563 2804

This brand name, now owned by Southcorp, refers to one of the pioneers of fine wine production in Australia. It fell behind in the 1980s but is making a spirited comeback. The Leonay Watervale Riesling has always remained a beacon of quality. This white wine has extraordinary aging qualities; enjoy its delicate floral aromas and searing acidity when young, or wait for the metamorphosis after as much as 20 years in bottle.

Best wines ★★★ Leonay Watervale Riesling ♀, ★★ Leonay Eden Valley Riesling ♀

Best years ♀1998, '97, '95, '94, '92, '91, '90, '87

CAPE MENTELLE, Margaret River, WA   08 9757 3266/9757 3233

David Hohnen is the founder and driving force of Cape Mentelle. While his Cabernet is a pace-setter, Cape Mentelle Shiraz is emerging as an important benchmark Western Australian wine. The Zinfandel is a quirky but highly seductive wine. Chardonnay and Semillon-Sauvignon are improving and on the verge of joining the Margaret River élite.

Best wines ★★★ Cabernet ♥, ★★ Shiraz ♥, ★ Semillon-Sauvignon ♀

Best years ♥1998, '96, '95, '92, '91, '90, '88, '86

CHAMBERS, Rutherglen, Victoria   03 6032 8641/6032 8101

Somewhere among the semi-chaos at this family winery are bottles of the extremely fine Old Liqueur Muscat and Tokay. With amazing concentration and power, the

Special and Rare blends are some of the finest wines of their kind.

Best wines ★★★ Old Liqueur Muscat ♀ and Old Liqueur Tokay ♀

CHAPEL HILL, McLaren Vale, SA   08 8323 8429/8323 9245

Pam Dunsford produces quintessential McLaren Vale Shiraz as well as fine Cabernet Sauvignon, Chardonnay and more recently, fascinating tropical fruity Verdelho. The Vicar is a highly regarded Cabernet/Shiraz blend.

Best wines ★★ The Vicar ♥, **★** Reserve Shiraz ♥ and Shiraz ♥

Best years ♥1998, '97, '96, '95, '94, '93, '91

CHATEAU REYNELLA, McLaren Vale, SA   08 8392 2222/8392 2202

Owned by BRL Hardy, this winery is the oldest in South Australia. Since 1997 the Chateau Reynella name has been used for export only, the wines using the Reynell name in Australia. Its former glory is now restored with Basket Pressed Cabernet Sauvignon and Shiraz, both massively concentrated wines combining value and quality.

Best wines ★★ Basket Pressed Cabernet Sauvignon ♥ and Basket Pressed Shiraz ♥

Best years ♥1997, '96, '95, '94

CLARENDON HILLS, McLaren Vale, SA   08 8364 1484

This controversial producer creates highly extracted red wines such as Astralis, a single-vineyard Shiraz which is astronomically expensive. Much of the production heads off to the USA and Asia. All the wines are opulent in style and packed with fruit.

Best wines ★★ Astralis ♥, Shiraz ♥ and Old Vine Grenache Blewitt Springs ♥

Best years ♥1997, '96, '95, '94

COLDSTREAM HILLS, Yarra Valley, Victoria   03 5964 9388/5964 9389

Coldstream Hills Reserve Chardonnay and Reserve Pinot Noir have played an important role in the development of these varietals in Australia. The latter is very consistent, with bright cherry meaty aromas, a silken palate and good flavour.

Best wines ★★★ Reserve Pinot Noir ♥ and Reserve Chardonnay ♀

Best years ♥1998, '97, '96, '94, '92; ♀1998, '97, '96

CULLEN, Margaret River, WA   08 9755 5277/9755 5550

Diana and Vanya Cullen form a formidable partnership that spans 12 years. The Cabernet/Merlot is gloriously scented and well-structured, while the Chardonnay is abundant with tropical fruit and nutty complexity.

Best wines ★★★ Cabernet/Merlot ♥, **★★** Chardonnay ♀

Best years ♥1999, '97, '96, '95, '94, '92, '91, '90, '88; ♀1999, '98, '97, '96, '95, '94, '93, '92

D'ARENBERG, McLaren Vale, SA   08 8323 8206/8323 8423

Another pioneering McLaren Vale winery which has transformed the quality and consistency of its wines recently. Characterful, old-vine reds based on Shiraz and Grenache are the main strength.

Best wine ★★ Dead Arm Shiraz ♥   **Best years** 1999, '98, '97, '96, '95, '94

DE BORTOLI,   03 5965 2423/5965 2464

Riverina, NSW and Yarra Valley, Victoria

This large, family-owned winery is known for exceptional, botrytis-affected Semillon. There is also fine Yarra Valley Chardonnay, Shiraz and Pinot Noir.

Best wines ★★★ Noble One Semillon ♀, **★★** Yarra Valley Chardonnay ♀ and Shiraz ♥

Best years ♥1998, '97, '96, '95, '94, '93, '92, '90; ♀1998, '97, '96, '95, '94, '93, '92, '91, '90

DEVIL'S LAIR, Margaret River, WA   08 9757 7573/9757 7533

Exciting, high-quality producer of opulent Chardonnay, fine Pinot Noir and elegant, lightly leafy Cabernet/Merlot. Production will rise dramatically following the winery's purchase by the giant Southcorp group in late 1996.

Best wines ★★ Pinot Noir ♥ and Chardonnay ♀

Best years ♥1999, '96, '94, '93, '92, '90; ♀1999, '98, '97, '96, '95, '94, '93

FREYCINET, East Coast, Tasmania   03 6257 8574/6257 8454

The Pinot Noir here, with lovely varietal definition, sappy palate and fruit sweetness, is one of Australia's best and suggests this variety may well find a natural home on this sheltered part of Tasmania's east coast. In warmer years the Chardonnay is good too.

Best wine ★★ Pinot Noir ♥   **Best years** 1998, '97, '96, '95, '94, '92, '91

GIACONDA, Beechworth, Victoria   03 5727 0246

This winery is a darling of wine scribes and consumers. Grilled nuts, tropical fruit aromas, complexity and creaminess are all hallmarks of the Chardonnay. The Pinot Noir is profoundly complex and very Burgundian in style.

Best wines ★★ Chardonnay ♀ and Pinot Noir ♥

Best years ♥1998, '97, '96, '95, '94, '92; ♀1999, '98, '97, '96, '95, '94, '93, '92

GROSSET, Clare Valley, SA   08 8849 2175/8849 2292

Jeffrey Grosset is best known for exceptional, intensely floral Riesling but is also not half bad at making creamy, oaky Piccadilly Chardonnay from Adelaide Hills fruit.

Best wines ★★★ Polish Hill Riesling ♀ and Watervale Riesling ♀, Piccadilly Chardonnay ♀

Best years 1999, '98, '97, '96, '95, '94, '93, '92

HENSCHKE, Eden Valley, SA   08 8564 8223/8564 8294

Attention to detail is a keynote for this husband-and-wife team. Top wine is stunning Hill of Grace Shiraz from old vines, full of dark exotic flavour. Abbotts Prayer is a fairly recent addition – a Cabernet-Merlot blend from the Adelaide Hills with excellent fruit purity and structure. Julius Riesling has highly defined fruit and linear acidity.

Best wines ★★★ Hill of Grace Shiraz ♥, Mount Edelstone Shiraz ♥, Cyril Henschke Cabernet Sauvignon ♥ and Julius Riesling ♀, ★★ Abbotts Prayer Cabernet Merlot ♥

Best years ♥1997, '96, '94, '92, '91, '90, '88, '86, '84, '82, '80, '78, '72; ♀1999, '98, '97, '96, '95, '94, '93, '92

HOLLICK, Coonawarra, SA   08 8737 2318/8737 2952

Producer of classic Coonawarra Cabernet with highly defined blackcurrant aromas, fine-grained tannins and good balance. The Ravenswood label has been around for quite some time and while it used merely to offer Bordeaux-like austerity, recent vintages have begun to display a far more exciting fragrance and depth of dark fruit.

Best wine ★★ Ravenswood ♥   **Best years** 1998, '96, '94, '93, '92, '91, '90, '88

HOWARD PARK, Great Southern, WA   08 9848 2345/9848 2064

Noted for its intense briary aromas, balance and structure, the Cabernet Sauvignon/Merlot is one of Western Australia's new stylistic leaders. Like the excellent Chardonnay, it needs several years to meld together. The Riesling has plenty of fruit purity and racy acidity.

Best wines ★★★ Cabernet Sauvignon Merlot ♥, Chardonnay ♀ and Riesling ♀

Best years ♥1997, '96, '94, '92, '90, '89, '88, '86; ♀1998, '97, '96, '95, '94, '93

LAKE'S FOLLY, Hunter Valley, NSW   02 4998 7507/4998 7322

Dr Max Lake had a reputation as something of an eccentric, his son Stephen less so. The Chardonnay here is designed for long aging and can reach Burgundian peaks of intensity and elegance. 'Cabernets' blends 4 Bordeaux varieties and can be excellent.
Best wines ★★ Cabernets ♥, Chardonnay ♀
Best years ♥1997, '96, '94, '91, '89; ♀1998, '97, '96, '95, '94, '92, '91

LEEUWIN ESTATE, Margaret River, WA   08 9757 6253/9757 6364

This Chardonnay was one of the first Australian examples to exhibit Burgundian style and complexity; the Cabernet is blackcurranty and lean. Also in the premium Art Series is a stylish Riesling. Keep the Chardonnay for at least 5 years, the Cabernet longer.
Best wines ★★★ Chardonnay ♀, **★★** Cabernet Sauvignon ♥ and Riesling ♀ (all Art Series)
Best years ♥1997, '96, '95, '94, '92, '91, '89, '87, '82; ♀1999, '98, '96, '95, '93, '92

LINDEMANS, Murray Darling, Victoria   03 5051 3333/5051 3390

This historic winery was once the flagship of the Hunter Valley – Bin 3100 Hunter River Burgundy was arguably one of the region's great wines. Today's Hunter River Shiraz and Semillons (once called Chablis) can be excellent. Now owned by the giant Southcorp group, the main production centre is at Karadoc on the Murray. The Hunter facility has recently been revamped so expect these wines to improve drastically.
Best wines ★ Hunter River Shiraz ♥, Hunter River Reserve Steven Vineyard Shiraz ♥, Hunter River Semillon ♀ and Limestone Ridge Shiraz/Cabernet ♥
Best years ♥1998, '96, '95, '94, '91, '87; ♀1999, '98, '96, '95, '94, '91, '90, '87, '86

MCWILLIAMS MOUNT PLEASANT, Hunter Valley, NSW   02 4998 7505/4998 7761

McWilliams' finest wines have tended to hide behind its portfolio of fortified and commercial wines (combined with a downmarket image). Its Hunter Valley Semillons, with honeyed straw aromas, deep set fruit and vitality, are beautifully made, and really consistent, lovely wines. The OP and OH Shiraz and Rosehill Shiraz are the best reds. McWilliams also produces fine Rutherglen Muscat, full of molasses richness and power.
Best wines ★★★ Lovedale Semillon ♀, **★★** Elizabeth Semillon ♀ and MCW11 Liqueur Muscat ♀, **★** Rosehill Shiraz ♥ and OP & OH Shiraz ♥
Best years ♥1998, '95, '94, '93, '91, '90, '89, '87; **Semillon** 1998, '96, '95, '94, '93, '92, '91, '90, '89, '86, '83, '82, '81, '79

CHARLES MELTON, Barossa Valley, SA   08 8563 3606/8563 3422

A gifted winemaker producing some of the most highly prized and undervalued wines in the Barossa. Nine Popes is quintessential Australian yet based on France's Châteauneuf-du-Pape, with ripe plummy aromas, deep set fruit and flavour. The Shiraz has intense gamy, spicy, blackberry aromas supported by American oak, a ripe palate packed with fruit sweetness, ripe tannins and length.
Best wines ★★★ Nine Popes ♥, **★★** Shiraz ♥   **Best years** 1998, '97, '96, '95, '94, '93, '92, '90

MITCHELL, Clare Valley, SA   08 8843 4258/8843 4340

A top Riesling producer rapidly regaining pre-eminence after a dull period. The Watervale Riesling is extraordinary – possessing mouthwatering properties and value. Peppertree Shiraz has licorice and blackberry aromas, ripe tannins and flavour.
Best wines ★★★ Watervale Riesling ♀, **★** Shiraz ♥
Best years ♥1998, '96, '95, '94, '93, '92, '90; ♀1999, '98, '97, '95, '91, '90, '87, '85

MORRIS, Rutherglen, Victoria   02 6026 7303/6026 7445

Probably the greatest of all Australian fortified producers, now owned by ORLANDO. The Old Premium Muscat has wonderful freshness and vitality with sweet 'rancio' aromas, marvellous syrupy richness and viscosity, but never cloying. The Old Premium Tokays are tighter but remain incredibly luscious.

Best wines ★★★ Old Premium Muscat ♀ and Old Premium Tokay ♀

MOSS WOOD, Margaret River, WA   08 9755 6266/9755 6303

An extraordinary vineyard site that justifies the current enthusiasm for regionality. The Margaret River Pinot Noir is perfumed and supple, arguably the best from the region. The Chardonnay demonstrates why Margaret River is a top region for this variety, while the Semillon has fresh lemony aromas with mouthquenching acidity and flavour.

Best wines ★★★ Cabernet Sauvignon ♥, ★★ Pinot Noir ♥, Chardonnay ♀ and Semillon ♀

Best years ♥1997, '96, '95, '94, '93, '91, '90, '87, '86, '85, '83; ♀1998, '97, '96, '95, '94, '92, '90, '86

MOUNTADAM, Eden Valley, SA   08 8564 1101/8564 1064

From vines planted high on the Mount Lofty Ranges come rich, buttery Chardonnay and sumptuous Pinot Noir, together with impressive Cabernet/Merlot blend, called The Red, and a rich Shiraz, called Patriarch. These wines have enough potential to be kept for 5 years or longer.

Best wines ★★ Pinot Noir ♥ and Patriarch Red ♥, ★ The Red ♥ and Chardonnay ♀

Best years ♥1998, '97, '96, '95, '94, '93, '91, '90; ♀1998, '97, '96, '94, '93, '92, '91, '90

MOUNT LANGI GHIRAN, Grampians, Victoria   03 5354 3207/5354 3277

There is no doubt that Trevor Mast makes one of Australia's top Shirazes. With ripe blackberry aromas, pronounced pepper and spice character, fruit sweetness, underlying oak and ripe but grainy tannins, it can last for 7 years or more. The well-structured Cabernet Sauvignon/Merlot and delightful perfumed, lemony Riesling are also good.

Best wines ★★★ Shiraz ♥, ★★ Cabernet Sauvignon/Merlot ♥, ★ Riesling ♀

Best years ♥1998, '97, '96, '95, '94, '93, '92, '90, '89, '86

MOUNT MARY, Yarra Valley, Victoria   03 9739 1761/9739 0137

This classic estate takes Bordeaux as its model, producing the dry white Triolet from Sauvignon, Semillon and Muscadelle, and Cabernets Quintet from all 5 Bordeaux red grape varieties. There is also impressive Pinot Noir. Keep the wines for 5 years or more.

Best wines ★★★ Cabernets Quintet ♥, ★★ Pinot Noir ♥, ★ Triolet ♀

Best years ♥1997, '96, '95, '94, '92, '91, '90, '88, '86, '85; ♀1998, '97, '96, '95, '94, '92, '91

ORLANDO, Barossa Valley, SA   08 8521 3111/8521 3100

The extraordinary success of the Jacob's Creek brand from Australia's second largest wine company is a double-edged sword in the world of fine wine but after a period in the 1990s when quality was sacrificed for quantity, it is back on song. The St Hugo Cabernet Sauvignon is very consistent and the Steingarten Riesling has had several brilliant vintages in the 1990s. Centenary Hill Shiraz is the expensive new flag waver.

Best wines ★★ St Hugo Coonawarra Cabernet Sauvignon ♥, Eden Valley Steingarten Riesling ♀ and Centenary Hill Shiraz ♥, ★ Jacaranda Ridge Cabernet Sauvignon ♥ and Lawson's Shiraz ♥

Best years Shiraz 1994, '93, '91, '90, '88; ♀1999, '97, '96, '95, '94, '92, '91, '90

PARKER ESTATE, Coonawarra, SA   08 8737 2946/8737 2945

Whenever one speaks to John Parker about his wine cheekily named First Growth, he bubbles with enthusiasm. Extraordinary depth of fruit, balance and structure are hallmarks of the style. It drinks well at 3 years but promises to age well also. Another decade or so of this performance may indeed see the wine become something of a legend.

Best wine ★★★ Coonawarra Estate First Growth ❢   **Best years** 1998, '96, '93, '91

PENFOLDS, SA   08 8560 9389/8560 9669

This flagship brand for the Southcorp Wines group has an enviable reputation for quality at every price level. Although the winery has existed since 1844, it is really only since the late 1940s that its reputation for red wine has been forged (see page 315). Overall the style is about defined fruit sweetness, ripe tannins, scented American oak, richness, power and concentration. Penfolds Grange, Bin 707 Cabernet Sauvignon, St Henri, Magill Estate and Bin 389 are all sought after on the investment market, with Grange, from Shiraz, generally considered Australia's greatest red wine and only showing its magnificence after at least 10 years in bottle. Bin 707 Cabernet Sauvignon is a brilliantly made wine and is already showing impressive aging characteristics. Experimentation is a keynote here, for both red and white wines. Penfolds has begun to establish a name for white wines in recent years, with new Chardonnay and Semillon from Adelaide Hills led by overpriced 'Yattarna'.

Best wines ★★★ Grange ❢ and Bin 707 Cabernet Sauvignon ❢, ★★ St Henri Shiraz ❢, Magill Estate Shiraz ❢, Bin 389 Cabernet/Shiraz ❢, Bin 407 Cabernet Sauvignon ❢ and Bin 94A Chardonnay ♀, ★ Bin 128 Coonawarra Shiraz ❢, Bin 28 Kalimna Shiraz ❢, Bin 2 Shiraz/ Mourvedre ❢ and Clare Estate ❢

Best years Grange 1995, '94, '93, '92, '91, '90 ,'88, '86, '84, '83, '80, '76, '71, '67, '66, '63, '62, '55, '53, '52

PENLEY ESTATE, Coonawarra, SA   08 8736 3211

Classic Coonawarra Cabernet, with cedary blackcurrant aromas, fine-grained but ripe tannins, fruit sweetness, concentration and length, is the focus here. The wine is always at the riper end of the Cabernet spectrum, but with enough structure to age.

Best wine ★★ Cabernet Sauvignon ❢   **Best years** ❢1998, '96, '94, '93, '92, '91, '90

PETALUMA, Coonawarra, SA   08 8339 4122/8339 5253

Brian Croser, probably Australia's most influential winemaker, has a passion for Merlot. At a time when Cabernet/Shiraz blends were the undisputed Australian favourite, he ripped out all his Shiraz vines and replanted with Merlot. The Cabernet/Merlot shows ripe plummy fruit underpinned by classy French oak. It is one of the few Australian wines offered 'en primeur'. There are also excellent whites, especially Chardonnay and Riesling. Single-vineyard Tiers Chardonnay is made in tiny quantities.

Best wine ★★★ Chardonnay ♀, ★★ Riesling ♀ and Merlot ❢

Best years ❢1998, '97, '96, '95, '94, '93, '92, '91, '90; ♀1999, '98, '97, '96, '95, '94, '93

PIERRO, Margaret River, WA   08 9755 6220/9755 6308

Pierro's Chardonnay has an exceptional reputation; classically made and full of fruit aromas and complexity, this wine is one of Australia's best examples. The fruity, crisp Semillon/Sauvignon Blanc blend is very drinkable and there is also an impressive Bordeaux-style red called Cabernets which repays a decade of aging.

Best wines ★★★ Chardonnay ♀, ★★ Cabernets ❗, ★ Semillon/Sauvignon Blanc ♀

Best years ❗1996, '94; ♀1998, '97, '96, '95, '94, '93, '92

PIPERS BROOK, Pipers River, Tasmania   03 6332 4433/6334 9122

In this marginal climate for ripening grapes Andrew Pirie has produced a range of highly sought-after wines. Steely, yet scented Riesling with keen acidity and elegant and stylist Chardonnay are the most impressive, but there is also attractive Pinot Noir, Gewürztraminer and barrel-fermented Sauvignon Blanc. Pirie is an acclaimed new Champagne-method sparkler – well structured, it shows a bready complexity.

Best wines ★★ Chardonnay ♀, Riesling ♀ and Pirie Vintage ♀, ★ Pellion Pinot Noir ❗

Best years ❗1998, '97, '94, '92; ♀1999, '98, '97, '95, '93, '92, '91

PLANTAGENET, Great Southern, WA   08 9851 2150/9851 1839

One of the top wineries of the region, Plantagnet is noted for extraordinarily well-made Cabernet, expressing a ripe spectrum of Cabernet with cassis aromas, underlying oak, ripe finely grained tannins and high concentration, ripe, balanced Shiraz and Pinot Noir, along with melony, nutty Chardonnay and limy Riesling. The reds in general benefit from a few years' aging.

Best wines ★★ Cabernet Sauvignon ❗, Shiraz ❗, Chardonnay ♀ and Riesling ♀

Best years ❗1998, '96, '95, '94, '93, '92, '91, '90, '89, '86, '85; ♀1998, '97, '95, '93, '91, '90

PRIMO ESTATE, Adelaide Plains, SA   08 8380 9442/8380 9696

A brilliant winemaker, Joe Grilli has created wonders using the traditional Italian method of making Amarone and Recioto wines with semi-dried grapes which has the effect of increasing the juice to skin ratio and therefore flavour and concentration: his Amarone Cabernet/Merlot is abundant in bitter-sweet fruit, ripe tannins and mouthfilling flavour. Keep for up to 10 years. La Magia is a botrytized fragrant, honeyed Riesling with fresh, crisp acidity.

Best wine ★★★ Joseph Moda Amarone Cabernet/Merlot ❗, ★★ Riesling ♀

Best years ❗1998, '97, '96, '95, '94, '93, '91, '90; ♀1998, '96, '95, '94, '93, '91

ROCKFORD, Barossa Valley, SA   03 8563 2720/8563 3787

The winery is a working museum right down to a functioning basket press made in the 1920s. Rocky O'Callaghan produces quintessential Barossa Shiraz, with opulent fruit, laden with ripe blackberry and prune aromas, ripe tannins, American oak, fruit sweetness and length of flavour. There is also a wild and whacky sparkling Black Shiraz.

Best wines ★★★ Basket Press Shiraz ❗, ★ Sparkling Black Shiraz ❗

Best years 1998, '97, '96, '95, '94, '92, '91, '90

ROSEMOUNT, Hunter Valley, NSW and McLaren Vale, SA   02 6547 2467/6547 2742

Rosemount's Mountain Blue Shiraz/Cabernet from Mudgee is fast becoming a collector's item and it illustrates the immense talent of the winemaking team headed by Phillip Shaw. The Rosemount Chardonnays are immensely complex and idiosyncratic in style with ripe tropical fruit aromas, high-toned new oak and a fleshy palate and flavour; and deserve recognition as some of Australia's great Chardonnays, having more in common with top white Burgundies than much Australian Chardonnay.

Best wines ★★ Mountain Blue Shiraz/Cabernet ❗, Show Reserve Chardonnay ♀ and Roxburgh Hunter Valley Chardonnay ♀

Best years ❗1998, '97, '96, '95; ♀1999, '98, '97, '96, '95, '93, '91, '90, '89, '87

ROTHBURY ESTATE, Hunter Valley, NSW   02 4998 7555/4998 7553
Once Len Evans' baby, but then swallowed up by corporate take over. Its early
Semillons were legendary wines. Unfortunately fashion, poor brand definition, too
many labels and a propensity for sales at any price dulled the Rothbury armoury. A
premium range of wines called Brokenback, together with the marketing power of the
owner Mildara Blass, may well bring this important estate back into focus.
Best wines ★ Shiraz ❢, Hunter Valley Semillon ♀ and Brokenback Semillon ♀
Best years ❢1998, '96, '94, '93, '91, '89; ♀1998, '97, '96, '94, '93, '89, '86, '84, '79

ST HALLETT, Barossa Valley, SA   08 8563 2319/8563 2901
A young company that has rapidly become one of the new wave leaders in Barossa.
The vines for Old Block Shiraz are 60–100 years old and this shows in the
extraordinary quality of this wine, full of ripe tannins. Unoaked, fruity whites from
Semillon, Sauvignon Blanc and Chardonnay are also impressive.
Best wines ★★★ Old Block Shiraz ❢, ★★ Blackwell Shiraz, ★ Semillon/Sauvignon Blanc ♀
Best years ❢1998, '96, '95, '94, '93, '91, '90, '88, '86, '84; ♀1999, '98, '97, '96

SEPPELT, Barossa Valley, SA   08 8568 6200/8562 8333
Seppeltsfield in the Barossa is an eyecatching folly, with its Seppelt family mausoleum,
palm tree-lined roads and beautifully preserved buildings. The fortified wines are some
of the best in Australia. The DP 117 Show Fino and DP 116 Show Amontillado are
excellent sherry styles, the equal of Spain's best. The Para Liqueur Ports are now
vintage-dated although the early years of 1947, '44, '39, '33, '30, '27 and '22 are not
necessarily entirely made from that vintage. You can't get better Tawny Ports than these.
Best wines ★★★ DP 117 Show Fino ♀, DP 116 Show Amontillado ♀, DP 38 Show
Oloroso ♀, Para Liqueur Port ❢ and Centenary Para Liqueur Port ❢

SEPPELT GREAT WESTERN, Grampians, Victoria   03 5361 2239/5361 2200
Part of the Southcorp cluster of wine brands, Great Western has always shown great
potential for Shiraz, although it is best known for its sparkling wines (Drumborg,
Harpers Range and Salinger are leading brands). The red Show Sparkling Shiraz is the
benchmark for this idiosyncratic wine style, which can age for up to 15 years.
Best wines ★★★ Show Sparkling Shiraz ❢, ★ Great Western Shiraz ❢
Best years ❢1998, '96, '95, '92, '91, '90, '88, '86, '85; **Show Sparkling Shiraz** 1990, '87,
'86, '85, '84, '83, '82

SHAW & SMITH, Adelaide Hills, SA   08 8370 9911/8370 9339
This combination of cousins Martin Shaw and Michael Hill Smith has made a strong
impression on the international market. The Reserve Chardonnay is always reliable
and made with classic proportions in mind. It demonstrates a benchmark restrained
style with tropical fruit aromas and grilled-nut complexity underpinned by new French
oak and a fleshy palate. There is also good unoaked Chardonnay and tangy Sauvignon.
Best wine ★★ Reserve Chardonnay ♀   **Best years** 1998, '97, '96, '94

TYRRELL'S, Hunter Valley, NSW   02 4998 7509/4998 7723
Vat 9 is arguably the most important and consistent Shiraz from this family-owned
and run winery. The wine shows distinctive regional character with its restrained but
obvious polished leather bouquet, sweet tannins and ripe fruit. Vat 1 Semillon is a
classic Hunter Valley Semillon, taking on great honeyed richness with age.

Best wines ★★★ Vat 9 Winemakers Selection Shiraz ❢, Vat 47 Chardonnay ♀ and Vat 1 Semillon ♀
Best years ❢1998, '97, '96, '95, '93, '92, '91, '89, '87; **Semillon** 1998, '97, '96, '95, '94, '92, '91, '87, '86, '79, '77, '76, '75

VASSE FELIX, Margaret River, WA   08 9755 5242/9755 5425

After a decade of rather disappointing vintages, the Cabernet Sauvignon, one of the wines that originally brought this region to prominence, has been revitalized completely – there is now plenty of ripe mulberry leaf Cabernet aromas along with complex berry fruit, fruit sweetness and oak. The Shiraz is also very stylish, with plenty of flavour and good balance. Heytesbury Red is a new flagship Bordeaux-style red. There is also fine botrytized Riesling and a deep-flavoured, barrel-fermented Semillon.
Best wines ★★★ Heytesbury Red ❢, **★★** Cabernet Sauvignon ❢, Shiraz ❢, Riesling ♀ and Semillon ♀
Best years ❢1998, '97, '96, '95, '94, '91, '90, '88, '86; ♀1999, '98, '97, '96, '95

GEOFF WEAVER, Adelaide Hills, SA   08 8272 2105/8271 0177

Geoff Weaver is an accomplished winemaker who provides excellent proof, along with PETALUMA and Knappstein, that Adelaide Hills Chardonnay is an emerging classic wine style. His Chardonnay has a grapefruit aroma with complexity and flavour.
Best wine ★ Chardonnay ♀   **Best years** 1997, '95, '96, '94, '93, '91, '90

WENDOUREE, Clare Valley, SA   Tel 08 8842 2896

Old vines are the key to quality here and the winemaking is old-fashioned too, with limited output and intense extract in spicy, concentrated Shiraz and powerful, long-lived Cabernet/Malbec. The excellent medium-sweet Muscat is for drinking young.
Best wines ★★★ Cabernet/Malbec ❢ and Shiraz ❢, **★** Muscat of Alexandria ♀
Best years ❢1997, '96, '95, '94, '92, '91, '90, '89, '86, '83, '80, '78

WYNNS, Coonawarra, SA   08 8736 3266/8736 3202

The name Wynns is synonymous with the Coonawarra region and its Cabernet Sauvignon and Shiraz are always good value and with plenty of aging potential. However the top wines, John Riddoch Cabernet and Michael Shiraz, are truly exceptional. Made only in the best years, they are both powerful and long-lived wines.
Best wines ★★★ John Riddoch Cabernet ❢ and Michael Shiraz ❢
Best years ❢1997, '96, '94, '93, '91, '90, '88, '86, '82

YALUMBA, Barossa Valley, SA   08 8561 3200/8561 3393

A lineage of 3 decades, proven aging potential, immense resources and a very fine winemaking team are all the hallmarks of Yalumba's success. Well known for its sparkling Angas Brut and Oxford Landing wines, as well as liqueur Muscat, Yalumba also makes some truly fine wines. Octavius is a remarkable oaky but concentrated Shiraz – with dollops of American oak, this wine will coax the fur off your tongue and needs aging for at least 5 years. The Reserve Signature, a blend of Coonawarra Cabernet and Barossa Shiraz, is made in classic Australian style. Here, the love affair with American oak is more restrained although still to the fore. The Menzies Cabernet Sauvignon is named after a famous wartime Australian Prime Minister who was very partial to Yalumba wine. White wines play less of a role, but there are some exceptional single-vineyard examples from the Barossa ranges.
Best wines ★★ Octavius Shiraz ❢ and Reserve Signature ❢, **★** Menzies Cabernet Sauvignon ❢
Best years ❢1996, '95, '94, '93, '92, '91, '90, '88, '86, '85, '81, '76, '75, '66, '62

Australia is an enormous continent with varying climatic conditions. The idea that a specific region can make wines of individual and unique quality is now the catchword. Barossa Shiraz is quite different from Hunter Valley Shiraz, as Coonawarra Cabernet differs from Margaret River Cabernet. Vintages can be markedly different even within a state. The so-called Distinguished Vineyard Site may also outperform other vineyards in its area.

Aging qualities

Australian winemakers are used to good ripening conditions. Barossa Valley Shiraz, for instance, needs an alcohol level of 13°–14° to give the wines scope to add complexity as they age. Hunter Valley Semillon is picked early and is lower in alcohol, yet it can age for 20 years or more. Coonawarra Cabernet comes in 2 guises: super-concentrated wine needing substantial bottle age or, wine which is drinkable after 4 years but has potential for longer aging. Margaret River Cabernet has fine tannins and fruit which show well after 5 years and can keep longer. Clare Valley Riesling has purity of fruit and good acidity for aging; the best live for 30 years or more. Australian Chardonnay is generally good to drink on release, but wines from cool climates can age 10 years.

Maturity charts

These are 2 Australian wine styles with fine track records for aging. Only the very best Cabernet wines will age and mature Semillon is unrecognizable from youthful Semillon.

Coonawarra Cabernet

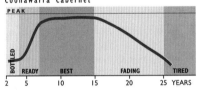

Hunter Valley Semillon (unwooded)

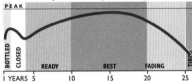

VINTAGE CHART

	99	98	97	96	95	94	93	92	91	90	89
NEW SOUTH WALES											
Hunter Valley Semillon (premium unoaked)	80○	90○	60○	80○	80○	70○	70◑	50◑	90○	60●	80◑
VICTORIA											
Yarra Valley Cabernet Sauvignon	70○	80○	90○	50○	70○	80◑	70●	60◑	90○	80●	40◑
SOUTH AUSTRALIA											
Barossa/Clare Shiraz	70○	80○	90○	90○	80○	90○	60◑	60◑	80◑	90●	50●
Coonawarra Cabernet	80○	90○	70○	80○	50○	80○	70◑	70◑	90○	100●	50◐
Clare/Eden Valley Riesling	80○	100○	100○	80◑	80○	80◑	60●	70◑	80●	80●	40◐
WESTERN AUSTRALIA											
Cabernet Sauvignon	80○	60○	90○	90○	80○	80◑	90○	60◑	90●	80●	80●

KEY ○= needs more time ◑= ready but will improve ●= at peak ◐= fading or tired

VINTAGES AT A GLANCE

Each state in Australia has vineyards with vastly differing natural conditions. Consequently vintage assessments must be taken as generalizations.

Great Years ★★★	NSW 1998, '95, '91, '86; **Victoria** 1998, '97, '94, '91; **SA** 1998, '97, '96, '95, '94, '91, '90; **WA** 1996, '94, '91, '86
Good Years ★★	NSW 1996, '94, '93, '89, '87; **Victoria** 1999, '96, '95, '93, '92, '90, '88, '86; **SA** 1999, '96, '95, '94, '93, '92, '91, '88; **WA** 1999, '97, '95, '93, '92, '90
Moderate Years ★	NSW 1999, '97, '92, '90; **Victoria** 1996, '95; **SA** 1999, '95, '93, '92, '89; **WA** 1999, '98, '89
Poor Years (No Stars)	NSW 1988; **Victoria** 1989; **SA** 1995

Annual vintage reports
New South Wales

1999★ Rain at the wrong times meant this was not a memorable year for reds. Chardonnay is probably the best variety. Only those producers who selected their grapes carefully will produce good wines.

1998★★★ Quality was above average to excellent, especially in the Hunter Valley. High sugar levels as well as high acids were attained, promising wines of exceptional potential longevity.

1997★-★★★ A near-perfect growing season was hampered by rain at harvest. Many growers experienced botrytis in the vineyard, so selective picking was the key to successful winemaking this year.

1996★★ This was a high-quality vintage following slow ripening during a cool summer, healthy vines and ideal harvest conditions; the Hunter reds have great concentration and good acidity.

1995★★★ Drought during 1994 ensured lower than average crops. Unseasonably cool conditions allowed the grapes to accumulate marvellous flavour; a very good year, sometimes a great one.

1994★★ A near-perfect growing season was marred later by scorching heat and stress for the vines. Most red wines have great intensity as a result.

1993★★ One of the coolest vintages experienced recently in the Hunter Valley,

creating an extended ripening period. The best reds and Semillons are still worth waiting for.

1992★ Drought conditions in 1991 meant low yields this year. Choose wines from top producers to be on the safe side.

1991★★★ One of the Hunter Valley's greatest recent vintages; early picking of Semillon made supremely elegant wines with high acidity.

1990★ Almost perfect conditions prevailed until the first week of February when rain poured down. Only those who picked early made fine wines.

1989★★ A hot spring followed by a cool summer ensured even ripening. The Semillons have great depth of flavour.

1987★★ The top Semillon wines are still showing well.

1986★★★ A superb year for Hunter Valley Semillon. A cool spring followed by a hot summer meant optimum maturity.

Victoria

1999★★ Reasonably good year with variable results: Geelong Pinot Noir and Cabernet Sauvignon look long-lived.

1998★★★ Victoria was very dry and harvested early in perfect conditions. Wines of excellent potential longevity.

1997★★★ Heatwave at harvest time; yields were quite low, notably in the Yarra and Great Western regions, but the reds produced were superbly concentrated.

1996★-★★ Great vintage in warm areas such as Rutherglen. In general, this is not a vintage for keeping.

1995★-★★ As elsewhere, this was a smallish crop with some attractive whites.

1994★★★ Good quality, but late cool weather reduced yields. Drinking well now.

1993★★ Cool conditions and rain resulted in a cluster of light, agreeable wines.

1992★★ Generally good but some wines lack richness and ripeness. Drink up.

1991★★★ Yields lower than average after a cool vintage. Elegant, balanced wines, with reds especially impressive now.

1990★★ Great year for Muscat and Tokay in Rutherglen. Also high yields in the Yarra Valley and good quality wines.

1989 A rather poor year.

1988★★ Deep, balanced and rich wines now at their peak.

1986★★ Excellent vintage conditions. Keep the best Cabernet and Shiraz a little longer.

South Australia

1999★-★★ A difficult vintage and wine quality very mixed. Reds will be lighter-bodied and for early drinking.

1998★★★ Quality may be variable but Clare Riesling looks set to rival the 1997s.

1997★★★ Intense heat in February caused some damage to vines but wine quality proved excellent, especially in rich Barossa and Coonawarra reds and Clare Riesling.

1996★★-★★★ Cool growing conditions meant excellent ripening for red grapes and consequent concentration and balance.

1995 0-★★★ Poor vintage for Coonawarra but Barossa Shiraz did well due to intense heat, reduced yields and top quality fruit.

1994★★-★★★ An above-average vintage with many producers picking late. The wines are classical in style with ripe tannins and fruit sweetness.

1993★-★★ A difficult growing season, with a wet spring and early summer. Dry weather came late but meant excellent wines were produced from older vines.

1992★-★★ An average year.

1991★★-★★★ Superb, early vintage after a long hot summer made rich, opulent red wines with great aging potential.

1990★★★ Some feel this was a 'vintage of the century'; a long season meant grapes built up flavour, yet kept their acidity.

1989★ Average quality. Drink up.

1988★★ A generally good vintage but only top Riesling can still be drunk.

Western Australia

1999★-★★ A mid-vintage cyclone means it's unlikely to be a year for long-term aging. Cabernet Sauvignon and Merlot are the best varieties.

1998★ The vintage was more variable than further east, hampered by mid-harvest rain in Margaret River and Great Southern.

1997★★ A good, occasionally excellent vintage. Low yields from old vines gave superb Margaret River Cabernet.

1996★★★ Perfect growing conditions produced full-blooded red wines and great Chardonnay.

1995★★ A hot summer meant good concentration in the red wines. Some outstanding whites were made too.

1994★★★ A superb vintage for Margaret River reds after a very dry summer.

1993★★ Hail during flowering cut yields but the summer brought good ripeness and flavour to Cabernets, which are set for long aging.

1992★★ Balanced wines from a mixed year. Drink now.

1991★★★ A text book vintage meant all grape varieties did well.

1990★★ Mild, dry summer meant slow ripening but good Cabernet which is drinking well now.

1989★ A reasonable year, though few wines have kept well.

NEW ZEALAND

The most exciting wines in New Zealand are characterized by intense and often brilliantly bright fruit flavours that, in the case of aromatic styles such as Sauvignon Blanc or Riesling, seem to leap from the glass. They are influenced by a cool climate, which increases their pungent zestiness, and a rather high-tech 'New World' approach to winemaking which places a strong emphasis on freshness and fruit flavour. The most impressive wines have subtle power and complexity that can sometimes owe as much to winemaking talent as to an ideal vineyard site and careful viticulture. Fine wines are as likely to be made by New Zealand's 3 largest wineries, Montana, Corbans and the Villa Maria/Vidals/Esk Valley group (which together crush nearly 90% of the nation's grapes), as by the 260 'boutique' producers.

WINE STYLES

The wine regions span nearly 1600km with a wide range of climatic conditions and soil types that favour many different wine styles. Red Bordeaux varieties (Cabernet Sauvignon, Cabernet Franc and Merlot) are more suited to the warmer North Island: Waiheke Island in Auckland Harbour and Hawke's Bay are the country's 2 top red wine regions. Sauvignon and Riesling are more suited to the cooler southerly regions, especially Marlborough, Martinborough (in Wellington) and North Canterbury. Pinot Noir performs best here and in Central Otago. Gewürztraminer is curiously suited to Gisborne in the North Island and Central Otago in the deep south. Chardonnay can make fine wine in every region, albeit in significantly different styles.

Cabernet Sauvignon
Fresh, bright berryfruit and cedar flavours, often with a mint/tobacco herbal influence.

Chardonnay
North Island Chardonnay, with its lush peach, melon and grapefruit flavours, is typically riper and more full-bodied than that from the cooler South Island. Here, Chardonnay becomes lighter and more aromatic with zestier acidity and the flavours of citrus/grapefruit and white peach as well as a mineral or herbal note.

Merlot
Plum-raspberry fruit flavours with gamy, leathery, savoury complexity with age.

Pinot Noir
Strong plum and cherry flavours, with the very best wines showing a sappy, almost animal complexity, as well as a mouth-filling richness and silken texture.

Riesling and Gewürztraminer
Aromatic floral wines often with the richness and concentration of Alsace wines even though most are made in a medium-dry style. There are also good dry and outstanding sweet wines.

Sauvignon Blanc
Pale, light, fresh wine with a pungent blend of ripe tropical fruit, passionfruit and sweet red capsicum flavours. It has less of the ripe gooseberry, green capsicum and cut grass flavours of French Sauvignon, along with crisp acidity.

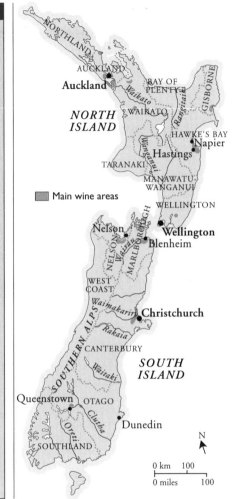

GREAT NEW ZEALAND WINES

Oz Clarke's selection

Pelorus ♀ (Cloudy Bay) A great sparkling wine, resplendent in its traditional flavours of nuts, yeast and cedarwood.

Sauvignon Blanc ♀ (Vavasour) All the gooseberry and limegrass attack you could wish for, yet wrapped in ripeness.

Reserve Chardonnay ♀ (Seresin) Majestic Burgundian style of oatmeal and hazelnuts and long-lingering richness.

The Terraces ! (Esk Valley) One of New Zealand's few world class reds – stunning pepper and black cherry depth from Bordeaux varieties in a Hawke's Bay suntrap.

Pinot Noir ! (Palliser) Beautiful, ripe and perfumed example of Pinot Noir, and consistently delicious.

The Navigator ♀ (Alpha Domus) Another superb example of how Hawke's Bay can ripen the Bordeaux varieties – rich, deep, full and impressive.

Steven Spurrier's selection

Sauvignon Blanc ♀ (Cloudy Bay) New Zealand's most famous Sauvignon Blanc, and a worldwide benchmark for this grape.

Chardonnay ♀ (Kumeu River) An intensely flavoured, classic Chardonnay made by the brilliant Michael Brajkovich, New Zealand's first Master of Wine.

Moutere Riesling ♀ (Neudorf) Limited production of the highest-quality grapes produce this textbook Riesling.

Pinot Noir ! (Ata Rangi) A world class Pinot Noir, with individuality and character behind the plummy, cherry fruit.

Cabernet blend ! (Goldwater Estate) A wine of extraordinary richness, depth and complexity from a unique mesoclimate and severely selected grapes.

Coleraine Cabernet Merlot ! (Te Mata) Ripe fruit and a very polished use of oak keep this wine at the top of the New Zealand Cabernets.

Top New Zealand producers

Cabernet Sauvignon, Merlot, Cabernet Franc & Bordeaux-style blends Alpha Domus, Clearview, Esk Valley, Fenton Twin Bays, GOLDWATER, Providence, St Nesbit, STONYRIDGE, TE MATA, Waiheke Vineyards, Vidal, VILLA MARIA, Waitakere Vineyards.

Chardonnay Clearview, CLOUDY BAY, KUMEU RIVER, MARTINBOROUGH VINEYARD, MORTON ESTATE, NEUDORF, Pegasus Bay, Seresin, TE MATA, The McDonald Winery (Church Road), VAVASOUR.

Pinot Noir Ata Rangi, Dry River, Fromm, MARTINBOROUGH VINEYARD, NEUDORF, Palliser.

Sauvignon Blanc CLOUDY BAY, HUNTER'S, Jackson Estate, Seresin, VAVASOUR, VILLA MARIA.

A–Z OF NEW ZEALAND WINE REGIONS

AUCKLAND

A large area of North Island around Auckland. Tiny Waiheke Island in Auckland Harbour makes many of the country's top reds and the Kumeu/Huapai districts north of Auckland also produce good reds, especially Merlot, and top Chardonnay (notably KUMEU RIVER). Matakana, north of Auckland, shows potential for top red wine, particularly Merlot and Cabernet Franc.

Best producers Collards, Fenton Twin Bays, GOLDWATER, KUMEU RIVER, MONTANA, MORTON ESTATE, Providence, St Nesbit, Selaks, STONYRIDGE, VILLA MARIA, Waiheke Vineyards, Waitakere Vineyards.

Best years 1999, '98, '96, '94, '93, '91.

CANTERBURY

This cool region on the South Island's east coast has 3 distinct districts: Canterbury Plains, Banks Peninsula and the most prestigious, Waipara. Predictably, the varieties that respond best to a cool climate are the top performers in this region. Pinot Noir produces the best results although fine Riesling, pungent Sauvignon Blanc and elegant Chardonnay are also made by the mostly small producers. The arid, sheltered Waipara Plains north of Christchurch is a relatively new area that promises to produce some of the country's finest wines.

Best producers Giesen, Pegasus Bay, St Helena, Sherwood, Waipara West.

Best years 1999, '98, '96, '95, '94.

CENTRAL OTAGO

New Zealand's only wine region with a continental rather than a maritime climate. Very cold winters, cool summer nights and very hot days produce fine-flavoured wines with fresh acidity. A high frost risk keeps producers on their toes during the growing season. Exquisite Pinot Noir and Gewürztraminer are produced in most years although the later-ripening Riesling can struggle in a cool vintage. Elegant, zesty Chardonnay is also a feature of this region.

Best producers Black Ridge, Chard Farm, Gibbston Valley, Rippon Vineyard.

Best years 1999, '98, '97, '96, '95, '94.

GISBORNE

Once New Zealand's 'bulk wine' region and home to large acreages of Müller-Thurgau. Much replanting of better varieties has occurred in the last 10 years and high-quality sites have emerged. Distinctively soft and charming Chardonnay with lush peach and pineapple flavours and powerful spicy Gewürztraminer are Gisborne's best-known fine wine styles.

Best producers Collards, Coopers Creek, CORBANS, Matawhero, Matua Valley, The Millton Vineyard, MONTANA, Revington.

Best years 1999, '98, '97, '96, '95, '94.

HAWKE'S BAY

The high number of sunshine hours and a wide range of soil types, aspects and vineyard altitudes have attracted a large number of small 'life-style' winemakers who produce a diverse range of fine wines. Hawke's Bay is best known for strong, ripe Cabernet Sauvignon and Merlot, together with intense, powerful Chardonnay. All have good aging potential. Intense, peppery Syrah is now making an appearance in hotter, drier sites while Pinot Noir shows promise in cooler, higher-altitude areas. Sauvignon Blanc can be a bit lacklustre although exciting new clones of Sémillon can contribute backbone to a blend with Sauvignon

Blanc, producing a style similar to dry white Bordeaux.

Best producers Alpha Domus, BABICH, Brookfields, Clearview, Collards, CORBANS, Delegat's, Esk Valley, The McDonald Winery, Matua Valley, Mills Reef, MORTON ESTATE, Ngatarawa, C J Pask, Sacred Hill, Stonecroft, TE MATA, Vidal.

Best years ❢1999, '98, '96, '95, '94, '91; ♀1999, '98, '96, '95.

MARLBOROUGH

This is New Zealand's largest and best-known wine region; it enjoys high sunshine hours, cool nights, relatively dry ripening conditions and free-draining, stony, low to moderately fertile soils. First planted with grape vines as recently as 1973, winemaking has now become one of the region's main industries.

Marlborough makes the world's most distinctive Sauvignon Blanc, with powerful, pungent passionfruit and herbal flavours and this was the style that first brought the region worldwide fame. The cool growing conditions are ideal for high-quality Champagne-method sparkling wine, as well as fine aromatic Riesling and elegant Chardonnay. Pinot Noir is a recent triumph although Cabernet Sauvignon and Merlot struggle to ripen fully most years.

Best producers Allan Scott, Cellier le Brun, CLOUDY BAY, CORBANS, Fromm, Grove Mill, HUNTER'S, Isabel, Jackson Estate, Lawson's Dry Hills, MONTANA, Nautilus, St Clair, Selaks, Seresin,

VAVASOUR, VILLA MARIA, Wairau River, Whitehaven, Wither Hills.

Best years 1999, '98, '97, '96, '94.

NELSON

This cool region, on the wetter westerly side of the northern tip of the South Island but sheltered to some extent by the Tasman Mountains, is made up of a series of small hills and valleys. It produces top Chardonnay, Sauvignon and Riesling with good Pinot Noir in favourable vintages.

Best producers Greenhough, NEUDORF, Seifried, Spencer Hill

Best years 1999, '98, '96, '94, '91.

WELLINGTON

Wellington is now the official region that covers the southern tip of North Island, including Wairarapa, a district that encompasses the well known sub-district, Martinborough. Low-yielding, free-draining, relatively infertile soils produce some of the country's most concentrated wines. Martinborough is famous for its impressively powerful Pinot Noir, once rated as New Zealand's best but now facing stiff competition from Marlborough, Canterbury and Central Otago. Rich, buttery Chardonnay, pungent Sauvignon Blanc, intense Riesling and inky Cabernet Sauvignon/Merlot blends also do well here.

Best producers Ata Rangi, Benfield & Delamare, Dry River, MARTINBOROUGH VINEYARD, Nga Waka, Palliser, Te Kairanga, Walnut Ridge.

Best years ❢1999, '98, '96, '94, '91.

WORLD CLASS CHAMPAGNE-METHOD SPARKLING WINE
New Zealand is now carving out a reputation for top-quality Champagne-method sparkling wine, now usually called Méthode Traditionelle. They are mostly a blend of Chardonnay and Pinot Noir, sometimes with the addition of Pinot Meunier. These wines are slightly riper and fruitier than Champagne itself but still have similar biscuity, bready yeast characteristics.
Best producers Cellier Le Brun, Cloudy Bay (Pelorus), Corbans (Amadeus), Hunter's (Miru Miru), Mills Reef, Montana (Deutz, Lindauer), Morton Estate.

A–Z OF NEW ZEALAND PRODUCERS

BABICH, Auckland   09 833 7859/833 9929

A family winery making wines from grapes grown in Hawke's Bay, Gisborne and
Marlborough, which is large enough to achieve competitive prices but still small
enough to inject some passion into developing high-quality, individual wines.
Best wines ★★ Irongate Chardonnay ♀, Irongate Cabernet/Merlot ❢, Mara Estate Syrah ❢,
Patriarch Cabernet Sauvignon ❢ and Patriarch Chardonnay ♀, ★ Marlborough Sauvignon
Blanc ♀ and Hawkes Bay Chardonnay ♀
Best years ❢1999, '98, '96, '95, '94; ♀1999, '98, '96

CLOUDY BAY, Marlborough   03 572 8914/572 8065

New Zealand's super-star producer of top wines from the Marlborough region.
Founded by Australian winemaker, David Hohnen, and now owned by VEUVE
CLICQUOT. Good vineyards, rigorous selection and skilled winemaking deliver top
wines in every vintage. All the wines are best within 2–3 years of the vintage.
Best wines ★★★ Sauvignon Blanc ♀, ★★ Chardonnay ♀, Late-Harvest Riesling ♀ and Pelorus
Méthode Traditionelle ♀, ★ Pinot Noir ❢
Best years 1999, '98, '97, '96

CORBANS, Auckland, Gisborne and Marlborough   09 837 3390/837 6778

New Zealand's second-largest producer has wineries in Auckland, Gisborne, Hawke's
Bay and Marlborough and makes a large range of wines with many gems. Brands
include Cooks, Cottage Block, Longridge, Private Bin, Robard & Butler and Stoneleigh.
Best wines ★★ Corbans Noble Riesling ♀, Corbans Private Bin Marlborough Chardonnay ♀
and Stoneleigh Riesling ♀, ★ Corbans Private Bin Merlot ❢, Stoneleigh Sauvignon Blanc ♀,
Cottage Block (Pinot Noir ❢, Chardonnay ♀ and Sauvignon Blanc ♀)
Best years Marlborough 1999, '97, '96; **Hawke's Bay** 1999, '98, '96

GOLDWATER ESTATE, Waiheke Island, Auckland   09 372 7493/372 6827

The winery that pioneered Waiheke Island, the country's top red wine district. Since
1994 Goldwater has made Chardonnay and Sauvignon Blanc from Marlborough grapes.
Best wines ★★ Cabernet Sauvignon/Merlot/Cabernet Franc ❢ and Marlborough Dog Point
Sauvignon Blanc ♀, ★ Marlborough Roseland Chardonnay ♀
Best years ❢1999, '98, '96, '94; ♀1999, '97

HUNTER'S, Blenheim, Marlborough   03 572 8489/572 8457

Established Marlborough winery, owned and managed by viticulturist Jane Hunter.
Selection in vineyard and winery preserve the consistency and integrity of its top wines.
Hunter's has benefited from the input of Dr Tony Jordan, general manager of Domaine
Chandon in Australia's Yarra Valley.
Best wines ★★ Sauvignon Blanc ♀, Oak-Aged Sauvignon Blanc ♀ and Chardonnay ♀
Best years 1999, '97, '96, '94

KUMEU RIVER, Auckland   09 412 8415/412 7627

Small family winery that unusually specializes in locally grown grapes, with spectacular
success. The wine is made by talented Master of Wine, Michael Brajkovich. The
Chardonnay is widely acclaimed as New Zealand's best and can be aged for at least 5
years in most vintages.

Best wines ★★★ Chardonnay ♀, ★★ Sauvignon Blanc/Sémillon ♀, ★ Merlot/Cabernet Sauvignon ❢ (replaced from 1998 by Melba, a Merlot/Malbec blend)
Best years Chardonnay 1999, '96, '94, '93

MARTINBOROUGH VINEYARD, Martinborough, Wellington   06 306 9955/306 9217
Since 1986 this has consistently been New Zealand's top Pinot Noir producer, though this status is now matched by others such as Ata Rangi. There is now also impressive Chardonnay, which like the Pinot Noir is made using the whole gamut of Burgundian winemaking techniques, as well as strong spicy Riesling. All 3 wines show an impressive capacity for aging – allow them at least 3 years.
Best wines ★★★ Pinot Noir Reserve ❢, ★★ Chardonnay ♀, ★ Riesling ♀
Best years 1999, '98, '96, '94

MONTANA, Auckland   09 570 8400/570 8440
New Zealand's largest wine company has wineries in Auckland, Gisborne, Hawke's Bay and Marlborough where it pioneered winemaking in the 1970s. Montana is using the Bordeaux firm of Cordier, to help it develop top Bordeaux-style reds, and works with the Champagne house DEUTZ to refine its very good Champagne-method 'fizz'. Brands include Brancott Estate, Fairhall Estate and Church Road.
Best wines ★★ Deutz Marlborough Cuvée Blanc de Blancs Vintage ♀, Deutz Marlborough Cuvee Brut Non-Vintage ♀, Montana 'F' Fairhall Estate Cabernet Sauvignon ❢, Montana 'O' Ormond Estate Chardonnay ♀ and Montana 'R' Renwick Estate Chardonnay ♀
Best years Marlborough 1999, '98, '97

MORTON ESTATE, Auckland   09 300 5053/300 5054
This winery has earned a reputation for producing top-quality Hawke's Bay wines, particularly robust, complex Chardonnay and vintage sparkling wines. Ideally drink the Black label white wines with 2–4 years' aging and the reds with 4–6 years.
Best wines ★★★ Black Label Hawke's Bay Chardonnay ♀, ★★ Black Label Hawke's Bay Merlot/Cabernet ❢ and Brut Vintage ♀, ★ Black Label Fumé Blanc ♀ and White Label Chardonnay ♀
Best years ❢1999, '98, '96, '95, '94; ♀1999, '98, '96, '95, '94

NEUDORF, Nelson   03 543 2643/543 2955
Nelson's top winery, making stylish and often innovative wines. Neudorf is also one of New Zealand's best producers of Chardonnay that in good years can resemble Puligny-Montrachet. Pinot Noir and Riesling are also excellent. Both the Chardonnay and Pinot Noir can improve for up to 5 years while the Riesling and Sauvignon Blanc are delicious young.
Best wines ★★★ Moutere Chardonnay ♀, ★★ Moutere Pinot Noir ❢ and Moutere Riesling ♀, ★ Moutere Sauvignon Blanc ♀
Best years 1999, '98, '96, '94

STONYRIDGE, Waiheke Island, Auckland   09 372 8822/372 8766
Small red wine specialist producing New Zealand's most expensive wine, Larose, a Bordeaux-style blend. Low yields from a warm, sheltered site on Waiheke Island in Auckland Harbour contribute concentration and complexity to this long-lived red that in good years can age well for 5–10 years. Organic viticulture methods are used.
Best wine ★★★ Larose Cabernet ❢   **Best years** 1998, '96, '94, '93, '91, '89, '87

TE MATA, Hawke's Bay   06 877 4399/887 4397

The star of Hawke's Bay and one of New Zealand's most respected premium winemakers. In the early 1980s Te Mata made Cabernet-based reds that were light years ahead of the field. There is also outstanding Chardonnay and stylish Syrah. Exeptional vintages of all 3 wines might last for 5–10 years.

Best wines ★★★ Coleraine Cabernet/Merlot ❗, ★★ Awatea Cabernet/Merlot ❗ and Elston Chardonnay ⚲, ★ Bullnose Syrah ❗

Best years ❗1999, '98, '96, '95, '94, '91, '90, '89; ⚲1998, '97, '96, '95, '94

VAVASOUR, Marlborough   03 575 7481/575 7240

Vavasour pioneered the Awatere Valley, an exciting district of Marlborough that has become very fashionable since its first vintage in 1989. The Chardonnay is one of New Zealand's best. A second label 'Dashwood' helps strengthen and maintain the quality of the premium 'Vavasour' label.

Best wines ★★ Vavasour Chardonnay ⚲, Sauvignon Blanc ⚲ and Cabernet Sauvignon ❗

Best years 1999, '98, '97, '96

VILLA MARIA, Auckland   09 255 0660/255 0661

Villa Maria's owner, George Fistonich, also owns the Hawke's Bay wineries Vidal and Esk Valley. Their combined production makes the group New Zealand's third-largest winery, although each operates independently. Hawke's Bay has traditionally been the prime source of grapes for Villa Maria although Marlborough is growing in importance.

Best wines ★★★ Reserve Cabernet Sauvignon ❗, ★★ Reserve Noble Riesling ⚲, Reserve Marlborough Chardonnay ⚲, Clifford Bay Marlborough Sauvignon Blanc ⚲, Reserve Cabernet/Merlot ❗, and Esk Valley The Terrraces ❗

Best years Marlborough 1999, '98, '97, '96; **Hawke's Bay** 1999, '98, '96, '94

NEW ZEALAND VINTAGES

Like many cool-climate wine countries New Zealand experiences considerable vintage variation. Variation is more obvious in marginal varieties such as Cabernet Sauvignon grown in the cooler South Island. Late-ripening Sauvignon Blanc can also experience ups and downs.

Aging qualities

New Zealand's wines have experienced such a rapid rate of development in quality over the past couple of decades that few people have given much thought to aging. However, consistent styles for regions, varieties and vintages are starting to take form and there's no doubt some wines will age well. Even so, it will depend on your personal taste. If you age Marlborough Sauvignon for more than a couple of years you'd better like the flavours of canned asparagus and gooseberries in syrup. Ideally, this is *the* white wine to drink young. Simple, unoaked New Zealand Chardonnay can be mature at 2 years while a serious, concentrated classic can last as much as a decade. As a general rule, Pinot Noir should be enjoyed within 5 years; Cabernet Sauvignon (and Merlot blends) may peak at between 5–10 years; most Riesling will reward aging for at least 4–5 years; botrytized dessert wines can last for 5–10 years.

VINTAGE CHART

HAWKE'S BAY	99	98	97	96	95	94	93	92	91	90	89
Cabernet Sauvignon	8○	10○	7○	8○	7○	9○	7●	6●	9●	7●	10●
Chardonnay	9○	9○	8○	8●	8●	8●	7◑	7●	9●		

MARTINBOROUGH	99	98	97	96	95	94	93	92	91	90	89
Pinot Noir	8○	9○	7○	8○	6●	9●	7●	7◑	9◑		

MARLBOROUGH	99	98	97	96	95	94	93	92	91	90	89
Sauvignon Blanc	9○	6●	8●	9◑	5◑	9●	8◑				
Chardonnay	8○	8○	8○	8○	6◑	9○	7○	6●	9●	8◑	9●

AUCKLAND, KUMEU	99	98	97	96	95	94	93	92	91	90	89
Cabernet Sauvignon/Merlot	8○	8○	7◑	8○	6◑	9●	10●	7◑	9●	7◑	9◑
Chardonnay	8○	9◑	7◑	8●	6●	9●	8●	7◑	9●		

KEY ○= needs more time ◑= ready but will improve ●= at peak ◐= fading or tired

VINTAGES AT A GLANCE

Diligence in the vineyard (or the lack of it) and different mesoclimates within a region can cause significant variation in results from grower to grower.

Great Years ★★★ Auckland 1998, '94, '93, '91; Hawke's Bay 1999, '98, '94, '91, '89; Martinborough 1999, '98, '96, '94, '91, '89

Good Years ★★ Auckland 1999, '97, '96, '89; Hawke's Bay 1997, '96, '95, '87; Martinborough 1997, '93, '92, ' 88; Marlborough 1998, '97, '96, '90, '88

Moderate Years ★ Auckland 1995, '92, '90; Hawke's Bay 1993, '92, '90; Martinborough 1995, '90; Marlborough 1993, '92

Poor Years (No Stars) Auckland 1988; Hawke's Bay 1988; Martinborough 1987; Marlborough 1995

Annual vintage reports

1999★-★★★ North Island regions suffered from heavy rain. Marlborough Sauvignon Blanc, Hawke's Bay Chardonnay and Waiheke reds among the best.

1998★-★★★ Hotter and drier conditions than normal have encouraged many winemakers to believe this will be the country's biggest and best vintage to date. Excellent Hawke's Bay reds.

1997★★ Moderately cool vintage helped by an Indian summer that greatly benefited late-ripening varieties, particularly reds. Flavour concentration was aided by a lower than normal yield.

1996★★-★★★ An abundant crop and good quality. The star region was Martinborough.

1995 ★-★★ Mostly poor results in Marlborough, particularly Sauvignon Blanc, but exceptional ones in Canterbury. Hawke's Bay and Gisborne Chardonnay variable but can be very good.

1994★★★ Good results in all regions and many outstanding wines in Gisborne and Auckland. Only Canterbury and Central Otago failed to perform very well.

1993★ A generally lacklustre vintage. The notable exceptions were Auckland reds and some good South Island Riesling.

1992★-★★ A cool vintage with some wet weather at harvest. Whites better than reds.

1991★★★ Hot dry conditions made this an excellent vintage in every region. Many classic wines produced.

1990★ A coolish vintage. Late varieties, particularly reds, failed to ripen fully.

1989★★★ A superb vintage although many wines failed to reach their potential.

SOUTH AFRICA

For the world's seventh-largest wine producer the creation of fine wine has been almost a marginal activity. South Africa's political isolation prevented the all-important exchange of ideas and information seen in rivals Australia and California. Only in the 1990s with the ending of Apartheid and the lifting of economic sanctions has a real surge in quality been possible. New cool-climate areas are finally being developed and a major programme of replanting with a better selection of clones and a wider variety of cultivars is well under way.

WINE STYLES

Red wines

Long-lived Bordeaux-style reds have long been South Africa's strongest hand but these old-fashioned and increasingly unappreciated reds have for the most part undergone a major transformation. In recent years there has been a move towards a more modern structure and fruit richness and a noteworthy few wines have real elegance and finesse. South Africa's own Pinotage is emerging as world class, alongside Pinot Noir and Shiraz.

White wines

The arrival of new oak in the 1980s transformed South African whites as much as the reds. More recently white winemaking has taken on a greater sophistication and the focus has been on using ever better quality fruit for improved concentration, structure, balance and complexity in the wines.

Sauvignon Blanc is often unwooded and bold with ripe melon fruit fighting it out with razor-sharp grapefruit and lime. Suggestions that the Cape was not suitable for Chardonnay have long since been consigned to the bin as a series of excellent cool-climate and lusher warm-climate examples have appeared.

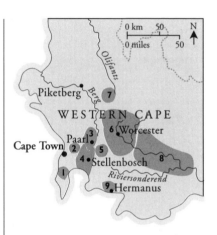

Main Western Cape wine regions

1 Constantia	6 Worcester
2 Durbanville	7 Tulbagh
3 Paarl/Wellington	8 Robertson
4 Stellenbosch	9 Hermanus/Walker Bay
5 Franschhoek	

Sweet wines

The Cape's historic Constantia sweet wine from Muscat grapes has been revived at KLEIN CONSTANTIA, complementing the outstanding sweet wines made at NEETHLINGSHOF, STELLENZICHT and NEDERBURG which are made mostly from Riesling, Sémillon or Chenin Blanc.

GREAT SOUTH AFRICAN WINES

Oz Clarke's selection

**Cabernet Sauvignon !
(Thelema)** Outstanding blackcurranty minty wine from South Africa's modern quality pioneer.

Sauvignon Blanc Reserve ♀ (Vergelegen) From a single-vineyard this is a marvellous example of fully ripe fruit intensity tempered by startling acidity.

Pinotage ! (Clos Malverne) Exotic mix of damson, coconut and toasted marshmallow from a top producer of South Africa's indigenous variety.

Kaaimansgaat Chardonnay ♀ (Bouchard Finlayson) Proof from unirrigated, cool-climate vineyards that South Africa can produce great barrel-fermented Chardonnays.

Sémillon ♀ (Fairview Estate) Leader of growing band of South African Sémillon producers creating quince, melon and custard-cream-flavoured barrel-fermented styles.

Chardonnay ♀ (Radford Dale) Tremendous oatmealy Chardonnay almost more Burgundian than New World in style.

Steven Spurrier's selection

Shiraz ! (Fairview Estate) A finely extracted fruit marks this excellent Shiraz made by Charles Back.

Pinotage ! (Kanonkop) Winemaker Beyers Truter is the leading exponent of deep-coloured, smoothly intense Pinotage from mostly old-bush vines.

Pinot Noir ! (Hamilton Russell) South Africa's first great Pinot Noir, and still leading the field despite some real competition from other producers.

Rubicon ! (Meerlust) The most classic Bordeaux-style blend from the Cape's most beautiful winery, now owned by the eighth generation of the Myburgh family.

Trilogy ! (Warwick Estate) A complex, Old-World-style, Bordeaux blend with ripe fruit and charm.

Vin de Constance ♀ (Klein Constantia Estate) From one of South Africa's showpiece estates, a re-creation of an intensely sweet, naturally concentrated wine, that brought fame to the Cape's vineyards over 300 years ago.

Fortified wines

Port styles have long been successful, and the widely planted Tinta Barocca is now being complemented by Touriga Nacional, the king of Port grape varieties. These powerful robust wines should show greater finesse and still greater complexity.

Classifications

The Wine of Origin (WO) laws, provide, by way of a seal on the neck of the bottle, official certification for area of origin, vintage and cultivar (grape variety). Origin is divided into regions, districts and wards. As in other New World winemaking countries there is still a strong emphasis on varietal labelling. The wine need only contain 75% of the cultivar stated on the label (85% for exported wines).

Top South African producers

Cabernet/Bordeaux-style BEYERSKLOOF, KANONKOP, MEERLUST, NEDERBURG, RUSTENBERG, SAXENBURG, THELEMA.

Chardonnay BOUCHARD FINLAYSON, De Wetshof, GLEN CARLOU, HAMILTON RUSSELL, MEERLUST, MORGENHOF, MULDERBOSCH, RUSTENBERG, THELEMA, VERGELEGEN.

Merlot MEERLUST, MORGENHOF, SAXENBURG, SPICE ROUTE, THELEMA, VERGELEGEN.

Pinot Noir BOUCHARD FINLAYSON, Cabrière, HAMILTON RUSSELL, SPICE ROUTE.

Pinotage KANONKOP, WARWICK.

Sauvignon Blanc KLEIN CONSTANTIA, MORGENHOF, MULDERBOSCH, RUSTENBERG, SAXENBURG, THELEMA.

Shiraz Fairview, SAXENBURG, SPICE ROUTE, STELLENZICHT.

Sweet wines KLEIN CONSTANTIA, NEDERBURG, NEETHLINGSHOF, STELLENZICHT.

Fortified wines Boplaas.

A–Z OF SOUTH AFRICAN PRODUCERS

BEYERSKLOOF, Stellenbosch   021 8822135/8822135

Small young winery focusing on South Africa's 2 leading red varieties, Cabernet
Sauvignon and Pinotage. Beyers Truter, KANONKOP's renowned winemaker, directs
operations and has quickly established the Cabernet Sauvignon as one of the country's
best. Intended as a lighter style, the Pinotage has rapidly become a serious wine.
Best wines ★★ Cabernet Sauvignon ♟, ★ Pinotage ♟
Best years Cabernet 1997, '96, '95, '94, '93, '92, '90, '89; **Pinotage** 1999, '98, '97, '96, '95

BOUCHARD FINLAYSON, Walker Bay   0283 23515/22317

The emphasis is on Chardonnay and Pinot Noir, perhaps unsurprisingly as Peter
Finlayson has teamed up with experienced Burgundian producer, Paul Bouchard.
Much has been made of the best bought-in grapes but new domaine-bottlings from
increasingly mature vineyards promise still more. The newest wines are a rich oaky
Chardonnay and a powerful firm Pinot Noir that needs aging for at least 3–5 years.
Best wines ★★ Pinot Noir Galpin Peak ♟ and Chardonnay Kaaimansgaat ♀
Best years ♟1998, '97, '96, '95, '94, '93; ♀1998, '97, '96, '95

BUITENVERWACHTING, Constantia   021 7945190/7941351

This estate is the quality leader in the exciting, relatively cool area of Constantia. In less
than 2 decades this run-down farm has been beautifully restored and has created wines
to match. The richly varietal wines are of a consistently high standard.
Best wines ★★ Christine (predominantly Cabernet) ♟, ★ Cabernet Sauvignon ♟,
Chardonnay ♀ and Sauvignon Blanc ♀
Best years Christine 1995, '94, '93, '92, '90, '91, '89; **Chardonnay** 1998, '97, '96, '95, '94

GLEN CARLOU, Paarl   021 8755528/8755314

Walter Finlayson, who proved himself one of South Africa's best winemakers, has now
been ably succeeded by his son David. Chardonnay is the star variety here with the
rich, toasty Reserve wine considered by many to be the Cape's finest. Donald Hess of
California's HESS COLLECTION bought into the winery in 1995, thus further boosting
its prospects.
Best wines ★★ Chardonnay ♀ and Chardonnay Reserve ♀
Best years 1998, '97, '96, '95

GRANGEHURST, Stellenbosch   021 8553025/8552143

Jeremy Walker established this label as recently as 1992. The grapes may all be bought-
in but the results are consistently impressive. There are now just 2 red wines. Both are
concentrated and best with 5–8 years' aging or more.
Best wines ★★ Cabernet Sauvignon/Merlot ♟ and Pinotage ♟
Best years 1998, '97, '95, '94, '93, '92

HAMILTON RUSSELL VINEYARDS, Walker Bay   0283 23595/21797

For many years the source of the Cape's top Pinot Noir which still continues to
improve due to new clones and increasing viticultural and vinification sophistication,
even though there is now some serious competition from other South African
producers. The 1997 and '96 are a real advance on admirable but simpler earlier
efforts. Chardonnay, too, is very good.

Best wines ★★ Ashbourne Pinot Noir ♥ and Ashbourne Chardonnay ♀, ★ Pinot Noir
Best years ♥1998, '97, '96, '95; ♀1999, '98, '97, '96, '95

KANONKOP ESTATE, Stellenbosch   021 8844656/8844719

Kanonkop has long produced the country's best Pinotage wine from mostly old bush vines. However, the Bordeaux blend Paul Sauer wine (predominantly Cabernet Sauvignon) sometimes outclasses it. Both wines show the hand of the formidable winemaker Beyers Truter, who also makes the wine at BEYERSKLOOF.

Best wines ★★ Pinotage Auction Reserve ♥, Paul Sauer ♥, Cabernet Sauvignon ♥ and Auction Reserve (Cabernet) ♥, ★ Pinotage ♥
Best years 1998, '97, '96, '95, '94, '92, '90, '91, '89

KLEIN CONSTANTIA ESTATE, Constantia   021 7945188/7942464

This beautifully restored showpiece estate has not only revived the famous non-botrytized Muscat dessert wine of Constantia but has also helped illustrate the potential of this relatively cool zone. The quality of the Sauvignon Blanc and other whites owes more than a little to winemaker Ross Gower's New Zealand experience.

Best wines ★★ Vin de Constance ♀, ★ Chardonnay ♀ and Sauvignon Blanc ♀
Best years Vin de Constance 1995, '94, '93, '92, '91, '90, '89, '88, '87, '86

MEERLUST ESTATE, Stellenbosch   021 8433275/8433513

Eight generations of the Myburgh family have nurtured this beautiful estate which is renowned for Rubicon, one of the Cape's first Bordeaux blends. This wine has long been at the very pinnacle of the South African red wine hierarchy. Italian winemaker Giorgio Dalla Cia also makes full, toasty Chardonnay and very good Merlot.

Best wines ★★ Rubicon ♥ and Chardonnay ♀, ★ Merlot ♥
Best years ♥1997, '96, '95, '94, '92, '91, '89; ♀1997, '96, '95

MORGENHOF, Stellenbosch   021 8895510/8895266

This 300-year-old estate is French owned and there is an absolute commitment to quality. Merlot, subject to a delayed release, is the top wine but the latest wines include exciting Chardonnay and Sauvignon Blanc as well as a rare quality Chenin Blanc.

Best wines ★★ Merlot ♥ and Première Selection ♥, ★ Sauvignon Blanc ♀ and Chardonnay ♀
Best years ♥1996, '95, '94, '93; ♀1998, '97

MULDERBOSCH VINEYARDS, Stellenbosch   021 8822488/8822351

Winemaker Mike Dobrovic sets the standard for South African Sauvignon Blanc, making a wine that is marvellously consistent, full and structured with a figgy richness from relatively low yields. The Bordeaux-blend Faithful Hound and Chardonnay reinforce the estate's quality image – there's even good, lightly oaked Chenin Blanc (called Steen-op-Hout) from old vines.

Best wines ★★ Sauvignon Blanc ♀, ★ Chardonnay ♀ and Faithful Hound ♥
Best years ♥1997, '96, '95, '94; ♀1999, '98, '97, '96, '95

NEDERBURG (AUCTION WINES), Paarl   021 8623104/8624887

Owned by the large Stellenbosch Farmers' Winery, Nederburg is run as a completely separate operation. The real interest lies in the Private Bin wines sold at the annual Nederburg auction – the most prestigious date in the South African wine calendar.

Best wines ★★ Edelkeur ♀, Noble Late Harvest Private Bin S316 (Riesling) ♀, ★ Cabernet Private Bin R163 ♥

Best years Edelkeur 1997, '96, '95, '93, '92, '91, '90, '89; **Noble Late Harvest Private Bin S316 Riesling** 1997, '96, '95, '92, '91, '90; **Cabernet Private Bin R163** 1988, '86, '84

NEETHLINGSHOF ESTATE, Stellenbosch   021 8838988/021 8838941

Sister estate to STELLENZICHT and making arguably the Cape's most outstanding botrytized dessert wine. The dry whites and reds are not of quite the same standard but investment over more than a dozen years by the owner, Hans-Joachim Schreiber, has led to an impressive range of wines.

Best wines ★★ Noble Late Harvest (Riesling) ♀, ★ Lord Neethling ▮ and Cabernet Sauvignon ▮

Best years ▮ 1997, '95, '94, '93, '91; **Noble Late Harvest** 1998, '97, '96, '95, '94, '93, '92, '91, '90

RUSTENBERG ESTATE, Stellenbosch   021 809 1200/809 1219

The wines from this great old estate were badly in need of improvement and a new cellar is part of the major overhaul taking place. The range of wines has been revamped and there are excellent examples under each label.

Best wines ★★ Peter Barlow ▮, ★ Rustenberg Five Soldiers ♀, Brampton Sauvignon Blanc ♀ and Rustenberg ▮

Best years ▮1997, '96; ♀1999, '98, '97

SAXENBURG, Stellenbosch   021 9036113/9033129

The headily scented, burly Private Collection Shiraz is the top wine at this renowned red wine estate. The Private Collection Cabernet Sauvignon and Merlot are rich, powerful wines too. Sauvignon Blanc and Chardonnay are showing real promise.

Best wines ★★ Shiraz Private Collection ▮ and Cabernet Sauvignon Private Collection ▮, ★ Merlot Private Collection ▮

Best years ▮1997, '96, '95, '94, '92, '91

SPICE ROUTE WINE COMPANY, Swartland   021 8632450/8632591

High profile operation now owned by Charles Back of Fairview. The real quality is to be found in the reds, especially the big, yet classically styled Flagship trio of wines.

Best wines ★★ Flagship Pinotage ▮, Flagship Merlot ▮ and Flagship Syrah ▮

Best years ▮1998

STELLENZICHT VINEYARDS, Stellenbosch   021 883 8988/883 8975

This Helderberg farm is under the same ownership as NEETHLINGSHOF on the other side of the valley. As at Neethlingshof, botrytized sweet wines are a strength but there is also outstanding rich, spicy Syrah and excellent dry whites, especially Sauvignon Blanc.

Best wines ★★ Syrah ▮ and Noble Late Harvest ♀, ★ Sauvignon Blanc ♀ and Sémillon Reserve ♀

Best years ▮1998, '97, '95, '94; **Noble Late Harvest** 1998, '96, '95

THELEMA MOUNTAIN VINEYARDS, Stellenbosch   021 8851924/021 8851800

No-one else in South Africa seems to be as obsessed with viticulture as Thelema's Gyles Webb and every varietal made here is at or near the top of the quality hierarchy.

Best wines ★★ Cabernet Sauvignon ▮ and Chardonnay ♀, ★ Merlot ▮ and Sauvignon Blanc ♀

Best years ▮1996, '95, '94, '93, '92, '91; ♀1998, '97, '96, '95, '94

VERGELEGEN, Stellenbosch   021 8471334/8471608

Winemaker André van Rensburg, previously at STELLENZICHT, has lost no time in creating a range of wines equal to their grand surroundings. The barrel-fermented

Chardonnay Reserve and dense, opulent Merlot are already impressively intense.

Best wines ★★ Chardonnay Reserve ♀ and Merlot ♚, ★ Sauvignon Blanc Reserve ♀

Best years ♚1998, '95, '94; ♀1999, '98, '97, '96, '95

WARWICK ESTATE, Simonsberg   021 8844410/8844025

Norma Ratcliffe is one of South Africa's most respected winemakers, concentrating on Bordeaux-style reds, including Trilogy. A varietal Cabernet Franc is not only unusual but a great success. The Pinotage is also fine.

Best wines ★★ Old Bush Vine Pinotage ♚, ★ Trilogy ♚ and Cabernet Franc ♚

Best years ♚1998, '97, '96, '95, '94, '93; ♀1999, '98, '97

SOUTH AFRICAN VINTAGES

Vintage assessments apply only to a very limited number of South African wines and are largely confined to the top reds. Traditionally these have been Cabernet-based wines from the Stellenbosch region but there is age-worthy Shiraz and even Pinot Noir from further afield.

Aging qualities

Recent vintages in South Africa have seen a trend to more modern soft, fruity styles of red wines which are accessible from an early date. A pre-1990 vintage date on a bottle is likely to indicate a wine that is more old-fashioned – big, bold and tannic with lots of extract. Pinot Noir shows increasing aging potential as do a handful of exceptional Pinotage wines. Shiraz has always shown considerable aging potential but now offers far more pleasure from the hands of a top producer. Merlot is likely to show a greater capacity for aging if blended with Cabernet Sauvignon in the Bordeaux style. The most concentrated, structured Cabernet-based reds will still keep for at least a decade but, unlike past vintages, can also often be broached with just 3–4 years of aging.

Most South African Sauvignon Blanc and Chardonnay wines are best drunk young. However, a growing number of barrel-fermented and oak-aged Chardonnays are better kept for 3–4 years and might last beyond 5 years.

VINTAGES AT A GLANCE

The Cape's Mediterranean climate serves to reduce more extreme vintage variation. A lack of adequate sunshine isn't a problem in terms of ripening, but a burst of excessive heat resulting in high sugars but leaving green tannins behind often is. However, among the numerous mesoclimates many have the right soils to promote slow, even ripening and top-quality fruit. While the quest for the ideal cultivar/site match is currently causing much interest and excitement, South Africa's grape-growers are working vigorously to improve the quality of their vine material too.

Great Years ★★★
Cape Cabernet Sauvignon-based 1997, '95, '91; Cape Chardonnay 1997

Good Years ★★
Cape Cabernet Sauvignon-based 1999, '98, '94, '93, '92; Cape Chardonnay 1999, '98, '96

Moderate Years ★
Cape Cabernet Sauvignon-based 1996

Poor years (No Stars)
None

INDEX

A

346

ACKNOWLEDGEMENTS

Editorial Director Fiona Holman; **Art Director** Nigel O'Gorman; **Editorial Assistant** Ingrid Karikari; **Maps** Andrew Thompson; **Indexer** Naomi Good; **Production** Kâren Connell.